Studies in Diversity Linguistics

Editor: Martin Haspelmath

In this series:

ISSN: 2363-5568

A grammar of Komnzo

Christian Döhler

language
science
press

This title can be downloaded at:
http://langsci-press.org/catalog/book/212
© 2018, Christian Döhler
Published under the Creative Commons Attribution 4.0 Licence (CC BY 4.0):
http://creativecommons.org/licenses/by/4.0/
ISBN: 978-3-96110-125-2 (Digital)
        978-3-96110-126-9 (Hardcover)

ISSN: 2363-5568
DOI:10.5281/zenodo.1477799
Source code available from www.github.com/langsci/212
Collaborative reading: paperhive.org/documents/remote?type=langsci&id=212

Cover and concept of design: Ulrike Harbort
Typesetting: Christian Döhler, Sebastian Nordhoff
Proofreading: Ahmet Bilal Özdemir, Ivica Jeđud, Jaime Peña, Jeffrey Pheiff, Jeroen van de Weijer, Jingting Ye, Kilu von Prince, Klara Kim, Lachlan Mackenzie, Laura Melissa Arnold, Ludger Paschen, Mykel Brinkerhoff, Sebastian Nordhoff, Sune Gregersen, Yvonne Treis
Fonts: Linux Libertine, Libertinus Math, Arimo, DejaVu Sans Mono
Typesetting software: X∄LATEX

Language Science Press
Unter den Linden 6
10099 Berlin, Germany
langsci-press.org

Storage and cataloguing done by FU Berlin

Freie Universität Berlin

For Nakre and Tayafe

Contents

Acknowledgments

This grammar of Komnzo started out as my PhD project at the Australian National University in Canberra. Since 2016, there have been many additions and revisions to this grammar, but the majority of the contents are the same as in the final version of my dissertation. These changes are the result of the comments given by reviewers, editors and proof-readers as well as the ever-increasing knowledge I receive from my Komnzo speaking friends.

This book would not have been possible without the support of the Farem people who took on the task of teaching me their language. I am deeply grateful to them for welcoming me in their community, for feeding me and keeping me safe at all times, for the patience they have had with my probing questions, and above all for sharing their language and culture with me. It is impossible to acknowledge everyone who assisted in teaching me Komnzo, for every exchange provided a contribution to my knowledge. Amongst my indigenous teachers were: Abia Bai, Nakre Abia, Daure Kaumb, Riley Abia, †Marua Bai, Lucy Abia, Sékri Karémbu, Janet Abia, Steven Karémbu, Caspar Mokai, Karo Abia, Kaumb Bai, Moses Abia and Albert Mokai.

My principal supervisor Nicholas Evans first suggested the Tonda languages as an area of research. Nick's enthusiasm and challenging criticism has helped me to sharpen my analysis and description of Komnzo. His open-mindedness about fieldwork and his holistic approach to language documentation made me see fascinating details of the language. I have greatly appreciated the contributions of I Wayan Arka, Andrew Pawley, Mark Ellison and Mark Donohue, who took over supervision at various periods over the years. I thank Ulrike Mosel, Ger Reesink and Martin Haspelmath for reviewing the dissertation. Their positive as well as their challenging comments have greatly improved this grammar. I am indebted to the administrative staff at the School of Culture, History and Language who have helped me navigating the bureaucracy. I would like to thank Jo Bushby, Penelope Judd, and Stephen Meatheringham. I am grateful to Kay Dancey at cartographic unit for the linguistic map of the Morehead district (see Figure 1.1).

There are a number of people who have helped me with specific knowledge and advice concerning virtually all aspects of carrying out research in the Morehead district. I would like to thank Mary Ayres who invited me to her house in Philadelphia and shared her fieldnotes from Rouku. Paul O'Rear and Risto Sarsa have answered many questions and requests about Rouku and Yokwa. Thanks also to Garrick Hitchcock and Kevin Murphy for sharing their knowledge about and experience in working in this part of the country. I also thank Jeff Siegel for his help both in Morehead and in other places where we have met. I want to thank Cezar Fernandez and the staff of New Century Hotel in Daru, who continue to make my brief stays in this town a pleasant experience, and Douglas Dawi,

Andrew Little, Peter Paradi, and Charlie Subam for transporting me and my equipment safely between Daru and the Morehead district.

Over the years, I have received financial support from the DOBES project of the Volkswagen Foundation, the Stephen and Helen Wurm Bequest at ANU, The Max Planck Institute for Evolutionary Anthropology and the ACR Centre of Excellence for the Dynamics of Language at ANU. I thank all these institutions for making language documentation and description possible. I thank especially Vera Szöllösi-Brenig for organising the DOBES project, as well as Paul Trijlsbeek, Han Sloetjes and Alexander König for providing technical training and assistance.

I thank the staff at Language Science Press, especially Sebastian Nordhoff and Martin Haspelmath. Moreover, I am grateful to the numerous volunteers who spent their valuable time during the publication process of this book. I embrace you in the spirit of true open-access publishing.

To my family and friends who have provided me with moral and practical support over the years, I am deeply grateful. Too many years and too many people have passed by to thank everyone, but particular thanks go to Darja Hoenigman, Aung Si, Charlotte van Tongeren, Sebastien Lacrampe, Penny Johnson, Gary Kildea, Matthew Carroll, Beth Evans, Alena Witzlack-Makarevich and Sonja Riesberg. Lastly, I want to thank my parents Regina and Jörg, my brother Matthias and his family for their continued support over the last years.

Abbreviations

∅	zero form
\.../	verb stem, e.g. y\fath/wr (§5.2, §5.3)
(.)	speech pause
.	multi-item gloss, e.g. old.man, be.standing, 3SG.MASC
|	used in cases of syncretism, e.g. 2|3 is second or third person
1	first person (§5.5.1)
2	second person (§5.5.1)
3	third person (§5.5.1)
α	alpha prefix series (§5.5.1.4, §6.2.1)
β	beta prefix series (§5.5.1.4, §6.2.1)
β1	beta 1 prefix series (§5.5.1.4, §6.2.1)
β2	beta 2 prefix series (§5.5.1.4, §6.2.1)
γ	gamma prefix series (§5.5.1.4, §6.2.1)
A	most agent-like argument (§5.4)
ABS	absolutive case (§4.4)
ABL	ablative case (§4.8.3)
ADJZR	adjectivaliser (§3.1)
ALL	allative case (§4.8.2)
ALR	iamitive ('already'), (3.4.1, §6.3.5)
AND	andative (§5.6.1)
ANIM	animate (§4.3, §4.18)
APPR	apprehensive (§3.5.2, §5.6.2, §6.3.2)
ASSOC	associative case (§4.15, §7.6)
BG	backgrounded (§6.2.4)
CHAR	characteristic case (§4.12)
COP	copula (§8.3.2)
DAT	dative case (§4.6)
DEM	demonstrative (§3.1.12)
DIM	diminutive (§4.17.5)
DISTR	distributive (§4.17.4)
DIST	distal demonstrative (§3.1.12)
DU	dual (§5.5.3)
DUR	durative (§6.2.4)

EMPH	emphatic (§4.17.1)
ERG	ergative case (§4.5)
ETC	et cetera ('and all'), (§4.17.3)
EXT	extended verb stem (§5.2, §5.3)
FEM	feminine (§3.1.3, §5.5.2)
FUT	future (§3.4.1, §6.3.4, §6.4.1)
FUTIMP	future imperative (§6.2, §6.2.4)
HAB	habitual (§3.4.1, §6.3.6)
IMM	immediate demonstrative (§3.1.12.5)
IMN	imminent (§3.4.1, §3.5.2, §6.3.1)
IMP	imperative (§5.5.1.1, §6.2.5, §6.4.3)
INDF	indefinite (§3.1.11)
INS	instrumental case (§4.10)
IO	indirect object (§5.4)
IPFV	imperfective (§6.2, §6.4.2)
IPST	immediate past (§3.5.2, §6.2, §6.3.1, §6.4.1)
IRR	irrealis (§6.2.2, §6.4.3, §10.5)
ITER	iterative (§6.2)
LK	linking consonant (§5.5.1.1)
LOC	locative case (§4.8.1)
LPL	large plural (§5.5.3.2)
M	middle (§5.4, §5.4.5)
MASC	masculine (§3.1.3, §5.5.2)
MED	medial demonstrative (§3.1.12)
ND	non-dual (§5.5.3)
NEG	negator (3.4.1, §8.5)
NMLZ	nominaliser (§3.2, §5.4.3, §9.1)
NPL	non-plural (§5.5.3)
NPST	non-past (§6.2, §6.4.1)
NSG	non-singular (§5.5.3)
OBJ	object (§5.4)
ONLY	exclusive marker ('only', 'just'), (§3.4.2, §4.17.2)
P	most patient-like argument (§5.4)
PFV	perfective (§6.2, §6.4.2)
PL	plural (§5.5.3)
POS	positional verb stem (§5.4.4.2)
POSS	possessive (§4.7)
POT	potential (§3.4.1, §6.3.3)
PRIV	privative case (§4.14)
PROP	proprietive case (§4.13)
PROX	proximal demonstrative (§3.1.12)
PST	past (§6.2, §6.2.3, §6.4.1)
PURP	purposive case (§4.11)

QUOT	quotative (§3.1.12.7, §9.7)
RECOG	recognitional pronoun (§3.1.12.6)
REDUP	reduplication (§4.2)
RPST	recent past (§6.2, §6.4.1)
RS	restricted verb stem (§5.2, §5.3, §5.5.3.4)
S	single argument of an intransitive verb
SBJ	subject (§5.4)
SG	singular (§5.5.3)
SIMIL	similative (§4.16)
STAT	stative (§5.4.4.2)
TEMP	temporal case (§4.9)
U	undergoer (§5.4)
VC	valency change (§5.4.2, §5.4.3, §5.5.3.3)
VENT	venitive (§5.6.1)

1 Preliminaries

1.1 Introduction

This grammar describes Komnzo, the language of the Farem people, who live in the Southern New Guinea area. The word *farem* is a proper name derived from an origin place (*farem kar* 'Farem place'). The concept of a shared place of origin overlaps with speech variety. Hence, the speakers of Komnzo sometimes refer to themselves as the "Farem tribe" when they speak English.

The proper name *Komnzo* must have had its origin in a mistranslation in the context of a visit by a patrol officer. Early sources are difficult to interpret because they only mention places along the Morehead River. The listed names for the Rouku area include *bangu* (Ray 1907: 292) and *perem/peremka* (Ray 1923: 334). The former is a section or clan name found throughout the region, while the latter looks like *farem kar*, because the grapheme <p> in early sources corresponds to the bilabial fricative [ɸ] in Komnzo. From the 1950s onwards, the label *komnzo zokwasi* 'Komnzo language' was used. It is unclear when and how this was introduced as the official language name. The word *komnzo* means 'just, only, still' in the sense of *komnzo käms!* 'just sit down!' or *komnzo ymarwé* 'I can still see him'. Thus, the phrase *komnzo zokwasi* literally means 'only language' or 'just speech'. It can be imagined as the reply to an outsider's question: "What language do you speak?" with the answer: "We speak only language" or "We say just words."

This naming pattern is pervasive in the area. With the exception of Ránmo, Wartha and Arammba, all varieties of the Tonda subgroup on the Papua New Guinean side of the border derive their name from the word for 'just, only'. These are Anta, Ara, Wára, Wèré, Blafe, Kémä and Kánchá. The map in Figure 1.1 provides a linguistic overview of the Morehead district. Members of the Yam family (Morehead-Maro group) are portrayed in different shades of grey according to their subgroup. We find Komnzo at the eastern edge of the Tonda subgroup.

Figure 1.1: Map of the languages of Southern New Guinea

1.2 Typological overview

1.2.1 Introduction

Komnzo is a Papuan language. The term Papuan is a negative category comprising those languages of the area near New Guinea which are neither Austronesian nor Australian. It was originally introduced by Sidney Ray (1926: 24). The number of distinct language families that have been proposed ranges from ten (Wurm 1975) to 23 (Ross 2005) up to 60 (Foley 1986: 3). Although authors acknowledge the incredible diversity within New Guinea, there have been some attempts at defining grammatical properties which are characteristic for Papuan languages (Foley 1986 and Foley 2000). Komnzo, the languages of the Yam family, and possibly the whole Southern New Guinea area deviate from this Papuan type. Other authors have shown that the languages of New Guinea do not share a set of typological features that set them apart from the languages of the world (Comrie & Cysouw 2012).

In the following sections, I will introduce the typologically most striking features of the language. Detailed information on each topic can be found in later chapters.

1.2.2 Phonology

The Komnzo phoneme inventory consists of eight vowels and 18 consonants. The vowels are the five cardinal vowels [i], [e], [a], [ɔ], [u] plus a low front unrounded vowel [æ] and, two front rounded vowels [y] and [œ], which are unusual for Papan languages.[1] The most frequent vowel is the epenthetic vowel, which is schwa.

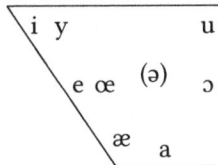

Figure 1.2: Vowels

The consonants follow a set of pairs of voiceless and prenasalised plosives at the alveolar and velar point of articulation: [t], [ⁿd], [k], [ᵑg]. There are labialised velars: [kʷ], [ᵑgʷ]. At the bilabial point of articulation there is only a prenasalised plosive [ᵐb], while its oral counterpart [b] only occurs in loanwords. There are three nasals [m], [n], [ŋ], one trill/tap [r], two semivowels [j], [w] and, again unusual for Papuan languages, three fricatives [ɸ], [ð], [s] and two affricates [ts], [ⁿdz]. It follows that we can identify three main points of articulation: bilabial, alveolar and velar. Further points of articulation include dental [ð], palato-alveolar [ts] and [ⁿdz] as well as palatal [j].

---

[1] Outside of the Yam family front rounded vowels are also found in Awyu-Dumut languages (van Enk & de Vries 1997: 60).

	t	ts		k	kʷ
ᵐb		ⁿd	ⁿdz	ᵑg	ᵑgʷ
m		n		ŋ	
ɸ	ð	s			
		r			
			j		w

Figure 1.3: Consonants

As in other Papuan languages, for example such as Kalam (Blevins & Pawley 2010), many syllables lack phonemically specified vowels. In this case, an epenthetic vowel may be inserted, usually a short central vowel [ə]. Many words lack phonemically specified vowels altogether such as *ymgthkwrmth* [jə̆mə̆ᵑğə̆θkʷə̆rə̆mə̆θ] 'they were feeding him'.

The syllable structure allows for complex onsets of the type CRV, as in *gru* 'shooting star' or *srak* 'boy'. Otherwise onsets are simply CV. Even though vowel-initial words exist, they are always produced with a glottal stop, as in *ane* [ʔane] 'that' or *ebar* [ʔeᵐbar] 'head'. Syllable codas are optional, but they consists of one consonant maximally.

1.2.3 Morphology

Komnzo morphology can be used to easily distinguish nominals from verbs. As in other Yam languages such as Nama (Siegel 2014) and Nen (Evans 2015a), Komnzo verb morphology exhibits a high degree of complexity. Verbal morphology is highly synthetic, while nominal morphology is almost entirely suffixing.

Komnzo nouns are inflected for number if their referent is animate. Otherwise number marking only takes place in the verb. Furthermore, nouns are marked for case by enclitics, which attach to the last element of the noun phrase. Table 1.1 shows the case markers for the inanimate noun *efoth* 'sun, day' and the animate noun *kabe* 'man, people'.

Nominal morphology in Komnzo is comparatively simple. Case marking is shown by enclitics that attach to the rightmost element of a noun phrase, which is usually a head noun as in (1a), but may sometimes be a modifier as in (1b).

(1) a. *kafar kabe=f=nzo*
         big   man=ERG.SG=ONLY
         'only the big man (did sth.)'
     b. *kabe kafar=f=nzo*
         man big=ERG.SG=ONLY
         'only the big man (did sth.)'

In contrast to nominals, verb morphology is highly synthetic. Verbs may index up to two arguments showing agreement in person, number and gender. Verbs encode 18 TAM categories, valency, directionality and deictic status. Complexity lies not only in the number of categories verbs express, but also in the categories are encoded.

Table 1.1: Cases

	inanimate	animate singular	animate non-singular
Absolutive	*efoth=∅*	*kabe=∅*	*kabe=é*
Ergative	*efoth=f*	*kabe=f*	*kabe=é*
Dative	*efoth=n*	*kabe=n*	*kabe=nm*
Possessive	*efoth=ane*	*kabe=ane*	*kabe=aneme*
Locative	*efoth=en*	*kabe=dben*	*kabe=medben*
Allative	*efoth=fo*	*kabe=dbo*	*kabe=medbo*
Ablative	*efoth=fa*	*kabe=dba*	*kabe=medba*
Temporal locative	*efoth=thamen*	n/a	n/a
Temporal purposive	*efoth=thamar*	n/a	n/a
Temporal possessive	*efoth=thamane*	n/a	n/a
Instrumental	*efoth=me*	n/a	n/a
Purposive	*efoth=r*	n/a	n/a
Characteristic	*efoth=ma*	*kabe=anema*	*kabe=anemema*
Proprietive	*efoth=karä*	*kabe=karä*	n/a
Privative	*efoth=mär*	*kabe=mär*	n/a
Associative[a]	*efoth=ä*	*kabe=r*	*kabe=ä*
Similative	*efoth=thatha*	*kabe=thatha*	n/a

[a]The associative forms encode DU versus PL (§7.6).

1.2.4 Distributed exponence

Komnzo verbs exhibit what may be called "distributed exponence". Distributed exponence is characterised by the fact that morphemes are underspecified for a particular
grammatical category. Therefore, morphological material from different sites has to be
taken into account. This phenomenon is different from multiple exponence (e.g. circum-
fixes) in that each morphological site can be manipulated independently. This is shown
in Table 1.2 in the expression of a few selected TAM categories for the verb *thoraksi*
'arrive, appear' in a third singular masculine frame.

Distributed exponence means that we cannot gloss the prefix *y-* for a tense value, because it is used for the inflections of non-past, recent past and past. Furthermore, glossing
the suffix -*m* as a durative is only half of its function as it backshifts tense as well from
non-past to recent past and again from recent past to past tense. In fact, the only morpheme in the example that serves only one function is the past suffix -*a*. As we can see
in the example, exponents of TAM include the verb stem (*thorak* versus *thor*). Indeed,
most Komnzo verbs possess two stems which are sensitive to aspect. Again, the stem
alone is not sufficient to express the aspectual values (imperfective, perfective, iterative,
durative), but it is the combination of stem type, prefix and suffix.

Distributed exponence is best explained with the way Komnzo marks number on verbs.
The four possible values are singular, dual, plural, and large plural. Note that only a small

Table 1.2: Distributed exponence - TAM

non-past imperfective	*y-thorak-wr*
recent-past imperfective	*su-thorak-wr*
recent-past durative	*y-thorak-wr-m*
recent-past perfective	*sa-thor*
past imperfective	*y-thorak-wr-a*
past durative	*su-thorak-wr-m*
past perfective	*sa-thor-a*
iterative	*su-thor*

subset of verbs can form large plurals. The exponents of number are distributed over two morphological slots. There is a binary distinction in the prefix (*y-* vs. *e-*) and the suffix (*-thgr* vs. *-thgn*). The four possible combinations of these exponents encode the four number values. This is shown with the intransitive verb *migsi* 'hang' in a third person frame in Table 1.3.

Table 1.3: Distributed exponence - number

singular	*y-mi-thgr*
dual	*e-mi-thgn*
plural	*e-mi-thgr*
large plural	*y-mi-thgn*

1.2.5 Syntax

Komnzo is a double-marking language. The case marking is organised in an ergative-absolutive system. In addition to three core cases (absolutive, ergative and dative), there are 14 semantic cases. Verbs index up to two arguments. The undergoer argument is indexed by a prefix and the actor argument is indexed by a suffix. One-place predicates split along the lines of stative versus dynamic event types. The latter employ the suffix for indexing, while the former make use of the prefix. Valency changing morphology enables the indexing of a goal, beneficiary or possessor in the prefix. This is shown below with the verbs 'stand', 'return', 'see' and 'give'. I use the term "template" to describe the different inflectional patterns in which verb stems are found.

(2)   a. *fi*   *y-rugr.*
          3.ABS 3SG.MASC-sleep
          'He sleeps.'

b. *fi   ŋabrigwr-th.*
3.ABS return-3PL
'They return.'

c. *nafa   fi   y-mar-th.*
3PL.ERG 3.ABS 3SG.MASC-see-3PL
'They see him.'

d. *nafa   yare   kabe=n   y-a-rithr-th.*
3PL.ERG bag(ABS) man=DAT 3SG.MASC-VC-give-3PL
'They give the man the bag.'

The most frequent word order in Komnzo is SOV, more accurately AUV[2], since there is only weak evidence for a subject category. At the same time, the flagging of noun phrases with case allows for considerable freedom in the word order patterns. Nominal compounds and noun phrases are typically head-final, although modifying elements in the noun phrase, for example adjectives or quantifiers, may occur after the head. Relative clauses follow their head.

Subordinate clauses in Komnzo are usually non-finite employing nominalised verbs with appropriate case markers. Verb chaining and the distinction between medial and final verb forms, which are typical for Papuan languages, are not found in Komnzo. The examples below show a phasal complement (3) and a complement of desire (4).

(3)   *nafa   with   rku-si   the-thkäfa-th.*
3NSG.ERG banana(ABS) knock.down-NMLZ 2|3PL-start-2|3SG
'They started knocking down the bananas.'

(4)   *fi   miyo   yé   nge   fatha-si=r.*
3.ABS desirous 3SG.MASC.be child hold-NMLZ=PURP
'He wants to hold the child.'

In addition to nominalised verbs, clauses can be connected with conjunctions (5), relative pronouns (6) or demonstratives flagged for case (7).

(5)   *fi   z   zebnaf-∅   o komnzo y-rugr?*
3.ABS ALR wake.up-3SG or still   3SG.MASC-sleep
'Did he wake up already or is he still sleeping?'

(6)   *kabe   sa-thor   kayé   mane sf-marwrm-e.*
man(ABS) 3SG.MASC-arrive yesterday which 3SG.MASC-see-1PL
'The man who we saw yesterday arrived.'

(7)   *ŋare   z   ze-far   bäne=ma   nafane kkauna*
woman(ABS) ALR 3SG.FEM-set.off DEM:MED=CHAR 3SG.POSS things
zwa-rithr-th.
3SG.FEM-give-3PL
'The woman has left already, because they gave back her belongings to her.'

---

[2] AUV: actor undergoer verb.

1.3 The Farem people and their language

1.3.1 Location

The area considered in this study is the southwestern corner of the Western Province of Papua New Guinea. This area used to be called "Trans-Fly" in the past, for example in Williams' ethnography of the Keraki people entitled "Papuans of the Trans-Fly" (1936). Mary Ayres rightly criticises this term for its geo-centrism (1983: 1). I use the administrative term "Morehead district" which encompasses the area between the Indonesian border to the west, the Fly River to the north, the boundary of the Yam language family in the east (see Figure 1.1), and the coastline in the south.[3] The area is named after Morehead station, the administrative center, and the Morehead River, which in turn was named after Boyd Dunlop Morehead, the premier of Queensland between 1888 and 1890. I use the term "Southern New Guinea" which encompasses a much wider region roughly from the Digul River in the west to the Fly River in the north and east.

Komnzo is spoken in the village of Rouku, which is located about 7km west of Morehead and about a kilometer north of the Morehead River. It is situated on the road that connects Morehead with Weam in the west. Traditional lands expand about 20km east-west and 25km north-south. There are four clans in Rouku village: *Mrzar Mayawa, Banibani Mayawa, Muthrata Sangara, Wazu Sangara.*[4] Further settlements include Morehead, Gunana, Firra, Kanathr, Ŋazäthe and Masu. Only Morehead and Gunana are settled permanently, while the others are garden places in some years. The map in Figure 1.4 shows Rouku and the surrounding places.

Gunana, the second largest settlement, is situated about 2km west of Rouku along the road. The present-day village was established around 10 years ago. Gunana is situated closer to the Morehead River. The name Rouku, from the Komnzo word *rokuroku* 'riverbank', was given to this place when the first missionaries arrived in the 1950s. Thus, Gunana is the original Rouku, and it is often referred to as Rouku-Gunana. The word *gunana* is a loanword from Motu which means 'old'. Two clans live in Gunana today: *Farem Sangara* and *Nümgar Bagu*. They speak mostly Wára and Anta for reasons which I address in §1.3.11. Morehead station includes the government administration, the aidpost, the primary school and the airstrip. A number of small settlements are built around Morehead station, and these virtually merge into one another. The largest of these is Garaita, a Nama-speaking village. Since Morehead station was built on land belonging to the Mayawa section from Rouku, some families from Rouku have settled in Morehead permanently. One small hamlet of this kind is Fsan. Moreover, some families from Rouku live in Morehead because they are employed in the local administration as teachers or public servants. With respect to clans, this population is mixed. The hamlet Firra

---

[3]The Morehead-Rural census division encompasses the same area, but the eastern border is further to the east including some of the Pahoturi River languages such as Idi.

[4]Mary Ayres avoids using the word 'clan' (1983: 142), instead she draws a distinction between "non-local sections" (*Bagu, Mayawa, Sagara*), which are found throughout the region, and "local-sections" (*Nümgar Bagu, Mrzar Mayawa, Muthrata Sangara*), which are found in one group only, for example the Farem. I will use 'clan' for the latter and 'section' for the former. This is discussed in §1.3.8.

Ŋazäthe

Gunana   Rouku

Masu   Kanathr

Morehead

Firra

1km

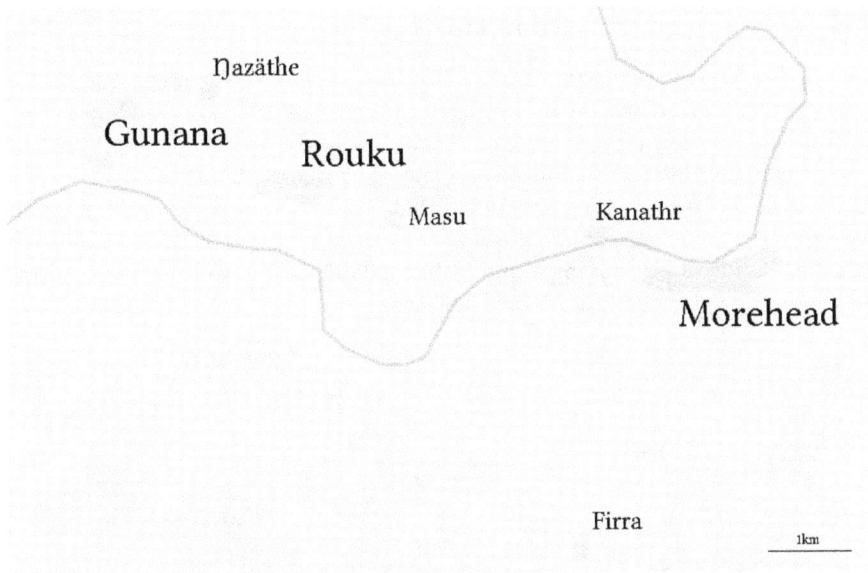

Figure 1.4: Rouku and surrounds

is situated about 7km south of Morehead. Only a few families of the *Banibani Mayawa* clan live there. Most of the people have shifted their residence to Morehead, but keep garden places at Firra. Kanathr is a small hamlet located 2km west of Morehead on the northern side of the river. Kanathr marks the point where the road crosses the river. As there is no bridge, people cross the river by canoe, and cars or motorcycles use a rusty old pontoon. Kanathr serves as a place where children from Rouku and Yokwa, the next village along the road to the west, stay overnight while they attend Morehead primary school. Kanathr was settled in the 1980s, and deserted in the 1990s, and has only been re-established over the last three years. Its population is mixed with respect to clans, but since the land belongs to the two Mayawa sections, they make up the majority.

There are many places around Rouku that used to be settled, but have now been abandoned or are used only as garden places. These include Ytkum, Dmädr, Faremkar, Ŋazäthe, Masu and Akrimogo. Two examples are Ŋazäthe and Masu. The map in Figure 1.4 shows Ŋazäthe, Rouku and Masu. Both used to be settled until about 10 years ago by clans of the *Sagara* and *Mayawa* section respectively. Today both are used as garden places, but they still play an important role as places of origin. Both places are very close to Rouku, about a 15-minute walk. Note that named places are densely clustered in the Morehead district, especially in the vicinity of settlements. More importantly, these places are perceived as being different despite their geographic proximity. This topic is discussed in §11.3.2.

1.3.2 Geography and environment

In its biota, the Morehead district is more similar to northern Australia than to the rest
of New Guinea. We find eucalypts, melaleuca, acacias and banksias combined with wallabies, bandicoots, goannas, taipans and termite mounds. The area consists of lowland
which a Papuan highlander or a European would describe as almost featureless. An early
visitor, Wilfred Norman Beaver, concluded that "there is nothing to induce settlement,
nor would I ever advice anyone to go there." (Murray 1912: 64). Francis Edgar Williams
described the landscape as having a "mild, almost dainty, attractiveness in detail, but [...]
on the whole the extreme of monotony" (1936: 1).

Figure 1.5: Rouku: the area to the right is inundated during wet season

I have measured differences in elevation between 12m and 41m above sea level.[5] However small these differences in elevation, they are significant over the monsoon cycle
with a long dry season (June - November) and an intense wet season (January - May).
Areas very close to settlements or gardens are inundated during the wet season, while
the larger villages are situated on higher ground. In fact, all villages along the road are
built on what is called the "Morehead ridge" (Paijmans et al. 1971: 15), thus keeping houses
and gardens safe from the annual flooding. The photo in Figure 1.5 was taken in Rouku.
During the previous wet season, the paperbark trees to the right were inundated to about
1m, while the bamboo groves on the left stayed dry.

The Morehead ridge is intersected by many small creeks, which carry little or no water
during the dry season. The Morehead River always carries water as it slowly meanders
towards the coast. The Morehead forms a narrow, deep channel whose riverbanks drop
off sharply 2-3m down to the water level. Close to Rouku village, I have measured 40m
width and 15-20m depth during the dry season. The Morehead is a tidal river, which
means that during the dry season, when it has virtually no flow, salt water pushes back
many kilometers upriver. During the wet season, the river overflows and turns the surrounding land into a wide swamp with many inlets and lagoons. See also Hitchcock
(2004: 100) for a description of the ecology of the region. Figure 1.6 shows the Morehead
River during the dry season.

---

[5]This was done with a GPS device: the 12m point was the water-level of the Morehead River close to Rouku;
the 41m point was measured in Rouku village.

Figure 1.6: The Morehead River near Rouku during dry season

There is a remarkable diversity of ecological zones (Paijmans 1970 and Paijmans et al. 1971). For the description of native land use, Ayres distinguishes four landscape types: "big bush", "open bush country", "clear places", and "seasonal swamps" (1983: 5). In what follows, I employ the respective Komnzo terms: (i) *kafar fz* 'big forest', which is a type of monsoon rainforest, (ii) *fz* 'forest', which is a much thinner forest type covered by a grass floor and dotted with red anthills, (iii) *ksi kar* 'bushy place', which is a type of savannah that lacks trees, but is covered with high grass, and (iv) *zra* 'swamp', which is a place entirely inundated during the wet season timbered by paperbark trees and a ground cover of dead leaves. Figures 1.7-1.10 show images of these types in the vicinity of Rouku village. As one would expect, these landscape types differ strongly in the kinds of plants that grow there. The collection of specimens and their identification was greatly facilitated by Kipiro Damas, who visited Rouku in 2011 and 2015.

The Morehead district is rich in wildlife. The main game species are pigs, cassowaries and wallabies. There are many other marsupial species including bandicoots, phalangers (cuscus) and gliders. The Morehead district is also abundant in birdlife. Attested species include birds of paradise, parrots, lorekeets, pidgeons, eagles, hawks, bush fowls, jaberoos, storks and brolgas. Thanks to the help of Chris Healey, who visited Rouku in 2012 and 2013, we were able to match around 100 Komnzo bird names to the corresponding scientific names of these species. The rivers and swamps are rich in fish and amphibious species, for example barramundis, mullets, catfish, eelfish, rainbowfishes, glassfishes, stingrays, river crayfish, prawns, crocodiles, water snakes and turtles. Other reptiles include various goanna species, frogs and snakes. Examples for the latter are the Papuan taipan, the New Guinea death adder, the New Guinea brown snake, the Papuan blacksnake as well as various python types.

Figure 1.7: *Kafar fz*: road cut through the monsoon rainforest

Figure 1.8: *Fz*: thin forest

Figure 1.9: *Ksi kar*: small patch of savannah

Figure 1.10: *Zra*: seasonal swamp during dry season

1.3.3 Agriculture and subsistence

The Farem people are agriculturalists. Their main crops are round and long yams, bananas, sweet potatoes, cassava, taro, coconut, sago, breadfruit and sugar cane. Additionally, there are many fruits and nuts available during the dry season. Although the Farem are skilled in hunting, trapping and fishing, they rely on their garden products. In this section, I will focus on their staple food: yam.

Figure 1.11: Yam garden two months after planting

Without a doubt yams are the most important crop for the Farem, and the role of this bland tasting tuber can hardly be overstated. Williams concludes his chapter on food production by stating that "the social significance of food among these people derives largely from the pride which individuals and groups feel in having plenty of it." (1936: 235). Large quantities of yams are exchanged at feasts, and sizeable tubers are often given as personal gifts. During the celebration of Independence Day in Morehead, there is a competition where individuals measure and weigh their biggest yams. On many occasions, people have shown off the content of their yam houses to me, and during harvest time some of my friends have peeked through the wall of other's yam house to examine the yield and compare it to their own, which would often become the talk of the day. In short, yams indicate a person's wealth and social status.

Yam cultivation involves hard labour. The cultivation cycle can be divided into three phases: (i) preparing and planting, (ii) tending, and (iii) harvesting. The preparations begin by clearing the land (between August and October). Good, well-drained soil is found on the high ground; either virgin forest or a piece of land that has lain fallow for some years. The gardener has to cut the overgrowth and clear the grass. Large trees are usually only ring-barked and one would wait for the tree to die and eventually to fall. The cleared area has to be burned. Depending on the quality of the soil, one may bring grass from elsewhere and burn it as fertiliser. The ground has to be ploughed thoroughly, and small roots and weeds are pulled out. Next, the garden plot has to be enclosed by a fence to keep out wallabies, deer and wild pigs. The most important material for fences is bamboo which is grown in small bamboo groves. During preparation, people are busy in their gardens every day. Planting may start as early as October, but it can last until January. Yams for planting are selected carefully, but the tiny yam suckers are usually planted in heaps in an old garden plot. Figure 1.11 shows a yam garden about two months after planting. Between January and June, there are many small jobs to be done. These include weeding or erecting and replacing yamsticks on which the vines climb up. The change of the season in June is also signalled by the changing colour of the yam leaves. Around this time, the harvest season begins, and it may stretch until August, when the cycle begins again. Harvested yams are counted, sorted and stored in yam houses. This involves shaving the shoots off each tuber; a time-consuming task that is usually done in the afternoon hours while sitting in conversation in front of the yam house. Because garden plots are subdivided into rows, one for each member of the family, the yams are sorted accordingly in the yam house. Figure 1.12 shows the inside of a yam house after the harvest.

Figure 1.12: Inside a yamhouse

There are many special customs around yam cultivation. Some men possess yam planting magic which helps them to compete with others. This usually involves particular spells and magic stones passed down from the father's generation. Others "steal the soil" from their competitors. Knowledge of this kind is usually kept secret and never admitted in public. Furthermore, there are a number of rules about handling yams, which everyone follows. One example is the belief in "female pollution", which is widespread in Southern New Guinea (Knauft 1993: 104). During a woman's monthly period, but also after having sexual intercourse, it is strictly forbidden to go to the garden plot for it will "spoil" the yams. This rule applies not only to the woman, but to anyone who sleeps in the same house, sometimes even the neighbouring house.

Yams play the most important role in exchange feasts. For example, an exchange marriage is consummated through a feast, sometimes called "pig dance". The two men who have exchanged sisters henceforth *fäms* 'exchange fellow', will raise a pig and invite their respective *fäms* and his associates for a dance. The host side will feed the guests, and in return the guests will entertain the hosts by singing and dancing through the night. The next day, the hosts will give the guests large quantities of yam tubers to take back to their village. The amount has to be recorded with great detail, because after a year has passed, the roles will be reversed. Nothing would be more embarrassing than falling short in the repayment. Often two villages have particularly strong marriage links. In the past this has led to competitive yam cultivation between the two groups.

Yams also play a role in the regulation of conduct. I have been told about a ritual called *mefa*. The culprit, usually someone who has treated his wife badly, is confronted by his *fäms* and other brothers of his wife (*ngom*). They will then put lime on the culprit's forehead and then strike him over the head with a small yam tuber. This is, however painful, only an immediate punishment. The bigger punishment comes in the form of a gift. The culprit is given a large quantity of yams, and it is expected that he repays the same amount and quality the next year. An individual can never achieve this, and thus the culprit is forced to ask people in and maybe even beyond his clan for help. If he fails to repay the expected amount, he will lose all respect and social status. Disputes about an individual's gardening abilities may become violent. The only time I had to witness a violent outbreak by one of my brothers, who is a calm and peaceful person, was when his aunt insulted him by accusing him of "being lazy" and a "bad gardener". After a tirade of insults, this was the last straw. In conclusion, it is difficult to find any aspect of life in which yam cultivation does not play some role.

1.3.3.1 Yam counting

For many of the customs described above, it is important to record the exact quantity of tubers. For the counting ritual a special base-six numeral system is used, which is unique to the Yam languages. This senary system has received some attention in the literature (Donohue 2008, Hammarström 2009 and Evans 2009). Williams was the first to describe the counting procedure, but he points out that it "is apparently a more or less recent fashion among the Keraki, having been imported from beyond the Morehead" (1936: 225). This area includes the Farem territory. In the following section, I describe the procedure as I have witnessed it many times in Rouku and surrounds.[6]

The counting procedure involves two men who move the yam tubers from a prepared pile. They take up three yams each, move a few meters and deposit them together in a new pile. One of the two is the designated counter and he shouts out *näbi näbi näbi*

---

[6] I have published two videos of the counting procedure. The interested reader can view them at the following URLs: https://zenodo.org/record/1404789 and https://zenodo.org/record/1208073

Figure 1.13: Ritual yam counting (left); counting tally *tiftif* (right)

'one one one'. This means that they have moved the first unit of six. Without pause they take up again three yams each and move them over, while the counter shouts out *yda yda yda* 'two two two'. Now two lots of six or 12 tubers have been counted. Again they pick up three yams each shouting *ytho ytho ytho* 'three three three'. The two men continue with this process until they reach *nibo* 'six'. Now 36 yams have been counted and the bystanders and observers cheer in agreement. This amount corresponds to one *fta* or 6^2. Each *fta* is marked by putting a single yam on the side of the new pile. The two men continue until all yams have been counted, and the little pile on the side which indicates the amount of *fta* slowly grows. Next, this pile is counted in the same fashion, only that each counting yam, that is put to the side, now markes one *taruba*, which corresponds to 216 or 6^3. One may continue in the same fashion. Six *taruba* make up one *damno* corresponds to the amount 1,296 or 6^4. For example, one *damno* is amount of yams that a man should store in order to bring his family through the year. Six *damno* make up one *wärämäkä* corresponding to 7,776 or 6^5. Finally, six *wärämäkä* make up one *wi* corresponding to 44,656 or 6^6. I should add that nobody in Rouku remembered the last time this number was actually reached. The recursive counting procedure gives rise to the senary system. I describe the numeral system in §3.1.6.2.

Figure 1.13 shows two men during the counting the procedure. The counting is always a public event accompanied by the loud, monotonous beat of a drum. I was told that neighbouring villages or travellers should be made aware of the ongoing counting procedure. In order to record and keep the amount for later proof, the Farem produce a counting tally made from a coconut frond. This is shown on the right side of Figure 1.13. The stalks indicate the number of different senary values, which are separated by small notches. The red arrows in the image point to the two notches. Figure 1.13 was taken during a yam counting ritual in Morehead in September 2010. The amount counted was 3 *damno*, 2 *taruba*, 3 *fta* or 4,428 tubers in total. This was the contribution of several clans to a pig dance that took place two weeks afterwards in Garaita. The counting had to be repeated two times because older men who observed the procedure closely said that mistakes had been made.

The largest amount of yams that I have seen was in the village of Yokwa in September 2013. Following the death of an older man, his relatives decided to built a *sirä mnz*, a communal yamhouse.[7] All the relatives of the deceased man, including my brother from Rouku, stored several *fta* up to one *taruba* of yams inside this house. The content was to be shared and exchanged during a feast in honour of the deceased at the height of the rainy season. Mary Ayres describes this practice in her chapter on mourning customs (1983: 289). The yamhouse in Yokwa can be seen in Figure 1.14. It measured 2,50m wide, 1,60m high and an astonishing 60m long. The floor was separated into compartments of equal size where each contributor stored his share. For some of the contributors there was a display shelf (*sirä*) for very large yams. I did not witness the whole counting procedure as it took more than a day, but I estimate that the *sirä mnz* held more than 10,000 yams.

Figure 1.14: Communal yamhouse in Yokwa: inside (left) / outside (right)

1.3.4 Demography and vitality

It proves difficult to determine the exact number of Komnzo speakers. I give a rough estimate here of about 150 to 250. For the most part, this inexactness is caused by particular

---

[7]Mary Ayres uses the word *kwitenz* for this, but my informants from Rouku and Yokwa did not know the word. They suggested *sirä mnz* 'sirä house'. The word *sirä* refers to the shelves that are found in these yam houses to hold especially large tubers.

social factors. For example, the system of exchange marriage fosters a high degree of multilingualism. A Farem child typically grows up speaking at least the varieties of her father and mother. Since the system of residence is virilocal only the father's language is Komnzo. Of course there are two sides to this, and there are many speakers of Komnzo in other villages, namely women who have married out and their children. What complicates matters further in the case of Rouku is that not all Farem men speak Komnzo as their daily language, and not all families have a Komnzo-speaking parent. I provide an explanation for this in §1.3.5.2. Furthermore, there is a small group of speakers who have moved further away to Daru, Kiunga, Port Moresby or other parts of Papua New Guinea.

Komnzo is vital in the sense that the language is being transmitted to children. At the same time, Komnzo is an endangered language because of its small number of speakers and its relatively low prestige compared to the lingua franca, which is English. Komnzo is not taught in the school system; there is no writing tradition, and it is not used in administration. For these reasons, it should be regarded as an endangered language from an academic point of view.

Komnzo speakers perceive their language to be under threat from what they call "mother's language". Mary Ayres notes that there are strong marriage links between particular villages because it is desirable for a daughter to marry back to her mother's village (1983: 226). In the case of Rouku, there are strong links to Yokwa, and what is meant by "mother's language" is almost always Wára. One line of reasoning about the perceived threat is that women from Yokwa fail to pass Komnzo on to their children. It should be noted that women are expected to switch their speech variety when they move to their husband's village. In reality this hardly ever occurs, because there are enough women from Yokwa to form small exclaves of Wára speakers. Moreover, all Komnzo speakers are fluent in Wára. Hence, there is little pressure on a woman to actually change her speech variety. This is different with women who come from more distant places. I discuss the topic of multilingualism and language ideology in §1.3.11.

1.3.5 History

1.3.5.1 Pre-contact history

Until the rise of the sea level during the Late Pleistocene, the island of New Guinea and the Australian continent were joined in a single landmass called Sahul (White & O'Connell 1982). Recent studies have highlighted that there is still a lack of research from the Southern New Guinea region (Pawley et al. 2005, Ballard 2010, and Evans 2012a). The geomorphological past of this lowland region has been turbulent over the last 20,000 years. A chronology of the changing coastlines is given by Chappell (2005).[8] Figure 1.15 shows the northern coastline of Sahul at the Last Glacial Maximum at 21,000 BP. Figure

---

[8]His methodology is as follows: "the procedure for reconstructing the coastlines at a given epoch is to compute the relative sea level field for a given region [...] by combining the ice-equivalent sea level with the regional departures that arise from the isostatic and gravitational factors. The results are then superimposed on the present topography in detail..." (2005: 529).

1.16 shows the coastline at 8,000 BP shortly after the sea breached the Torres Strait, thus disconnecting New Guinea and Australia. The thin black line shows the present coastline.

Figure 1.15: Coastline at 21,000 BP; adopted from (Chappell 2005: 527)

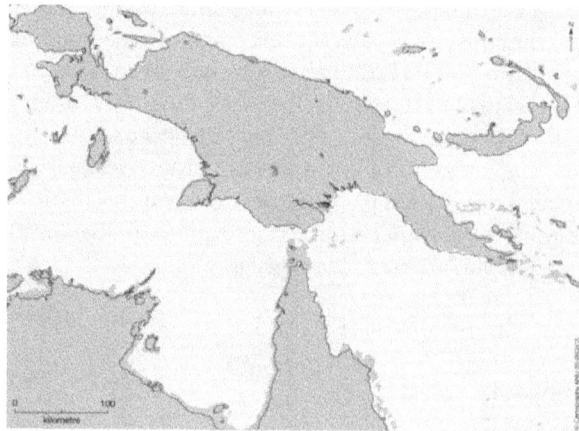

Figure 1.16: Coastline at 8,000 BP; adopted from (Chappell 2005: 528)

We can see from the figures that the separation of Sahul occurred only shortly before 8,000 BP. Keeping in mind that human presence on the Sahul continent goes back to at least 40,000 BP (Golson 2005), we can safely assume that what was later to become the Southern New Guinea region was already settled well before the separation. Chappell shows that large parts of the Fly-Digul platform, to which the Morehead ridge belongs, was submerged at the maximum height of the sea level at 6,000 BP. Figure 1.17 shows that this has affected the western part of the Southern New Guinea region.[9] This part of

---

[9]With regard to Figure 1.17, which is the result of a computer model, Chappell argues for a more conservative

the region was slowly rebuilt by the sediments carried by the Fly River and Digul River. Note that the Morehead ridge as one of the highest points of elevation on the Fly-Digul platform was not submerged during this period.

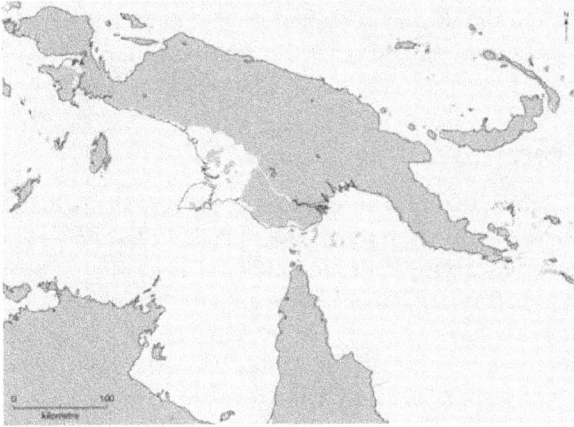

Figure 1.17: Coastline at 6,000 BP; adopted from (Chappell 2005: 528)

The geological scenario outlined by Chappell is reflected to some extent in the linguistic landscape of the region. For example, concerning the Trans-New-Guinea languages spoken in the west of the Fly-Digul platform, Pawley points out that the "homogeneity of the Asmat-Kamoro group is clear evidence that their expansion was comparatively recent" (2005: 10). Usher and Suter (2015) have recently shown evidence for the existence of the Anim language family which stretches from Ipiko in the east to Marind and Yaqayic in the west, thus encircling the area under investigation in this study. Evans argues that it is "unlikely that all language differences currently found in Southern New Guinea developed in situ. What seems more likely is that they represent the interaction of a number of unrelated groups entering the region from different regions" (2012a: 111). While this is evident for some of the linguistic units, for example the Trans-New-Guinea languages, we do not know how other linguistic units, for example the Yam languages or the Pahoturi River languages, fit into the chronology of events. I suggest that we should accept the possibility that the Yam languages represent a much older population, and – as Evans rightly point outs – we can only speculate from where this population entered the region.

Some suggestions come from recorded mythology, namely the myth of two brothers and the origin of people at a place called *Kwafar*. This myth was recorded by Williams (1936: 306) as well as Ayres (1983: 50). I have recorded a version of this myth told in Komnzo, which is given in the Appendix 11.3.4. What is noteworthy about the story is that the place *Kwafar* is located off the coast in an area that was last exposed well before 8,000 BP. According to this story, there was a flood, and one of the brothers escaped

---

estimate, in which the coastline at 6,000 BP does not extend all the way up to the Fly River (2005: 531).

northward. Eventually, he picked up the branches of *dödö* 'Melaleuca sp', beat the water with it, and the flood came to a halt. The myth suggests that the people retreated northwards from the rising sea level, i.e. the myth "reports" events which date back at least 8,000 years. Although I am not claiming linguistic continuity from the time of the sea level rise to present-day Komnzo – after all we know that populations may change languages – one cannot deny the fact that this myth is found in the area where the Yam languages are spoken, more precisely the languages of the Tonda subgroup.[10]

1.3.5.2 Modern history

The Southern New Guinea region was contacted relatively late, which led Knauft to claim that it has "remained effectively outside the purview of state political economies for longer than any other major non-arctic coastal population" (1993: 26). In 1890, Sir William MacGregor, the Administrator of Papua, discovered the Morehead River on an expedition. It took another six years for a second visit by MacGregor during which he collected a vocabulary list, which can be found in the Annual Reports (MacGregor 1890: 106).[11] Both expeditions travelled by ship. The first known white man to walk through the region was William Dammköhler in 1898 on an adventurous escape from Marind headhunters (Hitchcock 2009). Until 1921, sporadic patrols were conducted by A. P. Lyons, Resident Magistrate of the Western Division. Lyons recorded native customs, but his journals held at the National Cultural Council at Port Moresby were inaccessible to me. In 1926, F. E. Williams started to pay regular visits to the Morehead district in his role as "official government anthropologist". Until 1932, he visited the area almost every year, and his fieldwork culminated in the book Papuans of the Trans-Fly (Williams 1936), which is still the most comprehensive ethnographic description of a group in the Morehead district.

At the time of contact, Southern New Guinea was home to groups of very different sizes and political organisation. On the one end of the spectrum, there were small groups like the Farem, probably with no more than 100 people at that time. On the other end, we find large groups like the Kiwai (9,700), Marind (7,000) and Suki (3,500). Note that these three groups surround the area concerned with in this study. Although headhunting was practised by all groups, it was only those larger groups which could muster war parties and attack places far away from their home territory. This was especially true of the Marind (also known as Tugeri or Tugere). In his introduction to Williams' book, AC Haddon, who had led the British expedition in the Torres Strait in 1888, writes that he had "heard lurid stories about these head-hunting, cannibal marauders" (1936: xxiiv). The Marind were militaristic expansionists, who went on headhunting expeditions raiding villages along the south coast as far as Boigu Island. Since the Marind's home territory was in Dutch New Guinea, the British colonial administration was unable to act against them. The Marind's activity led to a joint Dutch-British expedition, which established the

---

[10]Both Williams and Ayres recorded these myths with speakers of Tonda languages. Among the origin myths of the Morehead district, this particular myth is only found in Tonda-speaking territory.

[11]Based on the verb forms in the list, I identify the variety as either Kánchá or Kémä. Nominalised verbs in these two varieties end in a bilabial fricative, and many verbs in the list have a final grapheme <p>. In Komnzo, Wára, Anta and Wèré nominalised verbs end in a vowel: [i] or [e].

border at the mouth of the Bensbach River. Eventually, in 1902, the Dutch administration set up a police post in Merauke.

The impact of the Marind is somewhat inconclusive. For example, Mary Ayres argues that their immediate role has been overstated by many Europeans who visited the area in this early period (1983: 19). She points to two confusing inferences that had been made. The first was the erroneous belief that a great number of settlement names given to MacGregor and various patrol officers must also mean that the population of the Morehead district must be very large. As I will explain below, the traditional settlement pattern was to live in small hamlets often comprising a single patriline. Secondly, the fact that the population density was actually very low was attributed to massive depopulation by the Marind. An example comes from MacGregor who describes that he met a group of people on the Morehead River: "Of this tribe we saw altogether about thirty to forty men, boys and women. They are probably the remains of a tribe that has been decimated by the Tugere" (1896: 74). Ayres criticises that MacGregor and others jump to conclusions here. The low population density in the Morehead district, especially along the coast west of the Wassi Kussa River, can be explained by geographical factors alone. She notes that "the accute scarcity of fresh water during the dry season was not readily observed" (1983: 22), because early visits always occurred during the rainy season, which is the best time to navigate the coast. Ayres concludes that there is no definite evidence for or against depopulation by the Marind. Nonetheless, if we consider the discrepancies in group sizes in Southern New Guinea over a longer period, it is easy to imagine that these larger groups would have assimilated the smaller ones sooner or later. Evans concludes that "we may not be exaggerating to say that without the arrival of colonial governments (and missionary endeavours eliminating headhunting and overt warfare) many of the small languages of the Trans-Fly may not have survived in the way they have." (2012a: 117).

In the remainder of this section, I will focus more on the local level. In 1951, the administration established a government station at Rouku. The name Rouku comes from Komnzo *rokuroku* 'riverbank'. This name was given to a place a few kilometers to the west of present-day Rouku, where a group of Farem people had lived in the 1920s (Ayres 1983: 14). This older Rouku is now settled again by Farem people who call it Gunana – a Motu word meaning 'old' – and sometimes it is called Rouku Gunana 'old Rouku'. The government station included a school, which was run by the London Missionary Society. Its successor, the United Church, is still the most influential denomination in the area west of Morehead, including Rouku. During the 1950s, the Australian Petroleum Company explored the Morehead district for oil. Many older Farem still remember their parents being employed as labourers with the company. A more tangible legacy of the company's operation is a network of roads in the Morehead district, although these have often reverted back to narrow tracks. In 1959, the station was moved to Morehead, where an airstrip was constructed. In the early 1960s, a government school was opened there, which is still operational to this day. Since that time, Morehead has been the administrative centre of the district.

Large bureaucracies like nation-states tend to organise their population by dividing and subdividing them into organisational units. The nation-state Papua New Guinea consists of 22 provinces, which consist of districts, which in turn consist of local level government areas, which are divided into wards. Rouku belongs to Ward 16 of the Morehead-Rural local level government area of the South Fly District of Western Province. Such organisational schemes are useful, but they fail to adapt to cultural peculiarities, an issue which seems of particular importance in a country as diverse as Papua New Guinea. During the 1950s and 1960s, the government began a policy of village consolidation. Small hamlets and related villages were asked to form combined larger villages. The concurrent establishment of churches, schools and roads provided some incentives for this policy to show some effect. I agree with Ayres when she writes that this "is antithetical to traditional settlement patterns of widely scattered very small villages where residence is not continuous" (1983: 17). It is no surprise that people returned to their traditional settlement patterns during the 1970s when the government patrols ceased. Thus, on a very local level we find a pulsating movement from dispersion to consolidation and back to dispersion. Ayres supports this observation by pointing out that – although Rouku was consolidated as "one village" during the 1950s – the Farem people lived scattered over several hamlets when she did fieldwork in 1980. The official census for Rouku in 1980 was 108, but only 30 people lived at Rouku then (1983: 17). The others lived at Ŋazäthe, Faremkar, Kafthéfr, Masu, Firra, Kanathr and Morehead.

30 years later, I can add my own observations to this. When I first visited Rouku in 2010, my main informant Abia Bai told me that he had lived in Kanathr in the 1980s and later at Masu together with his Mayawa clan (*Mrzar Mayawa*). In the mid-1990s, this clan moved from Masu to Rouku, thus Masu and Kanathr were not settled in 2010. Two Sagara clans (*Muthrata Sagara* and *Wazu Sagara*) had lived in Rouku more or less continuously with short intervals at Ŋazäthe and Faremkar. In 2010, the Bagu clan (*Nümgar Bagu*) was transitioning to Gunana from a place called Dmädr, about 5km northwest of Rouku. Gunana itself was established around the year 2000 by the third Sagara clan (*Farem Sagara*). Lastly, the second Mayawa clan (*Banibani Mayawa*) was split between one patriline living in Rouku and another patriline living in Morehead. The latter had moved to Morehead from Firra during the late 1990s. Hence, we could say that in 2010 the Farem people were "consolidated" in the two settlements of Rouku and Gunana. Over the last five years, some of the Mayawa people have established a new settlement at Kanathr. What started out with two families in 2012, has now grown to about four families which belong to both Mayawa and Sagara. Other people have built houses in Masu and Ŋazäthe. Yet others have moved to Morehead. The point I am trying to make is that settlement is not continuous and an individual may choose to move several times during his lifetime. During the annual cycle, movement is even more pronounced as one may stay for several weeks at a garden place during the planting and harvesting time, or at a sago, fishing or hunting camp. As a consequence, I would often arrive in Rouku wondering where all the people had gone.

An interesting epiphenomenon to oscillation between fragmentation and consolidation is that it did not always follow linguistic or cultural lines. For example, the closest village to Rouku is Yokwa (also called Safs) situated about 12km west along the road. During the first consolidation in the 1950s, people from the south who spoke Kánchá and Ara consolidated with the Wára speakers of Yokwa. Naturally, this may lead to problems in the documentation of a particular speech variety. While it is easy to find Kánchá speakers for comparison further to the south in other villages, Wára and Ara speakers are only found in Yokwa. I should add that I have not had the opportunity to study this in detail in Yokwa.

For the linguistic history of Rouku, this meant that some men of the father generation of the Bagu clan as well as two of the Sagara clans had shifted to Yokwa and lived there for almost a decade. Nowadays, their children live in Rouku and Gunana, and despite being bilingual in Komnzo and Wára they speak mostly Wára. This is not only a problem for the documenter, but it results in real political problems. As I point out in §1.3.11, the linguistic ideology in the Morehead district connects identity with land and language. Consequently, there is a strong feeling that one should speak the variety that in some sense belongs to the land. In other words, a Farem individual should speak Komnzo. It follows that for some individuals village consolidation has led to a disconnect between the daily language and the language of social identity.

1.3.6 Mythology and the origin of people

Ayres (1983: 146) uses the term "starting-place" to describe the place from which the apical ancestor of each group has spread. I will label these "origin places" henceforth. There are multiple origin places because there were multiple splitting events. The notion of spreading from a prior unity is pervasive in the Morehead district, and Ayres offers a spatial analysis of the foundational myths in her thesis.

Initially, all people lived at a mythical origin place called *Kwafar*. This place is said to be somewhere in the Arafura sea. There are several origin myths connected to *Kwafar*. In one version all people lived in a huge tree. They spread out after the tree burned down. In another version people lived inside a tree and the ancestor released them one after the other by chopping down the tree. Common to the different narratives is a movement of people – sometimes represented as a single character – from *Kwafar* towards the north. Some people went to *Zwäri* and some to *Komo*, both are located on the coast. From these places, some groups came directly towards the north, while others went to *Kuramogo*, a place close to Bebdbn in the east (Williams 1936: 292). The apical ancestor of the Mayawa section in Rouku was a man called *Mathkwi*. He came from *Komo* and wandered north. He was accompanied by the ancestor of the Sangara section of the village Mifne. After various stops, *Mathkwi* arrived at *Faremkar*, where he found the ancestor of the Sagara section of Rouku, who had settled there already. From *Faremkar*, he went to *Masu*, a few kilometers to the east. The ancestor of the Sagara section in Rouku also came from *Komo*, but he travelled to *Kuramogo* first and then came to *Faremkar*. Thus, people who claim one origin place need not trace their ancestry to the same person. It is sufficient to jointly identify with the most recent in a series of origin places. In this sense, all Komnzo speakers associate themselves with *Faremkar*.

Specific episodes in these narratives provide explanations of various natural phenomena. For example, the Morehead River and the web of smaller creeks are connected to the burning of the tree at *Kwafar*. In some versions, the burning roots of the tree formed canals, while other versions tell that the tree fell towards the north, and its trunk and branches shaped the Morehead River and the creeks. Likewise, the occurrence of red, coarse-grained sedimentary rock in certain spots is connected to the ancestor's path and his dropping of leftovers along the way. The existence of all crops is explained in a similar fashion.

In addition to these founding myths, there are many smaller stories, which make reference to a particular place. An example is a small rock layer along the Morehead River close to Morehead. This is explained by a story in which two 'story men' were fighting. After their quarrel, they agreed to cut down a stone passage across the river. Such places of mythological significance are called *menz kar* 'story places'. The word *menz* can refer to some mythological event as well as to some supernatural being that lives at and guards these places. In its latter meaning, I translate *menz* as 'story man'. Again, I refer the reader to Mary Ayres' excellent description and analysis of locality in the Morehead District (Ayres 1983).

1.3.7 Social organisation

Mary Ayres draws a distinction between the first and second order of segmentation of people (1983: 126). The first order of segmentation is one which aligns people with a specific origin place and, as I mentioned earlier, with a specific speech variety. Hence, all Komnzo speakers share the origin place *Faremkar* and, thus belong to the same group. The second order of segmentation are local groups. Ayres divides these groups into non-local and local sections. She avoids the word "clan" (1983: 142). There are three non-local sections, namely Bagu, Sagara and Mayawa, which are replicated in many villages in the Morehead District. I will refer to these simply as "sections".[12] Local sections, on the other hand, can be seen as local subsets of the three sections. I will use the term "clan" for these. For example, there is one Bagu clan, three Sagara clans and two Mayawa clans among the Farem. These have proper names, for example *Mrzar Mayawa* or *Farem Sagara*.[13] Finally, there are patrilines within the clans. An overview of the segmentation of the Farem is given in Table 1.4.

In addition to self-attribution, there is a web of more or less visible markers that distinguish a member of one group from that of another group regardless at which level. Markers include certain designs printed on grass skirts, particular patterns carved on arrows, special songs and dance styles. Furthermore, there are totemic animals which one may not hunt or eat. For example, the Brahminy Kite (*banibani*) is a totemic bird for the *Mrzar Mayawa* clan and the *Banibani Mayawa* clan. The latter derives its name from

---

[12]They are different from the terms "section" or "skingroup" as it is used in Aboriginal ethnographic descriptions.

[13]Note that I spell section names in upright font (e.g. Mayawa), because they are in some sense a hypernym, while I spell clan names in italic (e.g. *Mrzar Mayawa*). Another reason is that sections names are found in languages other than Komnzo, while clan names are proper nouns found only in Komnzo.

Table 1.4: Sections, clans and patrilines

section	clan name	gloss	number of patrilines
Bagu	*nümgar*	'crocodile'	1
Sagara	*farem*	place name	2
Sagara	*wazu*	place name	2
Sagara	*muthrata*	place name	1
Mayawa	*banibani*	'Brahminy Kite'	2
Mayawa	*mrzar*	proper name	1

it. Likewise, the Swamp Eel (*dobakwr*) is a totem for both Mayawa clans, but also for the three Sagara clans. It follows that some of these markers overlap between different clans. The web of similarities and differences is commonly employed in reasoning about group identity.

The most important fact about clans and sections lies in land ownership. While the land ownership within the same section is less important, it plays a big role between sections. For example, a man will not hunt, make a garden or collect building materials on territory that does not belong to his section. In this case, he will consult the rightful owners first. Land boundaries are often marked by creeks or other landmarks, and they are very much public knowledge. Finally, the system of segmentation plays an important role in exogamy, which I will address in the next section.

1.3.8 Exogamy

Within the Morehead district, a system of symmetrical sister-exchange is practised. This has been described by Mary Ayres for the Farem and surrounding groups (1983) and by Francis Edgar Williams for the Keraki (1936). Ayres' work is most relevant for the following description. Note that the following description reflects an ideal to which people generally aspire, even though it is at odds with reality in many instances.

The system of exogamy is shaped by the segmentation of people described above, and all levels of segmentation form exogamous groups. Thus, people who share an origin place may not intermarry. We may call this "place exogamy". An interesting fact about place exogamy is that it practically results in linguistic exogamy. Ayres notes that "Marriage between people who claim prior unity at a 'starting place' [CD: origin place], i.e. the dialect group, is prohibited. In the native model this rule is sometimes explained as a rule of dialect exogamy: "We should not intermarry because we talk the same language" is a phrase sometimes stated by informants" (1983: 186). The three sections also form exogamous groups. It follows that one may not marry a person of the same section, even if that person is from another place. We may call this "section exogamy". Lastly, the clan forms an exogamous group, and one may not marry a person from the same clan. We may call this "clan exogamy". As pointed out by Ayres, the rules of exogamy are an ideal. In her description, Ayres finds many attested marriages which violate place or section exogamy. I can confirm this from my own observations. Ayres concludes that place exogamy is ranked higher than section exogamy, i.e. there used to be more cases of same-section marriages than of same-place marriages. In my own data, these violations of rules of exogamy occur with the same frequency. There are no cases of same-clan or same-patriline marriages.

The ideal marriage is one of direct sister-exchange. In other words, two men of different place, section and clan exchange their respective sisters. The preferred option is to exchange a true sister, that is a woman of the same age in the clan or patriline. In many cases, this is not possible for demographic reasons, and there are indeed some unmarried older men. An alternative option is to "borrow a sister" from another group, preferably one's own section in another place, but this is not a precondition. One would not ask another group for a wife, but for a woman to exchange. This shows that it is the actual exchange which counts. The exchange initiates a link to another group of people and to another place, and this is corroborated by mutual invitations to feasts and the giving and taking of yam tubers. The least preferred, but often practised, option is to pay for a wife with a raised pig and a certain amount of yams. However, this payment does not cover the cost of a person. The exchange is only deferred to the next generation. In such a one-sided marriage, the man is expected to give his first daughter back to the family of his wife. The daughter is not given back as a wife, but to be exchanged to yet another group. In the past, neither husband nor wife had much of a say in this arrangement between clans. Women were often sent as young girls to the family of their future husbands (Williams 1936: 145). Polygamy used to be practised in the past, but it is virtually absent today. There is one man in Rouku, who is married to two wives, and this invites much laughter and gossip.

1.3.9 Kinship terminology

Although I have not much too add to Ayres' formidable analysis of kinship, I disagree with her on a few specific terms. Below, I use only Komnzo terms in the kinship diagrams, but I point out when there are coexisting terms from another language. The knowledge about one's relatives has been described by Ayres as "extremely shallow" (1983: 217) and I much agree with her. The mythological time of the first ancestor is often placed immediately before the generation of one's grandparents. Contact with the western world, biblical traditions and especially the education system has brought a change to this world view. Younger speakers often point out a few names along the patriline up to the apical ancestor.

The system of kinship terminology in Komnzo is a five generational system, which calculates from ego to the generation of grandparents and grandchildren, respectively. Interestingly, grandparents and grandchildren are equated by using the same kin term, *aki* or *zath*, reciprocally. Otherwise the system is characterised by special kin terms which are used only after the consummation of a sister exchange. It follows that kin terms can and often do change as result of affinal relations.

Figure 1.18 shows the consanguineal kin terms. The shaded individuals live in a different village. The asterisk indicates that the respective term is used reciprocally. Many kin terms can be used for co-residents of a different section or clan. A result of place exogamy is that all Farem men or women of the generation above ego can be called *ŋafe* 'father' or *ŋame* 'mother', and all coresidents in the same generation can use the appropriate sibling term. The terms for mother and father co-exist with the Nama loanwords *afa* and *ama*. An optional age distinction for the brothers of ego's father and their wives is *ŋafe katan* 'small father' and *ŋame katan* 'small mother'. Sibling terms only encode relative age, not sex: *nane* 'older sibling' and *ngth* 'younger sibling'. Children are referred to by *nge* 'child'. Mother's sisters are commonly called *ŋame* 'mother'. Mother's brothers are called *ŋäwi* '(maternal) uncle'. The word *babai* coexists with *ŋäwi*, but its origin is unclear. Both are used reciprocally. The relation between ego and mother's brother used to be of special importance for certain initiation ceremonies.

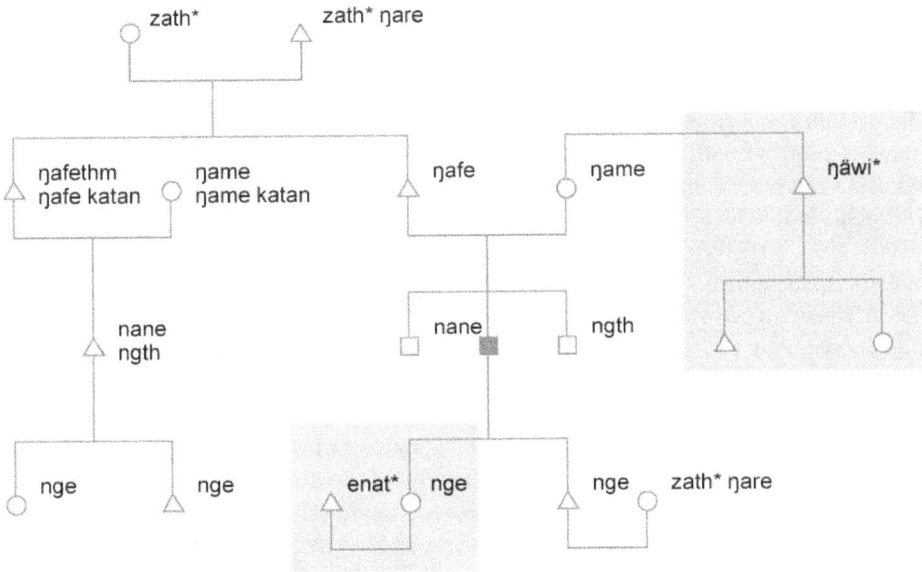

Figure 1.18: Consanguineal or co-resident kin terms

The spouses of ego's children are called *enat* 'son in-law' and *zath ŋare* 'daughter in-law'. Both words are used reciprocally, i.e. they mean 'parents-in-law' from the opposite perspective. The sex of the referent can be specified by adding *ŋare*. Ayres points out that grandparents and grandchildren are equated by the same word *zath*, which also means 'moon' and 'month', and as we have just seen 'daughter in-law'. However, *zath* is somewhat archaic, and the Nama loan *aki* with the same set of meanings is used in its place. Ayres explains this grouping of three meanings – grandparents, grandchildren and daughter in-law – by a "structural incompleteness that is felt to be generated by the original exchange" (1983: 226). She points out that the preferred arrangement for the daughter of an exchanged woman is to marry back to her mother's place. She concludes that the grouping of the three meanings in the same kin term encodes a cultural practise which "assures the continuity of a man's patriline not simply through his own children, but through their children" (1983: 227).

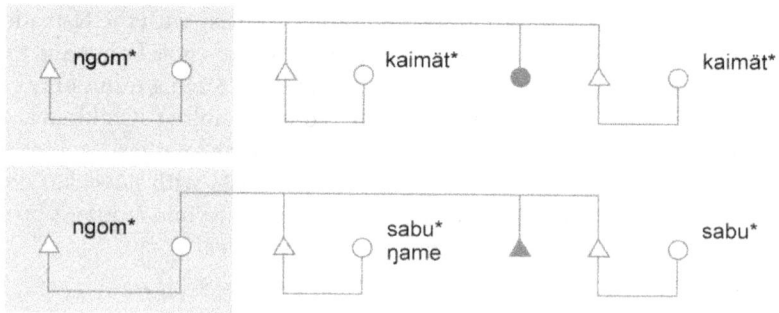

Figure 1.19: Same-generation, affinal kin terms for female and male ego

Figure 1.19 shows the affinal kin terms in the same generation. The word *ngom* 'brother-in-law' is used by both women and men, and for men it is used reciprocally. In (Ayres 1983: 214), the words *ntjufaré* and *nakimi* [her spelling] appear in a kinship diagram for 'brother-in-law'. The former is a Kánchá word and the latter is from Motu (Turner-Lister & Clark 1935: 107). While *nakimi* coexists with *ngom*, *ntjufare* is not used by Komnzo speakers. I suspect that this word was given to Ayres by Wára speaking women from Yokwa. There are strong marriage ties between Rouku and Yokwa, and the process of village consolidation (§1.3.5.2) has led to an influx of Kánchá speakers in Yokwa in the past. The term *kaimät* is used between a woman and her brother's wife, and both are in a joking relationship. The term *sabu* is used between a man and his brother's wife, and both are in a taboo relationship. The taboo is much stricter for the wife of the younger brother, who is always called *sabu*. As for the wife of the older brother, one may also use *ŋame* 'mother' if she is sufficiently older, and the taboo relation is somewhat lax.

After a consummated exchange marriage, a special set of terms is used. These are shown in Figure 1.20. The word *fäms* 'exchange fellow' is used between the two men who have exchanged sisters, and the exchanged woman is called *fäms ŋare* 'exchange woman'. The children of the exchange couple are called *fäŋame* or *fäŋafe* depending on their sex. These two words are archaic in Komnzo and instead *bäiŋame* or *bäiŋafe* are used. The last vowel of both is sometimes dropped resulting in *bäiŋam* or *bäiŋaf*. These words are used reciprocally, but the last part (*-ŋaf* and *-ŋam*) encodes the sex of the referent. It is unclear when and how the first part changed from *fä*- to *bäi*-, but the consonants /ɸ/ and /ᵐb/ stand in a paragidmatic relationship, because there is no voiceless counterpart of the prenasalised /ᵐb/. For this reason, I suspect that the first part is a contraction of *fäms*, and *fäŋame* or *fäŋafe* used to be *fäms ŋame* 'exchange mother' and *fäms ŋafe* 'exchange father'. Note that the same figure can be drawn for a female ego. We would only have to change the words for wife and husband, which are *fzenz* and *fis* respectively.

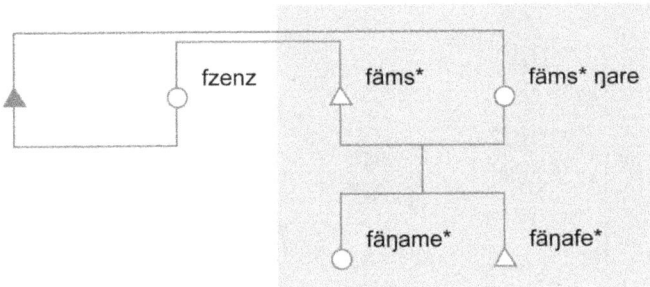

Figure 1.20: Sister-exchange kin terms: *fäms*

An exchange marriage also affects the children's generation. Ayres points out that cross-cousins are preferred marriage partners (1983: 217), but this excludes the children of an exchange. Cross-cousins from an exchange marriage refer to each other with the term *yamit*. The relationship between them is more like that between siblings, which is corroborated by the fact that ego employs the same kin term *ngom* for the husband of the *yamit*. The wife of ego's *yamit* is called *yumad*. This is shown in Figure 1.21.

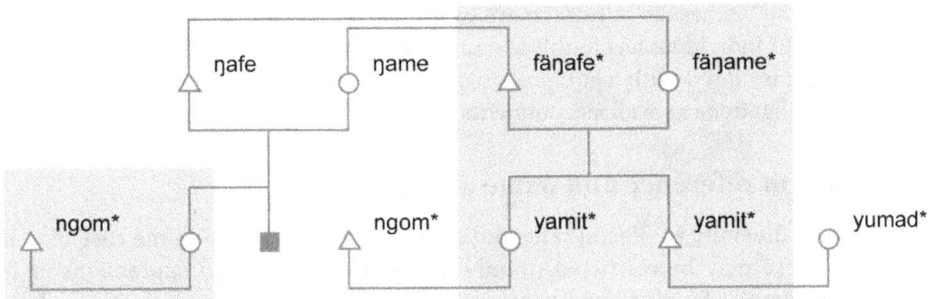

Figure 1.21: Sister-exchange kin terms: *yamit*

There is another special relation that holds between the affines and children of two sisters. Two men who are married to sisters refer to each other with the term *nakum*. The parallel-cousins in such an arrangement refer to each other as *naku*, and what holds for the *yamit* relation is also true for the *naku* relation. This is shown in Figure 1.22.

The rules and regulations are often explained in terms of space and Mary Ayres focusses on this aspect in her thesis. For example, informants would often explain that two individuals cannot marry because "they come from the same place", meaning that their mothers come from the same place in the case of a *naku* relationship. But it can also mean that they result from a direct exchange between places in the case of a *yamit* relationship.

There are other terms which function similarly to kin terms. One such example is the word *ngath*, which I translate as 'mate'. Two children who were born around the same time are considered to be like close relatives, even if they belong to different clans and/or

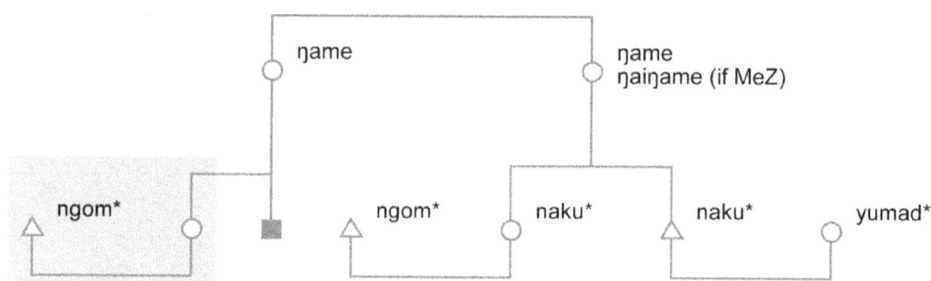

Figure 1.22: The *naku* relationship

sections. They will grow up as close mates and they will support each other. It is up to the parents to decide who will become *ngath*, but it is always children of the same sex. I know of two cases where the *ngath* relationship was inherited from the fathers who were also *ngath* to each other. Another example is the word *ngemäku*, which is used between the biological parents of a child and the ones who have adopted the child. Adoption is very common and it occurs shortly after the weaning period. The word *ngemäku* contains the word *nge* 'child', but the second part *mäku* has no meaning by itself. A third example is the word *nzäthe* 'namesake'. Children are given many names when they are born. As a consequence an individual has multiple namesake relationships.

This section is closed with a comprehensive list of kin terms in Table 1.5. Alternative terms and applications as well as comments are given in the rightmost column.

1.3.10 Person reference and name avoidance

There is some diversity in person referring expressions in Komnzo. In the case of name avoidance, these may be restricted to only a subset. The common expressions ar full names (given name + family name), personal names, nicknames, kin terms, other relation terms, reference via circumspection, and the recognitional demonstrative.

The kinship system as presented above lays out a number of rules of behaviour. Among them is a practise of name avoidance which holds between all affines. When recording genealogies, informants would often hestitate or refuse to utter the name of a particular person and instead ask some bystander or a child to pronounce the personal name for me. Name avoidance is seen as a way of showing respect. This was explained to me by my sister while transcribing a text in which she used the personal name of her sister-in-law. When I asked her, why she had not used the appropriate kin term *kaimät*, she replied that she was very angry with her at the time and showed her anger by using the personal name. Name avoidance impacts on the reference to other persons with the same personal name, to whom the speaker may not be in a name-avoidance relationship. In other words, name avoidance is independent of the referent in a particular situation. Instead name avoidance targets the personal name. This does not result in any practical problems because people have multiple names.

Table 1.5: Summary of kin terms and other relation terms

Komnzo	gloss	relation[a]	comment
ŋafe	father	F, FB	also *afa* (Nama loan)
ŋame	mother	M, MZ, FBW	also *ama* (Nama loan)
nane	brother, sister	eB, eZ	FBS and FBD (if older)
ngth	brother, sister	yB, yZ	FBS and FBD (if younger)
zath	grandparent, grandchild, parent-in-law, daughter in-law	FF, FM, MF, MM, SS, SD, DS, DD, HF, HM, SW, BSW, SSW	also *aki* (Nama loan), used reciprocally (rcpl.), can be specified for sex by adding *ŋare*
kaimät	sister-in-law	BW, HZ	female perspective, used rcpl.
sabu	sister-in-law	BW, HB	male perspective, used rcpl.
ngom	brother-in-law[b]	ZH, WB	also for husbands of cross-cousins[b], i.e. *yamit's* husband, used rcpl.
yumad	n/a	n/a	wife of parallel-cousin[b] (*yamit's* wife), used rcpl.
enat	parent-in-law son in-law	DS, WF, WM	used rcpl.
ŋäwi	uncle, niece, nephew	MB, ZS, ZD	also *babai*, used rcpl.
fäms	exchange[b]	ZH, BW	can be specified for sex by adding *ŋare*, used rcpl.
fäŋame	aunt, niece[b]	FZ, BD	also *bäiŋam*, used rcpl.
fäŋafe	uncle, nephew[b]	MB, ZS	also *bäiŋaf*, used rcpl.
yamit	cross-cousin[b]	MBS, MBD, FZS, FZD	used rcpl.
naku	parallel-cousin	MZS, MZD	used rcpl.
nakum	n/a	WZH	used rcpl.
thuft	in-law	n/a	also *nakimi* (Motu loan), used rcpl.
ngath	mate	n/a	between two (predetermined) mates of the same sex, used rcpl.
ngemäku	n/a	n/a	between true parent and adopted parent, used rcpl.
nzäthe	namesake	n/a	between two people with the same name, used rcpl.

[a]F=father, M=mother, B=brother, Z=sister, S=son, D=daughter, H=husband, W=wife

[b]only after a consummated sister exchange marriage

There are different solutions to ensure that the hearer understands who is meant. In addition to the appropriate kin term, one may use circumspection or a recognitional demonstrative. For example, the name of one of my brothers in-law is *Kurai*. I should not utter his name, but use the kin term *ngom* instead. In many situations, this term is sufficient to establish the correct reference. Alternatively, I can use circumspection strategy like *tokoafis* 'Toko's husband' or a teknonym *weweaŋafe* 'Wewe's father'. For teknonyms, it is usually the name of first-born child that is used, regardless of sex. A third solution is to use the recognitional demonstrative. The recognitional demonstrative can be roughly translated into English as 'the one that we both know about' (§3.1.12.6).

The different strategies of person reference can be ranked according to how much knowledge is presupposed on the part of the hearer. For example, a personal name requires very little contextual knowledge, whereas a recognitional demonstrative requires much more. We may rank these strategies like this: full name (*Kurai Tawth*) > personal name (*Kurai*) > circumspection/teknonym (*tokoafis* 'Toko's husband') > kin term (*ngom* 'brother-in-law') > recognitional (*baf* 'that one'). Note that using a full name is a recent adaptation to western culture, which is only employed in the context of a census or other administrative matters. It is a common practise in PNG to use the name of the father as family name. Hence, *Kurai's* father was *Tawth* and therefore his full name is *Kurai Tawth*. In daily interaction, this strategy is absent.

A person has a multitude of personal names or nicknames. Almost everyone has a set of five to ten names and the frequency of use of any one of these may come and go like a fashion. Shortly after birth, or sometimes even before birth, different relatives will propose names for the new-born. These may be their own names, which establishes a namesake relationship. In fact, the word *nzäthe* 'namesake' is the most frequent term of address. There is a special ceremony a couple of months after birth, where the name-giver presents gifts to his namesake and holds the baby for the first time. Names may also be created on the spot, as nicknames or as self-attributions. For example, the three elders of the *Mrzar Mayawa* clan in Rouku are *Marua*, *Kaumb* and *Abia*. Their respective nicknames are *oroman loŋ* 'old man long' because he prefers wearing long trousers, *afa kwanz* 'father bald head' because he is bald and *afa thwä* 'father catfish' because he has a big belly. The first of them, *Marua*, decided one day that he should be called *oroman zulai* 'old man July'. To my bewilderment, I found that everyone had accepted this name within a few weeks. Interestingly, a namesake relationship may transfer all of these names to the namesake. For example, a small baby boy was given the name *Marua*, thus establishing a namesake relationship. Today, the toddler is sometimes called *Marua*, *loŋ* or *zulai*.

1.3.11 Language ideology and multilingualism

Language ideology is characterised by a set of beliefs on the part of speakers about the role which language plays in constructing their social world (Silverstein 1979, Rumsey 1990 and Makihara & Schieffelin 2007). In the Morehead Region, people draw a strong connection between land and speech variety. This native linguistic ideology is similar to Aboriginal cultures, especially in Arnhem Land (Merlan 1981) and Cape York (Sutton 1978). As for the Farem people, this ideology surfaces through open statements and explanations, the expected behaviour of in-marrying women, ancestor stories, but it is also entailed in metaphors. I will briefly note some of my own observations on language ideology here.

In Rouku, there is strong social pressure on all members of the community to speak Komnzo. This is openly expressed during public speeches, but also by individuals in conversation or during interviews. One often hears that women should not talk in "their language" to the children, but in Komnzo. In practice, this is often violated and virtually everybody grows up in a multilingual context. We can take an example which is the result of the process of village consolidation described in §1.3.5.2. A number of older men originally from Rouku have stayed for a long time in Anta or Wára-speaking villages, and consequently their children grew up with those varieties as their main language. The children, now in their late 1940s, have moved back to Rouku. Some of them have married a woman from their natal villages and hence the dominant language of some Farem households is Anta or Wára. However, when I administered a socio-linguistic questionaire, they would deny speaking anything but Komnzo.

In an attempt to understand the situation, I conducted sociolinguistic interviews with about 40 people. Some of the questions targeted language ideology ("What is your language?", "What do think about language mixing in the village?", "What language do you want your children to learn?"). The conclusion from these interviews is that language and land form an inseparable bond. I defer the statistical analysis of the interviews to another point in time. The bond between language and land is identical to the bond between a group of people and their origin place. This bond is transmitted through the father's line. An example taken from the interviews is that of an older woman who lives in Rouku. She explained to me that she grew up in Yokwa, and consequently she speaks Wára most of the time. Although she speaks mostly Wára, she knows that this is not the language of the place. She wishes for her children to speak Komnzo. When asked about her language she answered Kánchá instead of Wára. She explained that her father had moved as a teenager from a Kánchá-speaking village to Yokwa. It follows that regardless of whether an individual uses predominantly mother's language or the language of the village, he or she will identify with the language of his or her father's place.

Mixing or shifting languages, although very common, is almost universally looked down upon. The answers as to why this behaviour is thought of as inappropriate often follow along the lines of matching language to place ("They should not speak Wára here because this is the language of Yokwa", "We should not mix languages because the children will not be able to name the places and animals that belong to our land").

Women who marry in are expected to shift to the local language, but this is often not followed because there are enough women from any one village to form small exclaves, for example of Wára-speaking women in Komnzo-speaking territory. It is hard to corroborate, but informants say this was enforced more in the past. For example, there are spells and rituals to enhance the language learning process on the side of the woman. One ritual involves splitting a thin bamboo behind a woman's head and whispering a spell. This procedure is said to facilitate the learning process. I asked many times to have this procedure performed on me, but people refused to do it because I would forget my native German. There are other customs and rules which connect land and language. For example, it is forbidden to talk another language at story places and men would introduce their new bride to a *menz* 'story man' at a particular place in order to avoid sickness. The policy of language shift expected from women is hardly ever enforced these days and one might wonder whether it ever was. Ayres (1983: 226) describes the preference for a daughter to marry back into her mother's village, which she calls a short marriage cycle. This pattern establishes strong ties between particular villages. In the case of the Rouku it is the village of Yokwa and the language is Wára. As mentioned above, groups of women from Yokwa would often speak Wára between themselves or to their children and there is no reason why this should have been different in the past. But when asked about this, they would look down on 'language mixing' and stress the importance of the correct language at the right place.

Ancestor stories almost always involve comments on language. For example, the Kuramonggo myth which is found across the Morehead Region involves an ancestor who heard voices coming from a tree. Different versions are found in (Williams 1936: 299) and (Ayres 1983: 102). In the myth, the ancestor starts to chop the tree into segments from the top to the bottom. With each little bit that he chopped, people speaking different languages came out and started running towards their respective places. The further he worked his way to the bottom of the tree, the more intelligible the words became to him. When he reached the base of the tree, he heard his own language and thus his own people emerged from the tree. A common metaphor that explains the language situation from a local perspective builds on this story. One often hears the local language being described as *zfth* 'base of a tree' and all the surrounding languages as *tuti* 'branches'. The tree metaphor is important in the local perspective. For example, women are jokingly described as *bidr* 'flying foxes' because they fly from tree to tree, and sometimes they are described as *fätü* 'a wild yam' or *saka* 'mustard vine' because the vines of these plants grow on trees.

1.4 Komnzo within the Yam languages

This section situates Komnzo within the Yam languages. This language family was formerly referred to as the "Morehead and Upper Maro Rivers languages", or "Morehead-Maro languages" (Wurm 1971). This name is misleading because its geographical boundary in the east, the Morehead River, excludes all the languages of the Nambu subgroup. I follow Evans in using the more precise term "Yam languages" (2012a: 124). Not only are yams the staple food, and of high cultural importance in exchange feasts, they also gave rise to the senary numeral system, which is unique to the languages of the family. In addition to the English word yam [jæm], there is a lexemes *yam* [jam] in many of the Yam languages, which carries high cultural significance. For example, in Komnzo it means 'footprint, custom, tradition' and in Nen it means 'law, tradition, culture'.

The Yam languages comprise three subgroups: Nambu in the east, Tonda in the west, and Yei, which has only a single member. A first attempt to reconstruct various aspects of the proto language can be found in (Evans et al. 2017). While it is relatively easy to place Komnzo in the Tonda subgroup, it is much harder to classify the units within Tonda; in other words to draw a boundary between language and dialect. Are Komnzo, Anta and Wèrè dialects of Wára as Ethnologue[14] portrays it or are they languages in their own right? Peter Mühlhäusler (2006) points out the difficulty and futility in answering such questions in Papua New Guinea and the contradictions that different researchers have produced in the past. As the preceding description of language ideology has highlighted, these are considered to be different languages from a local perspective. I remain agnostic throughout this section and offer a short conclusion at the end.

I discuss sound correspondences and sound changes first. Next, I show some lexico-statistic data from (Wurm 1971) and (Clifton et al. 1991). Last, I discuss case markers, pronouns and verb morphology. I include here the following Tonda varieties: Komnzo, Anta, Wára, Wèrè, Ránmo, Blafe, Wartha Thuntai and Kánchá. I refer the reader to Figure 1.1 for an overview of where these varieties are spoken. I do not include Arammba, which I take to be sufficiently different to be considered a separate language (Boevé & Boevé 2003). I have no data for the Tonda varieties spoken on the Indonesian side of the border (Baedi, Ngkolmpu, Smerky, Bakari, Taemer and Sota), and only very little data on Kémä.

With the exception of Komnzo, the spelling of the names of these varieties is adopted from Ethnologue, which in turn goes back to an orthography workshop held by SIL missionaries in Morehead in 2000. Note that the orthographies were developed for each variety with the result that the graphemes in the language names have different phonetic values: Komnzo [kĕmⁿdʒo], Anta [aⁿda], Wára [wæra], Wèrè [wĕrɛ], Ránmo [rænmo], Blafe [ᵐblæɸe], Wartha Thuntai [warða ðuⁿdã͡ɪ], Kánchá [kɔⁿdza]. To ensure comparability in this section, I will employ IPA for all language examples, including Komnzo.

1.4.1 Phonology

First, I will turn to phonological correspondences. In this section, the languages in the tables have been sorted geographically: west (left) to east (right). We find that only Blafe and Ránmo have an /l/ phoneme in their respective inventories. Table 1.6 shows that this phoneme corresponds to an interdental fricative in Komnzo, Anta, Wára, Wèrè, Wartha Thuntai and Kánchá. Note that final devoicing produces [θ] in coda position.

A second set shows the correspondence of bilabial stops, [ᵐb] and [b], in Blafe, Ránmo and Wartha Thuntai to lavio-velar stops, [ᵑgʷ] and [kʷ], in Komnzo, Anta, Wára, Wèrè and Kánchá in Table 1.7. We find that the labial part is sometimes realised as a rounded back vowel, [ᵑgo] and [ko], in Kánchá, Wèrè and Wartha Thuntai, for example in lines 3 ('butterfly') and 4 ('crow'). One possible explanation is a process of develarisation that has occurred in Blafe, Ránmo and Wartha Thuntai.

There is a small set of words in which the bilabial fricative corresponds to a pre-nasalised bilabial stop. The set in Table 1.8 once again groups Blafe, Ránmo and Wartha Thuntai against Komnzo, Anta, Wára, Wèrè and Kánchá. Interestingly, the form of the 2SG.ABS 'you' groups Blafe, Ránmo, Wartha Thuntai, Kánchá and Komnzo together.

---

[14]http://www.ethnologue.com/language/tci

Table 1.6: Correspondence set: [l] versus [ð]

item	Blafe, Ránmo	Wartha	Kánchá	Wèré	Anta	Komnzo, Wára
1 tongue	læmin	ðæmin	ðæmin	ðæmin	ðæmin	ðæmin
2 faeces	wəl	wəθ	wəθ	wəθ	wəθ	wəθ
3 wet	kilkil	kiθkiθ	tʃiθtʃiθ	tiθtiθ	tiθtiθ	tʃiθtʃiθ
4 armpit	ŋgəlki	ŋgəθki	kəθtʃi	ŋgəθki	ŋgəθtʃi	ŋgəθtʃi

Table 1.7: Correspondence set: [ᵐb/b] versus [ᵑgʷ/kʷ]

item	Blafe, Ránmo	Wartha	Kánchá	Wèré	Komnzo, Wára, Anta
1 nest	ᵐbəl	ᵐbəθ	ᵑgʷəθ	ᵑgʷəθ	ᵑgʷəθ
2 mosquito	ᵐbæ	ᵐbæ	ᵑgʷæ	ᵑgʷæ	ᵑgʷæ
3 butterfly	taᵐbam	taᵐburam	ᵐbæᵑgoram		ᵐbæᵑgʷərəm
4 crow	ᵐbaθ	kot	koθ	koθ	kʷaθ
5 light	praja	bæjan	kʷajan	kʷajan	kʷajan
6 sick	bik	bik	kʷik	kʷik	kʷik

Table 1.8: Correspondence set: [ᵐb] versus [ɸ]

item	Blafe, Ránmo	Wartha	Kánchá, Komnzo	Wára, Anta, Wèré
1 wife	ᵐbəᵑgeⁿt	ᵐbəᵑgeⁿts	ɸətʃeⁿts	ɸətʃeⁿts
2 husband	ᵐbi	ᵐbi	ɸis	ɸis
3 2SG.ABS 'you'	ᵐbæ	ᵐbæ	ᵐbæ	ɸe

A clear directional change is palatalisation before front vowels. In Table 1.9, I show only a subset of the varieties. Komnzo represents those in which palatalisation has oc-cured. This also holds true for Anta and Wára, but the forms are slightly different. Wartha Thuntai represents those in which palatalisation has not occured. This is also the case for Blafe and Ránmo. The table shows that Wèré and Kánchá are somewhat irregular. In lines 4 and 5 ('house' and 'one') palatalisation occurs in Wèré, but not in Kánchá. Line 6 ('armpit') shows the opposite. In lines 1-3 ('woman', 'I', 'people') palatalisation has oc-cured in both and in line 7 ('tree') in neither. I have included Nama, a Nambu language, to show that Nambu languages have preserved the original velar quality, for example in lines 1, 3, and 4 ('woman', 'people', 'house'). Note that in line 5 ('one'), Nambu has dropped the first consonant. The deletion of initial velar nasals is a regular change in

Nambu languages; for example, 'mother' is [ŋame] in Komnzo, but [ama] in Nama and Nen. Note that the conditioning context for palatalisation has been lost in line 4 ('house'), because the examples end in a consonant. Nama attests a vowel in this position.

Table 1.9: Palatalisation before front vowels

item	Wartha	Kánchá	Wèré	Komnzo	Nama
1 woman[a]	ᵐbroki	ᵐbrotʃi	ᵐbrasi	ᵐbratʃi	ᵐbrake
2 1SG.ABS	ᵑga	ⁿdʒæ	se	ⁿdʒæ	(jəⁿd)
3 people[b]	ᵑgɣⁿtəm	tʃœⁿtəm	sœⁿtmæ	tʃœⁿtmæ	ᵑgɣⁿtmæ
4 house	meⁿk	məⁿk	məⁿts	məⁿts	mæᵑgo
5 1 (one)	ŋæᵐbi	ŋæᵐbi	næᵐbi	næᵐbi	æᵐbiro
6 armpit	ᵑgəθki	kəθtʃi	ᵑgəθki	ᵑgəθtʃi	-
7 tree species	ᵑgœⁿt	ᵑgœⁿt	ᵑgoⁿt	ⁿdʒœⁿts	-

[a]a woman in the time after giving birth
[b]people who live to the west of one's own group

The last set shows the correspondence between stops and affricates. In Table 1.10, Blafe, Ránmo, Wèré and Anta are grouped against Komnzo, Wára, Wartha Thuntai and Kánchá.

Table 1.10: Correspondence set: stop versus affricate

item	Blafe, Ránmo	Wartha	Kánchá	Wèré	Anta	Komnzo, Wára
1 pain	ti	ⁿdʒi	tʃi	ti	ti	tʃi
2 right	tawe	tsowe	tsowe	tawe	tawe	tsawe
3 bowerbird	ⁿdojar	ⁿdʒojar	ⁿdʒojar	ⁿdʒojar	ⁿdojar	ⁿdʒœjar

Concluding the comparison of phonological correspondences, we find that Komnzo and Wára are almost always grouped together, and we may include Anta as well. Kánchá and Wèré share a number of correspondences with Komnzo, Wára and Anta, but they differ in some sets. Blafe, Ránmo and Wartha Thuntai are different in almost all sets. While Blafe and Ránmo are always grouped together, Wartha Thuntai can be grouped with the other varieties in some sets.

1.4.2 Lexicon

In this section, I will present data from (Wurm 1971) and (Clifton et al. 1991). I defer the statistical analysis of my own wordlists to a latter point in time.

A first calculation of cognate rates was offered by Wurm. His dataset comprised Tonda and Nambu languages as well as and Yei and Marori. In Table 1.11 only the Tonda varieties have been extracted. Wurm's language labels refer to different Tonda varieties: Upper Morehead (Komnzo, Wára, Anta, Arammba), Lower Morehead (Kánchá), Tonda (Blafe, Ránmo, Wartha Thuntai, Wèré) and Kanum (Baedi, Ngkolmpu, Smerky, Bakari, Taemer, Sota).

Table 1.11: Cognate rates (adopted from Wurm 1971: 159)

Upper Mhd			
71%	Lower Mhd		
60%	55%	Tonda	
39%	39%	40%	Kanum

A more fine-grained dataset comes from a SIL survey conducted by Clifton, Dyall and O'Rear (1991), who collected wordlists in 18 villages of both Tonda and Nambu languages. In Table 1.12, I will only show the Tonda varieties, but I exclude Arammba, Rema and Kémä, and I choose Bondobol as the village representative of Kánchá. Moreover, I have rearranged their data in order to present the varieties geographically from west to east.

Table 1.12: Rates of shared vocabulary (extracted from Clifton et al. 1991)

Blafe							
80%	Ránmo						
63%	59%	Wartha					
32%	40%	52%	Kánchá				
49%	55%	55%	59%	Wèré			
43%	51%	50%	70%	84%	Wára		
44%	51%	50%	61%	72%	82%	Anta	
41%	49%	46%	70%	72%	87%	88%	Komnzo

My own wordlists confirm the data in Table 1.12. We can draw some conclusions: (i) Blafe and Ránmo can be grouped together, (ii) Wartha Thuntai is different from all other varieties, (iii) Komnzo, Wára and Anta can be grouped together, (iv) Wèré and Kánchá, though different from each other, are close to Komnzo, Wára and Anta. If we compare these statements to the map in Figure 1.1, we find that the rates of shared vocabulary between Komnzo, Wára, Anta, Wèré and Kánchá roughly reflect geography. As for Blafe/Ránmo and Wartha Thuntai, this cannot be said. In other words, if we try to understand the relation of these varieties as a dialect chain, we would have to make two cuts. The first cut splits off Blafe and Ránmo. The second cut singles out Wartha Thuntai, while the remaining varieties belong to a single dialect chain.

1.4.3 Morpho-syntax

As an intermediate summary, we can conclude that Komnzo, Anta, Wára, Wèré and Kánchá are somewhat closer together as opposed to Blafe, Ránmo and Wartha Thuntai. Therefore, I will focus on the first group in this section.

Table 1.13 shows a comparison of case markers. We find that Komnzo deviates from the other varieties in the ergative singular and non-singular, and in the allative. Kánchá deviates from the others in the ablative and the locative for consonant-final words.

Table 1.13: Comparison of case markers

	Kánchá	Wèré	Wára	Anta	Komnzo
ERG.SG	-o	-o	-o	-o	-ɸ
ERG.NSG	-oi	-ai	-əɪ	-əɪ	-jə
ALL	-ɸ	-ɸ	-ɸ	-ɸ	-ɸo
ABL	-ɸo	-ɸa	-ɸa	-ɸa	-ɸa
LOC V_	-n	-n	-n	-n	-n
LOC C_	-i	-en	-en	-en	-en

Table 1.14 shows a comparison of free pronouns. We find that Komnzo and Kánchá share a number of forms or some element of a form. For example the first consonant of the first and second person in both absolutive and ergative case. In the possessive non-singular pronouns, only Komnzo and Kánchá attest a separate element which signals non-singular -*me* in addition to the vowel change found in all varieties. However, the first consonant of the third person ergative and possessive pronouns differs only in Kánchá.

As the last topic in this section, I will briefly address the marking of dual number. As in most Yam languages, dual number is marked on the verb. The affix encodes dual versus non-dual number, and its value has to be integrated with information from other morphological sites to yield the three number values singular, dual and plural. I address this topic in §5.3.2 and §5.5.3. For now, it is sufficient to compare the site of dual marking on the verb. In some varieties this depends on the type of verb stem which is employed. Most verbs have two stems which are sensitive to aspect. While multiple verb stems are attested in all Tonda varieties, the encoding of duality differs. In Komnzo, Anta, Wára and Kánchá, there are two options: duality is encoded in a suffix if the 'extended stem' is used, but in a prefix if the 'restricted stem' is used. The meaning of these labels in Komnzo is explained in §5.3. Only in Wèré, duality is always encoded in a suffix regardless of the type of stem. Blafe, Ránmo and Wartha Thuntai have lost dual marking on both stem types. In these three varieties, dual marking occurs only in high frequency verbs such as the copula or the verb 'walk', where it is usually suppletive. I sketch out a tentative historical explanation of this in §5.3.4.

1.4.4 Summary

In conclusion, we may say that the different levels of comparision converge. Sound correspondences, lexicostatistics are well as morphological differences single out at least three separate units: Blafe/Ránmo, Wartha Thuntai and a chain of dialects, which we may call 'Eastern Tonda'. The latter comprises Wèré, Wára, Kánchá, Anta, Komnzo and

Table 1.14: Comparison of free pronouns

		Kánchá	Wèré	Wára	Anta	Komnzo
ABS	1SG	^{n}dʒæ	se	tʃe	tʃe	^{n}dʒæ
	1NSG	ni	ni	ni	ni	ni
	2	^{m}bæ	ɸe	ɸe	ɸø	^{m}bæ
	3	ɸi	ɸi	ɸi	ɸi	ɸi
ERG	1SG	^{n}dʒən	sən	tsən	tsən	^{n}dʒe
	1NSG	nin	ni	ni	ni	ni
	2SG	^{m}bən	ɸən	ɸən	ɸən	^{m}be
	2NSG	^{m}bən	ɸe	ɸən	ɸən	^{m}bənə
	3SG	tʃaɸ	naɸo	naɸo	naɸo	naɸ
	3NSG	tʃaɸ	naɸ	naɸ	naɸ	naɸa
POSS	1SG	^{n}dzuni	^{n}done	^{n}dzone	^{n}done	^{n}dzon
	1NSG	^{n}dʒenme	^{n}dane	^{n}dzane	^{n}dane	^{n}dʒenme
	2SG	^{m}buni	^{m}bone	^{m}bone	^{m}bone	^{m}bone
	2NSG	^{m}benme	^{m}bane	^{m}bane	^{m}bane	^{m}benme
	3SG	tʃaɸani	naɸəne	naɸəne	naɸəne	naɸane
	3NSG	tʃaɸanme	naɸane	naɸane	naɸane	naɸanme

probably Kémä. Eastern Tonda shows characteristics which are typical of dialect chains: geographically distant varieties, for example Komnzo and Wèré or Anta and Kánchá, show the biggest differences. Close neighbours, on the other hand, like Komnzo and Wára or Anta and Wèré are very similar. That being said, I will remain cautious until more data has been gathered, and I will continue to refer to all of them as varieties. In this way, I pay respect to the native linguistic ideology which picks up on the slightest differences as being highly emblematic markers of socio-linguistic identity.

1.5 Previous work and methodology

1.5.1 Previous work

There has been no previous research on Komnzo that goes beyond the collection of wordlists. One example is the SIL survey discussed in the preceding section (Clifton et al. 1991). The activity of SIL missionaries in the area has led to a number of orthography worksheets, unpublished manuscripts, surveys or theses. Examples of work on the surrounding varieties include a grammatical sketch of Arammba (Boevé & Boevé 2003), a thesis on Wára verb morphology (Sarsa 2001) and a socio-linguistic survey of the Tonda subgroup (Grummit & Masters 2012).[15]

---

[15]I wrote a review of the survey, which can be found under the following URL: https://zenodo.org/record/1404752

The ethnographic perspective is much better covered in the case of Komnzo. Mary Ayres conducted research in Rouku around 1980, which culminated in her thesis on locality and exogamous group definition (Ayres 1983). While she states that she did acquire Komnzo during her time in the field, she did record a number of stories in Komnzo and other Yam languages. On top of that she provides a valuable description and analysis of specific terms and concepts. The ethnography of the Keraki people, the speakers of Nambu, written by Williams remains the most comprehensive description of any culture in Southern New Guinea (Williams 1936).

There has been a renewed academic interest in the region in recent years, and the present study is part of this. Nick Evans has gathered a team of scholars who work on various languages of the wider region, but also on different Yam languages. Matthew Caroll has written a PhD thesis on Ngkolmpu, a related language of the Tonda subgroup, with a special focus on distributed exponence (Carroll 2017). Bruno Olsson has published a descriptive PhD grammar of Marind (Olsson 2017). Jeff Siegel has published on the morphology of tense and aspect in Nama (Siegel 2014), the eastern neighbour of Komnzo. Wayan Arka has written on tense and agreement in Marori, an endangered isolate spoken on the Indonesian side of the border (Arka 2012). Nick Evans has published on many topics in Nen such as positional verbs (Evans 2014), valency (Evans 2015b), inflection (Evans 2015a) and quantification (Evans 2017). An overview of the linguistic situation of the Southern New Guinea Region has been published in (Evans et al. 2017).

1.5.2 This project

This project began with a pilot fieldtrip to the Morehead district in September of 2010. At the time, my goal was to establish contact to a community that speaks one of the Tonda languages. I did not know which village or variety I was going to work on. When I arrived in Daru, I met three members of the local level government from the Morehead district who had come for administrative work to the regional capital. The three were Augustin Bikaninis from Wando (Blafe), Bongai Njyar from Wämnefr (Kémä) and Abia Bai from Rouku (Komnzo). It was Abia Bai who invited me to accompany him to Rouku. I received a warm and friendly welcome to the community and I stayed for eight weeks. I explained my intentions and people agreed that I may return regularly. Abia Bai adopted me into his clan (*Mrzar Mayawa*) and I was given the local name *Bäi* after Abia's father.

My perspective on the culture and language of the Farem has been dominated by people of the Mayawa section. This is visible in the text corpus as most texts are from speakers who belong to this section. However, I took care that my presence and impact in the village was not limited to this group, and – more importantly for this work – that my description of the language be confirmed by all Farem people.

I spent a total of 16 months in Rouku: two months in 2010, six months in 2011, three months in 2012, three months in 2013 and two months in 2015. During this time, I visited villages along the Morehead highway from Wereaver in the west as far as Bimadbn in the east. I visited Mari in the south and Uparua in the north. I was not able to visit villages on the Indonesian side of the border, and I did not travel to the extreme southwest (Bula, Wando and Korombo) nor did I travel to the north (Setavi, Kiriwo) of the area.

In Rouku, I lived in the house of Abia Bai and his wife Lucy together with their children Nakre, Janet, Sukawi, Nema and Alan. The oldest children Elise and Riley had already moved out of the house. Elise married a man from Wando, far in the west. Riley lives with his wife in Rouku. In the beginning, I concentrated my work on Abia Bai who possesses a great deal of knowledge about history, mythology and the natural world. For elicitation and structural analysis I worked together with my brothers Riley Abia and Daure Kaumb. It was only during my second fieldtrip in 2011 that I discovered the interest and talent of my sister Nakre in linguistic work. She became my main informant together with her father Abia. Their complementary talents have contributed greatly to this project. Abia is not only a great story-teller, but he proved to be an unlimited resource of knowledge. Nakre is a diligent worker in the transcription and translation of recordings, and she patiently answered long lists of questions and worked through complex verb paradigms in elicitation with me.

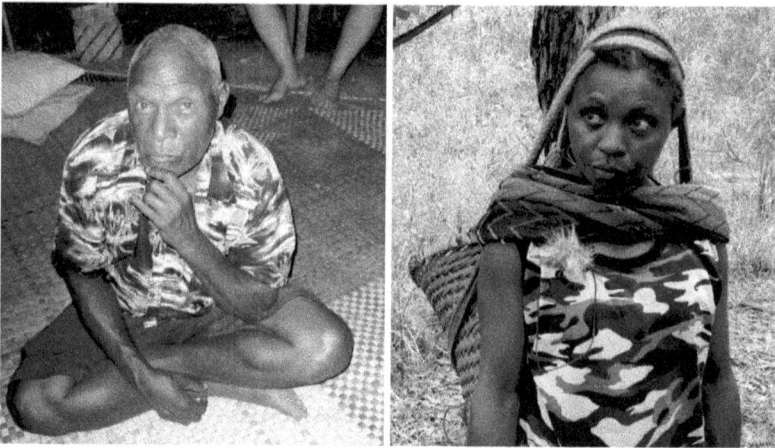

Figure 1.23: Abia and Nakre

From 2011 onwards, the documentation of Komnzo was funded and supported by the DOBES project of the Volkswagen Foundation.[16] The funding covered the basic documentation of two languages, namely Komnzo and Nen, the language of Bimadbn village, the latter of which is the language of the village Bimadbn which Nick Evans has been working on since 2008. The funding allowed us to buy a solar setup and ship it to both villages providing electricity for a computer, recording equipment and lights during the evening hours. Additionally, the DOBES project provided financial support to bring in academics who work in the field of biology. Kipiro Damas spent one week in Rouku in 2011 and again in 2015. He collected and later identified numerous plant specimens. Chris Healey identified and photographed over 100 bird species, thereby eliciting many fascinating narratives about cultural significance of birds. Julia Colleen Miller visited Rouku on two fieldtrips conducting socio-linguistic interviews as well as creating high-quality recordings suited for phonetic analysis.

---

[16] DOBES stands for German 'Dokumentation bedrohter Sprachen'.

1.5.3 The text corpus

The last decade has seen an exceptional increase in creating and archiving digital language material. Despite this positive development, linguists have pointed out that this is "unlikely to be parallelled by a significant acceleration in how long it takes field linguists to produce the sorts of careful translations and cross-questioning of semantic issues that are the hallmark of a well curated text collection" (Evans & Dench 2006: 25). The authors employ the metaphor of a Russian Matryoshka doll to propose a structure of several sub-corpora nested within each other, each one with an increasing depth of analysis. The Komnzo corpus follows this proposal. In fact, what I call the Komnzo corpus here is only one-sixth of the material collected and archived within the project. At present, the archive contains around 60 hours of audio-visual material. I estimate the total amount of text at around 40 hours.[17] The material that has been segmented, transcribed and translated amounts to 12 hours forming the Komnzo text corpus. These 12 hours constitute the data on which the description and analysis in this grammar rests. Hence, although around 60 hours have been archived, only 12 hours can be used for linguistic analysis. I hope that future speakers of Komnzo as well as researchers will benefit from the raw material.

The 12-hour corpus contains narratives, procedurals, conversations, public speeches, interviews as well as recordings from various stimulus tasks. Most recording sessions took place in somewhat articifical settings, whether it be a staged narration or a sociolinguistic interview. All conversational texts and public speeches are purely observational. At the present time, the Komnzo corpus consists of 65 texts with a total of 11hrs and 42min of transcribed material, and around 54,000 words. 34 speakers are featured in the age range from 20 to 68. The representation of speakers is skewed towards male speakers, 25 male versus 9 female. Furthermore, they are skewed towards speakers belonging to the Mayawa section. I acknowledge this as an artefact caused by the circumstances under which I was introduced to and later lived in Rouku.

The material has been placed in two locations. The complete material is archived at The Language Archive (TLA) which is a unit of the Max Planck Institute for Psycholinguistics, Nijmegen concerned with digital language resources and tools. The subset of files which make up the Komnzo text corpus are also archived at Zenodo.[18] At both locations, the materials are stored under an open-access policy. In order to access, browse and download the files, the reader can follow the links below:

- https://zenodo.org/communities/komnzo

- https://archive.mpi.nl/islandora/object/lat%3A1839_00_0000_0000_0017_B0AC_C.

---

[17] This applies a wide notion of what constitutes a text, thus including songs and wordlists for example.

[18] Zenodo is an open access repository for research related data belonging to the European Council's OpenAIRE initiative.

There are over 500 examples in this grammar, and around 90% of these are text examples. Text examples can be distinguished from elicited or overheard examples by an archive ID printed in [angled brackets] underneath the example sentence. Elicited examples are not marked, while overheard examples are marked with [overheard]. The archive ID allows the reader to find the example sentence in the text corpus and thereby view the example in its context. Archive IDs follow a fixed structure. An example is: [tci20110810-02 MAB #34]. The first three letters represent the ISO 639-3 code for Komnzo.[19] The next eight digits and the number after the hyphen refer to the date on which the recording was made. For example, tci20110810-02 refers to the second recording session on the 10th of August 2011. Hence, this information identifies the particular transcription file within the corpus. The last two elements of the archive ID help to find a particular example in the transcription file. First, there is a three-letter code which identifies the speaker, for example MAB for Marua Bai. If there are several speakers, each one is coded by a set of annotation tiers, all of which include the respective three-letter code. The speaker code is followed by the annotation number, which refers to the sequence of intonation units on a tier.

This information is needed to find a particular line of text in the archive. The reader of the electronic version of this grammar can simply click on the archive ID, which is printed below each text example. This will take her directly to the list of recordings in the appendix. The list of recordings in the appendix provides general information about each text (title, text genre, length, number of annotation units, number of tokens) as well as about each speaker (name, age, sex, section/clan). Moreover, the list of recordings contains a digital object identifier (DOI) that establishes a permanent link to the respective dataset on the Zenodo website. Practically, it should be no more than three mouseclicks to get from an example sentence to downloading the relevant transcription file. In this way, I enable the reader to access the original text without much effort.

---

[19]Note that Komnzo is listed, for example in Ethnologue, as a dialect of Wára. Hence, the code 'tci' includes more varieties than the one described in this grammar. More recent systems of language identification are more accurate in my opinion. For example, Glottolog lists Komnzo under the code: komn1238, which refers only to Komnzo.

2 Phonology

In this chapter, I describe the phonological system of Komnzo. The chapter begins with the segmental phonology of consonants in §2.1 and vowels in §2.2. Each section contains a list of minimal pairs which establish the phonemic status of the segments. As Komnzo phonology is characterised by widespread epenthesis, a discussion of the non-phonemic status of schwa is given in §2.2.2. Regular phonological processes are described in §2.3. I address phonotactics in §2.4. This section consists of a description of the syllable structure (§2.4.1), consonant clusters (§2.4.2), syllabification (§2.4.3), minimal word constraints (§2.4.4) and stress (§2.4.5). Morphophonology is addressed in §2.5. The chapter closes with a discussion of loanwords in §2.6 and an account of the development of the orthography in §2.7.

2.1 Consonant phonemes

Table 2.1 gives an overview of the consonant phonemes in Komnzo. Graphemes are given in <angle brackets>.

2.1.1 Obstruents

Obstruents in Komnzo are divided into stops, affricates, and fricatives. The stops and affricates belong to a chain of pairings of oral and prenasalised phonemes at four places of articulation: alveolar, palato-alvealor, velar, and labio-velar. This symmetry is broken at the bilabial place of articulation. The bilabial oral stop is lacking from the phoneme inventory. Since it occurs only in English loanwords and a handful of ideophones, I consider it a loan phoneme. As I will show below, the bilabial fricative /ɸ/ can be regarded as the structural counterpart of the prenasalised bilabial stop.

In the following section, I describe the oral and prenasalised stops, labialised velar stops, affricates and fricatives.

2.1.1.1 Stops

There are two voiceless stops (/t/ and /k/) and three prenasalised stops (/^{m}b/, /^{n}d/, and /^{ŋ}g/). The voiceless stops are phonetically slightly aspirated, but aspiration is not phonemic in Komnzo. The two labialised velar stops and the two affricates follow the same pairing of voiceless and prenasalised manner of articulation, but these will be discussed in separate sections below.

All stops occur in word-initial, medial, and final positions. In only a small number of lexical items, the bilabial /^{m}b/ occurs word-finally. This phoneme is also deviant as it lacks

Table 2.1: Consonant phoneme inventory

	bilabial	dental	alveolar	palato-alveolar	palatal	velar	labio-velar
stop/affricate			t̪~t	ts		k	kʷ
			\<t>	\<z>		\<k>	\<kw>
prenasalized stop/affricate	ᵐb		ⁿd	ⁿdz		ᵑg	ᵑgʷ
	\<b>		\<d>	\<nz>		\<g>	\<gw>
fricative	ɸ	ð	s				
	\<f>	\<th>	\<s>				
nasal	m		n			ŋ	
	\<m>		\<n>			\<ŋ>	
lateral			r~ɾ				
			\<r>				
semivowel					j		w
					\<y>		\<w>

a voiceless counterpart. There is evidence from loanword phonology (§2.6) and from surrounding Tonda languages that the bilabial fricative /ɸ/ occupies the same structural slot in the opposition of voiceless and prenasalised stops.

There is almost no allophonic variation within the stop series, but the prenasalised stops undergo final devoicing (§2.3.2). The /t/ phoneme varies between dental and alveolar points of articulation. In onset clusters where C_2 is /r/, /t/ is always alveolar. Elsewhere, it varies more or less freely.

/t/ →
- [t] / $_\sigma$[_ɾ   traksi   [trakɜ̆si]   'fall'
- [t]~[t̪] / elsewhere   tüf   [tɤɸ] ~ [t̪ɤɸ]   'soft ground'
-     rata   [ɾata] ~ [ɾat̪a]   'ladder'
-     kwot   [kʷɔt] ~ [kʷɔt̪]   'properly'

/k/ →
- [k]   kata   [kata]   'bamboo knife'
-     fokam   [ɸokam]   'grave'
-     safak   [saβak]   'saratoga'

/ᵐb/ → { [ᵐp] / _]σ   gb   [ᵑgə̆ᵐp]   'black palm'
       { [ᵐb] / elsewhere   bone   [ᵐbone]   2SG.POSS
                         gaba   [ᵑgaᵐba]   'storage yam'

/ⁿd/ → { [ⁿt] / _]σ   kd   [kə̆ⁿt]   'star'
       { [ⁿd] / elsewhere   deya   [ⁿdeja]   'tree wallaby'
                         rdiknsi   [rə̆ⁿdikə̆nsi]   'tie around'

/ᵑg/ → { [ᵑk] / _]σ   nag   [naᵑk]   'grass skirt'
       { [ᵑg] / elsewhere   gau   [ᵑgau͡]   'night heron'
                         sagara   [saᵑgara]   proper name

2.1.1.2 Labialised velar stops

The labialised velar stops /kʷ/ and /ᵑgʷ/ show no allophonic variation due to their restricted distribution. Both occur only in syllable onsets, not in the coda. Consequently, we do not find these phonemes in word-final position.[1]

/kʷ/ → { [kʷ] / σ[_   kwan   [kʷan]   'shout, voice'
                       ysokwr   [jə̆sokʷə̆r]   'rainy season'

/ᵑgʷ/ → { [ᵑgʷ] / σ[_   gwä   [ᵑgʷæ]   'mosquito'
                       fagwa   [ɸaᵑgʷa]   'width'

I argue in favour of an analysis whereby the labialised velar stops are complex phonemes rather than a sequence of two phonemes (velar stop + high back vowel /u/ or velar stop + /w/). This argument is based on two lines of evidence: onset consonant clusters and reduplication patterns.

Onset clusters are restricted to two consonants (C_1C_2V). If clusters occur, C_2 may only be /r/ or /w/ (§2.4.3). For this argument, only the /r/ is relevant. We do find words with an initial labialised velar stop (voiceless or prenasalised) in such a cluster, for example: kwras 'Brolga' or gwra 'MacCulloch's Rainbowfish'. If /kʷ/ and /ᵑgʷ/ were to be analysed as clusters of two phonemes, a separate syllable template (CCCV) would be required.

The second piece of evidence comes from reduplication. We find full and partial reduplication (§4.2). In full reduplication the entire word is repeated, as in yam 'footprint,

---

[1]In the neighbouring language Nama which belongs to the Nambu subgroup, labialised velar stops may occur in coda position, as in [aukʷ] 'morning'.

custom, event' → *yamyam* 'little feast'. Partial reduplication is more frequent, where only the first consonant of the initial syllable is copied, as in *zbär* 'night' → *zzbär* [tsɜ̆ts-sɜ̆ᵐbæɾ] 'dusk, twilight'. The domain of partial reduplication does not extend further than the first consonant. Thus, we get *frasi* 'hunger' → *ffrasi* [ɸɜ̆ɸɾasi] 'appetite, hunger', but not *frfrasi* [ɸɾɜ̆ɸɾasi]. If the labialised velar stops comprised two separate phonemes, we would expect that in partial reduplication only the velar stop is copied without the semivowel. On the contrary, we find that the whole phoneme is copied, as in *kwayan* 'light' → *kwkwayan* [kʷɜ̆kʷajan] ~ [kukʷajan] 'flickering light, dimmed light', but not *kkwayan* [kɜ̆kʷajan].

2.1.1.3 Affricates

The two consonant phonemes with the highest frequency are the affricates /ts/ and /ⁿdz/, which seem to give Komnzo its characteristic fricative sound. Both affricates occur initially, medially and finally, and show some allophonic variation. They are palatalised before front vowels, as in *zi* [tʃɪː] 'pain' and *nzikaka* [ⁿdʒɪkaka] 'Whistling Kite'. In all other environments they are alveolar. There is some degree of variation between speakers. Some speakers always palatalise, while most speakers follow the allophonic rules as formalised below. The prenasalised affricate is affected by final devoicing (§2.3.2).

/ts/ →	[tʃ] / _V$_{+\text{FRONT}}$	*zena*	[tʃena]	'now'
		ezi	[ʔetʃi]	'morning'
	[ts] / elsewhere	*zane*	[tsane]	DEM:PROX
		mazo	[matso]	'ocean'
		müz	[mʏts]	'phallocrypt'

/ⁿdz/ →	[ⁿdʒ] / _V$_{+\text{FRONT}}$	*nzigfu*	[ⁿdʒiⁿgɸu]	'rain stone'
		snzä	[sɜ̆ⁿdʒæ]	'crayfish'
	[ⁿts] / _]$_{\sigma}$	*mnz*	[mɜ̆ⁿts]	'house'
	[ⁿdz] / elsewhere	*nzun*	[ⁿdzun]	1SG.DAT
		rnzam	[rɜ̆ⁿdzam]	'how many'

2.1.1.4 Fricatives

There are three fricatives at the bilabial, dental and alveolar places of articulation. The dental fricative is voiced, while the other two are voiceless. The bilabial fricative has a voiced allophone, which occurs intervocalically. Although voiced in most environments, the dental fricative is affected by final devoicing (§2.3.2). The alveolar fricative is always voiceless in all environments. These rules are formalised below.

/ɸ/ → { [β] / V_V	*zafazafa*	[tsaβatsaβa]	'vine stick'
[ɸ] / elsewhere	*fid*	[ɸɪⁿt]	'bushrope'
	zarfa	[tsarɸa]	'ear'
	karaf	[karaɸ]	'paddle'

/ð/ → { [θ] / _]$_\sigma$	*süsübäth*	[sʏsʏᵐbæθ]	'darkness'
[ð] / elsewhere	*thamin*	[ðamin]	'tongue'
	ŋatha	[ŋaða]	'dog'

/s/ → { [s]	*saisai*	[sãĩsãĩ]	'drizzle (n)'
	fisor	[ɸisoɾ]	'turtle'
	fis	[ɸis]	'husband'

2.1.2 Nasals

There are nasal stops at three places of articulation: bilabial, alveolar, and velar. These three show differences in their frequency and distribution. The velar nasal /ŋ/ occurs only word-initially, while bilabial /m/ and alveolar /n/ are found initially, medially and finally. There is no allophonic variation with the nasals.

/m/ → { [m]	*mifum*	[miβum]	'nose ornament'
	zimu	[tʃimu]	'snot'
	thm	[ðɜ̃m]	'nose'

/n/ → { [n]	*no*	[no:]	'water, rain'
	mane	[mane]	'who' (ABS)
	minmin	[minmin]	'Emerald Dove'

/ŋ/ → { [ŋ] / WORD[_	*ŋazi*	[ŋatʃi]	'coconut'

2.1.3 Trill, tap - /r/

The alveolar trill /r/ is often realised as a single tap [ɾ] depending on speech rate and speaker. In onset consonant clusters where /r/ is occupying C$_2$ position, it is always tapped. Elsewhere, the trill and the tap are in free variation. Word-finally /r/ may also become voiceless. This variation between [ɾ] and [ɾ̥] seems to be conditioned by age. Older speakers use the voiceless variant more frequently.

$$/r/ \rightarrow \begin{cases} [\mathfrak{r}]\sim[\mathfrak{r}] \ / \ \underline{\quad}]_{\text{WORD}} & msar & [m\underset{\circ}{\mathfrak{e}}sa\mathfrak{r}] \sim [m\underset{\circ}{\mathfrak{e}}sa\underset{\circ}{\mathfrak{r}}] & \text{'green ant'} \\ [\mathfrak{r}] \ / \ _{\sigma}[\text{C}\underline{\quad} & frasi & [\phi rasi] & \text{'hunger'} \\ [\mathfrak{r}]\sim[\mathfrak{r}] \ / \ \text{elsewhere} & rnz & [r\underset{\circ}{\mathfrak{e}}{}^{n}ts] \sim [r\underset{\circ}{\mathfrak{e}}{}^{n}ts] & \text{'ember'} \\ & \eta are & [\eta are] \sim [\eta are] & \text{'woman'} \end{cases}$$

2.1.4 Approximants

The two approximants /w/ and /j/ occur in initial, medial and final position. In final position, they may be realised as a short offglide or become part of a diphthong. For both approximants, but especially for the palatal /j/, we find only a handful of lexical items where they do occur word-finally.

$$/w/ \rightarrow \begin{cases} [\widehat{}\widehat{u}]\sim[\underline{\quad}^w] \ / \ \text{V}\underline{\quad}]_{\sigma} & daw & [{}^{n}da\widehat{u}] \sim [{}^{n}da^w] & \text{'garden'} \\ [\text{w}] \ / \ \text{elsewhere} & wm & [w\breve{\mathfrak{d}}m] & \text{'stone, gravel'} \\ & fewa & [\phi ewa] & \text{'odour, stench'} \end{cases}$$

$$/j/ \rightarrow \begin{cases} [\widehat{}\widehat{\imath}]\sim[\underline{\quad}^j] \ / \ \text{V}\underline{\quad}]_{\sigma} & f\ddot{a}y & [\phi æ\widehat{\imath}] \sim [\phi æ^j] & \text{'payment'} \\ [\text{j}] \ / \ \text{elsewhere} & yusi & [jusi] & \text{'grass'} \\ & nz\ddot{o}yar & [{}^{n}d\mathfrak{z}œja\mathfrak{r}] & \text{'bowerbird'} \end{cases}$$

There are a number of reasons why the two approximants are analysed as consonants rather than high vowels which alternate according to their environment. Evidence comes from case allomorphy and phonotactics. In stem final position /w/ and /j/ select the same allomorph of the locative case as other consonants. This can be seen in the word *daw* [ⁿdaû] ~ [ⁿdaʷ] 'garden' which selects =*en* as its locative case marker, thus forming *dawen* [ⁿdawen] 'in the garden'. Words which end in a vowel select the =*n* allomorph of the locative case. Furthermore, the rules of syllabification (§2.4.3) treat these two phonemes like consonants. Thus, we find examples like *ys* [jĭs] 'thorn' and *ky* [kə̆ʲ] 'yam species', where epenthesis occurs after and before /j/, respectively.

2.1.5 Minimal pairs for Komnzo consonants

The following minimal pairs and near minimal pairs in Table 2.2 illustrate the phonemic contrast between consonants in initial, medial and final position.

Table 2.2: Minimal pairs of consonant phonemes

segments	examples			
/kʷ/ vs. /k/	*kwafar* place name	[kʷaβaɾ]	[kaβaɾ]	*kafar* 'big'
	sakwr 'he hit him'	[sakʷɤ̆ɾ]	[sakɤ̆ɾ]	*sakr* 'mustard vine'
	kwath 'crow'	[kʷaθ]	[kaθ]	*kath* 'ankle'
/ᵑgʷ/ vs. /ᵑg/	*gwra* 'rainbowfish'	[ᵑgʷra:]	[ᵑgra:]	*gra* 'tree sp'
/kʷ/ vs. /w/	*kwath* 'crow'	[kʷaθ]	[waθ]	*wath* 'dance (n)'
	kwf 'stone club'	[kʷɤ̆ɸ]	[wɤ̆ɸ]	*wf* 'shirt, blouse'
/ᵑgʷ/ vs. /w/	*gwth* 'nest'	[ᵑgwɤ̆θ]	[wɤ̆θ]	*wth* 'faeces'
/k/ vs. /w/	*kath* 'ankle'	[kaθ]	[waθ]	*wath* 'dance (n)'
/ɸ/ vs. /w/	*far* 'housepost'	[ɸaɾ]	[waɾ]	*war* 'top layer'
	kafar 'big'	[kaβaɾ]	[kawaɾ]	*kawar* pers. name
	tfitfi 'whirlwind'	[tɤ̆βitɤ̆βi]	[tɤ̆witɤ̆wi]	*twitwi* 'bird sp'
/s/ vs. /t/	*süfr* 'tree sp'	[svɸɤ̆r]	[tvɸɤ̆r]	*tüfr* 'many'
	kisr 'lizard sp'	[kisɤ̆r]	[kitɤ̆r]	*kitr* 'pandanus'
	wsws 'grass sp'	[wɤ̆swɤ̆s]	[wɤ̆twɤ̆t]	*wtwt* 'itchy'
/s/ vs. /ð/	*sirsir* 'glider'	[sirsir]	[ðirðir]	*thirthir* 'pig tusk'
	bis 'bird sp'	[ᵐbi:s]	[ᵐbi:θ]	*bith* 'honey bee'
	mus 'leech'	[mu:s]	[mu:θ]	*muth* '(sago) grub'
/s/ vs. /ts/	*si* 'eye'	[si:]	[tʃi:]	*zi* 'pain'
	srminz 'rainbow'	[sɤ̆rmints]	[tsɤ̆rmints]	*zrminz* 'roots'
	ksi kar 'savannah'	[kɤ̆si kar]	[kɤ̆tʃi]	*kzi* 'barktray'
	fs 'fish sp'	[ɸɤ̆s]	[ɸɤ̆ts]	*fz* 'forest'
/ð/ vs. /t/	*thruthru* 'bamboo sp'	[ðruðru]	[trutru]	*trutru* 'stream'
	füth 'rotten tuber'	[ɸɤθ]	[ɸɤt]	*füt* 'pouch'
/ð/ vs. /r/	*thusi* 'fold (v.t.)'	[ðusi]	[rusi]	*rusi* 'shoot (v.t.)'
	bthan 'magic'	[ᵐbɤ̆ðan]	[ᵐbɤ̆ran]	*bran* 'line'
	yathizsi 'die'	[jaðitsɤ̆si]	[jaritsɤ̆si]	*yarizsi* 'hear, listen'
	zithzith 'slickness'	[tʃiθtʃiθ]	[tʃirtʃir]	*zirzir* 'wetness'
	wath 'dance (n)'	[waθ]	[waɾ]	*war* 'top layer'
/r/ vs. /t/	*rar* 'for what'	[raɾ]	[taɾ]	*tar* 'friend'
	ŋarr 'bandicoot'	[ŋarɤ̆r]	[ŋatɤ̆r]	*ŋatr* 'rope'
	ft 'dead tree'	[ɸɤ̆t]	[ɸɤ̆r]	*fr* 'palm stem'
/r/ vs. /ts/	*rinaksi* 'pour'	[rinakɤ̆si]	[tʃinakɤ̆si]	*zinaksi* 'put down'
	wari 'plant sp'	[wari]	[watʃi]	*wazi* 'side'
	mür 'grass sp'	[myr]	[myts]	*müz* 'phallocrypt'
/ᵐb/ vs. /m/	*bith* 'honey bee'	[ᵐbiθ]	[miθ]	*mith* 'face'
	bä 2.ABS	[ᵐbæ:]	[mæ:]	*mä* 'where'
	züb 'depth'	[tʃɤᵐb]	[tʃɤm]	*züm* 'centipede'
/ⁿd/ vs. /n/	*dasi* 'bulge'	[ⁿdasi]	[nasi]	*nasi* 'long yam'
	badabada 'ancestor'	[ᵐbaⁿdaᵐbaⁿda]	[ᵐbana]	*bana* 'pitiful'

segments	examples			
	kd 'star'	[kɜ̃nt]	[kɜ̃n]	*kn* 'yam sp'
/ⁿg/ vs. /ŋ/	*gathagatha* 'bad'	[ⁿgaðaⁿgaða]	[ŋaðaŋaða]	*ŋathaŋatha* 'quoll'
	game 'tongs'	[ⁿgame]	[ŋame]	*ŋame* 'mother'
/m/ vs. /n/	*mä* 'where'	[mæ:]	[næ:]	*nä* 'some'
	mawan 'tree sp'	[mawan]	[nawan]	*nawan* 'waterhole'
/ⁿdz/ vs. /ⁿd/	*nzga* 'vagina'	[ⁿdzɜ̃ⁿga]	[ⁿdɜ̃ⁿga]	*dga* 'gills'
	ŋanz 'planting row'	[ŋaⁿts]	[ŋaⁿt]	*ŋad* 'rope'
	ymnz place name	[jɜ̃mɜ̃ⁿts]	[jɜ̃mɜ̃ⁿt]	*ymd* 'bird'
/ⁿdz/ vs. /n/	*nzä* 1SG.ABS	[ⁿdʒæ:]	[næ:]	*nä* 'some'
	gonz 'place name'	[ⁿgɔnts]	[ⁿgɔn]	*gon* 'hips'
/ᵐb/ vs. /ɸ/	*bä* 2.ABS	[ᵐbæ:]	[ɸæ:]	*fä* DIST
	bira 'axe'	[ᵐbiɾa]	[ɸiɾa]	*fira* 'betelnut'
	bis 'bird sp'	[ᵐbi:s]	[ɸi:s]	*fis* 'husband'
/ⁿd/ vs. /t/	*düfr* 'headdress'	[ⁿdʏɸɜ̃ɾ]	[tʏɸɜ̃ɾ]	*tüfr* 'plenty'
	drari 'container'	[ⁿdɾaɾi]	[tɾaɾi]	*trari* 'strong man'
	kadakada 'yamcake'	[kaⁿdakaⁿda]	[katakata]	*katakata* 'grass sp'
	sd 'yam sp'	[sɜ̃ⁿt]	[sɜ̃t]	*st* 'plant sp'
/ⁿdz/ vs. /ts/	*nzä* 1SG.ABS	[ⁿdʒæ:]	[tʃæ:]	*zä* PROX
	nzanza 'insect sp'	[ⁿdzaⁿdza]	[tsatsa]	*zaza* 'carrying'
	nzr 'leftover'	[ⁿdzɜ̃ɾ]	[tsɜ̃ɾ]	*zr* 'tooth'
	rbänzsi 'prohibit'	[ɾɜ̃ᵐbæⁿdzɜ̃si]	[ɾɜ̃ᵐbætsɜ̃si]	*rbäzsi* 'untie'
/ⁿg/ vs. /k/	*gd* 'mud'	[ⁿgɜ̃ⁿt]	[kɜ̃ⁿt]	*kd* 'star'
	gafar 'fish sp'	[ⁿgaβaɾ]	[kaβaɾ]	*kafar* 'big'
	gursi 'break off'	[ⁿguɾsi]	[kuɾsi]	*kursi* 'split'
	tag 'bee sp'	[taⁿk]	[tak]	*tak* 'pandanus'
	srag pers. name	[sɾaⁿk]	[sɾak]	*srak* 'boy'
/w/ vs. /j/	*warsi* 'chew'	[waɾsi]	[jaɾsi]	*yarsi* 'tired'
	wf 'shirt'	[wɜ̃ɸ]	[jɜ̃ɸ]	*yf* 'name'
	fäw 'arrow shaft'	[ɸæ͠u]	[ɸæ͠i]	*fäy* 'payment'

2.2 Vowel phonemes

The articulatory space for vowels can be divided into four levels of height (high, mid, mid-low, and low) and three levels of backness (front, central, and back). The absence versus presence of lip rounding is phonemic for front vowels. Figure 2.1 provides an overview of the vowel space, while Table 2.3 lists the segmental features and shows the graphemes with < >. Note that I include the epenthetic schwa in parentheses. This is because there is some evidence that schwa constitutes a marginal phoneme in word-final environment. That being said, in all other contexts it is created by epenthesis (§2.2.2).

Nasalisation is not phonemic, and nasal vowels are a marginal phenomenon. Only two words are attested, in which we find nasal vowels. These are the conjunctions *a* [ã:] 'and'

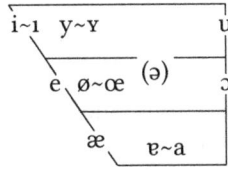

Figure 2.1: Komnzo vowel space

Table 2.3: Vowel phoneme inventory

	front		central	back
	unrounded	rounded		
high	i	y		u
	<i>	<ü>	<u>	
mid	e	œ	(ə)	o
	<e>	<é>	<o>	
mid-low	æ			
	<ä>			
low			a	
			<a>	

and *o* [ɔ:] 'or'. Both have a second, much rarer variant with an initial velar nasal: *ŋa* [ŋa:] and *ŋo* [ŋɔ:], respectively. This suggests that nasalisation of the vowel was caused by the loss of the preceding consonant.

There are no diphthongs in Komnzo. All diphthongs which occur on a phonetic level end in high offglides. These are analysed as allophones of the two approximants /w/ and /j/ in coda position (§2.1.4). In the practical orthography these are sometimes written as diphthongs, e.g. <ai> or <au>. Two words which exemplify this are *saisai* 'drizzle' and *kaukau* 'Mouth Almighty'.

2.2.1 Phonetic description and allophonic distribution of vowels

Table 2.4 shows that there this free variation for some most of the vowel phonemes.

There is no phonemic contrast between short and long vowels. However, vowels tend to be phonetically longer in monosyllabic roots, especially if the monosyllable is light/open, as in *nzä* [ⁿdʒæ:] 'I' or *se* [se:] 'bark torch'. This process of vowel lengthening is caused by minimal word conditions in combination with syllable weight. I address this topic in §2.4.1 and §2.4.4.

Table 2.4: Vowel allophones

phoneme	description	→ allophones
/i/	high front unrounded vowel	→ [i]~[ɪ]
/y/	high front rounded vowel	→ [y]~[ʏ]
/u/	high back rounded vowel	→ [u]~[ʊ]
/e/	mid front unrounded vowel	→ [e]~[ɛ]
/œ/	mid front rounded vowel	→ [ø]~[œ]
/o/	mid back rounded vowel	→ [o]~[ɔ]
/a/	low central unrounded vowel	→ [a]~[ɐ]
/æ/	low front unrounded vowel	→ [æ]

2.2.1.1 Allophones of /o/

There is further allophonic variation for /o/, which is related to vowel lengthening. In heavy, closed syllables, /o/ is realised as a short, centralised, rounded vowel [ŏ], whereas in light, open syllables it is realised as a mid back rounded vowel of normal length [ɔ]. Two words which show this allophonic variation are the language name *Komnzo* [kŏmⁿdzɔ] and *komon* [kɔmŏn] 'maybe'. We find the two allophones [ŏ] and [ɔ] conditioned by syllable weight in the syllables of the two words respectively. There are two rules which may override this allophonic distribution. The first is a minimal word constraint which produces [ɔ] even in closed syllables if the root is monosyllabic, as in *gon* [ⁿgɔn] 'hips'. The second rule overrides syllable weight and the impact of the minimal word constraint. After the labio-velar approximant (/w/) and the two labialised-velar stops (/kʷ/ and /ⁿgʷ/) /o/ is always realised as short, centralised, rounded vowel [ŏ], as in *woz* [wŏts] 'bottle'. Leaving the influences of the minimal word constraint to §2.4.4, we can formalise these observations in the following rule:

$$/o/ \rightarrow \begin{cases} [ŏ] / \_C]_\sigma & \begin{array}{lll} \textit{emoth} & [ʔeːmŏθ] & \text{'girl'} \\ \textit{ymorymor} & [jŏmŏɾjŏmŏɾ] & \text{'desire'} \\ \textit{thomgsi} & [ðŏmⁿgŏsi] & \text{'help'} \end{array} \\ \\ [ɔ] / \_]_\sigma & \begin{array}{lll} \textit{nibo} & [niᵐbɔ] & \text{'six'} \\ \textit{dokre} & [ⁿdɔkɾe] & \text{'frog'} \end{array} \\ \\ [ŏ] / C_{+\text{labio-velar}\_} & \begin{array}{lll} \textit{kwosi} & [kʷŏsi] & \text{'dead'} \\ \textit{woku} & [wŏku] & \text{'skin'} \end{array} \end{cases}$$

There are some irregularities with these rules when it comes to other bilabial consonants, like /ɸ/. There is *fofot* [ɸɔɸŏt] 'single child' which follows the rule, but there are a handful of words which do not follow the rule, like: *fothr* [ɸŏðŏr] 'eucalyptus species' or *fokufoku* [ɸŏkuɸŏku] 'small patch of vegetation'.

2.2.1.2 Analytic problems with /œ/

The vowel /œ/ poses a problem because there are no minimal pairs between /œ/ and some of its immediate neighbours (/e/, /o/, /æ/) in the corpus. There are minimal pairs distinguishing /œ/ from /i/, /y/, /u/, /a/. The lack of minimal pairs with the former group along with the effects of vowel harmony (§2.5.1) invites an analysis in which /œ/ is a variant of other phonemes, for example a rounded allophone of /e/ or a fronted allophone of /o/. However, no conditioning environment (e.g. vowel harmony or quality of adjacent consonants) can be established. The main problem lies in the fact, that occurences of /œ/ are much rarer than all other vowels.[2] For the current description, /œ/ is set up as an independent vowel phoneme. Further research will have to settle this question.

2.2.2 The non-phonemic status of schwa

The most frequent vowel in Komnzo is a short schwa [ə̆]. I will argue here that this is not a phoneme, but that it is inserted through epenthesis in order to create a syllable nucleus where there is none underlyingly. That being said, I will make an argument at the end of this section that schwa can be analysed as a marginal or emerging phoneme in word-final context. The rules of epenthesis will be laid out in §2.4.3.

Epenthetic vowels are known from many Papuan languages. The best documented case is certainly Kalam (Biggs 1963; Pawley 1966; Blevins & Pawley 2010), but epenthetic vowels have been described for other languages of the Yam family, e.g. Nen (Evans & Miller 2016). In Komnzo, the main arguments for schwa as an epenthetic vowel rather than a phoneme come from syllabicity alternations, the predictability of schwa, and its restricted distribution.

Syllabicity alternations which cause changes in the place of schwa insertion are influenced by affixation. Two examples are the verb *ttüsi* [tə̆tʏsi] 'print, paint' and the noun *fzenz* [ɸə̆tʃeⁿts] 'wife'. In both stems schwa occurs in the first syllable. When we inflect the verb with an undergoer prefix, the first consonant is syllabified as a coda and schwa needs to be inserted in a different position: *yttünzr* [jə̆ttʏⁿdzə̆ɾ] 's/he paints him'. When we add a possessive prefix to *fzenz*, e.g. *bufzenz* [ᵐbuɸtʃeⁿts] 'your wife', again the first consonant of the stem becomes a coda. In this case schwa disappears entirely because the possessive prefix ends in a vowel. It follows that schwa cannot be present in the underlying representation of these two lexemes.

Schwa has a very restricted distribution compared to specified vowels. It does not occur word-initially and it is very limited word-finally. I will show below that word-final schwas should be analysed as a marginal phoneme. Elsewhere, schwa is entirely predictable and therefore not represented in the orthography of Komnzo. The rules of schwa insertion are discussed as part of syllabification and possible consonant clusters (§2.4.3). There are many roots which lack specified vowels altogether.[3] A few examples

---

[2]Among the 1700 entries in the dictionary, only 30 contain /œ/. Compare this number with 730 for /a/. This is a conservative count, in which reduplications and their respective bases, as well as simple forms and compounds have been counted once.

[3]Among the 1700 entries in the dictionary, we find 105 without specified vowels. The number of entries in which the epenthetic vowel occurs together with specified vowels is much higher.

are: *mnz* [mɜⁿts] 'house', *zfth* [tsɜɸɜθ] 'base, reason', and *ggrb* [ⁿgɜⁿgɜɾɜᵐp] 'small, un-ripe coconut'. The quality of the epenthetic vowel shows only little variation. In almost all enviroments, it is realised as a mid central vowel of very short duration [ɜ]. However, there is one exception. When the epenthetic vowel is inserted preceding the two approx-imants /w/ and /j/, it is realised as a high back or high front vowel. respectively. Two examples are *thwak* [ðŭwak] 'shoulder' and *nyak* [nǐjak] 'we go'.

There is one caveat to the analysis of schwa as epenthetic: It cannot be predicted in word-final context. Although word-final schwa is very rare in terms of types, it cannot be dismissed as the aberrant behaviour of a few lexical items. This is because it is not rare at all in terms of tokens. For example, word-final schwa shows up in the verb morphology (1SG *-é*), in the case marking (ERG.NSG *=é*) and in the adjectivaliser suffix *-thé*.[4] For the first singular suffix on verbs, I argue in §5.5.1.1 that this is the result of vowel reduction (a>ə) because neighbouring varieties have a corresponding *-a* suffix. Moreover, the first person suffix *-é* disappears if other suffixal material is added to the verb. This is also found with some of the lexical items. For example, when *kayé* 'yesterday' is marked with a temporal possessive case (*=thamane*), word-final schwa disappears, as in *kaythamane dagon* 'yesterday's food'. This does not happen with full vowels, as in *ezithamane dagon* 'food from the morning' from *ezi* 'morning'. Thus, I analyse schwa in word-final contexts as a marginal phoneme, which emerged or is emerging from vowel reduction. In these word-final cases schwa is represented orthographically by <*é*>.

2.2.3 Minimal pairs for Komnzo vowels

The following minimal pairs and near minimal pairs illustrate the phonemic contrasts between vowels. Each vowel phoneme is set apart from its immediate neighbours in the vowel space. Each vowel phoneme is contrasted with the epenthetic vowel, i.e. the absence of a specified vowel (∅). Some combinations are redundant (e.g. /i/ vs. /e/ and /e/ vs. /i/) and not repeated in the table.

Table 2.5: Minimal pairs of vowel phonemes

phonemes	examples			
/i/ vs. /u/	*mith* 'face'	[miθ]	[muθ]	*muth* '(sago) grub'
	grigri 'maggots'	[ⁿgɾiⁿgɾi]	[ⁿgɾuː]	*gru* 'shooting star'
/i/ vs. /y/	*minzaksi* 'paint (vt.)'	[mi ⁿdzakɜsi]	[my ⁿdzakɜsi]	*münzaksi* 'allow'
	di 'back of head'	[ⁿdiː]	[ⁿdyⁿdy]	*düdü* 'in good shape'
/i/ vs. /e/	*si* 'eye'	[siː]	[seː]	*se* 'torch'
/i/ vs. /œ/	*di* 'back of head'	[ⁿdiː]	[ⁿdœː]	*dö* 'monitor lizard'
/i/ vs. ∅	*biribiri* 'plant sp'	[ᵐbiɾiᵐbiɾi]	[ᵐbɜɾiᵐbɜɾi]	*bribri* 'weeding'
	with 'banana'	[wiθ]	[wɜθ]	*wth* 'faeces'
/u/ vs. /y/	*futhfuth* 'scrapes'	[ɸuθɸuθ]	[ɸɣθɸɣθ]	*füthfüth* 'hatched bird'
	but 'kava sticks'	[ᵐbut]	[ᵐbɣt]	*büt* 'amputated limb'

[4]The latter could be historically related to the similative case marker (*=thatha*).

phonemes	examples			
	rusi 'shoot (vt.)'	[ɾusi]	[ɾʏsi]	*rüsi* 'rain (v.)'
/u/ vs. /o/	*muramura* 'medicine'	[muɾamuɾa]	[mɔɾamɔɾa]	*moramora* 'tree sp'
	muth '(sago) grub'	[muθ]	[mɤ̆θ]	*moth* 'path'
	tru 'palm sp'	[tɾu:]	[tɾɔ:]	*tro* 'python sp'
/u/ vs. ∅	*kursi* 'split (vt.)'	[kuɾsi]	[kɤ̆ɾsi]	*krsi* 'block (vt.)'
	fuk 'in a group'	[ɸuk]	[ɸɤ̆k]	*fk* 'buttocks'
/y/ vs. /e/	*fünz* 'arm muscles'	[ɸʏⁿts]	[ɸeⁿts]	*fenz* 'puss'
/y/ vs. /œ/	*nümä* 'one week away'	[nʏmæ]	[nœmæ]	*nömä* 'yamcake'
	düdü 'in good shape'	[ⁿdʏⁿdʏ]	[ⁿdœⁿdœ]	*dödö* 'plant sp'
/y/ vs. ∅	*sün* 'dirt, dust'	[sʏn]	[sɤ̆n]	*sn* 'yam sp'
	tüfr 'plenty'	[tʏɸɤ̆ɾ]	[tɤ̆ɸɤ̆ɾtɤ̆ɸɤ̆ɾ]	*tfrtfr* 'tree sp'
/e/ vs. /o/	*fethaksi* 'dip in'	[ɸeðakɤ̆si]	[ɸɔðakɤ̆si]	*fothaksi* 'take off (bag)'
	game 'tongs'	[ⁿgame]	[ⁿgamɔ]	*gamo* 'magic spell'
/e/ vs. /a/	*yem* 'cassowary'	[jem]	[jam]	*yam* 'event'
	fetr 'dangerous'	[ɸetɤ̆ɾ]	[ɸatɤ̆ɾ]	*fatr* 'shoulder'
	gwre 'bird sp'	[ⁿgʷre:]	[ⁿgʷra:]	*gwra* 'fish sp'
/e/ vs. /æ/	*fenz* 'puss'	[ɸeⁿts]	[ɸæⁿts]	*fänz* pers. name
	nze 1SG.ERG	[ⁿdʒe:]	[ⁿdʒæ:]	*nzä* 1SG.ABS
/e/ vs. ∅	*menz* 'story man'	[meⁿts]	[mɤ̆ⁿts]	*mnz* 'house'
	fethaksi 'dip in'	[ɸeðakɤ̆si]	[ɸɤ̆ðakɤ̆si]	*fthaksi* 'take from fire'
	ŋakwire 'we run'	[ŋakʷiɾe]	[ŋakʷiɾɤ̆]	*ŋakwiré* 'I run'
/æ/ vs. /a/	*näbi* 'one'	[næᵐbi]	[naᵐbi]	*nabi* 'bow, bamboo'
	fätr 'left'	[ɸætɤ̆ɾ]	[ɸatɤ̆ɾ]	*fatr* 'shoulder'
	mafä 'with whom'	[maɸæ]	[maɸa]	*mafa* 'who'
/æ/ vs. /o/	*bärbär* 'half'	[ᵐbæɾᵐbæɾ]	[ᵐbɤ̆ɾ]	*bor* 'rat'
	nä 'some'	[næ:]	[nɔ:]	*no* 'water'
/æ/ vs. ∅	*fäk* 'jaw'	[ɸæk]	[ɸɤ̆k]	*fk* 'buttocks'
	märmär 'slope'	[mæɾmæɾ]	[mɤ̆ɾmɤ̆ɾ]	*mrmr* 'inside'
	bnä 'with you'	[ᵐbɤ̆næ]	[ᵐbɤ̆nɤ̆]	*bné* 2NSG.ERG
/a/ vs. /œ/	*namä* 'good'	[namæ]	[nœmæ]	*nömä* 'yamcake'
/a/ vs. /o/	*zan* 'fight'	[tsan]	[tsɔn]	*zon* 'plant sp'
	karfa 'from village'	[kaɾɸa]	[kaɾɸɔ]	*karfo* 'to village'
	far 'house post'	[ɸaɾ]	[ɸɤ̆ɾ]	*for* 'riverbank'
/a/ vs. ∅	*ngath* 'friend'	[nɤ̆ⁿgaθ]	[nɤ̆ⁿgɤ̆θ]	*ngth* 'young sibling'
	tharthar 'next to'	[ðaɾðaɾ]	[ðɤ̆ɾðɤ̆ɾ]	*thrthr* 'intestines'
	sakwra 'I hit him' (PST)	[sakʷɤ̆ra]	[sakʷɤ̆ɾɤ̆]	*sakwré* 'I hit him' (RPST)
/o/ vs. ∅	*borsi* 'laugh'	[ᵐbɤ̆rsi]	[ᵐbɤ̆rsi]	*brsi* 'scoop water'
	fothaksi 'take off'	[ɸɔðakɤ̆si]	[ɸɤ̆ðakɤ̆si]	*fthaksi* 'take from fire'
	rgosi 'poke through'	[rɤ̆ⁿgosi]	[rɤ̆ⁿgɤ̆si]	*rgsi* 'wear clothes'
	monz 'trench, ditch'	[mɔⁿts]	[mɤ̆ⁿts]	*mnz* 'house'
	nzigom 'chain smoker'	[ⁿdʒiⁿgɤ̆m]	[ⁿdʒiⁿgɤ̆m]	*nzigm* 'stickyness'

2.3 Regular phonological processes

2.3.1 Gemination

Gemination occurs with a subset of the consonantal phonemes (/t/, /k/, /ɸ/, /ð/, /m/, /n/, and /r/). We find geminates in medial heterosyllabic consonant clusters, where the rules of syllabification specify that no epenthetic vowel needs to be inserted (§2.4.3). Phonetically, geminates are characterised by a prolonged realisation of fricatives, nasals, and alveolar trill. Geminate stops are realised with a delayed release of the airflow. Although gemination is caused by affixation in most cases, I discuss the topic here rather than as a morphophonemic rule because we also find monomorphemic roots with geminates. The list in Table 2.6 provides some attested examples from the corpus. In some of the examples, we find minimal pairs based on gemination, as can be seen in the rightmost column.

Table 2.6: Geminate consonants

segment	geminate	non-geminate
/t/	*yttünzr* [jə̆t:yⁿdzə̆r] 's/he paints him'	n/a
/k/	*yakkarä* [jak:aræ] 'quickly' yak=karä walk=PROP	*yakarä* [jakaræ] 'in tears' ya=karä cry=PROP
/m/	*yamme* [jam:e] 'through this event' yam=me event=INS	*yame* [jame] 'mat'
	fammäre [ɸam:ære] 'without thinking' fam=märe thoughts=PRIV	n/a
/n/	*yannor* [jan:ə̆r] 'he shouts hither' ya-n-nor 3SG.MASC-VENT-shout	*yanor* [janə̆r] 'he shouts' ya-nor 3SG.MASC-shout
/ɸ/	*fiyaffa* [ɸijaɸ:a] 'from the hunt' fiyaf=fa hunt=ABL	n/a
/ð/	*yththagr* [jə̆θ:aⁿgə̆r] 'it is sticking (on sth.)'	n/a
/r/	*firra* [ɸir:a] 'place name' *kwrro* [kʷr:o] 'Blue-winged Kookaburra'	*fira* [ɸira] 'betelnut' n/a

Gemination is not attested for complex consonants, including the prenasalised stops (/ᵐb/, /ⁿd/, and /ᵑg/) as well as the two affricates (/ts/ and /ⁿdz/) and /s/. Gemination is not relevant for the labialised velar stops (/kʷ/ and /ᵑgʷ/) and the velar nasal (/ŋ/) because these do not occur in coda position.

2.3.2 Final-devoicing

The process of final devoicing affects only those consonants which occur in final position, excluding non-final /kʷ/, /ᵑgʷ/, and /ŋ/. Moreover, it affects only those consonants which are voiced in all other environments, excluding voiceless /t/, /k/, /ɸ/, /s/, and /ts/. The nasal stops and the approximants are also not affected by final devoicing. This leaves us with the following phonemes, which are targetted by final devoicing: /ᵐb/, /ⁿd/, /ᵑg/, /ⁿdz/, /ð/, and /r/.

The domain of final devoicing is the syllable. In onset position, these phonemes are always voiced, for example /ⁿdz/ in *nzafar* [ⁿdzaɸar] 'sky' and *knzun* [kə̆ⁿdzun] 'parallel'. In coda position, they are voiceless, as /ⁿd/ in *bodkr* [ᵐbə̆ⁿtkə̆r] 'stinking' and /ð/ in *wathknsi* [waθkə̆nsi] 'pack up'. In word-final position, they are also voiceless, for example /ᵐb/ in *gb* [ᵑgə̆ᵐp] 'pandanus species' and /ⁿdz/ in *mnz* [mə̆ⁿts] 'house'.

We find further evidence in suffixation and encliticisation that the process is targetting the right edge of the syllable rather than the (phonological) word. *Mnz* [mə̆ⁿts] 'house' may take the vowel-initial locative enclitic *=en*, in which case /ⁿdz/ occurs in onset position and is voiced: *mnzen* [mə̆ⁿdzen] 'in the house'. This contrasts with the consonant-initial formatives *=fa* (ABL) and *=wä* (EMPH). In both cases, /ⁿdz/ is syllabified in coda position and is voiceless: *mnzfa* [mə̆ⁿtsɸa] 'from the house' and *mnzwä* [mə̆ⁿtswæ] 'really the house'. We can formalise final devoicing in the following rule:

$$/\text{ᵐb}/, /\text{ⁿd}/, /\text{ᵑg}/, /\text{ⁿdz}/, /\text{ð}/ \rightarrow \{\ [\text{-voiced}]\ /\ \_]_\sigma$$

The only excepion is /r/, where final devoicing occurs only word-finally. However, final devoicing of /r/ is optional and more commonly found with older speakers.

2.3.3 Glottal stop insertion

There are only few lexemes with an initial vowel. Among the 1700 entries in the dictionary, there are 54 vowel-initial lexemes: /a/ (21), /e/ (17), /o/ (8), /æ/ (4), /u/ (3), /i/ (1). Three of these are loanwords. In addition, there is a vowel-initial undergoer prefix in one of the five prefix series.[5] Thus, vowel-initial lexemes are a marginal phenomenon. Moreover, there are no vowel-initial syllables word-internally. A possible explanation for the occurence of vowel-initial words in Komnzo, as compared to other Tonda languages in the west, might be contact with the Nambu languages to the east, where vowel-initial words seem to be more frequent.

---

[5]In the alpha prefixes, 2|3NSG is *e-*.

For this marginal pattern we find a rule of glottal stop insertion, as in *ebar* [ʔeᵐbaɾ] 'head' or *ettünzr* [ʔettɤⁿdzˇɐɾ] 's/he paints them'. The glottal stop is predictable and not represented in the orthography. Its insertion is restricted to word-initial environments, because the rules of syllabification maximise onsets in almost all cases (§2.4.3). There is only one exception. Word-medial glottal stop insertion occurs with some of the vowel-initial enclitics like the associative *=ä*, or the possive *=ane*. When the possessive is attached to a word which ends in a vowel, a glottal stop is inserted at the morpheme boundary. An example is *kabe* 'man' → *kabeane* [kaᵐbeʔane] 'of the man'. However, there is a variant, whereby an approximant is inserted [kaᵐbejane].

2.4 The syllable and phonotactics

The phonotactics are best described in terms of the syllable. My description of the syllable is influenced by Blevins (1995). I begin by outlining different syllable templates and the constraints which help to define them. In §2.4.1, I provide evidence for the internal structure of the syllable. Consonant clusters are shown in §2.4.2. I offer a step-by-step analysis of syllabification and epenthesis in §2.4.3. The section closes with a discussion of the minimal word (§2.4.4) and stress (§2.4.5).

2.4.1 Syllable structure

The template for the maximal syllable in Komnzo is [CCVC]$_\sigma$. The minimal syllable is [CV]$_\sigma$ and in a more restricted environment [V]$_\sigma$. Thus, a syllable maximally consists of an onset, which may or may not be complex, a nucleus and a simple coda. Three constraints help to define the possible representations of the syllable in Komnzo:

1. Onsets are obligatory in word-medial and final position. There is a constraint against vowels in onset position: $^*{}_\sigma$[V. The only position where we find vowels in onsets is word-initially, but this is a marginal pattern. If the process of syllabification produces vowel-initial words, a glottal stop fills the onset position (§2.3.3).

2. Syllables may have complex onsets with a maximal number of two adjacent consonants: $_\sigma$[CC. There are constraints on the phonemes involved in CC onset clusters (§2.4.2.1).

3. Syllables may only have a simple coda: C]$_\sigma$. Post-vocalic consonsant clusters are always heterosyllabic VC]$_\sigma$C]$_\sigma$, never tautosyllabic *VCC]$_\sigma$. There are a number of constraints on the possibilities of heterosyllabic consonant clusters (§2.4.2.2).

From the three constraints given above, we can now derive the following possible syllable types: CV, CVC, CCV, CCVC. Word-initially, we also find V and VC. Figure 2.2 presents the syllable as a binary branching construct.

A branching syllable is chosen over a flat structure because there is evidence for the rhyme as a separate node of which nucleus and coda are subnodes. Such evidence includes the different shapes and constraints for onset and coda. Onsets may be complex.

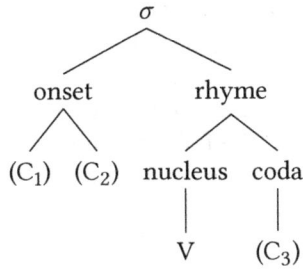

Figure 2.2: The internal structure of the syllable

Codas can only be simple. Onsets are obligatory in almost all cases, while codas are optional. Onsets and rhyme combine freely, thus capturing the generalisation that onsets rarely influence the nucleus. All consonant phonemes may appear in a simple onset (C_1). There are some restrictions, but these are internal to the onset (§2.4.2.1). The coda position (C_3) on the other hand is more limited as to which consonant phonemes may appear. The labialised velar stops /k^w/ and /^{n}g^w/ and the velar nasal /ŋ/ never appear in a coda.

The strongest evidence for an independent rhyme comes from syllable weight, which impacts on vowel length of the nucleus. When there is a specified vowel in the nucleus, the vowel will be realised long in open/light syllables, and it will be realised as short in closed/heavy syllables. This affects different vowels to varying degrees. We find a good example of this in the distribution of the two allophones of /o/, which are [ɔ] and [ŏ]. In the language name *Komnzo* [kŏm^{n}dzɔ] the first vowel is very short (although stressed), and the second vowel is of normal length. It follows that syllable weight influences the length (and sometimes quality) of the vowel in the nucleus. The shortening or lengthening of nuclei may be overridden by minimal word constraints (§2.4.4), but these rules hold for all polysyllabic roots. Consequently, for an adequate description, we require the rhyme as an independent subnode of the syllable.

2.4.2 Consonant clusters

We find tautosyllabic and heterosyllabic consonant clusters in Komnzo. These have very different restrictions on their combinations.

2.4.2.1 Tautosyllabic clusters

Tautosyllabic clusters are restricted to the onset of a syllable. No more than two consonants may occur and they only involve a subset of the phonemes. In a $_\sigma[C_1C_2$ template, C_2 may only be /r/ or /w/.

In a cluster with /r/ we find all consonant phonemes except for the three nasal stops ($^*_\sigma$[mr, $^*_\sigma$[nr, $^*_\sigma$[ŋr), the approximants ($^*_\sigma$[wr and $^*_\sigma$[yr), and /r/ itself ($^*_\sigma$[rr). This points to an explanation in terms of a sonority hierarchy in which nasal and approximants are more sonorous than the trill/tap. Some examples of Cr clusters are *brüzi* [^{m}brytʃi] 'catfish species', *frar* [ɸɞ̌rar] 'small fishtrap', *krüfr* [krɣɸɞ̌r] 'cold', *gru* [ᵑgru:] 'shooting star', *kwras* [kʷras] 'Brolga', *srima kabe* [srima kaᵐbe] 'scout, spy', *thruthru* [ðruðru] 'bamboo species', *trisi* [trisi] 'scratch (v)', and *zra* [tsra:] 'swamp'.

In a cluster with /w/, the restrictions on C_1 are more severe and roots, in which it is attested, are rare. We only find the following phonemes in C_1 position: /k/, /ᵑg/, /ts/, /ⁿdz/, /ð/, and /s/. The first two phonemes in the list pose a problem because one has to find a distinction between a Cw cluster and the labialised velar stops /kʷ/ and /ᵑgʷ/. This is impossible to do for roots, but we find some evidence in a morphophonemic rule in §2.5.3, where the vowel /u/ is realised as [w] and becomes part of a Cw cluster. Some examples of lexemes with Cw clusters are *swäyé* [swæjɞ̌] 'anchoring place', *zwäf* [tswæɸ] 'luke-warm', and *bzwär* [ᵐbɞ̌zwær] 'place name'.

2.4.2.2 Heterosyllabic clusters

Heterosyllabic clusters are much harder to pin down because there are syllabicity alternations, where a coda consonant may become an onset by inserting epenthetic schwa, which breaks up the cluster (§2.4.3). For the following description, I label the two consonants involved C_a (the coda of the first syllable) and C_b (the onset of the following syllable).

We find that where C_a and C_b are identical the consonants are never broken up but always realised as geminates. The attested geminate patterns are described as a phonological rule in §2.3.1. These patterns exclude a number of logically possible geminates: labialised velar stops (/kʷ/ and /ᵑgʷ/), velar nasal (/ŋ/), and all the prenasalised phonemes (/ᵐb/, /ⁿd/, /ᵑg/, and /ⁿdz/).[6] Other heterosyllabic clusters are rather unrestricted. Table 2.7 shows the possible cluster types.[7] Table 2.8 lists examples of these types.

Table 2.7: Heterosyllabic consonant clusters

	/r/	oral stop	pren. stop	nasal	affr.	fric.	approx.	labio-velar
/r/	✓	✓	n/a	✓	✓	✓	✓	✓
oral stop	n/a	✓	n/a	✓	n/a	✓	✓	✓
pren. stop	n/a	✓	n/a	✓	n/a	✓	✓	n/a
nasal	✓	✓	✓	✓	✓	✓	✓	✓
affr.	n/a	✓	n/a	✓	n/a	✓	✓	n/a
fric.	n/a	✓	n/a	✓	✓	✓	✓	✓
approx.	n/a	✓	n/a	✓	✓	✓	n/a	n/a
lab-velar	n/a	n/a	n/a	n/a	n/a	n/a	n/a	n/a

---

[6] The labialised velar stop and the velar nasal may not occur as C_a because these never occur in coda position.
[7] The column and the row labelled "pren. stop" includes prenasalised stops and the prenasalised affricate.

Table 2.8: Examples of attested heterosyllabic consonant clusters

C_a	C_b	example	phonetic	gloss
/r/	[+nasal]	ker.ma	[kerma]	'from tail'
		tr.nä	[tɤ̆rnæ]	'palm frond'
/r/	[+oral]	for.tu	[ɸɤ̆rtu]	'scar'
		ker.ko	[kerko]	'headdress'
/r/	[+affr.]	zr.zü	[tsɤ̆rtʃɤ]	'knee'
/r/	[+fric.]	war.fo	[warɸɔ]	'above'
		kr.si	[kɤ̆rsi]	'block (v)'
		tr.tha	[tɤ̆rða]	'life'
/r/	[+approx.]	kar.wä.si	[karwæsi]	'lie (v)'
		yar.yom.g.si	[jarjɤ̆mⁿgɤ̆si]	'scream (v)'
/r/	[+lab-vel]	ŋa.far.kw.re	[ŋaɸarkʷɤ̆re]	'we leave'
[+oral]	[+oral]	wät.ku	[wæ tku]	'pelican'
[+oral]	[+nasal]	dek.ni.ni	[ⁿdeknini]	'praying mantis'
		rt.maksi	[rɤ̆tmakɤ̆si]	'cut'
[+oral]	[+fric.]	f.rk.thé	[ɸɤ̆rɤ̆kðɤ̆]	'red'
		et.fth	[ʔetɸɤ̆θ]	'sleep (n)'
[+oral]	[+approx.]	thik.ya.si	[ðikjasi]	'build fence'
		zok.wa.si	[tsɤ̆kwasi]	'speech'
		mit.wa.si	[mitwasi]	'swing (v)'
[+oral]	[+lab-vel]	tat.kwo.nam	[tatkʷɔnam]	'tree species'
[+pren.]	[+oral]	gb.ka.rä	[ⁿgɤ̆ᵐpkaræ]	'with pandanus'
[+pren.]	[+nasal]	ŋad.me	[ŋaⁿtme]	'with rope'
[+pren.]	[+fric.]	bad.fo	[ᵐbaⁿtɸɔ]	'to the ground'
[+pren.]	[+approx.]	mnz.wä	[mɤ̆ⁿtswæ]	'house (EMPH)'
[+nasal]	/r/	nin.rr	[ninrɤ̆r]	'with us'
[+nasal]	[+oral]	am.kf	[ʔamkɤ̆ɸ]	'breath'
		thun.t.nä.gwr	[ðuntɤ̆næⁿgwɤ̆r]	'he lost them'
[+nasal]	[+nasal]	kan.motha	[kanmɔða]	'river snake'
[+nasal]	[+pren.]	yar.yom.g.si	[jarjɤ̆mⁿgɤ̆si]	'scream (v)'
		kum.da	[kumⁿda]	'basket'
		kän.brim	[kænᵐbrim]	'come here!'
[+nasal]	[+affr.]	san.zin	[santʃin]	'put him down!'
[+nasal]	[+fric.]	zan.fr	[tsanɸɤ̆r]	'far'
		kam.tha.tha	[kamðaða]	'like a bone'
[+nasal]	[+approx.]	nze.nm.wä	[ⁿdʒenɤ̆mwæ]	'for us (EMPH)'
[+nasal]	[+lab-vel]	ŋan.kwir	[ŋankʷir]	'run hither'
[+affr.]	[+oral]	ez.kn.wr	[ʔetskɤ̆nwɤ̆r]	'he moves them'
[+affr.]	[+nasal]	käz.nob	[kætsnɤ̆ᵐp]	'drink (it)!'
[+affr.]	[+fric.]	fz.fo	[ɸɤ̆tsɸɔ]	'to forest'

C$_a$	C$_b$	example	phonetic	gloss
[+affr.]	[+approx.]	*fz.wä*	[ɸɜ̆tswæ]	'forest (EMPH)'
[+fric.]	[+oral]	*mnz.wä*	[mɜ̆ⁿtswæ]	'house (EMPH)'
[+fric.]	[+affr.]	*buf.zenz*	[ᵐbuɸtʃeⁿts]	'your wife'
[+fric.]	[+fric.]	*ef.thar*	[ʔeɸðaɾ]	'dry season'
		füs.füs	[ɸʏsɸʏs]	'wind'
[+fric.]	[+approx.]	*nzf.wi.yak*	[ⁿtsɜ̆ɸwljak]	'we walked'
		naf.wä	[naɸwæ]	'they (EMPH)'
		fith.wo.g.si	[ɸiθwɔⁿgɜ̆si]	'take out'
[+fric.]	[+lab-vel]	*math.kwi*	[maθkʷi]	'personal name'
		y.ra.kth.kwa	[jɜ̆rakɜ̆θkʷa]	'he put on top'
[+approx.]	[+oral]	*faw.ka.rä*	[ɸaʷkaɾæ]	'with payment'
[+approx.]	[+nasal]	*faw.ma*	[ɸaʷma]	'from payment'
[+approx.]	[+affr.]	*bäw.zö*	[ᵐbæʷtʃœ]	'paperbark'
[+approx.]	[+fric.]	*wy.thk*	[wɜ̆ʲðɜ̆k]	'comes to end'

We can make a number of observations from Table 2.8. The prenasalised phonemes do occur in C$_a$ as well as C$_b$. In the latter case, C$_a$ may only be another nasal, as in *kum.da* [kumⁿda] 'basket', *kum.g.si* [kumⁿgɜ̆si] 'smell (v)', *dm.gu* [ⁿdɜ̆mⁿgu] 'waterhole', *tin.gwä* [tinⁿgʷæ] 'tree species'. If C$_a$ is a phoneme other than a nasal, the cluster will be broken up: *ga.r.da* [ⁿgarɜ̆ⁿda] 'canoe', *ä.th.gam* [ʔæðɜ̆ⁿgam] 'Parinari nonda', *th.f.gar.w.r.mth* [ðɜ̆ɸɜ̆ⁿgarwɜ̆rɜ̆mɜ̆θ] 'they were breaking them'. There are no attested cases of a prenasalised phoneme in C$_b$ with a homorganic nasal in C$_a$, i.e. /m/ + /ᵐb/, /n/ + /ⁿdz/, /n/ + /ⁿd/.

There are only few clusters which involve /r/ in the C$_b$ position. This is caused by maximizing onsets during syllabification, which creates complex onsets clusters of the type Cr. As a consequence, the only heterosyllabic clusters with /r/ in C$_b$ position are the ones which are illegal as onset clusters (e.g. *$_σ$[mr, *$_σ$[nr, *$_σ$[rr). In other words, because *$_σ$[nr is illegal as an onset, we do find it as a heterosyllabic cluster (*nin.rr* [ninrɜ̆r] 'with us'). Likewise, because $_σ$[fr is a legal onset cluster, we never find it as a heterosyllabic cluster.

We do find heterosyllabic clusters which involve /w/ in C$_b$ position and a velar (prensalised) stop in C$_a$ position. Evidence that these clusters are indeed heterosyllabic as opposed to an instantiation of the labialised velar stop /kʷ/ and /ⁿgʷ/ comes from two sources. First, we find examples like *zok.wa.si* [tsɜ̆kwasi] 'speech' where the short, centralised allophone of /o/ shows that the first syllable is a closed syllable (§2.2.1 and §2.4.1). Since the labialised velar stops cannot occur in coda position, we have to assume a syllable boundary between /k/ and /w/. Secondly, verb stems ending in /k/ and /ⁿg/ select the -wr allomorph of the non-dual suffix (§5.5.3.3). In inflected verbs like *ŋa.th.wek.wr* [ŋaðɜ̆wekwɜ̆r] the verb stem *thwek-* and the non-dual suffix *-wr* are separate morphemes and should be analysed as separated syllables. Consequently, heterosyllabic clusters /kw/ and /ⁿgw/ as well as the complex phonemes /kʷ/ and /ⁿgʷ/ are required for an adequate description of the phonological system.

2.4.3 Syllabification and epenthesis

Syllable structure is generally understood not to be defined at the underlying representation (Blevins 1995: 221). Thus, we do not find minimal pairs based on syllabicity. As was explained in §2.2.2, schwa is not a phoneme but an epenthetic vowel inserted in order to break up consonant clusters. There is some degree of free variation in syllabicity and schwa insertion. An example is the word *mrn* 'family, clan' with the locative suffix *-en*. The resulting word *mrnen* 'in the family' may be realised either [mɜɾnen] or [mɜɾɜnen]. There is no phonemic contrast and speakers find it difficult to perceive the difference in syllabicity.

The process of syllabification will be outlined here in the form of three ordered rules, which predict epenthesis and syllable structure:

1. Associate each specified vowel with a syllable nucleus.

2. Establish and maximise onsets in accordance with syllable templates (See constraint number 2 in §2.4.1 on onset clusters). A phonological rule will insert a glottal stop if there is no consonantal onset in word-initial position (§2.3.3).

3. Break-up unsyllabified consonants with epenthetic vowels:

    a) Exception: suffixes which allow no other syllabification than inserting the epenthetic vowel in final position. This includes the adjectivaliser *-thé*, non-singular ergative case marker *-yé* and the first singular actor verb suffix *-é*.

    b) Elsewhere: proceed from right to left breaking up consonant clusters.

    c) After each schwa insertion, establish codas in accordance with possible heterosyllabic consonant clusters. Otherwise, maximise onsets. Exception: word-initial segments are always recognised as onsets.

    d) The epenthetic vowel is [ŭ] and [ĭ] if followed by heterosyllabic /w/ and /j/, respectively. In all other instances it is [ɜ].

The process of syllabification attempts to map the minimal syllable CV onto the underlying representation. The rules give preference to onsets rather than codas. Consequently, we do not find vowel-initial syllables word-medially or word-finally.

I have modelled the process of syllabification as being divided into two steps. Syllables which contain full vowels are recognised first. In a second step epenthetic vowels are inserted to break up unsyllabified consonant clusters. This algorithm proceeds from right to left and inserts epenthetic schwas between unsyllabified consonants to create syllable nuclei. The insertion ensures that onsets are maximised. After each onset, the processs checks against the list of possible heterosyllabic consonant clusters (§2.4.2.2) whether another insertion occurs right away or only after a coda has been recognised. In the latter case, it "jumps" one consonant and breaks up the next pair of unsyllabified consonants. An exception is the word-initial position, where the segment is automatically recognised as an onset. The rules ensure that no word-initial schwa insertion occurs. The direction (right to left) explains why we never find schwa in word-final position. There are only a handful of lexemes in which schwa is attested word-finally, for example *kayé* [kajə̆] 'yesteray|tomorrow'.

The direction is important in order to explain forms like *wonrsoknwr* [wĕnə̆rsɔkə̆n-wə̆r][8] 's/he is bothering me' which is syllabified as *wo.nr.so.kn.wr*. The algorithm is applied from right to left. This is why the cluster *r.s* is first recognised as a possible heterosyllabic consonant cluster. Next, schwa is inserted to form the syllable [nə̆r]. If the process was applied from left to right, one would expect that *n.r* is first recognised as a possible heterosyllabic cluster and schwa would be inserted to form the syllable [rə̆], which yields the incorrect form *won.r.so.kn.wr*. There is some degree of optionality. For example, informants accepted schwa insertion in both places [wĕnə̆rə̆sɔkə̆nwə̆r] in elicitation.[9]

The algorithm specifies that schwa is inserted between consonants disregarding possible onset clusters (§2.4.1), whereas syllables with specified vowels maximise their onsets and produce onset clusters. Indeed, we do not find the possible onset clusters Cr or Cw with epenthetic vowels. There are only two exceptions for Cr. The first is the verb *frm.nz.si* 'fix, prepare', in which the onset cluster /fr/ is never broken up even if the verb is fully inflected, as in *ya.frm.nzr* 's/he prepares him'. The second exception occurs with all verbs in a specific inflection: Word-initially, the irrealis prefix *ra-* becomes part of an onset cluster with the undergoer prefix. This syllable usually contains a specified vowel, for example in *thra-* (2|3NSG) or *kwra-* (1SG). However, when the restricted verb stem is used, dual marking is encoded in the vowel of the syllable. The dual value is encoded by a zero-morpheme, as in *thr.th.bth* [ðrə̆ðə̆ᵐbə̆θ] 'they (2) put them inside'.[10] In this inflection, the Cr cluster is never broken up.

In Figures 2.3-2.6, I present four examples spelling out the algorithm step by step.

2.4.4 Minimal word

We find some constraints on the minimal size of a word in Komnzo. I describe this here, because the minimal word helps to explain a number of phenomena. It has an impact on allophonic variation of /o/ (§2.2.1), vowel length in general, and epenthesis.

Compared to polysyllables, monosyllabic roots have a slightly longer vowel if the syllable is closed, and a very long vowel if they consist of an open syllable. This is relevant for roots with specified vowels only, not for roots with an epenthetic vowel. Three examples are: *fk* [ɸə̆k] 'buttocks', *fäk* [ɸæk] 'jaw', and *fä* [ɸæ:] 'there (DIST)'. In moraic theory, we could rephrase the minimal word constraint as: "Words with specified vowels need to be at least two morae long".

We saw in §2.2.1 that the phoneme /o/ has two allophones: a short centralised rounded vowel [ə̆], which occurs in closed syllables, and a rounded back vowel [ɔ], which occurs

---

[8] The allophone [ə̆] of the phoneme /o/ occurs here not because this might be a closed syllable, but because it follows a labio-velar approximant (§2.2.1)

[9] This might be an artefact introduced by elicitation, because in fluent speech this hardly ever occurs.

[10] This verb is glossed as: th-r-∅-thb-th 2|3NSG-IRR-ND-put.inside.RS-2|3NSG It it a rare inflection because three things have to come together: irrealis mood, restricted verb stem, dual number marker (which is a zero-morpheme in this case).

/kwark/	underlying representation
	↓
/kw$_\sigma$[a]rk/	Rule 1: Associate each specified vowel with a nucleus.
	↓
/$_\sigma$[kwa]rk/	Rule 2: Maximise onsets. → establishes the syllable $_\sigma$[kwa]
	↓
/$_\sigma$[kwa]$_\sigma$[rk]/	Rule 3b: Break up consonant clusters. → schwa is inserted between /r/ and /k/ and creates a CVC syllable
	↓
/kwa.rk/	syllabified form: [kʷaɾə̆k]

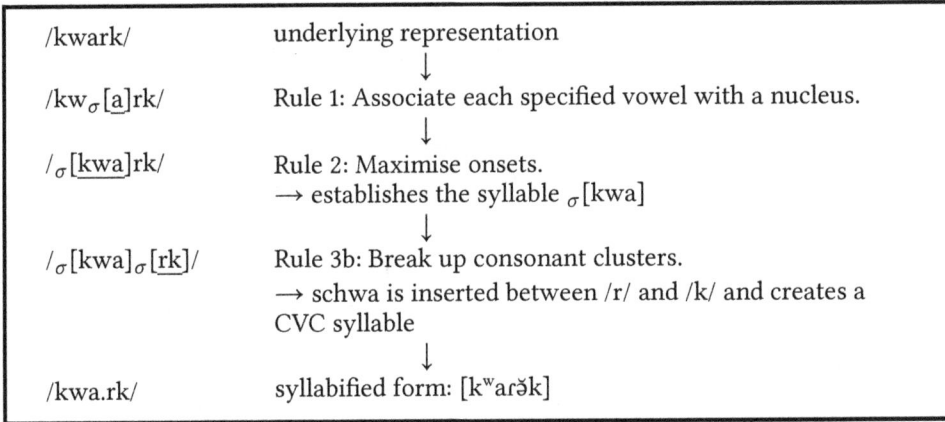

Figure 2.3: Syllabification of *kwark* 'deceased'

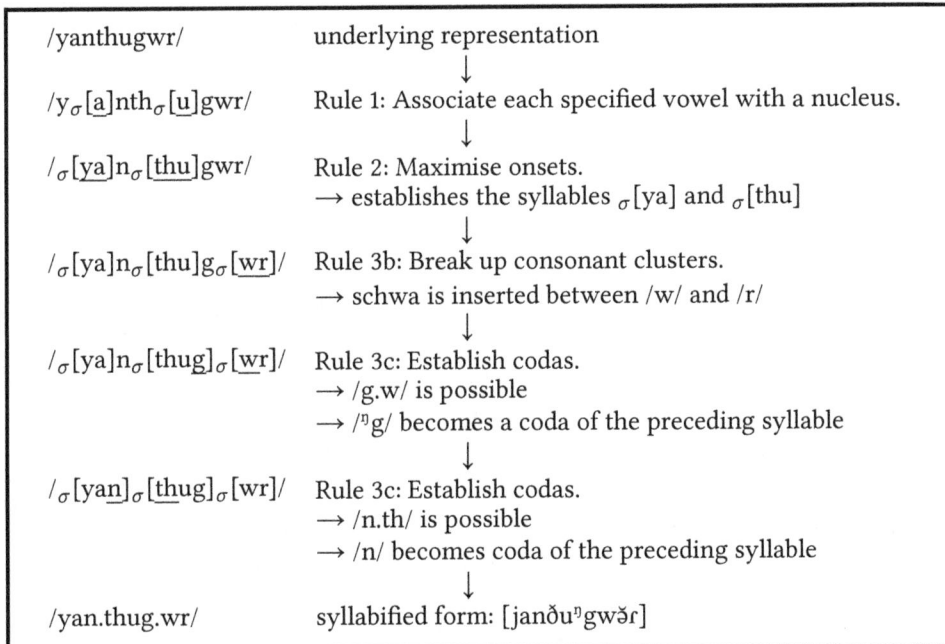

/yanthugwr/	underlying representation
	↓
/y$_\sigma$[a]nth$_\sigma$[u]gwr/	Rule 1: Associate each specified vowel with a nucleus.
	↓
/$_\sigma$[ya]n$_\sigma$[thu]gwr/	Rule 2: Maximise onsets. → establishes the syllables $_\sigma$[ya] and $_\sigma$[thu]
	↓
/$_\sigma$[ya]n$_\sigma$[thu]g$_\sigma$[wr]/	Rule 3b: Break up consonant clusters. → schwa is inserted between /w/ and /r/
	↓
/$_\sigma$[ya]n$_\sigma$[thug]$_\sigma$[wr]/	Rule 3c: Establish codas. → /g.w/ is possible → /ŋg/ becomes a coda of the preceding syllable
	↓
/$_\sigma$[yan]$_\sigma$[thug]$_\sigma$[wr]/	Rule 3c: Establish codas. → /n.th/ is possible → /n/ becomes coda of the preceding syllable
	↓
/yan.thug.wr/	syllabified form: [janðuⁿgwə̆ɾ]

Figure 2.4: Syllabification of *yanthugwr* 's/he tricks him here'

/zwäfiyokw$_\sigma$[é]/	underlying representation: final schwa (1SG) is prespecified as nucleus
	↓
/zw$_\sigma$[ä]f$_\sigma$[i]y$_\sigma$[o]kw$_\sigma$[é]/	Rule 1: Associate each specified vowel with a nucleus.
	↓
/$_\sigma$[zwä]$_\sigma$[fi]$_\sigma$[yo]k$_\sigma$[wé]/	Rule 2: Maximise onsets. → establishes: $_\sigma$[zwä], $_\sigma$[fi], $_\sigma$[yo], $_\sigma$[wé]
	↓
/$_\sigma$[zwä]$_\sigma$[fi]$_\sigma$[yok]$_\sigma$[wé]/	Rule 3c: Establish codas. → /k.w/ is possible → /k/ becomes coda of the preceding syllable
	↓
/zwä.fi.yok.wé/	syllabified form: [tswæɸɩjɔkwɜ̌]

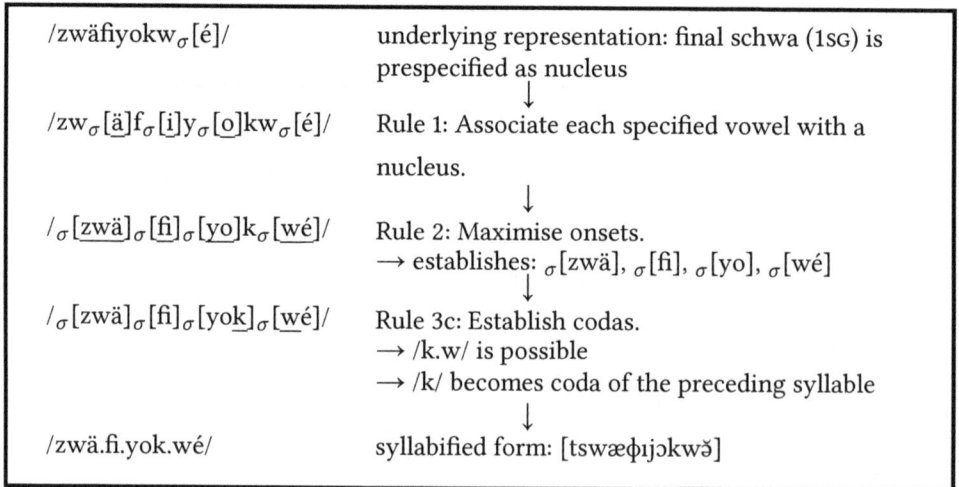

Figure 2.5: Syllabification of *zwäfiyokwé* 'I finished sth. for her'

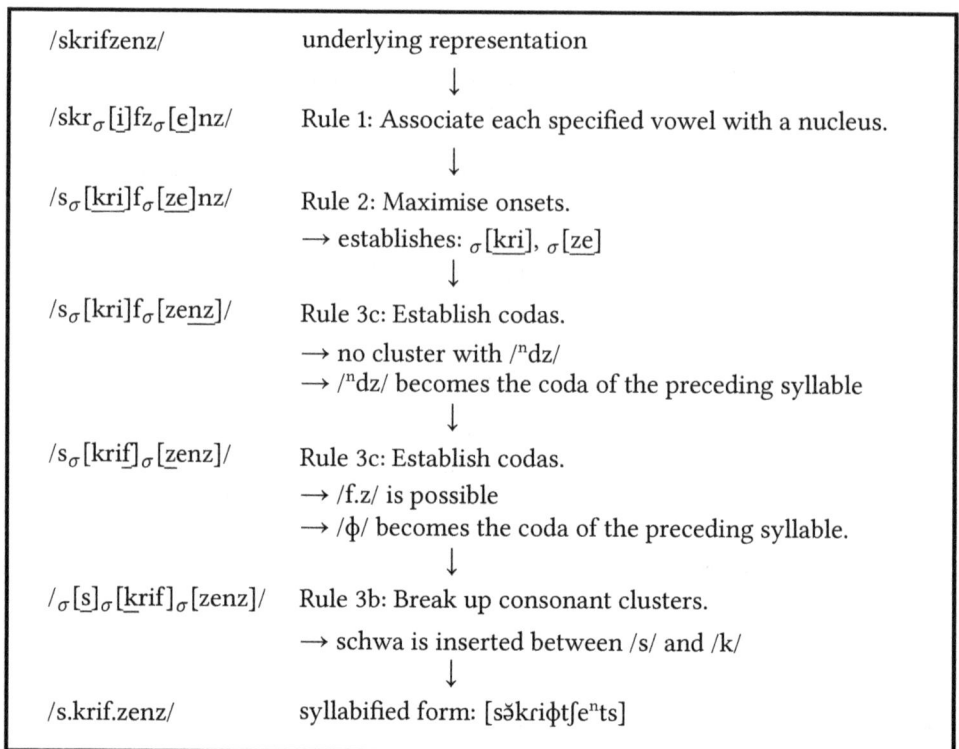

/skrifzenz/	underlying representation
	↓
/skr$_\sigma$[i]fz$_\sigma$[e]nz/	Rule 1: Associate each specified vowel with a nucleus.
	↓
/s$_\sigma$[kri]f$_\sigma$[ze]nz/	Rule 2: Maximise onsets. → establishes: $_\sigma$[kri], $_\sigma$[ze]
	↓
/s$_\sigma$[kri]f$_\sigma$[zenz]/	Rule 3c: Establish codas. → no cluster with /^{n}dz/ → /^{n}dz/ becomes the coda of the preceding syllable
	↓
/s$_\sigma$[krif]$_\sigma$[zenz]/	Rule 3c: Establish codas. → /f.z/ is possible → /ɸ/ becomes the coda of the preceding syllable.
	↓
/$_\sigma$[s]$_\sigma$[krif]$_\sigma$[zenz]/	Rule 3b: Break up consonant clusters. → schwa is inserted between /s/ and /k/
	↓
/s.krif.zenz/	syllabified form: [sɜ̌kɾiɸtʃe^{n}ts]

Figure 2.6: Syllabification of *skrifzenz* 'Skri's wife'

in open syllables. I employed this phenomenon in §2.4.1 to justify the need of syllable weight as a concept. As for the phoneme /o/, in monosyllabic roots the difference between these syllable types is suspended and we do find [ɔ] in closed syllables, as in *gon* [ⁿgɔn] 'hips' or *rot* [rɔt] 'fence type'. Thus, the minimal word constraint overrides these allophonic rules. The constraint applies at the root level and not the level of the inflected word. For example, we find [ɔ] instead of [ŏ] in the verb *thorsi* [ðɔrsi] 'put inside' because *thorsi* is multimorphemic (*thor-* 'put inside' + *-si* NMLZ). With polysyllabic roots, this is not the case and the two variants of /o/ follow the allophonic rule as was layed out in §2.2.1. An example is: *thomonsi* [ðɔmǝ̥nsi] 'pile up firewood', which consists the stem *thomon-* and the nominaliser *-si*.

The minimal word constraint impacts on syllabification because there are two variants for monosyllabic roots of the type CrV(C). These kinds of roots may be realised with a lengthened vowel in the nucleus. Alternatively, an epenthetic vowel may be inserted to break up the onset cluster thus creating a disyllabic form. In this case the specified vowel is of normal length and stress does not shift to the initial epenthetic vowel but remains with the specified vowel. Examples are: *srak* ['srak] ~ [sɜ̆'rak] 'boy' and *zra* ['tsra:] ~ [tsɜ̆'ra] 'swamp'.

2.4.5 Stress

Stress is a syllable-level phenomenon in Komnzo. A stressed syllable is marked by higher intensity and sometimes higher pitch. Vowel duration is not an acoustic correlate of stress. The epenthetic vowel [ɜ̆] is frequently stressed. That being said, specified vowels usually become more centralised and shortened in word-final position, which is always unstressed.

The prosodic domain of stress asignment is the phonological word. Primary stress (marked by preceding ' in the examples) is assigned to the initial syllable of a word. There are a number of exceptions to initial stress which I will describe below. Secondary stress (marked by preceding , in the examples) carries little function in Komnzo and it is often hard to distinguish from unstressed syllables. Secondary stress only occurs in words with more than three syllables. Only few roots have more than three syllables and none have more than four. An example of a four-syllable root is *ngemäku* ['nɜ̆ⁿge̩mæku] 'term of address between foster parent and real parent'. It follows, that all words with more than four syllables are polymorphemic. For example, inflected verbs often comprise more than four syllables, as in *kwamnzokwrmth* ['kʷamⁿdzĕk̩wɜ̆rɜ̆mŏθ] 'they were dancing.'

There are some exceptions to initial stress. For example, in partial reduplication (§4.2) the first syllable is unstressed, as in *rrokar* [rɜ̆'rokar] 'things'. In full reduplication, we find initial stress *rokarrokar* ['rokar̩rokar] as with the corresponding singleton form *rokar* ['rokar]. Another example comes from verbs with a proclitic. In the verb form *bŋatrakwr* [bɜ̆'ŋatrakʷɜ̆r] 's/he falls there', the proclitic *b=* (MED) attaches to the outer layer of the fully inflected verb. Cases like partial reduplication and verbal proclitics should be seen as exceptions to the rule of initial stress.

Stress is assigned from left to right. Words with two, three, and four syllables construct a trochee, dactyl, and ditrochee, respectively. In Table 2.9, I present templatic stress patterns for words between two and four syllables of length.

Table 2.9: Stress patterns of words with two to four syllables

syllable structure	example	phonetic	gloss
$'\sigma\sigma$	nzäthe	['ⁿdʒæðe]	'namesake'
	ebar	['ʔeᵐbaɾ]	'head'
	nzrm	['ⁿdʒɘ̆rɘ̆m]	'flower'
$'\sigma\sigma\sigma$	kafara	['kaβara]	'river pandanus'
	bägwrm	['bæⁿgʷɘ̆rɘ̆m]	'butterfly'
	krbu	['kɘ̆rɘ̆ᵐbu]	'swelling'
$'\sigma\sigma\,\sigma\sigma$	nänzüthzsi	['næⁿdʒɤθˌtsɘ̆si]	'cover with soil/mud'
	kukufasi	['kukuˌɸasi]	'Grey Shrike-trush'
	kdewawa	['kɘ̆ⁿdeˌwawa]	'firefly'

Words with more than four syllables vary in their assignment of secondary stress. Most five-syllable words assign secondary stress to the third syllable, but some assign it to the fourth. Most six-syllable and seven-syllable words assign secondary stress to the fourth syllable, but there are also exceptions. The variation of stress assignment in words with more than four syllables might be explained in terms of open vs. closed syllables, or in terms of specified vs. epenthetic vowel nucleus. The nature of secondary stress in Komnzo remains to be investigated in more detail.

2.5 Morphophonemic Processes

The following section addresses morphophonemic processes which occur through affixation or cliticisation.

2.5.1 Vowel harmony after =wä

Effects of vowel harmony can be found with the emphatic clitic =wä. Encliticisation of =wä causes a change in the quality of the vowel of the preceding syllable regardless whether this syllable is part of the root or another suffix or enclitic. Depending on the vowel quality its impact can be described as fronting or rounding. Some examples are given in Table 2.10.

The vowel harmony does not affect vowels in a closed syllable: *kafarwä* 'really big' not *kafärwä* or *dö kerwä* 'really the lizard tail' not *dö körwä*. The process is blocked by two intervening consonants. Vowel harmony of this type is restricted to morphophonemics

Table 2.10: Vowel harmony caused by =*wä*

process	example	example with =*wä*
fronting of /o/	*karfo* 'to the village'	*kar=fö=wä* village=ABL=EMPH
	bobo 'towards there'	*bobö=wä* MED.ALL=EMPH
raising of /a/	*nima* 'this way'	*nimä=wä* like.this=EMPH
	bafanema 'because of that one'	*baf=ane=mä=wä* RECOG=POSS=CHAR=EMPH
rounding of /e/	*zafe* 'long ago'	*zafö=wä* long.ago=EMPH
	etfthme 'overnight'	*etfth=mö=wä* sleep=INS=EMPH

because we do find lexemes where the vowels in question occurs in adjacent syllables, as in *namä* 'good' or *dowä* 'Wompoo Fruit Dove'.

2.5.2 Dissimilation between prefix and verb stem

We find a number of verb stems in which the vowel quality of the prefix is raised from /æ/ to /e/. This occurs only in inflections which build on the restricted stem, i.e. it is the prefix vowel which encodes the dual versus non-dual contrast. The vowel /æ/ marks usually non-dual, whereas /a/ or zero mark dual number. See §5.3 for stem types and §5.5.3.4 for a description of pre-stem dual marking. Dissimilation targets the non-dual /æ/ and raises it to /e/. The trigger is the first vowel of the verb stem. Raising takes place when the first vowel is either /a/ or /æ/; for two verb stems it is /œ/. Some examples are: *mar-* 'see', *far-* 'set off', *faf-* 'hold' and *wär-* 'crack, happen', *rä-* 'be, do', *räs-* 'erect', *söbäth-* 'ascend' and *sörfäth-* 'descend'.[11] Thus, for verbs like *marasi* the non-dual of a recent past perfective is not realised as **zämar* but *zemar* 'he looked at himself'. Depending on syllabification and intervening prefixes, the trigger vowel in the verb stem and the prefix can be separated by another syllable. In most cases, this is a syllable created by epenthesis. Verb stems like *mräs-* 'stroll', *thfär-* 'jump' and *thkäf-* 'start' have an epenthetic vowel after the first consonant in their nominalisations, for example *m.rä.z.si* 'stroll'. In the

---

[11]The majority of Komnzo verbs have two verb stems, a restricted and an extended stem (§5.3). I list the restricted stems here, because the first vowel of the stem is relevant here. Elsewhere in this grammar, I use the extended stem or the nominalisation to refer to verbs. Therefore, I provide the respective extended verb stems here: *mar-* 'see', *fark-* 'set off', *fa-* 'hold', *wä-* 'crack, happen', *rä-* 'be', *räz-* 'erect', *mrä-* 'stroll', *thfä-* 'jump', *thkäfak-* 'start', *sog-* 'ascend', *rsör-* 'descend'.

inflected verb form, the initial consonant is syllabified as a coda: *zemräs* 'he strolled around'. If the venitive prefix *n-* is added to the inflection, the trigger vowel and prefix vowel are separated by another syllable, but the raising still takes place: *ze.nm.räs* 'he strolled towards here'. The raising pattern described here applies to inflections of various TAM categories (irrealis, imperatives, iteratives). They all share the use of the restricted stem and, consequently the encoding of duality takes place in the vowel of the prefix.

A special case is the copula *rä-*. Although highly irregular in many ways, it follows the dissimilation pattern just described. What is special about the copula is that the past suffix *-a* triggers the same kind of raising in the stem of the copula. Thus, we find *erera* 'they were' instead of *ˣerära*. Without the the past suffix, raising takes not place: *erä* 'they are'.

Raising of the prefix vowel is a morphophonemic process, not a general phonological process. For example, we do find lexemes where /æ/ and /a/ occur in adjacent syllables, as in (*atätö* 'tree species', *mätraksi* 'bring out'). The same is true for /æ/ and /æ/ in adjacent syllables, as in (*krätär* 'tree species', *thäfäm* 'ripples'). Moreover, the /æ/ vowel is not raised to /e/ in verb inflections that build on the extended stem. Consider the 2|3NSG *e-* and the 3SG.FEM *w-* of the alpha prefix series (§5.5.1.4). The valency changing prefix *a-* follows in the next slot and it merges with these two prefixes, i.e. they are realised as *ä-* and *wä-*, respectively. However, the /æ/ vowel in the prefixes is not raised to *e-* if the first vowel of the stem is /æ/. For example, the verb *fänzsi* 'show' is realised as *wäfänzr* 's/he shows her' and not *ˣwefänzr*. One reason for this might be that raising the vowel to /e/ would neutralise the valency changing prefix *a-*. Another explanation might be that the raising pattern developed together with pre-stem dual marking, which is found only with restricted stem (§5.5.3.4). Restricted stems in turn do not combine with the prefixes of the alpha series (§6.2.1), which explains why these are not affected.

2.5.3 Approximant ↔ high vowel

In two different parts of the verbal inflectional paradigm, a change from the approximants to high vowels ([w] → [u]/[ü], and [y] → [i]) and the reverse is found.

All of the verbal proclitics consist only of a consonant, e.g. the immediate past *n=* or the three deictic proclitics *z=* PROX, *b=* MED, and *f=* DIST. These are cliticised to otherwise fully inflected verbs. In most cases, this creates an extra syllable word-initially, as in *b.ŋa.trak.wr* 's/he falls there'. Some of the verb prefixes in the alpha series begin with an approximant, for example (*wo-* 1SG, *w-* 3SG.FEM, and *y-* 3SG.MASC). When the clitics are attached to these prefixes, the approximants are realised as high vowels: *u-* 1SG, *ü-* 3SG.FEM, and *i-* 3SG.MASC. A few examples are given in (1-3).

(1)   *burera*
     b=wo-rä-ra
     MED=1SG.α-COP.ND-PST
     'I was there.'

(2) *zimithgr*
z=y-mi-thgr
PROX=3SG.MASC.α-hang-STAT.ND
'It hangs here.'

(3) *zürugr*
z=w-rugr
PROX=3SG.FEM.α-sleep.ND
'She sleeps here.'

Another change which involves high vowels and approximants is attested only for [u] ↔ [w]. The formatives of the beta-2 prefix series (β2) end in a [u] vowel, for example *ku-* 1SG, *su-* 3SG.MASC, *thu-* 2|3NSG. The valency changing prefix *a-* occurs in the following slot, for example *ku-a-* 'for me', *su-a-* 'for him', *thu-a-* 'for you/them'. In its presence, the [u] vowel becomes part of an onset consonant cluster and is realised as a high back approximant [w]. An example is given in (4-5).

(4) *thufsinzr*
thu-fsi-nzr-∅
2|3NSG.β2-count.EXT-ND-2|3SG
'S/he counted them.'

(5) *thwafsinzr*
thu-a-fsi-nzr-∅
2|3NSG.β2-VC-count.EXT-ND-2|3SG
'S/he counted for them.'

2.6 Loanwords and loanword phonology

A number of speech sounds are restricted to loanwords. These are the voiced oral stops [b], [d], and [g], the lateral approximant [l] and a few diphthongs. The "donor languages" of almost all loanwords found in Komnzo are either English or Hiri Motu. Only few loanwords come from Bahasa Indonesia, for example the terms for introduced fish species: *ikan lele* 'Clarias batrachas', *mujair* 'Oreochromis mossambicus', *gastor* 'Channa striata'. An increasing number of people start to learn the third offical language of Papua New Guinea - Tok Pisin - and sometimes expressions like *maski* 'nevermind' can be heard among younger Komnzo speakers. Otherwise Tok Pisin plays only a minor role in loanwords.

From the degree of indigenisation of loanwords we can distinguish at least two periods: an early phase which lasted until the 1960s and a second phase from that time until today. The boundary between the two periods is rather fuzzy. The first period was characterised by English speaking patrol officers and officials who visited the area for very short periods. The second period began with the opening of a Mission school in Rouku in the mid 1960s. At the beginning, the language of instruction was Hiri Motu. In the 1970s the school was moved to Morehead and since then, the language of instruction is English.

We find linguistic evidence for the two periods. Loanwords from the first period have undergone indigenisation in order to adapt to Komnzo phonology. Loans which entered the language during the second period are much closer to the original English or Motu pronunciation. An example is the word *doctor*. While it is pronounced [dokta] nowadays, some older speakers still use a second variant *nzokta* [ⁿdzokta] which they report was common in their parent's and grandparent's generation.

Words from the first period are: *frayn misin* [ɸrajə̆n mɪsɪn] 'plane, flying machine', *kas raba* [kas ɾaᵐba] 'gas lamp', *dis* [ⁿdiːs] 'dish, plate', *damaki* [ⁿdamakɪ] 'dynamite'. We find regular correspondences of English phonemes mapping onto Komnzo phonology. The bilabial stop [p] becomes a bilabial fricative [ɸ] in *frayn misin*, but in a cluster with the bilabial nasal [m] in *kas raba* it becomes a prenasalised voiced bilabial stop [ᵐb]. The velar voiced stop [g], also in *kas raba*, comes out as a voiceless velar stop [k]. The lateral approximant [l] in English *flying* becomes an alveolar tap or trill [ɾ ~ r] in Komnzo *frayn* and again in *kas raba*. The English diphthong [aɪ̯] in 'dynamite' is monophthongised in *damaki*. The voiced alveolar stop [d] becomes prenasalised [ⁿd] in *damaki* and *dis*[12]. In the same word, the post-alveolar fricative [ʃ] turns into an alveolar fricative [s]. However, there are too few loans from this early period to make a systematic comparison of all English phonemes in different environments.

The second period, which lasts until today, is characterised by loan phonemes. Indigenisation is found to a lesser degree. The second period is also characterised by the influx of loans from Hiri Motu. We find loan phonemes in the oral voiced stops [b], [d] and [g], as in *bara* 'paddle', *durua* 'help', *dibura* 'prisoner', *gunana* 'place name'[13] from Hiri Motu, and *baisikol* 'bicycle' from English. Note that the English diphthong [aɪ̯] is retained and not monophthongised and the lateral approximant [l] also does not change.

There are two correspondences which we find in both periods. The first is between the voiceless bilabial stop [p] in English and the voiceless bilabial fricative [ɸ] in Komnzo. The second correspondence is between the lateral approximant [l] and the alveolar trill/flap [ɾ ~ r]. In the early period, [l] was changed in all environments, but in the second period this only occurs in [pl] clusters in English. Elsewhere, [l] is taken over into Komnzo as a loan phoneme. We have seen some examples from the first period above. Examples from the second period are: *fren* 'plane', *fenzil* 'pencil', and *sosfen* 'saucepan'.

2.7 Orthography development

There is no writing tradition in Komnzo, but most people can read and write in one of the official languages, namely English and Motu. The mission school, which was based at Rouku during the 1960s, operated in Motu, but today English is the teaching language at the primary school in Morehead. Thus, reading and writing in Komnzo has not been promoted in the past. As a consequence, literacy in one's mother tongue is an alien concept for most Komnzo speakers.

---

[12]There is no explanation for the change from English [t] > Komnzo [k] in *damaki* 'dynamite'.

[13]*Gunana* means 'the former (one)' in Hiri Motu. In Komnzo, it designates a place 'where old Rouku used to be' as informants put it. A new hamlet was founded there a few years ago.

  The first attempt to develop an orthography for Komnzo was during an alphabet workshop organised by Marco and Alma Bouvé at Morehead Station in 2000.[14] It brought together representatives from a dozen villages. The two representatives from Rouku were Greg Marua and Wendy Yasii. When I began my work in Rouku, this orthography was not used except for a few words that were written on the blackboard in the elementary school. Regrettably, the Rouku elementary school has been dysfunctional since 2010. During my fieldwork I have organised two orthography meetings. The outcome of these meetings was the Komnzo Language Council, which includes representatives of all clans. The language council has remained an abstract administrative body overseeing my work. In practice, I concentrated most translation and elicitation work on 4-5 interested individuals. Together, we have revised the orthography several times. Table 2.11 and Figure 2.7 show the differences between the orthography from the workshop in 2000 and the current orthography. Changes are shown with an arrow ($\rightarrow$).

Table 2.11: Comparison of orthographies: consonants

	bilabial	dental	alveolar	palato-alveolar	palatal	velar	labio-velar
stop & affricate	b $\rightarrow$ □		t	ts $\rightarrow$ z		k	□ $\rightarrow$ kw
prenasalised stop & affricate	mb $\rightarrow$ b		nt $\rightarrow$ d	nj $\rightarrow$ nz		nþ$\rightarrow$ g	□ $\rightarrow$ gw
fricative	f	th	s				
nasal	m		n			ng $\rightarrow$ ŋ	
lateral			r				
semivowel					y		w

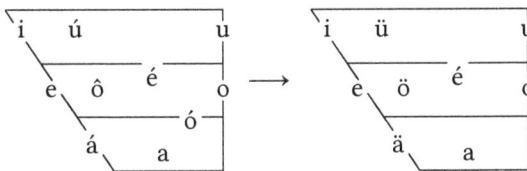

Figure 2.7: Comparison of orthographies: vowels

---

[14]The workshop was supported by the Summer Institute of Linguistics (SIL).

3 Word classes

In this chapter, I describe the major and minor word classes of Komnzo. I provide the necessary criteria to determine the word class of a given lexical item based on its morphological possibilities, syntactic distribution and semantic content. This chapter contains detailed information on smaller word classes or subclasses which will not be discussed elsewhere in the grammar. For these, I list all known members for quick reference.

The eight word classes include nominals (§3.1), verbs (§3.2), adverbs (§3.3), particles (§3.4), clitics (§3.5), connectives (§3.6), ideophones (§3.7), and interjections (§3.8). Nominals constitute a superclass comprising a variety of subclasses: nouns (§3.1.2), property nouns (§3.1.4), adjectives (§3.1.5), quantifiers and numerals (§3.1.6), locationals (§3.1.7), temporals (§3.1.8), personal pronouns (§3.1.9), interrogatives (§3.1.10), indefinites (§3.1.11), and demonstratives (§3.1.12).

I categorise Komnzo word classes along a number of lines. The clearest distinction is between inflecting (nominals and verbs) and uninflecting word classes (all other). The distinction between open and closed word classes is more difficult to define. Only a few nominal subclasses (nouns, property nouns, numerals) and interjections accept new members in the form of loanwords or neologisms. Although large in terms of members, verbs are not an open word class. Major words classes are nouns, property nouns and verbs, each with more than 300 members in the current dictionary. All other word classes have less than 30 members and are considered minor classes.

3.1 Nominals

Nominals are the largest word class, consisting of a number of subclasses. The largest are the open subclasses of nouns (§3.1.2) and property nouns (§3.1.4), which both readily accept borrowings from other languages, particularly English and Motu. Adjectives (§3.1.5) constitute a minor, closed class. The nominal superclass includes a number of other small, closed word classes. These are quantifiers and numerals (§3.1.6), locationals (§3.1.7), temporals (§3.1.8), personal pronouns (§3.1.9), interrogatives (§3.1.10) and demonstratives (§3.1.12).

The unifying characteristic of nominals is their ability to serve as the host of case marking clitics. However, not all nominal subclasses can take the full set of case distinctions. For example, while nouns and personal pronouns are prototypical nominals and take all case, demonstratives, temporals, and locationals are more limited in the ability to receive case clitics.

3.1.1 Criteria for distinguishing between nouns, property nouns and adjectives

Before addressing each subclass, it is necessary to give an overview of the distinction between nouns, property nouns and adjectives. The two main criteria involved are the ability to act as the head of a noun phrase and the ability to trigger agreement in both gender and number. Further criteria are the ability to enter into a possessive construction, the possibility of taking the adjectivaliser *-thé* and the different functions of the instrumental case *=me*. This section only lists the criteria. Examples are given in the following sections, which address each subclass in turn (§3.1.2-3.1.5).

Nouns and property nouns can act as the head of a noun phrase, whereas adjectives cannot. See §7.5 for further discussion of headedness. An adjective may be the only visible element of a noun phrase, but this is possible only if the omitted head can be established through context. This first criterion groups property nouns with nouns and singles out adjectives.

Agreement in gender and number is only triggered by nouns. Gender in Komnzo is covert (§3.1.3), and the agreement target for gender is the 3rd singular prefix of the verb. Number agreement is marked at various morphological sites on the verb including the undergoer prefix, the actor suffix, and the duality affix (§5.5.3). Adjectives fail to trigger gender or number agreement. Property nouns also fail to trigger gender agreement, because they are not indexed in the prefix. However, property nouns trigger a default SG number agreement in the suffix, for example in experiencer-object constructions where a property noun can be the stimulus flagged with the ergative case (§8.3.10). Nouns trigger both gender and number agreement. Hence, the criterion of agreement groups property nouns with adjectives and singles out nouns.

As far as the other criteria are concerned, possessive constructions are only possible with nouns and property nouns and not with adjectives. The adjectivaliser *-thé* is common with nouns of a particular semantic field, i.e. nouns which can used to described a more general characteristic. For example, *frk* 'blood', *nzafar* 'sky' for deriving colour terms. The adjectivaliser is optional with property nouns, but ungrammatical with adjectives. The instrumental case marker *=me* serves its prototypical function with nouns, but property nouns and adjectives function as adverbials when marked with the instrumental case. Table 3.1 provides an overview of the criteria.

3.1.2 Nouns

Nouns constitute a large, open class of lexical items which readily accepts new members by forming neologisms or adding loanwords from other languages. Nouns are typically referential and denote objects, locations, abstract notions, kinship relations, and proper names.

Semantically nouns can be subdivided into common nouns, kinship nouns, and proper nouns. Common nouns depict the natural world (*no* 'rain', *ttfö* 'creek', *ymd* 'bird') as well as artefacts (*mnz* 'house', *nag* 'grass skirt', *kufraru* 'bamboo flute') or abstract concepts (*bthan* 'magic', *wath* 'dance (n)', *dradr* 'taboo'). Common nouns are syntactically least

Table 3.1: Feature matrix for nominals

	nouns	property nouns	adjectives
gender agreement	+	−	−
number agreement	+	−[a]	−
head of NP	+	+	−
possessive construction	+	+	−
adjectivaliser -*thé*	+	+/−	−
INS case	instrument	adverbial	adverbial

[a]There is default number agreement (SG) in experiencer-object constructions (§8.3.10)

restricted, i.e. they enter into most nominal constructions and can be marked for all cases compared to the other nominal subclasses. Kinship nouns can intrinsically be specified for gender (*ŋafe* 'father', *ŋame* 'mother') or be flexible as to which gender is assigned (*nane* 'elder sibling', *ngth* 'younger sibling'). Many kinship terms are self-reciprocal (*ŋäwi* 'maternal uncle ↔ sister's child', *yamit* 'exchange cousin ↔ exchange cousin'). Kinship nouns frequently enter the close possessive construction (§4.7.2). Proper nouns consist of personal names and place names. Place names are always feminine and they are often compounds made up of a plant name and the word *zfth* 'base, stem, reason' like in the place name *gani zfth* ('Endiandra brassii + base'). Proper nouns are hardly ever modified by demonstratives, quantifiers or adjectives.

Nouns are distinct from other nominals in being the only lexical items which trigger gender agreement. The agreement target is the third person singular prefix of the verb (§5.5.2). The semantics of the gender system is described in the following section (§3.1.3). Additionally, nouns trigger number agreement, in this they resemble other nominal subclasses such as pronouns. The agreement target for number depends on the type of argument, but it involves three distinct verbal affix slots (the undergoer prefix, the actor suffix, and the duality marker). The verb morphology will be laid out in chapter 5, but we get a glimpse of the agreement system in examples (5-8).

Nominal number marking takes place on the level of the noun phrase, leaving aside the use of numerals. Nominal number marking is underspecified for three reasons. First, only animates are marked for number, especially humans. Example (1) shows the allative case marker on several nominals, and only the animate referents are marked for number. Note that the spatial cases (locative, allative, ablative) have special formatives for animate referents (§4.8). Secondly, number marking on the noun only occurs when the respective noun phrase is flagged with a case marker. Thus, nouns out of syntactic context or noun phrases in the absolutive case, which is zero, have no nominal number marking. Thirdly, nominal number marking is based on a singular versus non-singular distinction.[1] The full three-way distinction between singular, dual and plural is encoded in the verb. It

---

[1]The associative case is an exception. With animate referents it is used for the inclusory construction (§7.6), and there the values are dual and plural, instead of singular and non-singular.

follows that the majority of nouns or noun phrases are underspecified for number, and for core case arguments, number is assigned morpho-syntactically via the agreement system of the verb.

(1) *wati **nzedbo** zanrifthath **mayawanmedbo** rouku **bänefo** ... **masufo**.*
wati nzedbo zan\rifth/ath   mayawa=nmedbo   rouku
then 1NSG.ALL 2|3PL:SBJ>3SG.FEM:OBJ:PST:PFV/send mayawa=ALL.ANIM.NSG rouku
bäne=fo   (.) masu=fo
RECOG=ALL (.) masu=ALL
'Then they send the word to us ... to the Mayawas in Rouku ... to there ... to Masu.'

[tci20120814 ABB #34-35]

Nouns may undergo reduplication, which signals plurality and/or non-prototypicality, as in *yawiyawi* 'money, coins' from *yawi* 'seed' or *yamyam* 'marks' from *yam* 'footprint'. An example is given in (2) and (3). Example (2) shows the noun *znsä* 'work', while the reduplicant *znsäznsä* was often used for the kind of elicitation, recording and transcription work that I was doing (3).

(2) *znsä kwabznwrme dagon fawr.*
znsä kwa\bz/nwrme   dagon faw=r
work 1PL:SBJ:PST:DUR/work food   payment=PURP
'We worked for food.'   [tci20120924-01 TRK #50]

(3) *thrma n kwot thräre bänema **znsäznsär** thwanyan.*
thrma n   kwot   thrä\r/e   bäne=ma   znsä-znsä=r
later   IMN properly 1PL:SBJ>2|3PL:OBJ:IRR:PFV/do MED=CHAR REDUP-work=PURP
thwan\yan/
2|3DU:SBJ:RPST:IPFV:VENT/walk
'Later, we will get them out properly because you came for work.'

[tci20130907-02 JAA #251]

In order to derive adjectives, some nouns take the adjectivaliser suffix *-thé*. We can see this most clearly in the colour terms: *kwayanthé* 'white' from *kwayan* 'light' or *frkthé* 'red' from *frk* 'blood'. The productivity of *-thé* is rather limited and there are a number of lexical items which show frozen morphology. For example, *yfrsé* 'black' from *yfr* 'Syzygium sp' (used for black paint) shows an irregular variant, *-sé* instead of *-thé*. For *dbömsé* 'blunt' there is no corresponding noun without the suffix. The restrictions in terms of productivity can be explained by the presence of a class of property nouns to be discussed in §3.1.4. There is an alternative strategy for deriving colour and shape adjectives. This involves the formation of a compound with the word *woku* 'skin' which takes the adjectivaliser suffix. The Komnzo equivalent for English 'green' is expressed by *wämne taga wokuthé* (lit. 'tree leaf skin-like') or the translation of 'round' is *aki wokuthé* (lit. 'moon skin-like'). An example of this strategy is given in (4), where the speaker characterises a man as looking a bit 'boyish'.

(4) *fi sraksrak wokuthé yara.*
    fi   srak-srak woku-thé ya\r/a
    3.ABS REDUP-boy skin-ADJZR 3SG.MASC:SBJ:PST:IPFV/be
    'He was a bit boyish.'   [tci20131013-02 ABB #211]

All common nouns can serve as the host for case clitics (ergative, dative, possessive, locative, allative, ablative, instrumental, characteristic, purposive, associative, proprietive, privative, similative) or receive other nominal morphology (exclusive, emphatic). As I describe in §4.3, case markers operate at the level of the noun phrase. Noun phrases headed by a noun can function as arguments or adjuncts, as well as complements of the copula. This is illustrated by the ergative and absolutive-marked arguments in example (5).[2] Example (6) shows a locative-marked noun which functions as an adjunct.

(5) *brbrf garda bifnza.*
    brbr=f   garda   b=y\fn/nza
    spirit=ERG.SG canoe(ABS) MED=2|3SG:SBJ>3SG.MASC:OBJ:PST:IPFV/hit
    'The spirit was hitting (against) the canoe there.'   [tci20120904-02 MAB #87]

(6) *masun ni fä nzwamnzrm.*
    masu=n   ni   fä   nzwa\m/nzrm
    masu=LOC 1NSG DIST 1PL:SBJ:PST:DUR/dwell
    'We were staying in Masu over there.'   [tci20120821-02 LNA #100]

Nouns typically function as the head of a noun phrase or as the head of a nominal compound. Compounds are described in §7.5.3. Example (7) shows the noun *waniwani* 'picture, shadow' as the head of the noun phrase modified by the demonstrative *zane* and the adjective *katan*. Nouns may act as modifiers within a noun phrase. In the nominal compound in (8) the two nouns act as head (*kam* 'bone') and modifier (*tauri* 'wallaby'). In the examples NPs are marked off by [].

(7) *fof zäbth zane katan waniwani.*
    fof   zä\bth/   [zane   katan waniwani]
    EMPH 2|3SG:SBJ:RPST:PFV/finish DEM:PROX small picture
    'This little movie is finished.'   [tci20120914 RNA #63]

(8) *ŋathayé tauri kam yanathrth.*
    ŋatha=yé   [tauri   kam] ya\na/thrth
    dog=ERG.NSG wallaby bone 2|3PL:SBJ>3SG.MASC:OBJ:NPST:IPFV/eat
    'The dogs are chewing a wallaby bone.'   [tci20120818 ABB #42]

---

[2] The absolutive case is zero-marked in singular, and the non-singular formative *-é* is rare throughout the corpus. In example (5), the word *garda* 'canoe' is glossed with the absolutive case in brackets. Note that for most examples in this grammar, I do not gloss the absolutive if it is zero-marked. Exceptions are those examples, where the case value is important for the decription.

3.1.3 The semantics of the gender system

The gender system is covert as there are no formal elements on a given noun showing its gender. Instead, the two categories, feminine and masculine, are shown in the verb prefix. Nouns have either fixed gender (most nouns) or flexible gender (kin terms, certain animals).

Animate nouns, for which sex can be determined easily, for example dogs, pigs, wallabies, and of course humans, are placed in the respective category. Words with fixed gender allow us to set up some general semantic principles of classification. For example, elongated, big objects are usually masculine, while small round objects are feminine. Lexemes related to place and land are usually feminine. Abstract concepts or nominalised verbs are usually feminine. Most fish species are masculine, with the exception of the numerous catfish species, which are all feminine. Other species, like birds, are much more varied. Speakers often use the phrases *srak yé* 'it's a boy' or *matma rä* 'it's a girl', when being asked about the gender category of a particular word. Table 3.2 gives an overview of the semantic characteristics and lists some examples as well as exceptions.

A number of words always occur in plural, which means that no gender is triggered in the agreement target. Only some of them are clear mass nouns, like *kithuma* 'sago pulp' and *grau* 'red clouds'. Others can be visually perceived as mass nouns, for example *ŋarake* 'fence' and *nag* 'grass skirt'. On the other hand, words like *no* 'water' are feminine and not plural. Interestingly, body parts that exist in pairs, like arms legs, and eye, are often used in the plural, even though the language has a dual number category.

A few stems differ in their meaning depending on gender. For example, *mni* means 'fire' when feminine, but 'firewood' when masculine. Other examples are: *ekri* (FEM) 'flesh' vs. *ekri* (MASC) 'meat', *no* (FEM) 'water' vs. *no* (MASC) 'rain' and *efoth* (FEM) 'day' vs. *efoth* (MASC) 'sun'.

Words with flexible gender are mostly kin terms, for example sibling terms, which encode relative age difference, but not gender. Thus, the word *nane* can mean 'older brother' or 'older sister'. Many kin terms are reciprocal and may hold between a man and a woman. For example *ŋäwi* is used between a person and her/his mother's brothers. In other words, a young girl or boy calls her/his mother's brother *ŋäwi*, and he uses the same term back to her/him. The same is true for a man's parents-in-law. He calls both of them *enat* and they call him the same. Sometimes this can be specified by adding the word for 'woman' or 'man', for example *enat ŋare* 'mother-in-law' (lit. 'parent-in-law woman').

Other nouns with flexible gender are animals for which a sex distinction is noticeable, for example *tauri* 'wallaby', *ruga* 'pig' or *ŋatha* 'dog'. Yet other species like fish or insects are not flexible. Birds for which there is a visible difference between male and female adults are assigned different lexemes altogether. For example, the male Eclectus Parrot (Eclectus roratus) is referred to as *krara*, and the female as *tiŋa*, but in Komnzo both lexemes are masculine. Mismatches between biological gender and grammatical gender are quite common with birds. Two more examples are *nzöyar*, the Fawn-breasted Bowerbird (Chlamydera cerviniventris) and *ythama*, the Raggiana Bird-of-paradise (Paradisaea raggiana). For both species, the lexemes seem to refer only to the male birds, which can be

Table 3.2: The semantics of the gender system

semantics	gender	examples	exceptions
big, elongated objects	MASC	*naifa* 'bush knife' *wämne* 'tree' *nabi* 'bow' *turama* 'python' *with* 'banana' *nasi* 'long yam'	*sifren* 'grass knife' *waga* 'leg'
small, round objects	FEM	*yawi* 'seed, fruit' *wawa* 'yam' *yare* 'bag' *brnze* 'lips' *riwariwa* 'ring' *kwanz* 'bald head'	*nzagum* 'fly' *tora* 'dog whistle' *tef* 'spot'
plants, trees	MASC	*rugaruga* 'tree species' (Gmelina ledermannii) *withwith* 'vine species' (Pseuduvaria sp) *mür* 'grass species' (Cyperus sp)	*ŋazi* 'coconut' *gb* 'palm species' (Livistona sp)
fish	MASC	*find* 'Giant Glassfish' (Parambassis gulliveri) *kwazür* 'Narrow-fronted Tandan' (Neosilurus ater) *wifaza* 'Seven-spot Archerfish' (Toxotes chatareus)	catfish species *katif* 'Trout Morgunde' (Mogurnda mogurnda)
catfish	FEM	*zök* 'Broad-snouted Catfish' (Potamosilurus latirostris) *thrfam* 'Daniel's Catfish' (Cochlefelis danielsi)	*ikan lele* 'Walking Catfish' (Clarias batrachus)
events	FEM	*zan* 'fighting' *borsi* 'game, laughter' *si zübraksi* 'prayer'	*wath* 'dance'
landscape	FEM	*mni* 'fire' *kar* 'place, village' *zra* 'swamp' *daw* 'garden' *ŋars* 'river'	

explained by the fact that the females are less visible both in their plumage as well as in their behaviour. The Komnzo words, *nzöyar* and *ythama*, are assigned to the feminine category, and they are often talked about as being female birds.

3.1.4 Property nouns

There is a class of lexical items in Komnzo which shares features of both nouns and adjectives. Henceforth, I will refer to them as "property nouns" because they denote either physical properties (*fagwa* 'width', *dambe* 'thickness', *zrin* 'heaviness') or abstract mental states (*noku* 'anger', *miyo* 'desire', *miyatha* 'knowledge', *weto* 'happiness'). A few property nouns are more event-oriented and express behavioural patterns (*mogu* 'concentration', *ofe* 'absence', *müsa* 'restlessness', *zirkn* 'persistence', *waro* 'theft, deception'). Note that I translate property nouns in the glosses sometimes as abstract nouns (*miyamr* 'ignorance', *züb* 'depth') and sometimes as adjectives ('ignorant' and 'deep' respectively). I see no analytic gain in choosing one over the other and applying it consistently to all glosses in this grammar. The term "property noun" is chosen because most members of this word class express some physical or non-physical property, only a minority of them are event-oriented.

Property nouns can act as the head of a noun phrase and as such they behave as host for all case clitics just like nouns. However, with respect to agreement, they are syntactically inert in two ways. First, property nouns do not register in the undergoer prefix of verbs and consequently do not trigger gender agreement. Consider the two elicited examples in (9). In (9a), the undergoer slot of the verb is filled by an invariant middle marker, an *ŋ*- prefix.[3] Only the subject argument is indexed, which is a zero marker in suffix position. Thus, the object is not indexed in the verb.[4] This especially occurs with property nouns, which creates an indeterminacy as to the argument status of *twof* 'heat' in (9a). Both translations given in (9a) are possible. In the first, the property noun is the object, in the latter it is a nominal predicate. Example (9b) shows that this ambiguity is resolved, if an object argument is indexed in the undergoer slot, in this case a *w*- prefix. However, the verb prefix does not index property noun like *twof*. The object argument must be a different noun, for example *bad* 'ground, earth', which is put into backets in (9b). Note that, irrespective of whether or not the object noun phrase is present or omitted from the clause, the third singular feminine indexed in the verb cannot refer to the property noun *twof*.

(9) a. *efothf **twof** ŋafiyokwr.*
         efoth=f   twof   ŋa\fiyok/wr
         sun=ERG heat 2|3SG:SBJ:NPST:IPFV/make
         'The sun creates the heat.' or 'The sun makes (something) hot.'

---

[3]See §5.2 for an explanation of the glossing conventions of verbs in this grammar.
[4]The middle construction has a number of functions described in §5.4.5. One of these functions is the suppressed-object function shown in (9a).

b. *efothf (bad)* **twof** *wäfiyokwr.*
efoth=f (bad) twof wä\fiyok/wr
sun=ERG (ground) heat 2|3SG:SBJ>3SG.FEM:OBJ:NPST:IPFV/make
'The sun makes (the ground) hot.'

Note that with intransitive verbs, like the copula, property nouns function as nominal predicates. A clause like (10) can only be interpreted as having an omitted subject noun phrase which is third person singular masculine. It cannot be analysed in a way that *frasi* 'hunger' is the argument of the copula.

(10) **frasi** *yé.*
frasi \yé/
hungry 3SGMASC:SBJ:NPST:IPFV/be
'He is hungry.' not: 'It is hunger.'

Hence, we could say that property nouns escape indexation in the undergoer prefix and as a consequence there is no gender agreement. If informants are asked directly whether a given noun is feminine or masculine, they can answer this promptly, but with property nouns, they hesitate and often answer: "it depends". In an example like (10), it depends on the intended meaning: 'she is hungry' or 'he is hungry'. Thus, it depends on the gender of the referent indexed in the copula, not on the property noun.

Secondly, property nouns indexed in the actor suffix trigger a default singular number agreement. This occurs in experiencer-object constructions (11) or in the middle template (12). In (11), the property noun *thkar* 'hardness' is flagged with the ergative case, and it is indexed in the suffix of the verb *fiyoksi* 'make'. This example is from a myth in which a crocodile creates a large pool of water, because it got stuck, which translates literally as 'hardness made it'. In (12), the property noun *twof* 'heat' is in the absolute case, and it is indexed in the suffix of the middle verb *sogsi* 'ascend'. In both examples, the indexed person/number value is 2|3SG. See §8.3.10 for experiencer-object constructions and §5.4.5 for a description of the middle template.

(11) *ŋanraknza zbo zf ziyé. zä zf fthé* **thkarf** *yafiyokwa ziyé.*
ŋan\rak/nza zbo zf z=\yé/
2|3SG:SBJ:PST:IPFV:VENT/crawl PROX.ALL IMM PROX=3SG.MASC:SBJ:NPST:IPFV/be
zä zf fthé thkar=f ya\fiyok/wa
PROX IMM when hardness=ERG 2|3SG:SBJ>3SG.MASC:OBJ:PST:IPFV/make
z=\yé/
PROX=3SG.MASC:SBJ:NPST:IPFV/be
'It crawled here to this place. That is when it got stuck right here.' (lit. 'Hardness did it.') [tci20120922-09 DAK #17-18]

(12) *nafane* **twof** *kresöbäth nzafarfo.*
nafane twof kre\söbäth/ nzafar=fo
3SG.POSS heat 2|3SG:SBJ:IRR:PFV/ascend sky=ALL
'Its heat rose up to the sky.' [tci20110810-01 MAB #45-46]

Example (12) shows that property nouns can enter into a possessive construction. This is another characteristic they share with nouns and which sets them apart from adjectives. In this case, *twof* is the possessed. Although there are no examples attested in the corpus where a property noun is the possessor, this is confirmed by data from elicitation.

In both predicative and attributive constructions, property nouns take the adjectivaliser *-thé* optionally. An attributive construction in English like 'the embarrassed man' could be expressed as *fäsi kabe* or *fäsithé kabe*. The former could be translated as a compound 'embarrassment man' and the latter 'embarrassed man'. Hence, when it comes to property nouns no clear distinction can be drawn between attributive constructions and nominal compounds in a predicative construction. Moreover, a predicative construction like English 'The man is ashamed' can also be expressed with or without the adjectivaliser *-thé* as either *kabe fäsi yé* or *kabe fäsithé yé*.

In addition to nominal modification, property nouns can have a coverb function. Property nouns may occur with light verbs (*rä-* 'do', *fiyoksi* 'make', *ko-* 'become') or phasal verbs (*thkäfsi* 'start', *bthaksi* 'finish'). In (13), a malevolent spirit is trying to lure a traveller to stay the night at her camp. In the construction, the property noun *garamgaram* 'sweet talk' expresses most of the semantics of the event while the phasal verb *thkäfksi* 'start' takes the inflection and indexing.

(13) **garamgaram** *srethkäf. "kwa ŋabrigwr? efoth byé!"*
garamgaram   sre\thkäf/   kwa
sweet.talk   2|3SG:SBJ>3SG.MASC:OBJ:IRR:PFV/start FUT
ŋa\brig/wr   efoth b=\yé/
2|3SG:SBJ:NPST:IPFV/return sun   MED=3SG.MASC:NPST:IPFV/be
'She started sweet-talking him: "Will you go back? The sun is already setting!"'
[tci20120901-01 MAK #88-89]

Coverb + light verb constructions of this kind have been described for a number of Australian languages. For example, in Jaminjung (Schultze-Berndt 2000) or Bilinarra (Meakins & Nordlinger 2014) we find a division of labour in complex predicates whereby a distinct word class of coverbs contributes most of the meaning of an event while a light verb carries most of the inflectional material, In Komnzo, there are a few property nouns which seem to be more event-oriented in their semantics. However, there is insufficient morphological or distributional evidence for setting up a distinct word class of coverbs. In addition to the coverb function in example (13), property nouns can be used as secondary predicates. An example is provided in the use of *wri* 'intoxication' in (14), where an angry man is tranquilised by giving him kava to drink.

(14) *krärme srärirfth.* **wri** *kwosi sfthnm.*
krär=me   srä\rirf/th   wri   kwosi
kava=INS 2|3PL:SBJ>3SG.MASC:OBJ:IRR:PFV/kill intoxicated dead
sf\thn/m
3SGMASC:SBJ:PST:DUR/lie.down
'They put him down with kava. Then he was lying down dead drunk.'
[tci20120909-06 KAB #95-96]

Property nouns marked with the instrumental case have an adverbial function. In example (15), the property noun *ktkt* 'narrow' is the single argument of the intransitive verb. In the text, a group of headhunters prepare to attack a hamlet. The sentence is accompanied by a gesture which resembles the movement of the arms as if embracing a person. Here *ktkt* is does not function as a secondary predicate and it would be incorrect to translate it as 'They became narrow'. Note that the verb indexes 2|3SG and not 2|3NSG. Hence, a more literal translation is adequate 'narrowness became/happened' or with a dummy subject 'it became narrow'. In example (16), the same property noun *ktkt* takes the instrumental case and functions adverbially. Here the speaker explains how the plant *grnzari* (Chantium sp) grows.

(15) *kwot kar fthé wkrkwath wkrkwath wkrkwath a **ktkt** zäkora fof.*
      kwot   kar   fthé   3x(w\krk/wath)   a   ktkt
      properly village when 3x(2|3PL:SBJ>3SG.FEM:OBJ:PST:IPFV/block) and narrow
      zä\kor/a   fof
      2|3SG:SBJ:PST:PFV/become EMPH
      'They were blocking and blocking the village by narrowing (the circle).'
                                                                    [tci20111119-03 ABB #134]

(16) ***ktktme** erfikwr. nima fefe fof yrfikwr.*
      ktkt=me   e\rfik/wr   nima fefe fof
      narrow=INS 2|3PL:SBJ:NPST:IPFV/grow like.this really EMPH
      y\rfik/wr
      3SG.MASC:SBJ:NPST:IPFV/grow
      'They grow closely together. This one really grows like that.'
                                                                    [tci20130907-02 RNA #705]

3.1.5 Adjectives

Adjectives form a small class of lexical items in Komnzo. Semantically, adjectives denote size (*kafar* 'big, great', *katan* 'small', *yabun* 'fat, big', *tnz* 'short', *zanfr* 'tall'), quality (*namä* 'good', *gathagatha* 'bad'), age (*zafe* 'old', *zöftha* 'new'), physical property (*kwosi* 'rotten, dead', *kwik* 'sick', *tayo* 'ripe, dried', *gauyé* 'fresh, unripe') and human propensity (*dmnzü* 'silent', *yoganai* 'tired', *zäzr* 'exhausted'). Colour adjectives, as seen in §3.1.2, are derived from nouns by suffixing *-thé*. There are a few adjectives which take irregular forms of this suffix (*zisé* 'painful' from *zi* 'pain') and/or which lack a corresponding noun or property noun (*dbömsé* 'blunt'). Hence, these are treated as adjectives with frozen morphology. There are about two dozen members in the adjective word class. The low number can be explained by the presence of a class of property nouns (§3.1.4).

Syntactically, adjective usually precede their head. However, this is only a tendency, as they may be follow the head too. There are three adjectives which are special in that they occur only in postposed position. Two denote human propensity: *bana* 'poor, pitiful, hapless' and *kwark* 'deceased, late' (18). The third denotes quality: *fefe* 'true'.

Morphological evidence is provided by the adjectivaliser *-thé*, which cannot be suffixed to an adjective: **katanthé* 'small', **namäthé* 'good' or **tnzthé* 'short'. Some nouns, for example *kayanthé* 'white' (from *kwayan* 'light'), and all property nouns can take the adjectivaliser.

Adjectives may serve as the host for any case enclitic if they occur in the rightmost position of the noun phrase. This occurs if (i) the head of noun phrase has been omitted as in (17) or (ii) if an adjective has been postposed, as in (18). See §7.5 for further discussion of headedness and ellipsis. Example (19) shows an adjective preceding the head of the noun phrase. We see from these examples, combined with the argument of ellipsis, that adjectives cannot function as the head of a phrase. This is supported by the observation that it is the head of a phrase which triggers agreement in the verb prefix and not the adjective.

(17) *wati, kofä fthé brigsir n krär, **katanf** kwa ynbrigwr zbo.*
      wati kofä fthé \brig/-si=r   n   krä\r/   katan=f   kwa
      then fish when return-NMLZ=PURP IMN 2|3SG:SBJ:IRR:PFV/do small=ERG FUT
      yn\brig/wr   zbo
      2|3SG:SBJ>3SG.MASC:OBJ:NPST:IPFV:VENT/return PROX.ALL
      'When the fish tries to get out, the small (basket) will bring them back here.'
      [tci20120906 MAB #56-57]

(18) *nzwamnzrm fof ... oromanä fof ... oroman **kwarkä**.*
      nzwa\m/nzrm   fof   (.) oroman=ä   fof   (.) oroman
      1SG:SBJ:PST:DUR/dwell EMPH (.) old.man=ASSOC.PL EMPH (.) old.man
      kwark=ä
      deceased=ASSOC.PL
      'We stayed with the old man ... with the late old man.'   [tci20130911-03 MBR #72-73]

(19) *bobomrwä arufe krathfänzr ... **zagr** karfo.*
      bobomr=wä arufe kra\thfä/nzr   (.) zagr kar=fo
      until=EMPH arufe 2|3SG:SBJ:IRR:IPFV/fly (.) far village=ALL
      'He flies all the way to Arufe ... to a distant village.'   [tci20130903-04 RNA #144-145]

As with property nouns, adjectives with an instrumental case can function adverbially. In (20), the adjective *gathagatha* 'bad' modifies the verb. In the example, a mother is scolding her daughter because she walks carelessly through the long grass. In (21), the adjective *katan* 'small' modifies the predicate 'be rotten'. In this procedural text, the speaker demonstrates how to roll a little whistle from a coconut leaf. However, the first attempt to blow the whistle fails because the coconut leaf was not fresh.

(20) *kabothma! tayafe **gathagathamenzo** niyak! kabothma!*
      kaboth=ma   tayafe gathagatha=me=nzo n\yak/   kaboth=ma
      snake=CHAR tayafe bad=INS=ONLY   2SG:SBJ:NPST:IPFV/walk snake=CHAR
      'Tayafe, you walk in a bad way! (Watch out) for snakes!'   [tci20130907-02 JAA #143]

(21) *keke kwot yanor. zane **katanme** kwosi yé.*
      keke kwot   ya\nor/   zane   katan=me kwosi
      NEG properly 3SG.MASC:SBJ:NPST:IPFV/shout DEM:PROX small=INS dead
      \yé/
      3SG.MASC:NPST:IPFV/be
      'It doesn't whistle properly. This one is a little rotten.'   [tci20120914 RNA #55-56]

3.1.6 Quantifiers and numerals

The quantifier subclass typically contains lexical items that are "modifiers of nouns that indicate quantity and scope" (Schachter & Shopen 2007: 37). Quantifiers in Komnzo fall into two subclasses: non-numerical quantifiers (§3.1.6.1) and numerical quantifiers (§3.1.6.2), henceforth referred to as quantifiers and numerals, respectively.

Both subclasses show similarities to adjectives. What unites them as a distinct subclass is the ability to take the distributive suffix (*-kak*). Quantifiers and numerals are the only roots that take the distributive suffix. Like adjectives, they can be flagged for case and may take the instrumental case (*=me*) with an adverbial function, for example indicating how many times a particular event occurred.

3.1.6.1 Quantifiers

There are five quantifiers in Komnzo: *matak* 'nothing', *frü* 'alone, single', *etha* 'few', *tüfr* 'many, plenty', and *bramöwä* 'all'.

Quantifiers may precede or follow the noun which they modify. That being said, it is much more common for a quantifier to follow the noun, as in (22) and (23). Instances of a preceding quantifier are not attested in the corpus, but only verified through elicitation. But see (28) below and footnote 5 for a possible example.

(22) *kofä **bramöwä** fthé kränmtherth watik zzarä kwot threnthfär ... nä totkarä.*
      kofä bramöwä fthé   krän\mther/th   watik zzar=ä   kwot
      fish all   when 2|3PL:SBJ:IRR:PFV:VENT/come.up then net=ASSOC properly
      thren\thfär/   (.) nä   tot=karä
      2|3PL:SBJ:IRR:PFV:VENT/jump (.) other spear=PROP
      'When all the fish come up, then they jump in with the nets ... others with spears.'
      [tci20110813-09 DAK #28]

(23) *sitauane ŋare mane erna minu erna ... nge **matak**.*
      sitau=ane   ŋare   mane e\r/na   minu
      sitau=POSS.SG woman which 2|3DU:SBJ:PST:IPFV/be barren.woman
      e\rn/a   (.) nge   matak
      2|3DU:SBJ:PST:IPFV/be (.) child nothing
      'As for Sitau's two wives, they were barren women without children.'
      [tci20120814 ABB #469]

Quantifiers may take the distributive suffix (*-kak*) which can be translated as 'each' to English. For semantic reasons, neither *matak* 'nothing' nor *bramöwä* 'all' take this suffix. Two examples of the distributive suffix are given in (24) and (25). In the first example, the speaker describes a ritual for starting the harvesting season, during which 'each person' brings a tuber for cooking and tasting the first yams. In the second example, the speaker shows me her catch of the day: a lizard, several fish and a turtle. Thus, she emphasises that she caught plenty of different food.

(24) *we kwot we **näbikakme** ... we nä wawa thfrärmth katan o kafar.*
we kwot   we   näbi-kak=me   (.) we   nä   wawa
also properly also one-DISTR=INS (.) also INDF yam
thf\rä/rmth   katan o kafar
2|3PL:SBJ>2|3PL:OBJ:PST:DUR/do small or big
'Again, they took them out (of the garden plot) one by one ... small or big ones.'

[tci20131013-01 ABB #364]

(25) *watik, faso **tüfrkak** erä.*
watik, faso tüfr-kak   e\rä/
then, meat plenty-DISTR 2|3PL:SBJ:NPST:IPFV/be
'Okay, there is plenty of different meat.'   [tci20120821-01 LNA #68]

Quantifiers may take an instrumental case (*=me*) in order to derive adverbs, as is shown in example (26).

(26) *kabe ane **frümenzo** tnägsi zethkäfath.*
kabe ane frü=me=nzo   tnäg-si   ze\thkäf/ath
man DEM single=INS=ONLY lose-NMLZ 2|3PL:SBJ:PST:IPFV/start
'The people began to scatter.' (lit. 'They began losing themselves alone.')

[tci20131013-01 ABB #54]

The distributive and the instrumental may also be suffixed to the same quantifier. In this case, their order is fixed: the instrumental follows the distributive, as shown in example (27). The example also shows that, like other nominals, quantifiers can be reduplicated to indicate plurality. Here, the speaker talks about types of bows and how different men use these according to their abilities and preferences.

(27) *zawe **ffrükakmenzo** erä.*
zawe   f-frü-kak=me=nzo   e\rä/
preference REDUP-single-DISTR=INS=ONLY 2|3PL:SBJ:NPST:IPFV/be
'They each have their preferences.'   [tci20120922-23 MAA #104]

Example (28) shows *etha* meaning 'few'. Note that the word *etha* can also mean 'three', which I describe in §3.1.6.2.

(28) ***tüfrmär** kafarkafar nrä ... komnzo **ethanzo**.*
tüfr=mär   kafar-kafar n\rä/   (.) komnzo etha=nzo
plenty=PRIV REDUP-big 1PL:SBJ:NPST:IPFV/be (.) only   few=ONLY
'We are not many old people ... just a few.'   [tci20121019-04 ABB #187-188]

Note in passing that in (28)[5] the quantifier *tüfr* 'plenty' is negated by using the privative case =*mär*. This is also possible with *etha*.

The two quantifiers *matak* 'nothing' and *bramöwä* 'all' deviate in their behaviour from other quantifiers. As mentioned above, they do not take the distributive suffix. Furthermore, they do not take the instrumental case =*me*. At least for *bramöwä* there might be an explanation as to why this is the case. The emphatic marker =*wä* forces the preceding morpheme to harmonise its vowel. If the preceding morpheme is the instrumental marker, it changes from =*me* to =*mö*. It follows that, historically, *bramöwä* could be *bra=me=wä*. Since there is no corresponding lexical item *bra*, we are left to speculate, and accept it as a case of frozen morphology.

3.1.6.2 Numerals

The numerals of the Yam languages have received some attention in the literature because of their unique senary (base-6) system (cf. Donohue 2008, Hammarström 2009, and Evans 2009). In fact, Komnzo has two numeral systems: the senary system is unrestricted, but there is a second system with an upper limit of counting of four or five. This is similar to Donohue's description of Kanum, where an unrestricted system coexists with a restricted system (Donohue 2008). Nowadays, one should include English numerals which constitute a third system commonly used in Komnzo. For the remaining description, I will concentrate on the senary system and the restricted system only.

The senary system is predominantly employed in ritualised counting as described in §1.3.3.1. The number of yams counted during a feast quickly runs up to several thousands, for large feasts even tens of thousands. On the other hand, everyday counting hardly ever goes above four or five, and English numerals are borrowed in situations where approximation of larger numbers is insufficient, for example when trading goods, charging one's mobile phone credit, or counting the eleven members of a soccer team. Hence, we find a double numeral system in Table 3.3.[6] One set of numerals is commonly used, but it is restricted to low numbers. A second set is employed only in ritualised counting, but it is unrestricted.

Beyond the observation of cultural practices, evidence for this double system comes from the lexical items themselves. In everyday counting, the words for 'two' and 'three' are *eda* and *etha*. In ritualised counting, the words are *yda* and *ytho* respectively. The latter pair reflects older forms which have not undergone the loss of word-initial *y*. This

---

[5]In example (28) we can see that *tüfr* 'plenty' precedes the reduplicated adjective *kafarkafar* 'big'. The example is interpreted to have an elided noun *kabe* 'man' as its head, thus *kafarkafar* means 'the big ones'. This then constitutes a corpus example of a quantifier preceding its head.

[6]In the table, the term for 'five' shows two variants. The term for 'six' also shows two variants one of which is a combination of *tabuthui* 'five' and *nibo* 'six'. Outside of ritualised yam counting, I have overheard this only a few times by younger speakers. Older speakers did not produce a term for 'six' or were reluctant to do so. The combination *tabuthui nibo* might be explained by the way how ritualised counting works: While two men move a set of six yams, one of them will shout out the numbers. He continues to shout the current number as long as it takes to move to the next one (e.g. 'two two two three'). This means that each cycle of six ends with *tabuthui nibo* 'five six'. It seems that some speakers have taken this collocation and reinterpreted it to mean 'six'. I take this as being indicative for the fuzzy upper limit of the restricted set.

Table 3.3: The numeral system

value		restricted	ritualised
1		*näbi*	*näbi*
2		*eda*	*yda*
3		*etha*	*ytho*
4		*asar*	*asar*
5		(*tabuthui, tabru*)	*tabuthui*
6	6	(*tabuthui nibo, nibo*)	*nibo*
36	6^2		*fta*
216	6^3		*taruba*
1,296	6^4		*damno*
7,776	6^5		*wärämäkä*
46,656	6^6		*wi*

sound change (jə > e /#_) is attested in many pairs of lexical items between Komnzo and the neighbouring Tonda varieties, e.g. Wära *ymoth* 'girl' corresponds to Komnzo *emoth*. Another piece of evidence comes from the fact that the numeral *etha* 'three' can also mean 'a few' (28). I take this as evidence for the fuzzy upper limit of the restricted set.

Large quantities can be constructed in the following way: a quantity of 72 is expressed as *eda fta* '2 36' (or '2 6^2'). A quantity of 73 would simply add *a näbi* 'and one' to the expression: *eda fta a näbi* '2 36 and 1'. Thus, the fact that *eda* precedes *fta* means '2 times 36', whereas the fact that *a näbi* follows *fta* means '36 plus 1'. This has the effect that values which are relatively simple in a decimal system result in a long string in Komnzo, for example English 'fifty' corresponds to Komnzo *näbi fta a eda nibo a eda* (lit. '1 times 36 and 2 times 6 and 2'). A senary system differs from a decimal system only in the location of simple and complex points in the number space, but not in its overall complexity. Consequently, there are values which require a very long string in English, but have a short expression in Komnzo, for example 'forty-six thousand and six hundred and fifty-six' corresponds to *wi* in Komnzo.

Numerals can take the same morphology as quantifiers (§3.1.6.1). There are no corpus examples of a numeral taking either the distributive suffix or the instrumental case clitic, but example (29) illustrates the use of both. I was taught the phrase *näbikakme käznob!* 'drink it one by one!' before I administered pain relief tablets to my friends and informants. I was corrected whenever I falsely used only the instrumental *näbime käznob*, which means 'drink it in one go!' (lit. 'with one').

(29)   *nä kabe **näbikakmenzo** ... finzo miyatha thfrärm fof.*
     nä   kabe näbi-kak=me=nzo   (.) fi=nzo   miyatha   thf\rä/rm
     some men one-DISTR=INS=ONLY (.) 3.ABS=ONLY knowledge 2|3PL:SBJ:PST:DUR/be

fof
EMPH
'Only some people for themselves ... only they held that knowledge.'

[tci20120909-06 KAB #13]

Ordinal numerals can be derived from cardinal numerals by attaching the characteristic case marker *=ma*. This is shown in examples (30) and (31).

(30) *fi sraksrak wokuthé yara **ethama** mane yara.*
fi   srak-srak   woku-thé   ya\r/a   etha=ma   mane
3.ABS REDUP-boy skin-ADJZR 3SG.MASC:SBJ:PST:IPFV/be three=CHAR which
ya\r/a
3SG.MASC:SBJ:PST:IPFV/be
'As for the third one, he looked a bit boyish.'   [tci20131013-02 ABB #211]

(31) ***ethama** bäne mane zrarä fof... wfathwr ane fof.*
etha=ma   bäne   mane   zra\rä/   fof   (.)
three=CHAR RECOG which 3SG.FEM:SBJ:IRR:IPFV/be EMPH (.)
w\fath/wr   ane fof
2|3SG:SBJ>3SGFEM:OBJ:NPST:IPFV/hold DEM EMPH
'At the third attempt she will really hold her up.'   [tci20110817-02 ABB #106-107]

The numeral *näbi* 'one' can be used in the sense of 'one way' or 'for good'. The latter meaning is exemplified in (32).

(32) *wati, fi **näbi** zäbrima. zbo yamnzr ane woga oten.*
wati fi   näbi zä\brim/a   zbo   ya\m/nzr
then 3.ABS one SG:SBJ:PST:PFV/return PROX.ALL 3SGMASC:SBJ:NPST:IPFV/dwell
ane woga ote=n
DEM man ote=LOC
'He returned for good. This man now lives here in Ote.' [tci20120901-01 MAK #210-211]

3.1.7 Locationals

Komnzo has a small closed class of lexical items which I call locationals. Historically, some members of this subclass are derived from nouns. Locationals may act as hosts of case clitics, but for spatial cases only (locative, allative, and ablative). Table (3.4) lists all nine members.

Locationals occur always as modifiers which follow the head of the noun phrase. A typical example is provided in (33) with *banban* 'underneath'. The speaker describes how people reacted when the Imperial Japanese Air Service flew attacks on Merauke in Dutch New Guinea during the Second World War.

Table 3.4: Locationals

form	gloss	historical derivation
warfo	above	*war* 'top layer' *=fo* (ALL)
banban	underneath	-
zfthen	below	*zfth* 'base' *=en* (LOC)
mrmr	inside	-
zrfa	in front	*zr* 'tooth' *=fa* (ABL)
tharthar	next to	-
kamfa	behind	*kam* 'bone, backbone' *=fa* (ABL)
bobathm	at the end of	-
kratr	in between	-

(33) *fi fthé fof duga taga **banbanen** boba kwatharwrmth fof.*
fi   fthé   fof   duga taga banban=en   boba
3SG.ABS when EMPH taro   leaf underneath=LOC MED.ABL
kwa\thar/wrmth   fof
2|3PL:SBJ:PST:DUR/go.underneath EMPH
'That was really when they went underneath the taro leaves.'

[tci20131013-02 ABB #231-232]

I analyse these as locational nominals rather than postpositions, because like all nominals, they are marked for case. Additionally, as we can see in the third column of Table 3.4, some of the locational nominals are historically derived from nouns. For these, I propose a path of development from a nominal compound to a lexical item of a different nominal subclass. As an example, let us hypothesise about the origin of *warfo* 'above'. In the first stage, there would have been a nominal compound *mnz war* 'house top' made up of two nouns *mnz* 'house' and *war* 'top'. Nominal compounds are described in §7.5.3. This compound can be marked with the allative case productively, thus, producing *mnz warfo* 'to the top of the house'. In the second stage, *warfo* became a single lexical item 'above' and lost the specific allative semantics. As a consequence, it can now be marked for spatial cases, for example the locative case (*=n*), producing *mnz warfon* 'on top of the house'. This is commonly found in Komnzo, although presently there is no example in the corpus. Lexicalisation of this kind has progressed to varying degrees with the four locationals where a nominal origin is a possible scenario. While *warfo, kamfa* and *zrfa* are commonly marked with the locative case clitic, this does not occur with *zfthen*. Hence, *zfthen* is at a transitional stage between a noun with productive morphology (the locative case *=en*) and a locational. The choice depends on whether one analyses *zfth* in expressions like *mnz zfth* 'house base' as part of a noun+noun compound or as a noun+locational construction.

Two characteristics unite locationals as a word class. Locationals always follow the head of the noun phrase, and they take only spatial cases. As we will see in §4.8, spatial cases can be extended to cover temporal semantics, as in (34).

(34) *zena kwa ŋatrikwé fof ... nimame zrethkäfé zane ezi **mrmren**.*

     zena kwa ŋa\trik/wé   fof (.) nima=me   zre\thkäf/é

     today FUT 1SG:SBJ:NPST:IPFV/tell EMPH (.) like.this=INS 1SG:SBJ:IRR:PFV/start

     zane   ezi   mrmr=en

     DEM:PROX morning inside=LOC

     'Today, I will tell (a story) ... I will start like this in this morning.'

                                  [tci20110802 ABB #28-29]

3.1.8 Temporals

Temporals are a functional class with members from different nominal subclasses which encode temporal semantics. Beyond the shared reference to time, the unifying characteristic is their ability to act as hosts for a special set of temporal case clitics. Syntactically, these lexemes are flexible with respect to their position in the clause, but they occur most commonly in initial position.

Temporals comprise a set of lexical items which cross-cut three word classes. First, there are nouns denoting different times of the day (*ezi* 'morning', *efoth* 'day', *zizi* 'afternoon, dusk', *zbär* 'night'). Secondly, there is a group of time adverbials (*zena* 'now, today', *kayé* 'yesterday, tomorrow', *nama* 'two days ago, two days in the future', *nümä* 'a week ago, a week ahead'). Except for *zena*, these are bidirectional in their semantics. Thus, *kayé* could be glossed as '± 1 day', *nama* as '± 2 days' and *nümä* as '± a few days'. As for the latter two, the edges of the time interval are less clearly demarcated. Note that bidirectionals are also found in other Papuan languages, for example in Usan (Reesink 1987: 70). Thirdly, there are three adjectives *zöftha* 'before, first', *zafe* 'old, long time ago', and *thrma* 'later, after', all unidirectional in their semantics.

The uniting characteristic of this class is its ability to inflect for temporal cases. There are three temporal cases in Komnzo: the temporal locative (=*thamen*) 'at that time', the temporal possessive (=*thamane*) 'that time's', and the temporal purposive (=*thamar*) 'for that time'. Temporal cases are discussed in §4.9. In the following examples, the temporal purposive case is used on the noun *ezi* (35), on the time adverbial *nama* and the English loanword 'Friday' (36), and on the temporal adjective *thrma* (37). In (35), the speaker tells his friends to leave the work on a sago palm for the next day. In (36), the speaker begins his description of a namesake ceremony which is about to be held two days later. Finally, in (37), two speakers go through a set of stimulus pictures and try to sort them into a narrative.

(35) *nze thäkora "fefe yé **ezithamar**. ezi n kwot sräfrmnze."*

     nze   thä\kor/a   fefe \yé/

     1SG.ERG 1SG:SBJ>2|3PL:OBJ:PST:PFV/speak really 3SG.MASC:SBJ:NPST:IPFV/be

     ezi=thamar   ezi   n   kwot

     morning=TEMP.PURP morning try properly

     srä\frm/nze

     1PL:SBJ>3SG.MASC:OBJ:IRR:IPFV/prepare

     'I told them: "It is there for the morning. We will try and prepare it in the morning."'

                                   [tci20120929 SIK #65]

(36) *fam monme erä ... **namathamar fraidethamar** ... nge fathasi yamyam monme kwa ŋankwir.*

fam   mon=me e\rä/   (.) nama=thamar
thought how=INS 2|3PL:SBJ:NPST:IPFV/be (.) +|-2days=TEMP.PURP
fraide=thamar   (.) nge fath-si   yam-yam   mon=me kwa
friday=TEMP.PURP (.) child hold-NMLZ REDUP-event how=INS FUT
ŋan\kwir/
2|3SG:SBJ:NPST:IPFV:VENT/run

'(My) thoughts for the day after tomorrow, for Friday, are like this. This is how the children's ceremony will take place.'   [tci20110817-02 ABB #3-5]

(37) *zane mane rä **thrmathamar** zane rä.*

zane   mane \rä/   thrma=thamar   zane
DEM:PROX which 3SG.FEM:SBJ:NPST:IPFV/be later=TEMP.PURP DEM:PROX
\rä/
3SG.FEM:SBJ:NPST:IPFV/be

'As for this one, this is for later.'   [tci20111004 RMA #236-237]

Temporals can also take spatial cases, as in (38) with the temporal noun *ezi* 'morning' and in (39) with the time adverbial *zena* 'now'. The three adjectives of this subclass may also take spatial cases when they are in the final position of a noun phrase, as in (40). In all of these cases, what is otherwise spatial marking is extended to express temporal semantics.

(38) *frasinzo nzwamnzrm **ezifa** bobomr mor efoth.*

frasi=nzo   nzwa\m/nzrm   ezi=fa   bobomr mor efoth
hunger=ONLY 1PL:SBJ:PST:DUR/dwell morning=ABL until   neck day

'We were staying very hungry from the morning until midday.'   [tci20120924-01 TRK #37]

(39) *wati, **zenafa** ... ni tüfr nagayé kwakonzre.*

wati zena=fa   (.) ni   tüfr   nagayé   kwa\ko/nzre
then today=ABL (.) 1NSG plenty children 1PL:SBJ:RPST:IPFV/become

'Nowadays, we, the children, have become plenty.' (lit. 'From now on ...')   [tci20111107-01 MAK #149-150]

(40) *twofthé fthé krafiyokwr. ane **thrmafa** zränthore.*

twof-thé   fthé   kra\fiyok/wr   ane thrma=fa
heat-ADJZR when 2|3SG:SBJ:IRR:IPFV/make DEM after=ABL
zrän\thor/e
1PL:SBJ>3SG.FEM:IRR:PFV:VENT/carry

'It has dried then. After that we bring it (the drum) here.'   [tci20120824 KAA #78-79]

Temporal nouns may also enter into a noun+locational construction (41), again a temporal interpretation of the locational.

(41) *zane namä **ezi mrmren** nzä kwa trikasi ŋatrikwé.*
    zane   namä ezi   mrmr=en   nzä   kwa trik-si
    DEM:PROX good morning inside=LOC 1SG.ABS FUT tell-NMLZ
    ŋa\trik/wé
    1SG:SBJ:NPST:IPFV/tell
    'In this beautiful morning, I will tell a story.'   [tci20111119-01 ABB #2-3]

3.1.9 Personal pronouns

Personal pronouns form a closed subclass of nominals distinguishing three persons in both singular and non-singular number. Personal pronouns have distinct forms for case (absolutive, ergative, dative, possessive, associative, characteristic, locative, allative, ablative, and purposive), although some cases are not found in the pronouns (proprietive, privative, instrumental, and similative). The full set of formatives is listed in Table 3.5.

Table 3.5: Personal pronouns

case	1SG	1NSG	2SG	2NSG	3SG	3NSG
ABS	*nzä*	*ni*	*bä*		*fi*	
ERG	*nze*		*be*	*bné*	*naf*	*nafa*
DAT	*nzun*	*nzenm*	*bun*	*benm*	*nafan*	*nafanm*
POSS	*nzone*	*nzenme*	*bone*	*benme*	*nafane*	*nafanme*
LOC	*nzudben*	*nzedben*	*budben*	*bedben*	*nafadben*	*nafanmedben*
ALL	*nzudbo*	*nzedbo*	*budbo*	*bedbo*	*nafadbo*	*nafanmedbo*
ABL	*nzudba*	*nzedba*	*budba*	*bedba*	*nafadba*	*nafanmedba*
PURP	*nzunar*	*nzenar*	*bunar*	*benar*	*nafanar*	
CHAR	*nzonema*	*nzenmema*	*bonema*	*benmema*	*nafanema*	*nafanmema*
ASSOC[a]	*ninrr*	*ninä*	*bnrr*	*bnä*	*nafrr*	*nafä*

[a]The associative forms encode DU versus PL (§7.6).

We can see from Table 3.5 that, as with the case markers, there is no number distinction in the absolutive. Only the first person is an exception here. On the other hand, in the first person non-singular, the absolutive and ergative categories are neutralised. Furthermore, Table 3.5 shows that the characteristic pronouns are built from the possessive forms by suffixing *-ma*. The three local cases and the purposive pronouns share formal similarity with the dative pronouns, namely the [u] vowel in the singular forms. Personal pronouns typically constitute a complete noun phrase (§7.1). Unlike nouns, personal pronouns cannot be modified by demonstratives or quantifiers.

3.1.10 Interrogatives

Cross-cutting the division of nominals is the subclass of interrogatives. These are roots used to indicate that the speaker does not know the (full) identity of a referent. Interrogatives belong to the following nominal subclasses: pronouns (*ra* 'what', *mä* 'where', *mane* 'who, which', *rma* 'why, for what'), quantifiers (*rnzam* 'how many'), temporals (*rthé* 'when') or interrogative adverbs (*mon* 'how'). The degree to which these can be marked for case varies. Interrogatives may constitute a full noun phrase (42) or fill the determiner slot (43) of a noun phrase. In the following examples NPs are enclosed by square brackets.

(42) *ŋafyf **ra** kwa nm enzänzr?*
　　　ŋafe=f　　　[ra]　kwa nm　　en\zä/nzr
　　　father=ERG.SG what FUT　maybe 2|3SG:SBJ>2|3PL:OBJ:NPST:IPFV:VENT/carry
　　　'What might the father be carrying?'　　　　　　　　　　[tci20111004 RMA #79]

(43) *eh, **ra** gru zane ŋamitwanzr nabi tutin?*
　　　eh [ra　gru　　　　zane]　　　ŋa\mitwa/nzr　　　　　　nabi　　tuti=n
　　　eh what shooting.star DEM:PROX 2|3SG:SBJ:NPST:IPFV/swing bamboo branch=LOC
　　　'Hey, what shooting star is swinging here on the bamboo branch?'

　　　　　　　　　　　　　　　　　　　　　　　　　　　　　　[tci20111119-03 ABB #127]

　　　The roots which are syntactically most active are the interrogative pronouns *ra* 'what, what (kind)' and *mane* 'who, which'. Both can host almost all case clitics as we can see in Table 3.6.[7]

We can make two observations from Table 3.6. First, as with other nominal morphology, only animates are marked for number. Secondly, the root *rma* 'why' patterns with *ra*. Thus, it reflects a reduction of an earlier more transparent form *rama* consisting of *ra* with the characteristic case marker *=ma* (lit. 'for what').

　　　The interrogatives *mä* 'where', *mobo* 'whither', *moba* 'whence' are not shown here because these interrogatives - along with *mane* 'which' - are part of a paradigm of demonstratives. As I will show below, Komnzo demonstratives make a fourway distinction between proximal, medial, distal, and interrogative. Compare Table 3.8 in §3.1.12 for the full set of demonstratives. The interrogative *mane* in Table 3.6 can also be used for inanimates, as in *mane kar* 'which village'.

　　　Other interrogatives show a behaviour that aligns them with their respective nominal subclass. The temporal interrogative *rthé* 'when' may be marked for temporal case, for example *rthéthamane* 'of what time' in (44), where the speaker explains that he will move his garden plot closer to the road each year.

(44) *highway kwa wthayfakwé fi **rthéthamane**? ... ysokwren?*
　　　highway kwa w\thayfak/wé　　　　　　　　　　　　　　fi rthé=thamane　(.)
　　　road　　FUT 1SG:SBJ>3SG.FEM:OBJ:NPST:IPFV/bring.out but when=TEMP.POSS (.)

---

[7]Some cases are impossible on semantic grounds, for example the instrumental case with animate referents, or the associative case with inanimate referents.

Table 3.6: Interrogative pronouns

case	inanimate	animate SG	animate NSG
ABS	*ra* what, what kind	*mane* who, which	
ERG	*raf* what, what (kind)	*maf* who, which	*mafa* who
DAT	*rafn* to what	*mafn* to whom	*mafnm* to whom
POSS	-	*mafane* whose	*mafanme* whose
LOC	*rafen* at what place	*mafadben* at whose place	*mafanmedben* at whose place
ALL	*rafo* to what	*mafadbo* to whom	*mafanmedbo* to whom
ABL	*rafa* from what	*mafadba* from whom	*mafanmedba* from whom
INS	*rame* with what	-	-
PURP	*rar* for what	*mafanar* for whom	*mafanmenar* for whom
CHAR	*rma* for what, why	*mafanema* because of whom	*mafanemema* because of whom
ASSOC[a]	-	*mafrr* with whom	*mafä* with whom

[a]The associative forms encode DU versus PL (§7.6).

> ysokwr=en
> rainy.season=LOC
> 'I will bring (the garden) up to the road, but when ... in which year (will I get there)?' [tci20130823-06 STK #164-165]

The interrogative adverb *mon* 'how' frequently occurs with an instrumental case (=*me*). This is entirely optional and does not change its meaning (45). *Mon* or *monme* are the interrogative counterpart to the manner demonstrative *nima* 'this way' (§3.1.12.7).

(45) *bä **monme** miyatha zäkor komnzo fi nimäwä miyatha zfrärm ... komnzo zokwasi.*
bä mon=me miyatha zä\kor/ komnzo fi nima=wä
2.ABS how=INS knowledge 2|3SG:SBJ:RPST:PFV/become komnzo 3.ABS like=EMPH
miyatha zf\rä/rm (.) komnzo zokwasi
knowledge 3SGFEM:SBJ:PST:DUR/be (.) komnzo language
'How you have learned Komnzo, she also knew it ... the Komnzo language.'
[tci20130911-03 MBR #18]

The interrogative quantifier *rnzam* 'how many, how much' occurs with a nominal head. It is possible for *rnzam* to be marked for case if it follows its head. However, there are no occurrences of this in the corpus. (46) shows an example where the nominal head (*kabe* 'man') has been elided and consequently *rnzam* is flagged with the ergative case. In the example, the speaker explains how a piece of wallaby skin is glued onto a kundu drum.

(46) **rnzamé** *thzé krekarth ... asar kabe o tabuthui kabe? ... neba thrakogr krekarth*
      bäne ... tauri woku.

      rnzam=é   thzé kre\kar/th   (.) asar kabe o tabuthui kabe (.)
      how.many=ERG.NSG ever 2|3PL:SBJ:IRR:PFV/pull (.) four man or five   man (.)
      neba   thra\kogr/   kre\kar/th   bäne   (.) tauri
      opposite 2|3PL:SBJ:IRR:STAT/stand 2|3PL:SBJ:IRR:PFV/pull RECOG.ABS (.) wallaby
      woku
      skin
      'However many will pull ... four or five people? They will stand opposite and pull
      that one ... the wallaby skin.'   [tci20120824 KAA #89-92]

3.1.11 Indefinites

The indefinite determiner in Komnzo is *nä*, and it covers the meaning of 'some, other, another'. It behaves syntactically like a demonstrative, i.e. occurs in the same slots of a noun phrase (§7.2). Note that the numeral *näbi* 'one' is etymologically related to the indefinite. Historically, this analysis is supported by other Yam languages, for example Nen where *ämb* means 'some' and *ämbs* means 'one' (Evans 2017). *Nä* is used to form the indefinite pronoun *nä bun* 'someone, some other'. In example (47), there are two occurrences of *nä bun* in the dative case and in the characteristic case. The speaker explains the way how people used to exchange the yams from the first harvest.

(47) *fi **nä bunn** saro! **nä bunanema** be zawob!*
      fi   nä.bun=n   sa\r/o
      but someone=DAT.SG SG:SBJ>3SG.MASC:IO:IMP:PFV:AND/give
      nä.bun=ane=ma   be   za\wob/
      someone=POSS.SG=CHAR 2SG.ERG 2|3SG:SBJ:IMP:PFV/eat
      'But you give it (the yam) to someone else! You eat from someone else's!'
                                                                          [tci20120805-01 ABB #763-764]

Historically, *nä bun* seems to derive from a combination of *nä* and the second person singular dative pronoun *bun* (see Table 3.5), but it is unclear how this has happened. Synchronically, speakers no longer parse the two components as separate items.[8] This is reflected in its grammatical behaviour: *nä bun* can be marked for the same range of cases as personal pronouns, and like personal pronouns it may constitute a complete noun phrase. Table 3.7 lists all the case forms of *nä bun*.

---

[8]Hence, it might also be written as one word, *näbun* instead of *nä bun*.

Table 3.7: The indefinite pronoun

case	SG	NSG
ABS	*nä bun*	
ERG	*nä bunf*	*nä buné*
DAT	*nä bunn*	*nä bunnm*
POSS	*nä bunane*	*nä bunaneme*
LOC	*nä bundben*	*nä bunmedben*
ALL	*nä bundbo*	*nä bunmedbo*
ABL	*nä bundba*	*nä bunmedba*
PURP	*nä bunar*	*nä bunmenar*
CHAR	*nä bunanema*	*nä bunanemema*
ASSOC[a]	*nä bunrr*	*nä bunä*

[a]The associative forms encode DU versus PL (§7.6).

Like the demonstratives (§3.1.12), the indefinite *nä* can stand alone and take a subset of case clitics. These are the instrumental (*näme* 'with some other'), characteristic (*näma* 'because of some other'), purposive (*nämr* 'for some other'), proprietive (*näkarä* 'with some other'). More commonly *nä* functions as an indefinite determiner, as in *nä kar* 'some, other place' → 'somewhere' or *nä rokar* 'some, other stuff' → 'something' or *nä kayé* 'some yesterday|tomorrow' → 'sometime'. This can be extended to *nä kabe* 'some, another man' → 'someone'. Two examples of the determiner use are given in (48) and (49). In the first example, the speaker just explained that it is possible to 'borrow a sister' for exchange marriage from a clan, with whom one shares a land boundary. In the second example, he talks about tall posts, which were used to show off a clan's success in competitive yam cultivation.

(48) *wati ane **nä kayé** thräkorth "ft kabe."*
     wati ane nä   kayé   thrä\kor/th   ft kabe
     well DEM INDF yesterday 2|3PL:SBJ>2|3PL:OBJ:IRR:PFV/say ft people
     'Sometimes they call those ones "*ft people*".'   [tci20120814 ABB #322]

(49) *masu mane rera **nä far** fä yrästhgra.*
     masu mane \rä/ra   nä far fä
     masu which 3SG.FEM:SBJ:PST:IPFV/be INDF post DIST
     y\räs/thgra
     3SG.MASC:SBJ:PST:STAT/be.erected
     'As for Masu, there was another post planted over there.'   [tci20120805-01 ABB #472]

Negative indefinites are expressed by adding the negator *keke*. Thus, *nä zokwasi* means 'some words', but if negated by *keke* it expresses 'no words whatsoever'. This is the way how the speaker describes the shameful reaction of one of the characters in (50).

(50) *zokwasimär ŋafiyokwa ... **keke nä zokwasi.***
zokwasi=mär ŋa\fiyok/wa (.) keke nä zokwasi
word=PRIV 2|3SG:SBJ:PST:IPFV/make (.) NEG INDF words
'He was speechless ... no words whatsoever' [tci20110802 ABB #115-116]

Negative indefinites can also be constructed with interrogatives. This is a strategy attested in many languages (Haspelmath 1997, Haspelmath 2013). Thus, the concept of 'nobody' can be expressed by *kabe nä keke* (lit. 'people some not') or with an interrogative, for example *mane nä keke* (lit. 'who some not'). The order of elements is somewhat fixed in that the indefinite always follows the interrogative. In example (51), the speaker describes a ritual, whereby an arrow is shot into a tree trunk to mark a particular woman for marriage.

(51) ***keke mane nä** yanyaka keräfi fumaksir fof.*
keke mane nä yan\yak/a keräfi fumak-si=r
NEG who INDF 3SG.MASC:SBJ:PST:IPFV:VENT/walk arrow pull.out-NMLZ=PURP
fof
EMPH
'Nobody came to pull out that arrow.' [tci20120814 ABB #144]

In example (52), the speaker talks about *tütü* 'Pheasant Coucal', who was the guardian of fire before people knew about its existence. The first token of *nä* has scope over *kabe miyatha* ('people knowledge') and literally means 'no people's knowledge whatsoever'. The second token of *nä* is with the interrogative *ra* (what.ABS) and literally means 'she made them knowledgeable about nothing'.

(52) *zwärifthmo ... **kabe miyatha keke nä** ... **keke ra nä** miyatha thfkonzrm. finzo miyatha zfrärm.*
zwä\rifthm/o (.) kabe miyatha keke nä (.) keke
SG:SBJ>3SG.FEM:OBJ:RPST:PFV:AND/hide (.) people knowledge NEG INDF (.) NEG
ra nä miyatha thf\ko/nzrm fi=nzo
what INDF kowledgeable 2|3SG:SBJ>2|3PL:OBJ:PST:DUR/become 3.ABS=ONLY
miyatha zf\rä/rm
knowledge 3SG.FEM:SBJ:PST:DUR/be
'She hid away (the fire) ... no one knew ... she told them nothing. Only she knew.'
[tci20131008-01 KAB #27-29]

Positive indefinites are expressed without the use of *nä*. Instead, the particle *thzé* 'ever' is postposed to an interrogative, resulting in *ra thzé* 'whatever', *mane thzé* 'whoever, whichever'. An example with *rnzam* 'how many' was shown in (46). An example with *maf* 'who' is given in (53), where the speaker has just shown be a particular, but then leaves it on the path.

(53) *zbo kwa sräzine **maf thzé** srewakuth.*
zbo kwa srä\zin/e maf thzé
PROX.ALL FUT 1PL:SBJ>3SG.MASC:OBJ:IRR:PFV/put.down who.ERG ever

sre\wakuth/

2|3SG:SBJ>3SG.MASC:OBJ:IRR:PFV/pick.up

'We will put it down here (for) whoever will pick it up.'   [tci20130907-02 RNA #479]

3.1.12 Demonstratives

Komnzo has a rich set of demonstratives. These form a functional class comprised of pronouns, determiners, adverbials, and verbal (pro-)clitics. They are treated as a subclass of nominals because all can be marked for a subset of the cases. Only the verb clitics and the immediate demonstrative cannot be marked for case.

Dixon defines a demonstrative as "any item, other than 1st and 2nd pronouns, which can have pointing (or deictic) reference" (2003: 61-62). We can see in Table 3.8 that among the more typical functions of demonstratives, i.e. spatial functions, there are some which border the notion of 'deictic reference'. These functions are recognitional ('shared knowledge'), anaphoric ('tracking'), immediate ('attention'), interrogative ('lack of knowledge'), and apprehensive ('warning'). In spite of this diversity of functions, the main formatives constitute a neat paradigm with a four-way distinction between proximal, medial, distal and interrogative. This quadripartite structure builds formally on the initial consonants: *z, b, f* and *m* respectively. The structure of the system is quite similar to Japanese demonstratives, as described by Coulmas (1982).

Table 3.8: Demonstratives

	pronoun	adverbial	adv.ALL	adv.ABL	verb clitic
PROX	*zane*	*zä*	*zbo*	*zba*	*z=*
	DEM:PROX 'this'	PROX 'here'	PROX.ALL 'hither'	PROX.ABL 'hence'	PROX= 'here'
MED	*bäne*	*bä*	*bobo*	*boba*	*b=*
	DEM:MED 'that'	MED 'there'	MED.ALL 'thither'	MED.ABL 'thence'	MED= 'there'
DIST	*ane*	*fä*	*fobo*	*foba*	*f=*
	DEM	DIST 'yonder'	DIST.ALL 'to over there'	DIST.ABL 'from over there'	DIST= 'yonder'
INTERROG	*mane*	*mä*	*mobo*	*moba*	*m=*
	'which'	'where'	where.ALL 'whither'	where.ABL 'whence'	where=, APPR=
IMM		*zf*			
		IMM 'right here'			
RECOG	*baf*				
	RECOG 'that one'				

Following Diessel (1999), I outline the syntactic distribution of demonstratives first. In Table 3.8, a number of demonstratives appear in shaded cells. These have additional functions and to some extent different syntactic distributions. They will be discussed in separate sections to follow.

Diessel (1999) defines four syntactic contexts in which demonstratives occur: as independent pronouns that occupy an adpositional or verbal argument position ("pronominal"); with nouns in noun phrases ("adnominal"); as verb modifiers ("adverbial"); and in copula and non-verbal clauses ("identificational"). Some languages have distinct lexical categories for each function. Diessel calls the four categories demonstrative pronominals, demonstrative determiners, demonstrative adverbs, and demonstrative identifiers (1999: 3). See Himmelmann (1996) who makes similar distinctions. Demonstratives in Komnzo occur in all four syntactic contexts. Below, I use the proximal in order to illustrate the different syntactic contexts.

3.1.12.1 Pronominal and adnominal demonstratives

Demonstratives can be used pronominally (54) or adnominally (55).

(54) *moba zane nm nzyaniyak?*
       moba   zane   nm   nz=yan\yak/
       where.ABL DEM:PROX maybe IPST=3SG.MASC.SBJ:NPST:IPFV:VENT/walk
       'Where might this (man) have come from?'   [tci20120901-01 MAK #87]

(55) *zane namä ezi mrmren nzä kwa trikasi ŋatrikwé.*
       zane   namä ezi   mrmr=en nzä   kwa trik-si
       DEM:PROX good morning inside=LOC 1SG.ABS FUT tell-NMLZ
       ŋa\trik/wé
       1SG.SBJ:NPST:IPFV/tell
       'In this beautiful morning, I will tell a story.'   [tci20111119-01 ABB #2-3]

When used pronominally, demonstratives serve as the host for a subset of the case clitics. The examples below show case marking with the instrumental (56), purposive (57), and characteristic case (58). Rarely, they occur with the proprietive (59), and there are no corpus examples with the privative case. Demonstratives are not marked for other cases, but they can take other nominal morphology like the exclusive clitic *=nzo* or the emphatic clitic *=wä*.

(56) *arammba yare zaneme zf äfiyokwre.*
       arammba yare zane=me   zf   ä\fiyok/wre
       arammba bag DEM:PROX=INS IMM 1PL:SBJ>2|3PL:OBJ:NPST:IPFV/make
       'We make the Arammba bags with this one right here.'   [tci20130907-02 JAA #410]

(57) *ebar fobo fof zäbtha. zanemr zena znrä.*
       ebar fobo   fof   zä\bth/a   zane=mr   zena
       head DIST.ALL EMPH 2|3SG:SBJ:PST:PFV/finish DEM:PROX=PURP today
       z=n\rä/
       PROX=1PL:SBJ:NPST:IPFV/be
       'From this time onwards, the head-hunting finished. For this (reason), we are
       here today.'   [tci20111107-01 MAK #148-149]

(58) *nafanmedben keke znsä rä. **zanemanzo** ŋathwekwrth … yusi fathasimanzo.*
nafanmedben   keke znsä \rä/   zane=ma=nzo
3NSG.ANIM.LOC NEG work 3SG.FEM:SBJ:NPST:IPFV/be DEM:PROX=CHAR=ONLY
ŋa\thwek/wrth   (.) yusi fath-si=ma=nzo
2|3PL:SBJ:NPST:IPFV/be.happy (.) grass hold-NMLZ=CHAR=ONLY
'The (hard) work is not theirs (but ours). They are happy with doing just this …
just the weeding.'   [tci20130823-06 STK #109-111]

(59) *zane fthé keke srarä ziyarä keke kwa sräthorth moneyme. **zanekaräsü** ane srarä
kwot.*
zane   fthé   keke sra\rä/   z=ya\rä/   keke
DEM:PROX when NEG 3SG.MASC:IRR:IPFV/be PROX=3SG.MASC:IO:NPST:IPFV/be NEG
kwa srä\thor/th   money=me zane=karä=sü   ane
FUT 2|3PL:SBJ>3SG.MASC:OBJ:IRR:PFV/carry money=INS DEM:PROX=PROP=ETC DEM
sra\rä/   kwot
3SG.MASC:SBJ:IRR:IPFV/be properly
'If this (root) is not here, they won't buy it. Only with all of this will, they buy it.'
                                                       [tci20130907-02 RNA #471-473]

Case marked demonstratives are frequently used as conjunctions to connect the following clause, especially demonstratives marked for the characteristic (*zanema, bänema,
anema* 'therefore, because'), the instrumental (*zaneme, bäneme, aneme* 'with this/that,
thereby') and the purposive (*zanemr, bänemr, anemr* 'therefore'). See (60) for an example with *bänema*.

(60) *naf nima "samg! **bänema** nä buné fof yruthrth byé … keke kwosi yathizr."*
naf   nima sa\mg/   bäne=ma
3SG.ERG QUOT 2SG:SBJ>3SG.MASC:OBJ:IMP:PFV/shoot DEM:MED=CHAR
nä bun=é   fof   y\ru/thrth
INDF=ERG.NSG EMPH 2|3PL:SBJ>3SG.MASC:OBJ:NPST:IPFV/shoot
b=\yé/   (.) keke kwosi ya\thi/zr
MED=3SG.MASC:SBJ:NPST:IPFV/be (.) NEG dead 3SG.MASC:SBJ:NPST:IPFV/die
'He said: "Shoot it! Because others are shooting hard and it is not dying."'
                                                       [tci20131013-01 ABB #101-103]

What has been mentioned above about case marked demonstratives also holds for the
interrogative *mane* 'who, which' in Table 3.8. Like other interrogatives, it can be used
as a relative pronoun, and it can be marked for a subset of the case clitics: absolutive
mane 'who, which', characteristic *manema* 'because of which', instrumental *maneme*
'with which', and purposive *manemr* 'for which'.[9] An example with *maneme* is given in
(61).

---

[9]The animate referents for cases other than the absolutive are expressed by the interrogatives in Table 3.6.

(61) *ane fathnzo zfrärm. ... wämne keke ... dödönzo ... dödö **maneme** ŋarenwre fath.*
ane fath=nzo   zf\rä/rm   (.) wämne keke (.) dödö=nzo   (.)
DEM clearing=ONLY 3SG.FEM:SBJ:PST:DUR/be (.) tree   NEG   (.) dödö=ONLY (.)
dödö mane=me ŋa\ren/wre   fath
dödö which=INS 1PL:SBJ:NPST:IPFV/sweep clearing.
'It was a clear place ... no trees ... only *dödö* ... that *dödö* with which we sweep
the place.'   [tci20120821-02 LNA #25-27]

     The description of demonstratives leaves us with an analytic problem. Is there justifica-
tion for setting up two separate subcategories: demonstrative pronouns and demonstrative determiners? The fact that they can stand for a whole noun phrase is not sufficient
evidence for setting up an independent subcategory of demonstrative pronouns because
the head of a noun phrase can be omitted and leave only a modifier including a demonstrative determiner. The demonstratives described here do not take the full range of cases
as other pronouns, for example the personal pronouns (3.1.9), the indefinite (3.1.11) and
recognitional pronoun (3.1.12.6). Therefore, I describe them simply as demonstratives
with a pronominal and adnominal function.

3.1.12.2 Adverbial demonstratives

Table 3.8 includes a column of adverbial demonstratives (e.g. *zä* 'here') with a dedicated
form for the allative (*zbo* 'hither') and the ablative case (*zba* 'from here'). These are used
for verbal modification, as in example (62) with *zä* 'here' and in example (63) with *foba*
'from there' and *zbo* 'hither'.

(62) *taurianeme moth **zä** wnthn.*
tauri=aneme   moth zä   wn\thn/
wallaby=POSS.NSG path   PROX 3SG.FEM:SBJ:NPST:IPFV:VENT/lie.down
'The wallabies' path lies here.'   [tci20130903-01 MKW #35]

(63) *wati, ane **foba** ŋanmonziknwr. **zbo** wänyak. zane mnz zf wrwr.*
wati ane foba   ŋan\monzikn/wr   zbo
then DEM DIST.ABL 2|3SG:SBJ:NPST:IPFV:VENT/prepare PROX.ALL
wän\yak/   zane   mnz zf
3SG.FEM:SBJ:NPST:IPFV:VENT/walk DEM:PROX house IMM
w\r/wr
2|3SG:SBJ>3SG.FEM:OBJ:NPST:IPFV/build
'Then, this (bird) prepares over there and she comes here to build her nest right
here.'   [tci20120815 ABB #48]

     The allative adverbials are often found with an /mr/ element attached to them: *zbomr,
bobomr* and *fobomr*. I take this as frozen morphology of the purposive case marker *=r*.
These forms are often used as connectives to mean 'until' (§3.6).

3.1.12.3 Clitic demonstratives

Diessel (1999) includes the syntactic context of identification (identificational demonstratives) and finds a distinct class (demonstrative identifiers) in a number of languages. We find both the syntactic context as well as the distinct class in the language.

Komnzo possesses a set of deictic verbal proclitics which I call clitic demonstratives (Table 3.8). These clitics are used for identification and can attach to any inflected verb. In example (64), two brothers are trying to kill a creature by shooting an arrow into its heart.

(64) *naf nima "keke fi miyamr erä fofosa mä rä. nze komnzo **zimarwé** fof."*
    naf   nima keke fi   miyamr   e\rä/   fofosa mä
    3SG.ERG QUOT NEG 3.ABS ignorance 2|3PL:SBJ:NPST:IPFV/be heart where
    \rä/   nze   komnzo
    3SG.FEM:SBJ:NPST:IPFV/be 1SG.ERG only
    z=y\mar/wé   fof
    PROX=1SG:SBJ>3SG.MASC:OBJ:NPST:IPFV/see EMPH
    'He said: "They don't know where its heart is. I can see it here."'
                                                  [tci20131013-01 ABB #104-105]

While they can attach to any verb, clitic demonstratives are found with the copula in 90% of the tokens. Usually, the copula follows the main verb, as in example (65) and (66). The clitic demonstrative plus copula stands in apposition to the main clause, but they often form one intonational unit.

(65) *fi zena zane zf dö sakwré **zyé**.*
    fi   zena zane   zf   dö   sa\kwr/é
    but today DEM:PROX IMM goanna 1SG:SBJ>3SG.MASC:OBJ:RPST:PFV/hit
    z=\yé/
    PROX=3SG.MASC:SBJ:NPST:IPFV/be
    'But today I have killed this goanna here.'   [tci20120821-01 LNA #67]

(66) *yasifa foba fof ni zane zewärake zena **znrä**.*
    yasi=fa foba   fof   ni   zane   ze\wär/ake   zena
    yasi=ABL DIST.ABL EMPH 1NSG DEM:PROX 1PL:SBJ:PST:IPFV/crack today
    z=n\rä/
    PROX=1PL:SBJ:NPST:IPFV/be
    'From Yasi, we originate from him and (therefore) we are here today.'
                                                 [tci20111107-01 MAK #86]

The clitic demonstrative plus copula is the primary strategy to make an identificational reference much like English 'there it is' or 'here you go'. This is usually accompanied by a pointing gesture. Diessel points out that in other languages "demonstrative identifiers are often functionally equivalent to a demonstrative plus copula" (1999: 10). Komnzo confirms this pattern and, therefore, I analyse the clitic demonstrative plus copula as one unit. I adopt the label demonstrative identifier from Diessel. I address this topic in the description of verb morphology (§5.6.2).

The demonstrative identifier always agrees with some element in the main clause. Hence, if the argument in the clause is modified by a medial demonstrative, that same medial category will be used in the demonstrative identifier. An example with the proximal is given in (67). Note that the medial demonstrative identifier *byé* instead of the proximal *ziyé* would render the sentence ungrammatical.

(67) *zane kabe zf yé **zyé**.*
      zane   kabe zf \yé/   z=\yé/
      DEM:PROX man IMM 3SG.MASC:SBJ:NPST:IPFV/be PROX=3SG.MASC:SBJ:NPST:IPFV/be
      'It is this man right here.'   [tci20111004 RMA #51]

The verbal clitic *m=* is a special case. It can be attached to a copula, which will produce a question. In example (68), the speaker looks around for a particular tree species to show to me. Then she suddenly finds it.

(68) ***myé** yorär? yorär zyé ... zikogr.*
      m=\yé/   yorär yorär z=\yé/
      where=3SG.MASC:SBJ:NPST:IPFV/be yorär yorär PROX=3SG.MASC:SBJ:NPST:IPFV/be
      (.) z=y\kogr/
      (.) PROX=3SG.MASC:SBJ:NPST:STAT/stand
      'Where is *yorär*? *Yorär* is here ... It stands here.'   [tci20130907-02 JAA #449-451]

The same *m=* clitic, when attached to verb forms in imperative or irrealis mood, receives an apprehensive interpretation: 'don't do X' or 'you might X'. An example is given in (69). The *m=* clitic is discussed in §3.5.2 and again in §6.3.2 as part of the description of the TAM system.

(69) *aya msar **mkrätrth**!*
      aya msar m=krä\tr/th
      oh ant APPR=2|3PL:SBJ:IRR:PFV/fall
      'Oh, the ants might fall down!'   [tci20130907-02 RNA #678]

3.1.12.4 Anaphoric *ane*

In Table 3.8 *ane* has been glossed as a general demonstrative (DEM), even though it is placed in the paradigm position where one would expect the distal demonstrative. However, *ane* has no spatial reference, but it is used for anaphoric reference. It marks a referent which has been established in the preceding context. Consequently, *ane* marks definiteness and is the opposite of the indefinite *nä* (§3.1.11). Both cannot occur in the same noun phrase.

There is evidence from several sources that *ane* is the result of phonological reduction and semantic bleaching. Recordings from the 1980s by Mary Ayres contain a number of occurrences of a demonstrative *fane*, and older speakers today identify this as 'the way, how old people used to speak'. Indeed, the position in the paradigm would suggest an initial consonant *f*. This is attested in other Tonda varieties, e.g. Wartha Thuntai *fana*. We can conclude that this demonstrative has undergone phonological reduction from *fane* to *ane* over the last two generations of speakers. Moreover, we can infer semantic bleaching from spatial (distal) to anaphoric (tracking) from its position in the paradigm. However, we cannot put a time frame to the process of semantic bleaching, because it is unclear whether or not *fane* had a spatial meaning in the old recordings in addition to its anaphoric use.

The anaphoric demonstrative behaves in other respects like the demonstrative pronouns and determiners (§3.1.12.1). One exception is the agreement described in §3.1.12.3 between the demonstrative in the main clause and the demonstrative identifier. Since *ane* has no spatial reference, it may combine with the proximal and the medial demonstrative identifier as can be seen in example (70) and (71), respectively.

(70) *fintäth **ane ziyé** ... yemaneme dagon.*
    fintäth ane z=\yé/   (.) yem=aneme   dagon
    fintäth DEM PROX=3SG.MASC:SBJ:NPST:IPFV/be (.) cassowary=POSS.NSG food
    'This *fintäth* (fruit) here is the cassowaries' food.'   [tci20130907-02 RNA #316]

(71) *watik, nge **ane** zefar **byé** ruga monegsir.*
    watik nge ane ze\far/   b=\yé/   ruga
    then child DEM 2|3SG:SBJ:RPST:PFV/set.off MED=3SG.MASC:SBJ:NPST:IPFV/be pig
    moneg-si=r
    wait-NMLZ=PURP
    'Then the boy there set off to take care of the pig.'   [tci20130901-04 YUK #7]

3.1.12.5 Immediate *zf*

The immediate demonstrative *zf* is related to the proximate series on the basis of it sharing the first consonant. The immediate adds a pragmatic component to the spatial function of demonstratives, in that it draws the addressee's attention to someone or something in close proximity. It is often accompanied by a pointing gesture. Therefore I translate *zf* as 'right here' to English. We have seen *zf* already in examples (56), (63) and (67).

Zf is syntactically inert as it cannot be marked for case. It occurs in preverbal position and only the TAM particles or the negator may occur between the immediate demonstrative and the verb, as in example (72).

(72) *zane zf kwa esinzre zöbthé.*
    zane   zf kwa e\si/nzre   zöbthé
    DEM:PROX IMM FUT 1PL:SBJ>2|3PL:OBJ:NPST:IPFV/cook first
    'We will cook these (yams) here first.'   [tci20121001 ABB #62]

3.1.12.6 Recognitional *baf*

Following Himmelmann (1996), I use the term "recognitional demonstrative" for *baf*. Himmelmann describes a distinct recognitional use of demonstratives, which has become grammaticalised in some languages. Among them are a number of Australian languages, for example Nunggubuyu (Heath 1984) and Yankunytjatjara (Goddard 1985). See Himmelmann (1996: 231ff.) for further discussion. Komnzo *baf* counts as another example for this grammaticalisation. I analyse *baf* as a pronoun because it can be marked for all cases. In contrast to other demonstratives, there are both animate and inanimate forms (Table 3.9).

Garde characterises the recognitional demonstrative in Bininj Gunwok as reflecting "a belief on the part of the speaker that sufficient common ground exists for hearers to make the necessary inferences" (2013: 250). In Komnzo *baf* has a number of uses which all echo the notion of common ground. A speaker may use *baf* to introduce a referent which he believes the hearer to know about. This can be a first mention of a referent which is not topical or in focus (i.e. from an earlier part of a narrative). Moreover, the recognitional is often used as a filler in tip-of-the-tongue situations like 'whatchamacallit' in English. The recognitional can be described as an invitation to the addressee to ask for the referent or, more commonly, to fill in herself the appropriate word. Hence, the recognitional can be used pragmatically to keep a conversation going and assure the addressee's attention. Often the recognitional is employed as a strategy of circumspection, for example if the speaker is in a taboo relationship with a specific person and, therefore, has to avoid using her proper name.

Example (73) is a first mention of a particular person in a narrative. Although not required, it is quite common for the speaker to fill in the 'missing' referent after a short lapse. Thus, the phrase *masenane mezü* 'Masen's widow' refers back to *bafane mezü* 'that one's widow'.

(73)   *mabata fi mezü zwamnzrm.* **bafane** *mezü rera ... masenane mezü.*
         mabata fi   mezü   zwa\m/nzrm   baf=ane   mezü
         mabata 3.ABS widow 3SGFEM:SBJ:PST:DUR/dwell RECOG=POSS.SG widow
         \rä/ra   (.) masen=ane   mezü
         3SGFEM:SBJ:PST:IPFV/be (.) masen=POSS.SG widow
         'Mabata stayed as a widow. She was that one's widow ... Masen's widow.'
                                              [tci20120814 ABB #18-20]

The recognitional demonstrative is built on the medial demonstrative, as we can tell by the initial consonant *b*. It follows that the recognitional must have emerged through semantic extension from the medial demonstrative, and only later developed distinct forms for all the cases. We find that a number of forms serve a double function. For example, *bäne* can function as demonstrative pronoun ('that') and as recognitional pronoun ('the one I presume that you know about'). But the two differ in their combinatorics. While the demonstrative can modify as well as replace a nominal head of a phrase, the recognitional operates only pronominally. I have already shown in example (73) that it is quite common for a speaker to fill in the intended referent of a recognitional herself, sometimes after the clause, sometimes after a short pause. This leaves us with the problem of distinguishing the medial demonstrative from the recognitional in a phrase like *bäne kabe*. However, prosody signals which of the two it is. If both words belong to the same intonation contour, it is the medial demonstrative: 'that man'. If there is short break in the intonation or a longer pause, it is the recognitional: 'that one ... the man'. The other case forms which are formally identical are impossible to distinguish in a clear way. For example, *bänema* 'therefore, because' is often used to connect another clause (§3.1.12.1). In this case we always find a break in the intonation. It is best to interpret the formal identity as a signal of the semantic extension of the medial demonstrative. That being said, it would be wrong to conclude that the recognitional is merely a function of the medial demonstrative.

Table 3.9: The recognitional pronoun

case	inanimate	animate SG	animate NSG
ABS	*bäne*		
ERG	*baf*		*bafa*
DAT	-	*bafn*	*bafnm*
POSS	-	*bafane*	*bafanme*
LOC	*bafen*	*bafadben*	*bafanmedben*
ALL	*bänefo*	*bafadbo*	*bafanmedbo*
ABL	*bänefa*	*bafadba*	*bafanmedba*
INS	*bäneme*	-	-
PURP	*bänemr*	-	-
CHAR	*bänema*	*bafanema*	*bafanemema*
PROP	*bänekarä*	-	-
PRIV	*bänemär*	-	-
ASSOC[a]	-	*bafrr*	*bafä*

[a]The associative forms encode DU versus PL (§7.6).

As we can see in Table (3.9), the recognitional can be marked for all cases. In this respect, the recognitional surpasses even personal pronouns in the richness of its distinctions because there are animate and inanimate case forms.

3.1.12.7 Manner demonstrative *nima*

Komnzo has a manner demonstrative *nima* which is best translated as 'like this' or 'do this way'. In some languages this demonstrative is assigned to the class of verbs, for example in Boumaa Fijian and Dyirbal (Dixon 2003: 72). In other languages it is a nominal, for example in Kayardild (Evans 1995: 214). *Nima* falls in the latter category. It is a nominal which can be marked for a subset of cases (instrumental, characteristic, purposive, proprietive, and privative). It shares no morpho-syntactic characteristics with verbs, but may either modify a verb (74) or express a whole event (75). Example (74) is from a pig hunting story and *nima* is accompanied by the appropriate gesture describing how and where the person was standing. In (75) it expresses the whole following clause ('that I was walking towards them').

(74)   *ruga ŋankwira **nima** sankuka bä byé.*
      ruga ŋan\kwir/a   nima san\kuk/a   bä
      pig 2|3SG:SBJ:PST:IPFV:VENT/run like.this 3SG.MASC:SBJ:PST:PFV:VENT/stand MED
      b=\yé/
      MED=3SG.MASC:SBJ:NPST:IPFV/be
      'The pig came running, and he stood like this over there.'   [tci20110810-02 MAB #34]

(75)   *fi miyamr thfrärm **nima** ... nzä we ane fof kwofiyakmo nafanmedbo ... we nzä miyamr kwofrärm.*
      fi   miyamr thf\rä/rm   nima   (.) nzä   we ane fof
      3.ABS ignorant 2|3PL:SBJ:PST:DUR/be like.this (.) 1SG.ABS also DEM EMPH
      kwof\yak/mo   nafanmedbo (.) we   nzä   miyamr
      1SG:SBJ:PST:DUR:AND/walk 3NSG.ALL   (.) also 1SG.ABS ignorant
      kwof\rä/rm
      1SG:SBJ:PST:DUR/be
      'They did not know about this ... (that) I was walking towards them ... and I did not know either.'   [tci20111119-03 ABB #136-137]

Nima is used for three functions: deictic reference (actual or mimicked), anaphora, or introducing direct speech. When introducing direct speech *nima* may occur with a speaking verb (76) or just by itself (60). In these instances, it is glossed as a quotative marker (QUOT). This function is further described in §9.7.

(76)   *nzä **nima** zukorth "be fafä zane nagayé fäth zä thamonegwé!"*
      nzä   nima zu\kor/th   be   fafä   zane
      1SG.ABS QUOT 2|3DU:SBJ>1SG:OBJ:PST:PFV/speak 2SG.ERG after.this DEM:PROX
      nagayé fäth zä   tha\moneg/wé
      children DIM PROX 2SG:SBJ>2|3PL:OBJ:IMP:IPFV/take.care
      'The two told me: "You take care of these small children here!"'
                                                [tci20121019-04 ABB #91-92]

When marked with the instrumental case *=me*, *nima* is often used as an emphatic affirmative, as English 'Just like this!'. In (77), the speaker explains how his grandmother grew very old because she followed all the food taboos.

(77)   *nafaŋamane zokwasi nafaŋafane zokwasi naf mon zekarisa. **nimame** fof!*
      nafa-ŋame=ane   zokwasi nafa-ŋafe-ane   zokwasi naf   mon
      3.POSS-mother=POSS.SG language 3.POSS-father=POSS.SG language 3SG.ERG how

ze\karis/a   nima=me   fof
2|3SG:SBJ:PST:PFV/hear   like.this=INS EMPH
'She listened to her mother's words and to her father's words. Just like this!'

[tci20120922-26 DAK #60]

3.2 Verbs

Verbs are by far the most complex lexical items in Komnzo with respect to morphology. Here, only a brief overview and some of the definitional criteria for identifying a particular item as a verb are given. For a full discussion of verbal morphology in Komnzo the reader is referred to chapters 5 and 6.

With around 380 members, verbs are the second largest word class after nouns. In spite of its inventory size, verbs constitute a closed word class. There are no observed cases of loanwords or neologisms. Evidence for the closed status comes from two observations. First, the lack of derivational morphology (and shared roots) within the word class, but also between verbs and other word classes. Secondly, the fact that loanwords which are verbs in the donor language never end up in the verb class in Komnzo.

Within the word class of verbs there is no productive derivational morphology. Only a few non-productive patterns can be discerned, but the interpretation of these remains highly speculative. One such example is the pair of verbs *knsi* 'roll' and *myuknsi* 'roll, twist'. The former is often used for rolling cigarettes, while the latter is used for rolling up a tape measure. Hence, we could translate them as *knsi* 'roll lengthwise' and *myuknsi* 'roll widthwise', ignoring the second sense of *myuknsi* 'twist'. Without the nominaliser, the stems are *kn* and *myukn*, and a possible hypothesis is that the *myu* says something about the orientation of the object that is rolled up. However, *myu* is not a word in Komnzo, nor is the pattern attested elsewhere in the verb lexicon. Another example is the pair *misoksi* 'look up' and *risoksi* 'look down'. The formal difference lies only in the first consonant. I analyse these as idiosyncrasies of particular stems which might reflect frozen derivational morphology.

The same observation can be made for the relation between the verb class and other word classes. There are currently only four examples where a verb stem is identical or similar to a nominal element and a semantic bridge can be established. The first is the verb *rmrsi* 'rub, grind' and the property noun *rmr* 'roughness'. The second is the verb *miyogsi* 'beg, ask for' and *miyo*, which can be either a property noun 'desire' or a noun 'wish, taste'. The third is the verb *wasisi* 'shine light on' and the word for the masked owl *wasi*.[10] The last example is the verb *fokusi* 'miss out on sth.' and the word *fokufoku* which describes a patch of bush that was not burned or a patch of grass that was not cut down. There is a clear semantic overlap in the nominal and verbal semantics, but we cannot determine the direction of derivation. However, the scarcity of such examples is striking.

---

[10] The Masked Owl (Tyto novaehollandiae), like most owls, has large eyes.

One wonders then how new verb meanings enter the language. The clearest answer to this question comes from loanwords. Komnzo speakers were exposed to Hiri Motu during a short period in the 1950s when the local Mission school was run by Motu-speaking teachers. Since the 1960s the dominant educational as well as administrative language has been English. All loanwords which are verbs in Hiri Motu or English end up in the nominal subclass of property nouns, not in the verb class. Some Komnzo examples are *durua* 'help' and *tarawat* 'law, rightfulness' from Motu, *senis* 'change' and *boil* 'boil' from English. It is the complex verb morphology, for example stem types sensitive to aspectual distinctions, which prevents new material from being incorporated into the verb class. Instead, these loan verbs are property nouns in Komnzo, and they are employed in a light verb construction (§8.3.12). Cross-linguistically, this is a common strategy to integrate loan verbs (Wichmann & Wohlgemuth 2008).[11]

Morpho-syntactically, we can define verbs as those lexemes which inflect for gender, person, number, tense, aspect, mood, valency, and directionality, as can be seen in examples (78) and (79). With the exception of person and number, these are only found in verbs. The glossing of these grammatical categories, however, cannot be done straightforwardly, because a number of them can only be understood after unifying values from different morphological slots. For example, the aspectual value PST:DUR in (78) is encoded simultaneously in the verb stem, the prefix and the durative suffix. Prior to this unification, each morpheme taken by itself is underspecified with respect to any particular grammatical category. The only exceptions are the two directional affixes. In this subsection, I will employ a double glossing style as in the chapters on verb morphology (chapters 5 and 6). A segmented, itemised glossing line is given first, while a second line shows the unified gloss in smaller print. Morphological complexity in verbs is discussed in §5.2, where the reader also finds a more detailed justification for the double-lined glossing convention.

(78) *nafane nagayé **thfrärm**. naf **thwamonegwrm**.*
    nafane nagayé thf-rä-rm   naf
    3SGPOSS children 2|3NSG.β2-COP.ND-DUR 3SG.ERG
           2|3PL:SBJ:PST:DUR/be

    thu-a-moneg-wr-m-$\varnothing$
    2|3NSG.β1-VC-take.care.EXT-ND-DUR
    2|3SG:SBJ>2|3PL:OBJ:PST:DUR/take.care
    'They were her children. She took care of them.'   [tci20120901-01 MAK #47]

(79) *fi fthé **enthorakwa** … mnz kabe fof. nima **thäzigrthma** "nä tmatm fefe **nzŋawänzr**. manema kabe zä naf **nziyanathr**?"*

---

[11]From observation it is clear that younger speakers have already begun to replace some Komnzo verbs with English loans using a light verb construction with 'do'. For example, *thofiksi* 'disturb' is commonly expressed as *disturb ŋarär*, whereby *ŋarär* is the inflected verb 'do', and the expression can be literally translated as 'he does the distraction/disturbing'. One may predict that this pattern will become more dominant in the future. The shift from minor to major patterns in contact situations has been described by Heine and Kuteva (2005: 44).

fi   fthé   e-n-thorak-w-a-∅   (.) mnz   kabe   fof   nima
3.ABS when 2|3NSG.α-VENT-arrive.EXT-ND-PST-2|3SG (.) house people EMPH QUOT
          2|3PL:SBJ:PST:IPFV:VENT/arrive

th-ä-zingrthm-a   nä   tmatm fefe
2|3NSG.γ-VC.ND-look.around.RS-PST some event   real
2|3PL:SBJ:PST:PFV/look.around

nz=ŋ-a-wä-nzr-∅   mane=ma   kabe zä   naf
IPST=M.α-VC-break.EXT-ND-2|3SG which=CHAR man PROX 3SG.ERG
IPST=2|3SG:SBJ:NPST:IPFV/break

nz=y-a-na-thr-∅
IPST=3SG.MASC.α-VC-eat.EXT-ND-2|3SG
IPST=2|3SG:SBJ>3SG.MASC:OBJ:NPST:IPFV/eat

'At that time the house owners returned to the village. They looked around and said, "Something terrible has happened. From which village was the man who she ate here?"'   [tci20120901-01 MAK #106-111]

Examples (78) and (79) show the intricate architecture of Komnzo verbs. The verb forms in both examples are inflected for various grammatical categories. The agreement target for gender is the third person singular prefix on the verb, as can be seen in the last verb 'eat' in example (79). Person and number are encoded in the undergoer prefix as well as the actor suffix. However, these slots are underspecified: the second and third person in the non-singular are neutralised in both slots. The first non-singular and second singular are neutralised in the prefixes. These can be disambiguated by the free pronouns. In both slots, dual and plural are neutralised. The system of number marking combines a singular vs. non-singular opposition in the prefix and suffix with a dual vs. non-dual opposition in the duality affix. Thereby, one arrives at the three number values (SG, DU, PL). For about half a dozen high frequency verbs, such as the copula (78), the stem itself is sensitive to duality. For all other verbs, duality is either encoded by a prefix, as in the second verb 'look around' in (79) or by a suffix as in all other verbs in (78) and (79). The morphological site of duality marking depends on the stem type. Almost all verbs in Komnzo have two stems from which aspectual distinctions can be build. I label the two stem types 'restricted' (RS) and 'extended stem' (EXT). It follows that tense, aspect and mood are expressed by a combination of verb stem, prefixes, and further suffixal material. As for the prefixes, there are five different prefix series labelled α, β, β_1, β_2, and γ and an immediate past proclitic (for example in the last two verbs of 79). Beyond TAM, the prefixes encode information about person, number, and gender. Examples for the suffixal material are the durative suffix (DUR) in both verb forms in (78) and the past suffix (PST) in the first two verb forms in (79). The TAM value is calculated by unifying these different exponents. As the final category to mention here, the first verb 'arrive' in (79) is inflected for directionality. The two values of direction are venitive 'towards' (VENT) and andative 'away' (AND).

Verbs are the only lexical items which can take the nominalising suffix (-*si*). Nominalisations or infinitives are used as a citation form in the dictionary. Frequently, nominalisations were frequently given to me as *zokwasi ebar* 'head words' for an inflected verb form. Nominalisations are non-finite forms without inflectional material. Nominalisations can be treated like underived nouns. They can function as complements of phasal verbs (*finish, start, become*) (80) or infinitival adjuncts (81). Example (80) is taken from a story in which two birds have a competition on how long each one can hold its breath under water. Thus, *fsisi zäbthath* can be translated as 'the counting finished'. Example (81) can be translated as 'in the planting (season)'.

(80) *ane zwafsinzrm kwot e boböwä bäne zefafath … **fsisi** zäbthath.*

  ane zu-a-fsi-nzr-m-∅   kwot e bobo=wä
  DEM 3SG.FEM.*β*2-VC-count.EXT-ND-DUR-2|3SG properly until MED.ALL=EMPH
    2|3SG:SBJ>3SG.FEM:IO:PST:DUR/count

  bäne   z-ä-faf-a-th   (.) fsi-si
  RECOG.ABS M.*γ*-VC-ND-hold.RS-PST-2|3NSG (.) count-NMLZ
       2|3PL:SBJ:PST:PFV/hold

  z-ä-bth-a-th
  M.*γ*-VC-ND-finish.RS-PST-2|3NSG
    2|3PL:SBJ:PST:PFV/finish
  'He counted for her until he reached that number. Then the counting was finished.'
                                                                    [tci20130923-01 ALA #28-30]

(81) *fä fof sfrugrm … nima eftharen zf … nima **worsin** zf.*

  fä   fof sf-rug-rm   (.) nima efthar=en   zf (.) nima
  DIST EMPH 3SG.M.*β*2-sleep.EXT.ND-DUR (.) like.this dry.season=LOC IMM (.) like.this
          3SG.M:SBJ:PST:DUR/sleep

  wor-si=n   zf
  plant-NMLZ=LOC IMM
  'He slept over there … like this in the dry season … like this in the planting
  season.'   [tci20131013-02 ABB #140-142]

In other respects, nominalised verbs can be treated like any other noun. They can take case, for example the ergative (82) or the instrumental in a resultative construction (83). They can be reduplicated, as in (84). They can enter into possessive constructions either as possessed (84) or as possessor (85).

(82) *zarfa surmänwrm ane **wäsifnzo**.*

  zarfa su-rmän-wr-m-∅   ane wä-si=f=nzo
  ear 3SG.MASC.*β*2-close.EXT-ND-DUR-2|3NSG DEM break-NMLZ=ERG=ONLY
       2|3SG:SBJ>3SG.MASC:OBJ:PST:DUR/close
  'That breaking noise was blocking his ears.'   [tci20120818 ABB #68]

(83) *ŋafyf frthé bant wäfiyokwa, kidn ane rifthzsime zfrärm.*

  ŋafe-f   fthé bant w-a-fiyok-w-a-∅   kidn   ane
  father-ERG.SG when ground 3SG.FEM.*α*-VC-make.EXT-ND-PST-2|3SG ancient.fire DEM
                         2|3SG:SBJ>3SG.FEM:OBJ:PST:IPFV/make

rifthz-si=me   zf-rä-rm
hide-NMLZ=INS 3SG.FEM.*β*2-COP.ND-DUR
3SG.FEM:SBJ:PST:DUR/be
'When God made the Earth, the ancient fire was hidden.' [tci20120909-06 KAB #62-63]

(84) *fi miyomär yé. wri kabeaneme **ttrikasi** naf krarizr.*
fi   miyo=mär   \yé/   wri   kabe=aneme
3.ABS desire=PRIV 3SG.MASC.*α*.COP.ND   drunk man=POSS.NSG
3SG.MASC:SBJ:NPST:IPFV/be

t-trik-si   naf   k-ra-ri-zr-∅
REDUP-tell-NMLZ 3SG.ERG m.*β*-IRR.VC-hear.EXT-ND-2|3SG
2|3SG:SBJ:IRR:IPFV/hear
'He doesn't want to listen to those drunk people's stories.'   [tci20111004 RMA #140]

(85) *... **tharisiane** efoth fthé zfrärm.*
(.) thari-si=ane   efoth fthé   zf-rä-rm
(.) dig-NMLZ=POSS.SG day   when 3SG.FEM.*β*2-COP.ND-DUR
3SG.FEM:SBJ:PST:DUR/be
'... when it was harvesting season.'   [tci20120805-01 ABB #356]

Almost all verbs have an infinitive derived by means of the nominaliser (*-si*). However, there are a few exceptions where either an underived noun is used or an nominal form is lacking altogether. For the most part, these are verbs of high frequency. In the following three examples, the noun meaning is given first and the verb meaning second: *zan* 'fight, war (n); hit, kill (v)', *wath* 'dance, song (n); dance, sing (v)', *zrin* 'heaviness, burden (n); carry (v)'.

There are two options to analyse nominalisations. While I stress their verbal character, one could argue that they should be analysed as (deverbal) nouns. I believe that this is an analytic decision and that there are good arguments for both sides. I address this question here because the decision impacts several other parts of the grammar, for example the description of the interclausal function of the case markers (§4.3) and subordinate clauses (chapter 9), both of which involve infinitives. As shown above, nominalised verbs behave like nouns in terms of morphology, that is they can form reduplications and nominal compounds. Moreover, they can serve as hosts for the case enclitics. This supports the analysis of nominalisations as nouns. However, nominalised verbs retain particular verbal features, for example their argument structure. The agent (or most agent-like argument) of the finite verb can be expressed with the non-finite verb by means of a possessive construction. In *nafane tharisi* 'her digging', the third singular possessor refers to the agent argument. The patient (or most patient-like argument) can be expressed by the modifying element of a nominal compound. In *wawa tharisi* 'yam digging', the word for 'yam' is the patient of the event. Noun phrases of this type can be captured by the notion of an action nominal, which Comrie & Thompson describe as "a noun phrase that contains, in addition to a noun derived from a verb, one or more reflexes of a proposition or predicate" (2007: 343).

The verbal character of nominalisations in Komnzo is clearest in raising constructions. In example (86), the speaker demonstrates how to produce a children's toy from a coconut leaf. She uses a raising construction ('start rolling') with a nominalised form of 'roll'. This is followed by the finite form of 'roll'. We find that argument indexing of the finite 'roll' (1SG:SBJ>3SG.MASC:OBJ) has been raised to the phasal verb 'start'. In conclusion, I acknowledge that nominalised verbs can be analysed as either (deverbal) nouns or infinitives. I have made explicit why I choose the latter option.

(86) *myuknsi srethkäfe ... zane zf ymyuknwé.*
      myukn-si s-rä-thkäf-é   (.) zane   zf
      roll-NMLZ 3SG.MASC.γ-IRR-ND-start.RS-1SG (.) DEM:PROX IMM
          1SG:SBJ>3SG.MASC:OBJ:IRR:PFV/start

      y-myukn-w-é
      3SG.MASC.α-roll.EXT-ND-1SG
      1SG:SBJ>3SG.MASC:OBJ:NPST:IPFV/roll
      'I (usually) start rolling (the leaf). I roll this one right here.'   [tci20120914 RNA #45]

Word order in Komnzo is predominantly SOV, or more accurately AUV (agent undergoer verb). For pragmatic reasons, elements may follow the verb, but they are usually part of a separate intonation group. The only exceptions are the emphatic particle *fof* (§3.4.2) and the demonstrative identifier (§3.1.12.3).

Verbs can be subcategorised along both grammatical and semantic lines. As for the latter, we find a class of positional verbs, which take a special stative suffix and encode postural or positional semantics, for example *migsi* 'hang', *thorsi* 'be inside', *rngthksi* 'be in a tree fork' (§5.4.4.2). Morphologically, one interesting fact is that only a small part of intransitive verbs are purely prefixing. Most intransitive verbs employ both the prefix and the suffix. In this case, an invariant middle prefix is used and the single argument is indexed in the suffix (§5.4.5). Transitive verbs index their subject in the suffix and the object in the prefix (§5.4.6). Most stems can be applicativised by adding the *a-* prefix. In this case, the reference of the person prefix changes from the object (or subject of a prefixing verb) to an indirect object (usually a recipient, beneficiary, or raised possessor). I label the *a-* prefix VC for 'valency change'. This is because *a-* is used to increase as well as to decrease the valency of a verb. For example, the middle template, which can be used to form reflexives from transitive verbs, always takes the *a-* prefix (§5.4.2). A general feature of Komnzo verbs is a high degree of flexibility, whereby most stems may enter various morphological templates and a handful of stems can be cycled through all. This is discussed in detail in §5.4.

3.3 Adverbs

Adverbs make up a small closed class of about a dozen lexical items. A number of nominals, such as temporals and demonstratives have an adverbial function. Moreover, the instrumental case (*=me*) on adjectives and property nouns marks an adverbial function.

Some of the adverbs show remnants of frozen morphology. For example, *watmame* 'for a daytrip' shows a *=me* element, but the corresponding form *watma* is missing.

Temporals have been discussed in §3.1.8. They are a functional subclass of nominals, which can have an adverbial function. Spatial adverbials are expressed by the rich set of demonstratives discussed in §3.1.12.2. Hence, only manner adverbs comprise a word class in their own right. These are uninflecting words which are fairly free with respect to their position in the clause. Most commonly, they occur in preverbal position. Table 3.10 lists the currently attested manner adverbs.

Table 3.10: Manner adverbs

Komnzo	gloss
eräme	'together'
kwot	'properly'
matar	'quietly'
minzü	'very, too much'
nezä	'in return'
nm, nnzä	'perhaps, maybe'
ŋarde	'for the first time'
gaso	'badly'
gräme	'slowly'
dmnzü	'silently'
rürä	'alone, lonely'
watmame	'for a daytrip'
yakme	'fast, quickly'
nzagoma	'in advance'
ŋwä	'instead (of)'

3.4 Particles

There are two types of particles; TAM particles and discourse particles. Both are morphologically invariant, but differ slightly in their syntactic distribution. The TAM particles are discussed in more detail in §6.3.

3.4.1 TAM particles

There are five particles which are part of the tense-aspect-mood system. Most frequently, they occur in preverbal position, but other elements may intervene. These are important for TAM because even though Komnzo has a rich set of TAM related inflections on the verb, some categories can only be expressed by means of the particles, for example *kwa* for futurity and *z* for completion. The five particles are shown in Table 3.11. Note that there are the proclitics *n=* and *m=*, which play a role in TAM marking as well. Depending on their morpho-syntactic context they can be analysed as clitics or as particles. This point is discussed in §3.5.2.

Table 3.11: TAM particles

Komnzo	gloss	function	translation
kwa	FUT	future	'will'
z	ALR	iamitive	'already'
nomai	HAB	habitual	'often', 'always'
kma	POT	potential	'might', 'could'
keke or *kyo*	NEG	negator	'not'

The future marker *kwa*, sometimes just *ka*, is the only way of expressing the futurity of an event. It occurs with the non-past tense and the irrealis mood (87), both of which are insufficient for indicating that a particular event will take place in the future. The particle may occur just by itself, in which case it is an imperative that means 'wait!' (87). The future particle *kwa* is discussed in §6.3.4.

(87) *katakatan **kwa** zöbthé thrängathinzth nima: "**kwa**! komnzo **kwa**!"*
      kata-katan   kwa zöbthé thran\gathi/nzth   nima kwa
      REDUP-small FUT first   2|3PL:SBJ>2|3PL:OBJ:IRR:PFV:VENT/stop QUOT wait
      komnzo kwa
      only   wait
      'First, they will stop the small children (from jumping in). They will say: "Wait!
      Just wait!"'   [tci20110813-09 DAK #25]

The iamitive marker *z* functions as a completive marker. I adopt the term "iamitive" from Olsson (2013), who has coined it based on Latin *iam* 'already'. I use the gloss label ALR. The iamitive combines with all tense-aspect-mood categories, except for the imperative. The TAM system and the distinction between imperfective and perfective does not focus on completion, rather it draws a distinction between durative versus inceptive/punctual. The iamitive particle is the only way to indicate completion. It may be used in declarative sentences (88) or with a rising intonation in polar questions (89). The particle *z* is discussed in more detail in §6.3.5.

(88) *foba yakkarä enrera "oh, firran z thäkwrth."*
      foba   yak=karä en\rä/ra   oh firra=n   z
      DIST.ABL walk=PROP 2|3PL:SBJ:PST:IPFV:VENT/be oh firra=LOC ALR
      thä\kwr/th
      2|3PL:SBJ>2|3PL:OBJ:RPST:PFV/hit
      'They came fast from there (and said:) "Oh, they already killed them in Firra."'
                                                              [tci20131013-02 ABB #80]

(89) *z safäs?*
   z   sa\fäs/
   ALR 2|3SG:SBJ>3SG.MASC:IO:RPST:PFV/present
   'Did you show him already?'   [tci20130907-02 RNA #540]

The habitual marker *nomai* either indicates that an event happened regularly or that it took place for an extended time (90). There is a variant *nomair*, which expresses 'forever' or 'for a very long time' (91). The final /r/ element might be related to the purposive case. Its origin is still unclear, as particles cannot host case clitics. The habitual particle *nomai* is discussed in §6.3.6.

(90) *fi swathugwrm gaso. nimanzo **nomai** swafiyokwrm e **nomai nomai nomai**.*
   fi   swa\thug/wrm   gaso nima=nzo   nomai
   3SG.ABS 2|3SG:SBJ>3SG.MASC:OBJ:PST:DUR/trick badly like.this=ONLY HAB
   swa\fiyok/wrm   e   3x(nomai)
   2|3SG:SBJ>3SG.MASC:OBJ:PST:DUR/make until 3x(HAB)
   'He tricked him badly. He kept on doing this to him for a long, long time.'
                                                   [tci20110802 ABB #95-96]

(91) ***nomair** kwa namnzr kwot kwot kwot kwot e namä kakafar kwot käkorm.*
   nomair kwa na\m/nzr   4x(kwot) e   namä k-kafar   kwot
   HAB   FUT 2SG:SBJ:NPST:IPFV/dwell 4x(properly) until good REDUP-big properly
   kä\kor/m
   2SG:SBJ:FUTIMP:PFV/become
   'You will live forever ... all the time until you really grow old.'
                                                   [tci20120922-26 DAK #16]

The potential marker *kma* occurs with verbs of different aspect values. It marks counterfactuality with deontic or epistemic interpretation, for example potentiality of an event ('could' or 'could have') or obligation ('should' or 'should have'). In example (92), the speaker blames his wife for not telling him about a bushfire. In example (93), the speaker describes how he fought a bushfire in his garden. The particle *kma* is discussed in §6.3.3.

(92) *nzä tosaiaŋama **kma** kwräkor "käthf!" nzä nima fefe kwamnzrm kifa sfrwrmé.*
   nzä   tosai-a-ŋame   kma kwrä\kor/
   1SG.ABS baby-POSS-mother POT 2|3SG:SBJ>1SG:OBJ:IRR:PFV/speak
   kä\thf/   nzä   nima fefe kwa\m/nzrm   kifa
   2SG:SBJ:IMP:PFV/walk 1SG.ABS like.this really 1SG:SBJ:PST:DUR/sit rattan.wall
   sf\r/wrmé
   1SG:SBJ>3SG.MASC:OBJ:PST:DUR/weave
   'The baby's mother could have told me "You go!" but I was just sitting like this and weaving the rattan wall.'   [tci20120922-24 STK #8-10]

(93) ***kma** wämne ane fof kwakarkwé ane fof ... wämnef mane thänarfa ... keke ... watikthémäre.*

kma wämne ane fof   kwa\kark/wé   ane fof   (.) wämne=f mane
POT tree   DEM EMPH 1SG:SBJ:RPST:IPFV/pull DEM EMPH (.) tree=ERG which
thä\narf/a   (.) keke (.) watik-thé=märe
2|3SG:SBJ>2|3PL:OBJ:PST:PFV/press.down (.) NEG (.) enough-ADJZR=PRIV
'I should have pulled that tree off ... the one that was pushing down (the fences).
No (it was) not enough'.   [tci20120922-24 MAA #42-43]

With verbs in imperative or irrealis mood, *kma* frequently occurs together with the clitic *m*, which is discussed in more detail (§3.5.2). This combination of clitic, particle and verb inflection expresses a prohibitive. In this case, the clitic *m* may encliticise to *kma*. In fact, the resulting word *kmam* can stand as an utterance by itself meaning: 'Don't!' or 'Don't do it!'. In (94) one such example is given, which comes from a public speech during a dance. For further discussion, the reader is referred to §3.5.2 and §6.3.2.

(94) *gatha fam **kmam** gnräré monwä z fam thäkuke.*
      gatha fam   kma=m   gn\rä/ré   mon=wä   z   fam
      bad   thought POT=APPR 2SG:SBJ:IMP:IPFV/be how=EMPH ALR thought
      thä\kuk/e
      1PL:SBJ>2|3PL:OBJ:RPST:PFV/erect
      'You must not think bad about how we made up our minds.'
                                              [tci20121019-04 ABB #243-244]

The negator *keke* occurs in preverbal position (95). In rapid speech it is sometimes shortened to *ke*. There is a second negator *kyo* (96), which is mostly used by older speakers. Both negators can stand alone in an exclamation or as the answer to a question. Example (95) comes from a story about the speaker's father's generation. Example (96) is taken from a conversation about food taboos.

(95) *tüfr kabe **keke** thfrärm.*
      tüfr   kabe   keke thf\rä/rm
      plenty people NEG 2|3PL:SBJ:PST:DUR/be
      'They were not many people.'   [tci20120805-01 ABB #517]

(96) ***kyo** kwa nr kabeyé thranathrth ... nima ivanaŋame brä.*
      kyo kwa nr   kabe=é   thra\na/thrth   (.) nima
      NEG FUT belly people=ERG.NSG 2|3PL:SBJ>2|3PL:OBJ:IRR:IPFV/eat (.) like.this
      ivan-a-ŋame   b=\rä/
      ivan-POSS-mother MED=3SG.FEM:SBJ:NPST:IPFV/be
      'The pregnant people will not eat them ... like Ivan's mother there.'
                                              [tci20120922-26 MAB #38]

I was told that the teachers in the mission school during the 1960s discouraged their students from using *kyo* [kǯjo] because "it is a bad word". At the time, the teachers were Motu speakers and this was also the language of instruction. In Motu, the word *kio* [kijo] means 'vagina'. We can only hypothesise that the teachers of the mission school enacted pressure strong enough to replace the word *kyo* with the word *keke* whose origin is thus far unknown. Alternatively, the two negators might have existed simultaneously and the teachers' pressure only skewed their respective frequency of use. Negation is described in §8.5.

3.4.2 Discourse particles

There are three discourse particles in Komnzo: *we* 'also', the intensifier *fof* and the word from which the language name is derived, *komnzo* 'only, still'. These are used for different types of focus.

The particle *we* 'also' functions as an additive focus marker. It usually has scope over a whole proposition. It is rather flexible with respect to its position, and it may occur several times in a clause. Semantically, it always presupposes some event that has been established in the previous discourse. We can see this in example (97), where the speaker makes an additional comment as to why his time as a busy yam gardener has come to an end.

(97) *kafar z zäkora fof ... kafar ... watik, nzone tmä **we** katanme ŋarsörém.*
kafar z zä\kor/a fof (.) kafar (.) watik nzone tmä we
big ALR 1SG:SBJ:PST:PFV/become EMPH (.) big (.) then 1SG.POSS strength also
katan=me ŋa\rsör/m
small=INS 2|3SG:SBJ:RPST:DUR/recede
'I have grown old ... and my strength has also gone down a little.'
[tci20120805-01 ABB #662-664]

The particle *fof* is the word which occurs with the highest frequency in the corpus (around 2,000 tokens). It marks presentational focus of quite a wide range of elements. It always follows the element over which is has scope. This may be an adjunct (98), an argument (99), or the whole clause if it occurs after the verb (second *fof* in 99). In the examples below, the square brackets indicate the scope of the particle. Both examples come from a procedural text, in which the speaker presents his yam storage house. He explains the system by which the yams are piled up and sorted.

(98) *watik zanenzo fthé **fof** krägathinzth zethn ... dagonma **fof**.*
watik zane=nzo [fthé fof] krä\gathinz/th
then DEM:PROX=ONLY [when EMPH] 2|3PL:SBJ:IRR:PFV/stop
z=e\thn/ (.) dagon=ma fof
PROX=2|3PL:SBJ:NPST:STAT/lie.down (.) food=CHAR EMPH
'That is the time when only these ones are left. These lying here ... (are) really for eating.' [tci20121001 ABB #107]

(99) *ŋazäthema wawa ane **fof** erä **fof**.*
[ŋazäthe=ma [wawa ane fof] e\rä/ fof]
[ŋazäthe=CHAR [yam DEM EMPH] 2|3PL:SBJ:NPST:IPFV/be EMPH]
'These yams are really from Ŋazäthe.' [tci20121001 ABB #158]

The particle *komnzo* functions as a contrastive focus marker which has scope over the predicate. The clitic *=nzo* is its nominal counterpart, which is described in §3.5. The formal relationship between *komnzo* and *=nzo* holds true for other Tonda varieties. For example, Anta to the north has a corresponding particle *anta* and a clitic *=nta*.

In example (100), we see that *komnzo* has scope over the predicate, the copula in this case. I have often overheard women scolding their children by saying *komnzo kämés* 'Just sit down!'. In the example, a man returns to the place where the people of Firra took revenge on his wife after she had killed one of them.

(100) *wati nagawa ŋabrigwa sir.* **komnzo** *rä o z kwarsir mnin?*
wati nagawa ŋa\brig/wa   si=r   [komnzo
then nagawa 2|3SG:SBJ:PST:IPFV/return eye=PURP [only
\rä/]   o z kwa\rsir/   mni=n
3SG.FEM:SBJ:NPST:IPFV/be] or ALR 2|3SG:SBJ:RPST:IPFV/burn fire=LOC
'Then Nagawa returned to check: was she still alive or did she burn in the fire?'
[tci20120901-01 MAK #167-170]

3.5 Clitics

Proclitics and enclitics are attested in Komnzo. The former are found only with verbs, whereas the latter attach to nominals. I follow selected criteria based on the literature on clitichood, especially Zwicky & Pullum (1983) and chapter 8 of Anderson (1992). The relevant criteria in Komnzo are (i) clitics operate on a phrase rather than a word level, (ii) clitics show a low degree of selectivity with respect to their hosts and (iii) clitics can attach to other clitics. A further criterion which pertains only to the verbal proclitics and the (nominal) exclusive enclitic is (iv) clitics are reduced forms of independent lexical items.

3.5.1 Nominal enclitics

All the case markers in Komnzo are analysed as clitics. Evidence for the first two criteria is given in examples (101) and (102), where the ergative attaches to the rightmost element of an NP. The phrase boundaries are marked by square brackets in the examples. In (101), the noun phrase is *eda kwayan kabe* 'two white men'. In (102), the adjective is postposed and consequently is the last element of the phrase. Although case markers are attached only to nominals, they show a low degree of selectivity within this macro-word class. For a detailed discussion of the case markers, the reader is referred to §4.3.

(101) *waniwanime* [*eda kwayan* **kabeyé**] *yzänmth.*
waniwani=me eda kwayan kabe=yé
picture=INS   two white   man=ERG.NSG
y\zä/nmth
2|3DU:SBJ>3SG.MASC:OBJ:NPST:IPFV/carry
'The two white people are taking a picture of it.'   [tci20120821-01 LNA #35]

(102) *famé wathofiyokwrmth fof ... zbomr e [eda kabe **kafaré**] zukorth "paituaf nima*
bänemr ŋarär."

fam=é	wa\thofiyok/wrmth		fof (.) zbomr e eda
thought=ERG.NSG	2|3PL:SBJ>1SG:OBJ:RPST:DUR/disturb	EMPH (.) until until two
kabe kafar=é	zu\kor/th		paitua=f nima
men big=ERG.NSG	2|3DU:SBJ>1SG:OBJ:RPST:PFV/say	old.man=ERG.SG like.this
bänemr	ŋa\rä/r		
RECOG.PURP	2|3SG:SBJ:NPST:IPFV/do		

'These thoughts were disturbing me until the two big men told me: "The old
man thinks like this."'   [tci20121019-04 SKK #22-24]

The other nominal enclitics are no case markers: exclusive =*nzo* (ONLY), empathic =*wä*
(EMPH) and et cetera =*sü* (ETC). The first forms the nominal counterpart of the particle
komnzo (§3.4.2). This clitic satisfies criteria (iv) in that it is a reduced form of an independent lexical item. It functions as a contrastive focus marker and I translate it to with
English 'only'. Hence, in example (103), the woman picks up the yamstick with only one
thing on her mind. Note that this example shows that the clitic =*nzo* satisfies criteria (iii):
the ability to attach to other clitics. The exclusive enclitic =*nzo* will be discussed again
§4.17.2.

(103) *yaka **zanrnzo** srewakuth.*

yaka	zan=r=nzo	sre\wakuth/
yamstick	fight=PURP=ONLY	2|3SG:SBJ>3SG.MASC:OBJ:IRR:PFV/pick.up

'She picked up the yamstick to kill him.'   [tci20120901-01 MAK #86]

The emphatic enclitic =*wä* shows similar behaviour. It will be addressed in §4.17.1. The
et cetera enclitic =*sü* only attaches to the associative or proprietive case markers. It will
be discussed in §4.17.3.

3.5.2 Verbal proclitics

Verbal clitics are exclusively proclitics. They do not fully satisfy the criteria given above.
For example, they only attach to one word class (verbs) and they have scope only over
the inflected verb. On the other hand, all but one verbal proclitic are reduced forms of
independent lexical items.

Additional evidence against analysing them as prefixes comes from phonology. In
those cases where the proclitic creates an initial syllable through epenthesis, this syllable does not receive stress. For example, *bŋasogwr* 'he is climbing there' is marked with
the medial proclitic *b=*. Since all proclitics only consist of a single consonant, through syllabification an epenthetic vowel is inserted: [ᵐbə̌ŋˈasoⁿgʷə̌r]. On the surface, the second
syllable is stressed. However, stress remains word-initial, because the clitic is not a part
of the phonological word. Stress in Komnzo verbs is strictly word-initial and prefixes
which create an initial syllable (even if filled with the epenthetic vowel) are stressed, for
example *ŋazi wsogwr* 'he climbs the coconut' is realised as [ŋatʃi wˈɟ̆soⁿgʷə̌r].

The first set of verbal proclitics are the clitic demonstratives. These are deictic pro-clitics which attach to an inflected verb form: *z=* PROX, *b=* MED, and *f=* DIST. They are described in §3.1.12.3 and §5.6.2.

The second set of verbal proclitics comprises *m=* and *n=*. Depending on their morpho-syntactic context, they can be classified as either clitics or particles. The *m=* proclitic was briefly addressed in §3.1.12.3. We saw in Table 3.8, that *m=* patterns with the inter-rogatives. Thus, it patterns with the three deictic proclitics. However, this is a marginal function, because it is found only with the copula. More frequently, *m=* occurs with verb forms in irrealis or imperative mood. In this case it adds the meaning of apprehension ('X might happen!'), as in (104). Furthermore, with imperative verb forms only <u>and</u> with the potential particle *kma* it expresses prohibition ('don't do X!'), as in (94). In this latter function, *m* is analysed as a particle rather than a proclitic. This is discussed in detail in §6.3.2.

(104)   *thambrnzo **mthäkwr** fafä.*
        thambr=nzo m=thä\kwr/   fafä
        hand=ONLY APPR=2SG:SBJ>2|3PL:OBJ:IMP:PFV/hit afterwards
        'You might go home empty-handed afterwards.' (lit. 'You might hit only your hands afterwards.')   [tci20121019-04 ABB #126]

The second clitic *n=* also serves a double function. If attached to a verb inflected for non-past, it marks immediate past.[12] I gloss it IPST and analyse it as a proclitic. See ex-ample (105), which was uttered at the end of a recording.

(105)   *trikasi mane **nŋatrikwé** fof… ngafynm … badafa ane fof ŋanritakwa fof.*
        trik-si   mane n=ŋa\trik/wé   fof (.) ŋafe=nm   (.)
        tell-NMLZ which IPST=1SG:SBJ:NPST:IPFV/tell EMPH (.) father=DAT.NSG (.)
        bada=fa   ane fof   ŋan\ritak/wa   fof
        ancestor=ABL DEM EMPH 2|3SG:SBJ:PST:IPFV:VENT/cross EMPH
        'As for the story that I have just told, it was passed on to (our) fathers from the ancestors.'   [tci20131013-01 ABB #403-405]

The second function of *n* occurs with verbs in one of the past tenses or in irrealis mood. In this function, *n* is analysed as a particle because it can occur in various positions. This is shown in (106), where *n* occurs in preverbal position, and in (107), where it occurs freely in the clause. It expresses that an event was 'about to occur' or that someone was 'trying to do' something, and I use the gloss IMN for "imminent". In (106), the speaker reports how she saw something moving in the grass in her garden. In (107), the speaker talks about trying to extinguish a fire in his garden. I refer the reader to §6.3.1 for further discussion of *n*.

---

[12]Note that this is shown in the unified gloss: both non-past (NPST) and immediate past (IPST) are marked on the verb. This is because the latter is expressed by a clitic, whereas the former is part of the verb morphology proper.

(106) *wati foba fof **n** zäbrimé ... wati nzun nima "kaboth kma zamath."*
wati foba   fof   n   zä\brim/é   (.) wati nzun   nima kaboth
then DIST.ABL EMPH IMN 1SG:SBJ:RPST:PFV/return (.) then 1SG.DAT QUOT snake
kma za\math/
POT 2|3SG:SBJ:RPST:PFV/run
'Well, I was about to return from there ... and I thought to myself "This must be
a snake running off."'   [tci20120821-01 LNA #9-10]

(107) *kwankwiré zbo **n** fam zäré damaki yföfo ... "keke watikthémär zagr fefe rä."*
kwan\kwir/é   zbo   n   fam   zä\r/é
1SG:SBJ:NPST:IPFV:VENT/run PROX.ALL IMN thoughts 1SG:SBJ:RPST:PFV/do
damaki   yfö=fo   (.) keke watik-thé=mär   zagr fefe
dynamite.well hole=ALL (.) NEG enough-ADJZR=PRIV far   really
\rä/
3SG.FEM:SBJ:NPST:IPFV/be
'I was running around here considering (going to) the water well, but I thought
"No, not enough, it is too far."'   [tci20120922-24 MAA #49-50]

3.6 Connectives

There are a number of small words which I label connectives. These serve to connect
various constituents: noun phrases, clauses, discourse, etc. The most common ones are *a*
'and', *o* 'or', and *e* 'until'. The last of the three is usually a long, stretched out vowel. See
examples (108), (109), and (110), respectively.

(108) *nagayé zbo thgathinzako ... mantma kafarwä **a** srak nge ... katanwä.*
nagayé zbo   th\gathinz/ako   (.) mantma kafar=wä
children PROX.ALL SG:SBJ>2|3DU:OBJ:PST:PFV:AND/leave (.) female   big=EMPH
a   srak nge   (.) katan=wä
and boy   child (.) small=EMPH
'He left the two children here ... the big girl and the small boy.'
                                                          [tci20100905 ABB #21-23]

(109) *nafaŋamaf wnfathwr **o** ynfathwr.*
nafa-ŋame=f   wn\fath/wr   o
3.POSS-mother=ERG.SG 2|3SG:SBJ>3SG.FEM:OBJ:NPST:VENT/hold or
yn\fath/wr
2|3SG:SBJ>3SG.MASC:OBJ:NPST:VENT/hold
'(The child's) mother holds her or holds him.'   [tci20111004 RMA #327-328]

(110) *nzä nima waniyak **e** srn kränrsöfthé zrafo.*
nzä   nima   wa\niyak/   e   srn krän\rsöfth/é
1SG.ABS like.this 1SG:SBJ:NPST:IPFV/come until srn 1SG:SBJ:IRR:PFV:VENT/descend

zra=fo
swamp=ALL
'I came like this until I walked down to the swamp in Srn.' [tci20111119-03 ABB #96]

The three adverbial demonstratives in the allative case may also be used to express meaning 'until' both in a spatial and temporal sense. However, they have to marked for the purposive case, thus producing the forms *zbomr* from *zbo*, *bobomr* from *bobo*, and *fobomr* from *fbo*. This is not possible with the corresponding ablative forms, i.e. *zbamr*, *bobamr* and *fobamr* are all ungrammatical. Example (111) shows one occurrence of *bobomr* with a temporal meaning of 'until'. Here, the speaker describes her daily routine in the high school in Daru.

(111) *frasinzo nzwamnzrm ezifa **bobomr** mor efoth.*
       frasi=nzo   nzwa\m/nzrm   ezi=fa   bobomr mor efoth
       hunger=ONLY 1PL:SBJ:PST:DUR/sit morning=ABL until   neck day
       'We were staying very hungry from the morning until midday.'

       [tci20120924-01 TRK #37]

The word *fthé* 'when' may be used to connect clauses as causal, temporal or conditional sequences (§9.4.2 and §9.6). It may also be used without reference to another clause, in which case it can be translated as 'at the time when'. See example (112), where the speaker talks about food taboos.

(112) *kafar ŋarr **fthé** srarä, nzmärkarä **fthé** srarä ... zöftha nagayé keke kwa sranathrth.*
       kafar ŋarr   fthé sra\rä/   nzmär=kará fthé
       big   bandicoot when 3SG.MASC:IRR:IPFV/be grease=PROP when
       sra\rä/   (.) zöftha nagayé keke kwa
       3SG.MASC:IRR:IPFV/be (.) new   children NEG FUT
       sra\na/thr
       2|3SG:SBJ>3SG.MASC:OBJ:IRR:IPFV/eat
       'If it is a big bandicoot, if it is one with grease, then the young children will not eat it.'   [tci20120922-26 DAK #82-83]

3.7 Ideophones

Komnzo ideophones depict almost exclusively sounds and, thus, cover the lower spectrum of the implicational hierarchy of sensory imagery as discussed in Dingemanse (2012: 663). Komnzo ideophones cover a range of auditory phenomena: sounds from nature, animal sounds, human made noises, bodily noises, human made signals. Table 3.12 groups them according to their semantics.

Example (113) introduces the topic in the context of a rather gruesome story about an unsuccessful headhunting expedition. The ideophone *grr kwan* depicts the gurgling or rasping sound of someone breathing, in this example someone dying.

Table 3.12: Ideophones

sounds from nature	
susu kwan	sound of a running stream of water
buku kwan	sound of splashing water (fish jumping, people washing)
ba kwan	sound of something heavy falling on the ground
bü kwan	sound of a coconut falling on the ground
rürü kwan	sound of thunder (in the distance)
wär kwan	sound of thunder (close)
u kwan	sound of strong wind

animal sounds	
sö kwan	sound of wallabies grunting
gu kwan	sound of an animal grunting (e.g. pigs, dogs)
gww kwan	sound of barking dogs

bodily sounds	
nzam kwan	sound of smacking one's lips
gwrr kwan	sound of swallowing something
thmss kwan	sound of someone snuffling, snorting
grr kwan	sound of stertorous or rasping breathing
thmdrr kwan	sound of snoring
thmdi kwan	sound of a sigh during sleep
brr kwan	bilabial trill (baby babbling or someone farting)

human made noises	
ta kwan	sound of something that breaks or cracks, e.g. twigs
tä kwan	sound of chopping trees
yo kwan	sound of an arrow hitting something
tütü kwan	sound of steps, someone walking
rrr kwan	sound of rustling through dried leaves
suku kwan	sound of someone walking in water

human made signal sounds	
bübü kwan	sound of a hunter hitting the ground to attract wallabies
ws kwan	sound made to send the dogs after some animal
äs kwan	sound made to call the dogs
knzu kwan	sound of people shouting out for someone (usually [uː])
fifiya kwan	sound of whistling (a song)
siya kwan	sound of someone signalling by whistling
ti kwan	sound of someone singing in the distance
si kwan	hissing sound [s] in order to attract someone's attention
dm kwan	a signal of amazement produced as a series of alveolar clicks
mü kwan	a signal of approval or a backchannel marker produced as [mː]

(113) *wgathiknath fobo fof. frknzo zwanorm.* **grr kwannzo fobo zwanorm.**
w\gathik/nath   fobo   fof   frk=nzo
2|3DU:SBJ>3SG.FEM:OBJ:PST:IPFV/leave DIST.ALL EMPH blood=ONLY
zwa\nor/m   grr.kwan=nzo   fobo
3SG.FEM:SBJ:PST:DUR/shout rasping.sound=ONLY DIST.ALL
zwa\nor/m
3SG.FEM:SBJ:PST:DUR/shout
'The two left her while she was bleeding from there (the throat). She was just gurgling.'
                                                      [tci20111119-01 ABB #154]

Ideophones occur as a compound with the word *kwan* 'noise, shout, sound'. This should not be taken as evidence that speakers are merely mimicking a particular auditive phenomenon in an ad hoc way. On the contrary, ideophones are conventionalised lexical items like any other word. I will use the term ideophone only for those lexical items which do not have a lexical meaning other than the sound they depict. We can observe a gradient from lexical items to ideophones. For example *wth kwan* 'fart' consists of *wth* 'excrete, faeces' + *kwan*. It is a noun + noun compound and it would be wrong to call *wth* an ideophone. On the other end of the spectrum we have *brr kwan* 'the sound of a bilabial trill' which consists of *brr* + *kwan*. The former refers only to the particular sound and I will therefore call *brr* an ideophone. There are some transitional cases like *thmdi kwan* 'sound of a sigh during sleep', which is in principle decomposable as *thm* 'nose' + *di* 'back of the head' + *kwan*. However, speakers do not decompose this word anymore, but understand *thmdi* as one lexical item that refers to a particular sound.

There are only two exceptions, which do not fit the above description: *buay* means 'someone taking off in a hurry, fleeing, running away' and *bra* means 'something is finished, depleted, or gone'. Both lexical items differ in their semantics from other ideophones, i.e. *buay* expresses movement and *bra* expresses a visual state. They also differ in that they do not occur with *kwan*. However, I analyse them as ideophones following Dingemanse who defines ideophones as "marked words that depict sensory imagery" (2012: 655).

There are a few special phonological characteristics of ideophones. For example, I have shown in §2.6 that the bilabial stop [b] is not an indigenous phoneme in Komnzo. We find [b] in a number of ideophones, for example *bübü kwan* 'the sound a hunter makes when hitting the ground to attract wallabies'.

Ideophones can be modified by another nominal, an adjective or another noun. In example (114), we see the ideophone *ta kwan* 'a high-pitched clicking, breaking sound' as part of a compound modified by *zr* 'tooth'.

(114) *mnzfa boba kwanrizrmth nzarwonaneme zr ta kwan.*
mnz=fa   boba   kwan\ri/zrmth   nzarwon=aneme   zr
house=ABL MED.ABL 2|3PL:SBJ:PST:DUR:VENT/hear barramundi=POSS.NSG tooth
ta.kwan
clicking.sound
'They were hearing the snapping of the barramundis from the house.'
                                                        [tci20120922-21 DAK #8]

3.8 Interjections

Interjections in Komnzo are a small class of uninflecting words used to express delight, bewilderment, a negative attitude, approval or refusal, commands, greetings, or vocatives. Interjections form a separate intonation group, and they stand as an utterance by themselves. Table 3.13 gives an overview of the most common interjections.

Table 3.13: Interjections

form	translation (and context)
aiwa	'oh no' (used to signal compassion, negative surprise, emphasizing with another person's misfortune)
awe	'come!'
awkot	(used as a sudden surprise, e.g. somebody trips over a log)
awow	'ok' (used to signal agreement)
ayo	'watch out' (used as a warning sign)
kare	'go (away)!'
kiwar	'good hunting luck' (used to wish a successful hunting either a person or ritually after setting a trap, hanging a fishnet, etc.)
monzé	'yes, of course' (used as a sign of agreement)
razé	'yeah' (used as a sign of emphatic agreement or approval)
si rore rore	(shouted out by women during poison-root fishing)

4 Nominal morphology

4.1 Introduction

This chapter describes the nominal morphology of Komnzo. With the exception of the close possessive construction, all nominal morphology is encliticised or suffixed to the element over which it has scope, which is almost always the noun phrase. There is little to no allomorphy in the enclitic and affix formatives. There are no declension classes. There are special marking patterns for animate referents, which include a number distinction.

I begin by a description of reduplication, which is only found with nominals (§4.2). The remainder and bulk of this chapter describes case and further morphological markers. I introduce the reader to the 17 cases and their respective functions in §4.3. After this, each case is discussed in turn (§4.5 - 4.16). In §4.17, I describe three enclitics and one suffix which are not related to case. Finally, in §4.18, I offer a few concluding remarks on the formal and functional overlap between particular case markers.

4.2 Reduplication

There are two reduplication patterns in Komnzo. They differ only formally, not in their meaning, and words for which reduplication is a productive morphological process can form both patterns. I use the terms partial reduplication and full reduplication. In the former, the reduplicant is only the first consonant of the word. In the latter, the whole word is reduplicated.

Semantically, reduplication expresses non-prototypicality, plurality, or both. In (1), *ttrikasi* 'stories' is formed from *trikasi* 'story', and reduplication expresses plurality. In (2), the reduplication of *yawi* 'seed' refers to 'coins', i.e. it expresses non-prototypicality in addition to plurality.

(1) *komnzo nima fä zämnzerake nä **ttrikasi** keke.*
komnzo nima fä zä\mnzer/ake nä t-trika-si keke
only like.this DIST 1NSG:SBJ:PST:PFV/fall.asleep INDF REDUP-tell-NMLZ NEG
'We just fell asleep there, no more stories.' [tci20120922-25 ALK #45]

(2) *ŋareane **yawiyawime** kwa ŋonathr ane kabef.*
ŋare=ane yawi-yawi=me kwa ŋo\na/thr ane
woman=POSS.SG REDUP-seed=INS FUT 2|3SG:SBJ:NPST:IPFV/drink DEM
kabe=f
man=ERG.SG
'That guy is going to drink with his wife's money.' [tci20111004 TSA #182]

The nominal subclasses which can be reduplicated are nouns, adjectives, property nouns and quantifiers. Example (3) shows the quantifier *tüfr* expressing that many different jobs are involved in raising a pig. In (4), the adjective *tnz* 'short' is reduplicated, meaning that the man was just a bit short. In (5), the adjective *kafar* 'big' is reduplicated, meaning that the elders of the Mayawas of Firra had been killed in the headhunting raid.

(3)   *zena keke miyo worä ruga mgthksi ... znsä **ttüfr**.*
     zena   keke miyo wo\rä/   ruga mgthk-si   (.) znsä t-tüfr
     today NEG   desire 1SG:SBJ:NPST:IPFV/be pig   feed-NMLZ   (.) work REDUP-plenty
     'Today, I do not want to feed pigs ... (too) much work.'   [tci20120805-01 ABB #819-820]

(4)   *nafafis yf nagawa ... **tnztnz** kabe sfrärm.*
     nafa-fis   yf   nagawa (.) tnz-tnz   kabe sf\rä/rm
     3.POSS-husband name nagawa (.) REDUP-short man 3SG.MASC:SBJ:PST:DUR/be
     'Her husband's name (was) *Nagawa* ... he was a bit short guy.'
                                                            [tci20120901-01 MAK #17-18]

(5)   *nafanme mayawa **kkafar** z bramöwä thäkwrath firran.*
     nafanme   mayawa k-kafar   z   bramöwä thä\kwr/ath
     3NSG.POSS mayawa REDUP-big ALR all   2|3PL:SBJ>2|3PL:OBJ:PST:PFV/kill
     firra=n
     firra=LOC
     'All their Mayawa elders had been killed in Firra.'   [tci20111107-01 MAK 127]

In addition to productive reduplication with the above meanings, reduplications are found across the lexicon to form new meanings. There is a large number of reduplications in plant names and in the names for animals, especially bird and fish species. Often the pattern of reduplication establishes a semantic link between biota of different species, families or even kingdoms. I describe this phenomenon in §11.2.

Lastly, I want to mention that there are some reduplicative orphans which lack a corresponding simplex, for example *gwargwar* 'mud' or *ŋarŋar* 'bamboo paddle'.

4.3 The form and function of case markers

I follow Blake (1994) in making a distinction between core cases and peripheral cases. Core cases in Blake's typology "encode complements of typical one-place and two-place transitive verbs" (1994: 32), i.e. they are required by the verb's argument structure. I define core cases in Komnzo as those cases whose referent can be indexed in the verb. Thus, core cases are the absolutive, ergative and dative case. Note that the absolutive is zero-marked. The possessive is also counted as core case, because the possessor can be raised and indexed in the verb. Peripheral cases are those cases whose referents are not required by the structure of the verb, nor can they be indexed in the verb. I will use the term semantic cases for these.

Following Andrews (2007b), I understand semantic roles to refer to "thematic relations" or "deep cases" (Fillmore 1968). From these, one can derive grammatical functions

Table 4.1: The Komnzo case system

	case	semantic roles by function		
		adnominal	clausal	interclausal
core cases	ABS		agent, experiencer, theme, patient	agent, experiencer, theme, patient
core cases	ERG		agent	agent
core cases	DAT		recipient, beneficiary	
core cases	POSS	possessor		
semantic cases / spatial	LOC		location	simultaneity
semantic cases / spatial	ALL		goal of motion	
semantic cases / spatial	ABL		source of motion	
semantic cases / temporal	TEMP.LOC		location in time	
semantic cases / temporal	TEMP.PURP		goal in time	
semantic cases / temporal	TEMP.POSS	origin	origin in time	
semantic cases / other	INS		instrument, manner	result, manner
semantic cases / other	PURP		purpose	purpose
semantic cases / other	CHAR	origin	source, reason, purpose	reason, purpose
semantic cases / other	PROP		association	association, manner
semantic cases / other	PRIV		absence	
semantic cases / other	ASSOC		association, inclusion	association
semantic cases / other	SIMIL		comparison	

such as A, S, and P (Dixon 1972).[1] In the following, the terms core case and semantic case are used to refer to the cases, while the term semantic role is used to refer to the underlying semantics.

Following Evans and Dench (1988), who discuss the ways in which case can be used to establish three levels in Australian languages, I recognise three distinct levels at which cases operate in Komnzo. First, there is the adnominal level which relates one noun phrase within a matrix noun phrase. Secondly, there is the clausal level which operates directly below the clause level. Thirdly, there is the interclausal level which indicates that one clause is the argument of another clause. Table 4.1 provides an overview of the cases and their functions. Note that semantic cases can be subdivided into spatial, temporal and other.

As mentioned above, there is little allomorphy with the case markers. Examples are the locative, allative and ablative case, which have different formatives for animate and inanimate referents. It can be said that Komnzo nominal morphology is relatively simple, especially when compared to its verb morphology (see chapter 5). The formatives are given in Table 4.2.

---

[1]"I will use the term 'semantic role' to refer to both the specific roles imposed on NPs by a given predicate (..) and to the more general classes of roles, such as 'agent' and 'patient'. Semantic roles are important in the study of grammatical functions [A, S and P] since grammatical functions usually express semantic roles in a highly systematic way" (Andrews 2007b: 136).

Table 4.2: Case markers in Komnzo

case	inanimate	animate singular	animate non-singular
ABS	∅	∅	=é (=yé)
ERG	=f	=f	=é (=yé)
DAT	n/a	=n	=nm
POSS	=ane	=ane	=aneme
LOC	=en (=n)	=dben	=medben
ALL	=fo	=dbo	=medbo
ABL	=fa	=dba	=medba
TEMP.LOC	=thamen	n/a	n/a
TEMP.POSS	=thamane	n/a	n/a
TEMP.PURP	=thamar	n/a	n/a
INS	=me	n/a	n/a
PURP	=r	n/a	n/a
CHAR	=ma	=ane=ma	=aneme=ma
PROP	=karä / =kaf	=karä / =kaf	=karä / =kaf
PRIV	=märe	=märe	=märe
ASSOC[a]	=ä	=r	=ä
SIMIL	=thatha	n/a	n/a

[a]The associative forms encode DU versus PL (§7.6).

We find that case markers make a distinction between animate and inanimate referents. For certain cases, there are designated formatives for animate referents, for example all the spatial cases. Only with animate referents is there a number distinction (SG vs. NSG) in the case markers. Consider examples (6-8). The first example shows the locative case on *mnz* 'house', and the context of the story reveals that this is about several houses. The case marker, however, does not encode number. Examples (7) and (8) show that this is different for animate referents, and the case markers make a singular versus non-singular distinction.

(6)   *kwot namäme thfanakwrm ... **mnzen** thwarakthkwrmo.*
     kwot   namä=me thfa\nak/wrm   (.) mnz=en
     properly good=INS 2|3SG:SBJ>2|3PL:OBJ:PST:DUR/put.down (.) house=LOC
     thwa\rakthk/wrmo
     SG:SBJ>2|3PL:IO:PST:DUR:AND/put.on.top
     'She was sorting (the things) properly ... She put the things back in the
     houses.'   [tci20120901-01 MAK #38-39]

(7) **mizidben** *sokoro zewära.*
mizi=dben   sokoro ze\wär/a
pastor=LOC.ANIM.SG school SG:SBJ:PST:PFV/happen
'The school was at the pastor('s place).'   [tci20120904-02 MAB #16]

(8) **nafangthmedben** *byamnzr.*
nafa-ngth=medben   b=ya\m/nzr
3.POSS-younger.sibling=LOC.ANIM.NSG MED=3SG.MASC:SBJ:NPST:IPFV/dwell
'He stays at his small brothers' place.'   [tci20120814 ABB #216]

As Table 4.2 shows, most case markers employ an /m/ or /me/ element to mark non-singular number. I refrain from segmenting this element as a separate morph for two reasons. First, the /m/ or /me/ does not occur in all cases, for example not the ergative case. Secondly, its position is not fixed. With the possessive, /me/ follows the possessive marker *=ane*. With the dative, only /m/ follows the dative marker *=n*. With spatial cases /me/ precedes the locative, allative and ablative marker. I will offer an explanation of this in the final section of this chapter (§4.18).

These formatives attach to the rightmost element of the phrase, but have scope over the whole noun phrase. In example (9), the adjective *katan* 'small' precedes the noun *nzram* 'flower' and the case marker attaches to the latter. Example (10) shows the same adjective postposed to the noun *yfö* 'hole'. Again, the case marker attaches to the right-most element.

(9) **katan nzramma** *emarwr.*
katan nzram=ma   e\mar/wr
small flower=CHAR 2|3SG:SBJ>2|3PL:OBJ:NPST:IPFV/see
'You (can) identify them from the small flowers.'   [tci20130907-02 JAA #211]

(10) *watik* **yfö katanr** *kwa yarenzr.*
watik yfö katan=r   kwa ya\re/nzr
then hole small=PURP FUT 3SG.MASC:SBJ:NPST:IPFV/look
'Then, he will look around for a small hole.'   [tci20130903-04 RNA #26]

4.4 Absolutive

The absolutive case is almost always unmarked. The non-singular clitic (*=é*), (*=yé*) when it follows a vowel, is rarely used. On the clausal level the absolutive encodes the single argument of intransitive verbs (11), or the patient argument of transitive verbs (12).

(11) **nzä** *zä zf wamnzr.*
nzä   zä   zf   wa\m/nzr
1SG.ABS PROX IMM 1SG:SBJ:NPST:IPFV/dwell
'I live right here.'   [tci20130823-08 WAM #85]

(12) **nzä fthé fof afaf schoolen zwäthba.**
nzä   fthé   fof   afa=f   school=en
1SG.ABS when EMPH father=ERG.SG school=LOC
zwä\thb/a
2|3SG:SBJ>1SG:OBJ:PST:PFV/put.inside
'That was when father put me in school.'   [tci20120924-01 TRK #5]

When a nominalised verb functions as the patient of a matrix clause, it appears with no overt case marking. It could be analysed as being marked with absolutive case, though for reasons of parsimony I will not gloss it as such. This commonly occurs with phasal verbs, like in (13), where the speaker shows me how to make a whistle from a coconut leaf.

(13) **myuknsi srethkäfe. zane zf ymyuknwé.**
myukn-si sre\thkäf/e   zane   zf
roll-NMLZ 1PL:SBJ>3SG.MASC.OBJ:IRR:PFV/start DEM:PROX IMM
y\myukn/wé
1SG:SBJ>3SG.MASC.OBJ:NPST:IPFV/roll
'We would start twisting it. I am twisting this here.'   [tci20120914 RNA #45]

Overt marking of non-singular number is possible if the referent is animate. The formative is *=é* if the host is consonant-final, and *=yé* if it is vowel-final. Hence, there is a syncretism between absolutive and ergative non-singular. This pattern of syncretism is also found in the first person pronouns (§3.1.9), where *ni* is used for both ergative and absolutive non-singular. As a case marker on absolutive noun phrases it is very rare. One example is given in (14).

(14) **nzone amayé bä thfamrnm ksi karen.**
nzone   ama=é   bä   thfa\m/rnm   ksi   kar=en
1SG.POSS mother=ABS.NSG MED 2|3DU:SBJ:PST:DUR/dwell bush place=LOC
'My two mothers lived there in the bush.'   [tci20150919-05 LNA #240]

Only in the syntactic context of the inclusory construction is the absolutive non-singular obligatory (§7.6). Elsewhere it is optional, and tokens in the corpus are infrequent.

4.5 Ergative *=f*, *=è*

The ergative case marker is *=f* (SG) or *=é* (NSG). The ergative usually operates at the clausal level. It encodes the semantic role of actor or stimulus. Example (15) is taken from a "*Nzürna* story". These stories are widespread in the Morehead region. The main character *nzürna*, but also the plot of the stories, bears some resemblance to the classic European witch stories.

(15) *okay, ausi zakora "ŋame, **nzürna ŋaryf** wanmrinzr!" … **ausif** sakora "anema fof*
    gukonzé" nima "kmam foba gniyaké!"
    okay ausi za\kor/a   ŋame nzürna
    okay old.woman 2|3SG:SBJ>3SG.FEM:OBJ:PST:PFV/speak mother nzürna
    ŋare=f   wan\mri/nzr   (.) ausi=f
    woman=ERG.SG 2|3SG:SBJ>1SG:OBJ:NPST:IPFV:VENT/chase (.) old.woman=ERG.SG
    sa\kor/a   ane=ma fof
    2|3SG:SBJ>3SG.MASC:OBJ:PST:PFV/speak DEM=CHAR EMPH
    gu\ko/nzé   nima kma=m foba gni\yak/é
    1SG:SBJ>2SG:OBJ:RPST:IPFV/speak QUOT POT=APPR DIST.ABL 2SG:SBJ:IMP:IPFV/walk
    'Okay, he said to the old woman: "Mother, the *Nzürna* woman is chasing after
    me!" The old woman told him: "That is why I told you: Don't go there!"'
    [tci20120827-03 KUT #114-115]

Examples (16) and (17) show the ergative non-singular formative. This is =*é* when the
word is consonant-final and =*yé* when it is vowel-final. Example (16) is taken from a procedural text about a little whistle made from a coconut leaf. In example (17), the speaker
complains about some families whose children seem to be shifting from Komnzo to Wära.

(16) *rusa räkumgsir zane äfiyokwrth … **sraké**.*
    rusa räkumg-si=r zane ä\fiyok/wrth   (.)
    deer attract-NMLZ=PURP DEM:PROX 2|3PL:SBJ>2|3PL:OBJ:NPST:IPFV/make (.)
    srak=é
    boy=ERG.NSG
    'They make this one for attracting deer … the boys (make it).' [tci20120914 RNA #61]

(17) *… a **ŋameyé** nafanme zokwasimöwä thwasäminzrmth*
    (.) a ŋame=é   nafanme zokwasi=me=wä
    (.) and mother=ERG.NSG 3NSG.POSS speech=INS=EMPH
    thwa\sämi/nzrmth
    2|3PL:SBJ>2|3PL:OBJ:PST:DUR/teach
    '… and the mothers were teaching their own language (to the children).'
    [tci20120924-02 ABM #37-38]

The ergative case can be used to encode inanimate actors who for some reason are
attributed an actor-like behaviour. As with other case enclitics, there is no number distinction for inanimate referents, i.e. the non-singular -*é* is not used. Therefore, I do not
gloss the number value for =*f* when attached to inanimate referents. Example (18) comes
from a hunting story where the speaker reaches the camp of his family in the night and
sees a gaslamp hanging on the bamboos. Here, the wind (*füsfüs*) is marked with the
ergative.

(18) *nabi tutin fä fof zumirwanzrm **füsfüsf**.*
    nabi tuti=n fä fof zu\mirwa/nzrm   füsfüs=f
    bamboo branch=LOC DIST EMPH 2|3SG:SBJ>3SG.FEM:OBJ:PST:DUR/swing wind=ERG
    'The wind was swinging (the lamp) on the bamboo branch.' [tci20111119-03 ABB #117]

Example (19) is taken from a myth in which the island of New Guinea and the continent of Australia were still connected. The myth describes the rising sea-level and how the people had to take refuge on both sides. The inanimate referent *no* 'water' is flagged with the ergative case.

(19) **nof nä nima thärkothmako ... nä nima thänkothma nzezawe.**
no=f   nä   nima   thär\kothm\ako   (.) nä   nima
water=ERG some like.this SG:SBJ>2|3PL:OBJ:PST:PFV:AND/chase (.) some like.this
thän\kothm\a   nze-zawe
2|3SG:SBJ>2|3PL:OBJ:PST:PFV:VENT/chase 1NSG.POSS-right
'The water chased some away like this ... and it chased some here to our side like this.'   [tci20131013-01 ABB #125-126]

Experiencer-object constructions, in which the stimulus receives the ergative and the experiencer the absolutive, are quite common. Constructions of this type have been described for Kalam by Pawley et al. (2000) and for Nen by Evans (2015b). As in Kalam, experiencer-object constructions are often used to express bodily and mental processes. In example (20), after an evening by the fire, the speaker proclaims that she will go to sleep now because 'fear has already grabbed her'.

(20) **wtrif z zwefaf.**
wtri=f   z   zwe\faf/
fear=ERG ALR 2|3SG:SBJ>1SG:OBJ:RPST:PFV/hold
'I am already scared.' (lit. 'Fear already holds me.')   [tci20130901-04 RNA #164]

Example (21) comes from a story about a man who was angry and tried to shock people at a feast. The fact that he was infuriated is expressed literally as 'anger/grudges finished him'. Note that (21) is an exception to the rule that inanimate referents do not receive number marking for case enclitics. Such exceptions are rare in the corpus. There is one more example of this type in the grammar (page 300 example 41), which is also an experiencer-object construction. I take this as evidence, that experiencer-object constructions rank the stimulus argument higher in animacy, i.e. the stimulus is portrayed as being animate. See §8.3.10 for a more detailed discussion of experiencer-object constructions.

(21) **nokuyé fthé sabtha.**
noku=yé   fthé   sa\bth/a
anger=ERG.NSG when 2|3SG:SBJ>3SG.MASC:OBJ:PST:PFV/finish
'That is when he got really angry.' (lit. 'That is when anger finished him.')
[tci20120909-06 KAB #39]

The ergative case can also be attached to nominalised verbs, as in (22). This example is about a Marind headhunter who was trying to distract the people by imitating the sound that dogs make when they chew on bones. The poor guy was so busy making this noise that he did not hear how the villagers were approaching him. Hence, it is the infinitive of 'crack' which receives the ergative case in (22).

(22) *bäne thuwänzrm fof… zarfa surmänwrm **ane wäsifnzo***.
bäne   thu\wä/nzrm   fof (.) zarfa
DEM:MED 2|3SG:SBJ>2|3PL:OBJ:PST:DUR/crack fof (.) ear
su\rmän/wrm   ane wä-si=f=nzo
2|3SG:SBJ>3SG.MASC:OBJ:PST:DUR/close DEM crack-NMLZ=ERG=ONLY
'He was cracking those (coconut shells). This cracking was blocking his ears.'

[tci20120818 ABB #67-68]

Thus, the ergative case can also function at the interclausal level. Example (23) shows that the infinitive to which the ergative is attached may also take an object. In the example a malevolent spirit, who lives in a tree, is about to be burned by an angry mob. She does not notice the fire at first because she is too concentrated on weaving a mat. The 'mat weaving' receives the ergative.

(23) *mni wthomonwath a zräföfth … fi **yame yrsifnzo** zukonzrm boba wämne yfön fof*.
mni w\thomon/wath   a
fire 2|3PL:SBJ>3SG.FEM:OBJ:PST:IPFV/pile.firewood and
zrä\föf/th   (.) fi   yame   yr-si=f=nzo
2|3PL:SBJ>3SG.FEM:OBJ:IRR:PFV/burn (.) but mat   weave-NMLZ=ERG=ONLY
zu\ko/nzrm   boba   wämne yfö=n   fof
2|3SG:SBJ>3SG.FEM:OBJ:PST:DUR/do MED.ABL tree   hole=LOC EMPH
'They piled up the firewood and started to burn it … but she was concentrated on weaving the mat there in the tree hole.' (lit. 'The mat weaving did her.')

[tci20120901-01 MAK #155-156]

Contructions showing the ergative at the interclausal level are infrequent in the corpus. Note that in both examples above, the exclusive clitic *=nzo* is attached to the ergative-marked infinitive in order to highlight that it was "only that event" which acted on a person.

4.6 Dative *=n, =nm*

The dative case marker is *=n* (SG) or *=nm* (NSG). It operates at the clausal level and encodes the semantic role of (animate) recipient or goal. If it is attached to a place name, as in example (24), the people of that place are meant, not the place. The dative is categorised as a core case because a dative marked noun phrase is indexed in the verb, as in the verb form *thägathinza* in (24). Unlike in other Tonda languages, for example in Ngkolmpu (Carroll 2017), the dative case cannot be used adnominally to mark a possessor.

In example (24), the speaker talks about the different places where he used to own a garden plot. Example (25) comes from a set of stimulus videos.

(24) *nzone daw bä mane rera safsen … **nafanm** thägathinza … **safs karnm**.*
nzone   daw   bä   mane \rä/ra   safs=en (.) nafanm
1SG.POSS garden MED which 3SG.FEM:SBJ:PST:IPFV/be safs=LOC (.) 3NSG.POSS

thä\gathi/nza (.) safs kar=nm
SG:SBJ>2|3PL:IO:PST:IPFV/leave (.) safs village=DAT.NSG
'As for my garden there in Safs, I left it for them ... for the Safs people.'

[tci20120805-01 ABB #652-653]

(25) *emoth a srak markai no ŋarinth ... emothf yarithr* **srakn.**
emoth a srak markai no ŋa\ri/nth (.) emoth=f
girl and boy white.man water 2|3DU:SBJ:NPST:IPFV/pour (.) girl=ERG.SG
ya\ri/thr srak=n
2|3SG:SBJ>3SG.MASC:IO:NPST:IPFV/give boy=DAT
'The boy and the girl are pouring (each other) wine. The girl gives (it) to the boy.'

[tci20111028-01 RNA #27-28]

The formatives in Table 4.2 might suggest a syncretism between the dative case and the locative case. The singular marker of the dative is *=n*, and the locative marker is also *=n* when it attaches to a vowel-final word (for consonant-final words, it is *=en*). However, no syncretism takes place because (i) inanimates do not take dative *=(e)n*, and (ii) animate referents receive a special formative of the locative case (*=dben*). Moreover, there is some variation for the dative when it is attached to a vowel-final word. For example, the word *ŋafe* 'father' with the dative *=n* can be pronounced as [ŋaβen], [ŋaβeʔə̃n] or [ŋaɸjə̃n] (26).

In terms of meaning, there is some overlap between the allative and the dative case. Example (26) concludes an origin myth, and the speaker points out how the story was passed on from the ancestor. The noun phrase *ŋafynm* 'for/to the fathers' marks a goal. This could be equally expressed with an allative case marker *ŋafemedbo* 'to the fathers'.[2]

(26) *trikasi mane nŋatrikwé fof ...* **ŋafynm** *... badafa ane fof ŋanritakwa fof.*
trik-si mane n=ŋa\trik/wé fof (.) ŋafe=nm (.)
tell-NMLZ which IPST=1SG:SBJ:NPST:IPFV/tell EMPH (.) father=DAT.NSG (.)
bada=fa ane fof ŋan\ritak/wa fof
ancestor=ABL DEM EMPH 2|3SG:OBJ:PST:IPFV:VENT/pass EMPH
'The story which I have just told ... was really passed to the fathers from the ancestor(s).'

[tci20131013-01 ABB #405]

4.7 Possessive marking

4.7.1 Possessive *=ane, =aneme*

The possessive case is *=ane* (SG) or *=aneme* (NSG). It marks the semantic role of possessor, and the noun or noun phrase to which it attaches always functions adnominally. Examples (27) and (28) show animate possessors. Example (27) is taken from a story about marriage customs and (28) is from a procedural about traditional fishing baskets.

---

[2]Note that the verb *ŋanritakwa* 'it (was) passed' does not index the dative noun phrase *ŋafynm* 'for/to the fathers', but instead occurs in a suppressed-object construction (§8.3.7).

Note that all occurrences of the possessive case in (28) are within noun phrases whose nominal head is omitted because it can be recovered from the context.

(27) **bafane mezü** *rera ... masenane mezü.*
bafane   mezü \rä/ra   (.) masen=ane   mezü
RECOG.POSS.SG widow 3SG.FEM:SBJ:PST:IPFV/be (.) masen=POSS.SG widow
'She was this one's widow ... Masen's widow.'   [tci20120814 ABB #18-20]

(28) *wati, net ane mane erä* **markaianeme** *erä ane ... zane zf ...* **kar kambeaneme**
zfrärm ... **nzenme.**
wati net ane mane e\rä/   markai=aneme
then net DEM which 2|3PL:SBJ:NPST:IPFV/be white.man=POSS.NSG
e\rä/   ane (.) zane   zf   (.) kar   kambe=aneme
2|3PL:SBJ:NPST:IPFV/be DEM (.) DEM:PROX IMM (.) village man=POSS.NSG
zf\rä/rm   (.) nzenme
3SG.FEM:SBJ:PST:DUR/be (.) 1NSG.POSS
'As for those nets, they are the white man's (nets). This right here, this was the
village people's (fishbasket) ... ours.'   [tci20120906 SKK #53-56]

Examples (29) and (30) show the possessive case with inanimate possessors. When the host word is vowel-final, there are different variants. In careful pronunciation, a glottal stop is inserted, for example [ɸiraʔane] in (29). In fast speech, this does not occur. Either the vowel is lengthened (if the word ends in /a/) or a glide is inserted, for example [ɸira.ne] in (29) and [ðarisijane] in (30). However, sometimes a velar nasal is inserted, and example (29) could be realised as [ɸiraŋane].

(29) *faw wbrigwath ...* **firraane zanma** *fof.*
faw   w\brig/wath   (.) firra=ane   zan=ma
payback 2|3PL:SBJ>3SG.FEM:OBJ:PST:IPFV/return (.) firra=POSS.SG killing=CHAR
fof
EMPH
'They brought the payback ... because of the killing of Firra.' [tci20111119-01 ABB #5-6]

(30) *wati, nima fof kwafiyokwrme ... tharisi taemen ...* **tharisiane efoth** *fthé zfrärm.*
wati nima   fof   kwa\fiyok/wrme   (.) thari-si   taem=en (.)
then like.this EMPH 1PL:SBJ:PST:DUR/make (.) dig-NMLZ time=LOC (.)
thari-si=ane   efoth fthé   zf\rä/rm
dig-NMLZ=POSS.SG day   when 3SG.FEM:SBJ:PST:DUR
'Well, this is what we were doing ... in the harvesting time ... when it was the day
of harvesting.'   [tci20120805-01 ABB #354-356]

4.7.2 Close possession

There is a second possessive construction in Komnzo, which involves a prefix. The formatives are given in Table 4.3. Formally, these prefixes seem to be reductions of personal pronouns. Surprisingly, they originate not from the possessive but the dative pronouns (§3.1.9). This is evident from the vowel quality which signals the number distinction. For example, the first person singular possessive pronoun is *nzone* 'my', and the first singular dative pronoun is *nzun* 'for me'. The possessive prefixes of the first and second singular show the /u/ vowel of the latter, not the /o/ vowel of the possessive series. Note that the number distinction is lost in the third person. This is caused by the fact that in the third person pronouns (possessive as well as dative) there is no change in the vowel quality. The close possessive construction can also occur with other nominals, which are then treated like prefixes. I will discuss this at the end of this section.

Table 4.3: Possessive prefixes

person	SG	NSG
1	*nzu–*	*nze–*
2	*bu–*	*be–*
3	*nafa–*	

I label this type of possessive marking "close possession" rather than "inalienable possession". Although close possessive marking is used for entities which are characterised as being inalienable, for example kin terms or the origin of a person, close possessive marking is not obligatory for these concepts, but merely one of two options. Furthermore, some of the concepts which fall under the rubric of inalienability, for example body-part terms, rarely occur in the close possessive construction in Komnzo. Finally, for those lexical items which can be used in both possessive constructions, there is a semantic difference between normal versus close possession.

From a historical perspective, frequency can help to explain the emergence of the close possessive construction (see Bybee (2010: 142) for a discussion of frequency and language change). Given that some lexical items occur frequently in a possessive construction, we can assume that, in the course of time, the preceding pronoun reduced in form and turned into a prefix. Frequency is only one explanation and the inherently relational nature of some lexical items, such as kin terms, can also provide a pathway for the emergence of the close possessive construction. It is important to point out that the prefix pattern was not extended to all other nominals. On the contrary, the two marking patterns were associated with a semantic distinction between (normal) possession and close possession. Synchronically, this means that there is no clear-cut categorisation as there is with alienable/inalienable systems. Some lexical items are judged ungrammatical by my informants in a close possessive construction. For example, I was told that *nzumnz* 'my house' is ungrammatical, and *nzone mnz* should be used instead. However, I am cautious about these judgements, because I have overheard the very construction in conversation. On the other hand, informants agree that there are many lexical items which can alternate between the two possessive constructions, depending on how a speaker wants to frame the connection between possessed and possessor, for example *nzone kar* 'my village' (normal possession) or *nzukar* 'my village' (close possession). Finally, there is no class of words for which close possession is obligatory.

Example (31) shows the possessive prefix on the word *kar* 'village/place'. The example is taken from a myth, where the two protagonists are withholding a particular food source from each other.

(31) *"be nzun fof kwathungr!* **bukaren** *ane fof bä safak emgthkwa."*
   be   nzun   fof   kwa\thung/r   bu-kar=en   ane
   2SG.ERG 1SG.DAT EMPH 2|3SG:SBJ>1SG:IO:RPST:IPFV/trick 2SG.POSS-village=LOC DEM
   fof   bä   safak   e\mgth/kwa
   EMPH MED saratoga 2|3SG:SBJ>2|3PL:OBJ:PST:IPFV/feed
   "'You have played a trick on me! In your place there, you have been feeding these saratogas."'   [tci20110802 ABB #121-122]

Example (32) shows a double possessive construction 'their father's story' involving both types of possessive marking. Note that (32) could also be expressed using a possessive pronoun as *nafane ŋafeane trikasi.*

(32) **nafaŋafeane trikasi** *ŋariznth.*
   nafa-ŋafe=ane   trik-si   ŋa\ri/znth
   3.POSS-father=POSS.SG tell-NMLZ 2|3DU:SBJ:NPST:IPFV/hear
   'They are listening to their father's story.'   [tci20111004 RMA #164]

Close possession is also possible with personal names as possessors. In this case, the personal name is treated like a prefix, i.e. it is syllabified together with the possessed. This can be seen in example (33). The possessor is the personal name *Bäi* [ᵐbˈæ̃i], and the possessed is *fzenz* [ɸˈɜ̃tseⁿts] 'wife'. A normal possessive construction would add the possessive case to the possessor: *Bäiane fzenz* [ᵐbˈæjane ɸˈɜ̃tʃeⁿts] 'Bäi's wife'. Both words receive stress separately, and both are syllabified independently. In the close possessive construction, the two words are syllabified as one word: *Bäyfzenz* [ᵐbˈæjɜ̃ɸtʃeⁿts]. Note that the initial consonant of *fzenz* is resyllabified as a coda, the epenthetic vowel [ɜ̃] occurs between the two words, and *fzenz* does not receive separate stress. All this is evidence that the possessor (the personal name) is treated like the prefixes described above.

(33) *wati,* **bäyfzenzf** *zwäkor "bone dagon fof erä!"*
   wati bäi-fzenz=f   zwä\kor/   bone   dagon fof
   then bäi-wife=ERG.SG 2|3SG:SBJ>1SG:OBJ:RPST:PFV/speak 2SG.POSS food EMPH
   e\rä/
   2|3PL:SBJ:NPST:IPFV/be:
   'Then, Bäi's wife said to me "Your food is here!" '   [tci20120922-24 MAA #81]

Note that in this construction there is no morph signalling the possessive relation, i.e. there is no possessive case marker. Only the fact that the possessor and possessed are syllabified as one word shows the presence of possessive semantics. Consequently, there is no "possessive" in the gloss, and only the hyphen between the two words shows that they are in a (close) possessive relationship.

For some items in a close possessive construction, there is an /a/ element between possessor and possessed, as in example (34) *kowi-a-fis* 'Kowi's husband'. Thus, in these cases there is an overt marker of the close possessive construction. The /a/ element seems to be a reduction of the possessive case marker *=ane*. The example is taken from a conversation about food taboos. The speaker is joking about his sister – a young unmarried woman.[3]

(34) fi **kowiafisanemanzo** fthé z änathre ... kowiane kabe fthé srarä.
      fi   kowi-a-fis=ane=ma=nzo   fthé z
      but kowi-POSS-husband=POSS.SG=CHAR=ONLY when ALR
      ä\na/thre   (.) kowi=ane   kabe fthé
      1PL:SBJ>2|3PL:OBJ:NPST:IPFV/eat (.) kowi=POSS.SG man when
      sra\rä/
      3SG.MASC:IO:IRR:IPFV/be
      'Only from Kowi's husband we will eat (food) ... If Kowi had a husband.'

                                                    [tci20120922-26 DAK #137-138]

4.8 Spatial cases

There are three spatial cases in Komnzo: the locative (*=en*), allative (*=fo*) and ablative (*=fo*). All three cases have special formatives for animate referents with a number distinction (SG, NSG): locative (*=dben, =medben*), allative (*=dbo, =medbo*) and ablative (*=dba, =medba*). They function at the clausal level and are categorised as semantic cases. Unlike neighbouring languages, for example Nama and Nen, there is no perlative case in Komnzo. All three spatial cases have various semantic extensions. For example, they can be used in a temporal sense, even though there is a set of dedicated temporal case markers (§4.9).

All three animate non-singular case markers show some variation in their pronunciation. For example, *kabe=nmedben* and *kabe=medben* 'with/at the people' are both grammatical. The former contains an /n/, whereas the latter does not. I will offer an explanation for this in §4.18.

4.8.1 Locative *=en*

The locative case marker is *=en*, for example *mnz=en* 'in the house'. If the host word ends in a vowel, the formative is *=n*, for example *mni=n* 'in the fire'. There are designated formatives for animate referents, which make a singular versus non-singular contrast. Example (35) shows the locative case in its basic use. Example (36) comes from a text

---

[3]The fact that in example (34) the possessive case *=ane* is encliticised to *kowiafis* 'Kowi's husband' is not relevant for the point here. This always occurs when the characteristic case is attached to an animate referent (§4.12).

about a young boy who drowned in the Morehead river after he got stuck underwater in the mud. The example is a detailed description of how the body was recovered from the river.

(35) *nzone fäms byé **safsen***
      nzone   fäms   b=\yé/   safs=en
      1SG.POSS exchange.man MED=3SG.MASC:SBJ:NPST:IPFV/be safs=LOC
      'My exchange man is there in Safs.'   [tci20120805-01 ABB #269]

(36) *zä thabr thentharfa ... ŋakarkwa gwargwarfa ... srefzath ... neba thabr nima*
      *sfrärm **nagayedben** ... neba ... nebame kwansogwrm **nabin**.*
      zä   thabr then\tharf/a   (.) ŋa\kark/wa
      PROX arm   2|3SG:SBJ>2|3PL:OBJ:PST:PFV:VENT/put.under (.) 2|3SG:SBJ:PST:IPFV/pull
      gwargwar=fa (.) sre\fzath/   (.) neba   thabr
      mud=ABL   (.) 2|3SG:SBJ>3SG.MASC:OBJ:IRR:PFV/pull.out (.) opposite arm
      nima   sf\rä/rm   nagaye=dben   (.) neba   (.) neba=me
      like.this 3SG.MASC:SBJ:PST:DUR child=LOC.ANIM.SG (.) opposite (.) opposite=INS
      kwan\sog/wrm   nabi=n
      2|3SG:SBJ:PST:DUR/ascend bamboo=LOC
      'He put the arm underneath ... he pulled him from the mud ... he pulled him out
      ... one arm was like this on the boy ... the other ... with the other he climbed up
      on the bamboo.'   [tci20120904-02 MAB #189-193]

The locative can be translated to English with the prepositions 'in', 'on' or 'at'. In order to express that some entity is inside something else, one can use the locational nominal *mrmr* 'inside' (37). See §3.1.7 for locationals. Note that example (37) shows that the locative marker attaches to the last item *mrmr* 'inside' of the phrase *firra kar mrmr* 'inside the village of Firra'.

(37) ***firra kar mrmren** kabe thwamnzrm fobo.*
      firra kar   mrmr=en   kabe thwa\m/nzrm   fobo
      firra village inside=LOC man 2|3PL:SBJ:PST:DUR/dwell DIST.ALL
      'The people lived inside the village of Firra.'   [tci20120901-01 MAK #27]

The locative case can be extended to cover various abstract, non-spatial domains. In example (38) it is used temporally: 'on that day' and 'in the afternoon'. Example (39) shows a metaphorical use of the locative case: *zokwasi=n* 'in words'. This sentence was a description of a man who got infuriated at the demand of some of his relatives to give them his daughter as an exchange sister.

(38) ***ane efothen** ... **ane zizin** ... Kukufia we sathora fof.*
      ane efoth=en (.) ane zizi=n   (.) Kukufia we   sa\thor/a
      DEM sun=LOC (.) DEM afternoon=LOC (.) kukufia also 3SG.MASC:SBJ:PST:PFV/arrive
      fof
      EMPH
      'On that day ... in the afternoon, Kukufia arrived again.'   [tci20100905 ABB #105-107]

(39) *fi zokwasin kwanänzüthzr.*
  fi   zokwasi=n   kwa\nänzüth/zr
  3.ABS speech=LOC 2|3SG:SBJ:RPST:IPFV/bury
  'He got into a fuss.' (lit. 'He buried himself in words.')   [overheard]

The above functions of the locative were all at the clausal level. At the interclausal level, the locative can also be used with a nominalisation as the counterpart of an adverbial subordinator where it encodes an event that occurs simultaneously with that of the main clause. Example (40) is taken from a story about a malevolent spirit who had killed a man. In the example, she realises that others have discovered the truth.

(40) *wtri we z zära nima "z zwemarth ... **ane yam fiyoksin.**"*
  wtri we z   zä\r/a   nima z   zwe\mar/th   (.)
  fear also ALR 2|3SG:SBJ:PST:PFV/do QUOT ALR 2|3PL:SBJ>1SG:OBJ:RPST:PFV/see (.)
  ane yam fiyok-si=n
  DEM event make-NMLZ=LOC
  'She was already afraid and said: "They have already seen me doing that thing."'
                                              [tci20120901-01 MAK #150-152]

4.8.2 Allative *=fo*

The allative case marker is *=fo* for inanimate referents and *=dbo* (SG) or *=medbo* (NSG) for animate referents. It encodes a spatial goal. Example (41) describes how the speaker and his family received the news that a widow from the neighbouring village should get remarried (to one of his friends).

(41) *wati **nzedbo** zanrifthath **mayawanmedbo** rouku **bänefo** ... **masufo**.*
  wati nzedbo   zan\rifth/ath   mayawa=medbo   rouku
  then 1NSG.ALL 2|3PL:SBJ>3SG.FEM:OBJ:PST:PFV/send mayawa=ALL.ANIM.NSG rouku
  bäne=fo   (.) masu=fo
  RECOG=ALL (.) masu=ALL
  'Then they sent the word to us ... to the Mayawas in Rouku ... to there ... to Masu.'
                                              [tci20120814 ABB #34-35]

The allative can be translated as movement 'to' or 'towards' some entity (41), but also as movement 'inside' some entity (42).

(42) *zbo n zräthbé **yare kwosifo**.*
  zbo   n   zrä\thb/é   yare kwosi=fo
  PROX.ALL IMN 1SG:SBJ>3SG.FEM:OBJ:IRR:PFV/put.inside bag old=ALL
  'I will try and put it here ... in the old bag.'   [tci20130907-02 RNA #261]

The allative can also be used metaphorically, as in example (43), which is taken from a public speech.

(43) **zokwasifo** buthorakwr.
zokwasi=fo b=wo\thorak/wr
speech=ALL MED=1SG:SBJ:NPST:IPFV/arrive
'I get to the point now!' (lit. 'I arrive there to the words.')   [tci20121019-04 ABB #135]

The animate/inanimate distinction mentioned in §4.8 can be used to mark definiteness of animate referents, for example animals. In (44), the speaker points out that sorcerers usually do not attack a person directly, but they put a deadly spell on a person's dog or some other animal. Later, when the animal suffers and dies, the human victim will also die. Thus, in (44) 'the dog' and 'the wallaby' are generic, and therefore marked with the (inanimate) allative case marker. In contrast, example (45) is taken from a story about a dog and a crow. Both have been introduced previously and are known to the speaker as individual characters. Consequently, the dog in (45) is marked with the animate allative.[4]

(44) **taurifo** tmatm zrafiyokwr o **ŋathafo.**
tauri=fo   tmatm zra\fiyok/wr   o ŋatha=fo
wallaby=ALL event 2|3SG:SBJ:IRR:IPFV/make or dog=ALL
'(The sorcerer) does this to a wallaby or to a dog.'   [tci20130903-04 RNA #114-115]

(45) kofä ane zätr ... ymdane zr yföfa **ŋathadbo.**
kofä ane zä\tr/   (.) ymd=ane zr   yfö=fa   ŋatha=dbo
fish DEM 2|3SG:SBJ:RPST:PFV/fall (.) bird=POSS tooth hole=ABL dog=ALL.ANIM
'That fish fell down ... from the bird's mouth to the dog.'   [tci20111107-03 RNA #68-69]

Although it is possible to attach the allative to temporal nouns like *efoth* 'day', there are no corpus examples of this, and it is generally quite rare. The reason for this is the existence of a temporal purposive case marker =*thamar* (§4.9.2).

4.8.3 Ablative =*fa*

The ablative case marker is =*fa* for inanimate referents and =*dba* (SG) or =*medba* (NSG) for animate referents. Example (46) shows the (inanimate) ablative case marker, and example (47) shows the animate ablative case marker.

(46) **torres strait islandfa** thunrärm ... ane masis.
torres strait island=fa   thun\rä/rm   (.) ane masis
torres strait island=ABL 2|3PL:SBJ:PST:DUR:VENT/be (.) DEM matches
'Those matchboxes came from the Torres Strait Islands.'   [tci20120909-06 KAB #10]

(47) trikasi zane mane wnrä ... nzä mane ŋatrikwé ... **badabadamedba** wnrä.
trik-si   zane   mane   wn\rä/   (.) nzä   mane
tell-NMLZ DEM:PROX which 3SG.FEM:SBJ:NPST:IPFV:VENT/be (.) 1SG.ABS which
ŋa\trik/wé   (.) badabada=medba   wn\rä/
1SG:SBJ:NPST:IPFV/tell (.) ancestor=ABL.ANIM.NSG 3SG.FEM:SBJ:NPST:IPFV:VENT/be
'As for this story ... which I am telling ... it comes from the ancestors.'
[tci20110802 ABB #15-17]

---

[4]Unfortunately, there is no corpus example of a referent which undergoes a change from inanimate allative to animate allative when tracked through a discourse.

The ablative can be used with a temporal meaning. There is only one corpus example of the case marker *=fa* (48), but the deictic demonstratives are frequently used with temporal semantics. Example (48) concludes a headhunting story in which the speaker points out that the population has increased after this had ceased. The word *zenafa* ('from now') is best translated as 'nowadays'.

(48)   *wati, zenafa ... ni tüfr nagayé kwakonzre.*
       wati zena=fa   (.) ni   tüfr   nagayé kwa\ko/nzre
       then today=ABL (.) 1NSG plenty children 1PL:SBJ:RPST:IPFV/become
       'Nowadays, we have got plenty of children.'   [tci20111107-01 MAK #150-151]

Example (49) shows the use of the deictic demonstrative *foba* 'from over there' with a temporal meaning, i.e. it expresses a starting point. In the example, the speaker states why he does not know what happened to his family's rain magic stones, and *foba* means 'from that time onwards'.

(49)   *nzenme ŋafe fthémäsü kwosi yara ... watik foba ni miyamr nrä mafadben zena ethn.*
       nzenme   ŋafe   fthémäsü   kwosi ya\r/a   (.) watik foba
       1NSG.POSS father meanwhile dead   3SG.MASC:SBJ:PST:IPFV/be (.) then DIST.ABL
       ni   miyamr n\rä/   mafa=dben   zena
       1NSG ignorance 1PL:SBJ:NPST:IPFV/be who=LOC.ANIM.SG today
       e\thn/
       2|3PL:SBJ:NPST:IPFV/lie.down
       'In the meantime our father died ... and from then one we don't know with whom (the rain stones) are today.'   [tci20131013-01 ABB #399]

The allative can also be used metaphorically, as in example (50), which is taken from a picture task. In the picture story, a man refuses to drink with his mates, because his alcoholism had brought him to jail. Thus, the allative on the word *zrin* 'problem' means 'from this problem'.

(50)   *ane zrinfa watik ziyara.*
       ane zrin=fa   watik   z=ya\r/a
       DEM problem=ABL enough PROX=3SG.MASC:SBJ:PST:IPFV/be
       'He had enough of this problem here.'   [tci20111004 MAE #2]

4.9 Temporal cases

Komnzo has a set of temporal case markers: the temporal locative, purposive and possessive. All three temporal cases only attach to temporal nominals (§3.1.8), like *ezi* 'morning' or the interrogative *fthé* 'when'. I adopt the labels locative, purposive and possessive because of the formal and semantic similarities with the respective cases. Formally, the temporal case markers consist of *=tham(a)* plus the case marker after which they are named. For example, the temporal locative is *=thamen*. At the present time, there is no etymological explanation for the *=tham(a)* element.

4.9.1 Temporal locative *=thamen*

The temporal locative indicates that something took place in a particular time frame. It is the time frame, usually a temporal nominal, to which the temporal locative attaches. Hence, it overlaps with the locative case, which can also be used on temporal nominals. Expressions like *ane efoththamen* 'in that day' (with a temporal locative) and *ane efothen* (with a locative) are equivalent. There is only a handful of corpus examples of the temporal locative. Example (51) comes from a narrative in which a young boy was attacked by a sorcerer at night in his garden. The young man shot the sorcerer with an arrow, and the sorcerer ran away. The next day a trail of blood could be seen as far as until the garden entrance. In the example, the speaker points out that he was bleeding only at the beginning and the temporal locative attaches to *zöftha* 'first'. Thus, it locates the predicate 'bleed' into that time frame. In this case, the resulting form is not *zöfthathamen* as would be expected, but it is reduced to *zöfthamen*.

(51) **zöfthamen** *zamatho frk komnzo zä wtnägwrmo* ...
zöftha=thamen za\math/o   frk   komnzo zä
first=TEMP.LOC SG:SBJ:RPST:PFV:AND/run blood only   PROX
w\tnäg\wrmo
SG:SBJ>3SG.FEM:OBJ:RPST:DUR:AND/lose
'At first, when he started to run and he was just losing blood here ...'
[tci20130901-04 YUK #40]

4.9.2 Temporal purposive *=thamar*

The temporal purposive case indicates that something is meant for a particular point in time. The case marker attaches to a temporal nominal, which specifies that point in time. Example (52) comes from a procedural text about poison-root fishing. While the speaker explains all the steps, others in the background are busy preparing and cooking the fish. At the end of the recording, he points out how some of the food is 'for the afternoon' and the leftovers are 'for tomorrow'.

(52) *okay,* **zizithamar** *kwa ane fof erä ... nä thzé* **kaythamar** *thrägathinze.*
okay zizi=thamar   kwa ane fof e\rä/   (.) nä   thzé
okay afternoon=TEMP.PURP FUT DEM EMPH 2|3PL:SBJ:NPST:IPFV/be (.) some ever
kayé=thamar   thrä\gathinz/e
tomorrow=TEMP.PURP 1PL:SBJ>2|3PL:OBJ:IRR:PFV/leave
'Okay, those are for the afternoon ... whatever (is there), we will leave it for
tomorrow.'   [tci20110813-09 DAK #60]

4.9.3 Temporal possessive *=thamane*

The temporal possessive case indicates that something is from a particular point in time. It attaches to a temporal nominal, which specifies that point in time. Example (53) comes from a story in which the two protagonists are withholding a particular food source from each other. In (53a), one of them sees a ground oven in the other's camp and asks him about it. The other one responds in (53b) by saying that it is 'yesterday's oven'. Here the temporal possessive inherits the possibility of functioning adnominally from the possessive case.

(53) a. *"nzungath, rar karo zane erä?"*
       nzun-gath   ra=r   karo   zane   e\rä/
       1SG.POSS-friend what=PURP earth.oven DEM:PROX 2|3PL:SBJ:NPST:IPFV/be
       "My friend, what is this earth oven for?"

     b. *"keke ... kadakada sutränwé ... kayé. **kaythamane karo rä!**"*
       keke (.) kadakada su\trän/wé   (.) kayé
       NEG (.) yamcake 1SG:SBJ>3SG.MASC:OBJ:RPST:IPFV/slice (.) yesterday
       kayé=thamane   karo   \rä/
       yesterday=TEMP.POSS ground oven 3SG.FEM:SBJ:NPST:IPFV/be
       "No, I cut the yam cake ... yesterday. This is yesterday's oven."

                                                       [tci20110802 ABB #90-94]

In example (54), the temporal possessive case appears at the clause level, not within a noun phrase. The example is from a stimulus picture task. The last part of the task is to retell a story from a first-person perspective. In the example, one of the participants instructs the other one to retell the story 'from today onward'.

(54) *nima befe we zakwther! **zenathamane** be katrikwé!*
     nima   befe   we za\kwther/
     like.this 2SG.ERG.EMPH also 2SG:SBJ>3SG.FEM:OBJ:IMP:PFV/change
     zena=thamane   be   ka\trik/wé
     today=TEMP.POSS 2SG.ERG 2SG:SBJ:IMP:IPFV/tell
     'You change it like this! You tell it from today.'   [tci20111004 MAE #5]

4.10 Instrumental *=me*

The instrumental case is used for material and immaterial instruments. It usually operates at the clausal level. Example (55) is taken from a conversation about a sorcerer who – after being shot – received help from his friend. The friend closed the wound 'with mud'. Example (56) comes from the same story and shows an immaterial instrument. The origin of sorcerer could be identified because he spoke Wära or 'with Safis language'. Example (57) comes from a public speech, where the speaker announces that he speaks on behalf of two older men ('speak with their mouths').

(55) *naf we **gwargwarme** ane yfö yanrmänwa.*
     naf   we gwargwar=me ane yfö yan\rmän/wa
     3SG.ERG also mud=INS   DEM hole 2|3SG:SBJ>3SG.MASC:IO:NPST:IPFV/close
     'He also closed that hole on him with mud.'   [tci20130901-04 RNA #123]

(56) **safs zokwasime** *zenafthma.*
safs zokwasi=me ze\nafth/ma
safs language=INS 2|3SG:SBJ:PST:PFV/talk
'He talked in Wära.' (lit. 'He talked with Safs language.')   [tci20130901-04 RNA #57]

(57) **nafanme zr yföme** *ŋanafé ... sowai a karbu ... zena zbär.*
nafanme zr yfö=me ŋa\na/fé (.) sowai a karbu (.) zena
3NSG.POSS tooth hole=INS 1SG:SBJ:NPST:IPFV/speak (.) sowai and karbu (.) today
zbär
night
'Tonight, I am talking for them, for Sowai and Karbu.' (lit. 'I talk with their
mouths.')   [tci20121019-04 ABB #91-92]

At the interclausal level the instrumental case is used for resultative constructions
(58). Resultative constructions typically employ the copula and a nominalised verb form:
rfithzsime translates literally as 'with hiding'.

(58) *nge kwa erifthznth ... nafaŋamayé ...* **rifthzsime** *kwa enrn.*
nge kwa e\rifth/znth (.) nafa-ŋame=é (.)
child FUT 2|3PL:SBJ>2|3DU:OBJ:NPST:IPFV/hide (.) 3.POSS-mother=ERG.NSG (.)
rifthz-si=me kwa en\r/n
hide-NMLZ=INS FUT 2|3DU:SBJ:NPST:IPFV:VENT/be
'The mothers will hide the two children ... They will be hidden.'
[tci20110817-02 ABB #72-73]

The instrumental case is frequently used on property nouns (59) and adjectives (60)
with an adverbial function. In example (59) the speaker talks about customs surrounding
the yam harvest, and in (60) he explains why he is not planting big gardens anymore. In
both examples, the instrumental case derives a manner adverb.

(59) **zünzme** *befe fthé zanathé bonemäwä keke tüfr thrarä.*
zünz=me befe fthé za\na/thé bone=ma=wä keke
greed=INS 2SG.ERG.EMPH when 2SG:SBJ:IMP:PFV/eat 2SG.POSS=CHAR=EMPH NEG
tüfr thra\rä/
plenty 2|3PL:SBJ:IRR:IPFV/be
'If you eat greedily, your own (yams) will not be plenty.'   [tci20120805-01 ABB #760]

(60) *watik, nzone tmä we* **katanme** *ŋarsörm.*
watik nzone tmä we katan=me ŋa\rsö/rm
then 1SG.POSS strength also small=INS 2|3SG:SBJ:RPST:DUR/recede
'Well, my strength has gone down a little.'   [tci20120805-01 ABB #664]

The instrumental case can also be attached to demonstratives, as in (61), where the
speaker explains to me how to protect one's bamboo bow against insects. In (62), the
instrumental is attached to *mane* 'which' and used as a relative pronoun 'with which'.

(61) **ngazime** *o zaru ... nzanzama ... watik* **aneme** *zminzakwé zabth.*
ngazi=me o zaru (.) nzanza=ma (.) watik ane=me
coconut=INS or candlenut (.) woodworm=CHAR (.) then DEM=Ins
z\minzak/wé   za\bth/
2SG:SBJ>3SG.FEM:IMP:IPFV/paint 2|3SG:SBJ:RPST:PFV/finish
'With coconut or candlenut, because of the woodworm. Finally, you paint (the
bow) with that one and it is finished.'   [tci20120922-23 MAA #81-83]

(62) *kitr zane erä ... yame yrsima ... amaf* **maneme** *yame wrwr.*
kitr   zane e\rä/   (.) yame yr-si=ma   (.)
river.pandanus DEM:PROX 2|3PL:SBJ:NPST:IPFV/be (.) mat weave-NMLZ=CHAR (.)
ama=f   mane=me yame w\r/wr
mother=ERG.SG which=INS mat 2|3SG:SBJ>3SG.FEM:OBJ:NPST:IPFV/weave
'This is *Kitr*, for weaving mats ... with which mother weaves the mat.'
                 [tci20130907-02 JAA #235-236]

The instrumental attaches productively to several interrogative pronouns: *ra=me* 'with what' or *mane=me* 'with which'. The interrogative *mon* 'how' can occur with or without the instrumental case; both *mon* and *monme* can be used interchangeably.

4.11 Purposive =*r*

The purposive case is used at the clausal and interclausal level. It expresses someone's intention (63 and 64) or the inherent purpose of some entity (65). In example (63), a man informs his younger brothers about his plans for the night. Example (64) comes from a procedural about gardening and the speaker explains the purpose of the different steps involved.

(63) *naf ni nzräkor "ngthé ... nima nyak ŋarsfo etfthmöwä* **kofär** *... zbär kwa* **zuzir**
ŋarzre."
naf ni nzrä\kor/   ngthé   (.) nima
3SG.ERG 1NSG 2|3SG:SBJ>1PL:OBJ:IRR:PFV/speak younger.sibling (.) like.this
n\yak/   ŋars=fo etfth=me=wä kofä=r (.) zbär kwa
1PL:SBJ:NPST:IPFV/go river=ALL sleep=INS=EMPH fish=PURP (.) night FUT
zuzi=r   ŋa\r/zre
fishing=PURP 1PL:SBJ:NPST:IPFV/throw
'He said to us: "Hey small brothers! We will go to the river ... overnight ... for
fish. We will throw the fishing line in the night."' [tci120904-02 MAB #26-29]

(64) *efäefä krarzrth* **ŋaraker** *... wotuwotu räzsir.*
efäefä kra\r/zrth   ŋarake=r (.) wotu-wotu räz-si=r
aisle 2|3PL:SBJ:IRR:IPFV/throw fence=PURP (.) REDUP-stick erect-NMLZ=PURP
'They cut an aisle for the fence ... for erecting the sticks.' [tci20120805-01 ABB #51-52]

The last noun phrase in (64) and in (65) show the purposive case operating at the interclausal level. In both cases the purposive case marker is attached to an infinitival adjunct. In (65), the speaker talks about sorcerers who visit a deceased man's grave after the burial to extract certain body parts. In both examples, the clause marked with the purposive contains the infinitive as well as the object of the event in the ablative, for example *tmä yarisi* 'strength giving' in (65).

(65) *fi fenz ane **bänemrnzo** rä ... **tmä yarisir**.*
    fi   fenz   ane bänemr=nzo   \rä\   (.) tmä
    but body.liquid DEM RECOG.PURP=ONLY 3SG.FEM:SBJ:NPST:IPFV/be (.) strength
    yari-si=r
    give-NMLZ=PURP
    'but the body liquid is only for this ... for giving power.' [tci20130903-04 RNA #139-140]

The noun phrase or the infinitival adjunct marked with =r ascribes a specific purpose, and in this ascriptive function, the purposive overlaps with the characteristic case. Hence, in (65) both *tmä yarisir* and *tmä yarisima* would be grammatical and identical in meaning. I described the nature of this overlap in §4.12.

There is a set of purposive personal pronouns in Komnzo. All the pronouns share a -nar element, for example *nzunar* 'for me', *nzenar* 'for us'.[5] However, these pronouns are rarely used, in fact so rarely that I came accross them only very late in my fieldwork. Moreover, there is not a single token in the text corpus. As one would predict from the semantics of the purposive case, these pronouns encode a beneficiary or a goal. But this function is already covered by the dative case. I will offer a hypothetical semantic shift scenario at the end of this chapter which partly explains why the purposive pronouns are so rarely used.

4.12 Characteristic *=ma*

The characteristic case covers a number of semantic roles which are source, reason and purpose. The characteristic operates at all three levels: adnominal (66), clausal (67) and interclausal (68). In example (66), *karma* 'from the village' functions within a matrix noun phrase. In this example, the characteristic could be left out, and *ane karma kabe* or *ane kar kabe* are both grammatical.[6] In example (67), the characteristic case attaches to a separate noun phrase and functions at the clause level. In example (68), the speaker comments on the exhausting work of dragging a sago palm trunk. The characteristic case attaches to an infinitival adjunct ('dragging') and, thus, operates at a interclausal level.

---

[5]See Table 3.5 on page 99.
[6]In *zane kar kabe*, the phrasal head consists of a compound *kar kabe*. In *zane karma kabe*, the noun phrase *zane kar* is embedded in a matrix noun phrase. Thus, the reference of the demonstrative *zane* is different between the two examples. In the former case *zane* refers to the complex head, but in the latter case *zane* refers only to the head of the embedded noun phrase. See §7.5 for a discussion of noun phrases.

(66) *keke thufnzrm ...* **ane karma kabe**
    keke thu\fn/zrm   (.) ane kar=ma   kabe
    NEG 2|3SG:SBJ>2|3PL:OBJ:PST:DUR/hit (.) DEM village=CHAR man
    'She was not killing them ... the people from this village.'   [tci20120901-01 MAK #50]

(67) **zane karma** *minzü fefe nafa dagon swafiyokwrmth bänema z zbo ŋabrüza.*
    zane   kar=ma   minzü fefe nafa   dagon
    DEM:PROX village=CHAR very   real 3NSG.ERG food
    swa\fiyok/wrmth   bäne=ma   z   zbo
    2|3PL:SBJ>3SG.MASC:IO:PST:DUR/make RECOG=CHAR ALR PROX.ALL
    ŋa\brü/za
    SG:SBJ:PST:IPFV/drown
    'From this village, they made a lot of food for him because he drowned here.'
                                         [tci20150906-10 ABB #296-297]

(68) *festh tayo tayo nrä ...* **bäne thärkusima.**
    festh tayo tayo n\rä/   (.) bäne   thärku-si=ma
    body weak weak 1PL:SBJ:NPST:IPFV/be (.) DEM:MED drag-NMLZ=CHAR
    'Our bodies are weak from that dragging (of the sago).'   [tci20120929-02 SIK #66-67]

In example (68), the semantic role of spatial origin or source is extended to non-spatial origin, that is reason or cause. Note that the source of motion cannot be expressed using the characteristic case. Instead the ablative =*fa* has to be used. Non-spatial origin is also found at the clausal level, for example in (69) where the speaker explains why she was hesitant at first about working for the anthropologist Mary Ayres.

(69) *nzä* **ane markai zokwasima** *wtri kwarärm.*
    nzä   ane markai zokwasi=ma   wtri kwa\rä/rm
    1SG.ABS DEM outsider language=CHAR fear 1SG:SBJ:PST:DUR/be
    'I was afraid of that white man's language.'   [tci20130911-03 MAA #15]

Example (70) concludes a recording taken inside a yam house where the speaker has talked about the different types of yams and the sorting principle in the storage house. He launches a whole battery of noun phrases marked with the characteristic case to express what the story 'was about', and thus the case marker can also be used to express the topic of a conversation. In the example, the noun phrases are marked by angled brackets.

(70) *watik zane zizin* **[wawama]** **[trikasi tharisima]** **[tafoma]** **[sagusaguma]** *... mon eworthre ... mane* **[dagonma]** *erä ... mane tafo erä ... zbo zf zbthe brä trikasi ... eso kafar* **[bone namä yarizsima]**.
    watik zane   zizi=n   wawa=ma trik-si   thari-si=ma
    then DEM:PROX afternoon=LOC yam=CHAR tell-NMLZ harvest-NMLZ=CHAR
    tafo=ma   sagu-sagu=ma   (.) mon
    yam.type=CHAR REDUP-yam.type=CHAR (.) how
    e\wor/thre   (.) mane dagon=ma e\rä/   (.)
    1PL:SBJ>2|3PL:OBJ:NPST:IPFV/plant (.) which food=CHAR 2|3PL:SBJ:NPST:IPFV/be (.)

mane	tafo	e\rä/		(.) zbo	zf
which	yam.type	2|3PL:SBJ:NPST:IPFV/be		(.) PROX.ALL	IMM

z\bth/e   b=\rä/   trik-si   (.)
1DU:SBJ>3SG.FEM:OBJ:RPST:PFV/finish MED=3SG.FEM:SBJ:NPST:IPFV/be tell-NMLZ (.)
eso   kafar bone   namä yariz-si=ma
thanks big   2SG.POSS good listen-NMLZ=CHAR

'Well, in this afternoon ... (we talked) about yams, the story about harvesting, about Tafo yams and Sagu Sagu yams ... how we plant them ... which ones are for eating ... which ones are for Tafo (storing). We have finished it now there. Thank you for listening.'   [tci20121001 ABB #215-221]

Note that the last two tokens of *=ma* in example (70) are different in their semantics. The noun phrase *dagonma* does not translate as 'about the food', but as 'for eating'. The last token of *=ma* can be translated as both reason or purpose: *eso kafar [bone namä yarizsima]* 'thanks because of your listening' or 'thanks for your listening'. Without examples like these the labels 'source' and 'cause' would be sufficient descriptions for this case marker. However, quite frequently *=ma* encodes a purpose and, therefore, I prefer the cover term 'characteristic'.

Consider example (71) which comes from a walk through the forest. Along the path, the speaker shows me a particular grass. The leaf of this grass can be placed between the lips, and one can produce a high cheeping sound by blowing through it. She explains that this can be used 'for attracting snakes', thus, the characteristic is marking a purpose in (71a). After demonstrating how to produce the sound, she repeats in (71b) why the snake is coming (*kwanma* 'because of the sound') and concludes that she would not usually blow this grass (*anema* 'therefore'). Here the characteristic case marks a reason.

(71) a. ***kaboth räkumgsima** yé.*
         kaboth räkumg-si=ma   \yé/
         snake attract-NMLZ=CHAR 3SG.MASC:SBJ:NPST:IPFV/be
         'It is for attracting snakes.'   [tci20130907-02 RNA #612]

      b. *kaboth kwa ŋankwir **ane kwanma** ... **anema** fof keke efsgwre.*
         kaboth kwa ŋan\kwi/r   ane kwan=ma   (.) ane=ma
         snake FUT 2\|3SG:SBJ:NPST:IPFV:VENT/run DEM noise=CHAR (.) DEM=CHAR
         fof   keke e\fsg/wre
         EMPH NEG 1PL:SBJ>2\|3PL:OBJ:NPST:IPFV/blow
         'The snake will run here because of that sound ... therefore we do not blow them.'   [tci20130907-02 RNA #615-616]

In her analysis of Ancient Greek, Luraghi suggests that "the notion of Reason, which, as remarked by Croft (1991), mediates between Cause and Purpose, really constitutes a kind of undifferentiated area, in which the reason that motivates an agent to act is cognitively equivalent to the purpose of the action, so that the two notions overlap completely" (2003: 46). See also Luraghi (2001) for a cross-linguistic study of semantic roles. In Komnzo, this overlap does not play out as a diachronic process, but as coexisting uses of the characteristic case. Example (72) supports the point made by Luraghi. The noun *yasema* can be translated into English as cause/motivation ('because of meat') as well as purpose ('for meat'). The reason for the action and the purpose of the action are expressed by =*ma*.

(72) *nabimäre fthé gnräré bone nagayé kwa änor ... yasema.*
      nabi=märe fthé   gn\rär/é   bone   nagayé kwa
      bow=PRIV when 2SG:SBJ:IMP:IPFV/be 2SG.POSS children FUT
      ä\nor/   (.) yase=ma
      2|3PL:SBJ:NPST:IPFV/shout (.) game=CHAR
      'When you are without a bow, your children will cry for meat / because of meat.'

      [tci20120922-23 MAA #89-91]

The characteristic case competes with the purposive case in marking the semantic role of purpose. In many utterances, they can be used interchangeably. Consider examples (73) and (74), where both can be used to express an inherent purpose of some entity ('the leaf is for rolling cigarettes'). Likewise, in (71a), the purposive could be used (*kaboth räkumgsir yé* 'it is for attracting snakes'). An intentional purpose of some individual (e.g. 'he goes for hunting') is most frequently expressed by the purposive case, not by the characteristic.

(73) *zane mane yé ... bänemr yrärth ... sukufa knsir.*
      zane   mane \yé/   (.) bänemr
      DEM:PROX which 3SG.MASC:SBJ:NPST:IPFV/be (.) RECOG.PURP
      y\rä/rth   (.) sukufa kn-si=r
      2|3PL:SBJ>3SG.MASC:OBJ:NPST:IPFV/do (.) tobacco roll-NMLZ=PURP
      'As for this one ... they use it for that ... for rolling cigarettes.'

      [tci20130907-02 RNA #506-508]

(74) *ane taga mane erä sukufa knsima we erä.*
      ane taga mane e\rä/   sukufa kn-si=ma   we
      DEM leaf which 2|3PL:SBJ:NPST:IPFV/be tobacco roll-NMLZ=CHAR also
      e\rä/
      2|3PL:SBJ:NPST:IPFV/be
      'As for those leaves, they are also used for rolling cigarettes.'

      [tci20130907-02 RNA #567]

With animate referents, the dative is used to mark a goal or beneficiary. The purposive case can be used for more abstract animate referents, for example *fäms ŋare=r* 'for/as exchange woman'.[7] The characteristic case cannot serve for marking purpose in this sense. Instead, with animate referents it always marks a reason, origin or cause. Additionally, animate referents must take the possessive case first, and then the characteristic =*ma* attaches to the possessive. In example (75), a young man explains how the food will be

---

[7]Example (31) on page 205 provides a textual example of *fäms ŋarer*.

shared during an upcoming feast. The characteristic is attached to the possessive pronouns. Example (76) comes from a story in which the wife of a man had been killed, and at the end of the story he cries bitterly because of her. In both examples, the characteristic case attaches to a possessive: *nzenmema* and *nafaŋareanema*. It is ungrammatical to use the unmarked (absolutive) forms: *nima* and *nafaŋarema*.

(75)　*we nafa **nzenmema** sräthoroth ... ni **nafanmema** fof sränthore.*
　　　we　nafa　　nzenme=ma　　srä\thor/oth　　　　　　　　　　　　　(.) ni
　　　also 3NSG.ERG 1NSG.POSS=CHAR PL:SBJ>3SG.MASC:OBJ:IRR:PFV:AND/carry (.) 1NSG
　　　nafanme=ma　　fof　　srän\thor/e
　　　3NSG.POSS=CHAR EMPH 1PL:SBJ>3SG.MASC:OBJ:IRR:PFV:VENT/carry
　　　'They will take it from us and we will take it from them.'　[tci20120929-02 SIK #97-98]

(76)　*yanzo bobo yanora **nafaŋareanema**.*
　　　ya=nzo　　bobo　　ya\nor/a　　　　　　　　　nafa-ŋare=ane=ma
　　　cry=ONLY MED.ALL 3SG.MASC:SBJ:PST:IPFV/cry 3.POSS-woman=POSS=CHAR
　　　'He cried badly there because of his wife.'　　　　[tci20120901-01 MAK #208-209]

The characteristic suffix is used to derive cardinal numerals: *eda* 'two' → *edama* 'second' (§3.1.6.2). In example (77), the speaker explains what I have to do during an upcoming namesake ceremony.

(77)　*chrisf yathugwr keke kwa srefaf yakme ... **ethama** mane yé ... kwa fthé fof yfathwr.*
　　　chris=f　　　ya\thug/wr　　　　　　　　　　　　　keke kwa
　　　chris=ERG.SG 2|3SG:SBJ>3SG.MASC:OBJ:NPST:IPFV/trick NEG FUT
　　　sre\faf/　　　　　　　　　　　　　yakme (.) etha=ma　　　mane
　　　2|3SG:SBJ>3SG.MASC:OBJ:IRR:PFV/hold quickly (.) three=CHAR which
　　　\yé/　　　　　　　　　　　　　(.) kwa fthé　fof
　　　3SG.MASC:SBJ:NPST:IPFV/be (.) FUT when EMPH
　　　y\fath/wr
　　　2|3SG:SBJ>3SG.MASC:OBJ:NPST:IPFV/hold
　　　'Chris will trick him, he will not hold him quickly ... Only at the third (time) ...
　　　(that is) when he will really hold him.'　　　　[tci20110817-02 ABB #89-91]

The characteristic case is frequently used on demonstrative pronouns, as in (71b), meaning 'therefore'. In some words, the characteristic case has become lexicalised, for example: *rma* 'why' from *ra* 'what' plus *=ma* or *karama wath* 'karama dance' from *kara* which is a place in the West. Other lexical items show a *ma* element, but the connection to the characteristic case is hypothetical at the moment, for example *nzagoma* 'for later, in advance' and *madma* 'female'.

4.13 Proprietive *=karä*

The use the term "proprietive" for this case enclitic because it constitutes a functional opposition with the private case, i.e. 'having something' versus 'not having something'.

There are two variants for the proprietive *=karä* and *=kaf.* They operate at the clausal and interclausal level and express the semantic role of association ('with something' or 'with someone') or property ('having some quality', 'having some object'). The latter role often employs an existential construction, as in (80) and (81). In its semantics, the proprietive overlaps with the associative case. The main difference lies in the kinds of referents encoded. The associative often encodes animate referents, while the proprietive is rarely found with animate referents. See (79) for one such example. I discuss the difference between the associative and the proprietive in §4.15.

Although the proprietive *=karä* attaches to one noun phrase relating it semantically to another noun phrase, the two NPs do not form a syntactic constituent, i.e. the proprietive does not function adnominally. In example (78), the speaker is boasting about his big yam garden: 'I am the one with the biggest garden'. In example (79), a woman describes a namesake ceremony, where the mother 'with her child' are hidden behind a curtain of coconut leaves waiting to be officially presented to their relatives. In both examples, the NPs marked with the proprietive are printed in bold, and the NP to which it associates some entity is underlined.

(78) <u>*nzänzo zä zf worä*</u> **kafarwä dawkarä** *fof.*
    nzä=nzo   zä   zf   wo\rä/   kafar=wä daw=karä   fof
    1SG.ABS=ONLY PROX IMM 1SG:SBJ:NPST:IPFV/be big=EMPH garden=PROP EMPH
    'I am the only one here with a really big garden.'   [tci20120805-01 ABB #655]

(79) <u>*nzä*</u> *zweyafürath* **ngekarä** *... samtherath warfo "nge zyé!"*
    nzä   zwe\yafür/ath   nge=karä (.)
    1SG.ABS 2|3PL:SBJ>1SG:IO:PST:PFV/open child=PROP (.)
    sa\mther/ath   warfo nge
    2|3PL:SBJ>3SG.MASC:OBJ:PST:PFV/lift.up above child
    z=\yé/
    PROX=3SG.MASC:SBJ:NPST:IPFV/be
    'They opened it for me with the child. They lifted him up high (and said) "Here is the boy!"'   [tci20130823-08 WAM #43]

The proprietive is frequently used with the copula to express a property or quality of something: 'with dust' in (80), or someone: 'with facial hair' in (81). The kinds of properties assigned are usually portrayed as being of temporary nature.

(80) **gwrmgkarä** <u>*zane kar*</u> *rä.*
    gwrmg=karä zane   kar   \rä/
    dust=PROP   DEM:PROX place 3SG.FEM:SBJ:NPST:IPFV/be
    'This is a dusty place.'   [tci20121019-04 ABB #7]

(81) *kabe yé ...* **fäk thäbukarä** *yé.*
    kabe yé   (.) fäk thäbu=karä \yé/
    man 3SG.MASC:SBJ:NPST:IPFV/be (.) jaw hair=PROP 3SG.MASC:SBJ:NPST:IPFV/be
    'This is a man. He has a beard.'   [tci20111004 RMA #90]

Examples (82) and (83) contrast the proprietive case with the instrumental case. In example (82), the speaker talks about local medicine and how one has to mix the liquid of a particular plant with water. Hence, *nokarä* has to be translated as addition: '(together) with the water'. In example (83), the shallow water on the riverbank acts as an instrument making it easier to roll a heavy sago stem. Consequently, *nome* has to be translated as: 'with (the help of) the water'.

(82) **nokarä** *swathknwé! ... ane käznob!*
      no=karä   s\wathkn/wé   (.) ane käz\nob/
      water=PROP 2SG:SBJ>3SG.MASC:OBJ:IMP:IPFV/stir (.) DEM 2SG:SBJ:IMP:PFV/drink
      'You stir it with water and drink that!'   [tci20130907-02 RNA #189]

(83) *sathkäfake bi frezsi thenzgsi ...* **anemöwä** *töna sakorake ... zane* **nome***.*
      sa\thkäf/ake   bi   frez-si   thenzg-si (.)
      1PL:SBJ>3SG.MASC:OBJ:PST:PFV/start sago bring.up.from.river-NMLZ roll-NMLZ (.)
      ane=me=wä   töna   sa\kor/ake   (.) zane
      DEM=INS=EMPH high.ground 1PL:SBJ>3SG.MASC:OBJ:PST:PFV/become (.) DEM:PROX
      no=me
      water=INS
      'We started bringing up the sago from the river by rolling it ... with that we
      brought it to the high ground ... with the water.'   [tci20120929-02 SIK #57-58]

The proprietive case operates at the interclausal level when it is attached to a nominalised verb (84). Unlike the instrumental case, the proprietive does not form a resultative construction. In (84), the relationship between *borsi* 'laugh' and the predicate 'he looks' is one of association or simultaneity. It can also be translated as a manner adverbial ('He stands laughingly.'). In example (85) the father comes while telling a story. In contrast, in resultative constructions, the result of some previous event is emphasised. For example, in (86) the speaker points to a stack of yams in his storage house stressing the fact that he has piled up different types of yam tubers. This can be analysed as a pseudo-passive construction (§8.3.5).

(84) *gon z zefaf ...* **borsikarä** *efoth ymarwr.*
      gon z   ze\faf/   (.) bor-si=karä   efoth
      hip ALR 1SG:SBJ:RPST:PFV/hold (.) laugh-NMLZ=PROP sun
      y\mar/wr
      2|3SG:SBJ>3SG.MASC:OBJ:NPST:IPFV/see
      'He has his hands on his hips. As he looks up at the sun, he laughs.'
                                                        [tci20111004 RMA #502-503]

(85) *nafaŋafe* **trikasikarä** *yanyak.*
      nafa-ŋafe   trik-si=karä   yan\yak/
      3.POSS-father tell-NMLZ=PROP 3SG.MASC:SBJ:NPST:IPFV:VENT/walk
      'The father walks here while he is telling a story.'   [tci20111004 RMA #329]

(86) *zane fukthksime erä.*
zane   fukthk-si=me e\rä/
DEM:PROX mix-NMLZ=INS 2|3PL:SBJ:NPST:IPFV/be
'These ones have been mixed.'   [tci20121001 ABB #178]

At the clausal level, the proprietive can also attach to a nominalised verb. Example (87) is the description of a picture card which depicts a prisoner sitting in his cell. Example (88) comes from the same recording, when the prisoner is set free and handed back his belongings. These two examples presuppose some kind of result – 'has been tied' and 'has been opened', respectively – but the previous event remains implicit. For example, in (88) the speaker draws attention to the fact that the door is open with the help of a demonstrative identifier *brä*. If the instrumental case was used instead (*yafüsime*), the result of the opening event would be emphasised.

(87) *wati ane fóf yamnzr ... fam ngarär ... fafen **wäthsikarä** yé.*
wati ane fof   ya\m/nzr   (.) fam   nga\rär/   (.)
Then DEM EMPH 3SG.MASC:SBJ:NPST:IPFV/sit (.) thoughts 2|3SG:SBJ:NPST:IPFV/do (.)
fafen wäth-si=karä \yé/
during tie-NMLZ=PROP 3SG.MASC:SBJ:NPST:IPFV/be
'Well, that one is sitting ... he is thinking ... with his hands tied.'
                                                [tci20111004 RMA #133-134]

(88) *zrfö bana z seyafürth ... zrfö **yafüsikarä** brä.*
zrfö bana z   se\yafür/th   (.) zrfö yafü-si=karä
door poor ALR 2|3PL:SBJ>3SG.MASC:IO:RPST:PFV/open (.) door open-NMLZ=PROP
b=\rä/
MED=3SG.MASC:SBJ:NPST:IPFV/be
'They have already opened the door for the poor guy. There, the door is open!'
                                                [tci20111004 RMA #432-433]

There is a second variant of the proprietive marker, which is *=kaf*. In terms of frequency, the distribution of the two formatives is rather skewed: *=kaf* is attested 30 times in the corpus compared to 240 occurences of *=karä*. The distribution patterns neither with age or with the language portfolio of individual speakers. In the closely related varieties Wära and Anta both formatives are also attested.

4.14 Privative *=märe*

The privative case *=mär* or *=märe* expresses the opposite of the proprietive. It is used to indicate that some entity lacks something (90), someone (89) or some quality (91). The privative operates usally at the clausal level. Like the proprietive case, it can establish a semantic link between two noun phrases, but the two noun phrases do not form a syntactic constituent. In example (89), the speaker talks about older lineages of his clan. The example contrasts the proprietive and the privative case. The absence (*ngemär*) or existence (*ngekarä*) marked on *nge* 'child' relates those noun phrases to *fi* 'they' and *bäi*, respectively. In the following examples (90 and 91), the noun phrase to which the privative-marked noun phrase links is omitted.

(89) *sitau bagi fi zabthath **ngemär** ... bäinzo **ngekarä** yara fof.*
     sitau bagi fi   za\bth/ath   nge=mär   (.) bäi=nzo   nge=karä
     sitau bagi 3.ABS 2|3PL:SBJ:PST:PFV/finish child=PRIV (.) bäi=ONLY child=PROP
     ya\r/a   fof
     3SG.MASC:SBJ:PST:IPFV/be EMPH
     'Sitau and Bagi, they died without children ... only Bäi had children.'
                                                  [tci20120814 ABB #508]

(90) *frasi kwa nrä **ŋanzmäre** fthé gnräré*
     frasi   kwa n\rä/   ŋanz=märe fthé   gn\rä/ré
     hunger FUT 2SG:SBJ:NPST:IPFV/be row=PRIV   when 2SG:SBJ:IMP:IPFV/be
     'You will be hungry, if you don't have a row (of yams in the garden).'
                                                  [tci20130822-08 JAA #54]

(91) ***miyomäre** worä ... mrn ŋarake **miyomäre**.*
     miyo=märe wo\rä/   (.) mrn ŋarake miyo=märe
     desire=PRIV 1SG:SBJ:NPST:IPFV/be (.) clan garden desire=PRIV
     'I don't want to make a family/clan garden (anymore).'   [tci20130823-06 STK #77]

There is one lexeme where the privative case has become lexicalised. The property noun *miyatha* 'knowledge' or 'knowledgeable' is used in constructions expressing a positive epistemic state; usually of the structure *miyatha worä* 'I know', literally: 'I am with knowledge' or 'I am knowledgeable'. The negation of this statement is most commonly done by using the property noun *miyamr* 'ignorance' or 'ignorant', which contains *miya* and an element *mr*. The latter is a reduced and lexicalised form of the privative case marker *=mär*. We can see this in example (92), which comes from a myth where two brothers are trying to kill a creature by shooting an arrow into its heart.

(92) *naf nima "keke fi **miyamr** erä fofosa mä rä."*
     naf   nima keke fi   miyamr e\rä/   fofosa mä
     3SG.ERG QUOT NEG 3.ABS ignorant 2|3PL:SBJ:NPST:IPFV/be heart   where
     \rä/
     3SG.FEM:SBJ:NPST:IPFV/be
     'He said "No, they do not know where the heart is."'   [tci20131013-01 ABB #104-105]

4.15 Associative =ä

The associative case is used to express accompaniment at the clausal level or simultaneity with another event at the interclausal level. The formative is *=ä*. Like other case markers, the associative encodes number for animate referents. The enclitics are *=r* and *=ä*, and there is a set of pronominals shown in Table 4.4. These formatives differ in two points from the other case markers. First, the number distinction is between dual (=*r*) and plural (=*ä*). Secondly, the value encodes the number of the total set, i.e. someone in the company of one (dual) or more persons (plural). These forms are used in a construction for which I adopt the term "inclusory construction" based on Lichtenberk (2000) and Singer (2001). I describe the inclusory construction in the context of the syntax of the noun phrase (§7.6).

Table 4.4: Associative case / pronominals

	person	dual	plural
	1	*ninrr*	*ninä*
personal pronouns	2	*bnrr*	*bnä*
	3	*nafrr*	*nafä*
RECOG		*bafrr*	*bafä*
INDF		*nä bunrr*	*nä bunä*
interrogative		*mafrr*	*mafä*

The associative case overlaps in its function to mark accompaniment with the proprietive case (§4.13). Although both cases can be used for animate and inanimate referents, their distribution is rather skewed. The corpus contains 270 tokens of the proprietive case, of which 17% (46) are animate referents versus 83% (224) inanimate. Many of the animate referents can be accounted for by fixed expressions with a more ideosyncratic reading. For example, *ŋare=karä* 'with woman' and *nge=karä* 'with child' can also mean 'married' and 'having a family' respectively. For the associative case, the distribution is reversed. The corpus contains 159 tokens of the associative case, of which 85% (135) are animate referents versus 15% (24) inanimate. It follows that the associative case is mainly used to mark the accompaniment of a person, while the accompaniment of or the association with some inanimate entity is only a minor pattern. In spite of that I use only inanimate referents in the remainder of this section and refer the reader to the description of the inclusory construction in §7.6.

The associative case can operate at the clausal level (94) or at the interclausal level (93). Example (93) is taken from a storyboard picture task where the speaker describes one of the pictures as part of a narration. The associative is attached to the nominalised verb *thweksi* 'rejoice' which acts as an infinitival adjunct.

(93) *kfänrsöfth **thweksiä**.*
 kfän\rsöfth/   thwek-si=ä
 2|3SG:SBJ:PST:ITER:VENT/descend   rejoice-NMLZ=ASSOC
 'She always came down (the stairs) and was happy.'   [tci20120925 MKA #369]

Example (94) is taken from a story about a boy who drowned in the Morehead river. A group of policemen were on guard to deter crocodiles, while another man was trying to recover the body from the river. The phrase *markai nabiä* 'with shotguns' (lit. 'with white man bows') can also be marked with the proprietive case like the preceding phrase *gardakarä* 'with canoes' (93).

(94) *fath wäfiyokwath neba wazi neba wazi ... frisman fi gardakarä **markai nabiä** ...*
bara kwarafinzrmth ... nümgarma
fath   wä\fiyok/wath   neba   wazi neba   wazi (.)
clearing 2|3PL:SBJ>3SG.FEM:OBJ:NPST:IPFV/make opposite side opposite side (.)
frisman   fi   garda=karä markai   nabi=ä   (.) bara
policeman 3.ABS canoe=PROP white.man bow=ASSOC (.) paddle
kwa\rafi/nzrmth   (.) nümgar=ma
2|3PL:SBJ:PST:DUR/paddle (.) crocodile=CHAR
'They cleared the place along both sides ... the policemen with canoes and shotguns ... they were paddling because of crocodiles.' [tci20120904-02 MAB #162-165]

The third example (95) comes from visiting one of the many waterholes around Rouku, where people catch fish with poison-root during the dry season. The speaker points out how thoughtfully ('with thoughts') the ancestors looked after this place.

(95) *kofä kwot kwarkonzrmth namä yamme ... nä kafar zra zane zf **famä** zumarwrmth*
nafa zf ... kafar kwarké.
kofä kwot   kwa\rko/nzrmth   namä yam=me   (.) nä   kafar
fish properly 2|3PL:SBJ:PST:DUR/distribute good custom=INS (.) some big
zra   zane   zf   fam=ä   zu\mar/wrmth
swamp DEM:PROX IMM thought=ASSOC 2|3PL:SBJ>3SG.FEM:OBJ:PST:DUR/see
nafa   zf   (.) kafar kwark=é
3NSG.ERG IMM (.) big   deceased=ERG.NSG
'They shared the fish in a good way. They looked after this swamp here thoughtfully ... the late elders.'

[tci20120922-21 DAK #37-38]

4.16 Similative *=thatha*

The similative case functions at the clause level, and its semantics are quite comparable to the English expressions 'like X' or 'similar to X'. In example (96)[8], the speaker shows me a plant called *ŋaziŋazi* 'Exocarpus sp' and comments that its fruits taste a bit like chewing gum and that it is similar to *ŋazi* 'coconut'.

(96) *ŋaziŋazi ... **pikethatha** yé ... **ŋazithatha** ... nafane yawi.*
ŋaziŋazi (.) pike=thatha   \yé/   (.) ŋazi=thatha   (.)
ŋaziŋazi (.) chewing.gum=SIMIL 3SG.MASC:SBJ:NPST:IPFV/be (.) coconut=SIMIL (.)

---

[8] The word *pike* [pɪke] comes from Wrigley's PK® chewing gum, which has the initials of Philip Knight Wrigley printed in big letters on the package.

nafane   yawi
3SG.POSS fruit
'Ŋaziŋazi ... its fruit is like chewing gum ... like a coconut.'

[tci20130907-02 RNA #308-309]

Hence, the element marked with =*thatha* is portrayed as being similar to another element. Often enough that second element is established from context and the respective noun phrase is omitted, as in example (97), where the speaker describes a man hanging upside down from the branch of a tree.

(97)   **bidrthatha** *zbo sumithgrm ... wämnen.*
       bidr=thatha   zbo   su\mi/thgrm   (.) wämne=n
       flying.fox=SIMIL PROX.ALL 3SG.MASC:SBJ:PST:DUR:STAT/be.hanging (.) tree=LOC
       'He was hanging like a flying fox ... on the tree.'   [tci20130901-04 RNA #48]

There are a few cases where the similative case is attached to recognitional pronoun *bänethatha* 'like that one' or to the manner demonstrative *nimathatha* 'like in this way', as in example (98), where the speaker comments that some plants along the way look as if they had been planted by someone.

(98)   **nimathatha** *erä ... kma thuworthrth.*
       nima=thatha   e\rä/   (.) kma thu\wor/thrth
       like.this=SIMIL 2|3PL:SBJ:NPST:IPFV/be (.) POT 2|3PL:SBJ>2|3PL:OBJ:RPST:IPFV/plant
       'These (plants) look a bit like ... as if they planted them.'   [tci20130907-02 JAA #281]

4.17 Further nominal morphology

This section describes a number of nominal enclitics or suffixes that do not mark a semantic role.

4.17.1 Emphatic =*wä*

The emphatic enclitic =*wä* is used to intensify its host. For example, attached to the temporal adjective *zafe* 'old', it means 'really long ago' (99). If it is attached to a possessive pronoun, it is often translated as 'my own' instead of 'my' (100). As Komnzo has no dedicated marker for comparatives, the emphatic enclitic can be used for this (101).

(99)   *nze kwa natrikwé bun ... no kzima ...* **zaföwä** *ni monme no kzi thwafiyokwrme.*
       nze   kwa na\trik/wé   bun   (.) no kzi=ma   (.)
       1SG.ERG FUT 1SG:SBJ>2SG:IO:NPST:IPFV/tell 2SG.DAT (.) rain barktray=CHAR (.)
       zafe=wä ni   mon=me no kzi   thwa\fiyok/wrme
       old=EMPH 1NSG how=INS rain barktray 1NSG:SBJ>2|3PL:OBJ:PST:DUR/make
       'I will tell you ... about the rain-making barktray ... a really long time ago ... how
       we were making the rain-making barktray.'   [tci20110810-01 MAB #1-3]

(100) **nzonewä** *zane zf erä!*

nzone=wä   zane   zf   e\rä/

1SG.POSS=EMPH DEM:PROX IMM 2|3PL:SBJ:NPST:IPFV/be

'These ones right here are my own!'   [tci20121001 ABB #129]

(101) **katakatanwä** *thfrä. nzenme kafar erä.*

kata-katan=wä   thf\rä/   nzenme   kafar

REDUP-small=EMPH 2|3PL:SBJ:RPST:IPFV/be 1NSG.POSS big

e\rä/

2|3PL:SBJ:NPST:IPFV/be

'Those (yams) were smaller. Ours are big.'   [tci20120805-01 ABB #403]

Some words seem to have lexicalised the emphatic enclitic, i.e. they do not occur without =*wä*. One example is *nzüthamöwä* 'time' (in the sense 'instance of something happening'). This word can take the =*nzo* 'only' enclitic, for example *näbi nzüthamöwänzo* 'only one time'. Elsewhere, the emphatic enclitic =*wä* and the exclusive enclitic =*nzo* may not co-occur. Other examples are *bramöwä* 'all' and *gadmöwä* 'good fortune'. Note that all three contain a /mö/ element. I suspect that this is a lexicalised version of the instrumental case marker =*me*. The vowel of the instrumental =*me* is regularly rounded in the presence of =*wä*. However, removing these putative lexicalised enclitics from these words results in three non-words: *nzütha, *bra and *gad.

The emphatic enclitic can attach to lexical items preceding the case marker. Example (102) is from a story about two characters who each have a ford in the river where they place their fishing baskets. In *edawäneme*, the enclitic has scope over the numeral *eda* 'two'. Thus, it is emphasizing the fact that there are two, which suggests a distributive reading: 'each one had a trapping place'. If the enclitic was attached after the case marker (*edaanemöwä*), the possession would be emphasised: 'two of their own'. Example (102) is the only instance in the corpus where the emphatic enclitic occurs between a lexical item and a case marker. Hence, it is a possible yet very rare construction.

(102) *krsi zn we fä thwarnm … **edawäneme**.*

kr-si   zn   we fä thwa\rn/m   (.) eda=wä=aneme

block-NMLZ place also DIST 2|3DU:IO:PST:DUR/be (.) two=EMPH=POSS.NSG

'They also had a fishing place there … each had one.'   [tci20110802 ABB #58-59]

4.17.2 Exclusive =*nzo*

The exclusive enclitic =*nzo* has been described in §3.5. It forms the nominal counterpart to the discourse particle *komnzo* 'only' (§3.4.2) from which the language gets its name. The exclusive enclitic can attach to all nominals including pronouns, thus it occurs with a high frequency in the corpus. It usually attaches to the last element of the noun phrase over which it has scope. It is glossed as ONLY in the examples.

In example (103) the exclusive clitic attaches to a noun phrase with an adverbial function, *frme* 'straight'. In (104), it is attached to an adjective.

(103) *zokwasi mane rera komnzo **frmenzo** wyaka nzudbo.*
zokwasi mane re\r/a   komnzo fr=me=nzo
speech which 3SG.FEM:SBJ:PST:IPFV/be only   line=INS=ONLY
w\yak/a   nzudbo
3SG.FEM:SBJ:PST:IPFV/walk 1SG.ALL
'As for the message, it just came straight to me.'   [tci20120814 ABB #50-51]

(104) *zasath "bä **namänzo** nrä?" "keke nzä nimäwä worä."*
za\s/ath   bä   namä=nzo n\rä/   keke nzä
2|3DU:SBJ:PST:PFV/ask 2.ABS good=ONLY 2SG:SBJ:NPST:IPFV/be NEG 1SG.ABS
nima=wä   wo\rä/
like.this=EMPH 1SG:SBJ:NPST:IPFV/be
'They asked each other: "Are you alright?" "No, I am like this."'
[tci20120827-03 KUT #159]

4.17.3 Etcetera *=sü*

The enclitic *=sü* only attaches to either the associative or the proprietive case marker. It is often translated as "and all" by my informants. Consider example (105), in which a speaker reports how he and some of his brothers transported a heavy sago stem with a couple of canoes. The *=sü* enclitic expresses that there are more items than just the sago. Therefore, I label *=sü* as etcetera marker, and I gloss it with ETC.

(105) *masenffä fof nzräs "kwa känthfe **bikaräsü** zbo!" ... watik **bikaräsü** ŋarafinzake.*
masen=f   fä   fof nzrä\s/   kwa
masen=ERG.SG DIST EMPH 2|3SG:SBJ>1PL:OBJ:IRR:PFV/call FUT
kän\thf/e   bi=karä=sü   zbo   (.) watik bi=karä=sü
2PL:SBJ:IMP:PFV:VENT/walk sago=PROP=ETC PROX.ALL (.) then   sago=PROP=ETC
ŋa\rafi/nzake
1PL:SBJ:PST:IPFV/paddle
'Masen called out to us: "Come over here with the sago and all!" ... Then, we paddled with the sago and everything.'   [tci20120929-02 SIK #41-42]

Example (106) shows the etcetera enclitic attached to the associative case in an inclusory construction. The speaker describes how his friends slept in a camp where his father and other relatives were staying.

(106) *ni **ŋafyäsü** fä fof nrugra.*
ni   ŋafe=ä=sü   fä   fof n\rugr/a
1NSG father=ASSOC.PL=ETC DIST EMPH 1PL:SBJ:PST:IPFV/sleep
'We slept there with father and all the others.'   [tci20110810-02 MAB #11]

Example (107) is taken from an origin myth in which two brothers are fighting with a creature. One of them warns his brother that he is going to shoot the creature now and he should be prepared. Hence, the second clause literally translates as "you must be with thoughts and all".

(107) *watik ngth biruthé! famkaräsü gnräré!*
watik ngth   b=y\ru/thé
then   younger sibling MED=1SG:SBJ>3SG.MASC:OBJ:NPST:IPFV/shoot
fam=karä=sü   gn\rä/ré
thought=PROP=ETC 2SG:SBJ:IMP:IPFV/be
"Okay brother, I will shoot him now. You have to think and be prepared!"
[tci20131013-01 ABB #108-109]

4.17.4 Distributive *-kak*

I analyse the distributive marker *-kak* as a suffix rather than an enclitic because it does not operate on the level of the phrase. It can only be suffixed to numerals and some quantifiers. Its meaning can be translated into English with 'each' or 'individually'. The distributive is often followed by the instrumental, as in (108). In this example, the speaker had lost his dogs during hunting. The distributive highlights that the dogs came back individually.

(108) *ŋatha katakatan thunthorakwrm näbikakme.*
ŋatha kata-katan   thun\thorak/wrm   näbi-kak=me
dog   REDUP-small 2|3PL:SBJ:PST:DUR:VENT/arrive one-DISTR=INS
'The small ones were arriving one by one.'   [tci20111119-03 ABB #69]

In example (109), a woman has finished presenting to me what she has caught during the day. This includes different fish, a goanna and a turtle. She concludes with the words "There is plenty of meat". This could be translated as *faso tüfr erä* without the distributive. The distributive in (109) expresses that she has caught different kinds of meat.

(109) *watik, faso tüfrkak erä.*
watik faso tüfr-kak   e\rä/
then   meat plenty-DISTR 2|3PL:SBJ:NPST:IPFV/be
'Well, there is plenty of different meat.'   [tci20120821-01 LNA #68]

In example (110), the speaker tells me about different types of bows. He concludes by pointing out that different people like different types.

(110) *zawe ffrükakmenzo erä*
zawe f-frü-kak=me=nzo   e\rä/
talent REDUP-alone-DISTR=INS=ONLY 2|3PL:SBJ:NPST:IPFV/be
'People have different preferences.' (lit. 'There are different individual talents.')
[tci20120922-23 MAA #104]

4.17.5 Diminuitive *fäth*

I take the diminuitive *fäth* 'small one' as an example to describe a small group of lexemes which behave similar to the enclitics described above. However, I do not analyse them as enclitics but rather as lexemes on the verge of becoming grammaticalised. The two main reasons are: (i) they often occur by themselves without a host, and (ii) they have a more lexical meaning. Out of the four lexemes, two have to do with location: *zn* and *faf*, both mean 'place', and two have to do with smallness or compactness: *fäth* 'small one' (glossed as DIM) and *fur* 'bundle'.

Example (111) illustrates that *fäth* can occur as a free lexeme. However, *fäth* frequently occurs after a noun, as in (112) and (113). We could analyse *fäth* in (112) either as a compound of two nouns ('story' + 'small one'), or as a diminuitive enclitic which has scope over a preceding host. The latter analysis is supported by the fact that the two elements form an intonational unit.

(111) *nzone ŋafe fthé fof **katan fäth** sfrärm.*
       nzone   ŋafe   fthé   fof   katan fäth   sf\rä/rm
       1SG.POSS father when EMPH small DIM 3SG.MASC:SBJ:PST:DUR/be
       'My father was a small boy at that time.'   [tci20111107-01 MAK #34]

(112) ***trikasi fäth** fobo fof zwaythik fof.*
       trik-si   fäth fobo   fof   zwa\ythik/   fof
       tell-NMLZ DIM DIST.ALL EMPH 3SG.FEM:SBJ:RPST:IPFV/come.to.end EMPH
       'There, the small story comes to an end.'   [tci20111119-03 ABB #197]

If there is a case marker present, it will attach to *fäth* (113); a fact which supports both analyses.

(113) ***emoth fäthnm** thrätrif.*
       emoth fäth=nm   thrä\trif/
       girl DIM=DAT.NSG 2|3SG:SBJ>2|3PL:IO:RPST:PFV/tell
       'He told the small girls.'   [tci20120901-01 MAK #181]

On the basis of the arguments above, I decide to treat *fäth* as an independent lexeme. The same applies to *zn*, *faf* (both 'place') and *fur* ('bundle'). I analyse them as lexemes which are on the verge of becoming grammaticalised. Note that only for *fäth* I employ the gloss DIM instead of a more lexical one ('small one').

4.18 A few historical notes

The case markers presented in this chapter show some semantic and formal overlaps which invite speculations as to their emergence. I want to lay out some hypotheses here. My main point is that the dative and the possessive are historically related, and that the original form played some role in marking animacy.

In Table 4.5, we can see a subset of the personal pronouns for different cases and the respective case enclitics for animate referents. Note that only the first and second person are shown. The third person forms are not relevant for the argument advanced here. For reasons of comparison, the table includes the possessive prefixes, even though they are not case markers.

Table 4.5: Case marking with animate referents

| | personal pronouns | | | | case enclitics | |
	1SG	1NSG	2SG	2NSG	SG	NSG
CHAR	*nzonema*	*nzenmema*	*bonema*	*benmema*	*=anema*	*=anemema*
POSS	*nzone*	*nzenme*	*bone*	*benme*	*=ane*	*=aneme*
POSS-	*nzu-*	*nze-*	*bu-*	*be-*	n/a	n/a
DAT	*nzun*	*nzenm*	*bun*	*benm*	*=n*	*=nm*
LOC	*nzudben*	*nzedben*	*budben*	*bedben*	*=dben*	*=(n)medben*
ALL	*nzudbo*	*nzedbo*	*budbo*	*bedbo*	*=dbo*	*=(n)medbo*
ABL	*nzudba*	*nzedba*	*budba*	*bedba*	*=dba*	*=(n)medba*

One observation from the table is that the characteristic pronouns are built from the possessive pronouns. For example, the first singular possessive *nzone* 'my' is used to express the meaning 'because of me' by simply attaching the characteristic case marker *=ma*. In fact, the pattern is so transparent that instead of analysing a form like *nzonema* as 1SG.CHAR an alternative analysis would be to analyse it in a more compositional way: *nzone=ma* 1SG.POSS=CHAR. This also holds true for nouns. Note that the use of the possessive is only required for animate referents. For example, *no=ma* 'because of the rain' can do without the possessive, but *kabe=ma* 'because of the man' is ungrammatical, and it has to be *kabe=ane=ma* (man=POSS.SG=CHAR). Hence, the possessive functions as a marker of animacy. I want to argue that in the other case formatives, we find frozen morphology that points to a similar strategy.

A second observation from the table lies in the formal similarity of the possessive and the dative case enclitics. The dative formatives resemble the possessive ones, but they lack the vowels: *=ane* (POSS) vs. *=n* (DAT), and *=aneme* (POSS.NSG) vs. *=nm* (DAT.NSG). Furthermore, the table shows that all case enclitics share an element marking non-singular number. This is /m/ for the dative and /me/ for all other cases. Again, we may analyse this element as a separate morpheme, for example *=ane=me* (=POSS=NSG) and *=n=m* (=DAT=NSG). In the remainder of this section, I want to argue for three points: (i) that the possessive and the dative have developed from the same source, (ii) that the function of that source was to mark animacy, and (iii) that the source itself was segmentable into one morpheme marking animacy (*=n* or *=ane*) and a second morpheme marking non-singular number (*=m* or *=me*).

The main point of evidence comes from a variant of the non-singular formatives of the spatial cases. For example, the locative can be *=medben*, but there is a variant *=nmedben*. The latter includes an /n/ which is also found in the possessive and the dative enclitics. Note that for the possessive and the dative, /n/ is found in the singular and the non-singular formatives. For the non-singular formatives of the three spatial cases, I want to propose that the /n/-variant is the older one. Note that the /n/ element is also present in the singular formatives of the three spatial cases, but it is difficult to recognize it as a segment, because all three case enclitics begin with a prenasalised alveolar plosive [ⁿd]. Therefore, I want to suggest a more transparent analysis in Table 4.6.

Table 4.6: Revised analysis of case markers for animate referents

	=ANIM=case	=ANIM=NSG=case
POSS	=ane	=ane=me
DAT	=n	=n=m
LOC	=n=dben	(=n)=me=dben
ALL	=n=dbo	(=n)=me=dbo
ABL	=n=dba	(=n)=me=dba

The revised analysis in Table 4.6 suggests that the spatial case enclitics attached to an /n/ formative which was a marker of animacy. Moreover, there is the /me/ formative for marking non-singular number.

This analysis rests on the assumption that the dative and the possessive are historically related. There are four pieces of evidence to support this claim. First, the enclitics of the two cases are similar, if we assume that the dative formatives once had vowels: *=ane > =n* and *=aneme > =nm*. Secondly, the close possessive prefixes in Table 4.5 show that the vowel in the singular prefixes groups them with the dative, not with the possessive. The first person close possessive prefix is *nzu-* like the first person dative pronoun *nzun*, whereas the first person possessive pronoun is *nzone*. Thirdly, the argumentation in the preceding paragraph shows that the element *=nme*, which precedes the spatial case markers, is historically related to both the possessive and the dative. The fourth piece of evidence comes from a comparison with Ngkolmpu, a related Tonda language spoken in Indonesia. In Ngkolmpu, the dative marks the possessor role in its adnominal function (Carroll 2017).

This leaves us wondering about the pTonda or pYam system and the path of grammaticalisation in Komnzo. The scenario sketched out above suggests that the original system was more like Ngkolmpu, where one case marker serves both functions, dative and possessive. Alternatively, the predecessor could have had a much more general function. I have argued above that this function was to mark animacy. Although speculative at present, I want to point out that a possible source of the animacy marker could be the anaphoric demonstrative *ane*, which can occur in postposed position. For the moment, we can only speculate on the path of grammaticalisation. More data from the other Yam languages is needed to settle this question.

5 Verb morphology

5.1 Introduction

This chapter describes the verbal morphology of Komnzo, which is by far the most complex subsystem in the language, and reaches a scale of complexity which is comparable to polysynthetic languages.[1] Morphological complexity of the Komnzo verb arises not only from the number of affixes which the verb may host, but also from the way these combine to encode grammatical categories (§5.2). In its simplest form a verb exists as an infinitive, which is the stem plus a nominaliser suffix. At their most complex, verbs may host a large number of affixes and clitics. Table 5.1 gives an overview of the verb template, the inflectional categories and the formatives to be discussed in this chapter.

The central feature that reverberates throughout Komnzo verb morphology is its cumulative and distributed combinatorics. The particular values of most grammatical categories are only arrived at after unifying information from several morphological slots within the verb structure. This fact has shaped my descriptive approach which bounces back and forth between a functional and a formal perspective. I address alignment and valency in §5.4, person, gender and number in §5.5, and deixis and directionality in §5.6. At the same time, the functional perspective is interspersed with the description of structural phenomena like the two stem types in §5.3 or the suffixing subsystem in §5.5.1.1. Tense, aspect and mood will be described in Chapter 6. I describe the formatives and their possible combinations in §6.2, the contribution of TAM particles in §6.3, and the semantic nuances of the TAM categories in §6.4. In order to avoid too much repetition, related topics are linked by cross-references.

5.2 Morphological complexity

The relationship between the value of a grammatical category and its exponents exhibits varying degrees of complexity in Komnzo verbs. At its simplest, we find a one-to-one mapping between function and form, which exists for the directional affixes. For the most part, however, Komnzo verbs are characterised by complexity of exponence of the type one-to-many and many-to-many. Concerning the former, we find what Matthews (1974: 147-149) calls "cumulative exponence", whereby one exponent expresses several grammatical categories, as well as "extended exponence", whereby several exponents

---

[1]Most definitions of polysynthesis stress two main criteria: noun incorporation and the expression of syntactic relations by pronominal affixes (Baker 1996: 16; Evans & Sasse 2002: 2; and Mithun 2009). Komnzo lacks noun incorporation, but cross-references up to two participants with pronominal affixes. Typically, a verb consists of 3 up to 9 morphs.

Table 5.1: Templatic representation of verb inflection

	clitic	prefix slots			stem	suffix slots				
	-4	-3	-2	-1	√	1	2	3	4	5
valency			VC: *a-*							
person		undergoer: 1, 2, 3 or M								actor: 1, 2|3 or ∅
gender		undergoer: FEM, MASC								
number		undergoer: SG, NSG	DU: ∅- ND: *a-*				DU: *-n* ND: *-nzr, -wr, -r*			actor: SG, NSG
deixis & direction	PROX: *z=* MED: *b=* DIST: *f=*			VENT: *n-*					AND: *-o*	
TAM	APPR: *m=* IMN: *n=*	prefix: α, β, β1, β2, γ	IRR: *ra-*		stem type: EXT, RS	STAT: *-thgr*		PST: *-a* DUR: *-m*		IMP: actor suffixes

express one grammatical category. Note that the latter has also been called "multiple exponence" in the literature (Caballero & Harris 2012: 163). For example, the Komnzo verb prefixes are portmanteau realisations of the categories person, gender, number, tense and aspect. Conversely, a category like tense is encoded in three different slots on the verb. These slots can be independently manipulated, which results in a many-to-many mapping. Complex exponence of this type is a feature found in all Yam languages.

Let us take one inflected verb form to illustrate these types of exponence. Example (1) gives the inflected verb form *yfathwroth* 'they hold him away'.[2]

(1) *yfathwroth*
   y\fath/wroth
   2|3PL:SBJ>3SG.MASC:OBJ:NPST:IPFV:AND/hold
   'They hold him away.'

Here we find a one-to-one mapping between the directional value (andative) and the suffix *-o*. This is expressed in Figure 5.1 where the verb form has been segmented into morphs. A line indicates the exponence relationship between the value (AND) and the formative (*-o*).

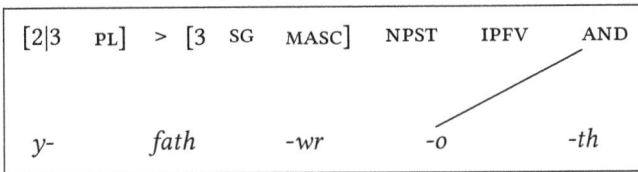

Figure 5.1: One-to-one mapping for the directional

Cumulative exponence is found in the verb prefix *y-* which fuses information on person (3), number (SG), and gender (MASC) of the object argument. In addition, *y-* contains information on tense (NPST) and aspect (IPFV). This is schematised in Figure 5.2.

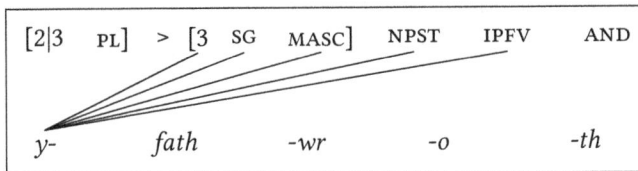

Figure 5.2: Cumulative exponence of person, number, gender, tense and aspect

Note that the prefix *y-* is necessary, but not sufficient, to establish the values for some of these categories. For example, the aspectual value of the verb (IPFV) is not expressed

---

[2]This verb form can have a stative as well as a dynamic reading: someone is holding a baby moving it away from the deictic centre (dynamic), or someone holds the baby in such a way that the toddler is facing away from the deictic centre (stative).

solely by *y-*. This is what Matthews calls "extended exponence" (1974: 147-149) and Caballero & Harris refer to as "multiple exponence" (2012: 163). It is essentially the mirror image of Figure 5.2. Thus, Figure 5.3 shows that aspect is distributed over three exponents in *yfathwroth*.

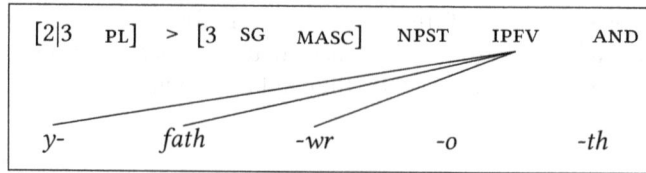

Figure 5.3: Extended exponence of aspect

A change in any one of the three slots above will cause a change in the TAM value. For example, the prefix *y-* can be replaced by *su-* to form a recent past imperfective (*sufath-wroth*) or a suffix *-m* can be added after *-wr* to form a recent past durative (*yfathwrmoth*). If both of these changes are made at the same time, we get a past durative (*sufathwrmoth*). It follows that we are not dealing with a circumfix where separated formatives always occur together, but rather with a circumfixal paradigm where the formatives in the different slots are quite independent. Although there are some combinatorial restrictions, it would be a distortion to describe this as a circumfix. The essence of the system is that only by unifying the information from each slot are we in a position to calculate the correct value of a given grammatical category.

Thus, the overall complexity of Komnzo verbs results from the co-ocurrence of different types of exponence relationships. Figure 5.4 captures all the dependencies between the values of a grammatical category and the morphs that make up *yfathwroth*. Quite literally, we find a web of tightly interwoven dependencies.[3]

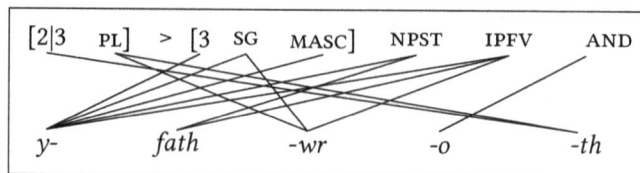

Figure 5.4: Reciprocal conditioning

Anderson uses the term "reciprocal conditioning" (1992: 55) for this phenomenon, whereby exponents depend on several grammatical categories while being underspec-

---

[3]In fact, the presence of the andative *-o* has the effect that the person value of the actor argument in the suffix is neutralised, i.e. the suffix *-th* only encodes non-singular number. Without a personal pronoun, the verb can mean 'we|you(PL)|they hold him away'. I have simplified this for the purpose of demonstration here. See §5.5.1.1 for neutralisations in the suffix subsystem.

ified for a single grammatical category.[4] I adopt the term "distributed exponence" from Caballero & Harris (2012: 170), who point out that it may be related to multiple/extended exponence. Although it is excluded from their survey, Caballero & Harris mention distributed exponence in the theoretical discussion by explaining some aspects of Georgian verb morphology (Gurevich 2006). Baerman (2012) describes a phenomenon that could also be called distributed exponence for Nuer, a Western Nilotic language. The complexity of marking case and number in Nuer builds on suffixes and stem alternations, which are independently manipulated and give rise to inflectional classes. Baerman stresses the noniconicity of the system "in that these operations characterise simply a contrast of meaning, without being linked to any particular meaning" (2012: 490). Similarly, Komnzo verb morphology must be understood as a system where morphs contribute to a grammatical category, but a specific value of a given grammatical category requires information from several slots. Carroll provides the most detailed study of distributed exponence in his grammar on Ngkolmpu (2017), a related Tonda language.

There are practical consequences for the description of such a system. I have used a glossing style which follows the Word-and-Paradigm model (Matthews 1974: 67) throughout this grammar to give the reader effortless access to the morpho-syntactic features of an inflected verb form. Since this chapter addresses verbal morphology, I will employ a double glossing and a verb like *yfathwroth* will be glossed as in (2). The first line gives a maximally segmented gloss in the Item-and-Arrangement style, while the second line in smaller print gives a unified gloss in the Word-and-Paradigm style.[5]

(2)   *yfathwroth*
      y-fath-wr-o-th
      3SG.MASC.*α*-hold.EXT-ND-AND-2|3NSG
      2|3PL:SBJ>3SG.MASC:OBJ:NPST:IPFV:AND/hold
      'They hold him away.'

The Item-and-Arrangement style provides more transparency in the morphological structure, which is the aim of this chapter. However, widespread underspecification means that the gain in structural transparency comes at the cost of somewhat opaque glossing labels. For example, in (2) we find established labels like SG (singular) and NSG (non-singular) to encode number, but we also need to recruit ND (non-dual). As for tense and aspect, we have to introduce even more abstract labels like *α* (alpha) in the prefixes or EXT (extended) with the verb stem. These will be explained in the following sections. A further drawback of the Item-and-Arrangement style is that some of the grammatical values, like non-past (NPST) or imperfective (IPFV) as well as subject (SBJ), object (OBJ) and indirect object (IO), cannot be shown on the gloss line because they can be inferred only after integrating several exponents.

---

[4]Morpheme underspecifiation does not stop at the word boundary in Komnzo. For example, future tense or event completion are expressed periphrastically with the particles *kwa* and *z*, respectively.

[5]Elsewhere in the grammar the verb stem is shown by slanted lines \.../ on the segmentation line: y\fath/wroth.

5.3 Stem types

Komnzo verbal stems have two forms: an "extended stem" (EXT) and a "restricted stem" (RS). This opposition is sensitive to aspect without encoding a specific aspectual category. For now it is sufficient to state that the labels refer to the temporal structure of the event, i.e. "extended in time" and "restricted in time". The two stems differ (i) in their form, (ii) in the order of slots with respect to dual marking and (iii) in their combinatorial possibilities with the prefix series. I describe each point below.

5.3.1 The formal relationship of extended and restricted stems

Komnzo has pairs of verb stems whose relationship is often unpredictable from any formal or semantic criteria. Nevertheless, there is a cline of similarity in form between the two stems which allows us to divide the verbal lexicon into seven classes (Table 5.2). The verb lexemes listed in the table, as well as the following numbers and percentages refer to a sample 322 verbs, which was compiled in 2016.[6] For around thirty percent, there is a rule-based relation between the shapes of the two stems. At the other end of the spectrum, we find suppletive pairs of stems in five percent of the verbal lexicon. For more than two thirds of the lexicon, the derivation of one stem from the other is unpredictable.

In class I, which makes up 13% of verbs, the two stems are identical (EXT=RS). Class II verbs (16%) derive their extended stems from the restricted stem with a suffix (EXT=RS-*ak*). Thus class I and class II make up the portion of the verb lexicon which has a rule-based relationship between the two stems. However, only a few generalisations can be made about the scope of the rule, i.e. given a particular lexeme, one cannot decide straightforwardly which class it belongs to. One observation is that most verbs in class I end in /n/. However, this is not true of all verbs in this class, and verbs ending in /n/ are found in other classes.

The majority of verbs involve unpredictable changes at the right edge of the stem. In class III, which makes up 25%, a consonant is added to the extended stem in order to form the restricted stem (RS=EXT-C). The stem pairs of class IV verbs (30%) involve final consonant mutation. In classes III and IV, the affected consonants are not conditioned by the phonological environment. Class V verbs (8%) are irregular, i.e. the difference involves more than the last consonant. The stems of class VI (5%) are fully suppletive. Finally, the handful of verbs in class VII are defective, and have only one of the two stems.

We can make a few observations from Table 5.2. First, we find a cline of similarity which ranges from identity of the two stems to suppletive pairs, with the bulk of verbs between the two extremes. Classes II–V all have in common that the difference in form occurs at the right edge of stem. Secondly, the classes and processes (consonant mutation, consonant addition, suffixation of -*ak*) are neither phonologically conditioned, nor can we detect a semantic basis for them. Thirdly, the system shows little productivity, which

---

[6]Since then, the total number of verbs in the dictionary has not increased much. At the present stage, around 330 verb lexemes have been documented.

Table 5.2: The formal relationship between EXT and RS stem

class	rule	EXT	RS	gloss	count
i	EXT=RS	mar- zik- rikn- rmän- matukn-		see turn off destroy close shake	42
ii	EXT⇐RS-ak	rfitfak- morak- bthak- ritak- msak-	rfitf- mor- bth- rit- ms-	answer lean finish cross sit	53
iii	EXT-C⇒RS	gar- fsi- tri- rni- thari-	garf- fsir- trinz- rnith- tharif-	break count scratch smile dig	81
iv	mutation	thwek- mthek- moneg- trakumg- bnaz-	thweth- mthef- mones- trakumth- bnaf-	be glad lift up wait smash wake up	96
v	irregular	rsör- thorak- myukn- rirkn- tur-	rsöfäth- thothm- myuf- rirkfth- turam-	descend search twist avoid kiss	26
vi	suppletive	re- ru- fn- na- zä- si-	zigrthm- mg- kwr- znob- thor- füs-	look around shoot, spear hit, kill drink carry cook	16
vii	RS only	-	-kuk[a]	stand	1
	EXT only	rug- rmug-	- -	sleep envy	7
TOTAL					322

[a]This verb has a second stem -kogr, which I analyse as a positional stem (§5.4.4.2).

I take as evidence for lexicalisation. In Table 5.2, it is only class II for which a regular process can be formulated: the suffixation of *-ak*. Finally, we find that for almost all verbs, both stems are attested. As a result, virtually all verbs can be inflected for the entire range of TAM categories, which leaves little role to play for lexical aspect (or Aktionsart) in Komnzo.

I offer a historical explanation in §5.3.4 as to how the two stems have evolved in Komnzo and in the Tonda subgroup more generally.

5.3.2 Dual marking with extended and restricted stems

The most salient difference between the two stems is the location of the dual marker, which follows the extended stem but precedes the restricted stem. I describe number marking in detail in §5.5.3. In the examples (3a-3c) and (4a-4c), I contrast the imperfective and perfective imperatives of 'hit'. The former often has a continuative interpretation ('keep on x-ing!') while the latter points to inception ('start doing x!'). In (3) and (4), all grammatical categories are held constant, and only the actor argument is cycled through the three number values; singular, dual and plural. In (3a-3c), dual is shown by a suffix (*-n*), which contrasts with a non-dual (*-z*). In (4a-4c), dual is expressed by a zero which contrasts with a non-dual prefix (*a-*).

(3)   a.   *be*   *fi*   *s-fn-z-é*
           2SG.ERG 3.ABS 3SG.MASC.β-hit.EXT-ND-2SG.IMP
                       2SG:SBJ>3SG.MASC:OBJ:IMP:IPFV/hit
           'Keep hitting him!'

     b.   *bné*   *fi*   *s-fn-n-e*
           2NSG.ERG 3.ABS 3SG.MASC.β-hit.EXT-DU-2NSG.IMP
                       2DU:SBJ>3SG.MASC:OBJ:IMP:IPFV/hit
           'Keep hitting him!'

     c.   *bné*   *fi*   *s-fn-z-e*
           2NSG.ERG 3.ABS 3SG.MASC.β-hit.EXT-ND-2NSG.IMP
                       2PL:SBJ>3SG.MASC:OBJ:IMP:IPFV/hit
           'Keep hitting him!'

(4)   a.   *be*   *fi*   *s-a-kwr-∅*
           2SG.ERG 3.ABS 3SG.MASC.β-ND-hit.RS-2SG.IMP
                       2SG:SBJ>3SG.MASC:OBJ:IMP:PFV/hit
           'Hit him!'

     b.   *bné*   *fi*   *s-∅-kwr-e*
           2NSG.ERG 3.ABS 3SG.MASC.β-DU-hit.RS-2NSG.IMP
                       2DU:SBJ>3SG.MASC:OBJ:IMP:PFV/hit
           'Hit him!'

     c.   *bné*   *fi*   *s-a-kwr-e*
           2NSG.ERG 3.ABS 3SG.MASC.β-ND-hit.RS-2NSG.IMP
                       2PL:SBJ>3SG.MASC:OBJ:IMP:PFV/hit
           'Hit him!'

The post-stem non-dual marker, *-z* in (3), has a number of phonologically conditioned allomorphs (§5.5.3.3). The dual marker is always *-n*. In terms of segmentation, the post-stem slot is simple to recognise. This is not the case with the pre-stem duality marker which is zero for dual and *a-* for non-dual in (4). For purposes of illustration, I have selected the imperatives here because the segmentation is clearest. In other parts of the paradigm, segmentation is messier because the dual marker fuses with the valency change prefix resulting in an ablaut contrast: *a-* for dual and *ä-* for non-dual (§5.5.3.4). From a historical perspective, this structural split between a pre-stem and a post-stem slot is a way of preserving dual marking after the original suffix had fused with the stem (§5.3.4).

5.3.3 The combinatorics of extended and restricted stems

Extended and restricted stems taken alone are underspecified for a particular TAM value and information from other morphological sites is required. With respect to the five prefix series α, β, β_1, β_2, γ (§5.5.1.1), the two stems differ in their combinatorial possibilities. For example, the α prefixes combine with the extended stem and the γ prefixes combine with the restricted stem, but not vice versa. The α series is recruited to form non-past, immediate past, recent past or past in imperfective or durative aspect depending on suffixal material. The γ series is employed for recent past or past, both perfective. The β prefixes combine with both stems to form imperatives and irrealis with imperfective and perfective aspect. The β_1 and β_2 prefixes combine with the extended stem (the latter exclusively so) to form recent past and past in imperfective or durative aspect, again depending on suffixal material. The β_1 prefixes combine with the restricted stem to form an iterative. The details of the five prefix series as well as the aspectual distinctions will be addressed in §6.2. For present purposes, it is sufficient to stress that there are some limitations on the combinatorial possibilities for extended and restricted stems.

5.3.4 A comparative note on multiple stems

Verb stem pairs which are sensitive to aspect are known from other Papuan languages, for example Mian (Fedden 2011: 245). In the Southern New Guinea region, Marind shows striking architectural similarities to the Komnzo system. Drabbe reports on 4 verb classes in Marind (1955: 31). The first two classes, which make up the main distinction, are labelled "momentaan" versus "duratief." Members of a third class can be both, and only the affixes signal the aspectual value of an inflected verb form. The fourth class is characterised as "momentaan", but it can be turned into "duratief" by suffixing *-a(t)*. The overall design of the Marind system looks similar once we equate "duratief" with extended and "momentaan" with restricted. Drabbe's third class in Marind bears resemblance to the group of Komnzo verbs where only one form is attested (class I in Table 5.2). The fourth class is very close to those stem pairs in Komnzo which add the suffix *-ak* to the restricted stem in order to form the extended stem (class II in Table 5.2). Moreover, the two suffixes, *-a(t)* in Marind and *-ak* in Komnzo, are formally similar. However, with the exception of Drabbe's groups three and four, the Marind system differs in that most verbs fall into either "momentaan" or "duratief." As we have seen above, almost all verbs in Komnzo have both stems.

Within the Yam family, multiple verb stems are found in the Nambu as well as the Tonda subgroup. However, the system as laid out here seems to be more developed in the Tonda languages. Pairs of verb stems are attested in Arammba, where Boevé & Boevé (2003) label them "common root" and "limited action root." In my own fieldwork, I found stem pairs in Anta, Wára, Wèré, Kámá, Kánchá, Blafe, Ránmo and Wartha Thuntai. As for Ngkolmpu[7], there are up to three stems for some verbs and these are sensitive to aspect as well as verbal number (Carroll 2017). More descriptive work is needed to understand how the two stems are employed in the respective TAM systems of these languages.

I will offer a first tentative historical explanation based on the comparison of duality/TAM marking and multiple stems within the Yam family. In the Nambu subgroup, aspect-sensitive stems are only a marginal phenomenon. However, part of the verb inflection is a suffix which combines aspectual information with dual marking. For example, in Nen (Evans 2015a) and Nama (Siegel 2014) a thematic suffix follows the verb stem encoding TAM plus dual versus non-dual. In Komnzo, the suffix following the stem encodes only duality, but the presence versus absence of this suffix slot is determined by the stem type. Thus, it is involved in marking aspect (§5.3.2).

I have shown above that the differences in form between the two stem types are located at the right edge. It is therefore a likely scenario that multiple stems have emerged through a process of demorphologisation (Hopper 1990: 154), i.e. through a fusion of suffixal material with the stem. Until more descriptive material is available, we are left to speculate on the nature of the original system. Logically, there are at least two possibilities: (i) the original suffix followed the Nambu pattern encoding TAM and duality simultaneously or (ii) there were separate suffixes for each category. Since both the occurrence of multiple stems as well as cognate forms are attested in all varieties of the Tonda languages, demorphologisation would constitute an innovation, which supports Tonda as a subgroup of the Yam family. This is of some importance, because other systematic differences between Nambu and Tonda, like word-initial velar nasals[8] or gender marking on verbs, can be explained by assuming the loss of a particular feature in Nambu rather than assuming an innovation in Tonda.

The historical scenario advanced above gave rise to different inflectional patterns within the Tonda subgroup. Languages further to the west, including Blafe, Ránmo, Wartha Thuntai and to some extent Kánchá, have lost dual marking except in some high frequency verbs like the copula. Other varieties, like Wára, Anta and Komnzo, have kept post-stem dual marking for one stem type, but requisitioned a different slot in the template for the other stem type. This would explain why, in terms of morphological segmentation, the pre-stem dual marking with restricted stems is much messier than post-stem dual marking with extended stems (compare §5.3.2 and §5.5.3.4). We could say that in a historical process, dual marking has "hijacked" a slot which was hitherto solely em-

---

[7]Ngkolmpu, as well as Bädi, Smerky and Sota, were classified as varieties of Kanum in the past.

[8]The Nambu language Dre, which is spoken close to other Tonda languages, has preserved initial velar nasals.

ployed for marking valency. A third pattern is attested in Wèrè, where dual marking is consistently post-stem for both stem types. However, irregularities involving a vowel change in the prefixes for some parts of the paradigm show that the Wèrè pattern is a case of regularisation of the Komnzo system rather than an independent development.

The scenario developed here has to be treated with some caution, as there are exceptions to the generalisations made above. For example, Nen has multiple stems for a few verbs like √*waram* versus √*warama* 'give', encoding imperfective and perfective aspect respectively (Evans forthcoming). Another exception is the Nambu language Nä, which has pre-stem dual marking for some middle verbs. Much more comparative work needs to be done to fully account for the emergence of multiple verb stems in these languages.

5.4 Alignment and verb templates

5.4.1 Grammatical relations

This section describes the argument structure in Komnzo. The term is understood as "the configuration of arguments that are governed by a particular lexical item" (Haspelmath & Müller-Bardey 2004: 1130). For the purpose of defining argument structure, we need to take into account particular constructions (Bickel 2011: 433). In Komnzo, these are case and agreement (i.e. verb indexing). There are no other constructions restricted to a set of arguments (e.g. control, relativisation, coordination, nominalisation of verbs).

First, I identify generalised semantic roles (GSRs) for each verb form. Following Bickel (2011), these roles are labelled as follows: A is the most agent-like argument and P is the most patient-like argument of a transitive verb, S is the sole argument of an intransitive verb. For ditransitive verbs, T is the most theme-like argument and R the most recipient-like argument.

In the following, I will outline the two parameters of argument structure in Komnzo. In (5a-5c), I show the basic structure for one-argument and two-argument predicates in a reduced glossing style. A is assigned ergative case, while S and P are assigned absolutive case. Example (5c) shows that A is indexed in the suffix and P is indexed in the prefix. S has to be split into S_P, which is indexed in the prefix (5a), and S_A, which is indexed in the suffix (5b). The underlying factor is the dynamicity of the predicate (§5.4.4).

(5) a. *fi   y-kogr*
       3(ABS) 3SG.MASC-stand
       'He stands.'

     b. *fi   ŋamränzr-th*
       3(ABS) stroll-3PL
       'They stroll around.'

     c. *nafa   fi   y-fnzr-th*
       3PL.ERG 3(ABS) 3SG.MASC-hit-3PL
       'They hit him.'

Examples (6a-6c) show the argument structure for three-argument predicates. Note that I discuss why there are some problems in describing ditransitives in §5.4.6. For case assignment, the examples show that P and T are marked by the absolutive case and R by the dative case. The R is always indexed in the prefix, not P nor T. Furthermore, the verb form is inflected with the *a-* prefix, which I label vc for valency change.

(6) a. *nafa   giri   nafan   y-a-rithr-th*
            3PL.ERG knife(ABS) 3SG.DAT 3SG.MASC-VC-give-3PL
            'They give him the knife.'

      b. *nafa   bone   zokwasi   nzun   w-a-rbänzr-th*
            3PL.ERG 2SG.POSS speech(ABS) 1SG.DAT 1SG-VC-explain-3PL
            'They explain your message to me.'

      c. *nafa   srak   nafan   y-a-brigwr-th*
            3PL.ERG boy(ABS) 3SG.DAT 3SG.MASC-VC-return-3PL
            'They return the boy for/to him.'

From the types of argument structure shown above, we can define the following grammatical relations in Komnzo:

1. The subject relation is characterised by either ergative or absolutive case assignment.

   a) If the noun phrase is in the ergative, it will always be indexed in the suffix.

   b) If the noun phrase is in the absolutive, it may be indexed in the suffix or the prefix. It is considered to be a subject, iff the clause contains no ergative-marked noun phrase.

2. The object relation is characterised by absolutive case assignment and indexation in the prefix. This only applies in the presence of another ergative noun phrase which is indexed in the suffix.

3. The indirect object relation is characterised by dative (or possessive) case assignment and indexation in the prefix. Additionally, the verb form receives the valency change prefix *a-*.

Similar to other grammatical categories, for example TAM and number, grammatical relations are constructed by unifying information from different sites. These are the person marking affixes and the diathetic prefix, but also the case assignment on the respective noun phrases. I describe the person marking affixes on the verb as the actor suffix and the undergoer prefix.[9] However, in the unified gloss, which is employed throughout this grammar, I use SBJ (subject), OBJ (object) and IO (indirect object). A reviewer suggested to use A (actor) und U (undergoer) and avoid using categories like subject and object. I agree that there is no strong evidence for a subject category in Komnzo. Nevertheless, I employ the terms subject, object and indirect object as metalinguistic labels

---

[9] I use a semantic definition of the term "undergoer": the argument which is affected by the event.

that I find useful in communicating with other linguists. I do not claim that these play an overly important role in the grammar of Komnzo. In addition, there are practical reasons for using SBJ (subject), OBJ (object) and IO (indirect object) in the gloss line. If I employ A (actor) und U (undergoer), it would be impossible to show the distinction between an object and an indirect object in the unified gloss line.

5.4.2 Morphological templates

This section describes the structure of verbs by looking at the slots involved in the indexation of arguments. More precisely, I describe the arrangement of slots, the presence vs. absence of slots, as well as their content.

Based on the inflectional pattern, Komnzo verbs can be classified into prefixing, middle and ambifixing verbs, depending on whether prefix, suffix or both are employed. I use the term "template" for the different inflectional patterns. Hence, we can say that a verb form occurs in "a prefixing template" or in "an ambifixing template". These templates are lexically determined for some verb lexemes, which means that we can speak of "a prefixing verb" or "a middle verb". For the majority of verb lexemes, the system is flexible and verbs occur in different templates. We can describe a particular verb lexeme by stating that "it occurs in the middle template and the ambifixing template, but not in the prefixing template".

The slots involved in the definition of templates are the following: (i) the undergoer prefix, (ii) the diathetic prefix, and (iii) the actor suffix. The undergoer prefix can index an argument, or its slot can be filled by the middle prefix, which is person-invariant. The diathetic prefix slot can be absent or be filled by the valency change prefix.[10] The actor suffix can be either absent or present. Figure 5.5 provides a first schematic overview of the possible templates. Note that there are more than the three templates mentioned above. This is because the prefixing and the ambifixing template can be further subdivided depending on the presence versus absence of the valency change prefix. Hence, there is a prefixing template and an indirect object prefixing template; and there is a transitive ambifixing template and a ditransitive ambifixing template.

I briefly describe each template here and refer the reader to the subsequent sections in which a detailed description follows (§5.4.4-6). In the prefixing template, only the undergoer prefix is used for person indexing. In the indirect object prefixing template also, only the undergoer prefix is used for person indexing. However, the undergoer prefix indexes an indirect object (beneficiary or possessor). This is formally marked by the valency change prefix *a-*. In the middle template, the prefix slot is filled by a middle marker which is invariant for person and number. The sole argument is indexed in the suffix. The middle marker is always followed by the valency change prefix *a-*. The middle template is used for a variety of functions, and depending on the function of the argument in the suffix it may index an agent or patient. The ambifixing transitive template uses both affixes for person indexing. The prefix encodes the object (patient, theme, experiencer)

---

[10]I use the neutral term "valency change" because its function is to either increase or decrease the valency of a verb.

and the suffix encodes the subject (agent, stimulus). The ditransitive ambifixing template follows the pattern of the transitive template with the addition of the valency change prefix *a-*. The undergoer prefix indexes the indirect object (goal, beneficiary, possessor).

I illustrate the five templates with the positional verb *migsi* 'hang' in examples (7a-e). Note that although the system is flexible, i.e. verbs occur in different templates, there is only a small amount of verb lexemes which can occur in all five templates. Positional verbs have a number of peculiarities, for example a special verb stem and a special stative suffix, which also encodes number (§5.4.4.2). This can be seen in (7a) and (7b).

(7) a. PREFIXING:
    y-mi-thgr
    3SG.MASC-hang.POS-STAT.ND
    'He is hanging.'

  b. INDIRECT OBJECT PREFIXING:
    y-a-mi-thgr
    3SG.MASC-VC-hang.POS-STAT.ND
    '(Something) is hanging for him.'

  c. MIDDLE:
    ŋ-a-mig-wr-∅
    M-VC-hang.EXT-ND-2|3SG
    'It hangs itself up.'

  d. TRANSITIVE AMBIFIXING:
    y-mig-wr-∅
    3SG.MASC-hang.EXT-ND-2|3SG
    'S/He hangs him up.'

  e. DITRANSITIVE AMBIFIXING:

prefixing:	undergoer prefix		stem	
indirect object prefixing:	undergoer prefix	vc	stem	
middle:	middle prefix	vc	stem	actor suffix[a]
transitive ambifixing:	undergoer prefix		stem	actor suffix
ditransitive ambifixing:	undergoer prefix	vc	stem	actor suffix

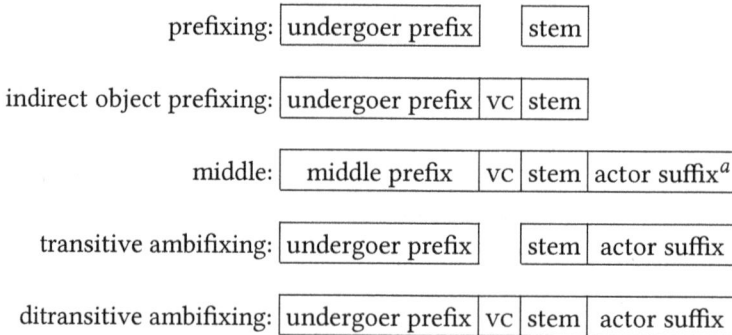

Figure 5.5: Morphological templates and argument structure

---

[a]The label 'actor suffix' is problematic with some lexemes which employ the middle template for a passive function, in wich case the suffix encodes a patient (§5.4.5).

y-a-mig-wr-∅
3SG.MASC-VC-hang.EXT-ND-2|3SG
'S/He hangs it up for him.'

The templates do not align neatly with transitivity. For example, only a small minority of intransitive verbs are prefixing (8a), while most employ a middle template (8b). The underlying semantic factor is the dynamicity of the event (§5.4.4). On the other hand, the middle template covers a wide range of functions including reflexives and reciprocals, passives, as well as antipassives (§5.4.5). Transitive verbs are usually expressed in the ambifixing template (8c). Ditransitive verbs occur in the ambifixing template with the addition of the valency change prefix *a-*, whereby an indirect object is introduced to the clause. The corresponding noun phrase is flagged with dative (8d) or possessive case, and it is indexed in the undergoer prefix (§5.4.6).

(8) a. *ktktme erfikwr.*
        kt-kt=me   e-rfik-wr
        REDUP-group=INS 2|3NSG.α-grow.EXT-ND
                        2|3PL:SBJ:NPST:IPFV/grow
        'They grow in groups.'

     b. *nagayé ŋakwinth.*
        nagayé ŋ-a-kwi-n-th
        children M.α-VC-run.EXT-DU-2|3NSG
                        2|3DU:SBJ:NPST:IPFV/run
        'The two children run.'

     c. *nafa ŋad yrbänzrth.*
        nafa   ŋad y-rbä-nzr-th
        3NSG.ERG rope 3SG.MASC.α-untie.EXT-ND-2|3NSG
                        2|3PL:SBJ>3SG.MASC:OBJ:NPST:IPFV/untie
        'They untie the rope.'

     d. *nze nafan wawa yarithé.*
        nze   nafan   wawa y-a-ri-th-é.
        1SG.ERG 3SG.DAT yam 3SGMASC.α-VC-give.EXT-ND-1SG
                        1SG:SBJ>3SG.MASC:IO:NPST:IPFV/give
        'I give him the yam(s).'

It follows that the valency change prefix *a-* (VC) has a double function. It increases and decreases the valency of a verb. This is exemplified with *migsi* 'hang' in examples (7a-7e). There are a number of deponent verbs attested, for example prefixing verbs or transitive ambifixing verbs which obligatorily take the *a-* prefix. I analyse them as deponent in the sense of Baerman et al. (2006) because in these cases the undergoer prefix indexes a direct object, although the presence of the VC prefix suggests an indirect object.[11]

Table 5.3 provides a fine-grained overview of the templates. I show the semantic roles of the arguments indexed in the affixes, the presence/absence of the valency change pre-

---

[11]Deponency is defined as a "mismatch between morphology and morpho-syntax" (Baerman et al. 2006).

Table 5.3: Argument marking

template	semantic role in the prefix	diathetic prefix	semantic role in the suffix	case frame	construction
prefixing (agent)[a]	experiencer	Ø	n/a	ABS	intransitive (stative)
indirect object prefixing	beneficiary or possessor	*a-*	n/a	DAT or POSS	intransitive (stative)
middle	n/a	*a-*	agent	ABS	intransitive (dynamic)
middle	n/a	*a-*	agent	ABS	impersonal
middle	n/a	*a-*	patient	ABS	passive
middle	n/a	*a-*	agent	ABS	reflexive & reciprocal
middle	n/a	*a-*	agent	ERG (ABS)[b]	suppressed-object
transitive ambifixing	patient, theme	Ø	agent	ERG ABS	transitive
transitive ambifixing	experiencer	Ø	stimulus	ABS ERG	experiencer-object
ditransitive ambifixing	beneficiary, goal	*a-*	agent	ERG ABS DAT	ditransitive
ditransitive ambifixing	possessor	*a-*	agent	ERG ABS POSS	ditransitive

[a]This is a marginal pattern as almost all prefixing verbs have stative semantics.
[b]In suppressed-object clauses, the object is suppressed from the indexation in the verb.

fix, the case frame and the name of the corresponding construction. These constructions are described in the section on clause types (§8.3).

5.4.3 Valency alternations

In Komnzo, valency alternations are achieved by placing the verb in different templates. There is only a handful of verbs which occur in all the templates. I choose the verb *msaksi* 'sit, dwell' to show its possibilities with textual examples (9-12). Note that *msaksi* deviates in two ways from other verbs. First, it takes the valency change prefix obligatorily when it occurs in a prefixing template, as can be seen in (9). Secondly, there is a special verb stem for the prefixing template: *m*. In other templates, *msaksi* has the extended stem *msak* and the restricted stem *ms*, i.e. it is a class II verb (compare Table 5.2).

In example (9), the speaker showed me a place which used to be inhabited by a spirit. He states that nobody knows where the spirit lives nowadays. Hence, the verb *msaksi* has a stative meaning in the prefixing template and can be translated into English with 'dwell, live, stay', or 'be sitting'.

(9) *watik ŋafäniza ... ni miyamr mä zena **yamnzr**.*
    watik ŋ-a-fäni-z-a-∅   (.) ni   miyamr   mä   zena
    then M.α-VC-shift.place.EXT-ND-PST-2|3SG (.) 1NSG ignorance where today
            2|3SG:SBJ:PST:IPFV/shift.place

    y-a-m-nzr
    3SG.MASC.α-VC-dwell.EXT-ND
    3SG.MASC:SBJ:NPST:IPFV/dwell
    'Then he shifted (location). We don't know where he lives today.'
                                [tci20120922-19 DAK #37]

Example (10) was uttered in the context of me visiting a garden place in the forest, where I was accompanied by the owner of the garden. The speaker happened to cycle past the garden place catching sight of me and the owner. The speaker comments on how he saw the two of us sitting down. Thus, *msaksi* in the middle template encodes a dynamic event and can be translated into English with 'sit down' or 'assume a sitting position'.

(10) *nze nimäwä! boba thnmaré **ŋamsakrnmth**.*
    nze   nima=wä   boba   th-∅-n-mar-é
    1SG.ERG like.this=EMPH MED.ABL 2|3NSG.γ-DU-VENT-see.RS-1SG
                             1SG:SBJ>2|3DU:OBJ:RPST:PFV:VENT/see

    ŋ-a-msak-rn-m-th
    M.α-VC-sit.EXT-DU-DUR-2|3NSG
    2|3DU:SBJ:RPST:DUR/sit
    'Me too! I saw you two from there and you were just sitting down.'
                                [tci20130823-06 STK #90]

Example (11) shows *msaksi* in a transitive ambifixing template. The example comes from a narrative, in which an angry man is forcefully seated and calmed down by giving him kava to drink.

(11) *wati **ymsakwrth** fof krär **yarinakwrth** bänemr fof nafane noku frazsir.*
    wati y-msak-wr-th   fof   krär y-a-rinak-wr-th
    then 3SG.MASC.α-sit.EXT-ND-2|3NSG EMPH kava 3SG.MASC.α-VC-pour.EXT-ND-2|3NSG
        2|3PL:SBJ>3SG.MASC:OBJ:NPST:IPFV/sit   2|3PL:SBJ>3SG.MASC:IO:NPST:IPFV/pour

> bänemr   fof   nafane   noku   fraz-si=r
> RECOG.PURP EMPH 3SG.POSS anger extinguish-NMLZ=PURP
> 'So they sit him down properly and pour kava for him to cool down his anger.'

[tci20120909-06 KAB 93-94]

Example (12) is an elicited example showing *msaksi* in a ditransitive ambifixing template, where the undergoer prefix indexes the possessor ('his child'). Note that the same template is found in *yarinakʷrth*; the second verb in (11), where the undergoer prefix indexes a beneficiary ('pour kava for him').

(12)   *nze nafange **yamsakwé**.*
  nze   nafa-nge   y-a-msak-w-é.
  1SG.ERG 3.POSS-child 3SG.MASC.*α*-VC-sit.EXT-ND-1SG
            1SG:SBJ>3SG.MASC:IO:NPST:IPFV/sit
  'I sit his child down.'

The above examples show that valency alternations are achieved by using the same verb in different templates. It is important to note that all the inflected verb forms share the same infinitive, which is formed by suffixing the nominaliser *-si* to the stem. In (13) and (14) I show the infinitive with a stative and a dynamic interpretation. Example (13) is the conclusion of a short narrative about taboos and customs that involve the bird of paradise. The speaker uses *msaksi* with a locative case suffix in a possessive construction to express 'in our life'. In example (14), the speaker showed me a beautiful place on the bank of the Morehead river. She comments that this is a good place to sit down and rest. Hence, the infinitive *msaksi* is used for both interpretations, a timeless state in (13) and a dynamic event in (14).

(13)   *nzenme trtha mrmren nzenme **msaksin** ... wtrikarä anema fof ŋamränzre.*
  nzenme   trtha mrmr=en nzenme   msak-si=n   (.) wtri=karä
  1NSG.POSS life   inside=LOC 1NSG.POSS sit-NMLZ=LOC (.) fear=PROP

  ane=ma   fof   ŋ-a-mrä-nzr-e
  DEM=CHAR EMPH M.*α*-VC-stroll.EXT-ND-1NSG
            1PL:SBJ:NPST:IPFV/stroll
  'In our way of life ... in our living ... we walk about with fear because of this.'

[tci20120817-02 ABB #40-43]

(14)   *camp rä ... zbo fthé nanyak **msaksir**.*
  camp rä   (.) zbo   fthé   n-a-n-yak
  camp 3SG.FEM.COP.ND   (.) PROX.ALL when 1NSG.*α*-VC-VENT-walk.EXT.ND
        3SG.FEM:SBJ:NPST:IPFV/be   1PL:SBJ:NPST:IPFV/come

  msak-si=r
  sit-NMLZ=PURP
  'This is a camp ... We come here to sit down (and rest).' [tci20130907-02 RNA #331-333]

The meaning of a verb stem in one template may differ substantially from its use in another template. For example, the verb *rfiksi* 'grow' occurs in the prefixing template

(8a), but it can be used in a transitive ambifixing template with the meaning 'nurture' (lit. 'grow somebody'). A second example is the verb *rbänzsi* 'untie' which usually occurs in a transitive ambifixing template (8c). Used in a ditransitive ambifixing template it has the meaning 'explain' (lit. 'untie for somebody'). Nevertheless, inflected verbs in different templates all share the same infinitive. In this aspect Komnzo differs from other Yam languages. For example, in Nen there are no infinitives for prefixing verbs, but instead valency-altered forms have distinct infinitives which include the relevant formatives from a set of diathetic prefixes (Evans 2015b). For example, one pair of infinitives is: *amzs* 'sit (v.i.)' versus *wamzs* 'set, sit (v.t.)'. There are even triplets: *aṇḡws* 'return (v.i.)' versus *waṇḡws* 'return (v.t.)' versus *wawaṇḡws* 'return to/for (v.t.)'. In Komnzo, there are no distinct infinitives for valency-altered forms. Hence, *rfiksi* is the infinitive of both 'grow' and 'nuture', and *rbänzsi* is the infinitive of 'untie' and 'explain'.

There are two ways of analyzing shared infinitives in Komnzo, and I argue that both are needed. On the one hand, we can understand it as a system where valency is fluid and lexemes are flexible. Under this analysis a lexeme can alter its valency by occuring in different templates. On the other hand, we could adopt the notion of heterosemy (Lichtenberk 1991 and Evans 2010: 524) to capture that different lexical items and meanings are expressed by different templates.[12] A verb like *msaksi* shows that we need both perspectives. On the one hand, $msaksi_1$ means 'dwell, live' in a prefixing template, while $msaksi_2$ means 'sit down' in a middle/ambifixing template. We would understand $msaksi_1$ as being heterosemous to $msaksi_2$ because there is a significant shift in meaning due to the template. The same holds for pairs like *rfiksi* meaning 'grow' or 'nuture' and *rbänzsi* meaning 'untie' or 'explain'. On the other hand, the system of valency alternations in Komnze is very productive. Especially the middle template and the ditransitive ambifixing template can be used for almost every verb which can also occur in the transitive ambifixing template. Thus, describing the alternation between *msaksi* in (11) 'sit someone down' and (12) 'sit someone's (child) down' in terms of heterosemy would fall short of an exhaustive description. It would not adequately capture the productivity of the system, nor would it fully explain shared infinitives for verb forms of different templates.

5.4.4 The prefixing template

5.4.4.1 Introduction

Prefixing verbs are a small class with around 20 lexical items attested so far. Some of them can occur in other templates, but most occur only in the prefixing template. Table 5.4 lists all the members of the prefixing class.[13] Furthermore, there is a class of 41 positional verbs, which can occur in the prefixing template (§5.4.4.2).

---

[12] This assumes a definition of the linguistic sign as having three parts: form, meaning and combinatorics (or syntax) as put forward by Mel'čuk (1973) and Pollard & Sag (1987: 51).

[13] Infinitives are marked with the nominaliser suffix *-si*. Prefixing verbs are irregular in many respects. Some of the verbs listed here lack an infinitive and only the extended stem is given, while others employ a common noun as their infinitive, for example *etfth* 'sleep', *moth* 'path, walk, come' and *kwan* 'noise, shout'. This does not correlate with whether there are other templates available. Where a nominalised form with *-si* is lacking, I give the extended stem. Another irregularity are verbs where the stem is sensitive to the dual versus non-dual distinction, for example 'walk' *-yak* (ND) versus *-yan* (DU) or 'shout' *-nor* (ND) versus *-rn* (DU). In these cases, the non-dual stem is listed.

Table 5.4: Prefixing verbs

infinitive or stem	gloss	possible templates	gloss
-rug	'sleep'	pref. only	-
-yak	'walk, go'	pref. only	-
[a]*-nyak*	'come'	pref. only	-
[a]*yathizsi*	'suffer'	pref. only	-
[a]*mthizsi*	'rest'	pref. only	-
[a]*-nor*	'shout, emit sound'	pref. only	-
wäksi	'be caught by daybreak'	pref. only	-
fogsi	'be caught by nightfall'	pref. only	-
rmigfaksi	'be in the middle of (doing) sth.'	pref. only	-
-thn	'be lying'	pref. only	-
[a]*yarenzsi*	'look around'	pref. only	-
-ythk	'be finished'	pref. only	-
[a]*namgsi*	'be panting, gasping'	pref. only	-
thfäsi	'jump'	pref./middle	'fly'
[a]*thgusi*	'forget'	pref./trans.	'confuse sth.'
thoraksi	'appear, arrive'	pref./trans.	'find, search'
wokraksi	'float'	pref./trans.	'make sth. float'
-rä	'be'	all templates	'do'
[a]*msaksi*	'dwell, live'	all templates	'sit (self or sb.)'
sufaksi	'grow old'	all templates	'bring to an end'
ziksi	'turn off, be on the side'	all templates	'put to the side'
rfiksi	'grow'	all templates	'nurture'

[a] These verbs are deponent, i.e. they use the vc prefix obligatorily.

Prefixing verbs are special in their morphology in that they can encode a fourth number value. The somewhat odd combination of a non-singular prefix and a dual suffix yields a large plural. This is attested in other Yam languages, for example for positional verbs in Nen and Nä (Evans 2014). I describe the four-way number contrast in §5.5.3.2.

Prefixing verbs are mostly stative in their semantics. Comparative work on split intransitivity has shown that differences in alignment are often semantically motivated (Merlan 1985, Mithun 1991 and Arkadiev 2008). In Komnzo, the semantic parameters involved are the dynamicity of the event and the volitionality of the participant, where the former plays the dominant role. As we have seen in §5.4.3, predicates in a prefixing template tend to be more stative (9), while predicates in middle or ambifixing templates tend to be more dynamic (10-12). In other languages of the Yam family, the split between stative and dynamic event types is congruent with the distinction between prefixing and middle intransitives, for example in Nen (Evans 2015a) and Nama (Siegel 2014).[14]

---

[14]Siegel uses different terminology in his description of Nama. What I call the prefixing template or stative intransitives equals "patientive intransitives", and what I label the middle template or dynamic intransitives equals "agentive intransitives" (Siegel 2014: 213).

In Komnzo, although all verbs in a middle or ambifixing template express dynamic event types, we find a somewhat mixed picture with prefixing verbs. Table 5.4 contains a few dynamic events, for example *-nor* 'shout', *thoraksi* 'appear, arrive' and *rfiksi* 'grow'. In some cases, volitionality is the semantic parameter involved in the prefixing/middle/ambifixing alternation: *thoraksi* and *rfiksi* in an ambifixing transitive template mean 'find' and 'nurture', respectively.[15] The verb *-nor* 'shout' allows no alternation, but occurs only in a prefixing template. Interestingly, *-nor* is often used in a pseudo-cognate object construction: *kwan yannor*[16] 'He shouts (the shout)' or *ya yannor* 'He cries (the tears)'. Hence, with this verb a less volitional meaning like 'emit a sound' might be licensed. Pseudo-cognate object constructions are described in §8.3.11. However, with other predicates in Table 5.4 such an explanation fails, for example *ziksi* 'turn off, go in' or *thfäsi* 'jump'. Keeping the unusually small size of the prefixing class in mind, I interpret these cases as exceptions to the overall rule. Furthermore, the existence of a class of positional verbs (§5.4.4.2) underscores the split along the lines of event dynamicity and volitionality.

All prefixing verbs can take the valency change prefix *a-*. This template was labelled indirect object prefixing in Table 5.3. However, in doing so they remain monovalent in their cross-referencing. The 'additional argument', usually a beneficiary or possessor, replaces the 'original argument', usually an experiencer. However, the event itself "is still about" the original argument. A common usage of this pattern involves the copula: When handing something to a person, one would say *bnarä!* 'There you are!' (lit. '(It) is there for you!'). A textual example comes from a stimulus task in which two speakers are describing the contents of picture cards (15). The picture in the example shows a policeman handing some personal belongings to another man. After describing the scene, one of the two speakers points to a few things on the side, asking what these were. The first verb in (15) 'be lying down' indexes the (assumed) possessor and not the things on the ground. The second clause is accompanied by a pointing gesture in order to draw the interlocutor's attention to the objects. Here, the copula indexes the things on the ground.

(15)   *mrmr ra **yathn**? zane **zerä**!*

mrmr ra   y-a-thn   zane   z=e-rä

inside what.ABS 3SG.MASC.α-VC-lie.EXT.ND DEM:PROX PROX=2|3NSG.α-be.EXT.ND

             3SG.MASC:IO:NPST:IPFV/lie   PROX=2|3PL:SBJ:NPST:IPFV/be

'What are these (of his) inside? These ones here!'   [tci20111004 TSA #29-30]

Table 5.4 indicates that eight out of 20 prefixing verbs obligatorily use the *a-* prefix without introducing an argument. I analyse these verbs as deponent (Baerman et al. 2006).

---

[15] In ambifixing templates, the case marking of a more agent-like argument is ergative. This is also found in middle templates with an suppressed-object function.

[16] *-nor* lacks a nominalised infinitive and instead the common noun *kwan* 'shout, call' is used.

5.4.4.2 Positional verbs

The class of 41 positional or postural verbs underscores the role of dynamicity in the alignment of S. Positional verbs express states of the type 'be in position X' ('be leaning', 'be standing', 'be submerged' etc). Example (16) shows the verb *migsi* 'hang'.

(16) *bidrthatha zbo **sumithgrm** wämnen.*
  bidr=thatha   zbo   su-mi-thgr-m   wämne=n
  flying.fox=SIMIL PROX.ALL 3SG.MASC.β1-be.hanging-STAT.ND-DUR tree=LOC
  3SG.MASC:SBJ:PST:DUR:STAT/be.hanging
  'He was hanging like a flying fox on the tree.'   [tci20130901-04 RNA #48]

Like most positional verbs, *migsi* can enter into other templates, for example a middle template ('assume a hanging position') or a transitive template ('hang something'). This is shown in examples (17) and (18) respectively. Example (17) is part of a plant walk around Rouku village. The speaker shows me a plant in the part of the land which is inundated during the rainy season. Example (18) comes from a procedural text in which the speaker shows me around his yam storage house. He remarks that small yam suckers are called *sagusagu* and they are stored by tying several yams into bundles.

(17) *bubukr zä zf kwa **ŋamigwrth** ... watik kofäyé zbo zf kwa erkunzrth.*
  bubukr zä   zf   kwa ŋ-a-mig-wr-th   (.) watik kofä=é   zbo
  insect PROX IMM FUT M.α-VC-hang.EXT-ND-2|3NSG (.) then fish=ERG.NSG PROX.ALL
  2|3PL:SBJ:NPST:IPFV/hang

  zf   kwa e-rku-nzr-th
  IMM FUT 2|3NSG.α-knock.down.EXT-ND-2|3NSG
  2|3PL:SBJ>2|3PL:OBJ:NPST:IPFV/knock.down
  'The insects will hang (themselves) from here and the fish will knock them down right here.'   [tci20130907-02 RNA #657]

(18) *nima yamme ane fof ŋafrmnzre bnrä ... **bemigwre** ane sagusagu.*
  nima   yam=me   ane fof   ŋ-a-frm-nzr-e
  like.this custom=INS DEM EMPH M.α-VC-prepare.EXT-ND-1NSG
  1PL:SBJ:NPST:IPFV/prepare

  b=n-rä   (.) b=e-mig-wr-e   ane sagusagu
  MED=1NSG.α-COP.ND (.) MED=2|3NSG.α-hang.EXT-ND-1NSG DEM sagusagu
  MED=1PL:SBJ:NPST:IPFV/be   MED=1PL:SBJ>2|3PL:OBJ:NPST:IPFV/hang
  'We prepare them in this way ... We hang up those *sagusagu*.' [tci20121001 ABB #38]

Positionals are attested in languages throughout the Yam family (Evans 2014). For Komnzo, I define them as a class of lexemes with positional or postural semantics which share the following morpho-syntactic properties: (i) the ability to occur in the prefixing template, (ii) the ability to take the stative suffix *-thgr*, (iii) the ability to form related middle and transitive verb forms, and (iv) the restriction to inflicet only for a subset of TAM categories in a prefixing template. Table 5.5 lists the 41 members of the class which are currently attested. We find both very general meanings (*rzarsi* 'be tied', *yufaksi* 'be bent over') and very specific meanings (*rngthksi* 'be stuck in a tree fork', *mgthksi* 'be in the mouth'). Some of these verbs occur with prototypical participants, for example *zaksi* 'be anchored' with *garda* 'canoe' or *thamsaksi* 'be spread out' with *yame* 'mat'.

Table 5.5 compares the extended (EXT) and restricted stem (RS) and shows that for some verbs a positional stem (POS) can be postulated. The positional stem is the lexical base to which the stative suffix *-thgr* attaches. In the first two groups of Table 5.5, the base is formally identical to the extended or restricted stem. Only in the third group is the base different from both, in that it is always shorter. The last group contains three lexemes which are irregular in a number of ways: (i) they take a slightly different form of the stative suffix, which is given in parentheses for each, (ii) the last two lexemes in this group occur only as positionals, (iii) the second lexeme in the group lacks an infinitive.

The data from Table 5.5 shows that for some of the verbs we need to posit a third stem type, the positional stem, in addition to the extended and restricted stems we already encountered. The formal difference or similarity between the positional stem and the other two stem types for a given lexeme cannot be predicted on semantic or phonological grounds, but must be seen as lexicalisation in a specific morpho-syntactic context. Furthermore, one should keep in mind that positional stems are not in a paradigmatic relationship of the kind we have seen with extended and restricted stems (§5.3). For example, the stative semantics of positionals blocks all perfective TAM categories.

Just like other verbs in the prefixing template, positionals may add a possessor or beneficiary by using the valency change prefix *a-*. An example of this is given in (19) where the speaker describes how he carried two fish up from the river. The first verb in (19) indexes the two catfish, but the second verb indexes a first singular, in this case the possessor ('on top of my shoulder'). Thus, although the predicate is about the two fish ('They were on top.'), the verb only indexes the first singular.

(19) *thwä **femithgrn** zane zazame **nwanwägr** ... fatren.*
      thwä   f=e-mi-thgrn   zane zaza=me
      catfish DIST=2|3NSG.α-be.hanging-STAT.DU PROX carrying.stick=INS
          DIST=2|3DU:SBJ:NPST:STAT/be.hanging

      n=wo-a-n-wä-gr   (.) fatr=en
      IPST=1SG-VC-VENT-be.on.top-STAT.ND (.) shoulder=LOC
      IPST=1SG:IO:NPST:STAT:VENT/be.on.top
      'Those two catfish are hanging there. I just brought them here on my shoulder
      with the carrying stick.'   [tci20121008-03 MAB #13]

As Table 5.5 shows, there are a five out of 41 positional verbs which I analyse as deponent, i.e. they take the *a-* prefix obligatorily without adding an additional argument to the clause.

5.4.5 The middle template

The majority of verb stems can enter into what I call the middle template. In the middle template, the prefix slot is filled by a person-invariant middle marker (glossed as M) and

Table 5.5: Positional verbs

infinitive	POS stem	EXT stem	RS stem	gloss
mosisi	*mosi-*	*mosi-*	*mosir-*	be gathered, piled
moyusi	*moyu-*	*moyu-*	*moyuth-*	be shrunk
rfakusi	*rfaku-*	*rfaku-*	*rfakuth-*	be sprinkled
ttüsi	*ttü-*	*ttü-*	*ttüth-*	be printed, carved
tharasi	*thar-*	*thar-*	*tharf-*	be underneath
worsi	*wor-*	*wor-*	*won-*	be planted
brüzsi	*brüs-*	*brüz-*	*brüs-*	be submerged
krsi	*kr-*	*krth-*	*kr-*	be blocked off
räzsi	*räs-*	*räz-*	*räs-*	be erected
[a]*rfuthraksi*	*rfuth-*	*rfuthrak-*	*rfuthr-*	be piled up
rmithraksi	*rmithr-*	*rmithrak-*	*rmithr-*	be joined together
rmnzüfaksi	*rmnzüf-*	*rmnzüfak-*	*rmnzüf-*	be side by side / parallel
rthbraksi	*rthbr-*	*rthbrak-*	*rthbr-*	be sticking (on sth.)
rzarsi	*rzaf-*	*rzar-*	*rzaf-*	be tied
thamsaksi	*thams-*	*thamsak-*	*thams-*	be spread out
[a]*yufaksi*	*yuf-*	*yufak-*	*yuf-*	be bent
zaksi	*z-*	*zak-*	*z-*	be anchored
fätfaksi	*fät-*	*fätfak-*	*fätf-*	be across sth.
fethaksi	*fe-*	*fethak-*	*feth-*	be dipped in water
fifthaksi	*fif-*	*fifthak-*	*fifth-*	be lying straight
migsi	*mi-*	*mig-*	*mir-*	be hanging
moraksi	*mo-*	*morak-*	*mor-*	be leaning
[a]*mgthksi*	*mg-*	*mgthk-*	*mgthm-*	be in the mouth
mreznsi	*mre-*	*mrezn-*	*mrezn-*	be straight
[a]*mtheksi*	*mthe-*	*mthek-*	*mthef-*	be lifted up
myuknsi	*myu-*	*myukn-*	*myuf-*	be twisted
nänzüthzsi	*nänzü-*	*nänzüthz-*	*nänzütham-*	be covered with soil
rafigsi	*rafi-*	*rafig-*	*rafinz-*	be on top of sth.
rakthksi	*rak-*	*rakthk-*	*rakthm-*	be on top of sth.
rinaksi	*ri-*	*rinak-*	*rin-*	be poured into
rngthksi	*rng-*	*rngthk-*	*rngthm-*	be in a tree fork
[a]*rgsi*	*rk-*	*rg-*	*rg-*	be wearing clothes
sisraksi	*si-*	*sisrak-*	*sisr-*	be sticking out of sth.
sümraksi	*süm-*	*sümrak-*	*sümr-*	be widened, be open
thäfrsi	*thäfrs-*	*thäf-*	*thäfrs-*	be covered
tharuksi	*tharu-*	*tharuk-*	*tharuf-*	be inside (open container)
ththaksi	*th-*	*ththak-*	*ththm-*	be pinned on sth.
wäthsi	*wä-*	*wäth-*	*wäf-*	be wrapped
thorsi	*th-(kgr)*	*thor-*	*thb-*	be inside (closed container)
yukrasi	*ko-(gr)*	n/a	*-kuk*	be standing
n/a	*wä-(gr)*	n/a	n/a	be up high

[a] These verbs are deponent, i.e. they use the vc prefix obligatorily.

the single argument is cross-referenced in the suffix. In addition, the valency change prefix *a*- is employed. As we will see below, the suffix in this template may cross-reference an A, S or P argument. The distinction between A vs. S/P is signalled by the case marking on the NP (ergative vs. absolutive).

I employ the term "middle", as defined by Kemmer (1993: 207-210) for situation types with a low degree of elaboration. Low degree of elaboration may refer to the event and/or to the participants involved in the event. The middle template in Komnzo covers a range of functions: intransitives, passive-impersonals, reflexives and reciprocals as well as suppressed-object middles (or antipassives). Kemmer describes these events as typical "middle situation types" (1993: 15).

Table 5.6: Intrinsic middle verbs

infinitive	EXT stem	gloss
borsi	*bor-*	'laugh, play'
bznsi	*bzn-*	'work'
farksi	*fark-*	'set off'
frezsi	*frez-*	'come up (from river)'
fsknsi	*fskn-*	'doze'
fänizsi	*fäniz-*	'shift location'
[a]*mni*	*rsir-*	'burn, cook' (v.i.)
[a]*moth*	*kwi-*	'run'
mränzsi	*mränz-*	'stroll'
müsinzsi	*müsinz-*	'glow'
rfeksi	*rfek-*	'limp'
risoksi	*risok-*	'look down'
rninzsi	*rninz-*	'smile'
rnäthsi	*rnäth-*	'get stuck'
rsörsi	*rsör-*	'descend, climb down'
rüsi	*rü-*	'rain'
sogsi	*sog-*	'ascend, climb up'
sufaksi	*sufak-*	'gulp down, guzzle'
thweksi	*thwek-*	'rejoice'
thärkusi	*thärku-*	'crawl'
[a]*wath*	*rnzür-*	'dance'
yonasi	*na-*	'drink'
n/a	*ko-*	'become'
n/a	*rä-*	'do, think'

[a] These verbs employ a common noun as their infinitive

Intransitive event types in Komnzo are distributed over the prefixing and the middle template (§5.4.4). The majority of syntactically intransitive verbs employ the middle template. As a consequence for the description of the middle template, we have to draw a distinction between intrinsic middle verbs and derived middle verbs. Intrinsic middles can only occur in the middle template. Derived middle verbs are derived from transitive verbs, whereby the middle template is used for different valency decreasing functions. There is a third group of verb stems, which almost always occur in the middle template, but with which a derived transitive or ditransitive is possible. These groups will be discussed below. For now, the main distinction is between verbs, for which the middle template is one strategy among others, and verbs which only occur in the middle template.

Some intrinsic middle verbs are listed in Table 5.6. In her cross-linguistic survey, Kemmer identifies a number of situation types which commonly occur with middle morphology (1993: 16-21). In Komnzo these are: translational motion ('run', 'climb up', 'climb down', 'shift location'), emotion middle ('laugh', 'rejoice', 'smile'), cognition middle ('think') and spontaneous events ('change', 'become'). The tendency to encode intransitive verbs with a dynamic event type in the middle template has been discussed in §5.4.4.

In addition to intrinsic middle verbs, most verb stems can occur in the middle template with various related functions. One such verb is *brigsi* 'return'. In the examples (20) and (21), the S argument is indexed in the suffix, while the prefix slot is filled by the middle morpheme. Since there is no formal difference in the middle template between intransitives, impersonals and reflexives, these should be understood as reflexiva tanta (Geniušienė 1987) and example (20) could also be translated as 'I return myself'.

(20)   *oh nzä karfo zena zf **ŋabrigwé**.*
     oh nzä   kar=fo   zena zf   ŋ-a-brig-w-é
     oh 1SG.ABS village=ALL today IMM M.α-VC-return.EXT-ND-1SG
                                    1SG:SBJ:NPST:IPFV/return
     'Oh, now I will go back to the village.'   [tci20111004 RMA 437]

(21)   *oh kaimätdbo fam **ŋabrigwrth**.*
     oh kaimät=dbo   fam   ŋ-a-brig-w-r-th
     oh sister.in.law=ALL.ANIM thoughts M.α-VC-return.EXT-ND-LK-2|3NSG
                                2|3PL:SBJ:NPST:IPFV/return
     'Oh, (my) thoughts are returning to my sister-in-law.'   [tci20130907-02 JAA 665]

Examples (22a-b) show *brigsi* in different templates. Both examples are taken from the same story about a headhunt which took place in the narrator's village Firra. In (22a), the ambifixing transitive template is used (lit. 'They returned the payback'). Just a few clauses later, the narrator concludes this part of the story in (22b) where the same referent, which was indexed in the prefix in (22a), is now indexed in the suffix with a passive or impersonal interpretation (lit. 'Revenge (was) returned').

(22)   a. *okay, nafa nezä z faw **wbrigrnath** ... bänema nafanme mayawa kakafar z*
        bramöwä thäkwrath firran.

okay nafa   nezä   z   faw   w-brig-r-n-a-th
okay 3NSG.ERG revenge ALR payment 3SG.FEM.*α*-return.EXT-LK-DU-PST-2|3NSG
2|3DU:SBJ>3SG.FEM:OBJ:PST:IPFV/return

(.) bäne=ma   nafanme mayawa ka-kafar   z   bramöwä
(.) DEM:MED=CHAR 3NSG.POSS mayawa REDUP-big ALR all

th-ä-kwr-a-th   firra=n
2|3NSG.*γ*-VC|ND-hit.RS-PST-2|3NSG firra=LOC
2|3PL:SBJ>2|3PL:OBJ:PST:PFV/kill
'Okay, then the two took revenge, because all their Mayawa elders had been
killed in Firra.'   [tci20111107-01 MAK 126-127]

b.   *watik, faw z ŋabrigwa ane … ane ebar nimame firran rera fof.*
    watik faw   z   ŋ-a-brig-w-a-∅   ane (.) ane ebar
    then   payment ALR M.*α*-VC-return.EXT-ND-PST-2|3SG DEM (.) DEM head
2|3SG:SBJ:PST:IPFV/return

    nima=me firra=n   rä-r-a   fof
    like.this=INS firra=LOC 3SG.FEM.COP-LK-PST EMPH
3SG.FEM:SBJ:PST:IPFV/be
    'Then, revenge was taken. This is really how the head(hunting) took place in
    Firra.'   [tci20111107-01 MAK 134-135]

Consequently, I refrain from using the terms 'middle voice' or 'passive voice'. It is more
adequate to speak of a middle template with a specific function. This function might be
reflexive, reciprocal, passive or impersonal. Consider example (23), in which the speaker
describes how he got home after a hard day of work in his garden. The first two verbs in
(23) are prefixing verbs. The last three verbs occur in the middle template and could be
translated as either reflexive ('wash self', 'change self', 'bring oneself up from river') or
intransitives ('wash', 'get changed', 'come up from the river').[17]

(23)   *yoganai worärm, kwofiyak, **kwamaikwé**, sänis **kwaräré, zänfrefé**.*
       yoganai wo-rä-r-m   kwof-yak   kw-a-mayk-w-é   sänis
       tiredness 1SG.*α*-be-LK-DUR 1SG.*β*2-walk.EXT-ND M.*β*1-VC-wash.EXT-ND-1SG change
1SG:SBJ:RPST:DUR/be   1SG:SBJ:RPST:IPFV/walk   1SG:SBJ:RPST:IPFV/wash

       kw-a-rä-r-é   z-ä-n-fref-é
       M.*β*1-VC-do.EXT-LK-1SG M.*γ*-VC-ND-VENT-come.up.from.river.RS-1SG
1SG:SBJ:RPST:IPFV/do   1SG:SBJ:RPST:PFV:VENT/come.up.from.river
       'I was tired. I walked. I washed myself. I got changed and I came up here from the
       river.'   [tci20120922-24 MAA 78-80]

We find the same ambiguity between reflexive and reciprocal interpretations. In (24),
the speaker describes how his ancestors used to live in small hamlets which comprised
a clan or often a single patriline. The reciprocal interpretation of the second verb only

---

[17]Note that 'get changed' is expressed with a nominal *sänis* (< English 'change') and a generic verb 'do',
literally 'I do the change'. The nominal is not indexed on the verb. I describe light verb constructions in
§8.3.12.

comes from the context. The verb form *kwamarwrme* in a different context could equally be translated as a reflexive: 'We were looking at ourselves'.

(24) *mrnmenzo nzwamnzrm. zagr sime **kwamarwrme**.*

mrn=me=nzo nzu-a-m-nz-r-m   zagr si=me
clan=INS=ONLY 1NSG.β1-VC-dwell.EXT-ND-LK-DUR far eye=INS
             1PL:SBJ:PST:DUR/dwell

kw-a-mar-w-r-m-e
M.β1-VC-see-LK-DUR-1NSG
1PL:SBJ:PST:DUR/see

'We used to stay in our clans. We saw each other only from a distance.'

                    [tci20120922-08 DAK 117-118]

We have seen an impersonal usage of the middle template in (22b). An example with a much clearer passive reading is provided in (25), where the speaker talks about sorting and selecting yam tubers in his storage house. The context reveals that it is the patient argument of the verbs ('choose', 'put down') which is indexed in the suffix. Keenan and Dryer include the entailment of an agent in their definition of passives setting them apart from middles (2007: 352). In Komnzo, this is dependent on the semantics of the verb. Prototypical transitive verbs, like 'choose' and 'put down' in (25), invite a passive interpretation rather than an impersonal one. However, in terms of morpho-syntax, there is no dedicated passive marking. Furthermore, the agent noun phrase cannot be included in the clause, because it would have to be indexed in the suffix of the verb, which is already occupied by the patient argument.

(25) *zane zf woksimär erä. gaba foba fof **kräwokthth** bobo we kwa **ŋanakwrth** a nima berä.*

zane   zf   wok-si=mär   e-rä   gaba   foba   fof
DEM:PROX IMM choose-NMLZ=PRIV 2|3NSG.α-COP.ND eating.yam DIST.ABL EMPH
                         2|3PL:SBJ:NPST:IPFV/be

k-ra-a-wokth-th   bobo   we kwa
M.β-IRR-VC|ND-choose.RS-2|3NSG MED.ALL also FUT
2|3PL:SBJ:IRR:PFV/choose

ŋ-a-nak-w-r-th   a   nima   b=e-rä
M.α-VC-put.down.EXT-ND-LK-2|3NSG and like.this MED=2|3NSG.α-COP.ND
2|3PL:SBJ:NPST:IPFV/put.down   MED=2|3PL:SBJ:NPST:IPFV/be

'These have not been selected. They will be selected over there and then put down there like those ones.'

                    [tci20121001 ABB 41-42]

A somewhat different function of the middle template is the suppressed-object middle. The formal difference with respect to the previous functions of the middle template lies in the marking of the NP, which receives ergative marking. Thus, the argument is an actor and the event is inherently transitive. Consider example (26), which is taken from a conversation between two young men. The speaker reports to his friend what his wife thinks about his plan to shift the garden place to another location. In (26), the pronoun *naf* is in the ergative case and agrees with the verb *ŋanafr* which is in the middle template. The object is suppressed from indexation and without context we are left to speculate what it might be: the goal ('she said to me') or the clausal theme ('to continue the old garden').

(26) *naf **ŋanafr** drdr mäyogsir.*
    naf   ŋ-a-na-f-r-∅   drdr   mäyog-si=r
    3SG.ERG M-VC-speak.RS-ND-LK-2|3SG old.garden repeat-NMLZ=PURP
           2|3SG:SBJ:NPST:IPFV/speak
    'She suggested/said to continue the old garden.'   [tci20130823-06 STK 161]

The suppressed-object middle is obligatory for a few lexemes, for example *na-* 'speak (v.t.)' in (26), *karksi* 'pull (v.t.)' or *yonasi*[18] 'drink (v.t.)'. For most verbs, the suppressed-object middle is a possible alternation and should be seen as derived from verbs which normally employ an ambifixing transitive template.

There are pragmatic reasons for suppressing the object, for example when the referent is common ground or when the event is somehow generic.[19] These motivations can be subsumed under Kemmer's criterion of low degree of (participant) elaboration with middle morphology. Consider example (27), where the speaker talks about how yams are stored. He says that the yams are heaped and sorted into separate piles and that the spatial layout signals the use of the yams. This last proposition is expressed as *naf ŋatrikwr* 'it indicates'. The verb *trikasi* 'tell' is usually used for story telling or for reporting on something, but the event depicted in example (27) is generic and less elaborated.

(27) *mnz mrmr fof enakwre zena monwä zane ethn zerä. **naf ŋatrikwr** zane zf ŋatr wawa erä zerä. zane gaba zf erä zerä.*
    mnz   mrmr fof   e-nak-w-r-e   zena mon=wä   zane
    house inside EMPH 2|3NSG.*α*-put.down.EXT-ND-LK-1NSG now how=EMPH DEM:PROX
                       1PL:SBJ>2|3PL:OBJ:NPST:IPFV/put-down

    e-thn   z=e-rä   naf
    2|3NSG.*α*-lie.down.EXT.ND   PROX=2|3NSG.*α*-COP.ND 3SG.ERG
    PROX=2|3PL:SBJ:NPST:IPFV/lie.down PROX=2|3PL:SBJ:NPST:IPFV/be

    ŋ-a-trik-w-r-∅   zane   zf ŋatr   wawa
    M.*α*-VC-tell.EXT-ND-LK-2|3SG DEM:PROX IMM rattan.vine yam
    2|3SG:SBJ:NPST:IPFV/tell

    e-rä   z=e-rä   zane   gaba   zf
    2|3NSG.*α*-COP.ND   PROX=2|3NSG.*α*-COP.ND DEM:PROX eating.yam IMM
    2|3PL:SBJ:NPST:IPFV/be PROX=2|3PL:SBJ:NPST:IPFV/be

---

[18]Interestingly, 'drink' and 'eat' share the same extended stem (*na*), but 'eat' almost always occurs in an ambifixing transitive template and it employs a common noun as its infinitive (*dagon* 'food'). The verb 'drink' on the other hand employs the infinitive *yonasi* with a regular nominaliser suffix and it always occurs in a (suppressed-object) middle template. The restricted stems of 'drink' and 'eat' are different: *nob* and *wob* respectively.

[19]During the translation of texts, consultants would often rephrase the suppressed-object middle with a generic event ('He did the X-ing') instead of a specific event ('He X-ed it').

e-rä   z=e-rä
2|3NSG.α-COP.ND   PROX=2|3NSG.α-COP.ND
2|3PL:SBJ:NPST:IPFV/be   PROX=2|3PL:SBJ:NPST:IPFV/be

'We put (the yams) down in the house, how these are laying here. That will indicate that these are measuring yams[20] here and these are eating yams here.'

[tci20121001 ABB 15-16]

Another motivation for suppressing the object, partly relevant to the previous example, lies in the relative salience of the referent. There is a tendency for inanimate referents not to be indexed, as we can see in example (28). This example is taken from a stimulus task about domestic violence. The speaker takes over the role of one of the characters in the story. He uses the verb *fiyoksi* 'make' twice, first in a middle template and then in a transitive template.[21] The crucial difference between the two situation types lies in the salience of the referent. In the first clause the referent is generic and inanimate (*yam* 'custom, event'), but in the second clause it is a close relative (*nzenme emoth* 'our sister').

(28)   *"be nima yam ŋafiyokwr. nzenme emoth be nima wäfiyokwr!"*
     be   nima   yam   ŋ-a-fiyok-w-r-$\emptyset$ nzenme   emoth   be
     2SG.ERG like.this event M.α-VC-make.EXT-ND-LK-2|3SG   1NSG.POSS sister   2SG.ERG
                               2|3SG:SBJ:NPST:IPFV/make

     nima   w-a-fiyok-w-r-$\emptyset$
     like.this 3SG.FEM.α-VC-make.EXT-ND-LK-2|3SG
               2|3SG:SBJ>3SG.FEM:OBJ:NPST:IPFV/make
     "You are behaving like this. You are doing this to our sister."

[tci20120925 MAE 89]

We can conclude that intrinsic middles are intransitive event types, but the middle template is used for various functions. The uniting characteristic of these functions is a relatively low degree of elaboration. This may apply either to the participants (28), i.e. they rank low in importance/salience, or to the event itself (27), i.e. the event is less elaborated.

5.4.6 The ambifixing template

The ambifixing template employs both affixes to index referents. The subject argument appears in the suffix, while the object argument is indexed in the prefix (29).

(29)   *gwamf nafangth sräkor: "muri zba känrit nzuzawe!"*
     gwam=f   nafa-ngth   s-ra-a-kor-$\emptyset$ muri zba
     gwam=ERG.SG 3.POSS-younger.sibling 3SG.MASC.β-IRR-ND-say.RS-2|3SG muri PROX.ABL
                               2|3SG:SBJ>3SG.MASC:OBJ:IRR:PFV/says

---

[20] *Natr* is a rattan piece which is often used to measure the dimensions of a particularly big tuber. Large yams are used in competitions or as special gifts.

[21] As we will see in §5.4.6, some transitive verbs like *fiyoksi* obligatorily take the valency change prefix *a-*. Since the argument is in absolute case, one would expect the inflected verb to be *wfiyokwr* (without the *a-* prefix). But this is ungrammatical and *fiyoksi* never occurs without the *a-* prefix. Thus, I regard *fiyoksi* and similar verbs as being deponent.

k-ä-n-rit-∅ nzu-zawe
M.*β*-ND-VENT-cross.over.RS-2SG.IMP 1SG.POSS-side
2SG:SBJ:IMP:PFV:VENT/cross.over
'Gwam said to his brother: "Muri, come over here to my side!"'

[tci20131013-01 ABB #96]

In most cases, the suffix indexes an agent, as in (29). Example (30) shows an experiencer-object construction, in which the suffix encodes a Stimulus. After an evening of stories about sorcery, the speaker announces that she will go to sleep now because 'fear has taken hold of her already'.

(30) *nze rokar kwa thräfrmsé. wtrif z zwefaf.*
nze rokar kwa th-ra-a-frms-é wtri=f z
1SG.ERG thing FUT 2|3NSG.*β*-IRR-VC|ND-prepare.RS-1SG fear=ERG ALR
1SG:SBJ>2|3PL:OBJ:IRR:PFV/prepare

zu-ä-faf-∅
1SG.*γ*-ND-hold.RS-2|3SG
2|3SG:SBJ>1SG:OBJ:RPST:PFV/hold
'I will prepare (my) things. I am already scared.' [tci20130901-04 RNA #164]

Since no more than two referents can be indexed on a verb, the same ambifixing template encodes transitive and ditransitive events. The differences lie in the presence versus absence of the valency change prefix *a-* and the case marking of that argument NP which is indexed in the prefix. In ambifixing transitives, the prefix encodes a patient ('prepare' in 30), theme (29) or experiencer ('hold' in 30), all in the absolutive. The prefix in ambifixing ditransitives encodes a goal (31) in dative case or a possessor (32) marked with a possessive.

(31) *nzun nafaemoth zwärath fof… bänemr … fäms ŋarer*
nzun nafa-emoth zu-ä-r-a-th fof (.) bänemr
1SG.DAT 3.POSS-sister 1SG.*γ*-VC-ND-give.RS-PST-2|3NSG EMPH (.) RECOG.PURP
2|3PL:SBJ>1SG:IO:PST:PFV/give

(.) fäms ŋare=r
(.) exchange woman=PURP
'They gave me their sister as that … as an exchange woman.'

[tci20120805-01 ABB #791-792]

(32) *nzone miyo kwa wabthakwr.*
nzone miyo kwa wo-a-bthak-wr-∅
1SG.POSS desire FUT 1SG.*α*-VC-finish.EXT-ND-2|3SG
2|3SG:SBJ>1SG:IO:NPST:IPFV/finish
'You will fulfil my wish.' [tci20130823-06 CAM #23]

Because the middle template is used for reflexives, the two argument slots of the ambifixing template may not be coreferential. Thus, if we wanted to change example (32) to an auto-benefactive ('I fulfil my wish / I fulfil the wish for me'), it would be ungrammatical to say *nzone miyo wabthakwé* (33a) because the first singular would occur twice in the verb affixes. Instead, one would have to employ a middle construction (33b).

(33) a. **nzone miyo wabthakwé.*
          nzone   miyo wo-a-bthak-w-é
          1SG.POSS wish 1SG.α-VC-finish.EXT-ND-1SG
                          1SG:SBJ>1SG:IO:NPST:IPFV/finish

      b. *nzone miyo **ŋabthakwé.***
          nzone   miyo ŋ-a-bthak-w-é
          1SG.POSS wish M.α-VC-finish.EXT-ND-1SG
                          1SG:SBJ:NPST:IPFV/finish
          'I fulfil my wish.'

Example (34) shows both a possessor and a goal in the first and second verb form, respectively. The example is taken from a story about sorcerers, who – according to local belief – visit the grave sites of recently deceased people. The first clause shows that the possessor noun phrase can be dropped. The noun *mitafo* 'spirit' is usually feminine, but the verb encodes a masculine referent ('his spirit').

(34) *befé mitafo **sabrim** nzun fefe **kwagathif!***
      be=wä   mitafo s-a-brim-∅   nzun   fefe
      2SG.ERG=EMPH spirit 3SG.MASC.β-VC.ND-return.RS-2SG.IMP 1SG.DAT body
                            2SG:SBJ>3SG.MASC:IO:IMP:PFV/return

      kw-a-gathif-∅
      1SG.β-VC.ND-leave.behind.RS-2SG.IMP
      2SG:SBJ>1SG:IO:IMP:PFV/leave.behind
      'You take his spirit back and leave the body for me!'   [tci20130903-04 RNA #92-93]

Example (34) highlights a problem that occurs with verb forms using the restricted stem. As I have shown in §5.3.2, with restricted stems the dual versus non-dual contrast and the valency change is expressed by a vowel change in the prefix. Although there are differences in the vowel pattern for different number combinations, which show the absence versus presence of the valency change prefix, there are a number of neutralisations (§5.5.3.4). The first verb *sabrim* in example (34) can mean both 'return him' (with a direct object) or 'return X for him' / 'return his X' (with an indirect object). Only the fact that *mitafo* 'spirit' is feminine, while the prefix is governed by a masculine referent, indicates that the indirect object is indexed ('return his spirit').

The valency change prefix *a-* attaches productively to almost all transitive verbs introducing a third argument into the clause, usually a beneficiary (dative) or possessor (possessive). A number of lexemes are deponent in the sense that they obligatorily take the valency change prefix *a-*, while the clause remains transitive and the referent indexed in the prefix is flagged with the absolutive case. Such deponent verbs are *frmnzsi* 'prepare' (30) or *fiyoksi* 'make' (28). Given the basic productivity of the ditransitive alternation, we may ask whether the category 'ditransitive' exists in Komnzo at all or whether it is better to view the phenomenon merely as applicativisation, in other words whether all ditransitives are derived.[22] Two counterarguments can be brought forward. First, there are a few verbs which only exist in an ambifixing ditransitive template, the obvious one being *yarisi* 'give'. Secondly, while the ditransitive alternation simply introduces a beneficiary for some verbs, there are rather idiosyncratic changes in meaning for other verbs. For example, *sáminzsi* means 'whisper' in the ambifixing transitive template, but 'teach' in the ambifixing ditransitive template. Another example was given in (8c) where *rbänzsi* means 'untie' as a transitive, but 'explain' in a ditransitive template. Although the meanings of the different templates share the same infinitive/nominalisation and are clearly related ('untie' → 'untie for sb.' = 'explain'), they often differ in idiosyncratic ways ('whisper' → 'whisper for sb.' = 'teach'). Thus, it is better to recognise ditransitive verbs as an independent category.

5.5 Person, gender and number

5.5.1 Person

Person marking in Komnzo verbs exhibits various patterns of syncretism and neutralisation in certain contexts. These patterns differ in the two sites of person marking: the prefix and the suffix. The suffixes show more complexity in their syntagmatic distribution: under certain conditions they are reduced to zero morphemes, and neutralise their person values. In addition, the existence of an independent first singular morpheme is questionable. The suffixes, on the other hand, show less paradigmatic complexity. They encode only two person values and there is only one suffix series. As for the prefixes, the opposite seems to be the case. Although they can be neatly separated and recognised, the prefix slot is equipped with five prefix series, and widespread syncretism within the paradigm is a central characteristic. I will address each subsystem of person marking below.

5.5.1.1 Person suffixes

The person suffix differentiates two person values: first and non-first person. Thus, second and third person are always neutralised and additional information from the personal pronouns or from context is required. As I will explain below, in certain morphological contexts, even this basic distinction is neutralised and only number marking is retained. Table 5.7 lists the suffix forms in the indicative and irrealis moods.

In the middle and ambifixing templates, the person suffixes are involved in marking imperative mood. Table 5.8 shows that the indexing of the addressee employs formatives which are identical to the first person suffixes in indicative or irrealis mood.[23]

---

[22] Please note that the *a-* prefix cannot be called an applicative prefix because it fulfils both functions: increasing and decreasing the valency. Thus, I prefer to label it valency change or valency switch.

[23] Evans (2012b) describes an inflectional category in Nen called the "assentive". The assentive is the second part of an adjacency pair (or dyadic sequence), and it follows an imperative ('Boil the water!' > 'I will boil the water.'). In the assentive, the person suffix deviates from indicative inflection in that it is identical to the preceding imperative; both being zero in perfective aspect. Although assentive inflections are not attested in Komnzo, the formal identity of the first person indicative and second person imperative suffixes can be explained by such conversational adjacency pairs.

Table 5.7: Person suffixes

gloss	formative	example	translation
1SG	-é	ŋakwiré	'I run'
1NSG	-e	ŋakwire	'we run'
2|3SG	-∅	ŋakwir	'you run' or 's/he runs'
2|3NSG	-th	ŋakwirth	'you run' or they run'

Komnzo imperatives can be imperfective ('Keep on doing X!') or perfective ('Do X!'). An example of this is shown in (35). This distinction is signalled by the stem type, but also by the fact that the second singular suffix in perfective imperatives is zero.

Table 5.8: Imperative person suffixes

	gloss	formative	example	translation
EXT stem	2SG.IMP	-é	kakwiré	'You keep running!'
	2NSG.IMP	-e	kakwire	'You (pl) keep running!'
RS stem	2SG.IMP	-∅	kamath	'You run!'
	2NSG.IMP	-e	kemathe	'You (pl) run!'

In Table 5.8, the middle verb -kwi 'run' is shown. The distinction between second singular and non-singular is expressed by the suffix. Another quirk in the system is that the suffix -é is used even if the verb is a prefixing verb, despite the fact that the number distinction is shown in the prefixes only: gn- 2SG vs. th- 2NSG (§5.5.1.4). A prefixing verb like -kogr 'stand' will be gnkogré 'You (SG) keep standing!' versus thkogré 'You (PL) keep standing!' In these cases I gloss -é as marking solely imperative mood, as in (35). However, prefixing verbs do follow the pattern in that only extended stems (imperfective imperative) receive the -é suffix, not the restricted stems (perfective imperatives). I show this in example (35), in which the speaker reports about the rough ways of going hunting with the Suki people.[24] See also §6.2.5 for further discussion of imperative marking.

(35) fiwä we nima ane kwa änor: "kwot fthé **gnäkuk** fathfathenwä **gnkogé!**"
      fi=wä   we nima   ane kwa e-a-nor   kwot   fthé
      3.ABS=EMPH also like.this DEM FUT 2\|3NSG-VC-shout.EXT.ND properly when
                                        3PL:SBJ:NPST:IPFV/shout

---

[24]The verb kuk-/kog- 'stand' is irregular in that it encodes dual versus non-dual in the positional stem, -kogr ND vs. -kogrn DU, but not in the restricted stem -kuk.

gn-ä-kuk	fath-fath=en=wä	gn-kog-é
2SG.*β*.IMP-ND-stand.RS	REDUP-clear.place=LOC=EMPH	2SG.*β*.IMP-stand.EXT.ND-IMP
2SG:SBJ:IMP:PFV/stand		2SG:SBJ:IMP:IPFV/stand

'They will also yell at one another like this "You stand properly in the clearing! Keep on standing!"'   [tci20130927-06 MAB #52-53]

5.5.1.2 The morphemic status of the first singular -*é*

I want to discuss the morphemic status of -*é* and provide evidence for the emergence of a marginal phoneme *é* [ɜ]. Both tables above include a suffix -*é* which for the purpose of the following discussion I will call 'first person singular suffix', disregarding that it may also signal a second singular in the imperative mood without person marking in the prefixing template. This suffix is realised as a short schwa [ɜ] and I have argued in §2.2.2 that schwa is the epenthetic vowel whose distribution is predictable. Schwa is not predictable in word-final position and, thus, has to be represented by a grapheme <é>. There are a handful of morphs in which schwa is attested word-finally, for example nominals (*kayé* 'tomorrow, yesterday', *megé* 'green coconut leaf'), function words (*fthé* 'when') and suffixes (-*thé* ADJZR, -*é* 1SG). The following discussion puts forward the argument that -*é* is the result of a truncation of the non-dual suffix in extended stems, which might have originated in some verbs and later generalised to all verbs. A possible historical explanation in terms of vowel reduction comes from neighbouring varieties in which the first person is marked by an -*a* suffix, for example in Wára and Anta. In Komnzo, there exists a suffix -*a*, but it is a past-tense marker.

As we can see in Tables 5.8 and 5.7, -*é* contrasts with -*e* (1NSG) and -Ø (2|3SG). The first singular -*é* could be analysed either as a morpheme in its own right or as the result of a truncation process of the non-dual suffix, which leaves no possible syllabification other than schwa in a word-final context. I am not claiming that truncation is a synchronic process, but I want to argue that truncation of the non-dual suffix plays a role in the explanation. I draw on evidence from more general properties of the suffix subsystem such as the non-dual suffix, the presence of a linking consonant and the neutralisation of person distinctions. As we will see below, the argumentation is only applicable to inflected forms which build on the extended stem. Restricted stems encode the duality contrast in pre-stem position. Hence, we have to assume that the result of the truncation process, the word-final schwa -*é*, has been extended to other morphological contexts.

First, let us turn to the non-dual marker for extended stems. The verb *kwi-* 'run' in Table 5.7 is irregular in that it employs -*r* for signalling the non-dual. The regular pattern, attested for 90% of verb lexemes, involves one of the three non-dual allomorphs -*wr*, -*nzr* and -*thr*. Consider the verb *marasi* 'see' in (36a-f), which takes the -*wr* allomorph. In first person singular (36a), the non-dual suffix is -*w* instead of -*wr*.

(36) a. *y-mar-w-é*
          3SG.MASC-see-ND-1SG
          'I see him.'

    b. *y-mar-n-e*
       3SG.MASC-see-DU-1NSG
       'We two see him.'

    c. *y-mar-wr-e*
       3SG.MASC-see-ND-1NSG
       'We see him.'

    d. *y-mar-wr-∅*
       3SG.MASC-see-ND-2|3SG
       'S/He sees him.' or 'You see him.'

    e. *y-mar-n-th*
       3SG.MASC-see-DU-2|3SG
       'They (two) see him.' or 'You (two) see him.'

    f. *y-mar-wr-th*
       3SG.MASC-see-ND-2|3NSG
       'They see him.' or 'You see him.'

In the examples, only the first singular (36a) deviates in that it takes a truncated form *-w*, from which final *-r* is deleted. This truncation in the first singular is attested for all three allomorphs of the non-dual suffix: *-wr* → *-w*, *-nzr* → *-nz* and *-thr* → *-th*. What weakens this particular piece of evidence is the fact that there is some variation between the non-truncated and the truncated formative even when other suffixal material follows, such as AND *-o*, 1NSG *-e* or 2|3NSG *-th*. For example, looking at the token frequency in the corpus of 2|3NSG *-th* preceded by *-nzr* (non-truncated) versus *-th* preceded by *-nz* (truncated), we find 91 verb forms with the non-truncated non-dual *-nzrth* and 13 with the truncated non-dual *-nzth*.[25] A similar distribution is found with the first non-singular *-e* suffix. There is no variation with the 2|3SG, which is a zero morpheme. The 2|3SG is never preceded by the truncated formative. In conclusion, the non-dual is never truncated with the 2|3SG zero morpheme, it shows some variation with other suffixes (but the non-truncated formative has a much higher frequency), and it is always truncated with the first singular.

Further evidence comes from person neutralisation patterns. The first singular *-é* disappears when further suffixes are added, for example the past suffix *-a*, the durative suffix *-m* or the andative suffix *-o*. Consider examples (37a, 37d and 37e), which neutralise the person value completely. In (36), the distinction between first and second/third person is basically a contrast between the surface result of a truncation process *-é* (36a) and a zero morpheme (36d). For examples (37a), (37d), and (37e), we have to postulate a zero marker, which now only encodes number (SG) and contrasts with 1NSG *-e* (37b) and 2|3NSG *-th* (37c).

(37)   a. *y-mar-wr-a-∅*
          3SG.MASC-see-ND-PST-SG
          'I saw him.' or 'You saw him.' or 'S/He saw him.'

---

[25]This search can be replicated by a simple search query: "nzrth" versus "nzth" in word-final context (in REGEX syntax: "nzrth\b" versus "nzth\b").

b. *y-mar-wr-a-k-e*
3SG.MASC-see-ND-PST-LK-1NSG
'We saw him.'

c. *y-mar-wr-a-th*
3SG.MASC-see-ND-PST-2|3NSG
'You saw him.' or 'They saw him.'

d. *y-mar-wr-m-∅*
3SG.MASC-see-ND-DUR-SG
'I was seeing him.' or 'You were seeing him.' or 'S/He was seeing him.'

e. *y-mar-wr-o-∅*
3SG.MASC-see-ND-AND-SG
'I see him that way.' or 'You see him that way.' or 'S/He sees him that way.'

A third piece of evidence comes from a linking consonant in the suffix subsystem. Example (37b) shows that the past suffix *-a* and the 1NSG *-e* are separated by *-k*. We have seen in §2.4.3 that the phonology of Komnzo allows strings of consonants which are broken up by epenthesis. However, the phonological system does not tolerate strings of vowels, which is demonstrated by the appearance of the linker in (37b). This can be used to strengthen the argument that the first singular *-é* deviates from other suffixes. We would expect (37a) not to neutralise the person value, and instead to insert the linker between the past suffix *-a* and *-é* analogous to (37b). However, the predicted inflection **ymarwraké* is ungrammatical.

The first singular *-é* occurs in other morphological contexts, where there is no truncated preceding element. As pointed out above, the template of restricted stems marks the dual versus non-dual contrast in pre-stem position and, thus, there is no non-dual marker to truncate (38a).[26] Likewise, there is no truncation of the dual marker *-n* in the template of extended stems (38b). However, the person neutralisations described above also occur in these contexts (38c and 38d).

(38) a. *s-a-mar-é*
3SG.MASC-ND-see(RS)-1NSG
'I saw him.'

b. *e-mar-n-é*
2|3NSG-see(EXT)-ND-PST-SG
'I see both of them.'

c. *s-a-mar-a-∅*
3SG.MASC-ND-see(RS)-PST-SG
'I saw him.' or 'You saw him.' or 'S/He saw him.'

d. *e-mar-n-a*
2|3NSG-see(EXT)-ND-PST-SG
'I saw both of them.' or 'You saw both of them.' or 'S/He saw both of them.'

---

[26]The verb *marasi* belongs to the class which has identical forms for restricted and extended stems (see Table 5.2), and only the template and the affixal material signal the aspectual value.

We have to conclude that a case for truncation or a negative morpheme as a synchronic process can only be made for a very circumscribed morphological context: for non-dual inflected verbs built from the extended stem. For other contexts, we have to postulate a suffix formative *-é*. This is best explained by a historical process of vowel reduction or syllable loss, which created a new marginal phoneme *é*. This can be used to explain word-final schwa in other items.[27] As I mentioned in the beginning of this section, surrounding varieties like Wára or Anta mark the first person singular with an *-a* suffix. Comparative material from other Tonda varieties is needed to settle this question.

5.5.1.3 Morpheme slots in the suffix system

In the preceding discussion, the linking consonant *-k* was introduced as a way of separating two adjacent vowel suffixes. This purely phonological explanation is insufficient and, on closer inspection, we find that the linker *-k* helps to arrange the suffixal material into morpheme slots. In addition to the first singular *-é*, the suffixal material includes the following morphemes: past *-a*, durative *-m*, andative *-o*, 1NSG *-e* and 2|3NSG *-th*. In the following section, I describe how these suffixes line up, which of them are mutually exclusive, and in which context person neutralisations occur.

First, the past suffix *-a* and the durative suffix *-m* never co-occur. The combinatorial system of Komnzo verb morphology employs a different strategy to express a past durative category, discussed in §6.2.

Secondly, the andative *-o* and the 1NSG *-e* stand in syntagmatic opposition to each other or, occupying the same slot. Consider examples (39a-d). In examples (39b) and (39d) the person value is fully neutralised, because the suffix *-th*, which was indexing 2|3NSG in earlier examples (36e-f and 37c), can now only be glossed as NSG.[28] The important observation in (39b) is that the linker *-k* is not used. If its appearance could be predicted on purely phonological grounds, we would expect a form like **ymarwroke*. But this is un-grammatical. Thus, I characterise the linking consonant in the following way: *-k* occurs (i) after the past suffix *-a*, (ii) if the following suffix consists of a vowel formative.

(39)   a. *y-mar-wr-e*
            3SG.MASC-see-ND-1NSG
            'We see him.'

    b. *y-mar-wr-o-th*
            3SG.MASC-see-ND-AND-NSG
            'We see him that way.' or 'You see him that way.' or 'They see him that way.'

    c. *y-mar-wr-a-k-e*
            3SG.MASC-see-ND-PST-LK-1NSG
            'We saw him.'

---

[27] The adjectivaliser *-thé* might be a reduced form of the similative case marker *-thatha*.

[28] An alternative would be to analyse *-th* as marking only number (NSG), not person. I reject this analysis, because (i) this would result in a system where only first person is marked overtly and (ii) the 1NSG in examples like (39a) would be an exception to the regular non-singular (*-th*).

d. *y-mar-wr-a-k-o-th*
    3SG.MASC-see-ND-PST-LK-AND-NSG
    'We saw him that way.' or 'You saw him that way.' or 'They saw him that way.'

Examples (39b) and (39d) also show that of the three categories (person, number, direction) it is person which is neutralised first. In the discussion of examples (37a-e), we found the same to be true for the person values of the singulars.

In (40), we find a textual example of the person neutralisation in (39d). In the example, a woman talks about her marriage and how she and her husband prepared a feast for her brothers and uncles. In (40) the first person interpretation of the actor of *tharakoth*[29] is clear from the preceding verb *yafiyokrnake* which lacks the andative *-o* suffix and, thus, is inflected with the first non-singular *-e* suffix.

(40) *dagon yafiyokrnake. babainm ane **tharakoth**.*
      dagon y-a-fiyok-rn-a-k-e   babai=nm   ane
      food 3SG.MASC-VC-make.EXT-PST-LK-1NSG uncle=DAT.NSG DEM
            1DU:SBJ>3SG.MASC:OBJ:PST:IPFV/make

      th-a-r-a-k-o-th
      2|3NSG.*y*-VC.DU-give.RS-PST-LK-AND-NSG
      DU:SBJ>2|3PL:IO:PST:PFV:AND/give
      'We prepared the food. We gave that to the uncles.'   [tci20130823-08 WAM #66-67]

The suffix subsystem of Komnzo verbs is summarised in Figure 5.6. The elements which share a column or an extended column in the figure are mutually exclusive. For example, if *-é* occurs, all the other material will not appear or if the durative suffix *-m* occurs, the past suffix *-a* (along with the linker *-k*) will not appear. The system as described here is applicable to both stem types. For the restricted stem the only difference lies in the fact that duality is marked in pre-stem position, as in *tharakoth* in (40). Therefore, some of the morphemes in the suffix system are optional: the dual/non-dual morphemes, the two TAM markers (PST *-a* and DUR *-m*) and the andative *-o*. Number (SG vs. NSG) is always marked.

The suffixing system is thus characterised by syntagmatic complexity, i.e. the chain of suffixes does not allow a straightforward segmentation into slots and respective functions. Moreover, the presence versus absence of individual suffixes affects the form and function of other suffixes.

5.5.1.4 Person prefixes

The person prefixes are syntagmatically less complex than the person suffixes. The prefix system comprises a single slot which is always filled with a formative, i.e. there are no zero morphemes.[30] On the other hand, the prefix system is paradigmatically more

---

[29]In *tharakoth* the pre-stem marker operates on a plural versus non-plural opposition. This pattern of pre-stem marking is discussed in §5.5.3.4.

[30]The only formative which occurs in the person marking slot, but does not encode person, is the middle marker, which is used for other purposes (§5.4.5).

stem	(duality)	(TAM)	(direction, person), number	
√	-*nzr, wr-, r-* -*n*	-*m*	-*é*	
			-*e*	
		-*o*	-*∅*	
		-*a*(-*k*)	-*th*	

Figure 5.6: Suffix subsystem of Komnzo verbs

complex. The prefix fuses person and number marking with information relevant to TAM. However, we have to draw on abstract glossing labels because the five prefix series are underspecified for a particular TAM value. Table 5.9 lays out the five prefix series: α, β, β_1, β_2, and γ.

Table 5.9: Person prefixes

gloss	α	β	β_1	β_2	γ
1SG	*wo-*	*kw-*	*ku-*	*kwof-*	*zu-*
1NSG	*n-*	*nz-* / *nzn-*	*nzu-*	*nzf-*	*nzn-*
2SG	*n-*	*nz-* / *gn-*	*gu-*	*gf-*	*nzn-*
3SG.FEM	*w-*	*z-*	*zu-*	*zf-*	*z-*
3SG.MASC	*y-*	*s-*	*su-*	*sf-*	*s-*
2|3NSG	*e-*	*th-*	*thu-*	*thf-*	*th-*
M	*ŋ-*	*k-*	*kw-*	*kf-*	*z-*

Before we look at the patterns of person marking, I will provide some justification as to why there are five independent series. Table 5.9 shows that there is widespread syncretism between the series, especially in the third person between the β and γ series. The formal difference between the α, β and γ series is clearest in the first person singular and the middle marker, each of which overtly distinguishes all five series. Furthermore, the table shows that we can speak of three main series: α, β, γ, plus two subseries: β_1 and β_2. These two subseries add an /u/ and /ɸ/ element to the β series. I will discuss in detail why I still treat them as independent series in §6.2.1. An additional quirk is added to the system by the fact that, within the β series, the first nonsingular and the second singular have two different formatives for the two modal categories: the imperative and irrealis.[31]

---

[31]The second singular differs in a number of ways which will be discussed in §6.2.1. Note that the second singular *gn-* is only used in the imperatives of prefixing verbs, where the addressee argument is encoded in the prefix. Verbs in the middle and ambifixing templates on the other hand employ the suffix to encode the addressee argument in the imperatives, leaving the prefix β series for the middle marker or the indexing of the undergoer argument.

The prefixes differentiate three person values in the singular: first, second and third. The values of second and third person in non-singular are always neutralised, leaving this ambiguity for either the context or the personal pronouns to resolve. The same holds true for the syncretism between the first non-singular and the second singular in the α and the γ series.[32] This pattern of syncretism is found in languages across the Yam family (Evans et al. 2017).

The overview of the verb template presented in the introduction of this chapter (Table 5.1) shows that the person prefix is followed by the valency change prefix *a-*, whose presence impacts on the formatives of the person prefixes in various ways. The α series shows a number of irregularities given in Table 5.10, for example with the first singular: /*wo-a-*/ → *wa-* or the second/third non-singular /*e-a-*/ → *ä-*. In a Komnzo recording from the 1980s made by the anthropologist Mary Ayres, I found a different realisation of the second/third non-singular prefix, which is [eja-]. In terms of segmentation, this is a much more transparent realisation. The recording was made with an older man, maybe in his late sixties. In modern Komnzo, there is no variation and the prefix is realised as given in the table as [æ-].

Table 5.10: Person prefixes: α-series with valency change prefix *a-*

gloss	formative	segmentation
1SG	*wa-*	*wo-a-*
1NSG	*na-*	*n-a-*
2SG	*na-*	*n-a-*
3SG.FEM	*wä-*	*w-a-*
3SG.MASC	*ya-*	*y-a-*
2|3NSG	*ä-*	*e-a-*
M	*ŋa-*	*ŋ-a-*

The other prefix series behave more regularly in the presence of the valency change prefix *a-*, but there is some influence of the valency change prefix. For example, the formatives of the β_2 series all end in a high back vowel [u], which turns into the corresponding glide when *a-* is present: 2SG *gu-* → *gwa-*. The β and β_2 series end in consonants. For both series, the *a-* prefix is simply added, for example 2\|3NSG *th-* → *tha-* for the β series and 2\|3NSG *thf-* → *thfa-* for the β_2 series.

As I have discussed in §5.3.3, the β, β_1 and γ series may combine with the restricted stem, the γ series exclusively so. With the restricted stem, dual marking takes place in pre-stem position (§5.3.2) and the *a-* prefix simultaneously encodes valency change and dual vs. non-dual. As the marking pattern does not impact on the formatives of the person prefixes, I will defer this topic to the discussion to §5.5.3.4.

---

[32] Table 5.9 also includes identical formatives *nz-* for first non-singular and second singular in the β series. The β series is used for irrealis inflection. The neutralisation is there on an abstract paradigmatic level, but the inflected verbs are never identical, because – unlike all other person/number combinations – the second singular does not take the irrealis prefix *ra-*. This will be further discussed in §6.2.1.

5.5.2 Gender

The agreement target of gender is the third singular prefix of the verb. There is a feminine and masculine gender value. Metalinguistic statements by speakers are often expressed as *madema rä* 'It is a girl' for feminine or *srak yé* 'It is a boy' for masculine. The formatives employed to encode gender across the prefix series are given in Table 5.9.

The discussion in §5.4 has shown that the prefix indexes the direct and indirect object in the ambifixing transitive template, and the subject of intransitives in the prefixing template. It follows that only those types of argument roles show agreement in gender, whereas the more agent-like arguments never show gender agreement.

The semantics of nominal gender classification in the noun lexicon is discussed in §3.1.3.

5.5.3 Number

Komnzo verbs encode three number values: singular, dual and plural. There exists an additional large plural value which is available only for prefixing verbs or verbs in the prefixing template. I describe the fourth number value in §5.5.3.2.

The peculiarity of number marking in Komnzo lies in the fact that it is distributed over two separate slots which, looked at individually, do not distinguish all three values, but operate on a binary opposition. Hence, the overall ternary number opposition is reduced to a binary opposition in the respective slots on the verb. There are three logical possibilities for this reduction because each of the three number values can be contrasted with its opposite: singular vs. non-singular; dual vs. non-dual; plural vs. non-plural. The combination of any two of the three binary oppositions is sufficient to encode all three number values. Figure 5.7 shows the principle behind this reduction.

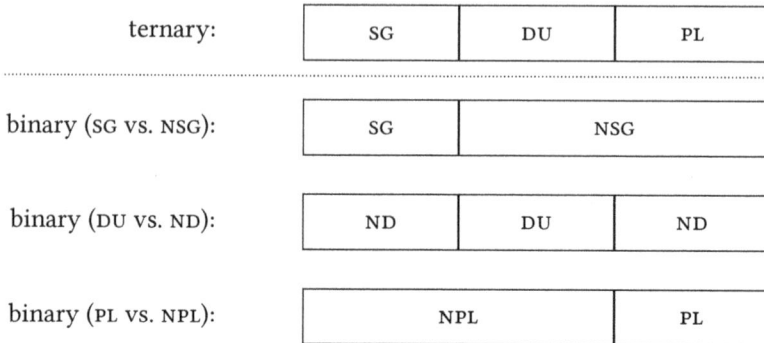

ternary:	SG	DU	PL

| binary (SG vs. NSG): | SG | NSG | |

| binary (DU vs. ND): | ND | DU | ND |

| binary (PL vs. NPL): | NPL | | PL |

Figure 5.7: Three ways of breaking up a ternary opposition

Komnzo makes use of all three oppositions, but only two of the possible combinations. The person affixes always operate on a singular vs. non-singular opposition. A separate affix, which I call the duality affix, makes a distinction between dual vs. non-dual. I will show below that under certain circumstances, the same affix encodes plural vs. non-plural, but this is a marginal pattern (§5.5.3.4). The basic system of distributed number marking integrates a SG-NSG opposition in the person affixes with a DU-ND opposition in the duality affix. Figure 5.8 provides an overview of this principle.

		DUALITY AFFIX	
		DU	ND
PERSON AFFIX	SG		singular
	NSG	dual	plural

Figure 5.8: Basic principle of distributed number marking on verbs

Figure 5.8 shows that out of four possible combinations, in fact only three are normally put to use, namely those that are logically compatible. Prefixing verbs and stems in a prefixing template, which includes positional verbs, are exceptional in that they utilise the fourth, seemingly nonsensical, combination SG-DU to encode a large plural (§5.5.3.2).

The two sites involved in number marking have very different properties. The binary opposition in the person prefixes and suffixes is much more stable in the sense that (i) the encoded value can be straightforwardly associated with an argument, because person and number marking are fused into one morpheme, (ii) the position of these affixes with respect to the stem is fixed and (iii) the values encoded are always SG and NSG. The duality affix differs in all three points and the subsequent discussion of number marking will focus on its peculiarities. But to give an overview here: first, if there are two participants indexed in the verb, the duality affix is ambiguous as to which of the two it is indexing. Secondly, duality is marked in a suffix with extended stems, but in a complex portmanteau prefix with restricted stems. Finally, as was mentioned above, in part of the paradigm, the DU-ND opposition is replaced by a PL-NPL opposition. I will discuss these points below.

5.5.3.1 Ambiguities in the reference of the duality affix

Examples (41a-g) show the verb *fathasi* 'hold' with different number combinations of the two arguments.[33] Only in example (41f) we find several possibilities with respect to number marking because both person affixes signal non-singular. The ambiguity stems from the fact that the duality marker is ambiguous as to which of the two arguments it is indexing. In other words, the dual morpheme *n-* in (41f) signals that one of the two participants is dual, but not which one. This does not create any ambiguities in cases

---

[33]Note, that the English translations are all in third person, although some of the person indexing morphemes neutralise the distinction between second and third person and, thus, could also be translated as second person.

where one of the two person affixes is singular (41a-e). Likewise, it is not a problem if both person affixes are non-singular and the duality affix in non-dual (41g). Although examples (41a-g) show the extended stem of the verb *fathasi*, this ambiguity is also found with restricted stems, where the duality affix occurs in pre-stem position.

(41)   a. *y-fath-wr-∅*
           3SG.MASC-hold.EXT-ND-2|3SG
           'S/He holds him.'

       b. *y-fath-n-th*
           3SG.MASC-hold.EXT-DU-2|3NSG
           'They (2) hold him.'

       c. *y-fath-wr-th*
           3SG.MASC-hold.EXT-ND-2|3NSG
           'They (3+) hold him.'

       d. *e-fath-n-∅*
           2|3NSG-hold.EXT-DU-2|3SG
           'S/He holds them (2).'

       e. *e-fath-wr-∅*
           2|3NSG-hold.EXT-ND-2|3SG
           'S/He holds them (3+).'

       f. *e-fath-n-th*
           2|3NSG-hold.EXT-DU-2|3NSG
           'They (2) hold them (3+).' or 'They (2) hold them (2).' or 'They (3+) hold them (2).'

       g. *e-fath-wr-th*
           2|3NSG-hold.EXT-ND-2|3NSG
           'They (3+) hold them (3+).'

For verbs in the transitive ambifixing and ditransitive ambifixing template, the distribution of the dual and non-dual markers can be expressed in an abstract way, as in Figure 5.9.

		ACTOR		
		SG	DU	PL
UNDERGOER	SG	wr	n	wr
	DU	n	n	n
	PL	wr	n	wr

Figure 5.9: The duality matrix with *fathasi*

For verb forms which index only one argument the marking pattern is simpler, as there is no referential ambiguity in the duality suffix. This is relevant for verbs in a prefixing or middle template. Examples (42a-c) show the verb *thoraksi* 'appear' in a prefixing template cycled through all three number values.

(42)   a. *wo-thorak-wr*
        1SG-appear.EXT-ND
        'I arrive.'

     b. *n-thorak-n*   (~ *n-thorak-rn*)
        1NSG-appear.EXT-DU
        'We (2) arrive.'

     c. *n-thorak-wr*
        1NSG-appear.EXT-ND
        'We (3+) arrive.'

Note that there are two variants for the dual morpheme, *-n* and *-rn* in (42b), which are attested for almost all members of the small class of prefixing verbs. This variation is both intra-speaker and inter-speaker and, thus far, no patterning along social lines could be detected (e.g. age of the speaker, speaker's exposure to other varieties, etc).

5.5.3.2 Large plurals with prefixing verbs

The prefixing template indexes the sole argument of the verb in the prefix, while the suffix slot is not used. We have seen that only a small number of verbs are inherently prefixing (§5.4.4), and about fifty stems may enter into this template. The latter group includes positional verbs (§5.4.4.2). I show below that because there is no ambiguity in the reference of the duality marker, all four cells in the paradigm can be exploited. This allows for a fourth number value, the large plural, which is formed by combining the dual marker with a singular. Figure 5.10 illustrates the pattern.

		DUALITY AFFIX	
		DU	ND
PERSON AFFIX	SG	large plural	singular
	NSG	dual	plural

Figure 5.10: Principle of distributed number marking for prefixing verbs

Consider example (43). The speaker in the story has been away from Rouku for a long time. He asks his brother whether the palm wine containers are still hanging, and the brother replies 'there are plenty'. This is expressed by the copula in dual and the prefix in singular. Note that the stem of the copula is sensitive to dual versus non-dual. I used the gloss label LPL for large plural.

(43) *"eh ngthé bana! sgeru komnzo emithgr?" "ah, segeru komnzo **yrn**"*

    eh ngthé bana sgeru   komnzo e-mi-thgr   ah

    hey brother poor palm.wine still   2|3NSG.α-hang.EXT-STAT.ND ah

                                          2|3PL:SBJ:NPST:STAT/hang

    segeru   komnzo y-rn

    palm.wine still   3SG.MASC.α-COP.DU

                              3LPL:SBJ:NPST:IPFV/be

    "Hey brother, are the palm wine (containers) still hanging?" "Yes, there are still plenty." [tci20130927-06 MAB #189]

Examples (44a-d) are elicited forms showing the positional verb *räzsi* 'erect, stand up' in all four number values.[34]

(44)   a. *woz*   *w-räs-thg-r*

          bottle 3SG.FEM-erect-STAT-ND

          'The bottle is standing.'

      b. *woz*   *e-räs-thg-n*   (~ *e-räs-thg-rn*)

          bottle 2|3NSG-erect-STAT-DU

          'The two bottles are standing.'

      c. *woz*   *e-räs-thg-r*

          bottle 2|3NSG-erect-STAT-ND

          'The bottles are standing.'

      d. *woz*   *y-räs-thg-n*   (~ *y-räs-thg-rn*)

          bottle 3SG.MASC-erect-STAT-DU

          'All the bottles are standing.' or 'Many bottles are standing.'

Example (44d) shows the large plural construction in which the seemingly non-sensical combination of a singular in the person prefix and a dual in the duality slot yields a large plural or exhaustive plural interpretation. There are some restrictions to the large pural. First, as we have seen, it only occurs in the prefixing template. Even though a stem like *räz-* 'erect' can appear in a middle or ambifixing template, it cannot form large plurals in these templates. Secondly, large plurals only occur in third person, not in first or second. Note that it is always the masculine prefix which is used in the large plural construction, even if the referent is feminine, as with *woz* 'bottle' (44a). In this way, the large plural construction substantiates the principle of distributed exponence, whereby the morphological material at the language's disposal is employed in ways that are not predictable by looking at individual morphemes.

---

[34]Note that we find the same variation in the dual morpheme (*-n* and *-rn*) as with other prefixing verbs. Compare with examples (42a-c).

Unfortunately, the large plural construction is attested only once in the corpus (43). The evidence presented above comes from eliciation.[35] Although the large plural is readily understood and judged grammatical by all my informants, I have not overheard it in daily conversation. Speakers commonly refer to this construction as 'a way the old people spoke'. Therefore, we have to assume that it will fade from the speakers' passive knowledge eventually and disappear altogether. In fact, the speaker in example (43) was an older man.

Although on different levels of comparison, dual marking in pre-stem position and the formation of large plurals are not compatible. This is partly caused by the stative semantics of verbs in the prefixing template. For example, positionals take the stative suffix *-thgr* which blocks all perfective semantics. Pre-stem dual marking on the other hand occurs only with restricted stems, and restricted stems are used to form perfectives. A positional verb like *räzsi* 'erect' can occur outside the prefixing template and form perfectives, but in this case the large plural does not apply. We saw in §5.4.4 that there are some prefixing verbs, which are not stative, for example *yarenzsi* 'look around' or *ziksi* 'turn to side'. These do form perfectives in the prefixing template. However, the large plural combination results in an ungrammatical inflection.

I suggest that a historical perspective explains why this is the case. I show in §5.5.3.4 that pre-stem dual marking is messier than post-stem dual marking in the sense that it is less segmentable and there are more patterns of syncretism. I have argued in §5.3.4 that pre-stem dual marking is an innovation, and that post-stem dual marking is an older pattern. Thus, the large plural construction has not survived the change in the pattern shift. Therefore, prefixing verbs with dynamic semantics cannot form large plurals in their perfectives.

5.5.3.3 Allomorphy in the post-stem duality slot

Before I turn to the dual marking in pre-stem position with restricted stems, I discuss the topic of allomorphy in post-stem position. The dual morpheme in the duality slot shows little variation. The above described variation between *-n* and *-rn* is found with prefixing verbs only; elsewhere the dual morpheme is always *-n*. As for the non-dual morpheme, the situation is different. There are three allomorphs (*wr-*, *nzr-*, *-r*) and their distribution is phonologically conditioned by the final element of the verb stem. The conditioning rules layed out in Table 5.11 account for 85% (275/322) of the attested verb lexemes.

The remaining 15% of verb lexemes are irregular (i) in taking a different formative to mark non-dual (e.g. *-thr* or *-∅*), (ii) in taking one of the three allomorphs under violation of the conditioning rules or (iii) in expressing the dual/non-dual contrast by irregular changes in the verb stem, for example *moth* 'walk' (*-yak* ND vs. *-yan* DU) or *kwan* 'shout' (*-nor* ND vs. *-rn* DU).

---

[35] I want to thank Nick Evans for pointing out the combinatorial possibility (SG+DU) in Nen (Evans 2014) which allowed me to test this pattern with Komnzo speakers.

Table 5.11: Allomorphs of the non-dual suffix

formatives	rule	count	example	gloss
-wr	/ k]$_{stem\_}$	92	mätrak-	'bring out'
			wek-	'invite'
	/ g]$_{stem\_}$	38	mäyog-	'repeat'
			brig-	'return'
	/ n]$_{stem\_}$	34	wathkn-	'pack up'
			myukn-	'twist'
	/ r]$_{stem\_}$	25	rsr-	'fish (poison)'
			wagr-	'meet'
-nzr	/ V]$_{stem\_}$	62	yagu-	'pour out'
			yafü-	'open'
			mrä-	'stroll'
			fsi-	'count'
			tha-	'uncover'
-r	/ z]$_{stem\_}$	24	brüz-	'submerge'
			rifthz-	'hide'
			räz-	'erect'
Total		275		

5.5.3.4 Pre-stem dual marking with restricted stems

The previous discussion concentrated on dual marking with extended stems. For restricted stems, this suffix slot is not available and the dual vs. non-dual contrast is marked by the vowel of the prefix, which changes to ä for non-dual. Pre-stem dual marking is relevant only for those TAM categories which build their inflection on the restricted stem. These are verbs inflected for iterative and perfective aspect. The latter include indicative (recent past and past tense), imperative or irrealis forms. In the following description, I use the irrealis perfective forms to explain the pattern and point to other TAM categories where they deviate.

Interestingly, it is the non-dual that receives a marker (ä-), while the dual is zero marked. At the same time, pre-stem dual marking is less segmentable and harder to gloss than post-stem dual marking, because the non-dual ä vowel superposes vowels from other prefixal material, for example the valency changer a- or the irrealis prefix ra-. This leads to patterns of syncretism which span several grammatical dimensions (valency, number, aspect, mood, etc.).

Irrealis mood is expressed by the prefix ra-, which directly follows the person/number prefix or the middle marker of the β prefix series (see Table 5.9 in §5.5.1.4). The non-dual marker ä replaces the vowel of the ra- prefix for all the person/number combinations which involve a non-dual participant. This pattern is uniform for prefixing as well as ambifixing verbs. In (45-51), I provide textual examples of the number combinations with a third person actor and a first person undergoer.[36] We find the *ä* vowel for the following actor>undergoer combinations: SG>SG (45), PL>SG (47), SG>PL (49) and PL>PL (50).

(45) *adif nima **kwräs** "ranzo?"*
      adi=f   nima kw-rä-s-∅   ra=nzo
      aunt=ERG.SG QUOT 1SG.*β*-IRR.ND-ask.RS-2|3SG what=ONLY
                        2|3SG:SBJ>1SG:OBJ:IRR:PFV/ask
      'Aunt asked me: "What is it?"'   [tci20120922-25 ALK #15-16]

(46) *yare kma nzä nafa **kwrakarth**.*
      yare kma nzä   nafa   kw-ra-kar-th
      bag POT 1SG.ABS 3NSG.ERG 1SG.*β*-IRR.DU-pull.RS-2|3NSG
                               2|3DU:SBJ>1SG:OBJ:IRR:PFV/pull
      'They (2) should take the bag from me.'   [tci20130907-02 JAA #10]

(47) *ngatha fäth ferä nafa **kwränbrmth**.*
      ngatha fäth f=e-rä   nafa   kw-rä-n-brm-th
      dog   DIM DIST=2|3NSG.*α*-COP.ND 3NSG.ERG 1SG.*β*-IRR.ND-VENT-follow.RS-2|3NSG
             DIST=2|3PL:SBJ:NPST:IPFV/be   2|3PL:SBJ>1SG:OBJ:IRR:PFV:VENT/follow
      'The small dogs over there, they started following me.'   [tci20111119-03 ABB #94]

(48) *foba **nzrans** "bä mon ern?"*
      foba   nz-ra-n-s-∅   bä   mon e-rn
      DIST.ABL 1NSG.*β*-IRR.DU-VENT-ask.RS-2|3SG 2.ABS how 2|3NSG.*α*-COP.DU
               2|3SG:SBJ>1DU:OBJ:IRR:PFV:VENT/ask   2|3DU:SBJ:NPST:IPFV/be
      'He asked us (2): "Who are you?"'   [tci20120904-02 MAB #125]

(49) *paituaf **nzräkor** "nzä fiyafr wiyak."*
      paitua=f   nz-rä-kor-∅   nzä   fiyaf=r
      old.man=ERG.SG 1NSG.*β*-IRR.ND-speak.RS-2|3SG 1SG.ABS hunting=PURP
                     2|3SG:SBJ>1PL:OBJ:IRR:PFV/speak

      wo-yak
      1SG.*α*-walk.EXT.ND
      1SG:SBJ:NPST:IPFV/walk
      'He said to us: "I will go hunting."'   [tci20120821-02 LNA #11-12]

(50) *kar zf rä zf masu ... manema **nzräkorth** masu kar.*
      kar   zf rä   zf masu (.) mane=ma
      place IMM 3SG.FEM.COP.ND   IMM masu (.) which=CHAR
                3SG.FEM:SBJ:NPST:IPFV/be

---

[36]Irrealis mood may be used in narratives for pragmatic reasons (backgrounding) and refer to events which actually took place (§6.4.3)

nz-rä-kor-th   masu kar

1NSG.*β*-IRR.ND-speak.RS-2|3NSG masu place.

2|3PL:SBJ>1PL:OBJ:IRR:PFV/speak

'This place right here is Masu, which is why they call us Masu people.'

[tci20120922-08 DAK #87]

(51) ni **nzrakorth** *"bä!" … oroman babua … "bä kwa ŋakwinth zmbär aki kwayanen!"*

ni   nz-ra-kor-th   bä   (.) oroman babua (.) bä   kwa

1NSG 1NSG.*β*-IRR.DU-speak.RS-2|3NSG 2.ABS (.) old.man babua (.) 2.ABS FUT

2|3PL:SBJ>1DU:OBJ:IRR:PFV/speak

ŋ-a-kwi-n-th   zmbär aki   kwayan=en

M.*α*-VC-run.EXT-DU-2|3NSG night moon light=LOC

2|3DU:SBJ:NPST:IPFV/run

'They said to us (2): "You!" to old man Babua "You two will run at night in the moonlight."'   [tci20120904-01 MAB #135-137]

Note that just like in post-stem dual marking (§5.5.3.1), pre-stem dual marking is ambiguous as to which of the two arguments is dual or non-dual. The verb *nzrakorth* 'they said to us' in (51) could be any of the three possible actor>undergoer combinations (PL>DU, DU>DU or DU>PL) because both person affixes index a non-singular participant. Thus, the absence of the *ä* vowel indicates that one of the two participants is dual, but not which one. Only context may solve this structural ambiguity, which in (51) is clear from the second verb *ŋakwinth* 'you two go'. For verbs in a prefixing template, there is no ambiguity since they index only one argument. Non-dual participants receive the *ä* vowel, while dual participants do not. The same holds for verbs in the middle template.

The marking pattern can be expressed in an abstract matrix, as in Figure 5.11. In terms of structure, not in its formatives, this matrix is identical to post-stem duality marking (see Figure 5.9).

		ACTOR		
		SG	DU	PL
UNDERGOER	SG	ä	∅	ä
	DU	∅	∅	∅
	PL	ä	∅	ä

Figure 5.11: The duality matrix without VC prefix

There are some exceptions for the third singular prefixes (both feminine and masculine). The combination of SG>3SG in the ambifixing template and 3SG in the prefixing template receive the vowel *a* rather than *ä* in all relevant TAM categories. In the imperatives, it is *a* for both of the combinations SG>3SG and PL>3SGInflections involving a dual participant would receive a zero marker. In a discussion with two informants after listening to old recordings made by the anthropologist Mary Ayres in the 1980s, I was able to elicit one inflectional form that is relevant to this topic. The informant contrasted the modern Komnzo inflection *santhor* 'He arrived here' with an older form of the same verb *snäthor*.[37] A first observation is that the *ä* does occur in the older form. Interestingly, it occurs after the venitive *n-* prefix. At the current stage of documentation, not much can be said about the time frame during which this change has occured. The informant who provided this information is now in his mid-sixties and remembers "old people" using this form. I was not able to elicit a full paradigm of these older inflections and, thus, we are denied insight into the changes that took place in the verb template. As for now, we can only state that the non-dual *ä* vowel existed at some point in time with third singulars in the prefix.

As I mentioned above, since pre-stem duality marking involves the *ä* vowel, it occupies a slot in the template which may be filled by other prefixal material, for example the irrealis prefix *ra-* and the valency changer *a-*, or both. We saw in the examples above that the non-dual *ä* vowel superposes the irrealis *ra-* prefix which results in the form *rä-*. This is not the case for the imperatives and indicative inflected verbs. As we have seen in §5.3.3, restricted stems combine only with prefixes of the *β*, *β2* and *γ* series. Most formatives of these series are composed of only a consonant (See Table 5.9 in §5.5.1.4). Only the 1SG.*γ* (*zu-*) and all formatives of the *β2* series end in /u/, which resyllabifies as part of a complex onset (*zw-*) in the presence of *ä* or *a*. For example, the 1SG.*γ* *zu-* in (52) is followed by a zero. Therefore, the verb is inflected for dual. In (53), the 1SG.*γ* is followed by the non-dual *ä* vowel and the prefix changes into *zwä-*. Therefore, I analyse the distribution of the *ä* vowel as was shown in Figure 5.11.

(52) *nzä nima **zukorth**: "be fafä zane nagayé fäth zä thamonegwé!"*
      nzä   nima zu-∅-kor-th   be   fafä   zane
      1SG.ABS QUOT 1SG.*γ*-DU-speak.RS-2|3NSG   2SG.ERG after.this DEM:PROX
                  2|3DU:SBJ>1SG:OBJ:RPST:PFV/speak

      nagayé fäth zä   th-a-moneg-w-é
      children DIM PROX 2|3NSG.*β*-VC-wait.EXT-ND-2SG.IMP
                        2SG:SBJ>2|3PL:IO:IMP:IPFV/wait
      'They (2) said to me: "You will look after these small children here later!"'
                                                               [tci20121019-04 ABB #97]

(53) *watik, naf **zwäkora**: "watik, nzone efoth fof zefafth."*
      watik naf   zu-ä-kor-a-∅   watik nzone   efoth   fof
      then 3SG.ERG 1SG.*γ*-ND-speak.RS-PST-2|3SG   then 1SG.POSS sun|day EMPH
                  2|3SG:SBJ>1SG:OBJ:PST:PFV/speak

      z-ä-faf-th
      M.*γ*-ND.VC-hold.RS-2|3NSG
      2|3NSG:SBJ:PST:PFV/hold
      'Then she said to me: "Well, my days are over now."'   [tci20130911-03 MBR #76]

---

[37] *s-a-n-thor*   *s-n-ä-thor*
3SG.MASC.*γ*-ND-VENT-arrive.RS   3SG.MASC.*γ*-VENT-ND-arrive.RS

Pre-stem duality marking co-occurs with the valency change prefix *a-*. The resulting vowel pattern is summarised in the matrix in Figure 5.12, which shows that the non-dual *ä* vowel (i) replaces the *a-* prefix and (ii) that it patterns differently to the forms given so far. Compare Figure 5.11 with Figure 5.12. Note that this neutralises the valency change prefix *a-* for some of the actor>undergoer combinations: PL>SG, SG>PL and PL>PL. For these combinations, it is only the case frame which identifies whether the undergoer argument is a direct object (ABS case) or an indirect object (DAT or POSS case).

		ACTOR		
		SG	DU	PL
UNDERGOER	SG	a	a	ä
	DU	a	a	a
	PL	ä	a	ä

Figure 5.12: The duality matrix with VC prefix

One exception is the combination of SG>SG. As we can see in Figure 5.12, this combination receives no *ä* vowel although both participants are non-dual. This pattern is regular for all persons. Thus, a PL>3SG would receive *ä*, whereas DU>3SG and SG>3SG would not receive it. For the last combination and all prefixing verbs with a 3SG this means that the valency change is neutralised and again only the case frame shows what type of undergoer is indexed. It is not neutralised for the other person values (SG>1SG, SG>2SG and 1SG, 2SG on prefixing verbs) precisely because SG>SG (and the SG in prefixing verbs) does not take *ä* but *a*.

Note that prefixing verbs with the valency change prefix *a-* show a pattern where *ä* only occurs on a plural, while *a* occurs with a singular and dual participant. At least on the surface, this results in the binary opposition of plural vs. non-plural. In (54), the prefixing verb *rfiksi* 'grow' occurs in the inflected form *zarfif* 'sth. grew for/over it'. From the context, it is clear that the speaker is talking about the grass growing over the path. The verb encodes a feminine undergoer, which can only be interpreted as being the pathway (*moth*), because *yusi* 'grass' is masculine. A dual number of the undergoer would be *tharfif* and a plural *thärfif*. Thus, under several conditions (presence of valency change, prefixing template, restricted stem), the duality marker marks an opposition between plural and non-plural.

(54) *gathagatha moth rä ... z wrfrwake we ane **zarfif**.*
  gathagatha moth rä   (.) z   w-rfr-w-a-k-e
  bad   path 3SG.FEM:COP:ND   (.) ALR   3SG.FEM.α-trim.EXT-ND-PST-LK-1NSG
                3SG.FEM:SBJ:NPST:IPFV/be   1PL:SBJ>3SG.FEM:OBJ:PST:IPFV/trim

we   ane   z-a-rfif
also DEM 3SG.FEM.γ-ND.VC-grow.RS
      3SG.FEM:IO:RPST:PFV/grow
'This is a bad path. We cut it already, but (the grass) grew over it again.'

                                      [tci20130907-02 RNA #39-41]

Before I conclude this section on number marking, I want to look at the behaviour of the *ä* vowel when the irrealis prefix *ra-* and valency change prefix *a-* come together. Since the irrealis prefix includes a vowel, the valency change prefix is neutralised in most parts of the paradigm. For extended stems, this neutralisation is complete, i.e. only the case frame indicates whether the undergoer argument is a direct object (ABS) or an indirect object (DAT or POSS). This will be further discussed in §6.2.2. For restricted stems, the valency change prefix *a-* is likewise neutralised, but the number marking pattern differs in those actor>undergoer combinations which involve SG>SG (Figure 5.12). Consider the vowel contrast between (45) and (55). The participant combination is held constant: 3SG>1SG. In (45) we find the *ä* vowel, because it is ditransitive and the valency change prefix *a-* is employed, but in (55) it is missing, because (45) is transitive and lacks the *a-* prefix. Compare (55) with (56) where the same verb *yarisi* 'give' shows the *ä* because the actor participant is plural.

(55)   *nafane bärbärnzo keke **kwrar**.*
       nafane   bärbär=nzo keke kw-ra-r-∅
       3SG.POSS half=ONLY   NEG 1SG.*β*-IRR.ND.VC-give.RS-2|3SG
                               2|3SG:SBJ>1SG:IO:IRR:PFV/give
       'She will not give me half of her (fish).'   [tci20120922-26 DAK #125]

(56)   *nä kwot **kwrärth** fafä.*
       nä   kwot kw-rä-r-th   fafä
       some again 1SG.*β*-IRR.PL.VC-give.RS-2|3NSG after.that
                   2|3PL:SBJ>1SG:IO:IRR:PFV/give
       'They might give me some more later.'   [tci20120805-01 ABB #226]

We can conclude from the examples that the irrealis inflection complies with the number marking patterns as they were shown in Figure 5.12. The only difference lies in the fact that the irrealis prefix *ra-* creates neutralisations in more combinations (with regard to the valency change) because *ra-* contains a vowel. However, there is one important caveat to this conclusion. As I have pointed out in §5.4.4 and §5.4.6, there are some verbs which are deponent in the sense that they obligatorily take the *a-* without a change in valency. Two examples are the transitive verb *fiyoksi* 'make' and the intransitive/prefixing verb *yarenzsi* 'look'. Consequently we would expect them to comply with the pattern in Figure 5.12. Consider example (57) with a SG>SG participant combination and example (58) with its single referent in SG. Both show the non-dual vowel *ä*, i.e. they violate the pattern in Figure 5.12, which predicts the vowel to be *a* and not *ä*. This violation occurs only with deponent verbs and only in irrealis mood. The natural explanation is that, for deponent verbs, the distinction between the presence vs. absence of the valency change prefix is redundant.

(57) *katan kwa **sräfiyothé**. kafar minzü yé.*

katan kwa s-rä-fiyoth-é   kafar minzü \yé/

small FUT 3SG.MASC.β-IRR.ND.VC-make.RS-1SG big   very   3SG.MASC.COP.ND

         1SG:SBJ>3SG.MASC:OBJ:IRR:PFV/make   3SG.MASC:SBJ:NPST:IPFV/be

'I will make it smaller. It is very big.'   [tci20120914 RNA #41-42]

(58) *wati, we nima n **kwräzigrthm** "eh, ra gru zane ŋamitwanzr nabi tutin?"*

wati we   nima n   kw-rä-zigrthm   eh ra   gru

then also QUOT IMN 1SG.β-IRR.ND.VC-look.RS eh what shooting.star

                 1SG:SBJ:IRR:PFV/look

zane   ŋ-a-mitwa-nzr-∅   nabi   tuti=n

DEM:PROX M.α-VC-swing.EXT-ND-2|3SG bamboo branch=LOC

          2|3SG:SBJ:NPST:IPFV/swing

'Then, I was about to look around and thought: "Hey, what is this shooting star swinging on the bamboo branch?"'   [tci20111119-03 ABB #126-127]

Another observation relevant for all TAM categories with pre-stem dual marking is the fact that the middle marker also obligatorily takes the valency change prefix *a-*. Likewise, a verb in the middle template which indexes a singular participant does not pattern along the lines of Figure 5.12, but instead it employs the *ä* vowel. Again, this can only be explained by taking into account that there is no need to make a distinction between the presence vs. absence of the valency change prefix, because it always occurs with the middle morpheme.

The patterning of *ä*, *a* and *∅* in the prefixes cannot be adequately captured by the traditional notion of a morpheme with a distinct meaning. Rather, it seems to be the case that the vowel change is employed only to mark a difference in meaning without being easily linked to a specific meaning. The vowel change or the *ä* vowel in the prefix can be glossed as a non-dual for only part of the paradigm. In other parts of the paradigm, the distribution is employed to maximise the possible grammatical categories that can be encoded. Thus, pre-stem duality marking is much messier than post-stem duality marking. Both show some ambiguities and neutralisations, and in both cases the duality marker has to be integrated with the singular vs. non-singular opposition of the person affixes. But at the same time, pre-stem dual marking is sensitive to more grammatical categories and shows more idiosyncrasies.

5.6 Deixis and directionality

Komnzo verbs may be inflected for deixis and directionality. Deictic inflection comprises the values of proximal, medial, distal and interrogative.[38] Directionality comprises a venitive ('hither') and an andative ('thither') category. Both deixis and directionality operate

---

[38]It might be odd to include the proclitic *m=* with deictics. The main reason for doing so, is that morphologically as well as morpho-syntactically it patterns with demonstratives. See 3.1.12 and Table 3.8.

from a deictic center, which is usually the speaker, but may be extended to cover a particular character or place in a narrative, or a point in time. Morphologically, both sets are simple in that there is a one-to-one mapping between form and function.

5.6.1 The directional affixes *n-* and *-o*

Directional inflection takes place in two slots on the verb: the venitive prefix *n-* precedes the verb stem, while the andative suffix *-o* occurs in the penultimate slot on the verb, preceding the person/number suffixes. Although it is in theory possible, the two morphemes do not co-occur, i.e. a verb is marked either as venitive or andative. In other Yam languages, for example in Nen (Evans 2015a), the two morphemes share one slot in the verb template. I have described in §5.5.1.1 how the presence of the andative suffix can lead to the neutralisation of the person value in the actor suffix. Example (40) in that section provided a text example of this neutralisation.

The use of directional marking is shown in example (59). The sentence concludes a mythical story which explains why two particular clans do not intermarry, but instead 'help each other out' with girls to be exchanged with other groups. The speaker assumes the position of one of the two clans, both spatially as well as in terms of kin relations. The verb *yarisi* 'give' is then marked with an andative in the first clause ('give away') and a venitive ('give towards') in the second clause. Additionally, both clauses contain a deictic in the ablative case (*zba* 'from here', *boba* 'from there').

(59) *zba nezä **ärithroth** fäms ŋarer. boba nezä **änrithrth** fäms ŋarer*
    zba   nezä   e-a-ri-thr-o-th   fäms
    PROX.ABL in.return 2|3NSG.α-VC-give.EXT-ND-AND-NSG exchange
                                PL:SBJ>2|3PL:IO:NPST:IPFV:AND/give

    ŋare=r   boba   nezä   e-a-n-ri-thr-th
    woman=PURP MED.ABL in.return 2|3NSG.α-VC-VENT-give.EXT-ND-2|3NSG
                                  2|3PL:SBJ>2|3PL:IO:NPST:IPFV:VENT/give

    fäms   ŋare=r
    exchange woman=PURP
    'From here, they give them girls to exchange. In return, they give them girls to exchange from there.'   [tci20110802 ABB #159-161]

The directional affixes can be used with dynamic events (59) or with stative verbs (60) The latter is taken from the description of a picture card, and the image depicts an older man, who is standing in the background watching what is happening. The venitive inflection on 'stand' refers to the direction of his posture, i.e. he is standing facing towards the deictic centre.

(60) *wotukarä ane **ynkogr**. sinzo foba **ynrä**.*
    wotu=karä ane y-n-kogr   si=nzo   foba
    stick=PROP DEM 3SG.MASC.α-VENT-stand.ND eye=ONLY DIST.ABL
                      3SG.MASC:SBJ:NPST:IPFV:VENT/stand

y-n-rä
3SG.MASC.*α*-VENT-COP.ND
3SG.MASC:SBJ:NPST:IPFV:VENT/be
'He stands there with his walking stick and he is just looking from there.'

[tci20111004 RMA #253]

The copula may receive a directional inflection, giving the interpretation of 'come' (60) and 'go' (61), literally translated as 'be hither' and 'be thither'.

(61) *watik, teacher zwäkor "keke kayé kwa **nrno**."*
    watik teacher zu-ä-kor-∅   keke kayé   kwa n-rn-o
    then teacher 1SG.*γ*-ND-speak.RS-2|3SG   NEG tomorrow FUT 1NSG.*α*-COP.DU-AND
             2|3SG:SBJ>1SG:OBJ:RPST:PFV/speak   1DU:SBJ:NPST:IPFV:AND/be
    'Then, the teacher said to me: "No, we will go tomorrow."'

[tci20130823-06 STK #67-68]

The spatial semantics of the directional inflection can be extended to cover metaphorical uses. Example (62) shows a temporal use where the speaker explains the old custom of tying a bowstring. Thus, he literally says that he 'follows the custom hither'. Example (63) is a description of a very old woman, who has outlived some of her own children. The speaker uses the andative inflection on the verb *yathizsi* 'die' which is best translated into English as 'pass away'.

(62) *nzenme bada nimame zf ŋatr thuzirakwrmth. watik, ni ane **wänbragwre** zenathamar.*
    nzenme   bada   nima=me   zf   ŋatr   thu-zirak-wr-m-th
    1NSG.POSS ancestor like.this=INS IMM bowstring 2|3NSG.*β*1-tie.EXT-ND-DUR-2|3NSG
                               2|3PL:SBJ>2|3PL:OBJ:PST:DUR/tie

    watik ni   ane w-a-n-brag-wr-e   zena=thamar
    then   1NSG DEM 3SG.FEM.*α*-VC-VENT-follow.EXT-ND-1NSG today=TEMP.ALL
                   1PL:SBJ>3SG.FEM:OBJ:NPST:IPFV:VENT/follow
    'Our ancestors where tying the bowstring this way. We have been following (this custom) until today.'   [tci20130914-01 KAB #1-3]

(63) *nagayé nafanemäwä nä z **äthizrako**.*
    nagayé   nafane=ma=wä   nä   z   e-a-thiz-r-a-k-o
    children 3SG.POSS=CHAR=EMPH some ALR 2|3NSG.*α*-VC-die.EXT-ND-PST-LK-AND
                          2|3PL:SBJ:PST:IPFV:AND/die
    'Some of her own children have already passed away.'

[tci20120922-26 DAK #54]

5.6.2 The deictic clitics *z=*, *b=*, *f=* and *m=*

Deictics include the three categories proximal *z=*, medial *b=* and distal *f=*. Additionally, there is an interrogative form *m=*, which behaves slightly differently. These morphemes are analysed as proclitics because they (i) attach to the outer layer of the verb, (ii) are not assigned stress (if they create an initial syllable through epenthesis) and (iii) are reduced forms of the demonstratives. In §3.1.12.3 and §3.5 I have labelled these clitic demonstratives.

Clitic demonstratives are always used situationally in order to point, direct or show the location of an event or a referent in relation to the deictic center. Example (64)[39] comes from a narrative. The deictic center of that part of the story is a man who is sitting in his camp and happens to hear someone shouting from the river. Note that both verbs ('hear' and 'shout') are inflected with a venitive marker. Thus, we can translate the second verb *byannor*, to which the medial clitic demonstrative (*b=* MED) is attached, as 'He shouts there towards here'.

(64) *nafafämsf srenkaris "oh, kabe **byannor** gardar."*
      nafa-fäms=f   s-rä-n-karis-∅   oh
      3.POSS-exchange.man=ERG.SG 3SG.MASC.β-IRR.ND-VENT-hear.RS-2|3SG oh
                                 2|3SG:SBJ>3SG.MASC:OBJ:IRR:PFV:VENT/hear

      kabe b=y-a-n-nor   garda=r
      man MED=3SG.MASC.α-VC-VENT-shout.EXT.ND canoe=PURP
           MED=3SG.MASC:SBJ:NPST:IPFV:VENT/shout
      'His exchange man heard him (and said:) "Oh, there is a man calling out for the canoe."'   [tci20111119-01 ABB #68]

If the inflected verb is vowel-initial or begins in a glide (only some formatives of the α series), the clitic demonstrative simply attaches as an onset, for example in (65)[40] or (67). Elsewhere, an initial syllable is created through epenthesis, as in (64) and (66).

(65) *frükakmenzo nzwamnzrm. ane mrn **fämnzr**. ane mrn **fämnzr**. ane mrn **fämnzr**.*
      frü-kak=me=nzo   nzu-a-m-nzr-m   3x[ane mrn
      alone-DISTR=INS=ONLY 1NSG.β2-VC-sit.EXT-ND-DUR 3x[DEM clan
                          1PL:SBJ:PST:DUR/sit

      f=e-a-m-nzr]
      DIST=2|3NSG.α-VC-sit.EXT-ND]
      2|3PL:SBJ:NPST:IPFV/sit
      'We used to live in groups. One clan lives over there, one clan lives over there and one clan lives over there.'   [tci20120922-08 DAK #114-117]

(66) *ane bä **bkwaruthrmth** büdisnen mnz znen.*
      ane bä   b=kw-a-ru-thr-m-th   büdisn=en   mnz
      DEM MED MED=M.β1-VC-bark.EXT-ND-DUR-2|3NSG büdisn=LOC house
                  MED=2|3PL:SBJ:PST:DUR/bark

      zn=en
      place=LOC
      'Those (dogs) were barking there in Büdisn at the house.'   [tci20111119-03 ABB #95]

---

[39] The verb -*nor* 'shout' is deponent and takes the valency change prefix *a*- prefix without an impact on the argument structure.

[40] The verb *msaksi* 'sit|dwell' is deponent and takes the valency change prefix *a*- without an impact on the argument structure.

Clitic demonstratives are found most frequently attached to the copula, which then follows the main verb of a clause. In the discussion of demonstratives, I have labelled this construction "demonstrative identifier" (§3.1.12.3). In (67), the speaker points to another person cutting off the branches of a tree. Note that the deictic value (MED) is held constant on the demonstrative pronoun *bäne*, the clitic demonstrative on *rtmaksi* 'cut' and the demonstrative identifier *byé*.

(67) *nima **bäne** birtmakwr byé.*

nima   bäne   b=y-rtmak-wr-∅   b=\yé/
like.this DEM:MED   MED=3SG.MASC.α-cut.EXT-ND-2|3SG   MED=3SG.MASC.COP.ND
                    MED=2|3SG:SBJ>3SG.MASC:OBJ:NPST:IPFV/cut   MED=3SG.MASC:SBJ:NPST:IPFV/be

'She cuts off that one there.'   [tci20130907-02 JAA #441]

I choose the label demonstrative identifier for the whole construction (clitic demonstrative plus copula), because the copula is unmarked for tense, i.e. it always occurs in non-past. In example (68), the speaker took me to a place on the riverbank which used to be a 'story place' a long time ago. Story places are always inhabited by spiritual beings and, therefore, they must not be disturbed by people. The verbs *rafisi* 'paddle' and *yak* 'walk, go' are in the past tense and only the copula is in the non-past tense.

(68) *gardame fthé kwarafinzrmth, boba wozinzo thfiyakm **berä**.*

garda=me fthé   kw-a-rafi-nzr-m-th   boba   wozi=nzo
canoe=INS when M.β1-VC-paddle.EXT-ND-DUR-2|3NSG   MED.ABL   side=ONLY
                2|3PL:SBJ:PST:DUR/paddle

thf-yak-m   b=e-rä
2|3NSG.β2-walk.EXT-DUR   MED=2|3NSG.α-COP.ND
2|3PL:SBJ:PST:DUR/walk   MED=2|3PL:SBJ:NPST:IPFV/be

'When paddling with the canoe, they only went there on the side there.'

                                                       [tci20120922-19 DAK #8]

Naturally, deictic markers are found mostly in situations where visual identification is important. Example (69) is taken from a plant walk, where the speaker points out two different kinds of trees: *mni bäwzö* and *fothr* (sometimes called *fothr bäwzö*).[41] In the recording, *fothr bäwzö* trees stood between the speaker and some *mni bäwzö* trees. Hence, the latter are marked as being further away and all deictic markers are medial: the deictic (*bä* 'there'), the proclitic on the verb (*bikogro* 'it stands there') and the deictic in ablative case (*bobafa* 'from there'). Note that the verb is also inflected with an andative suffix because more trees of the *mni bäwzö* kind were growing in that direction. As for the other tree, *fothr bäwzö*, it is marked by a proximal deictic (*zä* 'here'), a proximal demonstrative identifier (*zyé* 'it is here') and another proximal deictic in the ablative case (*zbafa* 'from here').[42]

---

[41]The words *bäwzö* and *fothr* are proper nouns. However, *mni* means 'fire' and the name *mni bäwzö* 'fire bäwzö' is used because the bark of this tree is hardened over the fire and later used for house walls.

[42]Both deictics *bobafa* and *zbafa* are doubly ablative, i.e. *boba* is already ablative and contrasts with allative *bobo*. This is the only example in the corpus of doubly marked deictics.

(69) **bä** *ane mni bäwzö* **bikogro.** *zä yé zyé fothr* **zbafa.** **bobafa** *mni bäwzö.*

    bä   ane mni bäwzö b=y-kogr-o   zä   \yé\

    MED DEM fire bäwzö MED=3SG.MASC.α-stand.ND-AND PROX 3SG.MASC.COP.ND

                            MED=3SG.MASC:SBJ:NPST:IPFV:AND/stand   3SG.MASC:SBJ:NPST:IPFV/be

    z=\yé\   fothr zba=fa   boba=fa   mni bäwzö

    PROX=3SG.MASC.COP.ND   fothr PROX.ABL=ABL MED.ABL=ABL fire bäwzö

    PROX=3SG.MASC:SBJ:NPST:IPFV/be

    'There, *mni bäwzö* is standing there. From here it is *fothr bäwzö* and from there (it

    is) *mni bäwzö.*'   [tci20130907-02 RNA #166-168]

The three proclitics *z=*, *b=* and *f=* can in principle attach to verb forms of all TAM categories. For example, in (66) the medial *b=* is cliticised to a verb in the past durative. Nevertheless, they occur most frequently with verbs in the present tense because of their situational use.

The clitic *m=* only occurs with the copula and the meaning 'where is X?', as in (70). As I will discuss in §6.3, *m=* can attach to verbs in the irrealis or imperative moods with an apprehensive ('you might do X!') and prohibitve interpretation ('you must not do X!'), respectively. Formally, the *m=* clitic patterns with the other demonstratives (See Table 3.8 in §3.1.12).

(70) **mern**? *ni wmägne zöbthé.*

    m=e-rn   ni   w-mäg-n-e   zöbthé

    where=2|3NSG.α-COP.DU 1NSG 3SG.FEM.α-lead.EXT-DU-1NSG first

    where=2|3DU:SBJ:NPST:IPFV/be   1DU:SBJ>3SG.FEM:OBJ:NPST:IPFV/lead

    'Where are they? We will lead (the path) first.'   [tci20130907-02 JAA #12]

6 Tense, aspect and mood

6.1 Introduction

Tense, aspect and mood is the most complex set of grammatical categories in the verb inflection, both in the way the categories are encoded and in the number of distinctions that can be expressed. Morphologically, there are 18 categories, which may be supplemented by a set of TAM particles. There are four morphological tense values (non-past, immediate past, recent past and past), four aspect values (perfective, imperfective, durative and iterative) and three mood values (indicative, imperative and irrealis).

I will begin this section with an overview of the morphological material that is involved in TAM inflection. Most of these building blocks and the idiosyncrasies in their behaviour have been addressed in the preceding chapter and I will refer to these sections where appropriate. In the following, I will focus on the combinatorics of the morphemes and stems (§6.2), the impact of clitics and particles (§6.3) and the semantics of the resulting TAM categories (§6.4). Aspect in Komnzo can at best be somewhat misleadingly captured with the traditional definition of perfective versus imperfective, which is often based on the completion of an event. Although I employ these labels, it should be noted that the perfective focusses more on the left edge of the event (inceptive) or expresses a momentaneous quality (punctual). With that in mind, I defer the discussion of the semantics of TAM to the end of this chapter (§6.4).

6.2 The combinatorics of TAM

The most basic element of TAM inflection is the distinction between an extended (EXT) and a restricted stem (RS). Both types are attested for almost every verb lexeme (§5.3). EXT and RS stems differ in their templates with respect to dual marking (§5.3.2) and in the possible combinations with the five prefix series α, β, β_1, β_2 and γ (§5.3.3). In addition to the five series, the irrealis prefix *ra-* and the immediate past proclitic *n=* are involved in TAM marking. The suffixal material includes a past suffix (*-a*) and a durative suffix (*-m*) and a special actor suffix series for the imperatives. Table 6.1 gives a full overview of the TAM categories and the way these are built up from the listed morphological material. An important distinction in the verb template, not expressed in Table 6.1, is the difference between post-stem dual marking with EXT stems and pre-stem dual marking with RS stems. This was described in detail in §5.5.3.

The combinations in Table 6.1 illustrate a feature of Komnzo morphology that reverberates throughout the verb inflection: the distribution of exponents. In other words, a grammatical category is encoded and manipulated by formatives that are scattered across the verb template. On the flip side of this phenomenon, most formatives lack a clear grammatical meaning, or have multiple grammatical functions depending on the combinatorics. Thus, they have to be glossed in an abstract manner. However, there are degrees of morpheme underspecification. For example, two morphemes in Table 6.1 can be assigned an unambiguous grammatical meaning. These are the irrealis prefix *ra-* and the past suffix *-a*. The *-a* morpheme only occurs in past tense inflections, and the label PST is a sufficient gloss for the *-a* suffix. However, the *a-* suffix is insufficient to describe the tense value "past" because other morphs, e.g. the prefix series, are required to form a past tense. A second group of morphemes is underspecified in the following way: they fulfil several functions, either simultaneously or in different morphological contexts. For example, the durative suffix *-m* encodes durative aspect, but it also "pushes back" the tense value. Thus, when suffixed to a non-past (imperfective), it will produce a recent past (durative), and when suffixed to a recent past (imperfective), it will produce a past (durative). One option would be to label it durative/backshifting suffix. However, in imperatives the *-m* suffix pushes the tense values "forward", producing a delayed imperative ('do X a little later'), and duration is not part of its meaning. Furthermore, the *-m* suffix may occur with perfectives as a means of backgrounding an event, again without encoding duration. Thus, the choice of the glossing label (DUR) for the *-m* suffix is somewhat arbitrary, and we could just as well label it "tense shifting" or "backgrounding". For a third group of morphemes, especially the five prefix series, all attempts to assign a grammatical meaning to them is futile and we have to draw on abstract labels like α, β and γ.

Not all logically possible combinations of morphs are grammatically acceptable. For example, the α and γ prefix series only combine with EXT and RS stems, respectively, but not vice versa. Likewise, the past suffix *-a* and the durative suffix *-m* are mutually exclusive and a verb form with both is rejected as ungrammatical. Third, the irrealis prefix *ra-* only combines with the β prefixes and not with the other prefix series. Lastly, the immediate past clitic *n=* can only attach to a verb form which employs the α prefix series, not to the other combinations. We can conclude from this observation that the combinatorial space is not fully exhausted, i.e. not all logically possible combinations of the morphological material are actually employed. Such a system is not surprising because all natural languages evolve incrementally without an overall design. What is remarkable about Komnzo in particular and the Yam languages in general is the fact that so many combinations are employed. In other words, the genius of the verb morphology lies in its extensive exploitation of combinations.

In the following section, I will describe the functions and some of the distributional characteristics of the morphemes in Table 6.1.

Table 6.1: The combinatorics TAM marking

TAM value			clitic $n=$	prefix series $\alpha, \beta, \beta1, \beta2, \gamma$	IRR prefix $ra\text{-}$	stem type EXT / RS	TAM suffix PST ($-a$) / DUR ($-m$)	IMPERATIVE suffix IMP/2SG($-\hat{e}$) / 2NSG-e
non-past	imperfective	indicative		α		EXT		
immediate-past	imperfective	indicative	$n=$	α		EXT		
immediate-past	durative	indicative	$n=$	α		EXT	$-m$	
recent-past	imperfective	indicative		$\beta1$ or $\beta2$		EXT		
recent-past	durative	indicative		α		EXT	$-m$	
recent-past	perfective	indicative		γ		RS		
past	imperfective	indicative		α		EXT	$-a$	
past	durative	indicative		$\beta1$ or $\beta2$		EXT	$-m$	
past	perfective	indicative		γ		RS	$-a$	
past	iterative	indicative		$\beta1$ or $\beta2$		RS	$-m$	
past	iterative/durative	indicative		$\beta1$ or $\beta2$		RS	$-m$	
n/a	imperfective	irrealis		β	$ra\text{-}$	EXT		
n/a	durative	irrealis		β	$ra\text{-}$	EXT	$-m$	
n/a	perfective	irrealis		β	$ra\text{-}$	RS		
n/a	imperfective	imperative		β		EXT		IMP
n/a	perfective	imperative		β		RS		IMP
future	imperfective	imperative		β		EXT	$-m$	IMP
future	perfective	imperative		β		RS	$-m$	IMP

6.2.1 The prefix series

The five prefix series α, β, β_1, β_2, γ were briefly addressed in §5.5.1.4. The table from page 214 is reproduced as Table 6.2.

Table 6.2: TAM prefixes

gloss	α	β	β_1	β_2	γ
1SG	*wo-*	*kw-*	*ku-*	*kwof-*	*zu-*
1NSG	*n-*	*nz-* / *nzn-*	*nzu-*	*nzf-*	*nzn-*
2SG	*n-*	*nz-* / *gn-*	*gu-*	*gf-*	*nzn-*
3SG.FEM	*w-*	*z-*	*zu-*	*zf-*	*z-*
3SG.MASC	*y-*	*s-*	*su-*	*sf-*	*s-*
2|3NSG	*e-*	*th-*	*thu-*	*thf-*	*th-*
M	*ŋ-*	*k-*	*kw-*	*kf-*	*z-*

The α prefixes combine only with the extended stem. They are used to encode non-past (1), recent past durative (2) and past imperfective (3). Example (1) comes from a hunting story, where the narrator meets a spiritual being in the forest. In (2), the speaker reports an incident from a neighbouring village involving a young boy who was attacked by a sorcerer in his yam garden. Example (3), is from an interview about the customs around the sister-exchange marriage system.

(1) *"nzä maf **wonrsoknwr**?"*
     nzä   maf   wo-n-rsokn-wr-∅
     1SG.ABS who.ERG 1SG.α-VENT-bother.EXT-ND-2|3SG
                     2|3SG:SBJ>1SG:OBJ:NPST:IPFV:VENT/bother
     "'Who bothers me here?'"   [tci20111119-03 ABB #165]

(2) *fthé zöfthamen zamatho frk komnzo zä **wtnägwrmo**.*
     fthé   zöftha=thamen z-a-math-o-∅   frk   komnzo zä
     when   first=TEMP.LOC M.γ-ND-run.RS-AND-SG blood only   PROX
                           SG:SBJ:RPST:PFV:AND/run

     w-tnäg-wr-m-o-∅
     3SG.FEM.α-lose.EXT-ND-DUR-AND-SG
     SG:SBJ>3SG.FEM:OBJ:RPST:DUR:AND/lose
     'At first, when he started to run, he was just losing blood here.'
                                                          [tci20130901-04 YUK #40]

(3) *nzun etha nzüthamöwä **warnzürwrath** wath.*
     nzun   etha nzüthamöwä wo-a-rnzür-wr-a-th   wath
     1SG.DAT three times   1SG.α-VC-dance.EXT-ND-PST-2|3NSG dance
                            2|3PL:SBJ>1SG:IO:PST:IPFV/dance
     'They danced three times for me.'   [tci20120805-01 ABB #769]

If the proclitic *n=* is attached to a verb employing the *α* prefixes, the resulting inflection is either immediate past imperfective (4) or immediate past durative (5) depending on the suffixal material. In other words, the immediate past is built from verbs inflected for non-past. This is preserved in the integrated glossing style, because the *n=* is analysed as a clitic. The *n=* is related to the imminent particle *n* (§6.3.1). Example (4) sums up a story about the origin of the Morehead people. In (5), the speaker talks about competitive yam cultivation and how older people assess a young man's status by the number and size of his crop.

(4) *trikasi mane **nŋatrikwé** fof… ŋafynm … badafa ane fof ŋanritakwa fof.*
   trik-si   mane n=ŋ-a-trik-w-é   fof (.) ŋafe=nm   (.)
   tell-NMLZ which IPST=M.*α*-VC-tell.EXT-ND-1SG EMPH (.) father=DAT.NSG (.)
               IPST=1SG:SBJ:NPST:IPFV/tell

   bada=fa   ane fof ŋ-a-n-ritak-w-a-∅   fof
   ancestor=ABL DEM EMPH M.*α*-VC-VENT-pass.EXT-ND-PST-SG EMPH
               2|3SG:SBJ:PST:IPFV:VENT/pass
   'The story which I have just told passed from the ancestors to (our) fathers.'
                                    [tci20131013-01 ABB #403-405]

(5) *fthé bone kafarwä **nefathwrmth** "eh yabun zane!" wtrikaräsü we gnrärm.*
   fthé bone   kafar=wä n=e-fath-wr-m-th   eh
   when 2SG.POSS big=EMPH IPST=2|3NSG.*α*-hold.EXT-ND-DUR-2|3NSG eh
               IPST=2|3PL:SBJ>2|3PL:OBJ:NPST:DUR/hold

   yabun zane   wtri=karä=sü we gn-rä-r-m
   big   DEM:PROX fear=PROP=ETC also 2SG.*β*-COP-ND-DUR
               2SG:SBJ:FUTIMP:IPFV/be
   'When they have just held your big (yam tubers) and say: "Hey, that (is) a big one!" then you have to be afraid!'   [tci20120805-01 ABB #378-380]

The *β* series is split into a basic series *β* and two related series *β1* and *β2*. The basic *β* series is used for all the non-tensed categories like the irrealis (6) and the imperatives (7). Example (6) comes from a procedural text about fish baskets and the speaker explains how the fish gets trapped inside. In (7), the narrator took over the role of a character in a stimulus picture task.

(6) *watik, fthé **kranbrigwrth** keke kwa zba we **krämätroth**.*
   watik fthé   k-ra-n-brig-wr-th   keke kwa zba   we
   then when M.*β*-IRR.VC-VENT-return.EXT-ND-2|3NSG NEG FUT PROX.ABL also
               2|3PL:SBJ:IRR:IPFV:VENT/return

   k-rä-mätr-o-th
   M.*β*-IRR.VC-ND-exit.RS-AND-NSG
   PL:SBJ:IRR:PFV:AND/exit
   'Well, when they turn around, they will not escape from here.'
                                    [tci20120906 SKK #45]

(7)   *"bné **käznobe!** nzä keke miyo worä."*

bné   k-ä-znob-e   nzä   keke miyo wo-rä
2NSG.ERG M.*β*-ND.VC-drink.RS-2NSG.IMP 1SG.ABS NEG desire 1SG.*α*-COP.ND
    2PL:SBJ:IMP:PFV/drink   1SG:SBJ:NPST:IPFV/be

"'You drink! I don't want to.'"   [tci20111004 RMA #282]

Table 6.2 shows that there are two formatives for the first person non-singular (*nz-* and *nzn-*) as well as the second singular (*nz-* and *gn-*) of the *β* series. For the first person non-singular, *nz-* is used for irrealis (8) and *nzn-* for the imperatives (9). In example (8), the speaker explains how a kundu drum is carved and prepared. Example (9) is taken from a conversation by the fire that involved a lot of hearsay information. In conclusion, the speaker tells the two addressees to go to Morehead and clarify the rumours.

(8)   *fiyafr **nzrayak** tauri woku thoraksir.*

fiyaf=r   nz-ra-yak   tauri   woku thorak-si=r
hunting=PURP 1NSG.*β*-IRR-walk.EXT.ND wallaby skin search-NMLZ=PURP
    1PL:SBJ:IRR:IPFV/walk

'We will go hunting and search for wallaby skin.'   [tci20120824 KAA #64]

(9)   *kanbrime! ... aneme nzenm **nznatrife!***

k-a-n-brim-e   (.) ane=me nzenm
M.*β*-VC.DU-VENT-return.RS-2NSG.IMP (.) DEM=INS 1NSG.DAT
2DU:SBJ:IMP:PFV:VENT/return

nzn-a-trif-e
1NSG.*β*-VC.DU-tell.RS-2NSG.IMP
2DU:SBJ>1DU:OBJ:IMP:PFV/tell

'You come back and tell us about it!'   [tci20130901-04 RNA #162]

For the second person singular, the situation is more complicated. The *gn-* formative is used for the imperatives of prefixing verbs, where the prefix encodes the imperative mood and the addressee simultanously (10). The second non-singular prefix is *th-* for all inflections that involve the *β* series. Note that for ambifixing verbs in the imperative, there is no overt marking of second person in the prefix because this would then be reflexive ('X yourself!') or auto-benefactive ('X for yourself!'). As pointed out in §5.4.5, reflexives and auto-benefactives are expressed in a middle template. Hence, the first verb in example (9) could be translated as a reflexive ('return yourselves!').

(10) *ezi **gnyako!***

ezi   gn-yak-o
morning 2SG.*β*.IMP-walk.EXT.ND-AND
    2SG:SBJ:IMP:IPFV:AND/walk
'You go there in the morning!'   [tci20120906 MAB #31]

The second formative for the second singular in Table 6.2 (*nz-*) is used for irrealis inflection of prefixing and ambifixing verbs. Interestingly, only the second person singular of ambifixing verbs does not employ the irrealis prefix *ra-* in the irrealis inflection (11). If it is a prefixing verb, the irrealis prefix *ra-* is employed (12).[1] Example (11) is taken from a procedural text in which the speaker shows me how to manufacture two children's toys. In (12), the malignant protagonist invites a stranger to stay with her.

(11) *gräthé znsä rä ... thrma **nzasämiré** bun.*

grä-thé	znsä	rä	(.) thrma	nz-a-sämir-é
slow-ADJZR	work	3SG.FEM.COP.ND	(.) later	2SG.β-VC.ND-whisper.RS-1SG
		3SG.FEM:SBJ:NPST:IPFV/be		1SG:SBJ>2SG:IO:IRR:PFV/whisper

bun
2SG.DAT
'It is easy work ... I will teach you later.'   [tci20120914 RNA #50-51]

(12) *nima zräzigrm "awe nzone moba **nzranyak**?"*

nima	z-rä-zigr-m	awe	nzone	moba
QUOT	3SG.FEM.β-IRR.VC.ND-look.around.RS-DUR	come	1SG.POSS	where.ABL
	3SG.FEM:SBJ:IRR:PFV/look.around			

nz-ra-n-yak
2SG.β-IRR.VC-VENT-walk.EXT.ND
2SG:SBJ:IRR:IPFV:VENT/walk
'She looks around and says, "Come my friend! Where are you coming from?"'
[tci20120901-01 MAK #74]

The β1 and β2 series are used for recent past imperfective (13), past durative (first verb in 14) and past iterative (second verb in 14). In example (14), the speaker talks about his experiences at the Rouku mission school in the 1960s.

(13) *kayé ama zuzir **zfyak**.*

kayé	ama	zuzi=r	zf-yak
yesterday	mother	fishing=PURP	3SG.FEM.β2-walk.EXT.ND
			3SG.FEM:SBJ:RPST:IPFV/walk

'Yesterday, mother went fishing.'   [tci20111107-03 RNA #40]

(14) *teste **nzwasäminzrm** bobomr kwarikwari efoth ... sokoro **kfäbth***

teste	nzu-a-sämi-nzr-m-∅	bobomr	kwarikwari	efoth
thursday	1NSG.β1-VC-whisper.EXT-ND-DUR-2|3SG	until	midday	sun
	2|3SG:SBJ>1PL:IO:PST:DUR/teach			

(.) sokoro kf-ä-bth-∅
(.) school M.β2-VC.ND-finish.RS-2\|3SG
2\|3SG:SBJ:PST:ITER/finish
'On Thursday, he was teaching us until midday and then school always ended (for the week).'   [tci20120904-02 MAB #14]

---

[1] Both verbs in this example are deponent employing, the valency change prefix *a-* without a change in valency. The second verb *yak* 'walk' is only deponent when it employs the venitive marker, meaning 'come', not when it is neutral or andative 'walk', 'go away'.

These two prefix series are derived from the β series by adding an element to it. For β_1, this is the vowel /u/ and, for β_2, it is the consonant /ɸ/. The only exceptions are the first person singular and the second person singular formatives (see Table 6.2). In a different analysis, the /u/ and /ɸ/ elements could be described as separate morphemes. Like the prefixes, these two morphemes would then have to receive an abstract label. Such an analysis would reduce the number of prefix series to three. Under the current analysis, there are three main series and two subseries. I retain the current analysis, but I do not see either as being more elegant or more parsimonious than the other. More important is the question regarding the difference between β_1 and β_2, which, for the moment, is unsettled. I will briefly discuss two possible explanations.

First, the difference might be understood in terms of sociolinguistic variation, i.e. the use of either variant is determined by an individual's linguistic biography. Although all Komnzo speakers are multilingual, the strongest influence comes from two close varieties, namely Wära and Anta. In my preliminary survey of the surrounding varieties, I found that β_1 and β_2 exist in Wära as well as Anta. My impressionistic view is that the β_2 prefix series occurs much more frequently than β_1. However, comparative work and documentation on both varieties is needed.

A second explanation is a true difference in meaning. Although β_1 and β_2 are almost always interchangeable without a clear change in meaning, there are some hints that semantics may play a role. For example, the copula can only take β_2 and not β_1, and the same is true for the verb *yak* 'walk' (13). Only when the copula is used in an ambifixing template, both β_1 and β_2 are possible. However, in an ambifixing template the copula cannot be translated as 'be', but instead functions as a light verb with the meaning 'do'. For other verbs, β_1 and β_2 are interchangeable. This observation leads me to believe that the β_2 prefixes encode either a longer duration of the event or a greater degree of affectedness of the participants. However, targeted elicitation and close observation of natural texts did not lead to a clear pattern along these lines. Informants found it hard to give a characterisation or translation of the difference and often contradicted each other or themselves. For now I will leave this question open for future research.

The γ prefixes are used for the perfectives: the recent past perfective (15) and the past perfective (16). Example (15) comes from a spontaneous conversation in the yam garden when a friend happened to pass by on his bicycle. Example (16) describes a dance that took place in the nearby settlement of Forzitho.

(15) *watik, zä zf **zamse** bä **nznäthor**.*

watik zä   zf   z-a-ms-e   bä   nzn-ä-thor
then PROX IMM M.γ-VC.DU-sit.RS-1NSG 2SG 2SG.γ-ND-arrive.RS
         1DU:SBJ:RPST:PFV/sit   2SG:SBJ:RPST:PFV/arrive

'Then, we two sat down and you arrived.'   [tci20130823-06 CAM #31]

(16) *wati, mane änyaka forzitho wath **sathaifath**.*

wati mane e-a-n-yak-a   forzitho wath
then which 2|3NSG.α-VC-VENT-walk.EXT.ND-PST forzitho dance
             2|3PL:SBJ:PST:IPFV:VENT/walk

s-a-thayf-a-th
3SG.MASC.ɣ-ND-bring.out.RS-PST-2|3NSG
2|3PL:SBJ>3SG.MASC:OBJ:PST:PFV/bring.out
'Well, those who came to Forzitho brought the dance out (to the village square).'

[tci20120909-06 KAB #25]

6.2.2 The irrealis prefix *ra-*

The irrealis prefix *ra-* is used for the imperfective, perfective and durative irrealis inflections. We have seen examples of all three aspect values in (11) and (12). Example (11) showed that the only place in the paradigm where the irrealis prefix *ra-* is not used is the second person singular of an ambifixing verb.

The interaction of the irrealis prefix with the valency changing prefix *a-* and pre-stem dual marking is explained in §5.5.3.4. In that section, I pointed out that the irrealis prefix *ra-* overrides the valency changing prefix *a-* to the effect that the absence versus presence of the valency changing prefix is neutralised. For verb forms which employ the extended stem, this neutralisation is complete. For verb forms which employ the restricted stem, there are small changes in the pre-stem duality marking pattern (§5.5.3.4). In these cases, only the case frame indicates whether the undergoer argument is a direct object, such as the absolutive case on *szsi* 'calling' in (17), or an indirect object, such as the dative case on *ŋatha* in (18). Both examples are taken from the same hunting story in which the narrator talks about his usual routines when going on a hunting expedition.

(17) *ŋathar foba **szsi threthkäfé***
ŋatha=r foba sz-si th-rä-thkäf-é
dog=PURP DIST.ABL call.out-NMLZ 2|3NSG.β-IRR.ND-start.RS-1SG
1SG:SBJ>2|3PL:OBJ:IRR:PFV/start
'From there, I started calling out for the dogs.' [tci20111119-03 ABB #63]

(18) *watik wamnza **ŋathanm** biskar mni **threthkäfé***
watik wo-a-m-nz-a ŋatha=nm biskar mni
then 1SG.α-VC-sit.EXT-ND-PST dog=DAT.NSG cassawa fire
1SG:SBJ:PST:IPFV/sit

th-rä-thkäf-é
2|3NSG.β-IRR.ND-start.RS-1SG
1SG:SBJ>2|3PL:OBJ:IRR:PFV/start
'Then I sat and started to cook the cassava for the dogs.' [tci20111119-03 ABB #73]

6.2.3 The past suffix *-a*

The position of the past suffix *-a* within the suffixing subsystem is described in §5.5.1.1. The past suffix *-a* is employed for two TAM categories: the past imperfective (19) and the past perfective (20). Example (19) is taken from a text on oral history of the Morehead district. The narrator talks about conflcts caused by an alleged sorcerer in the 1940s. The second example (20) comes from a much more recent event, where aa woman is talking about camping at the Morehead river and going fishing only a week before the recording was made.

(19) *watik gathagatha zokwasi fä **ykonath.***
     watik gathagatha zokwasi fä   y-ko-n-a-th
     then bad   words DIST 3SG.MASC.α-speak.EXT-DU-2|3NSG
                              2|3DU:SBJ>3SG.MASC:OBJ:PST:IPFV/speak
     'Then, they cursed him there.'   [tci20131013-02 ABB #102]

(20) ***zukorath** "mama, bä bana ketharuf! zuzi käzir!"*
     zu-Ø-kor-a-th   mama bä bana k-ä-tharuf-Ø
     1SG.γ-DU-speak.RS-PST-2|3NSG mother 2SG poor M.β-VC.ND-enter.RS-2SG.IMP
     2|3DU:SBJ>1SG:OBJ:PST:PFV/speak   2SG:SBJ:IMP:PFV/enter

     zuzi   k-ä-zir-Ø
     fishing.line M.β-VC.ND-throw.RS-2SG.IMP
                 2SG:SBJ:IMP:PFV/throw
     'They said to me: "Mama, get on (the canoe) and throw the fishing line!"'
                                            [tci20120922-25 ALK #7-8]

6.2.4 The durative suffix -*m*

The durative suffix -*m* is described in §5.5.1.1 with regard to its position in the suffixing subsystem. It is employed for durative aspect, which expresses an ongoing event in the immediate past[2], recent past (21), past (22) and irrealis (23). In example (21), the speaker reports on how he fought a bushfire in his garden the preceding day. Example (22) is taken from a story about rain-making magic which the narrator acquired and practiced in his youth. The irrealis example (23) is taken from a conversation about local customs surrounding the sister-exchange system.

(21) *wthzak zane **ŋanrsirwrmth.***
     wthzak zane   ŋ-a-n-rsir-wr-m-th
     sole   DEM:PROX M.α-VC-VENT-burn.EXT-ND-DUR-2|3NSG
                    2|3PL:SBJ:RPST:DUR:VENT/burn
     'The soles of my feet here were burning.'   [tci20120922-24 MAA #63]

(22) *grigri zä **kwasogwrmth.***
     grigri   zä   kw-a-sog-wr-m-th
     maggot PROX M.β2-VC-ascend.EXT-ND-DUR-2|3NSG
               2|3PL:SBJ:PST:DUR/ascend
     'The maggots were climbing up here.'   [tci20110810-01 MAB #71]

(23) *fäms fthé **krakwinmth** ... fäms fämsnzo ...*
     fäms   fthé k-ra-kwi-n-m-th   (.) fäms
     exchange.man when M.β-IRR.VC-argue.EXT-DU-DUR-2|3NSG (.) exchange.man
                   2|3DU:SBJ:IRR:IPFV/argue

---

[2]The immediate past occur with a low frequency in the text corpus and, consequently, there is only a handful of examples in the immediate past durative. Example (5) on page 239 is one of these.

fäms=nzo   (.)
exchange.man=ONLY (.)
'When exchange men are fighting ... exchange man (against) exchange man ...'

[tci20120805-01 ABB #460]

Part of the function of the durative suffix is to shift back the tense. If we remove the -*m* suffix from a verb inflected for the recent past durative (21) or past durative (22), the resulting form would be a non-past imperfective and recent past imperfective, respectively. Figure 6.1 shows this with the verb *songsi* from example (22).

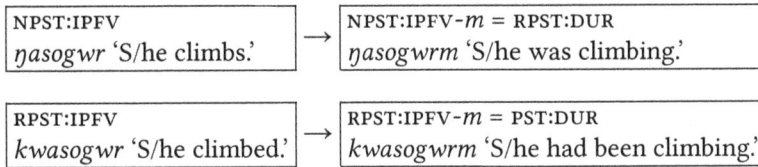

NPST:IPFV		NPST:IPFV-*m* = RPST:DUR
ŋasogwr 'S/he climbs.'	→	*ŋasogwrm* 'S/he was climbing.'

RPST:IPFV		RPST:IPFV-*m* = PST:DUR
kwasogwr 'S/he climbed.'	→	*kwasogwrm* 'S/he had been climbing.'

Figure 6.1: The backshifting function of the durative suffix -*m*

The durative suffix can also attach to an iterative inflection, in which case the iteration of the event is streched over a longer duration, as in (24) and (25). In (24), the speaker talks about the first fire which destroyed the world inhabited by humans. In (25), the speaker describes how the people used to avoid a particular place during the early and late hours of the day because it was inhabited by a story man.

(24) *zfth mni nä kayé **zwäsmth** kidn.*
   zfth mni nä kayé   zu-ä-s-m-th   kidn
   base fire some yesterday 3SG.FEM.*β*1-ND-call.RS-DUR-2|3NSG kidn
            2|3PL:SBJ>3SG:OBJ:PST:ITER:DUR/call
   'They always used to call the eternal fire Kidn.' [tci20120909-06 KAB #55]

(25) *kwamonegwrmth e efoth fthé zbo warfo **kwänkorm** fthé kwarafinzrmth zä zerä.*
   kw-a-moneg-wr-m-th   e efoth fthé zbo warfo
   M.*β*1-VC-wait.EXT-ND-DUR-2|3NSG until sun when PROX.ALL above
   2|3PL:SBJ:PST:DUR/wait

   kw-ä-n-kor-m-∅   fthé kw-a-rafi-nzr-m-th
   M.*β*1-VC.ND-VENT-become.RS-DUR-2|3SG when M.*β*1-VC-paddle.EXT-ND-DUR-2|3NSG
   2|3SG:SBJ:PST:ITER:DUR:VENT/become   2|3PL:SBJ:PST:DUR/paddle

   zä z=e-rä
   PROX PROX=2|3NSG.*α*-COP.ND
     PROX=2|3PL:SBJ:NPST:IPFV/be
   'They were waiting until the sun always reached highest point and then they paddled here.' [tci20120922-19 DAK #13]

The durative suffix -*m* can be suffixed to perfective verbs in the recent past, past and irrealis. In this case, the event is only backgrounded without encoding a longer duration.

However, these inflections are so rare that, at least for the recent past and past tenses, they are not attested in the corpus. For the irrealis perfective with the durative suffix, there are a handful of examples. In (26), the speaker talks about an old procedure for punishment which involved striking the culprit with a yam tuber over the head.[3]

(26) *nasime **sräkwrmth** ebaren "ah, miyatha käkor bä monwä zbrigwé!"*
      nasi=me   s-rä-kwr-m-th   ebar=en   ah miyatha
      long.yam=INS   3SG.MASC.*β*-IRR.ND-hit.RS-DUR-2|3NSG head=LOC ah knowledge
            2|3PL:SBJ>3SG.MASC:OBJ:IRR:PFV:BG/hit

      k-ä-kor-∅   bä   mon=wä   z-brig-w-é
      M.*β*-ND-become.RS-2SG.IMP   2.ABS how=EMPH 3SG.FEM.*β*-return.EXT-ND-2SG.IMP
      2SG:SBJ:IMP:PFV/become   2SG:SBJ>3SG.FEM:OBJ:IMP:IPFV/return
      'They would hit him on the head with the long yam (and say) "Now you come up
      with a plan to pay this back!"'   [tci20120805-01 ABB #236-240]

Irrespective of perfectivity, the durative suffix on any irrealis inflection can have a far future interpretation. In examples (27) and (28), it is clear from the context that the event is set in the future and the -*m* on the verb indicates that the event is further in the future (as opposed to an irrealis form without the -*m* suffix). In (27), the speaker showed me an old method of tying a bowstring. He then speculates whether and when these old practices will vanish. Example (28) is taken from a conversation about yam cultivation during which the speaker complains about young people's lack of interest in gardening.

(27) *ni miyamr mä kwa kräbth mane … mrnen **kräbthmo** frthé*
      ni   miyamr   mä   kwa k-rä-bth-∅   mane (.) mrn-en
      1NSG   ignorance where FUT M.*β*-IRR.VC.ND-finish.RS-2|3SG which (.) clan-LOC
            2|3SG:SBJ:IRR:PFV/finish

      k-rä-bth-m-o-∅   frthé
      M.*β*-IRR.VC.ND-finish.RS-DUR-AND-SG when
      SG:SBJ:IRR:PFV:BG:AND/finish
      'We do not know where it will finish … in which generation it will finish.'
      [tci20130914-01 KAB #43-44]

(28) *nzä miyamr thrma ra **sranathrmth** … nagayé*
      nzä   miyamr thrma ra   s-ra-na-thr-m-th
      1SG.ABS ignorance later what 3SG.MASC.*β*-IRR-eat.EXT-ND-DUR-2|3NSG
            2|3PL:SBJ>3SG.MASC:OBJ:IRR:IPFV:BG/eat

      (.) nagayé
      (.) children
      'I do not know what the children will eat later.'   [tci20120805-01 ABB #577]

If the durative suffix is attached to a verb in the imperative mood, it encodes a delayed or future imperative ('do X a little later!').[4] The future imperative is also a rare inflection,

---

[3]I will show the backgrounded status of the perfective verb in the unified gloss line with BG, as in the examples below. In the maximally segmented gloss line, I will continue to use the durative label DUR.
[4]I gloss the future imperative with FUTIMP in the unified gloss line.

and we have seen one text example in (5) on page 239. In example (29), the speaker describes how competitive yam harvesting took place in the old days. After harvesting and sorting, a piece of rattan was used to measure the size of the largest tubers. This measurement was then sent to the competitors as a sign of one's superior gardening skills.

(29) *wati, ŋatr **thärifthm** nafanmedbo!*
      wati ŋatr   th-ä-rifth-m-∅   nafanme=dbo
      then rattan 2|3NSG.*β*-ND-send.RS-DUR-2SG.IMP   3NSG=ALL.SG
           2SG:SBJ>2|3PL:OBJ:FUTIMP:PFV/send
      'Then, you send the measure string to them!'   [tci20120805-01 ABB #402]

6.2.5 The imperative suffixes

The formatives of the imperative actor suffix series were given in Table 5.8 on page 208, where I pointed out the syncretism with the first person indicative actor suffixes and the second person imperative suffixes, as well as the fact that the second singular suffix differs between perfective and imperfective imperatives. I refer the reader to section §5.5.1.1 for further information.

Here I describe the morphology of imperatives for the prefixing template. Prefixing verbs as defined here encode their single participant in the prefix. We saw in Table 6.2 on page 238 that imperatives are formed with the *β* prefix series. For prefixing verbs, the formatives are *gn-* (2SG.IMP) and *th-* (2NSG.IMP). A further suffix is added to prefixing verbs only. Consider example (30) in which the speaker quotes himself talking to his wife. The imperative inflected verb is marked with an *-é* suffix which resembles the actor suffix of an ambifixing imperfective imperative (2SG.IMP) or of an ambifixing indicative of any aspect class (1SG). In the morphological context of prefixing imperatives, this *-é* does not encode a person value, as can be seen in example (31) where the number of the addressee argument is plural. In other words, the *-é* suffix looks like a person/number suffix, but with prefixing verbs it is inert to those categories and it only encodes imperative mood.

(30) *bä znrä. zä **gnamnzé** kwot e nzä kränbrimé!*
      bä   z=n-rä   zä   gn-a-m-nz-é   kwot   e   nzä
      2.ABS PROX=2SG.*α*-COP.ND   PROX 2SG.*β*-VC-sit.EXT-ND-IMP   properly until 1SG.ABS
            PROX=2SG:SBJ:NPST:IPFV/be   2SG:SBJ:IMP:IPFV/sit

      k-rä-n-brim-é
      M.*β*-IRR.VC.ND-VENT:return.RS-1SG
      1SG:SBJ:IRR:PFV:VENT/return
      'Now you are here. You stay here until I return.'   [tci20130823-06 STK #221]

(31) *... zbär fiyafr mane eyak famäsü **thyaké**!*
      (.) zbär fiyaf=r   mane e-yak   fam=ä=sü
      (.) night hunting=PURP   who 2|3NSG.*α*-walk.EXT.ND thought=ASSOC=ETC
                                    2|3PL:SBJ:NPST:IPFV/walk

th-yak-é
2|3NSG.*β*-walk.EXT.ND-IMP
2|3PL:SBJ:IMP:IPFV/walk
'You (boys) who go hunting at night must be careful!'   [tci20130901-04 RNA #27]

The -*é* formative for imperatives, regardless of whether it occurs on prefixing or ambi-fixing verbs, shows the same idiosyncrasies as the first person singular suffix -*é*, which is described in §5.5.1.1. For example, it disappears when other suffixes are added, as we saw in example (10) on page 240, where the -*é* suffix does not appear because of the andative suffix -*o*.

6.3 The TAM particles

The rich system of TAM categories in Komnzo can be further supplemented by a set of preverbal particles. These include the future *kwa*, the habitual *nomai*, the potential *kma*, the iamitive z^5, the apprehensive or prohibitive *m* and the imminent *n*. The latter two are related to the deictic proclitic *m=* and the immediate past *n=*. These particles interact with the numerous TAM categories and there are only few limitations on the possible combinations.

6.3.1 The imminent particle *n*

The imminent particle *n* expresses the point in time just before the event takes place, usually without implying that it actually happened. This often gets translated by informants as 'try to do X' or 'be about to do X'. Both interpretations, the intentional and the imminent one, are possible and difficult to separate. In example (32), the speaker showed me how to weave a fish basket. He says that he will try and fetch me when the work is finished because he does not know whether or not it will be successful.[6]

(32) *n thrma **nzänmesé** ... fthé zräbthé zane kafar.*
      n   thrma nz-ä-n-mes-é   (.) fthé   z-rä-bth-é
      IMN later 2SG.*β*-ND-VENT-fetch.RS-1SG (.) when 3SG.FEM.*β*-IRR.ND-finish.RS-1SG
             1SG:SBJ>2SG:OBJ:IRR:PFV:VENT/fetch   1SG:SBJ>3SG.FEM:OBJ:IRR:PFV/finish

      zane   kafar
      DEM:PROX big
      'Later I will try and fetch you, when I have finished that big (basket).'
                                                                [tci20120906 SKK #18]

The imminent particle can occur with inflections of different TAM categories. The important part of its semantic contribution is twofold: (i) the point in time before the event and (ii) the fact that the action has not yet been carried out or – in most cases – is

---

[5]I adopt the term *iamitive* from Olsson (2013), who has coined the term based on Latin *iam* 'already'.
[6]Indeed, he never came and showed me the finished fish basket because I had already left the village. But he proudly presented it to me in the following year.

not or was not carried out. Example (33) is taken from a headhunting story in which two men are about to kill a young woman when they realise that the rest of their headhunting party has left already.[7]

(33) **n zfrnmth** *di kam garsir "awkwot! ngemäku, kabe matak erä!"*
  n zf-r-n-m-th di kam gar-si=r
  IMN 3SG.FEM.*β*2-do.EXT-DU-DUR-2|3NSG back.of.head bone break-NMLZ=PURP
    2|3DU:SBJ>3SG.FEM:OBJ:PST:DUR/do

  awkwot ngemäku kabe matak e-rä
  interjection foster.parent man nothing 2|3NSG.*α*-COP.ND
        2|3PL:SBJ:NPST:IPFV/be
  'They were about to break her neck. (He said:) "Oh no, my friend, all the people have left!"' [tci20111119-01 ABB #151-152]

There is an overlap in the semantics of the proclitic *n=* which encodes immediate past and the imminent particle *n*. I pointed out earlier that the immediate past clitic attaches to a verb which is otherwise inflected for non-past. Thus, it marks a point in time immediately before the present. The particle *n* occurs in front of verb forms of different TAM categories, marking a point in time immediately before the event. The semantic difference is in the implication as to whether or not the event was actually carried out. In the case of the immediate clitic, the event has happened, but with the particle *n* this is not the case. The difference between the two also lies in formal criteria. The particle *n* is syntactically independent in that it occurs free (32), or occur directly in front of the verb, where it is hard to say whether it is a proclitic or an independent element (33). On the other hand, the immediate clitic *n=* is always bound to the verb.

Speakers of Komnzo who have been brought up in a Wära-speaking family, and most young speakers of all backgrounds, have replaced the immediate past proclitic *n=* with its Wära equivalent *nz=*. This change only affects the proclitic and not the imminent particle *n*.

6.3.2 The apprehensive particle *m*

I point out in §5.6.2 that among the deictic proclitics there is one with a limited distribution. The *m=* proclitic can only attach to the copula, in which case it turns the clause into a question ('where is X?').[8] See example (70) on page 233. The *m* particle shows more syntactic flexibility as it can procliticise to the verb as *m=*, encliticise to the potential particle in the combination *kma=m* or occur by itself. The latter is only attested through elicitation and there are no corpus examples of independent *m*. Nevertheless, it can be classified as a particle and a clitic.

The particle *m* functions as an apprehensive marker. It is attested in the corpus with irrealis, imperative and perfective forms. Example (34) is from a story about a man who

---

[7]The word *ngemäku* in the example is an address term between two people where one has adopted the child of the other.

[8]I will gloss *m* as interrogative (where=) when it attaches to the copula. I will gloss it as apprehensive (APPR) in all other cases, including the cases where *m* and the potential particle *kma* express a prohibitive.

mocked a crowd of dancers by threatening them with a matchbox. They were afraid, as they did not know about matches and lighters.

(34) *krenafthth "sritüthe! sfafe! kidn mni **mzärfusir** ... frthe bramöwä ŋarsirwre."*

k-rä-nafth-th   s-∅-ritüth-e
M.*β*-IRR.VC.ND-say.RS-2|3NSG   3SG.MASC.*β*-DU-grab.RS-2|3NSG.IMP
2|3PL:SBJ:IRR:PFV/say   2DU:SBJ>3SG.MASC:OBJ:IMP:PFV/grab

s-∅-faf-e   kidn mni m=z-ä-rfusir-∅
3SG.MASC.*β*-DU-hold.RS-2|3NSG.IMP kidn fire APPR=M.*γ*-VC.ND-light.up.RS-2|3SG
2DU:SBJ>3SG.MASC:OBJ:IMP:PFV/hold   APPR=2|3SG:SBJ:RPST:PFV/light.up

(.) frthe bramöwä ŋ-a-rsir-wr-e
(.) when all   M.*α*-VC-burn.EXT-ND-1NSG
                    1PL:SBJ:NPST:IPFV/burn

'They said: "Grab him! Hold him! He might ignite the Kidn fire. (That is) when we will all burn."'   [tci20120909-06 KAB #82]

In these cases, the particle *m* seems to override the TAM value of the verb. In (34), the verb is in the recent past but lacks a therecent past reading. Likewise, I often heard the warning *mkätr*[9] '(watch out) you might fall!', where *m* is attached to an imperative form, but lacks an imperative reading. Naturally, if *m* occurs with an irrealis form, there is no such conflict. Example (35) is taken from a story about a bushfire. The speaker explains how he set a small controlled fire in order to stop the wild bushfire from spreading.

(35) *we ane nzefé zaföfé ... we **mkrärit** we fafä.*

we ane nzefé   z-a-föf-é   (.) we
also DEM 1SG.ERG.EMPH 3SG.FEM.*γ*-VC.ND-burn.down.RS-1SG (.) also
                          1SG:SBJ>3SG.FEM:OBJ:RPST:PFV/burn.down

m=k-rä-rit-∅   we fafä
APPR=M.*β*-IRR.VC.ND-pass.RS-2|3SG also after.that
APPR=2|3SG:SBJ:IRR:PFV/pass

'I also burned down this (grass) ... (the fire) might cross over later.'
                                                      [tci20120922-24 MAA #30-31]

If *m* occurs with an imperative inflected verb and the potential *kma*, it functions as a prohibitive. Example (36) is from the very beginning of a hunting story. The speaker tells his son to be quiet during the recording, while I am setting up the microphone.

(36) *zokwasi wzänzr ... daddyf. **kmam kanafré!***

zokwasi w-zä-nzr-∅   (.) daddy=f   kma=m
words   3SG.FEM.*α*-carry.EXT-ND-2|3SG (.) father=ERG.SG POT=APPR
        2|3SG:SBJ>3SG.FEM:OBJ:NPST:IPFV/carry

---

[9] *mkätr*
m=k-ä-tr-∅
APPR=M.*β*-VC.ND-fall.RS-2SG.IMP

k-a-naf-r-é
M.*β*-VC-speak.EXT-ND-2SG.IMP
2SG:SBJ:IMP:IPFV/speak
'Daddy is recording the words. You must not talk!'   [tci20130903-03 MKW #3-4]

In the prohibitive construction, the particle *m* is rather flexible. It can attach to the verb as a proclitic (37) or to the potential particle *kma* as an enclitic (36 and 38). What is important for the prohibitive reading is the co-occurence of *m* and *kma* in the clause, not the fact that they are conjoined. Example (37)[10] comes from a public speech at a dance in which the speaker tells the audience the rules for the night. Example (38) is taken from a text about food taboos.

(37) **kma** *wärir bä* **mgnanyaké** *zena zbär zbo!*
      kma wäri=r   bä   m=gn-a-n-yak-é   zena zbär zbo
      POT sex=PURP 2.ABS APPR=2SG.*β*-VC-VENT-walk.EXT.ND-IMP today night PROX.ALL
                      APPR=2SG:SBJ:IMP:IPFV/come
      'You must not come here for sex tonight!'   [tci20121019-04 ABB #46]

(38) *be* **kmam** *ŋazikarä* **kathafrakwé!**
      be   kma=m   ŋazi=karä   k-a-thafrak-w-é
      2SG.ERG POT=APPR coconut=PROP M.*β*-VC-mix.EXT-ND-2SG.IMP
      2SG:SBJ:IMP:EXT/mix
      'You must not mix it with coconut'   [tci20120922-26 DAK #12]

6.3.3 The potential particle *kma*

The potential particle *kma* can be employed with almost all TAM categories. We saw in §6.3.2 that it encodes a prohibitive when it occurs together with imperatives and the apprehensive particle *m*. This is the only construction in which *kma* and the imperative inflections occur together.

The potential particle *kma* is used to encode various types of speculation and counterfactuality with deontic or epistemic interpretation. Example (39) is taken from a public speech at a dance, where the guest side has brought too many people, and consequently the host side found it impossible to meet the needs of so many people. The speaker regrets that no proper arrangement has been made prior to the event. Thus, the clause "it should have been well" has a clear deontic reading.

(39) *namä* **kma** *nimame zrarenzrm fof ... fthé namä yamme nüfifthakwrme.*
      namä kma nima=me   z-ra-re-nzr-m   fof (.) fthé namä
      good POT like.this=INS 3SG.FEM.*β*-IRR.VC-look.EXT-ND-DUR EMPH (.) when good
                           3SG.FEM:SBJ:IRR:IPFV/look

---

[10] The verb *yak* 'walk' is deponent and employs the valency change prefix *a-* without a change in the valency of the verb. It is only deponent when it employs the venitive marker, meaning 'come', not when it is neutral or andative, meaning 'walk', 'go away'.

yam=me   n=w-fifthak-wr-m-e
custom=INS IPST=3SG.FEM.*α*-put.down.straight.EXT-ND-DUR-1NSG
IPST=1PL:SBJ>3SG.FEM:OBJ:NPST:DUR/put.down.straight
'It should have been well today, if we had straightened things out in a good way.'
[tci20121019-04 ABB #79]

Example (40) is taken from an origin myth in which the speaker speculates that one of the protagonists "must have had a shotgun", while his brother only had bow and arrow. This is a clear epistemic use of *kma*.

(40)   *nafangth **kma** markai nabikarä sfrärm.*
        nafa-ngth   kma markai nabi=karä sf-rär-m
        3.POSS-younger.sibling POT outsider bow=PROP 3SG.MASC.*β*2-COP.ND-DUR
3SG.MASC:SBJ:PST:DUR/be
        'His younger brother must have had a shotgun.'   [tci20131013-01 ABB #112]

6.3.4 The future particle *kwa*

Future tense is marked periphrastically in Komnzo with the particle *kwa*, which combines either with the non-past (41) or irrealis inflections (42).

(41)   *zena **kwa natrikwé** bun … no kzima.*
        zena kwa n-a-trik-w-é   bun   (.) no kzi=ma
        today FUT 2SG.*α*-VC-tell.EXT-ND-1SG 2SG.DAT (.) rain barktray=CHAR
1SG:SBJ>2SG:IO:NPST:IPFV/tell
        'Today, I will tell you about the rain-making barktray.'   [tci20110810-01 MAB #1]

(42)   *gb **kwa thrarfikwr** zba.*
        gb   kwa th-ra-rfik-wr   zba
        sprout FUT 2|3NSG.*β*-IRR-grow.EXT-ND PROX.ABL
2|3PL:SBJ:IRR:IPFV/grow
        'The sprouts will grow from here.'   [tci20120805-01 ABB #35]

The future particle can also be used by itself meaning 'wait', as in example (43), where the name of a particular plant has slipped from the speaker's mind.

(43)   ***kwa**! yf kwot keke miyatha worä.*
        kwa yf   kwot   keke miyatha   wo-rä
        wait name properly NEG knowledge 1SG.*α*-COP.ND
1SG:SBJ:NPST:IPFV/be
        'Wait! I don't quite know that name.'   [tci20130907-02 RNA #609]

When negated, the future particle *kwa* can express 'not yet', as in example (44), where the speaker points out that he has not yet heard the name that will be given to a particular person at an upcoming namesake celebration.

(44) *ni miyamr mane zrarä ane kar yf fof.* **keke kwa** *kar yf nä zamare fof.*

ni   miyamr   mane   z-ra-rä   ane kar   yf   fof   keke kwa
1NSG ignorance which 3SG.FEM.β-IRR-COP.ND DEM village name EMPH NEG FUT
                                  3SG.FEM:SBJ:IRR:IPFV/be

kar   yf   nä   z-a-mar-e   fof
village name some 3SG.FEM.γ-ND-see-1NSG   EMPH
                          1PL:SBJ>3SG.FEM:OBJ:RPST:PFV/see
'We do not know which local name it will be. We have not heard the name yet.'

[tci20110817-02 ABB #58-60]

Younger speakers of Komnzo are beginning to use the Wära equivalent *ka*, which which has a pure velar rather than labiovelar onset.

6.3.5 The iamitive particle *z*

I adopt the term "iamitive" from Olsson's (2013) comparative study of particles that express a perfect. Reesink (2009: 184) uses the term "perspectival aspect", which he adopts from Dik (1997). Komnzo speakers often translate the iamitive particle *z* as 'already', hence the gloss label ALR. An introductory example is given in (45). This is taken from a recording where two women took me on a plant walk. Example (45b) is the answer to the question in (45a).

(45) a. *zuyak z safäs?*
         zuyak z   s-a-fäs-∅
         zuyak ALR 3SG.MASC.γ-ND-show.RS-2|3SG
                      2|3SG:SBJ>3SG.MASC:OBJ:NPST:PFV/show
         'Have you shown him zuyak (Rhodania sp) already?'

[tci20130907-02 JAA #44]

      b. *z fof!*
         z   fof
         ALR EMPH
         'Yes, (I have) already.'

[tci20130907-02 RNA #121]

Example (45) shows that the function of the iamitive is to express "current relevance" of some past event. Consequently, the particle may combine with verbs inflected for different TAM categories. Example (45) shows a verb in recent past perfective. In (46), the iamitive particle is used with a past durative inflected verb. This combination is rarer, but well-attested in the corpus. In the example, the speaker is explaining which clans settled at which locations. He points out that his clan had already been living in Masu for a while.

(46) *fi fobo thwamnzrm nima … ni masun z nzwamnzrm.*
      fi   fobo   thu-a-m-nzr-m   nima (.) ni   masu=n   z
      3.ABS DIST.ALL 2|3NSG.β1-VC-sit.EXT-ND-DUR like.this (.) 1NSG masu=LOC ALR
                          2|3PL:SBJ:PST:DUR/sit

nzu-a-m-nzr-m
1NSG.β1-VC-sit.EXT-ND-DUR
1PL:SBJ:PST:DUR/sit
'They lived over there, this way ... and we had already been living in Masu.'

[tci20120922-08 DAK #97-98]

The iamitive particle can also be used with a non-past inflection. This is often restricted to interrogatives, as in (47), where the speaker is asking a crowd of people whether they can hear him speaking.

(47) *zbär bä zagrwä ämnzro. z wanrizrth?*
zbär bä   zagr=wä e-a-m-nzr-o   z
night MED far=EMPH 2|3NSG.α-VC-sit.EXT-ND-AND ALR
              2|3PL:SBJ:NPST:IPFV:AND/sit

w-a-n-riz-r-th
1SG.α-VC-VENT-hear.EXT-ND-2|3NSG
2|3PL:SBJ>1SG:IO:NPST:IPFV:VENT/hear
'Tonight you are sitting too far away. Can you hear me?'   [tci20121019-04 SKK #9]

The iamitive particle additionally expresses the completion of an event. Evidence for this come from different observations. First, it can express a current relevance meaning. Secondly, it never combines with iterative verbs, which express an ongoing repetition of some event in the past. Thirdly, it marks sequentiality of events in some narratives where the verb form which combines with it seems to be almost a prerequisite to the following verb. Example (48)[11] is a description of a path, which the speaker had taken the previous day. He describes the sequenced stages of his path to the location called Tümgo.

(48) *bä komnzo zwäzik ... ksi karen z kwanyak e zbo zwänthor tümgon.*
bä   komnzo zu-ä-zik   (.) ksi   kar=en   z
MED only   1SG.γ-ND-turn.off.RS (.) bush place=LOC ALR
              1SG:SBJ:RPST:PFV/turn.off

ku-a-n-yak   e   zbo   zu-ä-n-thor   tümgo=n
1SG.β1-VC-walk.EXT.ND until PROX.ALL 1SG.γ-ND-VENT-arrive.RS tümgo=LOC
1SG:SBJ:RPST:IPFV:VENT/walk   1SG:SBJ:RPST:PFV:VENT/arrive
'It turned off (the path) there ... I walked in the bushy place until I arrived here in Tümgo.'   [tci20120922-24 MAA #8-10]

The iamitive particle *z* in Komnzo shares a number of semantics characteristics with the forms described by Olsson (2013) in his comparative study. The main two characteristics of iamitives cross-linguistically are "the notion of a "new situation" that holds after a transition" and "the consequences that this situation has at reference time for the

---

[11]The verb *yak* 'walk' is deponent and employs the valency changing prefix *a-* without a change in the valency of the verb. Note that this occurs only with the venitive marker, in which case the verb means 'come', not when it is neutral ('walk') or marked with the andative ('go away').

participants in the speech event" (2013: 43). The former was described above as event completion, and the latter as current relevance. In fact, the iamitive particle is the main way to express event completion in Komnzo, because the perfective aspect does not explicitly set this boundary on an event.

There has been much discussion in the literature about the paths of grammaticalisation of perfects, for example in Bybee & Dahl (1989). In Komnzo, the iamitive particle *z* is formally closest to the proximal series of the deictic markers, and one might speculate about these as a source of grammaticalisation (§3.1.12).

6.3.6 The habitual particle *nomai*

The habitual particle *nomai* typically combines with durative inflections. In example (49), the cockatoo always warns the protagonist of another man who comes and visits him.

(49) *krara ymd suwägrm maf swatrikwrm **nomai** nima "oh, kabe yanyak."*
      krara   ymd su-wägr-m   maf
      cockatoo bird 3SG.MASC.β1-be.on.top.ND-DUR who.ERG
                   3SG.MASC:SBJ:PST:DUR/be.on.top

      su-a-trik-wr-m-$\varnothing$ nomai nima oh kabe
      3SG.MASC.β1-VC-tell.EXT-ND-DUR-2|3SG HAB   QUOT oh man
      2|3SG:SBJ>3SG.MASC:IO:PST:DUR/tell

      y-a-n-yak
      3SG.MASC.α-VENT-walk.EXT.ND
      3SG.MASC:SBJ:NPST:IPFV:VENT/walk
      'The cockatoo bird used to sit on top (of the tree), and told him always: "Oh, a man is coming."'   [tci20100802 ABB #80-82]

The habitual can also combine with verb forms inflected for other TAM categories, such as imperfectives (50). It only occasionally occurs with perfectives, as in (51), where the event is negated. In both examples, *nomai* expresses an extended period of time rather that a repeated habit.

(50) *yamnza yamnza ... **nomai** ... ysokwr tüfr.*
      2x[y-a-m-nz-a]   (.) nomai (.) ysokwr tüfr
      2x[3SG.α-VC-sit.EXT-ND-PST] (.) HAB   (.) year   plenty
      2x[3SG.MASC:SBJ:PST:IPFV/sit]
      'He stayed and stayed there for many years.'   [tci20120904-01 MAB #13]

(51) *keke **nomai** zämsath.*
      keke nomai z-ä-ms-a-th
      NEG HAB   M.γ-VC.ND-sit.EXT-PST-2|3NSG
                 2|3PL:SBJ:PST:PFV/sit
      'They did not stay (there) for long.'   [tci20131013-02 ABB #87]

6.4 Some remarks on the semantics of TAM

Following from our description of the morphology and combinatorics of TAM in Komnzo, I want to sketch out a coherent picture of the semantics of these categories and their extended uses. Although tense, aspect and mood are intertwined, I will discuss them separately in the following sections.

6.4.1 Tense

We saw that Komnzo has three or four morphological tenses depending on the analysis: the non-past, the recent past and the past. The immediate past is expressed by a clitic and builds on a verb form inflected for the non-past. Future reference is expressed periphrastically with the particle *kwa*.

The temporal reference of the immediate past and the recent past overlaps. The immediate past is used for events that took place a short while prior to the time of speaking, and it may be used to put extra emphasis on that fact. The recent past covers the same period of time, but it reaches further back, usually to the preceding day. Example (52) is taken from a hunting story, at the end of which the speaker returns home to find one of his dogs. He tells his wife that this is the dog which had disturbed him at the outset of the trip when he was about to cross the Morehead river. He had pushed the dog into the water, whereupon the poor dog ran back to the house. The whole episode in (52) is set in the same time frame with respect to the moment of speech. Only the 'pushing in the water' is expressed in the immediate past, while the other two verb forms are in the recent past.[12]

(52) *nzefe nima "ane ŋatha bä **nzwathofikwr** ... watik anema **nzibrüzé** bobo ... watik ane wtrime fi ŋatha **zanmath**."*

nzefe	nima	ane	ŋatha	bä	nzu-a-thofik-wr-∅	(.)	watik
1SG.ERG.EMPH	QUOT	DEM	dog	MED	1SG.β1-VC-disturb.EXT-ND-2|3SG	(.)	then
					2|3SG:SBJ>1SG:OBJ:RPST:IPFV/disturb		

ane=ma	nz=y-brüz-∅-é	bobo	(.)	watik	ane	wtri=me
DEM=CHAR	IPST=3SG.MASC.α-submerge.EXT-ND-1SG	MED.ALL	(.)	then	DEM	fear=INS
	IPST=1SG:SBJ>2|3SG.MASC.OBJ:NPST:IPFV/submerge					

fi	ŋatha	z-a-n-math-∅
3.ABS	dog	M.y-VENT-run.RS-2|3SG
		2|3SG:SBJ:RPST:PFV:VENT/run

'I said: "That dog disturbed me there and therefore I pushed him into the water. Well, full of fear he ran back here."' [tci20130903-03 MKW #188]

The bidirectional time adverbials discussed in §3.1.8 help to identify the appropriate time frames for each tense value. The term *kayé* expresses a moment in time which is removed by one day from the present time. Thus, *kayé* can mean 'tomorrow', when used

---

[12] The speaker uses the *nz=* formative of the immediate past clitic. As pointed out in §6.3.1, this formative is a borrowing from Wära. The Komnzo formative is *n=*.

with a non-past inflection, or it can mean 'yesterday', when used with a recent past. Events further back in time have to be expressed by the past tense. Likewise, one cannot use a recent past with the time adverbial *nama*, which indicates a point in time that is removed two days from the present time ('day before yesterday' or 'day after tomorrow'). In short, the recent past reaches back one day, whereas the past tense covers everything before yesterday, irrespective of whether it happened a week ago or in ancestral time. Example (53) shows the use of *kayé* and the recent past. Example (54) shows the use of *nama* and the past tense.[13]

(53) **kayé** *nzä boba* **zenfaré** *... kanathr.*
    kayé   nzä   boba   z-ä-n-far-é   (.) kanathr
    yesterday 1SG.ABS MED.ABL M.*γ*-VC.ND-VENT-set.off.EXT-1SG (.) kanathr
                                 1SG:SBJ:RPST:PFV:VENT/set.off
    'Yesterday, I set off from there towards here ... to Kanathr.'   [tci20120922-24 MAA #1]

(54) *zane nane dayr zbo* **nama** *mane* **wänyaka** *...*
    zane   nane   dayr zbo   nama   mane
    DEM:PROX elder.sibling dayr PROX.ALL two.days.ago which

    w-a-n-yak-a   (.)
    3SG.FEM.*α*-VC-VENT-go.EXT.ND-PST (.)
    3SG.FEM:SBJ:PST:IPFV:VENT/go
    'The older sister Dayr who came here two days ago ...'   [tci20130901-04 RNA #87]

Tense values can be used with a pragmatic motivation. It is quite common to foreground events in a narrative by putting them into the non-past, even though the story is set in the recent past or the past. Example (55) comes from a story that took place in the speaker's youth. In the example clauses, he describes walking with a friend during night time. The two boys rested along the way and smoked tobacco. Although the story is set in the past, only the first and the last verbs in (55) are inflected in the past tense ('walk' in both cases). The 'sitting down' and the 'setting off' are inflected for irrealis, and are thus tenseless. The rolling of the cigarettes and their smoking is told in the non-past, which moves this part to the foreground.

(55) *nyana ttfö bä rä ... bäne ... sazäthi fä kramse sukufa* **eknne änane** *boba krafare ...*
    zbär nzfyanm.
    n-yan-a   ttfö bä rä   (.) bäne   (.) sazäthi
    1NSG.*α*-walk.EXT.DU-PST creek MED 3SG.FEM.COP.ND   (.) RECOG.ABS (.) sazäthi
    1DU:SBJ:PST:IPFV/walk   3SG.FEM:SBJ:NPST:IPFV/be

    fä   k-ra-ms-e   sukufa e-kn-n-e
    DIST M.*β*-IRR.VC.DU-sit.RS-1NSG tobacco 2|3NSG.*α*-roll.EXT-DU-1NSG
        1DU:SBJ:IRR:PFV/sit   1DU:SBJ>2|3NSG:OBJ:NPST:IPFV/roll

    e-a-na-n-e   boba   k-ra-far-e   (.) zbär
    2|3NSG.*α*-VC-eat.EXT-DU-1NSG MED.ABL M.*α*-IRR.VC.DU-set.off.RS-1NSG (.) night
    1DU:SBJ>2|3PL:OBJ:NPST:IPFV/eat   1DU:SBJ:IRR:PFV/set.off

---

[13] *Nama* can also be used metaphorically to mean 'recently'.

257

nzf-yan-m
1NSG.β2-walk.EXT.DU-DUR
1DU:SBJ:PST:DUR/walk

'We walked. There is a creek there (called) Sazäthi. We sat down there, rolled the cigarettes and smoked. We set off from there. We were walking in the night.'

[tci20210904-01 MAB #140-143]

Future reference can be expressed by irrealis or non-past inflections combined with the future particle *kwa*. The main difference between the two strategies seems to lie in the anticipated degree of certainty: the non-past inflection is usually used when the speaker is more certain that the event is going to take place.

6.4.2 Aspect

I have labelled the principal aspectual distinction in Komnzo imperfective versus perfective. Durative aspect is understood as a subtype of the imperfective and we could label these two as 'basic imperfective' and 'durative imperfective'. I use the traditional labels imperfective and perfective, but I want to spell out the particular flavour that Komnzo gives to them.

Traditional accounts of perfectivity often take the completion of an event as a starting point (Frawley 1992: 296) or suggests that "perfectivity indicates the view of a situation as a single whole" (Comrie 1976: 16). In Komnzo, completion does not really play a role in the semantics of the perfective-imperfective distinction. The boundary set up by the perfective seems to concentrate more on the left edge, i.e. on the beginning of the event. Similar systems are found elsewhere in the Southern New Guinea region, for example in Marind (Drabbe 1955: 41), Nama (Siegel 2014) and Nen (Evans 2015b). In Komnzo, the main mechanism for expressing event completion, i.e. to set up a right edge event boundary, is the iamitive particle, which can occur with verb forms in perfective, imperfective and durative aspect (§6.3.5). It follows that imperfectivity does not entail that the event is open-ended. Example (56) is taken from a head hunting story. The quantifier *bramöwä* 'all' signals that the attack was full-scale and all inhabitants were killed, but the verb form in (56) is in the imperfective.

(56) *watik ebar kabe ane fof thäthora fof ... bramöwä ane fof **efnzath***
     watik ebar kabe ane fof   th-ä-thor-a   fof   (.) bramöwä ane
     then head man DEM EMPH 2|3NSG.γ-ND-arrive.RS-PST EMPH (.) all   DEM
                             2|3PL:SBJ:PST:PFV/arrive
     fof   e-fn-nz-a-th
     EMPH 2|3NSG.α-hit.EXT-ND-PST-2|3NSG
          2|3PL:SBJ>2|3PL:OBJ:PST:IPFV/hit

'Then, the head hunter arrived. They killed all of them.'   [tci20131013-02 ABB #143-145]

Likewise, perfectives do not entail that an event is finished, but rather that it has started or that its duration was of a punctual quality. The latter is shown in the first verb 'arrive' in example (56). The former is shown in example (57), which is taken from a story about a malignant being. At the end of the story this being tries to escape by entering a bird, but the villagers are quick to shoot down the bird. The entering event in (57) is expressed in the perfective, but the imminent particle *n* shows that the event has not started yet. Hence, completion of the entering event is not entailed, but excluded. Thus, a literal translation of *n zäthba* would be: 's/he was about to start to enter'.

(57)   *brbrnzo fof n zäthba bafen ... ymden fof.*

     brbr=nzo   fof   n   z-ä-thb-a-∅   baf=en   (.) ymd=en fof

     spirit=ONLY EMPH IMN M.ɣ-ND-enter.RS-PST-2|3SG RECOG=LOC (.) bird=LOC EMPH

                          2|3SG:SBJ:PST:PFV/enter

     'Only the spirit was about to go inside that one ... inside the bird.'

                                       [tci20120901-01 MAK #193-194]

Aspect in Komnzo seems to concentrate more on a punctual/inceptive versus ongoing/stretched-out distinction. I adopt the traditional labels perfective for the former and imperfective for the latter. The degree to which an event is "stretched out" would then decide whether the speaker chooses the imperfective or durative aspect. The basic binary distinction is clearest in the imperative forms. The imperfective imperatives often encode an ongoing action and, depending on the context, they can be translated as "keep on X-ing" or "do X for some time". Perfective imperatives, on the other hand, express inception "start X-ing" or punctuality "do X once/quickly". In example (58), the speaker has just produced a toy bullroarer from a coconut leaf and shows me how to hold it properly. In (58a), she tells me not to hit anything while swinging, and the imperative of 'hit' is in the perfective.[14] In (58b), she is already swinging the bullroarer, telling me to hold it away from the body. Consequently, all the imperative verb forms ('hold', 'blow', and 'swing') are in the imperfective.

(58) a. *fthé sakwr gwonyamen o festhen o wämnen ... keke kwa sranor.*

          fthé   s-a-kwr-∅   gwonyame=n o festh=en o wämne=n

          when 3SG.MASC.*α*-ND-hit.RS-2SG.IMP clothes=LOC   or body=LOC or tree=LOC

               1SG:SBJ>3SG.MASC:OBJ:IMP:PFV/hit

          (.) keke kwa s-ra-nor

          (.) NEG FUT 3SG.MASC.*β*-IRR.VC-shout.EXT

               3SG.MASC:SBJ:IRR:IPFV/shout

          'If you hit it on clothes, body or a tree, it will not make a sound.'

     b. *zagrwä nima sfathwé byé nima sfsgwé ... smitwanzé ... fi kwa yanor.*

          zagr=wä nima   s-fath-w-é   b=\yé/

          far=EMPH like.this 3SG.MASC.*β*-hold.EXT-ND-2SG.IMP MED=3SG.MASC.COP.ND

               2SG:SBJ>3SG.MASC:OBJ:IMP:IPFV/hold   MED=3SG.MASC:SBJ:NPST:IPFV/be

---

[14]This is a conditional construction which frequently employs imperative inflections together with *fthé* 'when/if' (§6.4.3 and §9.6).

nima   s-fsg-w-é   (.) s-mitwa-nz-é
like.this 3SG.MASC.β-blow.EXT-ND-2SG.IMP (.) 3SG.MASC.β-swing.EXT-ND-2SG.IMP
      2SG:SBJ>3SG.MASC:OBJ:IMP:IPFV/blow   2SG:SBJ>3SG.MASC:OBJ:IMP:IPFV/swing

(.) fi   kwa y-a-nor
(.) 3.ABS FUT 3SG.MASC.α-VC-shout.EXT.ND
          3SG.MASC.SBJ:NPST:IPFV/shout

'You have to hold it away like this and blow and swing it like this ... (then) it will make a sound.'   [tci20120914 RNA #25-28]

A number of authors have used a scale-based approach to model certain operators which change the structure of predicates (Kennedy & McNally 2005 and Kubota 2010). Such an approach is compatible with the TAM system of Komnzo, once we accept that the imperfective versus perfective distinction highlights different parts of event by manipulating the temporal scale. Applied to the Komnzo TAM system, such a model portrays perfectives as a means to (i) set an explicit initial boundary and to (ii) limit the temporal scale of the event. (Basic) imperfectives leave this initial boundary implicit, but highlight that the event was carried out for some time – a little further along the scale. The durative (imperfective) increases the temporal scale of the event. As shown above, none of these (morphological) aspectual categories sets an explicit boundary at the right edge of the event. The function of event completion is reserved for the iamitive particle. I will leave the theoretical modelling of the semantics of the Komnzo TAM system for future research.

The theoretical discussion of aspect has often focussed on the distinction between viewpoint aspect and situation aspect.[15] Despite all terminological confusion, the former is often called ASPECT, a term which is employed for "different ways of viewing the internal constituency of a situation" (Comrie 1976: 3). Situation aspect, on the other hand, has often been called AKTIONSART, and is associated with the internal structure of the event. Thus, situation aspect is something objective about the nature of the event, whereas viewpoint aspect is subjectively manipulated by the speakers, or as Smith puts it: "the categories of viewpoint aspect are overt, whereas situation aspect is expressed in covert categories" (1997: 5). We have seen that this does not apply to Komnzo. Aspectual categories, although highly grammaticalised, are based on the situation type rather than on viewpoint, i.e. they are about inception/punctuality, iteration and duration rather than completion. The fact that aspect is highly grammaticalised means that the categories are accessible to virtually all verb lexemes. I showed in §5.3 that the two stem types (RS and EXT) are attested for almost all stems. This supports the argument that the notion of an objective internal event structure, which is fed into the inflectional system, plays little role in Komnzo.

As we have seen in the discussion of verbal morphology, a central part of the inflectional system are the two stem types. The labels EXT and RS of course refer to "extended in time" and "restricted in time", respectively. All perfectives are built from the RS stem and all imperfectives are built from the EXT stem. However, a relabelling of the RS stem

---

[15]See Sasse (2002) for a formidable overview of the research on aspect.

as "perfective stem" and the EXT stem as "imperfective stem" would be misleading. For example, the RS stem is employed for iterative aspect, which is by definition not bounded in time. This contradiction can be resolved by assuming a more transparent contribution of the morphological mechanisms which participate in the iterative inflection. As shown in §6.2 (Table 6.1), the iterative builds on the RS stem, but it employs the *β1* or *β2* prefix series, which otherwise only occur with the EXT stem to build imperfectives and duratives. In other words, the iterative aspect limits the event structure by stem selection and simultaneously spreads out the event structure by the selection of the prefix series. This is an interesting scenario, which calls for further comparative research within the Yam languages to shed light on the grammaticalisation of iterative aspect.

6.4.3 Mood

There are three modal categories in Komnzo: indicative, imperative and irrealis. Further nuances can be expressed with the help of particles, especially the potential *kma*, the imminent *n* and the apprehensive *m* (§6.3). Here, I will only describe some of the ways in which two of the three basic categories – the imperative and the irrealis – deviate from their conventional definitions.

Imperatives can be used in a number of ways that fall outside the definition of 'giving an order'. In example (59), the speaker showed me the leaves of a pandanus plant pointing out that I can use the leaves to sleep on. The imperative form *gnyaké* 'you go' is thus not a command 'go without a mat', but more like a conditional 'if you go without a mat'. The conditional interpretation also comes from the word *fthé* which means 'when' or 'at the time when'. This type of conditional construction is an extended use of the imperative inflection. Most imperatives are used as commands, and there are conditional constructions without imperative inflections.

(59) *yamemäre fthé **gnyaké** ... etfthar.*
  yame=märe fthé gn-yak-é   (.) etfth=r
  mat=PRIV   when 2|3SG.*β*-walk.EXT.ND-IMP (.) sleep=PURP
             2SG:SBJ:IMP:IPFV/walk
  'If you go without a mat, (this one is) for sleeping.'

  [tci20130907-02 JAA #546-547]

As we have seen in §6.2.2, the irrealis is marked by the prefix *ra-*. There is no realis marker, hence no realis inflection. Beyond counterfactuality and futurity, the irrealis mood has a number of semantic extensions in Komnzo. Cross-linguistically irrealis mood is employed for a wide range of functions, which has led some authors to challenge its validity as a comparative category (Bybee et al. 1994). Others have suggested a prototype approach to irrealis mood, for example Givon (1994: 327). I will adopt the latter here. Example (60) and (61) show the irrealis mood in its more central functions, counterfactuality and futurity, respectively. Examples (60) is taken from a headhunting story which involved the speaker's father.[16] Example (61) is taken from a procedural in which the speaker shows me how to make a toy from a coconut leaf.

---

[16]The example also shows the 'relative use' of the immediate past. Although the events in the story happened

(60) *fi fthé niyamnzrm nafäsü kwa* **thräkwrth.**

fi   fthé   n=y-a-m-nzr-m   nafä=sü   kwa
3.ABS when IPST=3SG.MASC.*α*-VC-sit.EXT-ND-DUR 3ASSOC.PL=ETC FUT
       IPST=3SG.MASC:SBJ:NPST:DUR/sit

th-rä-kwr-th
2|3SG.*β*-IRR.ND-hit.RS-2|3NSG
2|3PL:SBJ>2|3PL:OBJ:IRR:PFV/hit

'If he had stayed, they would have killed him with all the others.'

[tci20111107-01 MAK #80]

(61) *katan kwa* **sräfiyothé** *... kafar minzü yé.*

katan kwa s-rä-fiyoth-é   (.) kafar minzü yé
small FUT 3SG.MASC.*β*-VC.ND-make.RS-1SG   (.) big   very   3SG.MASC.COP.ND
     1SG:SBJ>3SG:OBJ:IRR:PFV/make   3SG.MASC:SBJ:NPST:IPFV/be
'I will make it smaller. This is too big.'   [tci20120914 RNA #41]

Verbs inflected for irrealis can be used as habituals. This use, especially with past habituals, has been noticed in a cross-linguistic study by Cristofaro (2004). Example (62) comes from a procedural about poison-root fishing, which is a common activity during the dry season when the water recedes. The speaker talks about the preparations and the process of poison-root fishing, while his family is busy fishing in the background. All verb forms are in the irrealis mood.

(62) **thranäbünzrth** *... sam ane mane erä* **threthkäfth** *... zranrsrwrth fof no zrerärth
... thranor "si rore rore rore!!"*

th-ra-näbü-nzr-th   (.) sam   ane mane e-rä
2|3NSG.*β*-IRR-smash.EXT-ND-2|3NSG (.) liquid DEM which 2|3NSG.*α*-COP.ND
2|3PL:SBJ>2|3PL:OBJ:IRR:IPFV/smash   2|3PL:SBJ:NPST:IPFV/be

th-rä-thkäf-th   (.) z-ra-n-rsr-wr-th
2|3NSG.*β*-IRR.ND-start.RS-2|3NSG (.) 3SG.FEM.*β*-IRR-VENT-squeeze.EXT-ND-2|3NSG
2|3PL:SBJ>2|3PL:OBJ:IRR:PFV/start   2|3PL:SBJ>3SG.FEM:OBJ:IRR:IPFV/squeeze

fof   no   z-rä-rä-r-th   (.) th-ra-nor
EMPH water 3SG.FEM.*β*-IRR.VC-do.EXT-ND-2|3NSG (.) 2|3NSG.*β*-IRR-shout.EXT.ND
      2|3PL:SBJ>3SG.FEM:IO:IRR:IPFV/start   2|3PL:SBJ:IRR:IPFV/shout

si.rore.rore.rore
INTERJECTION

'They smash (the sticks). As for the juice that starts coming out, they squeeze it and mix it properly with the water ... and they shout out: "Si rore rore rore!!"'

[tci20110813-09 DAK #22-23]

Irrealis mood is frequently used in narratives which report factual truths. Foley (2000: 389) points out that Papuan languages often employ the realis-irrealis distinction for

---

a long time ago, the speaker uses the immediate past (*niyamnzrm* 'He was staying just before') to emphasise that the headhunt took place just after his father had left the village.

pragmatic purposes. In Komnzo, the pragmatic use comes from the alternation between irrealis and realis inflections especially in event sequencing. In this pattern, the irrealis is used for backgrounding. Example (63) is taken from a hunting story that occured many years ago. The story is told from a first-person perspective, thus, there is no reason to question the factual truth of what is being told. The clauses in (63) describe a sequence of events: fall asleep > be sleeping > wake up. Only the foregrounded clause ('sleep') is expressed in realis (past durative), whereas the backgrounded clauses ('fall asleep' and 'wake up') are expressed in irrealis (perfective). In that sense, the irrealis verb forms act as a backgrounding bracket around the foregrounded clause.[17]

(63) **krämnzeré** *efoth etfth* **kwofrugrm** *e zizi ...* **krebnafé.**
    k-rä-mnzer-é   efoth etfth kwof-rugr-m   e
    M.β-IRR.VC.ND-fall.asleep.RS-1SG sun   sleep 1SG.β2-sleep.EXT.ND-DUR until
    1SG:SBJ:IRR:PFV/fall.asleep   1SG:SBJ:PST:DUR/sleep

    zizi   (.) k-rä-bnaf-é
    afternoon (.) M.β-IRR.VC.ND-wake.up.RS-1SG
                   1SG:SBJ:IRR:PFV/wake.up
    'I fell asleep (for) a daytime nap. I was sleeping until the late afternoon ... and I
    woke up.'   [tci20111119-03 ABB #31-32]

The interaction of TAM categories with information structure was described by Hopper (1979). Hartzler describes a similar function of the irrealis mood in Sentani (1983). I defer the discussion of this topic to §10.5, where a detailed analysis is offered, drawing on a longer text segment.

---

[17]Note that example (55) on page 258 employs the same bracket-like use of the irrealis inflected verb forms. The only difference is that in (55), the foregrounded event is in the non-past, whereas in (63) the foregrounded event is in past durative.

7 Syntax of the noun phrase

7.1 Introduction

The noun phrase in Komnzo is defined as a group of nominals which jointly fulfil a functional role in the clause. Noun phrases may also contain a single nominal. The case markers which assign the specific functional role attach to the rightmost element of the noun phrase. Noun phrases in Komnzo cannot be scrambled. Therefore, case enclitics and the emphatic particle *fof* – if present – can be used to identify the right edge of a noun phrase. Typically one intonation contour covers a single noun phrase.

The head of a noun phrase can be a noun (§3.1.2), a property noun (§3.1.4), a personal pronoun (§3.1.9), the indefinite pronoun (§3.1.11), the recognitional demonstrative (§3.1.12.6) or an interrogative (§3.1.10). The head of a noun phrase can be omitted, leaving only a demonstrative, adjective, quantifier or locational. This is possible only if the head of the noun phrase can be recovered from context. Noun phrases can be dropped from the clause, in which case only the indexing in the verb provides information about the arguments. Consequently, inflected verbs can and often do stand alone as a clause.

This chapter begins with an overview of the structure of the noun phrase in §7.2. I describe the slots of a noun phrase and their respective fillers in §7.3 - §7.5. The chapter closes with a description of the inclusory construction in §7.6. In this construction, two or more noun phrases constitute a functional unit without forming a matrix noun phrase.

7.2 The structure of the noun phrase

I analyse noun phrases as flat structures made up by functional slots. Each slot may be filled by particular elements. The abstract structure is shown in Figure 7.1.

determiner slot	premodifier slot	head slot	postmodifier slot
determiner	adjective	noun	determiner
demonstrative	property noun	property noun	adjective
indefinite	numeral	nominalised verb	locational
interrogative	quantifier	pers. pronoun	numeral
POSS pronoun		RECOG pronoun	quantifier
noun phrase			

Figure 7.1: The structure of the noun phrase

I analyse the element in the HEAD slot as a semantic head which refers to the same entity as the whole phrase. This element is also the syntactic head, in that it governs the agreement in the verb form. However, this is only visible if the noun phrase has a core argument function. The HEAD slot can be complex, for example when it is filled with a compound. All other slots serve to limit the set of possible referents in the head. For this reason, proper nouns like personal or place names are rarely modified, and expressions like *ane Naimr* 'that Naimr' are only found if there are several individuals with that name and the speaker wishes to clarify which one is meant. Personal pronouns are never modified in that way.[1]

The DETERMINER slot is separate from the PREMODIFIER slot for two reasons. First, the elements in this slot are mutually exclusive. Hence, a noun phrase can contain either a possessive or a demonstrative in the DETERMINER slot, but not both. This contrasts with the elements in the PREMODIFIER slot, of which there can be multiple instances in the same noun phrase. Secondly, as we will see below, if the noun phrase is not case marked, the elements in the DETERMINER slot can be postposed. If there is a case marker, postposing the determiner is a rare exception. Such a restriction does not apply to elements in the PREMODIFIER slot.

There are two modifier slots because some word classes, for example locationals, can only occur in the POSTMODIFIER slot and not in the PREMODIFIER slot. Otherwise, almost all elements which are possible in the PREMODIFIER slot are also possible in the POST-MODIFIER slot.

Property nouns cannot be clearly assigned to the PREMODIFIER slot, because they can optionally take the adjectivaliser suffix *-thé*. In this case, they are derived adjectives in the PREMODIFIER slot, but derived adjectives show differences in their syntactic behaviour compared to non-derived adjectives. Without the adjectivaliser, property nouns can be a modifier element of a nominal compound. This is discussed in §7.5.3.

7.3 The DETERMINER slot

The DETERMINER slot can be filled with demonstratives (1), interrogatives (2), possessive pronouns (3) and whole noun phrases inflected for one of the adnominal cases. These include the possessive (4), temporal possessive (5) and characteristic case (6). In the following examples, noun phrases are marked by square brackets.

(1) *fi keke zä wrugr [**zane** gwthen].*
     fi   keke zä   w\rugr/   zane   gwth=en
     3.ABS NEG PROX 3SG.FEM:SBJ:NPST:IPFV/sleep DEM:PROX nest=LOC
     'She does not sleep in this nest here.'   [tci20120815 ABB #19]

---

[1]Two exceptions are the postposed adjectives *bana* 'hapless, poor, pitiful', which expresses a sympathetic emotion of the speaker towards the referent, and the postposed adjective *kwark* 'deceased'. Both frequently occur with proper nouns (e.g. personal names) as well as personal pronouns.

(2) *wayti erä o [ra yawi] erä?*
wayti   e\rä/   o ra   yawi   e\rä/
watermelon 2|3PL:SBJ:NPST:IPFV/be or what round thing 2|3PL:SBJ:NPST:IPFV/be
'These are watermelons or what fruits are these?'   [tci20111004 TSA #68]

(3) *[nzone trikasi] fobo fof zwaythk.*
nzone   trik-si   fobo   fof   zwa\ythk/
1SG.POSS tell-NMLZ DIST.ALL EMPH 3SG.FEM:SBJ:RPST:IPFV/come.to.end
'My story has come to an end there.'   [tci20111004 TSA #260]

(4) *wth fobo fof thämira ... [[ane kabeane] wth].*
wth   fobo   fof   thä\mir/a   (.) ane kabe=ane
intestines DIST.ALL EMPH 2|3SG:SBJ>2|3PL:OBJ:PST:PFV/hang (.) DEM man=POSS
wth
intestines
'She hung the intestines there ... that man's intestines.' [tci20120901-01 MAK #116-117]

(5) *[[kaythamane] karo] rä!*
kayé=thamane   karo   \rä/
yesterday=TEMP.POSS ground.oven 3SG.FEM:SBJ:NPST:IPFV/be
'It is yesterday's oven.'   [tci20110802 ABB #94]

(6) *[[baguma] kabe] ... foba ... zena mifnen zämnzr.*
bagu=ma   kabe (.) foba   (.) zena mifne=n   z=ä\m/nzr
bagu=CHAR man (.) DIST.ABL (.) now mifne=LOC PROX=2|3PL:SBJ:NPST:IPFV/dwell
'The Bagu people ... from over there ... live here in Mifne (or: Mibini)
today.'   [tci20131013-01 ABB #175-177]

These different fillers cannot co-occur. Consider example (7), which is taken from a
nzürna trikasi, a local equivalent to European witch stories. The example contains the
complex noun phrase *nä karma kabe*, in which the indefinite *nä* 'some, another' and
kar=ma 'from the village' are both candidates for the DETERMINER slot. However, the
indefinite does not refer to *kabe* 'man', but to *kar* 'village'. In other words, the indefinite
fills the DETERMINER slot of the embedded noun phrase, and the embedded noun phrase
fills the DETERMINER slot of the matrix noun phrase. This is shown with square brackets
in the example. Note that (4) shows the same structure.

(7) *[[nä karma] kabe] mane yanatha ... mogarkamma*
nä   kar=ma   kabe mane ya\na/tha   (.)
INDF village=CHAR man which 2|3SG:SBJ>3SG.MASC:OBJ:PST:IPFV/eat (.)
mogarkam=ma
mogarkam=CHAR
'It was a man from another village who she ate ... from Mogarkam.'
[tci20120901-01 MAK #225]

The determiner can appear in postposed position, which I analyse as non-prototypical order. The rest of this section describes this postposed position of the determiner. Example (8) is taken from the same story as the previous example. The noun phrase *tüfr yam nä* 'many other things' contains the quantifier *tüfr* in the PREMODIFIER slot, the noun *yam* 'event' in the HEAD slot, and the indefinite *nä* in postposed position. This noun phrase can be arranged in different orders, for example: *nä tüfr yam, nä yam tüfr*. However, the DETERMINER and PREMODIFIER slots cannot be exchanged. This order of elements, for example *tüfr nä yam*, would be split into two co-referential noun phrases, which is signalled by a break in the intonation contour and case marking on both noun phrases. Case markers would attach to *tüfr* as well as *nä yam*.

(8) [**tüfr yam nä**] *fefe thwafiyokwrm ... fi fathfa ane fof wäfiyokwa.*
tüfr   yam nä   fefe   thwa\fiyok/wrm   (.) fi   fath=fa
plenty event INDF really SG:SBJ>2|3PL:OBJ:PST:DUR/make (.) but clear.place=ABL
ane fof   wä\fiyok/wa
DEM EMPH SG:SBJ>3SG.FEM:OBJ:PST:IPFV/make
'She really did many other things ... but she did this in public.'

[tci20120901-01 MAK #223-224]

We saw in (7) that the determiner belongs to the head of the embedded noun phrase and not to the head of the matrix noun phrase. In such cases, the embedded noun phrase 'blocks' the DETERMINER slot, and postposing a determiner is the only option for it to refer to the head of the matrix noun phrase. This is shown in (9), where the postposed indefinite *nä* refers to the head of the matrix noun phrase. The embedded noun phrase *safsma* is marked with the characteristic case in adnominal function. It specifies the head of the matrix noun phrase: *safsma kabe* 'man from *Safs*'. Note that the same could be expressed by a nominal compound *safs kabe* '*Safs* man'. The semantic difference between an embedded noun phrase marked with the characteristic case and a nominal compound lies in the reference of the determiner: *ane safs kabe* 'that *Safs* man' versus *ane safsma kabe* 'man from that *Safs*' (i.e. not from some other place called *Safs*). It follows that the two elements in (9) restrict the reference of the head simultaneously: the embedded noun phrase *safma* and the postposed determiner *nä*. A postposed determiner usually occurs only if the noun phrase is not flagged with a case marker. But there are exceptions to this. See (13) discussed below.

(9) [[**safsma**] *woga nä*] *fobo swamnzrm ... gfi yf*
safs=ma   woga nä   fobo   swa\m/nzrm   (.) gfi yf
safs=CHAR man INDF DIST.ALL 3SG.MASC:SBJ:NPST:IPFV/dwell (.) gfi name
'Another man from Safs lived there ... by the name of Gfi.'   [tci20111107-01 MAK #76]

Although very rare, both DETERMINER slots – that of the embedded noun phrase and that of the matrix noun phrase – can be filled. In (10), the first non-singular possessive *nzenme* refers to *mayawa*, the head of the embedded noun phrase, and the indefinite determiner *nä* refers to *kabe*, the head of the matrix noun phrase.

(10) [[*nzenme mayawama*] *kabe nä*] *fä thägathizath.*
nzenme   mayawa=ma   kabe nä   fä   thägathizath
1NSG.POSS mayawa=CHAR man INDF DIST 2|3PL:SBJ>2|3PL:OBJ:PST:IPFV/leave
'They left some of our Mayawa people there.'   [tci20131013-01 ABB #170]

It follows from the discussion above that two determiners must belong to different noun phrases if they occur next to each other, like *zane* and *nä* in example (11). In this example, I analyse *zane* as a noun phrase with an omitted head.

(11) [*zane*] [*nä yawi*] *yé.*
zane   nä   yawi   \yé/
DEM:PROX INDF round.object 3SG.MASC:SBJ:NPST:IPFV/be
'This is another fruit.'   [tci20120815 ABB #39]

The elements in the DETERMINER slot cannot be inflected for the full range of cases. For example, demonstratives cannot be inflected for ergative, dative, possessive and the three spatial cases. In (12), the indefinite *nä* is interpreted as referring to the object argument, rather than the ergative marked argument.

(12) [*nof*] [*nä*] *nima thäkothmako.*
no=f   nä   nima   thä\kothm/ako
water=ERG INDF like.this SG:SBJ>2|3PL:OBJ:PST:PFV:AND/chase
'The flood chased away others like this.'   [tci20131013-01 ABB #125]

However, elicitation has shown that even this is possible, but such a structure is very rare. A textual example is shown in (13), where *ane* refers to the preceding noun, which is flagged with an ergative. Note that in this example, *ane* is followed by the emphatic particle *fof*, which has always scope over the preceding phrase (§3.4.2). Thus, *fof* may 'help' to mark the right edge of the noun phrase *gwamf ane*. This is, however, not the main function of *fof*.

(13) *wati* [*gwamf ane*] *fof ezi ŋatha thäsa thgathgen.*
wati gwam=f   ane fof ezi   ŋatha
then gwam=ERG.SG DEM EMPH morning dog
thä\s/a   thgathg=en
2|3SG:SBJ>3SG.MASC:OBJ:PST:PFV/call burned.place=LOC
'Well, that Gwam called the dogs to the burned place in the morning.'
[tci20131013-01 ABB #79]

The above description shows that there are some problems with the analysis of postposing elements in the DETERMINER slot. Determiners like *zane* or *ane* or *nä*, and even possessive phrases can stand alone if the head of the phrase is recoverable from the context. An alternative would be to analyse the postposed elements as independent noun phrases which are (i) co-referential with the preceding noun phrase, and which (ii) lack an element in the HEAD slot. This is always possible and, as we will see below, it is quite common to have co-referential noun phrases in one clause. Sometimes intervening material, for example adverbials, allows us to make a clear decision. If there is no intervening material, only the intonation contour indicates whether a particular example should be analysed as one or two noun phrases.

Syntactic evidence for the possibility of postposing the determiner comes from fronted relative clauses which are commonly used for topicalisation (§10.4). Fronted relative clauses of this type have the following structure: NP *mane* COPULA. They only allow a full noun phrase before the relative pronoun *mane* 'which, who'. In (14), the noun phrase includes the postposed indefinite determiner *nä* following its head *ŋatha* 'dog'. The fronted relative clause is marked by square brackets.

(14) *fi ([**kafar ŋatha nä**] mane erera) fi ane bä bkwaruthrmth büdisnen mnz znen.*
fi   kafar ŋatha nä   mane e\rä/ra   fi   ane bä
but big dog INDF which 2|3PL:SBJ:PST:IPFV/be 3.ABS DEM MED
b=kwa\ru/thrmth   büdisn=en mnz   zn=en
MED=2|3PL:SBJ:PST:DUR/bark PL=LOC   house place=LOC
'But, as for the other big dogs, they were barking there in Büdisn at the house.'   [tci20111119-03 ABB #95]

7.4 The MODIFIER slots

The elements in the MODIFIER slots are different from those in the DETERMINER slot. They can all be inflected for case if they happen to occur as the last element of the noun phrase. This is shown in (15) and (16). In example (15), the modifier is an adjective in the PREMODIFIER slot. In example (16), the adjective follows the head in the POSTMODIFIER slot, and consequently the adjective receives the case marker.

(15) *finzo fä fof **ane kafar emothf** thwathofiknm.*
fi=nzo   fä fof ane kafar emoth=f   thwa\thofik/nm
3.ABS=ONLY DIST EMPH DEM big girl=ERG.SG SG:SBJ>2|3DU:OBJ:PST:DUR/disturb
'Only they (were) there. That big girl was disturbing them.' [tci20111119-01 ABB #150]

(16) *watik **yfö katanr** kwa yarenzr.*
watik yfö katan=r   kwa ya\re/nzr
then hole small=PURP FUT 3SG.MASC:SBJ:NPST:IPFV/look
'Then, he will look around for a small hole.'   [tci20130903-04 RNA #26]

There are some restrictions for specific elements, for example the locationals can only inflect for spatial cases. Furthermore, all locationals (§3.1.7) and a few adjectives (§3.1.5) only occur in the POSTMODIFIER slot, not in the PREMODIFIER slot. One such adjective is *kwark* 'late, deceased' in (17). It occurs in the POSTMODIFIER slot, and therefore it is flagged with the ergative case. Note that the proper name *Wäni* is also inflected with the ergative and forms a noun phrase co-referential to *nafaŋafe kwark* 'his late father'.

(17) *wati ... **nafaŋafe kwarkf** ... wänif krekariso*
      wati (.) nafa-ŋafe   kwark=f   (.) wäni=f   kre\karis/o
      then (.) 3.POSS-father deceased=ERG.SG (.) wäni=ERG.SG SG:SBJ:IRR:PFV:AND/hear
      'Then, his late father, Wäni, heard (about it).'   [tci20120814 ABB #114]

Another difference between elements in the DETERMINER slot and the MODIFIER slots is that elements in the latter may be multiple. I can only give examples from elicitation here as there are no examples in the corpus, where (i) all slots are filled and (ii) multiple items occur in the MODIFIER slot.

(18) a. *ane kafar yfrsé wämne*
          ane kafar yfrsé wämne
          DEM big   black tree
          'that big black tree'

      b. *zane eda zanfr garda*
          zane   eda zanfr garda
          DEM:PROX two long canoe
          'these two long canoes'

      c. *nafane kafar mnz banbanen*
          nafane kafar mnz   banban=en
          3SG.POSS big   house underneath=LOC
          'underneath his big house'

The lack of textual examples which display all possible fillers at once is best explained by a strong tendency to distribute information over several co-referential noun phrases, either in the same clause or over a series of clauses. This can be seen in examples like (17), (14) or (19). I will address this topic in the following section.

7.5 The HEAD slot

As pointed out above in §7.2, the head of a noun phrase is both the notional head as well as the syntactic head. It is the notional head in the sense that it expresses what the whole noun phrase is about, and all other elements in a noun phrase serve to restrict the reference of the head. It is the syntactic head because it agrees in gender and number with the indexation in the verb. Below, I will address two points which sit at opposite ends of a spectrum: the ellipsis of the head, and complex heads involving compounds.

7.5.1 Introduction

However, before discussing those two points I want to make a general point about noun phrases in Komnzo. It is quite common to have multiple co-referential noun phrases. These can occur in the same clause or across a sequence of clauses. In example (19), the speaker talks about an old woman who was married to three men in her lifetime, but she had children only with one of them. Several noun phrases are co-referential. In the example, they are indexed with subscripted numbers.

(19) [*ausiane nagayé*]₁ ... [*anenzo*]₁ *fof ern* [*edanzo*]₁ ... [*nä*]₂ *mane yarako*
   [*ausiane kabe*]₂ [*nafafis*]₂ *ngemär yara* ... [*kafarkafar*]₂ *yara*
   ausi=ane   nagayé (.) ane=nzo fof e\rn/
   old woman=POSS.SG children (.) DEM=ONLY EMPH 2|3DU:SBJ:NPST:IPFV/be
   eda=nzo   (.) nä   mane ya\r/ako   ausi=ane   kabe
   two=ONLY (.) INDF which 3SG.MASC:SBJ:PST:IPFV:AND/be old woman=POSS man
   nafa-fis   nge=mär ya\r/a   (.) kafar-kafar
   3.POSS-husband child=PRIV 3SG.MASC:SBJ:PST:IPFV/be (.) REDUP-big
   ya\r/a
   3SG.MASC:SBJ:PST:IPFV/be
   'The old woman has only those two children. As for the other one, the old
   woman's man, her husband, he was without children. He was very old (when
   they got married)'   [tci20131013-02 ABB #334-336]

At the other end of the spectrum, noun phrases can be wholly omitted, since the indexation in the verb is sufficient. In this way, a single verb often stands as a whole clause. Example (20) describes the path which the ancestor took and what actions he did along the way. Since the protagonist is highly topical at this point in the story, the respective noun phrase is left out. Moreover, the last two verbs *zwafrmnzrm* 'he was preparing it (FEM)' and *zurzirakwa* 'he tied it (FEM)' occur without any noun phrases. That is because the object noun phrase (*nabi ŋatr* 'bowstring') was mentioned already.

(20) *nabi ŋatr fä fof zurärm zwafrmnzrm ... zurzirakwa fof.*
   nabi   ŋatr   fä fof zu\rä/rm
   bamboo bowstring DIST EMPH SG:SBJ>3SG.FEM:OBJ:PST:DUR/do
   zwa\frm/nzrm   (.) zu\rzirak/wa   fof
   SG:SBJ>3SG.FEM:OBJ:PST:DUR/prepare (.) SG:SBJ>3SG.FEM:OBJ:PST:IPFV/tie EMPH
   'Over there, he made his bowstring. He prepared it. He tied it.'
                                                    [tci20131013-01 ABB #235-236]

7.5.2 Ellipsis of the HEAD

The head of a noun phrase is often omitted. Consider example (21), where a mother tells me that she had sent two small children to dig for worms. The example starts out with the noun phrase *zane edawä kakatan* 'these two small (ones)'. Ellipsis of the head only occurs when the head is recoverable from previous context, or if it is common ground between speaker and hearer.

(21) *zane edawä kakatan ... fosam daisy fi zarath dd etharinath*
    zane   eda=wä   ka-katan   (.) fosam daisy fi   za\r/ath
    DEM:PROX two=EMPH REDUP-small (.) fosam daisy 3.ABS 2|3DU:SBJ:PST:PFV/do
    dd   e\thari/nath
    worm 2|3DU:SBJ>2|3PL:OBJ:PST:IPFV/dig
    'These two small (ones), Fosam and Daisy, they did that. They dug the worms.'
                            [tci20120922-25 ALK #5]

Example (22) shows the indefinite demonstrative *nä* used twice without a head. This is possible because the appropriate filler for the HEAD slot *zuzi* 'fishing line' was already mentioned.

(22) *zuzi thethkäfath migsi ... nä zba wazi ... nä boba wazi.*
    zuzi   the\thkäf/ath   mig-si   (.) nä   zba   wazi
    fishing.line 2|3PL:SBJ>2|3PL:OBJ:PST:PFV/start hang-NMLZ (.) INDF PROX.ABL side
    (.) nä   boba   wazi
    (.) INDF MED.ABL side
    'They started hanging the fishing lines ... some on this side and some on the other side.'   [tci20150906-10 ABB #52-53]

Example (23) is a description of a fish trap. These long bamboo baskets always consist of a larger basket and a smaller basket which is placed inside the bigger one. In the example, the speaker refers to the smaller basket as *nafane nge* 'its child' and later only with an adjective *katan* 'small' which is flagged with an ergative case marker.

(23) *nafane nge ... wati kofä fthé brigsir n krär ... katanf kwa ynbrigwr zbo ... keke kwa kränmätr.*
    nafane nge (.) wati kofä fthé brig-si=r   n   krä\r/   (.)
    3SG.POSS child (.) then fish when return-NMLZ=PURP IMN 2|3SG:SBJ:IRR:PFV/do (.)
    katan=f kwa yn\brig/wr   zbo   (.) keke
    small=ERG FUT 2|3SG:SBJ>3SG.MASC:OBJ:NPST:IPFV:VENT/return PROX.ALL (.) NEG
    kwa krän\mätr/
    FUT 2|3SG:SBJ:IRR:PFV:VENT/exit
    'Its child ... well, when the fish tries to return, the small (one) will bring it back here ... it will not get out.'   [tci20120906 MAB #55-58]

7.5.3 Compounds

An the other end of the spectrum are complex heads. The Komnzo lexicon contains a large number of nominal compounds. These may consist of nouns, property nouns or nominalised verbs. Table 7.1 shows a few examples of compounds with different nominal subclasses.

Compounds are always right-headed, that is, the rightmost element is not only the semantic head, but it determines the word class, number and gender of the whole compound. Although the first element in *wawa mnz* 'yam house' is masculine, it is the second

Table 7.1: Nominal compounds

type of compound	example	components		gloss
noun + noun	*wawa mnz*	*wawa* yam	*mnz* house	'yamhouse'
	wath kabe	*wath* dance	*kabe* man/people	'dancer(s)'
property noun + noun	*wri kabe*	*wri* intoxication	*kabe* man/people	'drunkard'
noun + property noun	*zan miyo*	*zan* killing	*miyo* desire	'bloodlust'
nom. verb + noun	*borsi zokwasi*	*bor-si* play-NMLZ	*zokwasi* words	'joke'
noun + nom. verb	*si zübraksi*	*si* eye	*zübrak-si* close.eye-NMLZ	'prayer'

element *mnz* 'house' which determines the gender (FEM in this case). Likewise, although the first element in *wri kabe* is a property noun – and property nouns do not show gender agreement – it is the second word *kabe* 'man' which enables gender agreement for the whole compound.

Compounds can be embedded within one another, which can lead to combinations of usually up to three elements. A rare example of a compound with four elements was coined by one of my informants to describe the botanist on our team: *wämne taga yf kabe* (lit. 'tree leaf name man'). Embedded compounds are always left-branching, and thus we can represent long compounds in this way: [[[*wämne taga*]₃ *yf*]₂ *kabe*]₁. Two corpus examples of longer compounds are given in (24) and (25).

(24) *ane **ksi kar emoth** thwanorm*
ane ksi kar emoth thwa\nor/m
DEM bush place girl 2|3PL:SBJ:PST:DUR/shout
'These bush girls were shouting.'   [tci20120821-02 LNA #36]

(25) *baf fthé sräbth nima ... **kabe zan miyof***
baf   fthé   srä\bth/   nima   (.) kabe
RECOG.ERG.SG when 2|3SG:SBJ>3SG.MASC:OBJ:IRR:PFV/finish like.this (.) man
zan   miyo=f
hitting desire=ERG
'That is when it overcomes him ... that bloodlust for people.'

[tci20130903-04 RNA #84-85]

Complex heads are different from complex noun phrases, that is, compounds in the HEAD slot are distinct from embedded noun phrases. The latter must be marked with adnominal case. Let us take the compound from example (24): *ane ksi kar emoth* 'those bush girls' (lit. 'bush place girls'). We can embed the noun phrase *ksi kar* 'bush place' into the matrix noun phrase by adding the characteristic case (*=ma*): *ksi karma emoth* 'girls from the bush'. In addition to case marking, the reference of the demonstrative *ane* in initial position depends on whether a noun phrase is embedded or the head contains a compound. In the former case, *ane* refers to the head of the embedded noun phrase: *ane ksi karma emoth* 'girls from that bush place'. If the head slot contains a compound, and no embedding takes place, the demonstrative refers to the compound, as in (24). The reference of the DETERMINER slot is described above in §7.3.

Property nouns can appear in both positions of a compound (see Table 7.1 above). If a property noun occurs as the first element, it modifies the head of the compound, for example *wri kabe* 'drunkard' in Table 7.1. Property nouns optionally take the adjectivaliser *-thé*. When this suffix is present, for example in *writhé kabe*, it is clear that the derived adjective appears in the MODIFER-1 slot, and is not part of a compound. The semantic difference is between *wri kabe* 'drunkard' – someone who is frequently drunk – and *writhé kabe* 'drunk man' – someone who is drunk. Syntactically, the derived adjective behaves like other adjectives, for example it can appear after the head in the POSTMODIFIER slot. Without the adjectivaliser, a change in order would change the meaning of the compound, e.g. *kabe wri* 'people's / men's intoxication'. However, as mentioned above, the adjectivaliser suffix is optional for property nouns. Additionally, property nouns can function predicatively (26). This creates some problems for the analysis of particular examples.

(26) *kabe **wri** kwosi sfthnm.*
      kabe wri   kwosi sf\thn/m
      man drunk dead 3SG.MASC:PST:DUR/lie
      'The man was lying down dead drunk.'   [overheard]

Lastly, I want to address compounds which involve nominalised verbs. Consider the compounds in (27) and (28). In (27), the speaker points out that these were *mgthksi ruga* 'raised pigs' as opposed to wild pigs. In (28), the speaker stresses that he has raised enough pigs in his life, and that *ruga mgthksi* 'pig feeding' is too much work.

(27) *ruga tabrunzo erera nima berä ... **mgthksi ruga***
      ruga tabru=nzo e\rä/ra   nima   b=e\rä/   (.)
      pig   five=ONLY 2|3PL:SBJ:PST:IPFV/be like.this MED=2|3PL:SBJ:NPST:IPFV/be (.)
      mgthk-si ruga
      feed-NMLZ pig
      'There were only five pigs like these ... raised pigs.'   [tci20120904-02 MAB #248-249]

(28) *zena keke miyo worä **ruga mgthksi** ... znsä ttüfr*
      zena keke miyo wo\rä/   ruga mgthk-si (.) znsä t-tüfr
      today NEG desire 1SG:SBJ:NPST:IPFV/be pig feed-NMLZ (.) work REDUP-plenty
      'Today, I do not want to feed pigs ... too much work.' (lit. 'I do not desire pig
      feeding.')
                                                         [tci20120805-01 ABB #819-820]

We find that compounds which involve nominalised verbs follow the same rule as other compounds: the rightmost element acts as the head of the compound. For example, *zan kabe* (killing+man) 'killer, headhunter' is a kind of man, whereas *kabe zan* (man+killing) 'war, fighting' is a nominalised activity.[2] For the following discussion, I will refer to the first pattern as noun-headed compounds, and the latter as verb-headed compounds.

In noun-headed compounds, the argument role of the noun with respect to the verb is less determined than in verb-headed compounds. The following argument roles are found: actor (*zan kabe* 'killer'), patient (*mgthksi ruga* 'feeding pig' in (27) above), instrument (*bi näbüsi wämne* 'sago beating stick'), location (*yonasi faf* 'drinking place'), or time (*tharisi efoth* 'harvesting time'). This variability contrasts with verb-headed compounds, where the noun is always a patient or theme, as in *kabe zan* 'war' (lit. 'people hitting'), *ruga mgthksi* 'pig feeding' in (28) above, or *wawa yarisi* 'yam exchange' (lit. 'yam giving'). Note that there is an implied agent in most of these examples. It follows that (nominalised) intransitive verbs do not participate in verb-headed compounds. For example, there can be a *mthizsi kabe* 'resting person' or a *yathizsi kabe* 'dying person'. But the reverse order is ungrammatical: **kabe mthizsi* or **kabe yathizsi*.

Some stems have been shown to be rather fluid in valency depending on the morphological template (§5.4.3), for example *msaksi* 'dwell, sit (v.i.), set (v.t.)'. It is no surprise that these verbs allow both types of compounds. The noun-headed compound *msaksi kabe* 'sitting people' can describe a group of people who stay behind, while others are attending a dance. The verb-headed compound *kabe msaksi* 'married life' takes on the transitive meaning of the verb, and it means literally: 'the sitting down of the man'.[3]

7.6 The inclusory construction

The inclusory construction builds on the associative case (§4.15). I adopt the term "inclusory construction" from Lichtenberk (2000) and Singer (2001). Singer defines the inclusory construction as "an endocentric construction in which some elements of a larger group are referred to along with the larger group itself" (2001: 1). Thus, we have a construction that involves a full set and one or more subsets. In Komnzo, the full set is always expressed in the verb form. Therefore, the inclusory construction only involves core arguments, that is, arguments flagged with the ergative, absolutive or dative case. For the following description, I introduce the terms "associative phrase" and "core phrase". The associative phrase expresses the participant who is included in the event. The core phrase expresses a subset different from the one expressed in the associative phrase or it may express the set. We will see below why this is sometimes difficult to determine with certainty. While the reference of the core phrase does not automatically include the subset expressed in the associative phrase, both are included in the full set which is expressed in the verb form. I choose the terms 'core phrase' and 'associative phrase' over more

---

[2] *Zan* 'hit, kill' is irregular in that its infinitive is not based on the normal stem-NMLZ pattern.

[3] From the perspective of a man, one could also use *ŋare msaksi* 'married life' (lit. 'the sitting down of the woman').

general terms like 'subset A' and 'subset B' because the core phrase is flagged with the case marker appropriate for the argument role of the set, while the associative phrase is flagged with the associative case.

What is special about the inclusory construction in Komnzo is that although both core phrase and associative phrase refer to distinct subsets, the number marking on each phrase has scope over the total set. Consider example (29) where the total set encoded in the verb is second/third dual. The two subsets are expressed by the personal names *Maureen* and *Kowi*. The core phrase is flagged with a non-singular ergative (*Maureen=é*), and the associative phrase is flagged with an dual associative (*Kowi=r*). The point here is that the scope of the number value is always the total set and not the respective subsets.[4]

(29) *Maureené bi ynäbünth Kowir.*
      maureen=é   bi   y\näbü/nth
      maureen=ERG.NSG sago(ABS) 2|3DU:SBJ>3SG.MASC:OBJ:NPST:IPFV/beat
      kowi=r
      kowi=ASSOC.DU
      'Maureen together with Kowi beats Sago.' (lit. 'Maureen with Kowi, they beat Sago.')

Example (29) shows that a non-singular attaches to a personal name. In example (30), the set encoded in the verb is first plural. Note that the core phrase is omitted here, but it could be expressed by the pronoun *ni* (1NSG). There are multiple associative phrases in the example: *nä srakä* 'with some boy(s)', *mafä thzé* 'with whoever' and *Mosesä* 'with Moses'. Since the total set is bigger than the minimal group, i.e. bigger than two, the associative phrase has to be marked as plural. Therefore, the personal name *Moses* is marked for plural.

(30) *nä srakä kwa nyak ... mafä thzé ... Mosesä.*
      nä   srak=ä   kwa n\yak/   (.) maf=ä   thzé (.)
      some boy=ASSOC.PL FUT 1PL:SBJ:NPST:IPFV/walk (.) who=ASSOC.PL ever (.)
      moses=ä
      moses=ASSOC.PL
      'We will go with some boy(s) ... with whoever ... with Moses.'
                                                        [tci20130907-02 RNA #749-750]

The abstract structure of the inclusory construction is shown in Figure 7.2. The circle represents the set, and the line in the middle cuts the total set into two subsets. The arrows on the left point to the referents expressed by each element. Note that there can be more than one associative phrase (30). Examples like (30) can be further elaborated by adding associative phrases, for example *Maureenä* and *Kowiä* to mean 'with Moses, with Maureen, with Kowi'. These additional associative phrases are not represented in Figure 7.2 because they would receive the same marking as the first associative phrase.[5]

---

[4]Note that literal translations of the inclusory construction are rather clumsy: 'Maureen with Kowi beat Sago', whereas idiomatic English translations imply that the verb is indexing a singular, as in (29).

[5]Naturally, this is only possible if there are more than two participants in the total set.

The arrow on the right shows that the number value encoded in each element tracks the number of the total set.

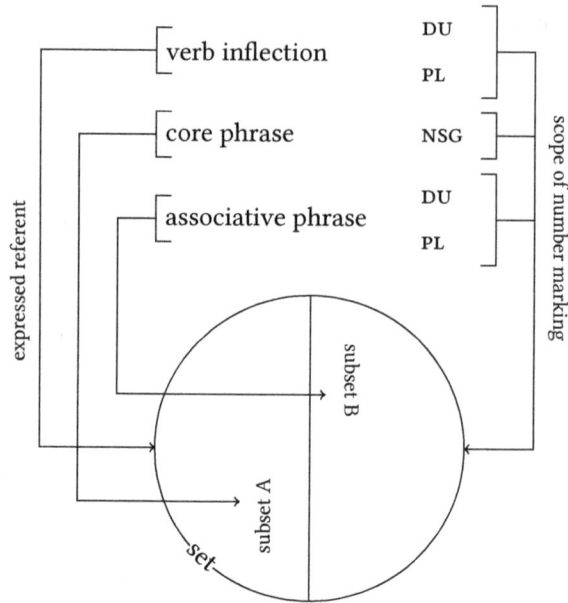

Figure 7.2: The inclusory construction

Figure 7.2 shows that the number values differ. The core phrase is always in non-singular. This is the expected behaviour of number marking on nominals (§4.3), which makes a distinction between singular and non-singular, leaving the subdivision between dual and plural to the verb inflection. As for the associative phrase, number marking is more specific, showing agreement with the verb inflection, thus encoding dual versus plural instead of singular versus non-singular. Because the set in the inclusory construction is minimally two, a singular on the core phrase or a singular in the verb inflection would be ungrammatical. For the associative case, there is no singular number value available. The enclitics =*r* and =*ä* encode dual and plural respectively.

The corresponding pronominal forms of the associative case are shown in Table 7.2.[6] The relevant pronominals are personal pronouns, the recognitional demonstrative, the indefinite pronoun and the interrogative. Two observations can be made from Table 7.2. First, all forms include a /rr/ element for dual and an /ä/ element for plural. Secondly, most forms are built from the ergative pronominal. For example, the third person absolutive is *fi*, whereas the third person ergative is *naf* (SG) or *nafa* (NSG). The associative third person forms, *nafrr* (DU) and *nafä* (PL) are formally closer to the ergative than to the absolutive. Another example is the interrogative, where the absolutive is *mane* 'who,

---

[6]I repeat here Table 4.4 in §4.15.

Table 7.2: Associative case / pronominals

	person	dual	plural
	1	*ninrr*	*ninä*
personal pronouns	2	*bnrr*	*bnä*
	3	*nafrr*	*nafä*
RECOG		*bafrr*	*bafä*
INDF		*nä bunrr*	*nä bunä*
interrogative		*mafrr*	*mafä*
case enclitic		*=r*	*=ä*

which' and the ergative is *maf* (SG) and *mafa* (NSG). The two exceptions are the first person and the indefinite pronoun. The first person non-singular is *ni*, and it neutralises the distinction between absolutive and ergative. The indefinite pronoun is *nä bun*, and it takes regular case enclitics just like nouns. Therefore, *nä bun* is analysed as being zero marked and thus absolutive.

Figure 7.2 shows that the core phrase always encodes non-singular number. As we have seen, this holds true for cases where there are only two participants and consequently the two subsets in the core phrase and the associative phrase refer to a single individual respectively. The examples below show this for an ergative-marked argument, *amayé nanyr* 'mother with big sister' (31), an absolutive-marked argument, *emothé bnrr* 'girl with you' (32), and a dative-marked argument, *sraknm nafrr* 'boy with him' (33). In contrasting examples without the inclusory construction, all of these would receive a singular marker of the respective cases. Note that the non-singular absolutive *=é* in (32) is the same as the non-singular ergative *=é* in (31). This syncretism is also found in the personal pronouns, where *ni* is both first person non-singular absolutive and ergative (§3.1.9). The absolutive singular is always zero-marked, and the non-singular formative *=é* is optional (§4.4). In the inclusory construction, however, non-singular number is obligatorily encoded on the core phrase.

(31) *mni ŋagarnth amayé nanyr.*
mni   ŋa\gar/nth   ama=é   nane=r
firewood 2|3DU:SBJ:NPST:IPFV/break mother=ERG.NSG elder.sibling=ASSOC.DU
'Mother together with big sister split firewood.' (lit. 'Mother with big sister, they split firewood.')   [tci20150919-05 LNA #140]

(32) *kabef emothé emarn bnrr.*
kabe=f   emoth=é   e\mar/n   bnrr
man=ERG.SG girl=ABS.NSG 2|3SG:SBJ>2|3DU:OBJ:NPST:IPFV/see 2.DU.ASSOC
'The man sees the girl together with you.' (lit. 'The man sees them, the girl with you.')

(33) *ŋafyf sraknm dunzi ärin nafrr.*
ŋafe=f   srak=nm   dunzi ä\ri/n   nafrr
father=ERG.SG boy=DAT.NSG arrow 2|3SG:SBJ>2|3DU:IO:NPST:IPFV/give 3.DU.ASSOC
'The father gives the arrow to the boy together with him.' (lit. 'Father gives them
the arrow, the boy with him.')

If the total set indexed in the verb is two, then it follows that the two phrases can
only refer to a single individual, even though the core phrase has to be marked for non-
singular, as in (29) and (31–33). If the total set indexed in the verb is plural, it is unclear
whether both subsets are bigger than one or whether one of them is singular and if
so, which one. Example (30) above is unambiguous because the associative phrase is
expressed by a personal name (*Moses*=ASSOC.PL). If the associative phrase it expressed by
a noun or pronoun, we are left with contextual clues. In example (34), the speaker talks
about marriage customs explaining that his clan will not exchange sisters with those
clans with which they share a land boundary. In this example, *nafä* has to be translated
as a plural 'with them'.

(34) *ni nafäwä bad wkurwre … fi neba erä … ni neba*
ni   nafä=wä   bad   w\kur/wre   (.) fi   neba
1NSG 3PL.ASSOC=EMPH ground 1PL:SBJ>3SG.FEM:NPST:IPFV/split (.) 3.ABS opposite
e\rä/   (.) ni neba
2|3PL:SBJ:NPST:IPFV/be (.) 1 opposite
'We really share a land boundary with them. They are there and we (are) here.'
(lit. 'we cut the ground with them.')   [tci20120814 ABB #307]

In contrast, in example (35) *nafä* refers to a singular 'with him'. This example is taken
from a text about grief, and the speaker justifies a particular mourning custom by pointing out that he and his family have shared a lifetime with the deceased person.

(35) *… bänema ni nafä kwamränzrme. ni nafä nzwamnzrm.*
(.) bäne=ma   ni   nafä   kwa\mrä/nzrme   ni   nafä
(.) RECOG=CHAR 1NSG 3PL.ASSOC 1PL:SBJ:PST:DUR/stroll 1NSG 3PL.ASSOC
nzwa\m/nzrm
1PL:SBJ:PST:DUR/dwell
'… because we walked around with him. We lived with him.'
[tci20120805-01 ABB #830-831]

It follows that out of context the pronoun *nafä* can refer to an individual or to a group
of people in (34) and (35). This is also true for the pronoun *ni* (1NSG) in both examples.
I pointed out above that the core phrase is always non-singular, even if the subset expressed by the core phrase is singular. Hence, the pronoun *ni* can refer to an individual
or a group of people, and out of context example (34) can be translated as 'I share land
with them', 'We share land with him' or 'We share land with them'. What it cannot mean

is 'I share land with him'. For this meaning, the verb would have to index a dual and the associative phrase would have to be marked for dual number.[7]

In the following discussion, I want to address the question whether or not the associative phrase and the core phrase form a constituent. From a semantic perspective, we can answer this question in the affirmative, but we can also find some structural evidence that the associative phrase and the core phrase form a functional unit. I have shown above that the associative phrase agrees with the verb in number. The core phrase, on the other hand, agrees with the verb in person and number. The number category is very telling because it is always non-singular. Additionally, the core phrase is assigned the appropriate case marker by the argument structure of the verb. I take these points as structural evidence that the associative phrase and the core phrase form a functional unit. However, they do not constitute a phrase. In other words, the associative case in the inclusory construction does not function in the way that adnominal case does. For example, the characteristic case signals that one noun phrase is embedded into a matrix noun phrase. There is a fixed structure for embedding, and scrambling of elements which belong to the matrix phrase is not possible in Komnzo (§7.2). There may be several instantiations of an argument in a clause, but these noun phrases are always marked for the same case. As we have seen above, the associative phrase can be moved independently of the core phrase. Moreover, most corpus examples lack a core phrase altogether. In conclusion, the inclusory construction is different from adnominal case, like the characteristic or possessive case. The core phrase and the associative phrase are not integrated into a matrix phrase.

The inclusory construction also differs from coordinative constructions (§9.2). Example (36) shows the same state-of-affairs as expressed in (29) above, but using a conjunctive coordination. The main structural differences are that in coordination: (i) a conjunction like *a* 'and' is required, (ii) the coordinated noun phrases have to precede and follow the conjunction, (iii) both noun phrases receive the same case marker, (iv) the case marker can be singular. Note that in (29) above the associative phrase *Kowir* could occur in all other positions. Nevertheless, the most natural positions are either after the verb or right after *Maureené*.

(36) *Maureenf a Kowif bi ynäbünth.*
      Maureen=f   a   Kowi=f   bi
      maureen=ERG.SG and kowi=ERG.SG sago(ABS)
      y\näbü/nth
      2|3DU:SBJ>3SG.MASC:OBJ:NPST:IPFV/beat
      'Maureen and Kowi beat sago.'

Furthermore, the elements in an inclusory construction can be coordinated, as in example (37), where the two associative phrases *nä oromanr* 'with another old man' and *nä kabe* 'with another man' are part of a disjunctive coordination connected by *o* 'or'.

---

[7]The inclusory construction can be seen as a syntactic equivalent to distributed exponence in the verb morphology (§5.2).

(37) *nä oromanr o nä kaber fi bämrn.*

nä oroman=r o nä kabe=r fi
INDF old.man=ASSOC.DU or INDF man=ASSOC.DU 3.ABS
b=ä\m/rn
MED=2|3DU:SBJ:NPST:IPFV/sit
'He is sitting there with another old man or another man.' (lit. '...with some old
man or with some man they two sit there.') [tci20111004 RMA #343]

There is no clear semantic difference between coordination and the inclusory construction, but the difference seems to be pragmatic. While coordination places the two
elements on the same rank, the inclusory construction may be used to highlight the referent expressed in the associative phrase. This is supported by the fact that in most corpus
examples, the core phrase is omitted, because its reference has been established earlier.
Example (37) above was uttered as the description of a set of picture cards. I reproduce
the example in a longer context in (38). The speaker talks about the protagonist of the
story who is drinking with his friends. While describing the picture card, the speaker
points out that the protagonist is sitting with another man. He then asks about the topic
of their conversation. This other man is expressed in the associative phrase. The same
state of affairs could be expressed by a coordinative construction ('He and another man
are sitting there'). The point is that the inclusory construction can be used to introduce
a new participant, and thus has a pragmatic function. Note that the associative phrase
occurs in the first position of the clause.

(38) *ane fof yamnzr byé. wri kabenzo ... ane bramöwä ... fof ausi fäth nä berä ... ttrikasi*
ŋatrikwrth ... nä oromanr o nä kaber fi bämrn ... skiski warfo. monme fi yatrikwr ...
nafan?

ane fof ya\m/nzr b=\yé/ wri
DEM EMPH 3SG.MASC:SBJ:NPST:IPFV/sit MED=3SG.MASC:SBJ:NPST:IPFV/be drunk
kabe=nzo (.) ane bramöwä (.) fof ausi fäth nä
man=ONLY (.) DEM all (.) EMPH old.woman DIM INDF
b=e\rä/ (.) t-trik-si ŋa\trik/wrth (.) nä
MED=2|3PL:SBJ:NPST:IPFV/be (.) REDUP-tell-NMLZ 2|3PL:SBJ:NPST:IPFV/tell (.) INDF
oroman=r o nä kabe=r fi b=ä\m/rn (.)
old.man=ASSOC.DU or INDF man=ASSOC.DU 3.ABS MED=2|3DU:SBJ:NPST:IPFV/sit (.)
skiski warfo monme fi ya\trik/wr (.) nafan
platform on.top how but 2|3SG:SBJ>3SG.MASC:IO:NPST:IPFV/tell (.) 3SG.DAT
'That is the one sitting there. (They are) drunkards ... all of them. There is some
woman. They are telling stories. He is sitting there with another old man or
another man ... on the platform. But what is he telling him?'

[tci20111004 RMA#340-345]

Lichtenberk suggests two parameters for a typology of inclusory pronominals: "(i) do
the inclusory pronominal and the included NP together form a syntactic construction, a
phrase, or not?; and (ii) is there or is there not an overt marker of the relation between the

inclusory pronominal and the included NP?" (2000: 3). This sets up a fourfold possibility space.[8] The second parameter is clear for Komnzo: the associative case is an overt marker of the inclusory construction. With respect to the first parameter, I hope to have shown above that Komnzo does not give a neat answer to these questions. In terms of agreement, we may say that the two elements agree, but they agree in their own ways. In terms of noun phrase syntax, it would be a rather aberrant noun phrase. Therefore, I suggest that Lichtenberk's typology should be expanded. A more fine-grained reformulation of his first parameter could help capture what constitutes a 'syntactic construction', for example verb agreement and phrase structure. Singer's typology (2001) concentrates on the locus of the encoding of the whole set. She draws a distinction between Type 1, in which the set of total participants is represented by an independent pronoun, and Type 2, in which it is represented by a verbal affix. Komnzo clearly belongs to the Type 2 category. But we can make a case for Komnzo also belonging to Type 1 because the associative phrase, which can be a pronoun, encodes the number of the total set.

Lichtenberk argues that the marker of inclusory constructions is often historically related to the coordinative conjunction or to the comitative case, but he adds that the inclusory construction differs from both.[9] We have seen in §4.15 that there is no inclusory construction and no number distinction with inanimates, and only =ä is attached as a case marker. With inanimates, =ä can be analysed as comitative case. On the other hand, the function of =r (DU) and =ä (PL) with animates is an inclusory function, which differs markedly from the associative with inanimates. I follow Lichtenberk by analysing =r and =ä as markers of a distinct inclusory construction, but for practical purposes I retain the label ASSOC in the gloss instead of introducing a separate label for the inclusory category.

---

[8]The four possibilities are: 1. +syntactic construction +overt marker, 2. +syntactic construction -overt marker, 3. -syntactic construction +overt marker, 4. -syntactic construction -overt marker.

[9]"In explicit inclusory constructions, the marker of the relation between the inclusory pronominal and the included NP is typically etymologically related either to the coordinate conjunction 'and' or to the comitative marker in the language." (Lichtenberk 2000: 4) and "The phrasal inclusory construction is neither coordinating nor comitative; it is a construction *sui generis*." (2000: 30, emphasis in original)

8 Clausal syntax

8.1 Introduction

This chapter addresses the syntax within simple clauses. In Komnzo, a large part of the argument structure is encoded in the verb morphology. This is described in §5.4, and summarised in Table 5.3. Therefore, the following description of clause types is brief for those types which have been addressed before, but more detailed for other types where the verb morphology plays a smaller role.

8.2 Constituent order

The dominant word order in Komnzo is AUV (actor undergoer verb). Recipients of ditransitives also precede the verb and follow the actor noun phrase, but there is no clear position with respect to the theme argument. Evidence for basic word order comes from the use of the recognitional demonstrative (§3.1.12.6). In example (1), the object argument is expressed first by the recognitional *bäne* 'those' and then by the noun *züm* 'centipedes'. The speaker uses the recognitional in the absolute case in the position where the constituent normally occurs. This is a tip-of-the-tongue situation, and therefore the speaker fills in the appropriate referent after the verb. Note that there is usually a break in the intonation contour if any constituent occurs after the verb.

(1) *nzürna ŋaref **bäne** sasryoftha **züm**.*
nzürna ŋare=f   bäne   sa\sryofth/a   züm
nzürna woman=ERG.SG RECOG.ABS SG:SBJ>3SG.MASC:IO:PST:PFV/send centipede
'The *nzürna* woman sent those ones after him ... the centipedes.'
[tci20120827-03 KUT #138]

Experiencer-object constructions (§8.3.10) deviate from the basic word order. The experiencer is placed almost always before the stimulus, i.e. the undergoer comes first and the actor follows (2). This can be explained by the relative salience of the experiencer in such constructions and the fact that it almost always ranks higher in terms of animacy.

(2) *ŋatha kawakawaf bthefaf.*
ŋatha kawakawa=f b=the\faf/
dog   madness=ERG MED=2|3SG:SBJ>2|3PL:OBJ:RPST:PFV/hold
'The dogs went crazy there.' (lit. 'Madness has grabbed the dogs.')
[tci20130907-02 JAA #488]

AUV word order is only a tendency in Komnzo. In fact, most clauses lack overt noun phrases for the respective constituents. The flagging of noun phrases with case allows for some flexibility in the arrangement of constituents. However, deviations from the basic word order are often pragmatically motivated. In example (3),[1] the speaker replies to a question whether a particular individual is his brother-in-law. He says 'really my brother-in-law' and then gives an explanation in the following clause, where the undergoer appears before the actor. The reversal of constituents can be explained as a strategy to focus the undergoer argument, that is *mayawa emoth* 'Mayawa sister' is focussed by fronting.

(3) *nzone ngom fof ... **mayawa emoth** naf zefafa fof.*
     nzone   ngom   fof (.) mayawa emoth naf   ze\faf/a
     1SG.POSS brother.in.law EMPH (.) mayawa girl   3SG.ERG SG:SBJ:PST:PFV/marry
     fof
     EMPH
     'My brother-in-law ... He married a Mayawa sister.'   [tci20120814 ABB #391-392]

In example (4), both constituents follow the verb. The undergoer comes first and after a short pause the actor follows. Examples like these are rare, but frequently one of the constituents follows the verb. This can occur because the speaker wants to clarify the state of affairs or because she wants to put emphasis on the referent. There is usually a break in the intonation contour after the verb form.

(4) *keke thufnzrm ane karma kabe ... naf.*
     keke thu\fn/nzrm   ane kar=ma   kabe (.) naf
     NEG SG:SBJ>2|3PL:OBJ:PST:DUR/kill DEM village=CHAR man (.) 3SG.ERG
     'She did not attack those village people.'   [tci20120901-01 MAK #50]

While the order of constituents is flexible to some extent, it is rarely the case that other elements follow the verb, like adverbs, TAM particles, or the negator. Komnzo supports a number of cross-linguistic generalisations found in verb final languages (Dryer 2007), for example that the possessor precedes the possessed. A second generalisation is that verb-final languages tend to have postpositions rather than prepositions. Komnzo does not have a category of adpositions, but locational nouns like *tharthar* 'side' or *mrmr* 'inside' always follow the noun whose location they specify (§3.1.7).

8.3 Clause types

8.3.1 Non-verbal clauses

Non-verbal clauses are a marginal phenomenon in Komnzo. This section describes the few types of verbless clauses. These are usually short, one or two word utterances including an element which has some verb-like semantics, for example TAM particles or property nouns.

---

[1]Note that the stem *fath-* means 'hold', but in a suppressed-object construction it means 'marry' (§8.3.7).

The TAM particles *kwa* FUT and *kma* POT can stand alone when they are used as commands. For example, *kma* can mean 'You have to!', and with the apprehensive clitic *=m* attached, it can mean the opposite: *kmam* 'You must not!'. In example (5), the future particle *kwa* is used in the sense of 'Wait!'. The speaker describes poison-root fishing and how they have to hold back the children from jumping into the water too early.

(5) *katakatan kwa zöbthé thrängathinzth nima "kwa! komnzo kwa!"*
kata-katan   kwa zöbthé thrän\gathinz/th   nima kwa
REDUP-small FUT first   2|3PL:SBJ>2|3PL:OBJ:IRR:PFV:VENT/stop QUOT wait
komnzo kwa
only   wait
'First, they will hold back the small ones and say: "Wait! Just Wait!"'
[tci20110813-09 DAK #25]

Another possible type of verbless clause is with the property nouns *miyo* 'desire' and *miyatha* 'knowledge' and their antonyms *miyomär* 'aversion, dislike' and *miyamr* 'ignorance'. These words are usually used as nominal predicates with light verbs or with the copula. As a consequence, we find examples like (6), where the last clause *nzä miyamr* does not contain a verb. It is possible to insert the copula in the appropriate inflection (*worera* 1SG:SBJ:PST:IPFV/be), but often it is left out. Apart from examples like these, there are no verbless clauses in Komnzo.

(6) *fi kafar mane erera näbi ane ofe ŋarerath. mobo erera? ... nzä miyamr*
fi   kafar mane e\rä/ra   näbi ane ofe
but big   which 2|3PL:SBJ:PST:IPFV/be one DEM disappearance
ŋa\rä/rath.   mobo   e\rä/ra (.)   nzä   miyamr
2|3PL:SBJ:PST:IPFV/do where.ALL (.)   2|3PL:SBJ:PST:IPFV/be 1SG.ABS ignorance
'As for the big dogs, they disappeared for good. Where did they go? ... I (do) not know.'
[tci20111119-03 ABB #70-72]

8.3.2 Copula clauses

Copula clauses are a subtype of non-verbal predication. They are described here in a separate subsection because the copula shows a number of idiosyncrasies. First, the copula has no restricted stem. Note that this can be predicted because the main function of the restricted stem is to express the perfective aspect. Secondly, the stem of the copula is sensitive to duality: the non-dual stem is *rä*, while the dual stem is *rn*. Thirdly, the third person singular inflections are irregular (in the non-past): masculine *yé*; feminine *rä*. Table 8.1 shows the copula forms in non-past, recent past and past tense. Finally, the copula stem *rä* can be used in an ambifixing template with the meaning 'do'. This last point is discussed as part of the description of light verbs in §8.3.12.

Table 8.1: Copula inflection

	NPST	RPST	RPST:DUR	PST	PST:DUR
1SG	*worä*	*kwofrä*	*worärm*	*worera*	*kwofräm*
1DU	*nrn*	*nzfrn*	*nrnm*	*nrna*	*nzfrm*
1PL	*nrä*	*nzfrä*	*nrärm*	*nrera*	*nzfrärm*
2SG	*nrä*	*nzfrä*	*nrärm*	*nrera*	*nzfrärm*
3SG.FEM	*rä*	*zfrä*	*rärm*	*rera*	*zfrärm*
3SG.MASC	*yé*	*sfrä*	*yrärm*	*yara*	*sfrärm*
2|3DU	*ern*	*thfrn*	*ernm*	*erna*	*thfrnm*
2|3PL	*erä*	*thfrä*	*erärm*	*erera*	*thfrärm*

The copula takes a copula subject and a copula complement. Copula clauses may express identity between two NPs (7). They are used in presentational constructions, usually with a clitic demonstrative (8).

(7) *ni fthé miyatha zäkorake "babai zane bthan kabe yé."*
ni   fthé   miyatha   zä\kor\ake   babai zane   bthan
1NSG when knowledge 1PL:SBJ:PST:PFV/become uncle DEM:PROX black.magic
kabe \yé/
man 3SG.MASC:SBJ:NPST:IPFV:COP
'That was when we realised "The uncle is this sorcerer."'   [tci20130901-04 RNA #45]

(8) *yorär ziyé ... zikogr.*
yorär z=\yé/   (.) z=y\kogr/
yorär PROX=3SG.MASC:SBJ:NPST:IPFV/be (.) PROX=3SG.MASC:SBJ:NPST:STAT/stand
'Yorär is here. It stands here.'   [tci20130907-02 JAA #450-451]

The complement may be marked with the proprietive case (§4.13) or the privative case (§4.14) to express the existence or non-existence of some entity in relation to the copula subject. The former is shown in (9), where the speaker literally says 'the village is with a name' to express that it has some reputation. The latter is shown in (10), where the speaker tells how he was looking for a creek that carried water.

(9) *zane kar mane rä yfkarä rä.*
zane   kar   mane \rä/   yf=karä
DEM:PROX village which 3SG.FEM:SBJ:NPST:IPFV:COP name=PROP
\rä/
3SG.FEM:SBJ:NPST:IPFV:COP
'As for this village, it has a (good) reputation.'   [tci20120805-01 ABB 447-448]

(10) *buyak we ttfö ane zräbrmé nimame ... keke ... nomär rä.*
b=wi\yak/   we ttfö ane zrä\brm/é   nima=me
MED=1SG:SBJ:NPST:IPFV/walk also creek DEM 1SG:SBJ:IRR:PFV/follow like.this=INS

(.) keke (.) no=mär   \rä/
(.) NEG (.) water=PRIV 3SG.FEM:SBJ:NPST:IPFV:COP
'I walked there, I followed another creek like this ... No ... (The creek) had no
water.'   [tci20130903-03 MKW #92-93]

Adjectives and property nouns may also be copula complements, as shown in (11) and
(12), respectively. In (11), the speaker reports how his fathers were comparing their yam
harvest. In example (12), the speaker talks about how as a teenager she was afraid of the
anthropologist Mary Ayres when she first visited Rouku.

(11) *katakatanwä thfrä! nzenme kafar erä!*
      kata-katan=wä   thf\rä/   nzenme   kafar e\rä/
      REDUP-small=EMPH 3PL:SBJ:RPST:IPFV:COP 1NSG:POSS big 3PL:SBJ:NPST:IPFV:COP
      'Their (yams) were a bit small! Our (yams) are big!'   [tci20120805-01 ABB 403]

(12) *nzä wwtri kwarärm ... markaianema ... nafanema fof.*
      nzä   w-wtri   kwa\rä/rm   (.) markai=ane=ma   (.)
      1SG.ABS REDUP-fear 1SG:SBJ:PST:DUR:COP (.) outsider=POSS.SG=CHAR (.)
      nafane=ma   fof
      3SG.POSS=CHAR EMPH
      'I was a bit afraid ... of the white woman ... really (afraid) of her.'
                                                            [tci20130911-03 MBR #10-11]

8.3.3 Intransitive clauses

In terms of verb morphology, intransitive clauses have been described in §5.4.2. The verb
inflection employs the prefixing or the middle template. Their single argument is always
in the absolutive case. Two examples are given in (13) and (14).

The two prefixing verbs in (13) have no overt subject noun phrases, but the second
clause contains an adjunct marked with the purposive case *karr* 'for a village' (or settlement place). In example (14), we see the middle verb *brigsi* 'return' and the subject
pronoun *nzä* in the absolutive case.

(13) *ŋarsenzo **swanyakm** ... karr **swanrenzrm**.*
      ŋars=en=nzo   swan\yak/m   (.) kar=r
      river=LOC=ONLY 3SG.MASC:SBJ:PST:DUR:VENT/walk (.) village=PURP
      swan\re/nzrm
      3SG.MASC:SBJ:PST:DUR:VENT/look.around
      'He was coming along the river ... he was looking for a place to settle.'
                                                            [tci20120922-09 DAK #14-15]

(14) *nzä boba fthé kanathrfa **zänbrima**.*
      nzä   boba   fthé kanathr=fa zän\brim/a
      1SG.ABS MED.ABL when kanathr=ABL SG:SBJ:PST:PFV:VENT/return
      'That was when I returned from Kanathr.'   [tci20120805-01 ABB #607]

8.3.4 Impersonal clauses

Impersonal clauses are expressed using the middle template of the verb, in which a person-invariant middle marker fills the prefix slot, while the suffix indexes the single argument of the predicate (§5.4.5). The indexed noun phrase, if present at all, occurs in the absolutive case. The salient feature of this clause type is that the referent of the verb indexing is impersonal, unclear or simply empty. Consider examples (15) and (16). In the first example, the speaker talks about rain-making magic, which involves a rotting mixture of meat and honey in bottles. These bottles or containers are opened and the rising odour is said to increase the rainfall. The third singular indexed by the verb form *kfäkor* refers to the changed weather conditions, and the English translation 'it was enough' exhibits the same general or impersonal meaning. The second example contains the noun *aki* 'moon', but it is unclear whether the verb really indexes this noun or whether its referent is empty. Hence, the two possible translations. During the transcription of example (16), the first translation was the preferred one in this particular context.

(15)   *watikthénzo fthé kfäkor ... we sgu thwäthbe woz thwärmäne.* watik-thé=nzo

   enough-ADJZR=ONLY

   fthé   kfä\kor/   (.) we sgu thwä\thb/e   woz
   when 2|3SG:SBJ:ITER/become (.) also plug 1PL:SBJ>2|3PL:OBJ:ITER/put.inside bottle
   thwä\rmän/e
   1PL:SBJ>2|3PL:OBJ:ITER/close
   'When it was enough, we put the lids back in and we closed the bottles.'

   [tci20110810-01 MAB #59-62]

(16)   *aki zbo kräkor.*
   aki   zbo   krä\kor/
   moon PROX.ALL 2|3SG:SBJ:IRR:PFV/become
   'It became moon(light) here.' or 'The moon came up here.'   [tci20120904-02 MAB #47]

Example (17) is a description of a picture as part of a stimulus task. The speaker takes on the role of a man in the picture and asks: 'What is going on?'. Again, the verb form *krewär* appears in the middle construction and indexes a third singular.

(17)   *sinzo foba ynrä nima "ra krewär bobo?"*
   si=nzo   foba   yn\rä/   nima ra
   eye=ONLY DIST.ABL 3SG.MASC:SBJ:NPST:IPFV:VENT/be QUOT what(ABS)
   kre\wär/   bobo
   2|3SG:SBJ:IRR:PFV/happen MED.ALL
   'He was just looking from over there and wondered: "What is going on there?"'   [tci20111004 RMA #353]

Impersonal constructions often involve light verbs, for example *rä-* 'do' and *ko-* 'become', which take a nominal predicate, for example a noun or property noun. In these cases, the nominal predicate will be unmarked for case, like the absolutive case. Therefore, it may be difficult to decide whether (i) it is a nominal predicate and the subject is empty, or (ii) whether the noun phrase in question is the subject indexed in the verb. Consider example (18), in which the speaker describes the location of the mythical place of origin *Kwafar*, which is located in the Arafura sea between Papua New Guinea and Australia. The verb form *ŋakonzr* 'it becomes' occurs in the relative clause, which is printed in boldface. The third singular indexed in the verb form could be *mazo* 'ocean' (lit. 'where the ocean becomes') or it could be an empty subject (lit. 'it becomes ocean').

(18) *thden rera ... zane zena mane bad mane wythk **mazo mä ŋakonzr** a ...*
      australiane bad mä wythk.
      thd=en   \rä/ra   (.) zane   zena mane bad   mane
      middle=Loc 3SG.FEM:SBJ:PST:IPFV/be (.) DEM:PROX today which ground which
      w\ythk/   mazo mä ŋa\ko/nzr   a   (.)
      3SG.FEM:SBJ:NPST:IPFV/come.to.end and (.) australia=POSS ground where
      australia=ane   bad mä w\ythk/
      3SG.FEM:SBJ:NPST:IPFV/come.to.end
      'It was in the middle ... this one, where the land ends ... where it becomes ocean until where Australia's land ends.'   [tci20131013-01 ABB #26-30]

Weather events often have empty or impersonal subjects. This can be shown with prefixing verbs as well as middle verbs. A common way to say 'It is going to rain' is shown in (19). It is clear that *nor* 'for rain' is not indexed in the verb because it is flagged with a non-core case, the purposive case. Therefore, the reference of the third singular in the verb form is empty.

(19) *nor yé.*
      no=r   \yé/
      rain=PURP 3SG.MASC:SBJ:NPST:IPFV/be
      'It will rain.' (lit. 'It is for rain')   [overheard]

Another example is the phrase *wär kwan yanor* 'it is thundering' in (20). The thunder is expressed by the ideophone *wär kwan* 'thundering noise', and all ideophones of this type are nominal compounds headed by *kwan* 'noise, sound' (§3.7). The verb *yannor* is inflected for a masculine subject, but *kwan* is feminine. Hence *wär kwan* is not the subject, and a literal translation would be: 'He shouts the thunder sound'. Again the reference of 'he' is empty.

(20) *wär kwan yanor.*
      wär kwan ya\nor/
      thunder 3SG.MASC:SBJ:NPST:IPFV/shout
      'It is thundering.'   [overheard]

Other weather or sound phenomena can be expressed by verbs in the middle template. In example (21), the verb 'start' is inflected for a 2|3SG subject, but its referent is unclear – partly because the verb does not index an object. Thus, the indexed argument could be (i) the sound of the fire ('The fire sound started'), or (ii) it could be an empty subject ('It started the fire sound').

(21) *fi mni zürnane u kwan zethkäfako.*
fi   mni zürn=ane   u kwan   ze\thkäf/ako
but fire smoke=POSS.SG roaring.sound SG:SBJ:PST:PFV:AND/start
'but the fire smoke's sound started (rumbling).'   [tci20120827-03 KUT #186-187]

8.3.5 'Passive' clauses

Passives meanings are expressed in two ways: (i) by a verb in the middle template which indexes a patient role; the indexed noun phrase occurs in the absolutive case (§5.4.5), or (ii) by a resultative construction, in which a nominalised verb is flagged with the instrumental case (§4.10). Note that both are not dedicated passive constructions. Instead, they should be understood as constructions which can express passive-like semantics.

Example (22) shows both constructions. The first two clauses are in a temporal relationship to the last clause, which is signalled by *fthé* 'when'. This is not a subordinate relationship because *fthé* can also be used in independent clauses with the meaning of 'that was when'. In the first clause, the single argument of the verb is *bad* 'ground, earth'. This can be translated either as an reflexive/impersonal 'the earth created (itself)' or as a passive 'the earth was created'. In the second clause, matters are clear because the verb is in a transitive template which shows actor agreement with 'father' (ERG) and undergoer agreement with 'earth' (ABS), thus: 'the father created the earth'. The last clause is a resultative construction. The nominalised verb *rifthzsi* 'hiding' takes the instrumental case ('with hiding'), which is best translated as a passive ('was hidden').

(22) **bad fthé ŋafiyokwa ... ŋafyf fthé bad wäfiyokwa ... kidn ane rifthzsime zfrärm.**
bad fthé ŋa\fiyok/wa   (.) ŋafe=f   fthé bad
earth when SG:SBJ:PST:IPFV/make (.) father=ERG.SG when earth
wä\fiyok/wa   (.) kidn   ane rifthz-si=me
2|3SG:SBJ>3SG.FEM:OBJ:PST:IPFV/make (.) eternal fire DEM hide-NMLZ=INS
zf\rä/rm
3SG.FEM:SBJ:PST:DUR/be
'When the earth was made ... when God made the earth ... that eternal fire was hidden.'   [tci20120909-06 KAB #61-63]

8.3.6 Reflexive and reciprocal clauses

Formally, reflexive/reciprocal clauses are encoded by (i) the verb form in the middle template and (ii) the argument noun phrase in the absolutive case. Ditransitives show exceptional grammatical behaviour in that the argument may be in the absolutive or ergative case. There is no distinction between reflexives and reciprocals other than the fact that singulars do not allow a reciprocal reading. Below I will describe how reflexive/reciprocals differ from intransitive and impersonal clause on the one hand, and from suppressed-object constructions on the other. This topic is also addressed in the description of the middle template (§5.4.5).

In example (23) the speaker talks about a ritual which chases away evil spirits. This rather gruesome ritual involves young men shooting at each other with blunt arrows. In the last clause of the example the noun phrase *kabe* 'man' is in the absolutive case and the verb employs the middle template and indexes one argument (2|3PL). The verb *rusi* 'shoot' has rather clear transitive semantics. Consequently, it invites a reciprocal interpretation in the middle template.

(23) *kabe kwaruthrmth frkkarä.*
kabe   kwa\ru/thrmth   frk=karä
man(ABS) 2|3PL:SBJ:PST:DUR/shoot blood=PROP
'The people were shooting at each other (until) they were
bleeding.'   [tci20150906-10 ABB #414]

In most cases only secondary information disambiguates between intransitive, impersonal and reflexive/reciprocal interpretations. By secondary information, I mean (i) context, (ii) grammatical devices which are not used solely for reflexive/reciprocal constructions, (iii) statistical tendencies of individual verbs. I will address these in turn. First, context is probably the most important, and it is evident that an example like (23) is usually preceded or followed by a description which disambiguates the state of affairs. Secondly, speakers may choose to repeat the absolutive noun phrase to make clear that the intended reading should be a reciprocal one. Consider example (24), which concludes a headhunting story. The pronoun *fi* occurs twice. Additionally, the utterance was accompanied by appropriate gestures to clarify the intended reciprocal meaning. The pronoun *fi* is marked with the exclusive enclitic *=nzo*. The repetition and the exclusive enclitic are secondary strategies which are not solely used to mark reflexive/reciprocal meanings. Note that the exclusive enclitic *=nzo* shows cognates in other Yam languages. In Nen, there is a set of reflexive/reciprocal pronouns which all end in *nzo*, for example *benzo* 2SG (Evans 2015b: 1072). In Komnzo, the exclusive clitic expresses the meaning of 'only' without reflexive/reciprocal semantics.

(24) *ni woga tüfrmäre nrä … bänema nzenme thden ane fof kwakwirm … woga **finzo finzo** kwafnzrmth.*
ni   woga tüfr=märe n\rä/   (.) bäne=ma   nzenme
1NSG man plenty=PRIV 1PL:SBJ:NPST:IPFV/be (.) DEM:MED=CHAR 1NSG.POSS
thd=en   ane fof kwa\kwir/m   (.) woga fi=nzo   fi=nzo
middle=LOC DEM EMPH 2|3SG:SBJ:PST:DUR/run (.) man 3.ABS=ONLY 3.ABS=ONLY
kwa\fn/nzrmth
2|3PL:SBJ:PST:DUR/kill
'We are not many … because this was going on in our middle … The people, this (group) and that (group) were killing each other.'   [tci20111107-01 MAK #157-158]

Although stems may alternate between different morphological templates there is a statistical tendency for a particular stem to occur in a particular template. For example, typically transitive meanings (*rusi* 'shoot', *zan* 'hit, kill', *marasi* 'see') occur most of the time in the ambifixing transitive template. If such stems occur in a middle template, it invites a reflexive/reciprocal reading rather than an impersonal or intransitive one. We will see in the following section that the middle template can also be used for the suppressed-object construction (§8.3.7). However, in the suppressed-object construction the noun phrase indexed in the verb form is marked for ergative case and not absolutive. On the other hand, stems which occur in the middle template most of the time (*maikasi* 'wash', *bringsi* 'return') should be analysed as reflexiva tanta (Geniušienė 1987), even though they may occur in the ambifixing transitive template ('wash someone', 'bring back someone'). Hence, there is a statistical tendency for stems to occur in a particular template, which helps to disambiguate between an impersonal or reflexive/reciprocal reading.

Next, I want to set reflexive/reciprocals apart from what I call the suppressed-object construction (§8.3.7). The state of affairs in reflexive/reciprocals is such that the actor and patient can be exchanged. In Komnzo, both are expressed by one noun phrase which occurs in the absolutive case. Herein lies the formal difference from the suppressed-object construction. If the noun phrase *kabe* 'people' in example (23) was in the ergative case – for example *kabe=yé* (man=ERG.NSG) – the sentence would mean 'they were shooting (at sth.)'. This is the suppressed-object construction, which I describe in the following section (§8.3.7). Note that the verb form *kwaruthrmth* remains the same, only the case marking changes.

For ditransitive verbs, the case marking is less fixed, and the argument noun phrase can appear in the absolutive as well as ergative case, both with a reflexive/reciprocal meaning. In example (25), the verb form *ŋarinth* indexes only the subject (2|3DU), while the prefix slot is filled with the middle marker. The subject argument appears in the ergative (*nafa*). A suppressed-object reading is not possible with ditransitive verbs. Note that the argument could also occur in the absolutive case (*fi*). This would create a clause with two absolutive noun phrases. Hence, the choice between ergative and abolutive seems to be dependent on the kinds of referents. In (25), both noun phrases are animate, and the use of the ergative case avoids confusion between agent ('they') and theme ('sisters').

(25) *emoth nafa ŋarinth fof.*
      emoth nafa   ŋa\ri\nth   fof
      girl   3NSG.ERG 2|3DU:SBJ:NPST:IPFV/give EMPH
      'They give each other sisters.'   [tci20120805-01 ABB #158]

At this stage, it is impossible to investigate this topic further, because (i) noun phrases are frequently omitted and (ii) as I have argued in §5.4.6, except for a few verbs (*yarisi* 'give', *trikasi* 'tell', *fänzsi* 'show') all ditransitive verbs are derived.

8.3.7 Suppressed-object clauses

Suppressed-object clauses employ the middle template of the verb. The argument indexed in the verb is treated like an actor by the case system, i.e. it is flagged with the ergative case. The object may be overtly expressed with a noun phrase, but it is suppressed from indexation in the verb form.

I describe in §5.4.5 how almost all transitive verbs can enter into the suppressed-object construction for semantic as well as pragmatic reasons. For example, most of the time, the referents of suppressed-objects rank low in the animacy hierarchy (Silverstein 1976). In example (26), the speaker searches for her shoes and complains that her friend has been wearing them. We only know about the object of *rgsi* 'wear' from the previous context since it is not expressed as a noun phrase, nor is the object indexed in the verb form. The semantics of *rgsi* renders a reflexive reading ('she wears herself') nonsensical. Additionally, the fact that the subject is in the ergative case (*naf*) rules out the reflexive/reciprocal interpretation. This is important because the verb form is identical between reflexive/reciprocals and the suppressed-object construction.

(26) *ebar zfthnzo! naf rar ŋargwrm?*
　　 ebar zfth=nzo　　naf　　ra=r　　　ŋa\rg/wrm
　　 head base=ONLY 3SG.ERG what=PURP SG:SBJ:RPST:DUR/wear
　　 'Thickhead! Why was she wearing (the flipflops)?'　　[tci20130901-04 RNA #173]

Objects can be suppressed for pragmatic reasons, often in addition to their low rank on the animacy hierarchy. That is because the suppression of the object has the pragmatic effect of focussing the subject. Example (27) is taken from a text about food taboos. This topic came up while talking about a very old woman, whose old age was ascribed to her respecting all food taboos. In the example, the speaker shifts the topic from the old woman to those people who did not respect food taboos. This shift of topic is achieved by (i) a fronted relative clause and (ii) the suppressed-object construction. As in the previous example, we only know about the object of *rirksi* 'respect, avoid' from the preceding context.

(27) *fi mafa keke kwarirkwrmth … watik tekmär esufakwa.*
　　 fi　　mafa　　　keke kwarirkwrmth　　　… watik tekmär
　　 but who.NSG.ERG NEG 2|3PL:SBJ:PST:DUR/respect (.) then duration=PRIV
　　 esufakwa
　　 2|3PL:SBJ:PST:IPFV/grow.old
　　 'But those who did not respect (the food taboos) … well, they grew old
　　 quickly.'　　[tci20120922-26 DAK #26-27]

Although the object is suppressed from indexation in the verb form, it may occur as a noun phrase in the clause. In example (28), the speaker talks about garden magic and people who steal the soil from other people's gardens. In the relative clause, the object *bad* 'ground' is suppressed from indexation in the verb, yet it appears as a noun phrase. The subject is indexed in the verb suffix and the corresponding noun phrase, the relative pronoun *mafa*, is in the ergative case.

(28) *nä kabenzo nnzä wawa gamokarä erä bad mafa ŋakarkwrth.*
　　 nä　　kabe=nzo nnzä　　wawa gamo=karä e\rä/　　　　　　bad
　　 INDF man=ONLY perhaps yam　spell=PROP 2|3PL:SBJ:NPST:IPFV/be ground

> mafa ŋa\kark/wrth
> who.ERG.NSG 2|3PL:SBJ:NPST:IPFV/take
> 'Perhaps only other people, who take the soil away, have yam magic.'
>
> [tci20130822-08 JAA #42]

The suppressed-object may also be a relative clause, as in example (29), which is taken from a picture stimulus task.

(29) *emothf ŋatrikwr monme zffnzr.*
emoth=f ŋa\trik/wr mon=me zf\fn/nzr
girl=ERG.SG 2|3SG:SBJ:NPST:IPFV/tell how=INS 2|3SG:SBJ>3SG.FEM:OBJ:RPST:IPFV/hit
'The girl tells (the story of) how he hit her.' [tci20120925 MAE #102]

There are a few verbs which always occur in the suppressed-object construction. A few examples are: *yonasi* 'drink', *fathasi* 'marry', *frzsi* 'fish/net (poison-root)', *naf-* 'talk, speak' and *karksi* 'pull'.[2] With other verbs there is only a statistical tendency to enter this construction. For example, *yarizsi* 'hear' occurs 104 times in the corpus; 25 times the object is indexed and 79 times it is suppressed. In other words, in only about a quarter of all tokens of *yarizsi* does the verb mean 'hear X'. In the other three quarters of tokens of *yarizsi*, it means 'hear (sth.)'. In (30), we see an example of *yarizsi* and *rfnaksi* 'taste' in the suppressed-object construction. The speaker explains how the news of the beginning yam harvest spread from East to West, from village to village.

(30) *watik, we masu karé kwekaristh "oh, nafa z zärfnth!"*
watik, we masu karé kwe\karis/th oh nafa z
then also masu village=ERG.NSG 2|3PL:SBJ:ITER/hear oh 2|3NSG.ERG ALR
zä\rfn/th
2|3PL:SBJ:RPST:PFV/taste
'Then the Masu people always heard (the other village): "Oh, they have already tasted (the yams)!"' [tci20131013-01 ABB #363]

8.3.8 Transitive clauses

This section deals with prototypical transitive clauses, which are transitive in their verb morphology, i.e. they are built from the ambifixing transitive template, as well as their noun phrase syntax, i.e. the actor argument is flagged with the ergative and the undergoer argument is in the absolutive. Therefore, suppressed-object constructions (§8.3.7) can be described as non-prototypical transitive clauses because (i) the verb appears in the middle template, and (ii) the object noun phrase is frequently omitted. However, noun phrases can generally be dropped in all clause types. The ambifixing verb template is described in §5.4.6. An example of a transitive clause is given in (31).

---

[2] The stem *karksi* can occur in a transitive template with the meaning 'take'. If it occurs in a suppressed-object construction, it means 'pull'. I analyse these as two different lexical items, because there is a difference in the semantics as well as the combinatorics of the stem.

(31) *nzürna ŋaref bäne ŋad yrtmakwa.*
nzürna ŋare=f bäne ŋad y\rtmak/wa
spirit woman=ERG.SG DEM:MED string(ABS) SG:SBJ>3SG.MASC:OBJ:PST:IPFV/cut
'The *nzürna* woman cut that string.' [tci20120827-03 KUT #142]

8.3.9 Ditransitive clauses

Ditransitive clauses employ the same template as transitive clauses. However, the valency changing prefix *a-* shifts the reference of the verb prefix from the direct object to the indirect object. The corresponding noun phrase appears in dative case. This is described in §5.4.6. Note that the *a-* prefix may increase as well as decrease the valency of a verb, hence, the label "valency changing prefix" (§5.4.2).

Example (32) shows the verbs *trikasi* 'tell' and *fänzsi* 'show'. The recipient arguments are flagged for dative case and the respective arguments are indexed in the two verbs.

(32) *nzone **ŋafyn bäin** ane trikasi **yatrikwath** ... nzunwä **ŋafyf bäif zwafäsa**.*
nzone ŋafe=n bäi=n ane trika-si
1SG.POSS father=DAT.SG bäi=DAT.SG DEM tell-NMLZ

ya\trik/wath (.) nzun=wä ŋafe=f bäi=f
2|3PL:SBJ>3SG.MASC:IO:PST:IPFV/tell (.) 1SG.DAT=EMPH father=ERG.SG bäi=ERG.SG

zwa\fäs/a
2|3SG:SBJ>1SG:IO:PST:PFV/show
'They told that story to my father Bäi ... and father Bäi showed (it) to me.'
[tci20110802 ABB #18-20]

Ditransitive clauses may also contain cognate objects, as in (32) *trikasi yatrikwath* 'they told him the story'. Another example is *yathugsi* 'trick (v)', which often occurs with *gaso* 'trick, lie'.

In §5.4.6, I argued that ditransitive should be recognised as a category even though most ditransitive verbs are derived from transitives by (i) adding the valency change prefix *a-*, which (ii) changes the reference of the verb prefix to an indirect object (goal, recipient, beneficiary) and (iii) putting the respective argument noun phrase in dative case. The same strategy can be used to raise possessors in the cross-referencing of the verb. In example (33) it is the possessor (*nzone* 'my' 1SG), which is indexed in the verb, and not the possessed (*miyo* 'desire/wish' 3SG.FEM).

(33) **nzone miyo** *kwa* **wabthakwr**.
nzone miyo kwa wo-a-bthak-w-r-∅
1SG.POSS desire FUT 1SG.α-VC-finish.EXT-LK-2|3SG
2|3SG:SBJ>1SG:IO:NPST:IPFV/finish
'You will fulfil my wish.' [tci20130823-06 CAM #23]

The ditransitive pattern is very productive and almost all transitive verbs can enter this construction. Most verbs retain their transitive semantics, but can index a beneficiary of the event. For example, in (34), the verb *fsisi* 'count' in the clause takes the object 'yam suckers'. The ditransitive pattern only adds a beneficiary which is indexed in the verb.

(34) *nä efothen ... wawa tafo yafsinzake ... babuan.*
nä   efoth=en (.) wawa tafo   yafsinzake   (.)
INDF day=LOC (.) yam   sucker 1PL:SBJ>3SG.MASC:IO:PST:IPFV/count (.)
babua=n
babua=DAT.SG
'Some day ... we counted yam suckers for him ... for Babua.'

[tci20120814 ABB #165-167]

As I pointed out in §5.4.4, prefixing verbs (intransitives) can enter the same pattern, in which a beneficiary or raised possessor, in dative and possessive case respectively, is indexed in the verb form. Example (35) is taken from a recording where two speakers discuss the content of a picture card. The prefixing verb *-thn* 'be lying' in the example does not index the objects that are lying on the ground, but the possessor instead.

(35) *ra kwa nm bäne wäthn? ... nafane nainai?*
ra   kwa nm   bäne   wä\thn/   (.) nafane
what FUT maybe DEM:MED 3SG.FEM:IO:NPST:IPFV/be.lying (.) 3SG.POSS
nainai
sweet.potato
'What (of hers) might be lying there? ... her sweet potatoes?' [tci20111004 RMA #108]

8.3.10 Experiencer-object constructions

Experiencer-object constructions express bodily, mental and emotional processes ('get sunburned', 'shiver in fear', 'be angry'). These are framed as transitive clauses in which the stimulus acts on the experiencer. Constructions of this type have been examined by Pawley et al. for Kalam (2000) showing that experiencer-objects as well as experiencer-subjects are found in the semantic domain of bodily and mental processes.[3] Komnzo confirms their findings. In terms of their morpho-syntax, experiencer-object constructions are characterised by the following criteria: (i) the stimulus argument appears in the ergative, (ii) the stimulus is indexed by a default 3SG in the verb suffix, (iii) the experiencer occurs in the absolutive case, and (iv) the word order is UAV (undergoer actor verb).

Consider the two ways of expressing a feeling of hunger in the elicited examples in (36). In (36a) the experiencer is the subject of the copula clause, but in (36b) it is the object of the verb *rmatksi* 'cut'. In the latter the feeling of hunger is portrayed as somewhat stronger. Note that the choice of verb is not entirely fixed. One can replace *rmatksi* 'cut' with a light verb, for example *rä-* 'do' ('hunger does me'), or with the phasal verb *bthaksi* 'finish' ('hunger finishes me'), thereby changing the degree or intensity of the experienced feeling. Thus, the experiencer-object construction is one possible way to express mental and bodily processes.

---

[3]Note that the notion of experiencer is slightly extended here to include bodily processes in addition to mental or emotional ones.

(36) a. *nzä frasi worä*
      nzä   frasi   wo\rä/
      1SG.ABS hunger 1SG:SBJ:NPST:IPFV/be
      'I am hungry.'

    b. *nzä frasif wortmakwr*
      nzä   frasi=f   wo\rtmak/wr
      1SG.ABS hunger=ERG. 2|3SG:SBJ>1SG:OBJ:NPST:IPFV/cut
      'I am hungry. / I am starving.' (Lit: 'Hunger cuts me.')

Examples like (36a) were given to me in elicitation, when asking 'How do I say 'I am hungry?'. I first encountered experiencer-object constructions in more natural situations, for example in overhearing conversations or when translating recordings. Komnzo speakers explicitly regard experiencer-object constructions as more original and creative language. Therefore, it seems natural that these were rarely offered in the context of elicitation. Experiencer-object constructions portray a situation in much more colourful terms. They often evoke some kind of emotional reaction (laughter or sympathy) from the audience, as in (37), where a woman describes what happened to her as a small child when she was hiding in a tree from a pig.

(37) *nzä **wthf** warfo bä **kwräbth**.*
      nzä   wth=f   warfo bä kwrä\bth/
      1SG.ABS faeces=ERG above MED 2|3SG:SBJ>1SG:OBJ:IRR:PFV/finish
      'I really had to take a dump there on top (of the tree).' (Lit: 'Excretions finish
      me.')   [tci20150919-05 LNA #117]

Experiencer-object constructions express bodily and mental processes, and it is this internal stimulus which 'acts' on the experiencer. Two text examples were given in the description of the ergative case (§4.5) and are repeated here as (38) and (39).

(38) ***nokuyé** fthé **sabtha**.*
      noku=yé   fthé   sa\bth/a
      anger=ERG.NSG when 2|3SG:SBJ>3SG.MASC:PST:PFV/finish
      'That is when he got really angry.' (lit. 'Anger finished him.')
                                            [tci20120909-06 KAB #39]

(39) ***wtrif** z **zwefaf**.*
      wtri=f   z   zwe\faf/
      fear=ERG ALR 2|3SG:SBJ>1SG:OBJ:RPST:PFV/hold
      'I am already scared.' (lit. 'Fear holds me.')   [tci20130901-04 RNA #164]

The stimulus noun phrase can be modified, for example with a nominal compound. In example (40) the stimulus *miyo* 'desire' is modified by two elements yielding *kabe zan miyo* 'desire to kill people'. This example is repeated from the discussion of complex heads in §7.5.3.

(40) *baf fthé **sräbth** nima ... **kabe zan miyof**.*
baf　　　　　 fthé　 srä\bth/　　　　　　　　　　　　　 nima　 (.) kabe
RECOG.ERG.SG when 2|3SG:SBJ>3SG.MASC:OBJ:IRR:PFV/finish like.this (.) man
zan　　 miyo=f
hitting desire=ERG
'That is when this overcomes him ... the bloodlust for people.' (lit. 'People killing
desire finishes him.')　　　　　　　　　　　　　　　　　[tci20130903-04 RNA #84-85]

Experiencer-object constructions differ in their basic word order from other clauses
in that the experiencer, the object, comes first. This can be explained by the special semantics of the experiencer-object construction, in which the most salient element is the
experiencer. However, most of the examples in this section do not include an overt noun
phrase. One example from the corpus is given in (41). Note that the speaker corrects himself in this example. He first uses the absolutive (*frfr*) 'shiver', but then repeats the same
noun in the ergative (*frfré*).

(41) *nge fäth frfr a **frfré** n safum.*
nge　 fäth frfr　 a　 frfr=é　　　　　 n　 sa\fum/
child DIM shiver ah shiver=ERG.NSG IMN 2|3SG:SBJ>3SG.MASC:OBJ:RPST:PFV/pull
'The small child was almost shivering' (lit. 'The shivers were about to pull
him.')　　　　　　　　　　　　　　　　　　　　　　　[tci20130901-04 YUK #26]

Note that in (41) and (38), the noun phrase is marked with the non-singular ergative
(=*é*), while the verb indexes a singular actor. All other examples in the corpus employ
the singular ergative (=*f*). In fact, these are the only examples in the corpus, where an
inanimate referent receives a non-singular ergative. Note that there is no number distinction for inanimate referent for all case enclitics. We can draw two conlcusions from
this observation. First, experiencer object construction give the stimulus are somewhat
elevated status of animacy, i.e. the stimulus is portrayed as being animate. Secondly, the
fact that the verb inflection is singular, rather than plural, is evidence for the limited
grammatical behaviour of property nouns. Property nouns do not trigger agreement in
the verb and the only construction in which property nouns show quasi-agreement is
the experiencer-object construction. I call this "quasi-agreement" because it is default
2|3SG in the suffix (§3.1.4).

The second domain of experiencer-object constructions is that of bodily processes, as
in (41). A few more examples of this type are given in (42-45).

(42) *zä zf fthé **thkarf** yafiyokwa ziyé.*
zä　 zf　 fthé　 thkar=f　　　　 ya\fiyok/wa
PROX IMM when hardness=ERG 2|3SG:SBJ>3SG.MASC:OBJ:PST:IPFV/make
z=\yé/
PROX=3SG.MASC:NPST:IPFV/be
'That is when it got stuck right here.' (lit. 'Hardness made it.')
　　　　　　　　　　　　　　　　　　　　　　　　　[tci20120922-09 DAK #18]

(43) **nzä sukufa zürnf wortmakwr.**
    nzä   sukufa zürn=f   wo\rtmak/wr   kwan=en
    1SG.ABS tobacco smoke=ERG 2|3SG:SBJ>1SG:OBJ:NPST:IPFV/cut throat=LOC
    'The tobacco is very strong.' (lit. 'Tobacco smoke cuts me.')   [overheard]

(44) **nzrmf wortmakwr** *kwanen.*
    nzrm=f   wo\rtmak/wr   kwan=en
    bitterness=ERG 2|3SG:SBJ>1SG:OBJ:NPST:IPFV/cut throat=LOC
    'It is very sour.' (lit. 'Bitterness cuts me.')   [overheard]

(45) *watik nzfrä ...* **efothf nfariwr.**
    watik   nzf\rä/   (.) efoth=f n\fari/wr
    enough 1PL:SBJ:RPST:IPFV/be (.) sun=ERG 2|3SG:SBJ>1PL:OBJ:NPST:IPFV/dry
    'We have done enough ... We are burning in the sun.' (lit. 'The sun dries
    us.')   [tci20111119-03 ABB #200]

8.3.11 Cognate and pseudo-cognate object constructions

Cognate objects are a common phenomenon in Komnzo. Examples (46-48) contain a nominalised verb and an inflected verb. In all three examples, the nominalisation and the inflected verb form are of the same lexeme. Hence, (46) translates literally as 'I tell them the telling'. The inflected verb indexes the indirect object (2|3PL) and as with other ditransitive verbs, *trikasi* is the direct object of the verb.

(46) *nze ane* **trikasi ätrikwé.**
    nze   ane trik-si   ä\trik/wé
    1SG.ERG DEM tell-NMLZ 1SG:SBJ>2|3PL:IO:NPST:IPFV/tell
    'I tell them the story.' (lit. 'I tell them the telling.')   [tci20111119-03 ABB #161]

There is an analytical problem with verbs which occur in the middle template. Example (48) translates literally as 'He laughs the laughter' or as 'He laughter-laughs'. The middle template used in (47) and (48) only indexes the subject argument, not the object. Because of this, it cannot be determined whether the nominalisations *maikasi* 'washing' and *borsi* 'laughing' function as objects or whether they function predicatively. We will see below that a predicative function is a possible analysis in some cases. From this perspective, cognate objects and predicative nominals in light verb constructions can be portrayed as contiguous phenomena. Light verb constructions are described in the following section (§8.3.12).

(47) **maikasi bä ŋamayukwro.**
    maik-si   bä   ŋa\maik/wro
    wash-NMLZ MED SG:SBJ:NPST:IPFV:AND/wash
    'I will wash there.' (lit. 'I washing-wash.')   [tci20130823-06 STK #53]

(48) **bor**si **ŋaborwr.**
borsi   ŋa\bor/wr
laugh-NMLZ 2|3SG:SBJ:NPST:IPFV/laugh
'He laughs.' (lit. 'He laughs the laughing.')   [tci20111004 TSA #128]

A second problem is that many verbs lack regular nominalisations, which are formed with the suffix -*si*. These verbs use a common noun, as in example (49). The adjective *kwosi* 'dead' functions adverbially and adds the meaning of a deep sleep. The noun *etfth* 'sleep', however, is semantically fully included in the meaning of the verb *rug*- 'sleep', just as the regular nominalisation *borsi* 'laugh' is included in the stem of the inflected verb in (48). As a consequence, *etfth* is optional and the sentence would be grammatical without it. Note that the same is true of examples (46-48).

(49) *fi **etfth** kwosi sfrugrm.*
fi   etfth kwosi sf\rugr/m
3.ABS sleep dead 3SG.MASC:SBJ:PST:DUR/sleep
'He was sleeping soundly.' (lit. 'He was dead sleep sleeping.')
                                          [tci20120904-02 MAB #98]

For want of a better term, I label examples like (49) 'pseudo-cognate object' constructions. They are unlike cognate objects because the verb stem and the nominal element are formally not related. Other examples are *rnzür*- 'dance, sing' and *wath* 'dance (n), song' and -*nor* 'shout, emit sound' and *kwan* 'shout (n)'. Although the verb stem and the noun are not cognate, distributional evidence shows that they stand in the same relationship as an inflected verb and the corresponding regular nominalisation with -*si*. For example, the phasal verb *bthaksi* 'finish' takes the noun *wath* 'dance (n), song' to mean 'finish singing'. This is because there is no regular nominalisation available for the verb *rnzür*- 'dance, sing'.

The noun in these constructions is not always redundant. For example, it can be modified as the head of a compound, thereby modifying the predicate. In (50), the noun *etfth* 'sleep' occurs in a compound modified by *efoth* 'day' indicating that the speaker was sleeping during the day.

(50) ***efoth etfth** kwofrugrm e zizi.*
efoth etfth kwof\rugr/m   e   zizi
day   sleep 1SG:SBJ:PST:DUR/sleep until afternoon
'I was sleeping during the day until the afternoon.' (lit. 'I was day-sleep sleeping.')
                                          [tci20111119-03 ABB #31]

This kind of predicate modification is developed to varying degrees. The best example is the intransitive verb *nor*- 'shout, emit a sound', which again lacks an infinitive and instead *kwan* 'shout (n), call' is used. Hence, *kwan yanor* 'He shouts the shout' or 'He emits the shout' is a common expression. The relatively large set of ideophones (§3.7) enter into compounds of the type ideophone + *kwan*, as in *sö kwan* 'sound of wallabies grunting' or *nzam kwan* 'the sound of smacking one's lips'. Most auditory sensations are expressed in this construction with the verb *nor-*. In example (51), the gurgling sound of a headhunter's victim is described.

(51) *grr kwannzo fobo zwanorm.*
  grr   kwan=nzo fobo   zwa\nor/m
  rasping.sound shout=ONLY DIST.ALL 3SG.FEM:SBJ:PST:DUR/shout
  'She was just gurgling.' (lit. 'She was shouting/emitting only the rasping sound.')
  [tci20111119-01 ABB #154]

Example (52) comes from a hunting trip, where I was instructed to imitate the sound of a jumping wallaby (*bübü kwan*) by hitting the ground with a thick stick.

(52) *bübü kwan gnanoré!*
  bübü   kwan gna\nor/é
  thumping.sound shout 2SG:SBJ:IMP:IPFV/shout
  'You must beat the ground!' (lit. 'You must shout/emit the thumping sound.')
  [overheard]

Lastly, the verb can be modified by using a different noun. This is a marginal pattern, and I can give only two examples. Instead of *kwan*, one can use the noun *frk* 'blood' with the verb *nor-* 'shout' to express that someone is bleeding, as in example (53), which comes from the description of a picture card.

(53) *ŋare frk neba komnzo wänor.*
  ŋare frk   neba   komnzo wä\nor/
  woman blood opposite only   3SG.FEM:SBJ:NPST:IPFV/shout
  'The woman is only bleeding on the other side.'   [tci20111004 RMA #402]

The second example is the noun *wanzo* 'dream' which can be used with *rug-* 'sleep' (instead of *etfth* 'sleep (n)'). In example (54), the speaker talks about the mythological significance of the bird of paradise, when it appears in one's dream.

(54) *... ythamama wanzo fthé nzrarugr.*
  (.) ythama=ma   wanzo fthé nzra\rugr/
  (.) bird.of.paradise=CHAR dream when 2|3SG:SBJ:IRR:IPFV/sleep
  '... when you are dreaming of the bird of paradise.'   [tci20120817-02 ABB #29]

There are a handful of (intransitive) verbs for which pseudo-cognate constructions are possible, even though there is a regular nominalisation with *-si* available. For example, *bznsi* 'work (v.i.)' can occur together with *znsä* 'work (n)'. Another example is *mthizsi* 'suffer', which can occur with *zi* 'pain', as in example (55).

(55) *zi swathizrm ... ekri zi ... kofä ysma.*
  zi   swa\thi/zrm   (.) ekri zi   (.) kofä ys=ma
  pain 3SG.MASC:SBJ:PST:DUR/suffer (.) flesh pain (.) fish thorn=CHAR
  'He was in pain ... body pain ... from the fish spike.'   [tci20100905 ABB #91-93]

We have seen above that cognate and pseudo-cognate constructions are similar to light verb constructions in that a nominal element contributes to the meaning of the predicate. They are markedly different in the degree of modification, because light verbs are much more general in their semantics (*rä-* 'do', *fiyoksi* 'make', *ko-* 'become'). It might be best to view this as a cline: at one end of the spectrum we have cognate object constructions, where the nominalisation of the verb occurs together with the same verb, as in examples (46-48). On the other end of the spectrum we have light verb constructions, where the nominal element not only carries most of the meaning of the predicate, but it always differs formally from the verb. Light verbs are described in the next section.

8.3.12 Light verb constructions

There are number of light verbs in Komnzo. These are *rä-* 'do', *ko-* 'become', *fiyoksi* 'make' and the two phasal verbs *thkäfsi* 'start' and *bthaksi* 'finish'. The first two are interesting from a lexical perspective. The light verb *rä-* is build from the same stem as the copula. In a prefixing template this stem means 'be', but in an ambifixing template it means 'do'. The second stem *ko-* only occurs in ambifixing templates, where it can mean 'speak' or 'become'. Although these are only statistical tendencies, in the middle template *ko-* usually means 'become', whereas in a transitive template it usually means 'speak'.

The light verb 'do' is usually used in the middle template indexing only the subject argument. A very frequent collocation is with *fam* 'thought', thus, literally: 'do thoughts' means 'think'. Examples (56) and (57) are taken from a picture stimulus task. Note that *fam* is not indexed in the verb form, even if the light verb indexes an object. In (57), *fam* functions predicatively, and a literal translation of 'He thinks of her' is 'He thought-does her'.

(56) *wati, ane fof yamnzr **fam** ŋarär.*
wati ane fof ya\m/nzr   fam   ŋa\rä/r
then DEM EMPH 3SG.MASC:SBJ:NPST:IPFV/sit thought 2|3SG:SBJ:NPST:IPFV/do
'Okay, this one is sitting. He is thinking.'   [tci20111004 RMA #133]

(57) ***zane emoth fam wrär** anema yatrikwr nafan.*
zane   emoth fam   w\rä/r   ane=ma
DEM:PROX girl   thought 2|3SG:SBJ>3SG.FEM:OBJ:NPST:IPFV/do DEM=CHAR
ya\trik/wr   nafan
2|3SG:SBJ>3SG.MASC:IO:NPST:IPFV/tell 3SG.DAT
'He thinks of that girl and he tells him about her.'   [tci20111004 RMA #52]

This is a general feature of light verbs. They require a nominal element which functions predicatively. Hence, we find predicative nominals in both intransitive (56) and transitive structures (57). In these examples, the predicative nominal was the noun *fam*, but very often property nouns are used for this function, especially property nouns with more event-oriented semantics. In example (58), the speaker remarks that his dogs have disappeared. The meaning of disappearing is expressed by the property noun *ofe* 'absent/absence'.

(58) *fi kafar mane erera näbi ane **ofe ŋarerath.***
      fi   kafar mane e\rä/ra   näbi ane ofe   ŋa\rä/rath.
      but big   which 2|3PL:SBJ:PST:IPFV/be one DEM absent 2|3PL:SBJ:PST:IPFV/do
      'But the big (dogs), they disappeared for good.'   [tci20111119-03 ABB #70]

The light verb *ko-* 'become' shows similar behaviour. It can appear with nominals as in (59) with the adjective *kafar* 'big'. But often 'become' occurs with property nouns which function predicatively. In (60), the property noun *wefwef* 'excited/excitement' contributes most of the meaning of the event.

(59) *wati fi zena ngemär ... **kafar z zäkor.***
      wati fi   zena nge=mär   (.) kafar z   zä\kor/
      then 3.ABS today child=PRIV (.) big   ALR SG:SBJ:RPST:PFV/become
      'Well, today she has become already old without (having) children.'
                                                          [tci20120814 ABB #214-215]

(60) *"Daddy skri, bun ane fof yé. be ane sawob!" watik skri ane **wefwefnzo kräkor.***
      daddy skri bun   ane fof \yé/   be   ane
      father skri 2SG.DAT DEM EMPH 3SG.MASC:NPST:IPFV/be 2SG.ERG DEM
      sa\wob/   watik skri ane wefwef=nzo
      2SG:SBJ>3SG.MASC:IMP:PFV/eat then   skri DEM excited=ONLY
      krä\kor/
      2|3SG:SBJ:IRR:PFV/become
      '"Daddy Skri, this one is for you. You eat this one!" Well, Skri got excited.'
                                                          [tci20120922-25 ALK #24-25]

The light verb 'become' together with the property noun *miyatha* 'knowledge' is used to express coming into the state of knowing something, literally 'become knowledge(able)'. In example (61) a man, who fell off a coconut palm in an attempt to steal palm wine, is badly insulted. The imperative *miyatha käkor* can be translated as both 'you know it!' or 'you feel it!'.

(61) *fof nrä! **miyatha käkor!** buŋame zakiyar!*
      fof n\rä/   miyatha   kä\kor/
      EMPH 2SG:SBJ:NPST:IPFV/be knowledgeable 2SG:SBJ:IMP:PFV/become
      bu-ŋame   za\kiyar/
      2SG.POSS-mother 2SG:SBJ>3SG.FEM:IMP:PFV/copulate
      'It is you! You feel it now! Fuck your mother!'   [tci20120904-01 MAB #95]

Example (62) is about the *tütü* bird (Pheasant Coucal), who used to be the custodian of fire before people knew about it. In the example, they find out about the bird's secret. Note that the light verb 'become' indexes the *tütü* bird (3SG.FEM). Thus, the predicative nominal *miyatha* 'knowledgeable' in the light verb construction can be used with an intransitive (61) or transitive sense (62).

(62) *nä kayé ... **miyatha wkonzath**. "oh budben mni rä fof."*
nä   kayé   (.) miyatha   w\ko/nzath   oh
INDF yesterday (.) knowledgeable 2|3PL:SBJ>3SG.FEM:OBJ:PST:IPFV/become oh
budben mni \rä/   fof
2SG.LOC fire 3SG.FEM:SBJ:NPST:IPFV/be EMPH
'One day ... they found out about her. "Oh, so the fire is really with you."'
[tci20131008 KAB #10-11]

The verb *fiyoksi* 'make' can occur as a prototypical transitive verb without the "semantic assistance" of a predicative nominal. However, it commonly occurs as a light verb. In
example (63), we find two occurences of *fiyoksi*. The first token indexes *zrin* 'problem,
burden' (3SG.FEM) as its object argument, and *fiyoksi* can be translated as 'create'. The
second token of *fiyoksi* indexes the subject. In the latter, the predicative nominal *durua*
'help' contributes most of the semantic content of the predicate.

(63) *nzä nima "bone zrin rä bone nagayf **ane zrin zwafiyokwr** keke kwa monme
durua ŋafiyokwre*"
nzä   nima bone   zrin   \rä/   bone   nagay=f
1SG.ABS QUOT 2SG.POSS problem 3SG.FEM:SBJ:NPST:IPFV/be 2SG.POSS child=ERG.SG
ane zrin   zwa\fiyok/wr   keke kwa mon=me durua
DEM problem 2|3SG:SBJ>3SG.FEM:OBJ:RPST:IPFV/make NEG FUT how=INS help
ŋa\fiyok/wre
1PL:SBJ:NPST:IPFV/make
'I said: "This is your problem. Your child has created this problem. We will not
help."'
[tci20120922-24 STK #22]

Analogous to the other light verbs, *fiyoksi* can be used in a transitive structure. In
example (64), an infamous sorcerer is annoyed by a few other men. The main semantic
contribution to the event comes from the property noun *thythy* 'nuisance', while the
object indexed in the light verb is the sorcerer (3SG.MASC).

(64) *wati **thythy** zä zf **swafiyokwrmth**.*
wati thythy   zä   zf   swa\fiyok/wrmth
then nuisance PROX IMM 2|3PL:SBJ>3SG.MASC:OBJ:PST:DUR/make
'Then, they were annoying him here.'
[tci20131013ß02 ABB #59]

The two phasal verbs usually take nominalised verbs as their complements (§9.3.1), but
they can also be supplemented by property nouns with more event-oriented semantics.
Hence, they exhibit the same double life as full verbs and light verbs as *fiyoksi*. Two
examples of *thkäfsi* 'start' functioning as a light verb are given below. In (65), a man is
trying to enter the house in which two children are hiding. The phasal verb indexes the
two children, while the semantic content of the event comes solely from the property
noun *zirkn* 'persistence'.

(65) *wati zänfrefa yanyak* **nagayé** *kma n zirkn thrathkäf ... zirkn.*
wati zän\fref/a   yan\yak/   nagayé kma
then SG:SBJ:PST:PFV/come.up 3SG.MASC:SBJ:NPST:IPFV:VENT/walk children POT
n   zirkn   thra\thkäf/   (.) zirkn
IMN persistence 2|3SG:SBJ>2|3DU:OBJ:IRR:PFV/start (.) persistence
'Then, he came up from the river, he walked. He was about to start hassling the
two children ... hassling (them).'   [tci20100905 ABB #111]

In example (66), a malevolent spirit is trying to persuade a man to stay the night in
her house. Again, the property noun *garamgaram* 'sweet-talk' expresses most of the
semantics of the event.

(66) **garamgaram** *srethkäf.*
garamgaram sre\thkäf/
sweet.talk   2|3SG:SBJ>3SG.MASC:OBJ:IRR:PFV/start
'She started sweet-talking him.'   [tci20120901-01 MAK #88]

As I have shown above, light verbs (*rä-* 'do', *ko-* 'become', *fiyoksi* 'make', *thkäfsi* 'start'
and *bthaksi* 'finish') require semantic assistance from nominal predicates. However, nominal predicates can be found with other verbs, i.e. full verbs. In the following examples,
the concepts of 'being concentrated' (67) and 'being locked in' (68) are expressed by
the property nouns *mogu* 'concentration' and *ttw* 'inertia', respectively. Both meanings
could be expressed with light verbs, for example (67) could be expressed as *mogu ŋarä̈ré*
'I am concentrating' (lit. 'I am concentration-doing'). The two examples employ full verbs
instead, which should be understood as a more idiosyncratic way of speaking.

(67) *biskar mnifnzo* **mogu** *kwofkämgwrm*
biskar mni=f=nzo   mogu   kwof\kämg/wrm
cassava fire=ERG=ONLY concentration 2|3SG:SBJ>1SG:OBJ:PST:DUR/block
'Cooking the cassava took all my attention. (lit. 'Cassava cooking concentration
blocked me.')'   [tci20111119-03 ABB #79]

(68) **ttw** *zwermänth. wati fobo thufnzrmth*
ttw   zwe\rmän/th   wati fobo
inertia 2|3PL:SBJ>3SG.FEM:OBJ:ITER/close then DIST.ALL
thu\fn/nzrmth
2|3PL:SBJ>2|3PL:OBJ:PST:DUR/kill
'They always closed off (the village). Then, they were killing them.'
                                                     [tci20120818 ABB #46-47]

I point out in §3.2 that verbs are considered to be a closed word class in Komnzo. Part
of the argumentation is based on the observation that loanwords, which are verbs in
the donor language, commonly end up as property nouns in a light verb construction.
One such example was shown in (63) with the property noun *durua* 'help', which is
a transitive verb in Motu (Turner-Lister & Clark 1935: 61). Below, two examples with

English loans are given. In (69), the verb *fiyoksi* indexes the object *zokwasi* 'words' (2|3PL), while the loanword *senis* 'change' expresses most of the semantics (lit. 'I will not change-make the words'). In (70), the middle verb *rä-* 'do' is supplemented by the English loan *zek* 'check' (lit. 'I check-do for water').

(69) **zokwasi ke kwa senis thräfiyothé.**
    zokwasi keke kwa senis   thrä\fiyoth/é
    words   NEG FUT change 1SG:SBJ>2|3PL:OBJ:IRR:PFV/make
    'I will not change my promise.'   [tci20121019-04 ABB #226]

(70) *kränsöfthé mäbri ttfö … **nor bobo zek kräré** … keke*
    krän\rsöfth/é   mäbri ttfö (.) no=r   bobo   zek
    1SG:SBJ:IRR:PFV/descend mäbri creek (.) water=PURP MED.ALL check
    krä\r/é   (.) keke
    1SG:SBJ:IRR:PFV/do (.) NEG
    'I went down to the creek in Mäbri to check for water, but no (water).'
                              [tci20130903-03 MKW #146-147]

For situations of language contact, Heine and Kuteva describe how minor patterns in a language can become major patterns (2005: 44). It is clear that light verb constructions are not a minor pattern in Komnzo. However, it seems evident that with more (verb) loans entering the language, light verb constructions will become even more widely used.

8.4 Questions

Content questions in Komnzo are formed by replacing the respective noun phrase with an interrogative. Word order may or may not be changed for pragmatic purposes. As content questions are always pragmatically motivated, the element which is asked about is automatically focussed. Therefore, the interrogative is often found in fronted position, but fronting is not part of question formation. Example (71) shows an example with the interrogative *ra* 'what'.

(71) *nafafis zräs "be ranzo kayé thwanfiyokwr?"*
    nafa-fis   zrä\s/   be   ra=nzo
    3.POSS-husband 2|3SG:SBJ>3SG.FEM:OBJ:IRR:PFV/ask 2SG.ERG what=ONLY
    kayé   thwan\fiyok/wr
    yesterday 2|3SG:SBJ>2|3PL:OBJ:RPST:IPFV:VENT/make
    'Her husband asked her: "Just what have you done to them yesterday?"'
                              [tci20120901-01 MAK #163]

Example (72) shows an example where the interrogative occurs inside a complex noun phrase 'whose sister'. Note that the noun phrase which contains the interrogative has been fronted for pragmatic reasons. This is an example of a rhetorical question, because it came up in a discussion about the type of punitive actions one would launch against one's brothers-in-law.

(72) *"mafane emoth be zufnzrm?" nima fof skonzé*
maf=ane emoth be   zu\fn/nzrm   nima fof
who=POSS sister 2SG.ERG 2|3SG:SBJ>3SG.FEM:OBJ:PST:DUR/hit QUOT EMPH
s\ko/nzé
2SG:SBJ>3SG.MASC:OBJ:IMP:IPFV/speak
"'Whose sister were you beating?" that is what you must say to him.'
[tci20120805-01 ABB #219]

Polar questions are often structurally identical to indicative statements but they have a rising intonation contour, as in (73) and (74). Additionally the iamitive particle *z* 'already' can be used even though the verb is in the non-past (73).

(73) *zbär bä zagrwä ämnzro. z wanrizrth?*
zbär bä   zagr=wä ä\m/nzro   z
night 2.ABS far=EMPH 2|3PL:SBJ:NPST:IPFV:AND/sit ALR
wan\riz/rth
2|3PL:SBJ>1SG.IO:NPST:IPFV:VENT/hear
'You are sitting far away. Can you hear me?' (lit. 'You hear my (words) already?')
[tci20121019-04 SKK #9]

(74) *ane wri kambeyé kma n yrärth "kwa kräznobe?" naf ekonzr "keke"*
ane wri   kambe=yé   kma n y\rä/rth
DEM intoxication man=ERG.NSG POT IMN 2|3PL:SBJ>3SG.MASC:OBJ:NPST:IPFV/do
kwa krä\znob/e   naf e\ko/nzr   keke
FUT 1PL:SBJ:IRR:PFV/drink 3SG.ERG 2|3SG:SBJ>2|3PL:OBJ:NPST:IPFV/speak NEG
'These drunkards are trying (to convince him): "Will we drink?" He says to them "No"'
[tci20111004 RMA #509]

Alternative questions are formed by a disjunctive coordination with *o* 'or'. In (75), the alternatives are expressed by two clauses, and in (76) by two noun phrases.

(75) *fam kwarärmth "kwa ywokrakwr o kwa ŋabrüzr?"*
fam   kwa\rä/rmth   kwa y\wokrak/wr   o kwa
thought 2|3PL:SBJ:PST:DUR/do FUT 3SG.MASC:SBJ:NPST:IPFV/float or FUT
ŋa\brüz/r
2|3SG:SBJ:NPST:IPFV/submerge
'They were thinking: "Will it float or will it sink?"'   [tci20120929-02 SIK #31]

(76) *zokwasi fefeme natrikwé o markai zokwasime?*
zokwasi fefe=me na\trik/wé   o markai   zokwasi=me
language real=INS 1SG:SBJ>2SG:IO:NPST:IPFV/tell or white man language=INS
'Will I tell you (the story) in Komnzo or in English?' (lit. '... in the real language or the white man's language?')   [tci20120901-01 MAK #1]

Question tags like *o keke* 'or not' can be added, which also receive a rising intonation.

(77) *kwa nm weto worär o keke?*
kwa nm   weto wo\rä/r   o keke
FUT maybe joy 2|3SG:SBJ>1SG:OBJ:NPST:IPFV/do or NEG
'Maybe he will be happy towards me or not?'   [tci20111004 RMA #477]

8.5 Negation

At the clause level, negation is expressed periphrastically with the negator *keke* in pre-verbal position, as in example (78). See §3.4.1 for more information on *keke* and its variant *kyo*.

(78) *nafanme emoth keke kränrit nzedbo.*
nafanme emoth keke krän\rit/   nzedbo
3PL.POSS girl NEG 2|3SG:SBJ:IRR:PFV:VENT/cross.over 1NSG.ALL
'They will not exchange sisters with us.'   [tci20120814 ABB #319]

One exception is the prohibitive construction (§6.3.2). This construction consists of the potential particle *kma*, the apprehensive clitic *m=*, and the verb in the imperative. The apprehensive clitic may attach either to the verb or to the potential particle. This construction is best translated into English as 'must not' as can be seen in example (79). Note that the negator cannot be included in this construction.

(79) *nznäbrimath "bä kmam thiyaké! kafarnzo ni nyak!".*
nznä\brim/ath   bä   kma=m thi\yak/é
2|3SG:SBJ>1PL:OBJ:PST:PFV/return 2.ABS POT=APPR 2PL:SBJ:IMP:IPFV/walk
kafar=nzo ni n\yak/
big=ONLY 1NSG 1PL:SBJ:NPST:IPFV/walk
'They brought us back and said: "You must not go! Only us big ones will go."'
                                  [tci20120904-02 MAB #232-233]

Negation at the level of the constituent can be expressed in a number of ways. The word *matak* 'nothing' is used to express non-existence, usually in a copula clause. This is shown in example (80) where a man takes notice that he is alone in the village. *Matak* can also be used in a non-verb predication, for example *nge matak* '(there were) no children'. Alternatively, any noun phrase can be negated by using the privative case marker *=mär*. This is described in §4.14.

(80) *kabe matak erä nima z bramöwä kwafarkwrth.*
kabe   matak e\rä/   nima z bramöwä
people nothing 2|3PL:SBJ:NPST:IPFV:COP like.this ALR all
kwa\fark/wrth
2|3PL:SBJ:RPST:IPFV/set.off
'There are no people (here). All of them have already left.' [tci20120901-01 MAK #77]

Negative indefinites expressing 'none whatsoever' or 'nothing at all' are constructed by adding the negator *keke* to a noun phrase that includes the indefinite marker *nä*. For example, *nä kabe* means 'some man' or 'someone', but *kabe nä keke* means 'nobody at all'. Note that the indefinite is always postposed in this construction. The same can be achieved by adding *nä* to an interrogative, as in (81). I describe this topic in more detail in §3.1.11.

(81)   *keke kwa ra nä zränzinth.*
       keke kwa ra   nä   zrän\zin/th
       NEG FUT what INDF 2|3PL:SBJ>3SG.FEM:IO:IRR:PFV:VENT/put.down
       'They will leave nothing for her.'   [tci20131004 RMA #9]

9 Complex syntax

9.1 Introduction

This section describes the combination of two or more predicates. There are three parameters involving the coding of complex clauses. The first parameter is the verb inflection. Are both predicates fully inflected or is one of them nominalised? The second parameter is the way, how an interclausal relationship between two fully inflected predicates is marked. This often involves demonstratives marked for case. The third parameter are syntactic restrictions in one of the two clauses. These parameters allow us to decide whether a particular clause combination should be analysed as coordination or subordination. Note that the first parameter supersedes the other two, in that nominalised predicates are always analysed as subordinate clauses, and the other two parameters do not apply. Only if two clauses contain inflected verbs, these two parameters help to identify the relationship between them. For example, relative clauses are structurally similar to content questions, but they differ in two points. First, they are usually headed by the relativised element, which is in some sense the answer to the question posed by the relative clause. Secondly, relative clauses have a more rigid structure than questions. Hence, they are analysed as a type of subordination. On the other hand, complements of knowledge consist of one clause with a predicative nominal (*miyatha* 'knowledge') and the copula. The epistemic content can be expressed by a separate clause, which shows no syntactic dependency to the first. It follows that in some cases these parameters fail and only semantic criteria can be applied.

I want to give a few examples, to show that there is a cline of syntactic integration between two clauses. Givón provides a functional explanation to the various degrees of syntactic integration: "the stronger the semantic bond between two events, the more extensive will be the syntactic integration of the two clauses into a single though complex clause" (2001: 41). As we will see, Komnzo supports this observation to some extent. I choose the domain of 'cause' to illustrate this below. The clearest way to mark a causer is by putting the element in the ergative case. In Komnzo nominalised verbs can be used in this way (1). In the example, a Marind headhunter tries to distract his victims by imitating the sound that dogs make when chewing bones, but he ends up only distracting himself. The phrase *ane wäsifnzo* 'only that cracking' functions as a clausal subject. The event 'crack' and the event 'close' are tightly integrated. They occur simultaneously and they stand in direct causal relation.

(1) *bäne thuwänzrm fof … zarfa surmänwrm **ane wäsifnzo**.*
      bäne   thu\wä\nzrm   fof (.) zarfa
      DEM:MED 2|3SG:SBJ>2|3PL:OBJ:PST:DUR/crack fof (.) ear

su\rmän/wrm   ane wä-si=f=nzo
2|3SG:SBJ>3SG.MASC:OBJ:PST:DUR/close DEM crack-NMLZ=ERG=ONLY
'He was cracking those (coconut shells) ... This cracking was blocking his ears.'

[tci20120818 ABB #67-68]

The characteristic case is used for adverbial adjuncts marking origin and cause. In example (2), *mni frazsi* functions as an adverbial clause. The predicate 'be weak' and the event 'extinguish' occurred at different times, but they stand in a causal relation.

(2) *komnzo tayo zwrä **mni frazsima**.*
     komnzo tayo z=wo\rä/   mni fraz-si=ma
     only   weak PROX=1SG:SBJ:NPST:IPFV/be fire extinguish-NMLZ=CHAR
     'I am just weak here from extinguishing the fire.'   [tci20120922-24 STL #21]

Komnzo has a recognitional demonstrative pronoun, which can function in a number of ways (§3.1.12.6). It is frequently used in 'tip-of-the-tongue' situations. Example (3) explains why a particular woman in Rouku grew very old, while her friends and some of her children have passed away already. The structure is the same as (2). The only difference is that the speaker uses the recognitional inflected with the characteristic case ('because of that one'). After a short pause, he fills in the referent *rirksima* 'because she respected'. The event 'survive' (lit. 'jump') and the event 'respect' occurred in different times, but they stand in a causal relation.

(3) *watik, fi komnzo zathfär **bänema** fof ... nima **rirksima** brä.*
     watik fi   komnzo za\thfär/   bäne=ma   fof (.) nima
     then 3.ABS only   3SG.FEM:SBJ:RPST:PFV/junp RECOG=CHAR EMPH (.) like.this
     rirk-si=ma   b=\rä/
     respect-NMLZ=CHAR MED=3SG.FEM:SBJ:NPST:IPFV/be
     'Well, she just lived on because of that ... because respected (the taboos). There
     she is.'   [tci20120922-26 DAK #22-23]

In discourse, the use of the recognitional creates some kind of expectation that something should follow. This something can remain empty, for example when the referent is common ground between the speaker and the addressee, but it can also be 'filled in' (3). This latent expectation explains why the recognitional is employed to introduce another clause (4). The function of that clause is determined by the case marker on the recognitional. In (4) it is the characteristic case, and consequently the function of the following clause is to mark a reason, in other words *bänema* can be translated with 'because'. The event in the first clause 'exit' and the event in the second clause 'close' stand in a causal relationship. However, the causal chain of events involves a number of steps.

(4) *keke kwamätrakwrm **bänema** ... **fam** z zwärmänth.*
     keke kwa\mätrak/wrm bäne=ma   (.) fam   z
     NEG SG:SBJ:PST:DUR/exit RECOG=CHAR (.) thought ALR

zwä\rmän/th
2|3SG:SBJ>3SG:.FEM:OBJ:RPST:PFV/close
'She did not come outside because they had already closed her thoughts (with
magic).'   [tci20120901-01 MAK #148-149]

Lastly, I want to contrast the use of the recognitional from other demonstratives. Consider example (5), which includes the general demonstrative *ane* in the characteristic case
in the second clause. The demonstrative *ane* functions anaphorically, and in that sense
it is the mirror image of the recognitional. The events 'disturb' and 'submerge' stand in
a causal relationship, but the components are reversed. We can translate it to English
with 'therefore' or 'that's why'. The two clauses are otherwise independent. This is also
supported by the paragraph marker *watik* 'well, then' which occurs at the beginning of
the second clause, but this is optional.

(5)   *ane ŋatha bä nzwathofikwr ... watik **anema** nzibrüzé bobo.*
      ane   ŋatha bä   nzwa\thofik/wr   (.) watik ane=ma
      DEM dog   MED 2|3SG:SBJ>1SG:OBJ:RPST:IPFV/disturb (.) then   DEM=CHAR
      nz=ybrüzé   bobo
      IPST=1SG:SBJ>2|3SG.MASC:OBJ:NPST:IPFV/submerge MED.ALL
      'That dog disturbed me there. Well, that's why I pushed him into the water.'
                                                                    [tci20130903-03 MKW #188]

The examples illustrate, that there is a cline between syntactically integrated clauses,
i.e. subordinated clauses, and independent clauses. While both ends of the cline are relatively easy to identify, the middle is a grey zone. It is clear that examples like (5) consists
of two independent clauses. Likewise, the nominalised predicates in (1 - 3) are clear cases
of subordination. But examples like (4) are somewhat indeterminate. On the one hand,
the recognitional pronoun creates a gap that needs to be filled. In other words, semantically, the second clause is subordinated to the first clause. On the other hand, the second
clause is syntactically independent. Therefore, I refrain from analysing the recognitional
as a subordinator, but rather as having a connecting function.[1]

The following description is functionally motivated, that is subsections are sorted the-
matically. For example, a subsection on purposive clauses will include clear cases of
subordination, but also constructions where the purpose is expressed in an independent
clause connected with the recognitional. I will describe coordinated clauses (§9.2), complement clauses (§9.3), adverbial clauses (§9.4), relative clauses (§9.5), conditional and
temporal clauses (§9.6) and direct speech and thought (§9.7).

9.2 Coordinated clauses

Coordination refers to syntactic constructions where two or more elements of equal
status are connected (Haspelmath 2007). Komnzo employs the same mechanisms for

---

[1]Note that the recognitional demonstrative can be inflected for following cases: characteristic *=ma* 'because',
instrumental *=me* 'thereby' and purposive *=mr* 'in order to, until'.

coordinating noun phrases as it does for coordinating clauses. The word *a* 'and' can be used for conjunctive coordination (6) and the word *o* 'or' can be used for disjunctive coordination (7).

(6) *mni wthomonwath a zräföfth.*
 mni w\thomon/wath   a
 fire 2|3PL:SBJ>3SG.FEM:PST:PST:IPFV/prepare.fire and
 zrä\föf/th
 2|3PL:SBJ>3SG.FEM:IRR:PFV/burn
 'They piled the fire and burn it.'   [tci20120901-01 MAK #155]

(7) *nafaŋamaf wnfathwr o ynfathwr.*
 nafa-ŋame=f   wn\fath/wr   o
 3.POSS-mother=ERG.SG 2|3SG:SBJ>3SG.FEM:OBJ:NPST:VENT/hold or
 yn\fath/wr
 2|3SG:SBJ>3SG.MASC:OBJ:NPST:VENT/hold
 '(The child's) mother holds her or holds him.'   [tci20111004 RMA #327-328]

For conjunctive coordination it is quite common to have no overt marker (8). Especially in sequences of events, two or more inflected verbs can follow each other. Example (8) describes the felling of a sago palm.

(8) *wati yfarwake … sabthake … safümnzake fof.*
 wati y\far/wake   (.) sa\bth/ake   (.)
 then 1PL:SBJ>3SG.MASC:PST:IPFV/chop (.) 1PL:SBJ>3SG.MASC:PST:PFV/finish (.)
 sa\fümnz/ake   fof
 1PL:SBJ>3SG.MASC:PST:PFV/pull.over EMPH
 'Then we chopped it (and) finished it (and) pulled it over.' [tci20120929-02 SIK #19-21]

Other ways of coordinating two clauses involve the manner demonstrative *nima* 'like this', which is commonly used to introduce direct speech (§9.7). In example (9), *nima* indicates the manner of movement (accompanied by an appropriate gesture), but it also connects the two following clauses.

(9) *nabi tutin fä fof zumirwanzrm füsfüsf … nima zfzänzrm fobo … nima zfzänzrm.*
 nabi   tuti=n fä fof zu\mirwa/nzrm   füsfüs=f
 bamboo branch=LOC DIST EMPH 2|3SG:SBJ>3SG.FEM:OBJ:PST:DUR/swing wind=ERG
 (.) nima zf\zä/nzrm   fobo (.) nima
 (.) like.this 2|3SG:SBJ>3SG.FEM:OBJ:PST:DUR/carry DIST.ALL (.) like.this
 zf\zä/nzrm
 2|3SG:SBJ>3SG.FEM:OBJ:PST:DUR/carry
 'The wind was swinging (the lamp) on the bamboo (and) it was moving it there (and) it was moving it here.'   [tci20111119-03 ABB #117-118]

9.3 Complement clauses

9.3.1 Phasal verbs

The most common complement taking predicates in Komnzo are the two phasal verbs *thkäfksi* 'start' and *bthaksi* 'finish'. Other verbs show similar behaviour, for example *gathiksi* 'stop, leave', *mäyogsi* 'continue, repeat'.

With phasal verbs, the indexation structure from the nominalised verb is raised into the matrix clause. The values of those categories expressed in the verb form are marked on the phasal verb. This may include number, person and gender of the arguments, but also tense, aspect, mood and direction. Example (10) shows the 'non-phasal' clause *bad wtharinzake* 'we were digging the ground'. The verb indexes the actor (1PL) and the undergoer *bad* 'ground' (3SG.FEM). In the first clause of the example, the same state of affairs is expressed, but the verb 'dig' occurs in its infinitive *tharisi*, and its argument structure is raised into the phasal verb *thkäfksi* 'start'. Now it is the phasal verb which indexes a first plural actor and a third singular feminine undergoer.

(10) *watik bad fof tharisi zathkäfake ... bad wtharinzake zabthake.*
watik bad   fof   thari-si   za\thkäf/ake   (.) bad
then   ground EMPH dig-NMLZ 1PL:SBJ>3SG.FEM:OBJ:PST:PFV/start (.) ground
w\thari/nzake   za\bth/ake
1PL:SBJ>3SG.FEM:OBJ:PST:IPFV/dig 1PL:SBJ>3SG.FEM:OBJ:PST:PFV/start
'Then we started to dig the ground. We were digging the ground and finished it.'
[tci20120929-02 SIK #72-73]

This is also found with ditransitive events, as in (11). The verb *thkäfksi* 'start' indexes the indirect object. Note that the dative noun phrase is omitted.

(11) *wri no n säthkäfath yarisi.*
wri   no   n   sä\thkäf/ath   yari-si
drunk water IMN 2|3PL:SBJ>3SG.MASC:IO:PST:PFV/start give-NMLZ
'They were about to give him alcohol.'   [tci20120925 MAE #158]

Verbs in the middle template also raise their respective indexation into the phasal verb. The middle template can be used with several functions (§5.4.5). Example (12) shows the verb *yonasi* 'drink', which always occurs in a middle template. In the example, *yonasi* occurs in the infinitive. Consequently, the phasal verb takes over this indexing pattern and only encodes the subject, but not the object.

(12) *nä kayé ... watik yonasi zethkäfa.*
nä   kayé (.) watik yona-si   ze\thkä/fa
some day (.) then   drink-NMLZ SG:SBJ:PST:PFV/start
'One day, he started to drink.'   [tci20120925 MAE #83]

In example (13), the prefixing verb *msaksi* 'sit, dwell' is used in its infinitive. Since, the phasal verb *thkäfksi* 'start' cannot enter the prefixing template, the middle template is used instead. As I describe in §5.4.4, the prefixing template is a minor pattern in Komnzo and most intransitive verbs are encoded using the middle template. Furthermore, the prefixing template usually has stative semantics.

(13) *wati foba msaksi fefe zathkäfake.*
      wati foba   msak-si   fefe   za\thkäf/ake
      then DIST.ABL dwell-NMLZ really 1DU:SBJ:PST:PFV/start
      'From there, we began our married life.' (lit. 'We began dwelling.')

                                                         [tci20130823-08 WAM #47]

Example (14) shows that for the middle verb *yak* 'run', the phasal verb takes over the indexation.[2] Note that the directional value (VENT) is also raised into the phasal verb.

(14) *kabe ane zenthkäfath yak.*
      kabe ane zen\thkäf/ath   yak
      man DEM 2|3PL:SBJ:PST:PFV:VENT/start run
      'The people started to run here.'   [tci20131013-01 ABB #91]

9.3.2 Complements of knowledge

Complements of knowledge are structured differently from phasal complements. They involve a property noun with predicative function plus the copula to form a predicate of knowledge (*miyatha* 'knowledge(-able)') or ignorance (*miyamr* 'ignorant/ignorance'). Note that the latter has probably developed from a more overt marking that involved the privative case marker *=mär*. The acquisition of knowledge is expressed by the property noun *miyatha* plus the light verb *ko-* 'become'. The epistemic content of these predicates of knowledge and ignorance – what is known or not known – can be expressed by a number of different strategies. Examples (15) and (16) show complements in which a nominalised verb form in the absolutive is added. In (15), the nominalised verb constitutes the head of a compound 'coconut climbing'.

(15) *nzä miyatha worä ŋazi sogsi.*
      nzä   miyatha   wo\rä/   ŋazi   sog-si
      1SG.ABS knowledge 1SG:SBJ:NPST:IPFV/be coconut climb-NMLZ
      'I know how to climbing coconut.' (lit. 'I am knowledgeable (about) coconut climbing')   [overheard]

The predicate of knowledge construction (*miyatha/miyamr* plus copula) is a frequent collocation. Therefore, it is possible to drop the copula altogether, as in (15).

---

[2]This verb is irregular: instead of a nominalised infinitive with *-si*, the third singular masculine form *yak* is used. However, *yak* is the third singular of 'walk' and not of 'run'. This would be *ŋakwir*. Thus, 'walk' employs the noun *moth* 'path, way' as its nominalisation and 'run' employs *yak*.

(16) *bäne ruga yfränzre ... afa fi miyamr ykwasi ... nzefénzo.*
bäne   ruga y\frä/nzre   (.) afa   fi   miyamr
DEM:MED pig   1PL:SBJ>3SG.MASC:NPST:IPFV/singe.off (.) father 3.ABS ignorance
ykwa-si   (.) nzefé=nzo
cut.meat-NMLZ (.) 1SG.ERG.EMPH=ONLY
'We burn the hair off that pig ... father doesn't know how to cut it ... only I
(know).'   [tci20120821-02 LNA #61-62]

As described in §4.12, the characteristic case can express a topic of conversation. Example (17) shows that the epistemic content can also be marked with the characteristic
case.

(17) *zf wthkärwé zokwasi nzä monme miyatha worä no kzima.*
zf   w\thkär/wé   zokwasi nzä   mon=me miyatha
IMM 1SG:SBJ>3SG.FEM:OBJ:NPST:IPFV/start speech 1SG.ABS how=INS knowledge
wo\rä/   no kzi=ma
1SG:SBJ:NPST:IPFV/be rain barktray=CHAR
'I will start the story how I know about the rain making (magic).'
                                                      [tci20110810-01 MAB #8]

The epistemic content can be expressed as a relative clause, which takes the predicate
of knowledge as its head, as in example (18).

(18) *bä z miyatha erä maf n zwämg?*
bä   z   miyatha e\rä/   maf   n
2.ABS ALR knowledge 2|3PL:SBJ:NPST:IPFV/be who.ERG IMN
zwä\mg/
2|3SG:SBJ>1SG:OBJ:RPST:PFV/shoot
'Do you know who almost shot me?'   [tci20130927-06 MAB #37]

The epistemic content can also be expressed in an independent clause, connected, for
example, with *nima* 'like this' (19). The use of *nima* in this example can also be analysed
as quoting inner thought (§9.7).

(19) *fi miyamr sfrärm nima fi zbo ern.*
fi   miyamr sf\rä/rm   nima   fi   zbo
3.ABS ignorance 3SG.MASC:SBJPST:DUR/be like.this 3.ABS PROX.ALL
e\rn/
2|3DU:SBJ:NPST:IPFV/be
'He did not know those two here.'   [tci20130927-06 MAB #123]

The acquisition of knowledge is expressed by replacing the copula with the light verb
ko- 'become'. Example (20) is taken from a text about a punitive custom, whereby the
perpetrator is humiliated by being given a large amount of yams, which he is expected
to pay back the following year. The epistemic content is expressed by a relative clause.

(20) *"miyatha käkor bä monwä zbrigwé bä ra nrä? daw kabe?" nima kwakonzrmth.*

miyatha	kä\kor/		bä	mon=wä

miyatha kä\kor/ bä mon=wä
knowledge 2SG:SBJ:IMP:PFV/become 2.ABS how=EMPH
z\brig/wé bä ra n\rä/ daw
2SG:SBJ>3SG.FEM:SBJ:IMP:IPFV/return 2.ABS what 2SG:SBJ:NPST:IPFV/be garden
kabe nima kwa\ko/nzrmth
man QUOT 2|3PL:SBJ:PST:DUR/say

"'You see how you pay this back! What are you? A gardener?" that is what they were saying.' [tci20120805-01 ABB #241]

Note that the phrase *miyatha käkor!* can be purely epistemic "(Now) you know it!" or it can express an experiential sensation "(Now) you feel it!".

9.3.3 Complements of desire

Much of what has been said about complements of knowledge, can be said about complements of desire. The property noun *miyo* 'desire' is used for this.[3] It can be negated with the privative case =*mär*: *miyomär*. Again, a property noun plus copula construction expresses the concept of 'want, wish or hope': *ra miyo erä?* 'What do you want' (lit. 'What desire you are?'). The clause encoding the desired (or undesired) can be expressed in a variety of ways. Example (21) shows a nominalised verb *mgthksi* 'feed' in the absolutive. The verb is heading a compound 'pig feeding'.

(21) *zena keke miyo worä ruga mgthksi ... znsä ttüfr.*

zena keke miyo wo\rä/ ruga mgthk-si (.) znsä t-tüfr
today NEG desire 1SG:SBJ:NPST:IPFV/be pig feed-NMLZ (.) work REDUP-plenty
'Today, I do not want to feed pigs ... too much work.' (lit. 'I am not desirous for pig feeding') [tci20120805-01 ABB #819-820]

In example (22), the word *zokwasi* is used as a nominalisation 'speaking'.

(22) *keke zokwasi miyo nzä worärm yoganai worärm.*

keke zokwasi miyo nzä wo\rä/rm yoganai wo\rä/rm
NEG speech desire 1SG.ABS 1SG:SBJ:RPST:DUR/be tired 1SG:SBJ:RPST:DUR/be
'I did not want to talk. I was tired.' [tci20120922-24 MAA #78]

The property noun *miyo* can also be used without the copula, as in (23).

(23) *frzsi miyomäre fthé kafara znfonzo kerafith thämther. sayäfianme rifthzsi fath zn rä.*

frz-si miyo=märe fthé kafara zn=fo=nzo
net-NMLZ desire=PRIV when river pandanus place=ALL=ONLY

---

[3]Note that *miyo* can also be a noun meaning 'wish' and 'taste'.

ke\rafith/   thä\mther/   sayäfi=anme
2SG:SBJ:IMP:PFV/paddle 2SG:SBJ>2|3PL:OBJ:IMP:PFV/lift.up river.crayfish=POSS.NSG
rifthz-si   fath   zn   \rä/
hide-NMLZ place place 3SG.FEM:SBJ:NPST:IPFV/be
'If you don't want to catch by net, you can paddle to the river pandanus and lift
up (the leaves). It is crayfish's hiding place.'   [tci20130907-02 RNA #450-451]

The desired proposition can also be expressed in an independent clause which is only
semantically connected to the desiderative proposition. In example (24), a man threatens
a young boy who shot an arrow at him.

(24)   *zbo z fefe saththma "nzä fthé miyo kwrarä zena zf mr kwa nwänzé."*
     zbo   z   fefe   sa\ththm/a   nzä   fthé   miyo
     PROX.ALL IMM really 2|3SG:SBJ>3SG,MASC:IO:PST:PFV/stick.on 1SG.ABS when desire
     kwra\rä/   zena zf mr   kwa n\wä/nzé
     1SG:SBJ:IRR:IPFV/be today IMM neck FUT 1SG:SBJ>2SG:OBJ:NPST:IPFV/crack
     'He stuck (the gun) right at him (saying): "If I wanted I could breack your neck
     right here and now."'   [tci20130927-06 MAB #45]

9.4 Adverbial clauses

Adverbial clauses show a wide range of possible constructions. These range from infinitival adjuncts to independent clauses. In the following section, purposive, temporal and
manner adverbial clauses are described. Note that the domain of cause was used to introduce the reader to the various levels of syntactic intregration of two clauses. Therefore,
I will not discuss this domain here, but refer to §9.1.

9.4.1 Purposive adverbials

Purposive adverbials are found in different construction. Example (25) is from a procedural about making a drum. The speaker explains how a bamboo ring will hold the
membrane in place after it is glued to the drum.

(25)   *nabi riwariwa kwa wäfiyokwre ... **narsir fof.***
     nabi   riwariwa kwa wä\fiyok/wre   (.)
     bamboo ring   FUT 1PL:SBJ>3SG.FEM:NPST:IPFV/make (.)
     nar-si=r   fof
     press.down-NMLZ=PURP EMPH
     'We make a bamboo ring ... for pressing down (the membrane).'
                                             [tci20120824 KAA #87-88]

In example (26), the speaker shows me a particular tree used for poison-root fishing.
The example shows that the purposive clause can take an object by forming a compound
'for swamp poisoning' > 'to poison the swamp'. Note that the recognitional pronoun is
used just before the nominalised verb.

(26) *nä kayé zane zf yirwre **bänemr** ... zra rsrsir.*
nä   kayé zane   zf   y\r/wre   bänemr   (.)
INDF day DEM:PROX IMM 1PL:SBJ>3SG.MASC:OBJ:NPST:IPFV/scrape RECOG.PURP (.)
zra   rsr-si=r
swamp poison.fishing-NMLZ=PURP
'Sometimes, we scrape (the root of) this one here for poisoning the waterholes.'

[tci20130907-02 RNA #340]

Purposive clauses can also be less syntactically integrated and form an independent
clause. In this case, they are usually introduced by the recognitional flagged with purposive case *bänemr*, which I translate with 'in order to'. Example (27) describes a tall
structure used to show off the amount of a group's yams harvest. This structure involved
a long post around which many layers of yam tubers were tied with thick rope.

(27) *wati far ane thden sfräzrmth **bänemr kwim ŋadme sfmthzgwrmth**.*
wati far   ane   thd=en   sf\räz/rmth   bänemr
then post DEM middle=LOC 2|3PL:SBJ>3SG.MASC:OBJ:PST:DUR/erect RECOG.PURP
kwim ŋad=me sf\mthzg/wrmth
kwim rope=INS 2|3PL:SBJ>3SG.MASC:OBJ:PST:DUR/encircle
'Then, they were erecting a post in the middle in order to wrap around the kwim
(Acacia mangium) rope.'

[tci20120805-01 ABB #463]

9.4.2 Temporal adverbials

Temporal adverbials are found in a number of constructions. Example (28) shows the
locative case attached to a nominalised verb. The clause *ane yam fiyoksin* 'doing that' is
therefore subordinated to the matrix clause. The relation between the two clauses is one
of simultaneity.

(28) *bäne zrazänzr ... fenz kzikaf ... mä ke kwa kabef sremar **ane yam fiyoksin**.*
bäne   zra\zä/nzr   (.) fenz   kzi=kaf   (.)
RECOG.ABS 2|3SG:SBJ>3SG.FEM:OBJ:IRR:IPFV/carry (.) body liquid barktray=PROP (.)
mä   keke kwa kabe=f   sre\mar/   ane yam
where NEG FUT man=ERG.SG 2|3SG:SBJ>3SG.MASC:OBJ:IRR:PFV/see DEM event
fiyok-si=n
make-NMLZ=LOC
'He will carry that one ... the body liquid with the barktray ... where no man will
see him while doing that.'

[tci20130903-04 RNA #49-52]

In order to connecting more independent clauses, the word *fthé* 'if, when' is used. This
is further described in §9.6 together with conditional clause. A close temporal connection
between the two clauses can be established by the word *fthémäsü* 'meanwhile, during'.
The words *fthé* and *fthémäsü* are historically related, but the etymology of the *mäsü* part
is unclear. In example (29), the speaker talks about a particular tree which flowers during

the planting season. Note that the first and last clause contain *fthé* and the middle clause contains *fthémäsü*: 'when X, while Y, that is when Z'.

(29) *efthar fthé kräkor minzü ... **fthémäsü wawa worsi threthkäfth** ... nzram fthé fof kwa ŋarär.*

efthar	fthé	krä\kor/		minzü (.)	fthémäsü	wawa
dry season	when	2|3SG:SBJ:IRR:PFV/become		very (.)	meanwhile	yam

wor-si	thre\thkäf/th		(.) nzram	fthé	fof	kwa
plant-NMLZ	2|3PL:SBJ>2|3PL:OBJ:IRR:PFV/start		(.) flower	when	EMPH	FUT

ŋa\rä/r
2|3SG:SBJ:NPST:IPFV/do

'When it reaches the height of the dry season ... while they are starting to plant the yams ... that is when this one will flower.' [tci20130907-02 JAA #220-221]

Fthémäsü is not a subordinator because it can be used on independent clauses with the translation 'in the meantime'. In example (30), the speaker explains that after his father's death, the stones for rain-making were lost.

(30) ***nzenme ŋafe fthémäsü kwosi yara** ... watik foba ni miyamr nrä mafadben zena ethn.*

nzenme	ŋafe	fthémäsü	kwosi	ya\r/a		(.) watik	foba
1NSG.POSS	father	meanwhile	dead	3SG.MASC:SBJ:PST:IPFV/be		(.) then	DIST.ABL

ni	miyamr	n\rä/		mafa=dben	zena
1NSG	ignorance	1PL:SBJ:NPST:IPFV/be		who=LOC.ANIM.SG	today

e\thn/
2|3PL:SBJ:NPST:IPFV/lie.down

'In the meantime our father died ... and from then one we don't know with whom (the rain stones) are today.' [tci20131013-01 ABB #399]

A third strategy to connect a clause temporally is by using the recognitional inflected with the locative case *bafen*. But this is an infrequent strategy because (i) the temporal function is an extension of the locative case and (ii) connecting clauses is only one function of the recognitional. Example (31) is about two men from Rouku who used to work on the Fly River. They run into another man from Rouku, who has been away for a long time. The recognitional occurs twice. First, is it coreferential with holiday: 'in that time ... during the holidays'. The second use is difficult to analyse because this is also a temporal/conditional construction, but one can assume that *bafen* introduces the second clause.

(31) *fthé nima bafen kabrigrnoth holidayen **bafen fefe katrife "fi bobo yé!"***

fthé	nima	baf=en	ka\brig/rnoth		holiday=en	baf=en
when	like.this	RECOG=LOC	DU:SBJ:IMP:IPFV:AND/return		holiday=LOC	RECOG=LOC

fefe	ka\trif/e		fi	bobo	\yé/
really	2DU:SBJ:IMP:PFV/tell		3.ABS	MED.ALL	3SG.MASC:SBJ:NPST:IPFV/be

'When you return in the holidays, then you have say: "He is there!"'
[tci20130927-06 MAB #206]

9.4.3 Manner adverbials

The proprietive and instrumental case on a nominalised verb can be used to express a manner adverbial clause. In the functional extension, the two case markers can also express a relation of association and temporal overlaps respectively. Hence, the nominalised verb flagged with the proprietive case in example (32) can be translated as 'He held hips while rejoicing' or 'He held hips rejoicingly.'

(32) **thweksikarä** gon z zefaf.
      thwek-si=karä   gon z   ze\faf/
      rejoice-NMLZ=PROP hip ALR 2|3SG:SBJ:RPST:PFV/hold
      'He held hips while rejoicing' or 'He held hips rejoicingly.'   [tci20111004 RMA #174]

The recognitional case also serves to introduce a clause which expresses a manner (or temporal association). In example (33), the speaker explains how he and his friends were loading a heavy sago stem on a canoe. Some people from Morehead Station were sceptical about this plan. Thus, *bäneme thfkogrm* 'They were standing with/like this' connects to the following clause which expresses 'They stood thinking ...'.

(33) *nä station kabe fä zämosirath* **bäneme** *thfkogrm ...* **fam kwarärmth "kwa**
      ywokrakwr o kwa ŋabrüzr?"
      nä   station kabe fä   zä\mosir/ath   bäne=me
      INDF station man DIST 2|3PL:SBJ:PST:PFV/gather RECOG=INS
      thf\kogr/m   (.) fam   kwa\rä/rmth   kwa
      2|3PL:SBJ:PST:DUR/stand (.) thought 2|3PL:SBJ:PST:DUR/do FUT
      y\wokrak/wr   o   kwa ŋa\brüz/r
      3SG.MASC:SBJ:NPST:IPFV/float or FUT 2|3SG:SBJ:NPST:IPFV/submerge
      'Some station people gathered there. They were standing thinking: "Will it float or will it sink?"'   [tci20120929-02 SIK #30-31]

The most common way to encode a manner adverbial is by a relative clause with *mon* or *monme* 'how' (§9.5). Example (34) is taken from a picture task, where the participants were asked to arrange picture cards into a story. In the example, the speaker explains the task to a bystander. Note that the recognitional *bäneme* 'with this, in this way' also appears in the first clause. The second recognitional *bäne* refers to *trikasi* 'story' as we can see in the last clause.

(34) *zena ane bäneme nzezinakwre* **monme bäne wyak brä ...** *trikasi monme kma*
      zrarä.
      zena ane bäne=me   nz=e\zinak/wre   mon=me
      now DEM RECOG=INS IPST=1PL:SBJ>2|3PL:OBJ:NPST:IPFV/put.down how=INS
      bäne   w\yak/   b=\rä/   (.)
      RECOG.ABS 3SG.FEM:SBJ:NPST:IPFV/walk MED=3SG.FEM:SBJ:NPST:IPFV/be (.)
      trik-si   mon=me kma zra\rä/
      tell-NMLZ how=INS POT 3SG.FEM:SBJ:IRR:IPFV/be
      'Now we are putting (the pictures) down how it goes there ... how the story should be.'   [tci20111004 RMA #313-314]

9.5 Relative clauses

I follow Andrews (2007a: 206) in defining relative clauses as a "subordinate clause which delimits the reference of an NP by specifying the role of the referent of that NP in the situation described by the RC [relative clause]". I adopt Andrews' label NP_{MAT} or matrix NP for the NP in the matrix clause, and NP_{REL} for the NP in the relative clause. The latter is always expressed by interrogative pronouns, which function as relative pronouns. Hence, Komnzo and other Yam languages employ the "relative pronoun strategy" for relativisation, which from a cross-linguistic perspective is found mostly in Europe (Haspelmath 2001).

Relative clauses in Komnzo are adjoined clauses in the sense of Hale (1976), who notes that adjoined relative clauses are "subordinate in some way, but [their] surface position with respect to the main clause is marginal rather than embedded" (1976: 78). Andrews defines them as having the relative clause appear outside the matrix NP. Relative clauses in Komnzo are almost always right-adjoined, i.e. they follow the matrix NP. Alternatively, they may refer to the whole preceding (matrix) clause. The matrix NP can be fronted together with the relative clause, which is a common strategy used for topicalisation (§10.4).

We can represent the structure of relative clauses schematically, as in Figure 9.1. The matrix element, $[...]_{MAT}$ in the figure, is usually a noun phrase, which can be omitted if it is understood from context. Alternatively, the matrix element can be a matrix clause. The relative clause, $[...]_{RC}$ in the figure, consists of the relative pronoun and the verb. There may be one noun phrase preceding the relative pronoun, but there cannot be more than one noun phrase in this position.

$$[NP_i]_{MAT} \ [(NP) \ REL.PRON_i \ V]_{RC}$$

Figure 9.1: Schematic representation of a relative clause (RC)

I begin by describing the formal structure of relative clauses. Formally, they are similar to content questions because the relative pronouns are identical to the interrogative pronouns.[4] We could say that interrogatives function as relative pronouns, which is why I do not gloss them as REL in the following examples. Instead, I gloss them in the same manner, in which pronouns in interrogative function are glossed. However, relative clauses are semantically distinct from content questions because the answer to the question is already given in the form of the NP_{MAT}. Relative clauses are also syntactically different from content questions in that the relative pronoun has to occur as the second element (Figure 9.1). Such a restriction does not apply to content questions. This is illustrated in (35-37), where the relative clause in each example is printed in bold face.

Example (35) comes from a hunting story where the narrator had encountered a spirit which began chasing him. In the example, the relative pronoun *maf* follows the pronoun *nzä*. The relative clause follows the NP_{MAT} *ane kabe* 'that man'.

---

[4]I refer the reader to §3.1.10 for a description of interrogative pronouns. See especially Table 3.6, but also the interrogatives in Table 3.8.

(35) *nze nima "byannor ane kabe fof **nzä maf wonrsoknwr**."*

nze   nima b=yan\nor/   ane kabe fof   nzä
1SG.ERG QUOT MED=3SG.MASC:SBJ:NPST:IPFV:VENT/shout DEM man EMPH 1SG.ABS
maf   won\rsokn/wr
who.SG.ERG 2|3SG:SBJ>1SG:OBJ:NPST:IPFV:VENT/bother
'I said: "He is shouting out there. This man who bothers me."'

[tci20111119-03 ABB #164-166]

In example (36), the speaker describes why he did not pay attention to a fire that almost burned his garden. In the example, the relative pronoun *mane* is preceded by the noun phrase *mnz tharthar* 'side of the house'. This is an adjoined relative clause because it is outside the NP$_{\text{MAT}}$, which in this case is *mni* 'fire', whose antecedent is understood from the context.

(36) *ni fi ane zumarwrme **mnz thartharen mane** zfrärm.*

ni fi ane zu\mar/wrme   mnz   tharthar=en mane
1NSG but DEM 1PL:SBJ>3SG.FEM:OBJ:PST:DUR/look house side=LOC   which(ABS)
zf\rä/rm
3SG.FEM:SBJ:PST:DUR/be
'But we were looking at that (fire), which was on the side of the house.'

[tci20120922-24 STK #5]

Finally, in (37) the speaker describes how he was trying to remove a burning tree from his garden fence. The relative pronoun *mane* follows the ergative marked *wämne* 'tree'. This is an adjoined relative clause because it is outside the matrix NP, which in this case is *ŋarake* 'garden fence', whose antecedent is understood from the context.

(37) *kma wämne ane fof kwakarkwé ane fof **wämnef mane** thänarfa … keke watikthémäre.*

kma wämne ane fof   kwa\kark/wé   ane fof   wämne=f mane
POT tree   DEM EMPH 1SG:SBJ:RPST:IPFV/pull DEM EMPH tree=ERG which(ABS)
thä\narf/a   (.) keke watik-thé=märe
SG:SBJ>2|3PL:OBJ:PST:IPFV/press.down (.) NEG enough-ADJZR=PRIV
'I should have pulled that tree (from the fence), which the tree was pushing
down. No, (I was) not (strong) enough!'   [tci20120922-24 MAA #42-43]

A second rule is needed for examples where the relative pronoun occurs in initial position of the relative clause. Although this is possible, such examples are much less frequent than the second position. The relative pronoun can occur in first position only (i) if it is preceded by the NP$_{\text{MAT}}$ (39 and 40), or (ii) if the only other element in the relative clause is the verb (38).

(38) *bundbonzo rä **mane** zawokth.*

bundbo=nzo \rä/   mane   za\wokth/
2SG.ALL=ONLY 3SG.FEM:NPST:IPFV/be which(ABS) 2SG:SBJ:IMP:PFV/choose
'It is up to you which one you choose!'   [tci20111004 RMA #528]

Example (39) is taken from a picture stimulus task. One of the participants is correcting the other. Note that the English translation is misleading. The noun phrase *mafanemäwä waniwani* is a complex noun phrase and the relative pronoun *mafanema* is marked flagged with the characteristic case in adnominal function. Thus, *mafanemäwä wani-wani* should be translated not as genitive 'whose picture', but as origin 'picture of/about who'.

(39) *sukawi, nima keke rä. zane fthéthamane yé ... ane kabe fof **mafanemäwä***
      waniwani zöbthé nzünmarwre.
      sukawi nima   keke \rä\   zane   fthé=thamane
      sukawi like.this NEG 3SG.FEM:SBJ:NPST:IPFV/be DEM:PROX when=TEMP.POSS
      \yé\   (.) ane kabe fof   mafane=ma=wä
      3SG.MASC:SBJ:NPST:IPFV/be (.) DEM man EMPH who.SG.POSS=CHAR=EMPH
      waniwani zöbthé nz=wn\mar\wre
      picture   first   IPST=1PL:SBJ>3SG.FEM:OBJ:NPST:IPFV:VENT/see
      'Sukawi, it is not like that. This is from that time ... really this man whose picture
      we just saw before.'   [tci20111004 RMA #194]

In example (40), the relative pronoun occurs initially following the NP$_{MAT}$ *dödö*.

(40) *ane fathnzo zfrärm wämne keke ... dödönzo ... dödö **maneme ŋarenwre fath.***
      ane fath=nzo   zf\rä\rm   wämne keke (.) dödö=nzo   (.) dödö
      DEM clearing=ONLY 3SG.FEM:SBJ:PST:DUR/be tree   NEG (.) dödö=ONLY (.) dödö
      mane=me ŋa\ren\wre   fath
      which=INS 1PL:SBJ:NPST:IPFV/sweep clearing
      'This was a clearing, no trees ... only dödö (Sida acuta) ... dödö, with which we
      sweep the clear places.'   [tci20120821-02 LNA #25-27]

Next, I describe which kinds of argument roles can be relativised in the matrix clause (NP$_{MAT}$), and which can occur in the relative clause (NP$_{REL}$). As the examples in this section show, there is virtually no restriction on the possible argument roles. NP$_{REL}$ is expressed by the relative pronoun, which can inflect for all cases (§3.1.10). The examples given in this section include the following cases: ergative (35), absolutive (36, 37, 38), characteristic (39), dative (45), locative (41), and instrumental (40).

It is harder to determine the argument role of NP$_{MAT}$ because its presence is optional. We saw in (37) that the relative pronoun *mane* referred to the fence, which the burning tree had pushed down. But this is not expressed by a noun phrase, nor is the fence indexed in the verb of the matrix clause. We only know about it from the preceding context of the story, and the plural prefix in the verb of the relative clause.[5] In (36), the fire is not expressed as a noun phrase, but the prefix of the verbs *zumarwrme* 'we were seeing it' and *zfrärm* 'it was', both indexing *mni* 'fire' (3SG.FEM). However, we can always determine the argument role of NP$_{MAT}$ from the context. The following argument roles are found in the examples given in this section: the single argument of an intransitive verb (35), patient (36), location (41), discourse topic (42), actor (43), and recipient (44).

---

[5]The word *ŋarake* 'fence' is frequently used in the plural.

(41) *mni wthomonwrth **yfö mä zfrärm.***

mni w\thomon/wrth   yfö mä   zf\rä/rm

fire 2|3PL:SBJ>3SG.FEM:OBJ:NPST:IPFV/pile.up.fire hole where 3SG.FEM:SBJ:PST:DUR

'They prepare the fire where the hole was.'   [tci20120901-01 MAK #153-154]

(42) *anema nä katan zokwasi nimamenzo fof zfrä ... nzone katan masisma ... ane*
      *mnima **zöbthé mane** zukonzrmth **kidn o zfth mni.***

ane=ma   nä   katan zokwasi nima=me=nzo   fof   zf\rä/

DEM=CHAR INDF small words   like.this=INS=ONLY EMPH 3SG.FEM:RPST:IPFV/be

(.) nzone   katan masis=ma   (.) ane mni=ma   zöbthé mane

(.) 1SG.POSS small matches=CHAR (.) DEM fire=CHAR before which(ABS)

zu\ko/nzrmth   kidn o zfth mni

2|3PL:SBJ>3SG.FEM:OBJ:PST:DUR/speak kidn or base fire

'This was another small story like this ... about my small matches ... about the
fire, which they were calling Kidn or base fire before.'   [tci20120909-06 KAB #126-127]

(43) *kabef tauri samg **ŋatha tüfrkarä mane yé.***

kabe=f   tauri   sa\mg/   ŋatha tüfr=karä

man=ERG.SG wallaby 2|3SG:SBJ>3SG.MASC:OBJ:RPST:PFV/shoot dog   plenty=PROP

mane   \yé/

who(ABS) 3SG.MASC:SBJ:NPST:IPFV/be

'The man who has many dogs shot the wallaby.'   [overheard]

(44) *be kmam nabi thar nafanm **mane wtri ŋarärth.***

be   kma=m   nabi tha\r/   nafanm mane   wtri

2SG.ERG POT=APPR bow 2SG:SBJ>2|3PL:IO:IMP:PFV/give 3NSG:DAT who(ABS) fear

ŋa\rä/rth

2|3PL:SBJ:NPST:IPFV/do

'You must not give a bow to those who are fearful.'   [overheard]

It is also possible that the relative clause is free in the sense that it refers to the whole
matrix clause and not to a particular nominal (Andrews 2007a: 213). Examples are given
in (38) and (45).

(45) *be fam kwot karäré **tosin mafan kwa yarithr.***

be   fam   kwot   ka\rä/ré   tosin mafan   kwa

2SG.ERG thought properly 2SG:SBJ:IMP:IPFV/do torch who.SG.DAT FUT

ya\ri/thr

2|3SG:SBJ>3SG.MASC:IO:NPST:IPFV/give

'You have to think properly to whom you will give the torch.'   [overheard]

The NP$_{MAT}$ can be fronted together with the relative clause, as in (46). This is commonly
used for topicalisation. After showing me a traditional fishing basket, the speaker shifts
the topic to more modern methods of fishing. The NP$_{MAT}$ is *net* in (46).

(46) *wati, net **ane mane erä** markaianeme erä ane.*

wati net   ane mane e\rä/   markai=aneme
then fishing.net DEM which 2|3PL:SBJ:NPST:IPFV/be outsider=POSS.NSG
e\rä/   ane
2|3PL:SBJ:NPST:IPFV/be DEM
'Okay, as for the fishing nets, they are the white man's (things).'

[tci20120906 SKK #53-54]

In example (47), the speaker talks about food taboos. He makes the point that a particular woman in the village has grown very old because she has always respected those food taboos. The relative clause (in bold) marks a shift in topic to all those people who did not respect the food taboos. The antecedent of the relative clause is omitted, since it is understood from context. It is different from the old woman, as can been seen by that fact that all following verbs index a plural argument, e.g. *kwarirkwrmth* 'they respected' and *thufathwrm* 'it grabbed them'.

(47) *watik, fi komnzo zathfär … bänema fof nima rirksima brä … nima kwarirkwrm …*
      *fi **mafa keke kwarirkwrmth** … watik, tekmär esufakwa kwikkwikf thufathwrm.*

watik fi   komnzo za\thfär/   (.) bäne=ma   fof   nima
then 3.ABS only 3SG.FEM:SBJ:RPST:PFV/jump (.) DEM:MED=CHAR EMPH like.this
rirk-si=ma   b\rä/   (.) nima
respect-NMLZ=CHAR MED=3SG.FEM:SBJ:NPST:IPFV/be (.) like.this
kwa\rirk/wrm   (.) fi   mafa   keke kwa\rirk/wrmth   (.)
2|3SG:SBJ:PST:DUR/respect (.) but who.NSG.ERG NEG 2|3PL:SBJ:PST:DUR/respect (.)
watik tek=mär   e\sufak/wa   kwik-kwik-f
then duration=PRIV 2|3PL:SBJ:PST:IPFV/grow.old REDUP-sickness=ERG
thu\fath/wrm
2|3SG:SBJ>2|3PL:OBJ:PST:DUR/hold
'She just lives on … because of her respect … she was respecting (the law) … but those who did not respect (the law) … well, they grew old quickly and they got sick.'

[tci20120922-26 DAK #22-27]

The fronted relative clause as a topicalisation strategy is described in detail in §10.4.

9.6 Conditional and time clauses

Conditional and time clauses are expressed in the same way, only the context resolves which of the two is meant. I will use the term conditional in the subsequent description to cover both. Conditionals are formed by using the word *fthé* 'when, if'. Note that *fthé* is not a subordinator per se because it can also occur in independent sentences with the meaning 'that is when'. Thus, *fthé* is required for a conditional, but it is not sufficient. The word *fthé* is used in the clause which sets up the conditional, often called the if-clause (Thompson et al. 2007: 255). The second clause, often called the then-clause, receives no special marking.[6] The clearest conditional reading is found with the second person. While an irrealis verb inflection is also possible, in most cases, the imperative is used in one of the two clauses, as in example (48) and (49).

(48) *ŋanzmäre fthé gnräré frasi kwa nrä.*
     ŋanz=märe fthé gn\rä/ré   frasi   kwa n\rä/
     ROW=PRIV when 2SG:SBJ:IMP:IPFV/be hunger FUT 2SG:SBJ:NPST:IPFV/be
     'If you are without a row (of yams in the garden), you will be hungry.'
                                      [tci20130822-08 LNA #17]

(49) *wati, zena fthé zanmar ... yusi fr mane rä ... ane fof nzone farsima rä.*
     wati zena fthé zan\mar/   (.) yusi fr   mane
     then today when 2SG:SBJ>3SG.FEM:OBJ:IMP:PFV/see (.) grass stem which
     \rä/   (.) ane fof   nzone far-si=ma
     3SG.FEM:SBJ:NPST:IPFV/be (.) DEM EMPH 1SG.POSS fell-NMLZ=CHAR
     \rä/
     3SG.FEM:SBJ:NPST:IPFV/be
     'If/When you look at it ... the grassland there ... that is from my cutting down
     (the trees).'   [tci20120805-01 ABB #614]

Both clauses can be marked for various TAM categories, for example imperative in the if-clause and irrealis in the when-clause in (50), where the speaker shows me the proper use of a toy bullroarer.

(50) *zbo fthé sakwr fefen o wämnen ... keke kwa srannor.*
     zbo   fthé sa\kwr/   fefe=n   o wämn=en (.)
     PROX.ALL when 2SG:SBJ>3SG.MASC:OBJ:IMP:PFV/hit body=LOC or tree=LOC (.)
     keke kwa sran\nor/
     NEG FUT 3SG.MASC:SBJ:IRR:IPFV/shout
     'If you hit it here against the body or against a tree, it will not make a sound.'
                                        [tci20120914 RMA #31-33]

In (51), all clauses are in past durative, yet the conditional construction can be interpreted as both actual (as in the translation) or counterfactual ('... the story man would have shot them with magic').

(51) *zizi zä keke kwarafinzrmth ŋoŋoyamkarä ... bänema fthé ŋoŋoyamkarä*
     kwarafinzrmth menzf thfruthrm ... bthanme.
     zizi   zä   keke kwa\rafi/nzrmth   ŋoŋoyam=karä (.) bäne=ma
     afternoon PROX NEG 2|3PL:SBJ:PST:DUR/paddle noise=PROP   ... RECOG=CHAR
     fthé   ŋoŋoyam=karä kwa\rafi/nzrmth   menz=f
     when noise=PROP 2|3PL:SBJ:PST:DUR/paddle story.man=ERG.SG

---

[6]Note that for time clauses, this would be the when-clause and then-clause respectively.

thf\ru/thrm (.) bthan=me

2|3SG:SBJ>2|3PL:OBJ:PST:DUR/shoot (.) magic=INS

'They did not paddle her with a lot of noise in the afternoon. If they were paddling making a lot of noise, the story man was shooting them with.'

[tci20120922-19 DAK #14-15]

9.7 Direct speech and thought

Direct speech is a common construction in Komnzo. In most cases, direct speech is introduced by a speech verb, for example *ko-* 'speak' or *na-* 'say', and the manner demonstrative *nima* 'like this' (§3.1.12.7). Direct speech receives a separate intonation contour and the whole clause is often produced at a slightly higher pitch to indicate that the speaker is taking on another person's role. An example is given in (52).

(52) a. *watik, srank kma **sakora** nima "srank, ni krafare!"*

watik srank kma sa\kor/a nima srank ni

then srank POT SG:SBJ>3SG.MASC:OBJ:PST:PFV/speak QUOT srank 1NSG

kra\far/e

2|3DU:SBJ:IRR:PFV/set.off

'Well, he tried to tell Srank: "Srank, we go!"'

b. *srankf **zenaftha** "keke efoth zizi fefe rä nzä kayé woräro."*

srank=f ze\nafth/a keke efoth zizi fefe

srank=ERG.SG SG:SBJ:PST:IPFV/say NEG sun afternoon really

\rä/ nzä kayé wo\rä/ro

3SG.FEM:SBJ:NPST:IPFV/be 1SG.ABS tomorrow 1SG:SBJ:NPST:IPFV:AND/be

Srank said: "No, it is late afternoon. I will go tomorrow."'

[tci20111107-01 MAK #44-45]

The manner demonstrative functions as a quotative marker. It can introduce direct speech without a speech verb, as in example (53).

(53) *naf **nima** "nakre! wimäsen mni bŋasog."*

naf nima nakre wimäs=en mni b=ŋa\sog/

3SG.ERG QUOT nakre mango.tree=LOC fire MED=2|3SG:SBJ:NPST:IPFV/climb

'He said: "Nakre! The fire is climbing up the mango tree."'

[tci20130901-04 RNA #152-153]

There is no dedicated construction for indirect speech. Indirect speech equivalents can be expressed by a speech verb with an adverbial adjunct (54) or a clause connected with *mon* 'how' (55).

(54) *naf ŋanafr **drdr** mäyogsir.*

naf ŋa\na/fr drdr mäyog-si=r

3SG.ERG 2|3SG:SBJ:NPST:IPFV/speak old.garden repeat-NMLZ=PURP

'She said to continue the old garden.'

[tci20130823-06 STK 161]

(55) *emothf ŋatrikwr **monme zfnzr**.*
emoth=f   ŋa\trik/wr   mon=me z\fn/nzr
girl=ERG.SG 2|3SG:SBJ:NPST:IPFV/tell how=INS 2|3SG:SBJ>3SG.FEM:OBJ:PST:IPFV/hit
'The girl reports how he hit her.'   [tci20120925 MAE #102]

An individual's inner thoughts are treated like direct and indirect speech. Hence, we find examples like (56) and (57), which mirror what has been described above for speech. The only difference lies in the framing expression, which is often the light verb construction *fam* 'thought' + *rä-* 'do'.

(56) *fam zära "kar bä rä a kar töna fobo fof wyak fof."*
fam   zä\r/a   kar bä \rä/   a   kar
thought SG:SBJ:PST:PFV/do village MED 3SG.FEM:SBJ:NPST:IPFV/be and place
töna   fobo   fof   w\yak/   fof
high.ground DIST.ALL EMPH 1SG:SBJ:NPST:IPFV/walk EMPH
'He thought "There is a village. I will walk there to the high ground."'
                                                         [tci20131013-01 ABB #259]

(57) *fam ane fof ŋarär monme sufnzrmth monme santhbath.*
fam   ane fof ŋa\rä/r   mon=me
thought DEM EMPH 2|3SG:SBJ:NPST:IPFV/do how=INS
su\fn/nzrmth   mon=me
2|3PL:SBJ>3SG.MASC:OBJ:PST:DUR/hit how=INS
san\thb/ath
2|3PL:SBJ>3SG.MASC:OBJ:PST:DUR:VENT/put.inside
'He is thinking how they were hitting him and how they locked him up.'
                                                         [tci20111004 RMA #457]

10 Information structure

10.1 Introduction

This chapter should be seen as a preliminary study of those linguistic structures captured under the rubric of information structure. I address a number of mechanisms which are employed to create textual cohesion, emphasis, and event sequencing. In linguistic theory, the notions of topicalisation, emphasis, focus, fore- and backgrounding have been used to analyse information structure. As in many other languages, the correlates of these abstract concepts are drawn from a wide range of linguistic phenomena. They may be expressed by nuances in intonation, designated morphology, specific particles, syntactic constructions, or an exploitation of the rich TAM system. Some of these mechanisms are typical of certain text genres while others are more pervasive.

I will describe different particles and enclitics that are used to mark focus, intensification and emphasis in §10.2 and briefly point to the narrative paragraph marker *watik* in §10.3. This is followed by a discussion of topicalisation in §10.4. The chapter closes with a description of how Komnzo speakers exploit their complex TAM system to sequence event descriptions in §10.5.

10.2 Clitics and particles

There are a number of particles, enclitics, and affixes that are used for focus. These are sometimes glossed as intensifiers, emphasisers, or they are sometimes translated into English by 'only' or 'also'. All of these interact with focus, but it might be premature to analyse them purely as focus markers. By looking at a longer piece of text, I will describe the intensifier *fof*, the emphatic enclitic *=wä*, the contrastive markers *komnzo* and *=nzo*, and the particle *we*. All of these elements are pervasive in the language and not preferred in any particular text genre.

Following König (1991), who discusses focus particles, I draw a distinction in function between presentational, contrastive and additive focus. König states that: "[a] focus particle relates the value of the focused expression to a set of alternatives" (1991: 32). A contrastive focus excludes all alternatives, while presentational focus emphasises whatever lies within its scope. Additive focus presupposes a previous proposition and highlights that the same applies to another referent. We find that Komnzo employs the particle *fof* and the enclitic *=wä* for presentational focus, the particle *komnzo* and the related enclitic *=nzo* for contrastive focus, and the particle *we* for additive focus.

These mechanisms may be categorised according to their scope. The particle *fof* usually has scope over the element which it follows. This may be a whole clause if it occurs post-verbally. More commonly, it is found after demonstratives, deictics or complete noun phrases in which case it has scope over these elements (§3.4.2). The enclitic *=wä* attaches to noun phrases, but is most commonly found with pronouns. The particle *komnzo* occurs pre-verbally and has scope over the predicate, while the enclitic *=nzo* attaches mostly to nominals and noun phrases and, thus, has scope over arguments or adjuncts. The particle *we* occurs in front of a clause over which it has scope or is sometimes used twice bracketing an element.

A third criterion for categorising these elements is according to their semantic content. König points out that English words like 'even, just, only' have a lexical meaning, whereas focus particles in other languages mark 'pure focus' (1991: 29ff.). He cites Somali (Saeed 1984: 21ff.) and Manam (Lichtenberk 1983: 476ff.) as languages where focus particles have been described as being lexically empty. We can attribute such a characteristic to the particle *fof*. It is the word which occurs with the highest frequence in the corpus. Informants often found it hard to give a separate translation of *fof*, and when pressed to do so often translated it with 'really'. As there are two adverbs *fefe* 'really' and *minzü* 'very' expressing the same, I take *fof* to have no lexical meaning. This holds not true for the other elements discussed here. The particle *komnzo* as well as the enclitic *=nzo* are often translated as 'only'. The particle *we* is, often translated as 'also' or 'too'.

I will make use of a text excerpt to explain how these mechanisms are put to use in Komnzo. The example text in (1) is the last part of a *nzürna* story which is a common narrative in the Morehead region with numerous local variants. The *nzürna* character is a female being who can change her appearance. Although these stories are often comical, the *nzürna* poses some kind of a threat to the protagonists of the story. She is said to kill and eat especially small children. Mary Ayres roughly translated *nzürna ŋare* as "devil woman" (1983: 93). In contrast to mythical stories, or knowledge about magic and sorcery, *nzürna* stories are public stories, which are often retold and joked about. This particular *nzürna* story is set in Firra, a now abandoned village about 15km south of Morehead. The narrator is Maraga Kwozi, a man who used to live in Firra. The *nzürna* used to help and look after the people of Firra until the day that she killed and ate a stranger who was visiting the village. Outraged at this vicious incident, the village people took revenge and burned the tree in which she and her husband Nagawa were living. Nagawa escaped from the fire, but his wife was killed. The text excerpt picks up where main action is over. Nagawa returns to their home in Waisam to find out if his wife has survived the attack by the villagers. The elements to be discussed are underlined:

(1)   1   *ane thrma mni fthé zäbtha.*
           'After this, the fire had finished.'

      2   <u>*wati*</u> *nagawa ŋabrigwa ... sir*
           'Then Nagawa returned ... to see'

      3   "<u>*komnzo*</u> *rä o z kwarsir mnin?*"
           "Is she still alive or did she burn in the fire?"

      4   *ŋabrigwa ... bobomr* <u>*we*</u> *waisam wäsü fthé sanmara.*
           'He went back ... there he also saw that Wäsü tree in Waisam.'

5 *watik fi "nafazfthenwä."*
'Then he (said): "It was all her own fault."'

6 *yanzo bobo yanora ... nafaŋareanema.*
'He was just crying ... for his wife.'

7 *wati, fi näbi zäbrima.*
'Thus, he went back for good.'

8 *zmbo yamnzr ane woga oten.*
'This man lives now here in Ote.'

9 *emoth fäthä ämnzr.*
'He lives with his daughters.'

10 *watik, kabeyé komnzo fä nomai sumarwre ... ymarwre fthé ...*
'Well, the people still see him there ... we see him when ...'

11 *fä ŋaritakwr nima firrafo yak ... we nima ŋabrigwr.*
'he crosses (the river) on his way to Firra ... and also when he returns.'

12 *tnz fäth ane kabe yé*
'He is a short man.'

13 *ane nzürna ŋareane zokwasi nimame fof rä fof.*
'That Nzürna woman's story is just like that.'

14 *mane bobo firran zwamnzrm.*
'the one, who was staying in Firra.'

15 *tüfr yam nä fefe thwafiyokwrm ...*
'She did many things, ...'

16 *fi fathfa ane fof wäfiyokwa ...*
'but this one thing she did in public ...'

17 *nä karma kabe mane yanatha mogarkamma*
'eating that man from another village ... from Mogarkam.'

18 *nafane zokwasi ... ane trikasi fobonzo wythk fof brä.*
'her story ... that story ends there. It is over.'

19 *ane nzürna ŋareanema*
'about that Nzürna woman.'

20 *watik, fobo fof zräkoré*
'Well, that is what I told you.'

21 *nä karen nima nä buné bänema ...*
'In other villages (there are) others ...'

22 *nä nzürna ŋare zokwasi trikasi bä räro ...*
'other Nzürna woman stories are there ...'

23 *fi ane kar woga mane erä fi ane miyatha erä*
'but it is those village people who know about these.'

24 *nzefé nzüwäbragwé nima ni miyatha nrä*
'I followed like we know (this story).'

25 *nzekaren ane yam kwafiyokwrm ...*
   'She did this in our village ...'

26 *nzenme ŋafyé mä thwamnzrm*
   'where our fathers lived.'

27 *ŋafyé <u>we</u> nzenm natrikwath*
   'The fathers also told us (about it).'

28 *nima zbo zf zakoré. <u>fof</u> zäbthé*
   'I have said it now. I am finished.'

[tci20120901-01 MAK #201-238]

The intensifier *fof* occurs in lines 13, 16, 18, 20, and 28. In line 13, the narrator marks the end of the story by stating the story is "just like that" and *fof* occurs twice. In the first instance, it has scope over *nima=me* 'like.this=INS'. In the second instance, it occurs postverbally and has scope over the whole proposition. It is very common to give an affirmative reply by saying *nima fof* or *nimame fof* 'just like this'. Such a reply rarely occurs without *fof*. In lines 16 and 20, *fof* occurs after the demonstratives *ane* (DEM) and *fobo* (DIST.ALL) which is also very common. In line 16, the narrator emphasises that amongst many things that she did, it was this one incident where she stepped out of line. In line 20, he literally says "<u>to there</u>, I spoke" emphasising the point where his story has come to an end now. In lines 18 and 28, *fof* has scope over the predicate which in this case is the whole proposition. In line 18, the verb form is *wythk* 'it comes to an end.' In 28, the verb *zäbthé* 'I am finished' follows and finally closes the narration. In each case, *fof* sets a mark which can be compared to a gesture like slamming one's hand on the table. It underlines and emphasises whatever lies in its scope.

The particle *komnzo* and the enclitic *=nzo* occur in lines 3, 6, and 18. In line 3, *komnzo* occurs in a question: 'Is she still alive or did she burn in the fire?' The first clause only contains *komnzo* and the copula *rä* which translates literally as 'she only exists'. In line 6, *=nzo* is cliticised to *ya* 'cry, wail' and thus translates literally as 'he was shouting out <u>only wails</u>'. In line 18, *=nzo* is attached to a demonstrative *fobo* DIST.ALL. The narrator stresses the fact that the story ends at that point and does not continue. Thus, with all three examples, we find *komnzo* and *=nzo* have a contrastive function, i.e. setting something apart from other options.

The particle *we* functions as an additive marker like the English particle *also*. It occurs in lines 4, 11, and 27. In line 4, it introduces the account of Nagawa's return: that of seeing the Wäsü tree. In line 11, the narrator talks first about Nagawa crossing the river and then adds another clause about his return trip when he crosses the river again. The function of additive focus becomes particularly clear in line 27. After the narrator explains that he is entitled and knowledgeable to tell the story because it took place in his village (lines 24-26), he adds another piece of justification, namely that his fathers told him the story.

The emphasising suffix *=wä* occurs only once in the text (line 5). In his pain and sadness, Nagawa realises that it was his wife's action that had led to the act of revenge. This comment could have been expressed as *nafa-zfth-en* 3.POSS-fault-LOC 'her fault', but the speaker adds *=wä nafa-zfth-en=wä* which can be translated as 'her <u>own</u> fault.' For a more detailed discussion of *=wä* (§4.17.1).

10.3 The paragraph marker *watik*

The word *watik* or sometimes *wati* means 'enough'. I often overhead it being used with together the adjectivaliser suffix *-thé* and the instrumental *=me*. Thus, *watikthéme* '(I have) enough' is a common reply to an offer to have more food or more tea. In narratives or procedural texts, *watik* is often used to mark a new thought or the begining of a paragraph. Its use is typically followed by a short pause similar to the English expressions 'well', 'and then', 'thus', or 'next'. We find such instances of *watik* or *wati* in the text excerpt (1) in lines 2, 5, 7, 10, and 20. *Watik* introduces new episodes in each of these lines.

10.4 Fronted relative clauses

Relative clauses are right-adjoined (§9.5), and an example of a relative clause is given in (2). The matrix noun phrase *bäne dgwr* 'that orchid' is followed by the relative clause [in square brackets]. Usually the relative clause follows the matrix clause.

(2) *dgwrfa enrgegwr bäne dgwr* [*boba mane themare*] *berä.*
dgwr=fa en\rgeg/wr   bäne   dgwr boba
orchid=ABL 2|3SG:SBJ>2|3PL:OBJ:NPST:IPFV:VENT/pull-off DEM:MED orchid MED.ABL
mane the\mar/e   b=e\rä/
which 1PL:SBJ>2|3PL:OBJ:RPST:PFV/see MED=2|3PL:SBJ:NPST:IPFV/be
'(The bowerbird) pulls them off the orchid. That orchid, which we saw over there.'
[tci20120815 ABB #32]

In public speeches, one often hears topic constructions such as (3) where the speaker proclaims to the people gathered at a feast that it is time to sing and dance (and not to fight). Literally, this sentence can be translated as: 'The drums which resonate, they resonate for the dance ... only for this.' Formally, this is a fronted noun phrase with a following relative clause. In most cases, the following relative clause consists of *mane* 'what, which' and the copula (4). As a convention, I translate this with the English phrases 'as for X', 'concerning X' or 'when it comes to X'.

(3) *brubru* [*mane änor*] *wathma änor ... zane frümöwä*
brubru mane ä\nor/   wath=ma   ä\nor/
drum   which 2|3PL:SBJ:NPST:IPFV/shout dance=CHAR 2|3PL:SBJ:NPST:IPFV/shout
(.) zane   frü=me=wä
(.) DEM:PROX alone=INS=EMPH
'As for the drums, they are resonating for the dance ... only for this.'
[tci20121019-04 ABB #46]

(4) *komnzo zokwasi* [*mane rä*] *... faremane zokwasi fefe ane fof rä ... komnzo.*
komnzo zokwasi mane \rä/   (.) farem=ane   zokwasi
komnzo language which 3SG.FEM:SBJ:NPST:IPFV/be (.) farem=POSS.SG language

fefe ane fof   \rä/   (.) komnzo
real DEM EMPH 3SG.FEM:SBJ:NPST:IPFV/be (.) komnzo
'When it comes to Komnzo, this is the Farem's real language ... Komnzo!'

[tci20120924-02 ABM #4-5]

As we see in (4), the relative clause often contains the copula (lit. 'Komnzo language which is ...'). The result is that it contributes nothing to the state of affairs, but its main function is pragmatic. Therefore, I analyse the fronted noun phrase together with the relative clause under the label fronted relative clause, i.e. fronted with respect to the matrix clause, and I put both together in bracket in the following examples. Note that there may also be no matrix noun phrase in cases where it is the event that is topicalised, for example in (5).

(5) [*mane ynzänza*] ... *büdisn mä nzrugrm ... oroman fä fof samara ... ŋafe*
     mane yn\zä/nza   (.) büdisn mä
     who SG:SBJ>3SG.MASC:OBJ:PST:IPFV:VENT/carry (.) büdisn where
     nz\rugr/m   (.) oroman fä   fof   sa\mar/a   (.)
     1PL:SBJ:PST:DUR/sleep (.) old.man DIST EMPH SG:SBJ>3SG.MASC:PST:IPFV/see (.)
     ŋafe
     father
     'As he was carrying him ... at Büdisn where we were sleeping ... the old man, father, saw him there.'

[tci20110810-02 MAB #55-56]

Fronted relative clauses are the main strategy to introduce or reactivate topics in the sense described by Keenan and Schieffelin (1976: 342). We find them not only in public speeches, but also in narratives, where speakers employ them to indicate a change in topic or to introduce a topic. I will describe this function by taking the reader through a particular narrative. Example sentence (6) introduces the protagonist of the story, a man named Kukufia.

(6) [*kukufia mane yara*] *masun swamnzrm.*
     kukufia mane ya\r/a   masu=n   swa\m/nzrm
     kukufia which 3SG.MASC:PST:IPFV/be masu=LOC 3SG.MASC:PST:DUR/dwell
     'Kukufia lived in Masu.'

[tci20100905 ABB #8-9]

In order to state the simple fact that Kukufia lived in Masu, it would be sufficient to say *kukufia masun swamnzrm* 'Kukufia lived in Masu'. But because the sentence establishes the topic (Kukufia), a fronted relative clause is used. This is a very common way to introduce a character to a story.

Kukufia is a malicious character who comes to Rouku and tortures two children while their parents are away at a sago camp. Kukufia takes the two children fishing in his canoe. He pokes the small boy with the bones of a fish. One day, the father of the two children returns looking for them. Example (7) shows, how this change in topic is expressed.

(7) a. *fafen nge zi swathizrm ... ekri zi ... kofä ysma.*

fafen   nge zi swa\thi/zrm   (.) ekri zi   (.) kofä
meanwhile child pain 3SG.MASC:SBJ:PST:DUR/die (.) body pain (.) fish
ys=ma
bone=CHAR
'In the meantime, the child was in pain ... body pain from the fish bones.'

b. *watik [nafaŋafe mane yanrá] nagayé thrathorthm.*

watik nafa-ŋafe   mane yan\r/a   nagayé
then 3.POSS-father which 3SG.MASC:SBJ:PST:IPFV:VENT/be children
thra\thorthm/
2|3SG:SBJ>2|3PL:OBJ:IRR:PFV/search
'Then ... As for their father, he was looking for the children.'

[tci20100905 ABB #90-95]

Again, the change in topic is marked by a fronted relative clause (7b). The construction is not purely pragmatic here, as there is a venitive marker on the copula (*yanra*) which indicates that the father is coming.

Further along in the story, the father finds his children locked inside the house. He finds out about Kukufia's visits and decides to hide underneath the house. When Kukufia returns later in the day, the father shoots him with an arrow. Kukufia runs away to Masu where his two wifes live. The father follows the trail of blood. In Masu, Kukufia transforms into a little baby boy hanging on the breast of one the wives. This is the point in the text where we find the next fronted relative clause (8b).

(8) a. *kukufia näbi zamatha dunzikarä ... ŋakwir e Masu kräkwther.*

kukufia näbi za\math/a   dunzi=karä (.) ŋa\kwi/r   e
kukufia one 3SG:SBJ:PST:PFV/run arrow=PROP (.) 3SG:SBJ:NPST:IPFV/run until
masu krä\kwther/
masu 3SG:IRR:PFV/change
'Kukufia ran away with the arrow (inside him) ... He was running until Masu where he changed (his appearance).'

b. *[nafane ŋare mane zfrärm] ... edama ... thrma ŋare. wati mämen fobo zämira fof.*

nafane   ŋare mane zf\rä/rm   (.) eda=ma (.) thrma
3SG.POSS woman which 3SG.FEM:SBJ:PST:DUR/be (.) two=CHAR (.) after
ŋare wati mäme=n fobo zä\mir/a   fof
woman then breast=LOC DIST.ALL 2|3SG:SBJ:PST:PFV/hang EMPH
'It was his wife ... the second ... the latter wife. He was hanging on her breast.'

[tci20100905 ABB #117-121]

The narrator first describes Kukufia's escape in (8a) and then changes the topic to the wife on whose breast the little baby boy is hanging (8b). The new topic is again introduced by a fronted relative clause. Kukufia's fate is sealed as the father quickly recognises the small boy. He kills Kukufia and his two wives on the spot and the story ends.

Fronted relative clauses of this type are used both to topicalise an expression, as in the introductory example to this section (3), but also to indicate a change in the topic, as in the examples above. The relative pronoun used for this type of construction is always *mane* 'who, which'.

10.5 TAM categories and event-sequencing

Foley points out that Papuan languages often exploit their rich TAM systems for pragmatic purposes (2000: 389). TAM marking and discourse notions such as foregrounding has been discussed by many authors, for example by Hopper (1979). One such example from the Papuan language Sentani comes from Hartzler (1983) who has shown that clauses in irrealis are commonly used for backgrounded, presupposed propositions, whereas realis is used for foregrounded, asserted propositions. Komnzo puts its TAM system to the same pragmatic use in order to create textual cohesion, but in Komnzo more TAM categories are involved (§6.4). This pragmatic use is often found in texts or parts of texts where the sequence of events is important, for example in procedurals, and descriptions of a path.

I will begin by comparing the above-mentioned realis-irrealis distinction. Consider the following text (9) which describes the first part of a wedding ceremony. This procedural was given by Abia Bai. The actual wedding took place two days after the recording was made. Therefore, the description of the event is set in the future, which reduces the number of possible TAM categories. The speaker may only choose between the indicative non-past and the irrealis verbal inflection.[1] In (9), I have underlined the verbs in irrealis mood in Komnzo as well as in the English translation. All other verbs are in non-past and indicative mood.

(9) 1 *wati foba nimame kwa ŋathkärwr.*
        'Well, it will begin like this:'

     2 *dagon rthé <u>thrarakthkwrth</u> <u>thräbthth</u>*
        'The food <u>will be placed</u> on the platform. That <u>will be finished</u>.'

     3 *zöbthé fefe kwa ... chris e nafaŋare maki ernth fof.*
        'First, they are putting the paint on Chris and his wife.'

     4 *maki fthé <u>thrarnth</u> ... fthé <u>thrabthth</u> ...*
        'When they <u>have put on</u> the paint ... when they <u>have finished</u> ...'

     5 *watik, foba kwa änrokonth.*
        'next they will escort them this way.'

     6 *fthé <u>thrnthbth</u> nima ...*
        'When they <u>will bring</u> them in ... '

     7 *faf mä kwa nge fathasi zn rä fof...*
        'to the place where the children's feast will take place ...'

---

[1]Future reference is expressed periphrastically with the particle *kwa* which may occur with non-past indicative and irrealis inflections.

8 *kwa änrokonth kwot bobomr ...*
'they will escort them up until ...'

9 *thranthaifth faf znfo.*
'they <u>will arrive</u> at the place.'

10 *watik kwa emsakrnth.*
'Next, they will sit them down.'

11 *thramsth kramsth*
'They <u>will sit</u> them down. They <u>will sit</u> down.'

12 *watik, zöbthé fefe kwa äyoknth a ätriknth nima:*
'Well, first, they will advise them and they will say:'

[tci20110817-02 ABB #22-40]

The content of this little excerpt is quickly summarised: After the food preparations, the bride and the groom will be decorated and painted. The women will escort the couple to the village square where they will be placed on a bench only to be lectured about codes of conduct and the expected behaviour.

We find that the speaker alternates between realis and irrealis mood. Realis occurs with the painting (line 3), the escorting (line 5), the escorting again (line 8), the sitting down (line 10) and the advising (line 12). Irrealis occurs with the finishing of the food preparations (line 2), the painting and the finishing thereof (line 4), the bringing (line 6), the arriving (line 8) and the sitting down (line 11). This alternation in TAM categories is congruent with an alternation between foregrounded, asserted events and backgrounded, presupposed events. In some instances, the verb in realis is repeated in irrealis, e.g. the sitting down in lines 11 and 12. Additionally, the repetition of one part of a proposition in the next proposition can be described as kind of tail-head-linkage.[2] Thus, we find a rhetorical device that is used both for textual cohesion and foregrounding.

As for stories in the past, speakers have more TAM values to choose from. They may alternate again between irrealis and realis, but they may also exploit the aspectual categories: perfective and imperfective. As was described in §6.4.2, the imperfective is divided again into a basic imperfective and durative. Thus, the richness of the TAM system allows speakers to make finer distinctions.

I will show this in another text excerpt (10). This text is part of a story about a man who fell off a coconut palm and died. It was told by Marua Bai who remembers this incident well. The protagonist of the story used to wander around in the night and steal other people's palm wine. Palm wine is produced by cutting a fresh shoot up in the palm. A bamboo container which is tied underneath the shoot captures the sap. The sap slowly ferments and turns into an alcoholic substance. The main character of the story sets off alone in the night. He climbs and raids a number of palms. At the third palm, a coconut leaf breaks and he falls some twenty meters into a pineapple plant. Even though he survives his severe injuries, he dies about a week later. For each verb in each of the

---

[2]De Vries (2005) offers a typology for tail-head-linkage in Papuan languages. However, for the most part his sample consists of languages where this is achieved by using (parts of) serial verb constructions.

lines of text, the TAM value is given on the right. Where there are two verbs in a line, the underlined segments show which verb belongs to which translation and TAM value.

(10)

1	*wati fam änatha:* He was thinking:	PST:IPFV
2	*"kwa ŋabrigwé skerur."* "I will go back for coconut wine."	NPST:IPFV
3	*zbär kretharuf gardafo.* In the night, he got into the canoe.	IRR:PFV
4	*kwanrafinzrm gardame.* He was paddling here with the canoe.	PST:DUR
5	*mane yanra zäzr mnz ... finzo ... kabe matak* When he got to Zäzr Mnz ... (it was) only him ... nobody else	PST:IPFV
6	*yokwa kar ane fof ... matak* the same thing in Yokwa ... nobody	no verb
7	*garda <u>sräzin</u> ... yaniyak aki kwayanen ... mnz.* He <u>put down</u> the canoe ... and came in the moonlight ... to the house.	IRR:PFV NPST:IPFV
8	*nä skeru ŋasongwr.* He climbed a (coconut) wine palm.	NPST:IPFV
9	*warfo ... fä ŋonathr.* Up there ... he was drinking.	NPST:IPFV
10	*zrämbth we nä ŋazifo kresöbäth.* He finished and climbed another coconut.	2x IRR:PFV
11	*fä ŋonathr.* He was drinking.	NPST:IPFV
12	*we nä kabeane ŋazifo kresöbäth* and again he climbed another man's coconut.	IRR:PFV
13	*mane ŋasogwa warfo ...* As he climbed on top ...	PST:IPFV
14	*<u>kräms</u> drari wrbr.* He <u>sat down</u> and untied the bamboo container.	IRR:PFV NPST
15	*fof n zäznoba.* He was about to drink.	PST:PFV
16	*zamthetha drari.* He lifted up the bamboo container.	PST:PFV

17	*bäw! ŋazi tafokarä ane zägarnza.*	PST:IPFV
	Bang! The coconut leaf broke off (with him).	
18	*zane zäkurfa ziyé*	PST:PFV
	This one here split.	
19	*zenta ŋagarwa*	PST:IPFV
	He split his crotch.	
20	*fainr fr sazika*	PST:PFV
	He went into the pineapple plant.	
21	*fä swanorm "ara ara" ... kambe matak*	PST:DUR
	There he was shouting "ah ah" ... no people (heard him)	

[tci20120904-01 MAB #42-69]

Several observations which pertain to event sequencing as well as foregrounding can be made from this text. First, the narrator uses non-past tense for several clauses: the walking to the house (line 7), the climbing (line 8), the drinking (lines 9 and 11) and the untying (line 14). In some cases, the non-past alternates again with the irrealis perfective forms (line 10, 12, and 14) as we have seen in the wedding text above. The use of a non-past tense in a story which is otherwise told in recent past or past is quite common. In these cases, the non-past is used to foreground or emphasise the clauses in question.

Secondly, we find that it is the past imperfective which is used for the foregrounded clauses (in lines 13, 17, and 19). In line 17, the breaking of the coconut leaf is in the imperfective, whereas the preceding events in lines 15 and 16 are in the perfective. This might seem to contradict the notion of perfectivity, but the reader should keep in mind that the perfective in Komnzo focusses more on the beginning of an event (inceptive, or punctual) rather than the completion of an event. See §6.4.2 for a description of the semantics of aspect in Komnzo. Lines 18 and 19 both describe the severe injury which the protagonist received from his fall. Again the imperfective aspect is used for the foregrounded clause which provides more detail about the injury (i.e. that he split his crotch).

Although preliminary at this stage of research, we may attempt to build a hierarchy of TAM values with respect to foregrounding. In such a hierarchy,s irrealis inflections are more backgrounding than realis inflections. All past tenses are more backgrounding than the non-past. Finally, as we have seen, the perfective is more backgrounding than the imperfective. It follows that the most foregrounding TAM value is the non-past, while the irrealis (perfective) is the most backgrounding TAM value. The pragmatic functions of the TAM system in Komnzo provide a rich field for future research.

11 Aspects of the lexicon

11.1 Introduction

This chapter brings together two topics which can be roughly subsumed under the rubric of lexicology. First, I describe sign metonymy and metaphor expressed by reduplication (§11.2). These are found especially in terms for plants and birds. The second part is a description of the conceptualisation of landscape (§11.3). These sections are sprinkled with anthropological comments.

11.2 Sign metonymies

11.2.1 Overview

This section builds on Evans (1997), who discusses 'sign metonymies' in Australian languages. He points out how biota of different species, families or even kingdoms are connected through sharing a linguistic sign, i.e. they are referred to by the same word or they share a stem. One observation that can be made for Komnzo is the high number of reduplications that are found in plant names, and to some extent in names for animals, especially bird and fish species. In some cases, we have a reduplicative orphan, because the base is missing. In other cases, the base exists only in another language. Most of the time, however, there is a base in the lexicon.

The semantic link between the two referents shows a wide range of complexity. At the lower end, reduplication can single out some salient part of one plant, usually the fruit, establishing a relation of non-prototypicality. For example, *mefa* and *mefamefa* refer to two chestnut species (Semecarpus sp), but the nuts of *mefa* are roasted and eaten, while the nuts of *mefamefa* are much smaller. Note that non-prototypicality is a general feature of reduplication in Komnzo (§4.2). At the upper end of complexity, the reduplication pattern links referents through several steps of technical or cultural practices. One example is *ruga* 'pig' and *rugaruga* 'tree species' (Gmelina ledermannii). The two biota are linked in the following way: *rugaruga* is the tree from which *brubru* 'kundu drums' are made. These drums are used for *wath* 'dance' or *ruga wath* 'pig dance', because a pig will be killed and distributed in the morning hours after the dance. Thus, the technical concept of 'drum' and the cultural practice of 'dance' mediate between *ruga* 'pig' and *rugaruga* 'tree species'.

Examples of this type have to be checked thoroughly with several speakers. Otherwise, we run the risk of either (i) documenting folk etymologies, or (ii) not recognizing existing links at all. In an early stage of my fieldwork, the connection between *ruga* and *rugaruga* was explained in terms of spatial relations: the pig is often found in the vicinity of this tree. We will see below that this is true for other connections, but not for this particular example. During a plant walk, I was shown the *rugaruga* tree, and when I invoked the spatial explanation, my informants ruled out that explanation by saying "pigs roam around anywhere".

In the cases involving reduplication, there is a clear direction from base > reduplication. In such cases, we may ask if there are any detectable patterns in the direction of the semantic extensions. Most examples follow the animacy hierarchy in the way that what ranks higher is the base and what ranks lower is the reduplicated form. A list of examples is given in the following sections. For now, we can list the *züm* 'centipede', which reduplicates to *zümzüm* 'grass species' (1b), or *kwazür* 'fish species', which reduplicates to *kwazürkwazür* 'grass species' (8a), or *zuaku* 'widow(er)', which reduplicates to *zuakuzuaku* 'Fly River Anchovy' (10c). Those examples which violate this rule involve inanimate referents, like *karo* 'anthill' and *karokaro* 'grassland goana' (9a). Some of them can be explained by invoking relative salience or importance in every-day life.

Patterns of shared stems not only allow us to gain insight into the local classification of plants and animals, but can also reveal culturally significant connections from plant usage to esoteric knowledge. The following description will group examples by the type of semantic connection. Note that, under Evans' definition, reduplication is only one type; identical forms or inflected forms are also included (Evans 1997: 136).

11.2.2 Metaphor

Metaphorical links between different biota can be based on movement (1), appearance (2), colour (3), taste (4), feeling (5), hearing/sounds (6), or patterns of human interaction (7). Note that a few examples link biota to non-biological concepts (2a, 2d, 5, 7a), and in example (2b) the base is a Nama word.

(1)   a.   *dö* 'monitor lizard'; *dödö* 'broom, plant species' (Melaleuca sp). MOVEMENT: the lizards "sweeps" the floor with its tail when it walks.

     b.   *züm* 'centipede'; *zümzüm* 'grass species'; MOVEMENT: the grass grows along the ground in curves and has little spikes like the centipede.

(2)   a.   *toku* 'piggy-back ride (but on the shoulders rather than the back)'; *tokutoku* 'Bar-shouldered Dove'; APPEARANCE: the bird has a thick brownish line on the back of its neck at the same place where one would carry a child.

     b.   *min* 'nose' in Nama; *minmin* 'Purple-tailed Imperial Pigeon'). APPEARANCE: the bird has large nose-like beak.

     c.   *msar* 'weaver ant'; *msarmsar* 'insect larvae, esp. bee larvae' APPEARANCE: the bee larvae look like little ants.

     d.   *garda* 'canoe'; *gardagarda* 'tree species'; APPEARANCE: the seeds ot this tree are long and thin; they crack open lengthwise resembling the shape of a canoe.

(3) *yem* 'cassowary' (Casuarius casuarius); *yemyem* 'tree species' (Aceratium sp); COLOUR: the fruit of this tree is bright red as the cassowary's skin on its throat.

(4) a. *thatha* 'sugarcane' (Poaceae sp); *thathathatha* 'grass species'; TASTE: the grass tastes as sweet as the sugarcane. In the neighbouring variety Wära, the grass species is *kthkokthko*, while the word for sugarcane is *kthko*.

  b. *with* 'banana'; *withwith* 'tree species' (Pseudouvaria sp); TASTE: fruit tastes sweet like a banana.

(5) *kata* 'bamboo knife'; *katakata* 'grass species' (Carex sp); FEELING: the grass is as sharp as a bamboo knife.

(6) *ŋatha* 'dog'; *ŋathaŋatha* 'Bronze Quoll' (Dactylopsila trivirgata); SOUND: the bronze quoll barks like a dog.

(7) a. *tafko* 'hat'; *tafkotafko* 'tree species' (Macaranga sp); INTERACTION: the large leaves of this tree can be used as a hat against rain or sun.

  b. *ŋazi* 'coconut' (Cocos nucifera); *ŋaziŋazi* 'grass species' (Exocarpus largifolius); INTERACTION: the grass is put on the flowers of a coconut when it flowers for the first time to make it grow strong.

11.2.3 Metonymy

Metonymic links between animals and plants can be of three types: temporal (8), spatial (9) and technical/cultural (10). Note that for some examples, the link involves a biological term and a non-biological term, as in *zuaku* 'widower, orphan' and *zuakuzuaku* 'fly river anchovy' (10c).

(8) a. *kwazür* 'Narrow-fronted Tandan' (Neosilurus ater); *kwazürkwazür* 'grass species' (Helminthostachis zeylanica). TEMPORAL: the flowering of this grass signals that the fish is greasy; HUMAN INTERACTION: fishnets and fishhooks are painted with the root of this plant to ensure a good catch.

  b. *tauri* 'wallaby'; *tauritauri* 'tree species' (Diplanchia hetrophila); TEMPORAL: In June/July, when the tree flowers, wallabies like to stay close to this tree; people set traps in its vicinity or hide there for hunting wallabies.

  c. *dbän* 'tree species (Lamiodendron sp)'; *dbän tayo* 'yam harvest season' (lit. 'weak, ripe *dbän*'); TEMPORAL: The dry leaves of this tree signal the begin of the yam harvest.

(9) a. *karo* 'anthill; ground oven'; *karokaro* 'monitor lizard (grassland)' SPATIAL: during the dry season, the grassland goanna likes to dig a hole and hide inside the anthill.

  b. *nzöyar* 'Fawn-breasted Bowerbird' (Chlamydera cerviniventris); *nzöyarnzöyar* 'tree species' (Elaeocarpus sp); SPATIAL: the bowerbird collects the branches and fruit of this tree to build its display area.

c. *dagu* 'tree species' (Banksia dentata); *dagu* 'python species'; SPATIAL: the python sleeps on the tree. APPEARANCE: the bark of the tree looks like the python.

More complex connections involve technical concepts (10a) or references to cultural concepts (10b-d).

(10) a. *tru* 'palm species' (Hydriastele sp); *kwartru* 'thin long trough which collects the sago'; *trutru* 'current, stream of water' TECHNICAL: *Kwartru* is made from the palm leaf. While washing the sago pulp, a stream of water runs along the trough collecting the sago flour.

b. *ruga* 'pig' > *rugaruga* 'tree species' (Gmelina ledermannii); CULTURAL: Pigs are killed during dances, which are often called *ruga wath* 'pig dance(s)'. At such dances, *brubru* 'kundu drum(s)' are used and the tree *rugaruga* provides the best timber for carving drums.

c. *zuaku* 'widow(er), orphan'; *zuakuzuaku* 'Fly River Anchovy' (Thryssa rastrosa); CULTURAL: Widows wear a woven mourning dress from one week up a year after the death of a relative. The bones of the fish look like the woven mourning dress.

d. *bidr* 'flying fox'; *bidr* 'joking name for woman'; CULTURAL: This builds on the tree metaphor in which the tree is the origin of people. It may stand for a mythical origin or for one's place of birth. Since women are expected to shift to their husband's village, they behave like flying foxes, who move from one tree to another.

The most complex connections involve esoteric knowledge. A particularly puzzling example involves the link between the names of two birds and the word for 'vulva'. The reduplications *ktikti* and *dirdir* refer to two birds, the 'Greater Streaked Lory' and the 'Red-cheeked Parrot', respectively.[1] Both words lack a corresponding base in Komnzo. However, the word *dir* [ⁿdɪr] means 'vulva' in Blafe and there is a cognate in Nen *kter* [kəter] 'vulva'. This is to say that the two bird names as well as the words in Blafe and Nen are cognate, while *nzga*, the Komnzo word for 'vulva', is probably not. Note that Blafe and Nen are spoken about 60km to the west and east, respectively.

The link between the two bird names and the word 'vulva' can be explained by the *fütha* myth, which talks about the origin of the bullroarer (Ayres 1983: 80). *Fütha* is a story place in Rouku. This story also appears in (Williams 1936: 307) as an episode of the Kwavaru myth. According to the myth, a man hears a roaring noise coming from his wife's belly. He wonders what is causing the noise. He wants to have this object. So he calls several birds to fetch that object from his wife's vagina. Many of them fail, but in their attempts, they spill blood on themselves. That is why their plumage contains patches of red. Finally, one of the birds is successful. It steals the bullroarer and brings

---

[1]*Ktikti* refers to either the Greater Streaked Lory (Chalcopsitta scintillata) or the Rainbow Lorikeet (Trichoglossus haematodus), or the term covers both. *Dirdir* is the Red-cheeked Parrot (Geoffroyus geoffroyi).

it to the man. Since then, the bullroarer is a sacred object, only for initiated men. In William's version, the woman breaks down bleeding and crying, and thus, the story also explains the origin of menstruation.

The reduplication pattern makes reference to the red plumage of the two birds *ktikti* and *dirdir*. Moreover, there are other small birds with red colour that involve these words. For example, *kti tharthar* 'Spangled Drongo' has bright red eyes, and the word *tharthar* means 'side, next to'. The 'Red-flanked Lorikeet' *ŋazi dirdir* has a red beak and red sides, but the connection to *ŋazi* 'coconut' can be explained by its behaviour rather than relating to the red colour. These birds like to sit in coconut palms. The 'Orange-breasted Fig-parrot' *kor dirdir* has red cheeks, but the meaning of *kor* is unclear.[2] The shared linguistic sign links these bird names to bases meaning 'vulva'. But this is esoteric knowledge, which should not be shared with women or uninitiated men. Therefore, the link is hidden by using words from distant languages: not from Komnzo, nor from neighbouring languages.

11.2.4 Conclusion

This has been a preliminary analysis of the data on sign metonymies. Many examples have been collected, but more comparative data is needed to explain the semantic links. Data from the surrounding languages can provide two kinds of evidence; first, there will be more cases in which the base comes from another language, as in (2b), or in the myth described above. Secondly, we may find that the same biota are linked in other languages. Two examples of this come from Wära and Blafe. In Wära, the link between sugarcane and a particular grass species (4a) is established by the reduplication of the non-cognate word *kthko* [kǝθko]. In Blafe, the temporal link between the fish and the grass species (8a) is established by the cognate word *bäwr* [bæwǝr].

11.3 Landscape terminology

11.3.1 Conceptualisation of landscape

Williams opens his monograph about the Morehead district with the following description of the landscape: "Its scenery often has a mild, almost dainty, attractiveness in detail, but represents on the whole the extreme of monotony" 1936: 1. The Komnzo terminology reflects Williams' observation. There are general terms for landscape types, but we also find words expressing very specific local arrangements. For example, while there is a general distinction between *fz* 'forest', *ksi kar* 'open grassland' and *fath* 'clear place', we also find fine-grained distinctions like *fokufoku* 'small patch of forest', *fz minz* 'thin strip of forest' (lit. 'forest vine'), *thaba* 'clearing surrounded by forest' and *morthr* 'edge of forest with a smaller patch forest close by'. Some of the more general terms are shown with pictures in §1.3.2.

---

[2] Spangled Drongo (Dicrurus bracteatus), Red-flanked Lorikeet (Charmosyna placentis) and Orange-breasted Fig-parrot (Cyclopsitta gulielmiterti).

Large parts of the Morehead district are inundated by rising water during the wet season. This usually takes place between January and June, but there is some fluctuation from year to year. It is hardly surprising that this regular cycle has found its way into the lexicon of Komnzo. I invite the reader on a walk from the high ground down to the river. I translate the term *töna* as 'high ground'. It is that part of the land, regardless of vegetation type, which is virtually never covered by water. Settlements and yam gardens are located on *töna*. Small hills are referred to by *märmär* or the Motu loan *ororo*.[3] These areas may become islands (*bod*) during high floods. Wide, gentle slopes (*rsrs*) lacerated by many small creeks (*ttfö*) lead to lower areas. It is often along creeks where people plant sago palms or sometimes taro. Closer to the river, the ground can be very uneven and bumpy due to running water. This is called *kore*. A little lower lies that part of the land which is always covered by water during the rainy season. Often backwater stays in stagnant pools, which dry up only during the height of the dry season. These places are called *zra*, which I translate with 'swamp', but maybe the term 'billabong', commonly used in Australian English, is more fitting. In this area, we find smaller pools of water which dry up (*nawan*) and larger pools which are permanent (*dmgu*). The ankle-deep, muddy water covered with leaves is called *nzäwi*. Walking towards the river, the land rises again in many places. This difference in elevation is almost unnoticeable, but it is enough so that this area dries up first at the end of the wet season. These area between the swamp and the river are called *for* and people plant cassava, sweet potato and taro here. The steep riverbanks along the Morehead river are called *rokuroku*, a word from which the village name Rouku originates. The sides of the river are covered with patches of *süfi* 'floating grass', and in some places this layer is called *tüf* when it is thick enough to support the cultivation of sweet potatoes. Finally, there is the river which is called *ŋars*. Although found only in the southwest around Bensbach, large open lagoons are called *füwä* in Komnzo.

Especially in dry season much of people's daily life involves coming and going from the high ground to the river. This movement has left some impact in the verb lexicon. For example, the stem *frezsi* usually means 'take something out of the water'. In a middle template it means 'come up from the river' and can be used when disembarking a canoe, or walking back from a river camp to the village.

There are numerous creeks leading to the Morehead river. The mouth of a creek or a river is referred to by *zfth* 'base'. This word can refer to the base of a tree, but it can also mean 'origin, reason'. Interestingly, the smaller creeks may be called *ttfö tuti* 'creek branches, creek twigs' or *ttfö minz* 'creek vines'. The place where the creeks start can be called either *ttfö ker* 'creek tail' or *ttfö zrminz* 'creek root'. The same can be said about the Morehead river. Thus waterways are often conceptualised by a tree metaphor. This stems from the *kwafar* myth, which associates the origin of all people with a tree. Kwafar is located somewhere in the Arafura Sea between Papua New Guinea and Australia. In the myth, the tree burns down and a flood caused by killing a mythical creature forces people to retreat northwards and southwards. The roots in the ground also burn and with the rising water they become creeks and rivers. In other versions of the myth, the tree

---

[3]Nowadays, Komnzo speakers refer to people from the highlands as *märmär kabe* 'hill people'.

falls northwards and the creeks and rivers are formed from the burned stem, branches, and twigs of the tree.

11.3.2 Place names

Place names in the Morehead district are both numerous and densely clustered (Ayres 1983: 129).[4] The village of Rouku alone consists of some three dozen named places. The knowledge of most place names is common knowledge, for example Williams notes that "if you ask your guide where you stand at any moment, he will be able to give a name to the land." (1936: 207). However, the details of every small track and the stories that belong to it is something only known by the rightful owners of that piece of land. In that sense, knowledge about place names can be compared to a proof of ownership. Therefore, I deliberately do not include a complete list of collected place names, nor do I provide a detailed map. Below, I address selected topics related to place names.

All place names in Komnzo are proper nouns, but they differ with respect to their meaning. Some place names have no meaning other than the places they designate, for example *fthi, kanathr* or *ŋazäthe*. At some point in the past, they might have been segmentable into meaningful parts or constitute a meaningful word in themselves, but this knowledge has faded away.[5] Place names commonly preserve features which have become non-productive or lexemes which have become archaic. This can also be found in Komnzo. For example, the place name *thmefi*, meaning 'moustache', can be split into the components *thm* 'nose' and *efi* 'hair'. However, the word *efi* is archaic, and instead *thäbu* is used. In fact, some speakers are unaware of the possible segmentation.

More commonly, Komnzo place names consist of two elements, which usually form a nominal compound. These compounds range from rather dry descriptions, like *gani zfth* 'base of the *gani* tree' (Endiandra brassii), to the most colourful illustrations, as in *nzga warsi* 'vulva chewing', *kwanz fath* 'bald head clearing'. Many nominal compounds consist of a plant name plus a landscape term or a term used for the part of a plant. The most common landscape terms are *zra* 'swamp, waterhole' and *ttfö* 'creek'. The most common plant part terms are *zfth* 'base' and *fr* 'stem, grove'.[6] A few examples are: *karesa zfth* '*karesa* base' (Melaleuca sp), *atätö fr* '*atätö* stem' (Pouteria sp), *wsws zra* '*wsws* swamp' (Combretum sp). These are not descriptions of places, but place names. A phrase like *karesa zfth* can refer to the base of any *karesa* tree, but it refers only to one named place.

A few place names are inflected verb forms, for example *karifthe* 'you two send each other off!'.[7] This place connects to a myth in which the ancestor of the Garaita people and the ancestor of the Rouku people were fighting. At the end of the story, they depart

---

[4]I would like to thank Mary Ayres for giving me access to her fieldnotes which proved to be enormously helpful during the elicitation and investigation of place names.

[5]Two of these examples look like inflected verb forms; *kanathr* is similar to an imperative form of 'eat' in a middle template: *kanathé* 'eat yourself!'; *ŋazäthe* contains the middle prefix *ŋ-*, a possible non-dual marker *-th* and the first non-singular suffix *-e*. However, the assumed verb stem *zä-* does not exist in modern Komnzo.

[6]The word *zfth* can mean (i) 'base of a plant, tree', (ii) 'rivermouth', (iii) 'origin' or (iv) 'reason'.

[7]ka\rifth/e
2|3DU:SBJ:IMP:PFV/send

in opposite directions from *karifthe*. Another name which includes an inflected verb is *kafthé fr*. The first element is means 'take off your bag!' and the second means 'stem, grove'. Interestingly, *kafthé* is not Komnzo, but Wartha.[8] I address the topic of mixed language place names in §11.3.3. For some place names, there is no etymology available, for example *yrn* 'they are many'.

Simpson and Hercus (2002) provide a list of differences between introduced and indigenous place names in Australia. In the following, I apply some points of their typology to the Morehead district. The first point which Hercus and Simpson discuss is the difference between a system and a local network. The former is meant to provide an overview, a kind of standardised template for naming places, which can be applied universally and is open to everyone. Komnzo place names, like indigenous place names in Australia, differ in that they often constitute smaller networks of place names. For example, the number of named places is much denser in the vicinity of inhabited places or previously inhabited places. Moreover, places or tracks of land belong to a particular clan, and the detailed knowledge about these places, which may sometimes include place names, is not meant for the public.

A second difference raised by Hercus and Simpson is that between local mnemonics and mnemotechnics. They point out that place names have developed organically over a long time as local mnemonics to refer to places. This applies to places in Europe and Australia (or the Morehead district) alike, but not to introduced place name systems. For example, the Komnzo place name *swäri zfth* 'swäri base' must have started as the description of a place with an especially large or beautiful *swäri* tree (Alstonia actinifila), but over time it has lost its descriptive function. Today it is used even though the *swäri* tree was cut down decades ago. Francesca Merlan has described place name systems of this kind as being "non-arbitrary", because they establish a direct relationship to the designated places (Merlan 2001). In contrast to local mnemonics, technological advances like writing and mapping provides a kind of mnemotechnics, which opens the possibility to include arbitrary place names like *Sydney* or *Port Moresby*.

Simpson and Hercus outline three naming strategies that are rarely found in indigenous Australia: commemoration strategies, topographic descriptors and relative location. Commemoration strategies are wholly absent in Komnzo place names. They are only found in those names introduced by Europeans. For example, the Morehead river was named after B. D. Morehead, who was the premier of Queensland between 1888 and 1890. The Bensbach river was named during a joint expedition in 1895 by W. MacGregor and J. Bensbach who was the Dutch Resident at Ternate at the time. While Hercus and Simpson point out that topographic descriptors are rare in indigenous Australia, they are quite common in Komnzo. However, as pointed out above, they include only a small set of words (*zfth* 'tree base', *fr* 'stem, grove' or *ttfö* 'creek'). Relative terms like *North Melbourne* or *West Berlin* are almost completely absent in Komnzo, as they are in Australian languages. The only example in which a place name establishes a relation to another place is *fthiker*. The link here is a creek which has its mouth at place called *fthi* and its

---

[8]Imperative perfectives in Komnzo mark dual versus non-dual with a vowel change in the prefix, and the suffix is zero for second singular. The corresponding Komnzo verb form would be *käthf*.

starting point at *fthiker* '*fthi* tail'. Note that creeks themselves are usually not named, but the word *ttfö* 'creek' can be added to a place situated on a creek.

11.3.3 Mixed place names

An interesting phenomenon that sheds some light on multilingualism is the fact that many place names are composed of words from two languages. I refer to these as mixed place names. Most of them involve one Komnzo word. But in a few place names both words are from different languages even though the place is located on Komnzo speaking territory. The basic principle of mixed place names is shown in Figure 11.1 for *fotnz*. This is a place near Rouku village, which can be parsed as one word from Wartha Thuntai and one word from Komnzo.

place name: *fotnz* 'short coconut'

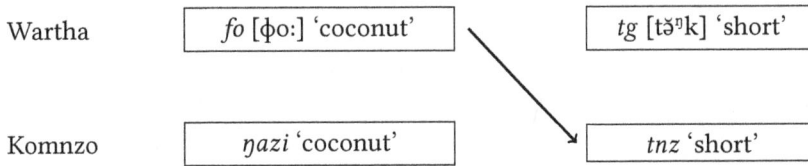

Wartha   *fo* [ɸoː] 'coconut'   *tg* [tɜ̃ᵑk] 'short'

Komnzo   *ŋazi* 'coconut'   *tnz* 'short'

Figure 11.1: The principle of mixed place names: *fotnz*

This principle is rather pervasive. A quarter of recorded place names involve a word from another language. I give a few examples in (11-13). These are sorted according to whether the Komnzo word is the first (11) or last element (12). I show the place name as a single word in most cases, because often speakers only realised their segmentability when I prompted them. This is followed by a literal English translation of the contributing elements, after which the two languages are given. In parentheses, I provide the two words in each language. Note that I follow the Komnzo orthography here, because with the exception of Nama there is no orthography available for these varieties. A few cases are problematic because one of the two words is identical in the contributing languages (13). However, all examples designate places on Komnzo speaking territory.

(11)   a.   *fotnz* 'coconut + short'; Wartha Thuntai (**fo** *tg*) + Komnzo (*ŋazi* **tnz**).

      b.   *säzäri* 'paperbark + bending over'; Wartha Thuntai (**sä** *ytho*) + Komnzo (*karesa* **zäri**); the word *zäri* 'bending (branches)' is considered archaic, but there is the modern word *zäre* 'shade'.

      c.   *tratrabäk* 'bird species + back'; Kánchá (**tratra** *bak*) + Komnzo (*drädrä* **bäk**).

      d.   *makozanzan* 'vagina + beating'; Arammba (**mako** *kamakama*) + Komnzo (*nzga* **zanzan**).

    e. *füsari* 'garden row + axe'; Nama (**fü** *bilé*) + Komnzo (*ŋanz* **sari**); The word *sari* is considered archaic.

    f. *düdüsam* 'broom + liquid'; Nama (**düdü** *wkwr*) + Komnzo (*dödö* **sam**).

    g. *fakwr* 'after + ashes'; Nama (**fa** *fak*) + Komnzo (*thrma* **kwr**).

    h. *wästhak* 'tree species (Ficus elastica) + place'; Nama (**wäs** *näk*) + Komnzo (*wäsü* **thak**); the word *thak* is archaic in Komnzo and only found in *mni thak* 'fire place'.

(12)   a. *zthékabir* 'penis + sleep(n)'; Komnzo (**zthé** *etfth*) + Wära (*zthk* **kabir**).

    b. *snzäzwär* 'river crayfish + base'; Komnzo (**snzä** *zfth*) + Wartha (*dawi* **zwär**).

    c. *ormogo* 'Emerald Dove + house'; Komnzo (**or** *mnz*) + Nama (*bänz* **mogo**).

    d. *yem gi faf* 'cassowary killing place'; Komnzo (**yem** *zan* **faf**) + Nama (awyé gi faf).

    e. *märofak* 'tree species (Dillenia ensifolia) + ashes'; Komnzo (**märo** *kwr*) + Nama (*mane* **fak**).

(13)   a. *sizwär* 'eye + base'; Komnzo (**si** *zfth*) + Wartha Thuntai (**si** *zwär*).

    b. *gawe* 'I + also'; Komnzo (*nzä* **we**) + Wartha Thuntai (**ga** *we*).

    c. *mnzärfr* 'ant + stem'; Nama (**mnzär** *fr*) + Komnzo (*msar* **fr**).

    d. *zöfäthak* 'bird + place'; Wära (**zöfä** *thak*) + Komnzo (*ymd* **thak**); the word *thak* is archaic in Komnzo and only found in *mni thak* 'fire place'.

Mixed place names pattern roughly according to geography. For example, place names containing Nama words are mostly found east of Rouku, while place names involving Wartha Thuntai words are mostly found to the southwest. There are many exceptions, where (i) the place does not fit geography or (ii) the 'foreign' word could be from more than one language. However, the overall pattern suggests that geography plays a role. Thus, if we showed these places on a map and marked them for the contributing 'foreign' languages, we could geographically visualise speech varieties. Data from other villages and their place names is needed to corroborate this observation.

The pattern of mixed place names calls for an investigation of naming customs. However, as with most place names, the point in time when such double language names were coined is far removed. Most of my informants did not remember anyone giving a name to these places. A common response was "we learned them from our fathers". In fact, most informants find the idea of naming a place somewhat strange. That being said, we can still draw some conclusions about naming customs. Mixed place names differ from the monolingual, descriptive place names in one important aspect. One can imagine a gradual transition from a description to a proper name like *swäri zfth* 'swäri base' mentioned above. With mixed place names such a transition is an unlikely scenario. Instead, a more deliberate act of coining the name has to be assumed. Note that we also find monolingual place names, where a transition from description to proper name can be ruled out on semantic grounds, for example *nzarga wth* ('tree species + faeces') or *zäzr mnz* ('lazy + house'). However, the point here is that a gradual transition is unlikely because two languages are involved, even if the name is of a more descriptive nature like (11h) and (12b). These observations authenticate the importance of place in Morehead culture, an argument that was put forward by Ayres (1983).

Mixed place names can shed some light on the degree of multilingualism in the language communities concerned. There are varying degrees of metalinguistic awareness both between different place names and between different speakers. That is to say that speakers differ in their language profiles, and ultimately differ in how much access they have to the word in the "foreign language". Moreover, some place names are easier to parse, while others have undergone phonological reduction or one of the segments has become archaic. Generally speaking, most speakers are aware of these double language names and the meaning in the respective languages. One observation that can be made is the complete absence of doublets, that is cases were both terms refer to the same referent, but in different languages. There are examples of doublets in Komnzo, but not for place names. For example, there is a cassava species called *ubi biskar*. The word *ubi* is from Malay and the word *biskar* is a Komnzo word, but both mean 'cassava'. This type of doublet is to be expected if the speakers who coined the name did not know the meaning of the foreign word. The pattern that we find with place names suggests the opposite. At the time of coinage, one has to assume a degree of multilingualism at least as high as today.

11.3.4 Social landscape

This section addresses the topic of social landscape, by which I mean the reference system used for people in relation to space. The Komnzo terms for this domain conceptualise either pure geography or what we may call kinship-dependent geography. The importance of place in the Morehead district has been described in great detail by Mary Ayres. I sketch out the sister-exchange system only where it is relevant to the discussion. Otherwise I refer the reader to Ayres (1983) and §1.3.8.

The purely geographic terms are based on an east-west axis. The people who live in the east are referred to with the word *nzödmä*, while the people in the west are called *smärki*. These labels are often only applied to people living two villages away. They are rarely used for one's immediate neighbours. The system is ego-centric in that the same labels or cognate terms are applied in other villages. If one moves further west, the term *güdmä* [$^{\eta}$gγ^ndmæ] is used for everyone to the east, including the people of Rouku.[9] Likewise the people in the east would call everyone who lives west of them *smärki*. Thus, the terms *nzödmä* and *smärki* do not refer to a specific group, but mean 'people from the east' and 'people from the west', respectively. This has caused some confusion for early ethnographers (Williams 1936: 36), but was explained by Ayres (1983: 132). Furthermore, the east-west axis is validated by the term *tharthar kabe* 'people on the side', which is

---

[9]The word *güdmä* in Nama and Blafe are cognate with Komnzo *nzödmä*. In Komnzo, Wära, Anta, and Wère velar stops have undergone palatalisation before front vowels, for example [$^{\eta}$g] > [^{n}dʒ].

used for the Arammba speakers in the north.[10] The naming system is a correlate of a fact about the region's geography. Most villages are built on what is called the "Morehead ridge" (Paijmans et al. 1971: 15), a slighty elevated ridge that runs in east-west direction. Further north, the speakers of Suki and Gogodala are collectively labelled with the proper name *wiram*. Also the people in the south do not fit in the east-west schema, but are instead referred to by proper names, for example *wartha*, or they may be called *mazo kabe* 'coast people'. Groups which live further away have proper names, for example the Kanum and Marind speakers in the west are called *kodomarid*, and the speakers of Kiwai are called *turéd*.

As pointed out by Ayres, people define themselves as belonging to a particular origin place. The ancestors of different clans and sections might have arrived from different directions, but they "spread out" from the same origin place. Hence, people can be referred to by their origin place. For Komnzo speakers, this is *farem kar* 'farem place', which is situated about 3km northwest of Rouku. Other examples are *mät* for the people of Yokwa or *thamga* for the people of Uparua.[11] Origin places usually overlap with language variety, in that a speaker of Wära belongs to *mät kar*, whereas a speaker of Anta belongs to *thamga kar*.

The kinship system gives rise to yet another, very common way of referring to people. The rules of exogamy involve a number of factors. Some are related to place, for example identification with a particular origin place establishes an exogamous group. Some are related to the section system, for example the Mayawa section regardless of place forms an exogamous group. The section classification cross-cuts the place system, i.e. one may not marry people from the same origin place, but also not from a different place if they belong to the same section. Additionally, people who "share a land boundary" may not intermarry. That is to say that two individuals may not marry even if they belong to different places and different sections, if their land is adjacent. Ayres argues convincingly that locality forms the most important factor in the complicated definitions of exogamous groupings (1983: §5). If kinship is conceptualised in terms of space, it follows that kinship terms can be used to refer to people of a particular place. I often overheard people talking about their *ngom kar* 'brother-in-law place' or *thuft kar* 'in-law place'. Note that the calculations one has to make to arrive at the correct referent are rather complex. Not only does one individual normally have several brothers-in-law, but that different individuals have different in-laws. Nevertheless, such knowledge is common ground for the people of Rouku. Although I often found it difficult to identify the referent in an utterance like (14), every child in Rouku could make the correct deduction without effort.

(14) *watik kraritth bern ... sukufa ärithr **nafathufthnm** ... **nafangom karnm**.*
      watik kra\rit/th   b=e\rn/   (.) sukufa
      then 2|3DU:SBJ:IRR:PFV/go.across MED=2|3DU:SBJ:NPST:IPFV/be (.) tobacco
      ä\ri/thr   nafa-thufth=nm   (.) nafa-ngom
      2|3SG:SBJ>2|3PL:IO:NPST:IPFV/give 3.POSS-in.law=DAT.NSG (.) 3.POSS-brother.in.law

---

[10] Often the Arammba phrase *sarsar ŋar* is used, which has the same meansing.
[11] *mät* is a term referring to the red colour of the ground, and the villaga *Mata* in the east derives its name from the same word. There is no etymology for *thamga* or *farem*.

kar=nm
village=DAT.NSG
'Then they went across there ... He shared tobacco with his in-laws ... with the
people of his brother-in-law place.'   [tci20111119-01 ABB #88-91]

Sample text: Nzürna trikasi

Nzürna trikasi

This text belongs to a genre called *nzürna trikasi* 'nzürna stories'. I translate *nzürna* with 'devil', 'spirit' or 'witch'. Although all of these translations fall short of a full description, the *nzürna* character has some resemblance to witches in a western context. They are malevolent beings, usually old women, who live in the forest. They have long eyebrows and sharp fingernails, with which they disembowel people to devour them. They can change their appearance to look like a human being. They can summon and control animals, especially the centipede (*züm*). They often trick people who foolishly walk alone in the forest. [1]

Although *nzürna* stories belong to a particular place, they are very much public stories. The *nzürna* character is often joked about openly. For example, one may call a person or a dog "*nzürna*", when it roams around in the dark. Although there are many local variations of the *nzürna* theme, we can identify some recurring elements. First, the *nzürna* often lives in a tree, usually a *wäsi* tree. Secondly, most stories involve some innocent person who is killed and eaten. Third, relatives and friends of the victim take revenge by burning the *nzürna*.

The following *nzürna* story belongs to the hamlet of Firra. The narrator is Maraga Kwozi. He was born in Firra, but he told me the story in Morehead. This *nzürna* story deviates in two points. First, the *nzürna* character lives together with a husband, and they have children. Secondly, the *nzürna* character lived in harmony with the people of Firra up until she kills and eats a visitor.

This text can be accessed under: https://zenodo.org/record/1294666

---

[1] All texts in the appendix have been edited in the following way: (i) I corrected mistakes that came up during the transcription (ii) I have removed overly long speech pauses and (iii) I have lumped together some annotations and split others. All editorial changes were kept to a minimum. The unedited versions can be found in the archive.

1   *zaföwä ... fthé kabe keke kwot tüfr thfrärm*
    zafe=wä   (.) fthé   kabe keke kwot   tüfr   thf\rä/rm
    before=EMPH (.) when man NEG properly plenty 2|3PL:SBJ:PST:DUR/be
    'Long time ago, that is when there were not many people'

2   *thwamnzrm zane kafar baden thé z kabe enrera*
    thwa\m/nzrm   zane   kafar bad=en   thé   z kabe
    2|3PL:SBJ:PST:DUR/dwell DEM:PROX big   ground=LOC when ALR man
    en\rä/ra
    2|3PL:SBJ:PST:IPFV:VENT/be
    'and they were living here on this land. That is the time when people came.'

3   *nä kabe thfamnzrm ... mogarkamen ... kar nima rä ... mogarkam*
    nä   kabe thfa\m/nzrm   (.) mogarkam=en (.) kar   nima
    INDF man 2|3PL:SBJ:PST:DUR/dwell (.) mogarkam=LOC (.) village like.this
    \rä/   mogarkam
    3SG.FEM:NPST:IPFV/be mogarkam
    'Some people lived in Mogarkam ... There is a village there ... Mogarkam.'

4   *okay, nä thfamnzrm firran*
    okay nä   thfa\m/nzrm   firra=n
    okay INDF 2|3PL:SBJ:PST:DUR/dwell firra=LOC
    'Okay, others lived in Firra.'

5   *okay, nä fä fefe thwamnzrm mänwä kar bramöwä erä*
    okay nä   fä   fefe   thwa\m/nzrm   mä=wä   kar   bramöwä
    okay INDF DIST really 2|3PL:SBJ:PST:DUR/dwell where=EMPH place all
    e\rä/
    2|3PL:SBJ:NPST:IPFV/be
    'Okay, others lived right there, where all the villages (and hamlets) are.'

6   *firra mrmren ... mane zfrärm ... nzürna ŋare bobo zwamnzrm*
    firra mrmr=en   (.) mane zf\rä/rm   (.) nzürna ŋare   bobo
    firra inside=LOC (.) which 3SG.FEM:SBJ:PST:DUR/be (.) nzürna woman MED.ALL
    zwa\m/nzrm
    3SG.FEM:SBJ:PST:DUR/dwell
    'As for Firra, a nzürna woman lived in the village.'

7   *nzürna ŋare nafafisrwä thfrnm*
    nzürna ŋare   nafa-fis=r=wä   thf\rn/m
    nzürna woman 3.POSS-husband=ASSOC.DU=EMPH 2|3DU:SBJ:PST:DUR/be
    'The nzürna woman was with her husband.'

8   *nafafis yf nagawa ... tnztnz kabe sfrärm*
    nafa-fis   yf   nagawa (.) tnz-tnz   kabe sf\rä/rm
    3.POSS-husband name nagawa (.) REDUP-short man 3SG.MASC:SBJ:PST:DUR/be
    'His name (was) Nagawa ... He was a short guy.'

9   *nafane ŋare ... nzürna ŋare fof yf mane zfrärm zafo ... nafrr thwamrnm*

nafane   ŋare   (.) nzürna ŋare   fof   yf   mane zf\rä/rm

3SG.POSS woman   (.) nzürna woman EMPH name which 3SG.FEM:SBJ:PST:DUR/be

zafo (.) nafrr   thwam\rn/m

zafo (.) 3DU.ASSOC 2|3DU:SBJ:PST:DUR/be

'His wife ... the nzürna woman whose name was Zafo ... He lived with her.'

10   *wati, mä fefe thwamrnm wäsü ... nafanme mnz zfrärm*

wati, mä   fefe   thwam\rn/m   wäsü (.) nafanme mnz

then where really 2|3DU:SBJ:PST:DUR/dwell wäsü (.) 3NSG.POSS house

zf\rä/rm

3SG.FEM:SBJ:PST:DUR/be

'Where they really lived (was) the wäsü tree (Ficus elastica) ... it was their house.'

11   *wäsü kafar sukogrm ... ane yfön thuthkrnm*

wäsü kafar su\kogr/m   (.) ane yfö=n

wäsü big   3SG.MASC:SBJ:PST:DUR:STAT/stand (.) DEM hole=LOC

thu\thkr/nm

2|3DU:SBJ:PST:DUR:STAT/be.inside

'There was a big wäsü tree standing ... They were inside that hole.'

12   *boba mnz nafanme zfrärm mä thwamrnm*

boba   mnz nafanme zf\rä/rm   mä   thwa\m/rnm

MED.ABL house 3NSG.POSS 3SG.FEM:SBJ:PST:DUR/be where 2|3DU:SBJ:PST:DUR/dwell

'This was their house, where they were living'

13   *firra kar mrmren kabe thwamnzrm fobo*

firra kar   mrmr=en   kabe thwa\m/nzrm   fobo

firra village inside=LOC man 2|3PL:SBJ:PST:DUR/dwell DIST.ALL

'People were living over there in the village of Firra.'

14   *kabe fthé kwarfakunzrmth fthé thfyakm*

kabe fthé   kwa\rfaku/nzrmth   fthé   thf\yak/m

man when 2|3PL:SBJ:PST:DUR/sprinkle when 2|3PL:SBJ:PST:DUR/walk

'When the people spread out, when they went ...'

15   *nima ŋarake znfo o fiyafr o ... nima efothen ... etfthmöwä fthé thfyakm*

nima   ŋarake zn=fo   o fiyaf=r   o (.) nima   efoth=en (.)

like.this fence   place=LOC or hunting=PURP or (.) like.this day=LOC (.)

etfth=me=wä   fthé   thf\yak/m

sleep=INS=EMPH when 2|3PL:SBJ:PST:DUR/walk

'like this to the garden place or hunting or during the day ... or when they went overnight'

16   *ane nzürna ŋare ausi fof kwänzinzr ... fi zwanyakm*

ane nzürna ŋare   ausi   fof   kwän\zinzr/   (.) fi

DEM spirit   woman old woman EMPH 2|3SG:SBJ:ITER:VENT/replace (.) 3.ABS

zwan\yak/m
3SG.FEM:SBJ:PST:DUR:VENT/walk
'that nzürna woman, that old woman always took over the place ... she came.'

17   *gatha kar fthé thumarwrm ... gathagathame thfnakwrmth mnz gatha kar.*
gatha kar fthé   thu\mar/wrm   (.) gathagatha=me
rubbish   when 2|3SG:SBJ>2|3PL:OBJ:PST:DUR/see (.) bad=INS
thf\nak/wrmth   mnz   gatha kar
2|3PL:SBJ>2|3PL:OBJ:PST:DUR/put.down house rubbish
'When she saw the rubbish ... they had carelessly put down the rubbish in the house'

18   *dödö thfefaf ane zurenwrmo mnz fath thwafiyokwrm*
dödö   thfe\faf/   ane zu\ren/wrmo
broom 2|3SG:SBJ>2|3PL:OBJ:ITER/hold DEM SG:SBJ>3SG.FEM:PST:DUR:AND/sweep
mnz   fath   thwa\fiyok/wrm
house clear.place SG:SBJ>2|3PL:IO:PST:DUR/make
'She always grabbed the broom, swept the house and cleaned it for them.'

19   *nafanme kkauna monme gathagathame thfnakwrmth kwot namäme thfanakwrm*
nafanme k-kauna   mon=me gathagatha=me
3NSG.POSS REDUP-stuff how=INS bad=INS
thf\nak/wrmth   kwot   namä=me
2|3PL:SBJ>2|3PL:IO:PST:DUR/put.down properly good=INS
thfa\nak/wrm
2|3SG:SBJ>2|3PL:OBJ:PST:DUR/put.down
'How they had dropped their things carelessly, she was sorting them properly.'

20   *mnzen thwarakthkwrmo ... mni tnztnz rä ... kwanbrigwrm nafanemäwä mnzfo*
mnz=en   thwa\rakthk/wrmo   (.) mni   tnz-tnz
house=LOC SG:SBJ>2|3PL:IO:PST:DUR:AND/put.on.top (.) firewood REDUP-short
\rä/   (.) kwan\brig/wrm   nafaneme=wä
3SG.FEM:SBJ:NPST:IPFV/be (.) 2|3SG:SBJ:PST:DUR/return 3NSG.POSS=Emph
mnz=fo
house=ALL
'She put their (things) back in the house ... for example the small pices of firewood ... She brought them back to their house.'

21   *fthé we thwanyakm thwänthor ... ane mnz woga fthé swänthor*
fthé we   thwan\yak/m   thwän\thor/   (.) ane mnz
when also 2|3PL:SBJ:PST:DUR:VENT/walk 2|3PL:SBJ:ITER:VENT/arrive (.) DEM house
woga fthé   swän\thor/
man when 3SG.MASC:SBJ:ITER:VENT/arrive
'When they were coming back, each time they arrived ... each time when the houseowner arrived'

22   *"oh zane ŋare z nzwänyak mnz fath zf nzürenwro zrä."*

oh zane   ŋare   z   nz=wän\yak/   mnz   fath

oh DEM:PROX woman ALR IPST=3SG.FEM:NPST:IPFV:VENT/walk house clear place

zf   nz=w\ren/wro   z=\rä/

IMM IPST=SG:SBJ>3SG.FEM:NPST:IPFV:AND/sweep PROX=3SG.FEM:SBJ:NPST:IPFV/be

'(he said) "Oh, this woman already came. She has swept the houseyard just now."'

23   *zafe kabe miyatha thfrärm nafanme rzarsi monme zfrärm ... ane kar woganzo*

zafe   kabe miyatha   thf\rä/rm   nafanme rzar-si   mon=me

before man knowledgeable 2|3PL:SBJ:PST:DUR/be 3NSG.POSS tie-NMLZ how=INS

zf\rä/rm   (.) ane kar   woga=nzo

3SG.FEM:SBJ:PST:DUR/be (.) DEM village man=ONLY

'Before, the people people knew about their ties (to her) ... only those village people.'

24   *nafä fi monme nzürna ŋareyä kwarzarwrmth*

nafä   fi   mon=me nzürna ŋare=ä   kwa\rzar/wrmth

3PL.ASSOC 3.ABS how=INS spirit   woman=ASSOC.PL 2|3PL:SBJ:PST:DUR/tie

'how they were behaving towards the *nzürna* woman.'

25   *keke thufnzrm ane karma kabe naf ... bänema fi nar wogathatha bäne thfrärm nima*

keke thu\fn/nzrm   ane kar=ma   kabe naf   (.)

NEG 2|3SG:SBJ>2|3PL:OBJ:PST:DUR/hit DEM village=CHAR man 3SG.ERG (.)

bäne=ma   fi   nar   woga=thatha bäne   thf\rä/rm   nima

DEM:MED=CHAR 3.ABS friend man=SIMIL   DEM:MED 2|3PL:SBJ:PST:DUR/be like.this

'She did not attack the people from that village ... because they were like friends ...'

26   *miyatha thfrärm ... nafane nagayé thfrärm naf thwamonegwrm ... kabe fefe*

miyatha   thf\rä/rm   (.) nafane   nagayé thf\rä/rm

knowledgeable 2|3PL:SBJ:PST:DUR/be (.) 3NSG.POSS children 2|3PL:SBJ:PST:DUR/be

naf   thwa\moneg/wrm   (.) kabe fefe

3SG.ERG 2|3SG:SBJ>2|3PL:IO:PST:DUR/look.after (.) man really

'They knew about this. They were her children. She looked after them ... really the people.'

27   *wati, nä kayé ... mogarkamma kabe nima sfyakm firrafo*

wati nä   kayé   (.) mogarkam=ma   kabe nima

then INDF yesterday (.) mogarkam=CHAR man like.this

sf\yak/m   firra=fo

3SG.MASC:SBJ:PST:DUR/walk firra=ALL

'Well, one day, a man from Mogarkam walked this way to Firra.'

28   *wati, fi mane yara nama zokwasi woga yara*

wati fi   mane ya\r/a   nama zokwasi woga

then 3.ABS which 3SG.MASC:SBJ:PST:IPFV/be nama language man

ya\r/a
3SG.MASC:SBJ:PST:IPFV/be
'As for this one, he was a speaker of Nama.'

29 *firran mane thwamnzrm mema zokwasi woga yara ... fthé thwamnzrm kabe*
firra=n   mane thwa\m/nzrm   mema zokwasi woga
firra=LOC which 2|3PL:SBJ:PST:DUR/dwell mema language man
ya\r/a   (.) fthé thwa\m/nzrm   kabe
3SG.MASC:PST:IPFV/be (.) when 2|3PL:SBJ:PST:DUR/dwell man
'As for the ones who lived in Firra, they were speaker of Mema. That'a when the people lived in Firra.'

30 *wati, fi mane yaka e "krara krara krara"*
wati fi   mane \yak/a   e   3xkrara
then 3.ABS which 3SG.MASC:SBJ:PST:IPFV/walk until 3xsound.of.coockatoo
'Well, when he walked. "krara krara krara"'

31 *firra sathora fof with fren fof "krara krara krara"*
firra sa\thor/a   fof   with   fr=en   fof   3xkrara
firra 3SG.MASC:SBJ:PST:PFV EMPH banana stem=LOC EMPH 3xsound.of.coockatoo
'He arrived in Firra (and he went) between the banana trees "krara krara krara"'

32 *fi zära yakme we senis zära ... kabe wokuthé zäkora nima kabe*
fi   zä\r/a   yakme we senis zä\r/a   (.) kabe
3.ABS 2|3SG:SBJ:PST:PFV/do quickly also change 2|3SG:SBJ:PST:PFV/do (.) man
woku-thé zä\kor/a   nima   kabe
skin-ADJZR 2|3SG:SBJ:PST:PFV/become like.this man
'He quickly changed. He became like a human being ... like a man.'

33 *ane si thäbu zanfr ra zane thfrärm ... ofe ŋarerath ... zäwthefa ... kabe zäkora*
ane si thäbu zanfr ra   zane   thf\rä/rm   (.) ofe
DEM eye hair   long what DEM:PROX 2|3PL:SBJ:PST:DUR/be (.) absence
ŋa\rä/rath   (.) zä\wthef/a   (.) kabe
2|3PL:SBJ:PST:IPFV/do (.) 2|3SG:SBJ:PST:PFV/change (.) man
zä\kor/a
2|3SG:SBJ:PST:PFV/become
'These long eyebrows and whatever else there was, it disappeared. He changed. He became a human.'

34 *watik ŋare nima zräzigrm "awe nzone moba nzranyak?"*
watik ŋare   nima zrä\zigrm/   awe nzone moba
then woman QUOT 3SG.FEM:SBJ:IRR:PFV/look.around come 1SG.POSS where.ABL
nzran\yak/
2SG:SBJ:IRR:IPFV:VENT/walk
'Well, the woman was looking around and said "Come my friend, where do you come from?"'

35 *naf we komnzo zära nima "oh zane ausinzo zf zagathifth"*
    naf   we   komnzo zä\r/a   nima oh zane   ausi=nzo
    3SG.ERG also only   2|3SG:SBJ:PST:PFV/do   QUOT oh DEM:PROX old woman=ONLY
    zf   za\gathif/th
    IMM 2|3PL:SBJ>3SG.FEM:OBJ:RPST:PFV/leave
    'He was also thinking "Oh, they have left only this old woman behind."'

36 *"kabe matak erä nima z bramöwä kwafarkwrth nima erä ŋarsfo" ... "awow"*
    kabe matak   e\rä/   nima z bramöwä
    man nothing 2|3PL:SBJ:NPST:IPFV/be   like.this ALR all
    kwa\fark/wrth   nima e\rä/   ŋars=fo (.) awow
    2|3PL:SBJ:PST:IPFV/set.off   like.this 2|3PL:SBJ:NPST:IPFV/be   river=ALL (.) okay
    ' "Nobody is here. All the people left this way to the river." ... "Okay"'

37 *yamenzo srathams ... kramath with tayo yanrkunzr ... yarithr*
    yame=nzo sra\thams/   (.) kra\math/
    mat=ONLY 2|3SG:SBJ>3SG.MASC:IO:IRR:PFV/spread.out   (.) 2|3SG:SBJ:IRR:PFV/run
    with   tayo yan\rku/nzr   (.)
    banana ripe 2|3SG:SBJ>3SG.MASC:IO:NPST:IPFV/knock.down   (.)
    ya\ri/thr
    2|3SG:SBJ>3SG.MASC:IO:NPST:IPFV/give
    'She spread (the mat) for him, ran and knocked down some ripe banana for him
    ... and gave them to him.'

38 *kafar famä zäkora nima "nzone dagonma zane zf yé. z nzyanyak"*
    kafar fam=ä   zä\kor/a   nima nzone   dagon=ma
    big   thought=ASSOC 2|3SG:SBJ:PST:PFV/become   QUOT 1SG.POSS food=CHAR
    zane   zf   \yé/   z
    DEM:PROX IMM 3SG.MASC:SBJ:NPST:IPFV/be   ALR
    nz=yan\yak/
    IPST=3SG.MASC:SBJ:NPST:IPFV:VENT/walk
    'She had big thoughts "This one here is my dinner. He came already."'

39 *bänema yrgfakwa nima "zane karma keke yé. moba zane nm nzyanyak?"*
    bäne=ma   y\rgfak/wa   nima zane
    DEM:MED=CHAR   2|3SG:SBJ>3SG.MASC:OBJ:PST:IPFV/recognise QUOT DEM:PROX
    kar=ma   keke \yé/   moba   zane   nm
    village=CHAR NEG 3SG.MASC:SBJ:NPST:IPFV/be   where.ABL DEM:PROX maybe
    nz=yanyak
    IPST=3SG.MASC:SBJ:NPST:IPFV:VENT/walk
    'because she realised "He is not from this village. Where might he have come
    from?"'

40 *garamgaram srethkäf "kwa ŋabrigwr? efoth byé!"*
    garamgaram   sre\thkäf/   kwa
    sweet.talk   2|3SG:SBJ>3SG.MASC:OBJ:IRR:PFV/start   FUT

365

ŋa\brig/wr   efoth b=\yé/
2|3SG:SBJ:NPST:IPFV/return sun   MED=3SG.MASC:SBJ:NPST:IPFV/be
'She started sweet-talking him "Will you return today? The sun setting already?"'

41   *"keke, zä zf kwa worugr. kwa fof thrämonesé kayé fthé thräthor."*
      keke zä   zf   kwa wo\rug/r   kwa fof
      NEG PROX IMM FUT 1SG:SBJ:NPST:IPFV/sleep FUT EMPH
      thrä\mones/é   kayé   fthé   thrä\thor/
      1SG:SBJ>2|3PL:OBJ:IRR:PFV/wait tomorrow when 2|3PL:SBJ:IRR:PFV/arrive
      ' "No, I will sleep right here. I will wait until they return tomorrow."'

42   *zbär ... faf ŋathamsakrnth ... etfth kramnzerth*
      zbär   (.) faf   ŋa\thamsak/rnth   (.) etfth
      night (.) place 2|3DU:SBJ:NPST:IPFV/spread.out (.) sleep
      kra\mnzer/th
      2|3DU:SBJ:IRR:PFV/fall.asleep
      'The night came and they spread the mats. They fell asleep.'

43   *etfth kwosi krämnzer ... ausi nzürna ŋare krebnaf "züm züm züm züm"*
      etfth kwosi krä\mnzer/   (.) ausi   nzürna ŋare
      sleep dead 2|3SG:SBJ:IRR:PFV/fall.asleep (.) old woman spirit   woman
      kre\bnaf/   4x(züm)
      2|3SG:SBJ:IRR:PFV/wake.up 4x(centipede)
      'He was fast asleep! The nzürna woman woke up (and called out) "centipedes!
      centipedes! centipedes! centipedes!"'

44   *subnazrm fof ... sain swarithrm ... wati*
      su\bnaz/rm   fof   (.) sain
      SG:SBJ>3SG.MASC:OBJ:PST:DUR/wake.up EMPH (.) sign
      swa\ri/thrm   (.) wati
      SG:SBJ>3SG.MASC:IO:PST:DUR/wake.up (.) enough
      'She was really waking him up, giving him a sign ... but no.'

45   *keke zethäkna ane*
      keke ze\thäkn/a   ane
      NEG SG:SBJ:PST:PFV/shake DEM
      'That guy did not move.'

46   *yaka zanrnzo srewakuth.*
      yaka   zan=r=nzo   sre\wakuth/
      yam.stick hit=PURP=ONLY SG:SBJ>3SG.MASC:OBJ:IRR:PFV/pick.up
      'She picked up the yam stick to kill him.'

47   *di fof safrnza kwosi.*
      di   fof sa\frnz/a   kwosi
      back.of.head EMPH SG:SBJ>3SG.MASC:OBJ:PST:PFV/uproot dead
      'She whacked him on the head and killed him.'

48 *kwot yanatha fä fof ... bramöwä.*
    kwot   ya\na/tha   fä   fof   (.) bramöwä
    properly SG:SBJ>3SG.MASC:OBJ:PST:IPFV/eat DIST EMPH (.) all
    'She ate him there ... all of him.'

49 *sabtha wthnzo ezänzr. füni komnzo bikogr firran.*
    sa\bth/a   wth=nzo
    SG:SBJ>3SG.MASC:OBJ:PST:PFV/finish intestines=ONLY
    e\zä/nzr   füni komnzo
    2|3SG:SBJ>2|3PL:OBJ:NPST:IPFV/carry füni still
    b=y\kogr/   firra=n
    MED=3SG.MASC:SBJ:NPST:STAT/stand firra=LOC
    'She finished him and carried away only the intestines. The füni tree still stands
    in Firra.'

50 *wämne ... yf füni yé ... firran bä ykogr.*
    wämne (.) yf   füni \yé/   (.) firra=n   bä
    tree (.) name füni 3SG.MASC:SBJ:NPST:IPFV/be (.) firra=LOC MED
    y\kogr/
    3SG.MASC:SBJ:NPST:STAT/stand
    'The name of the tree is füni. It stands there in Firra'

51 Maraga addresses me directly now.
    nä kayé fthé boba gnyako nima kwa ymarwr ... ane kafar wämne.
    nä   kayé   fthé boba gn\yak/o   nima   kwa
    INDF yesterday when MED.ALL 2SG:SBJ:IMP:IPFV:AND/go like.this FUT
    y\mar/wr   (.) ane kafar wämne
    2|3SG:SBJ>3SG.MASC:NPST:IPFV/see (.) DEM big   tree
    'When you go there some day, you will see it ... that big tree.'

52 Marua, who sits in the back, tells him that I have been to Firra in the previous week.
    z nyakako? ... zba mothfa mane ykogr füni.
    z   n\yak/ako   (.) zba   moth=fa mane
    ALR 2SG:SBJ:PST:IPFV:AND/walk (.) PROX.ABL path=ABL which
    y\kogr/   füni
    3SG.MASC:SBJ:NPST:STAT/stand füni
    'You already went? It is here on the road, where the füni tree stands.'

53 *ane bafen ... yakan dganzo saräsa.*
    ane baf=en   (.) yaka=n   dga=nzo
    DEM RECOG=LOC (.) yamstick=LOC bifurcation=ONLY
    sa\räs/a
    SG:SBJ>3SG.MASC:OBJ:PST:PFV/erect
    'At that place ... on the yamstick ... she rammed it in the ground.'

54 *wth fobo fof thämira ... ane kabeane wth. fi zäbrimako ... zäthbako mnzen.*
wth   fobo   fof   thä\mir/a   (.) ane kabe=ane
intestines DIST.ALL EMPH SG:SBJ>2|3PL:OBJ:PST:PFV/hang (.) DEM man=POSS
wth   fi   zä\brim/ako   (.) zä\thb/ako
intestines 3.ABS SG:SBJ:PST:PFV:AND/return (.) SG:SBJ:PST:PFV:AND/enter
mnz=en
house=LOC
'She hanged the intestines up there ... that guy's intestines! Then she went back.
She went inside the house.'

55 *nafafis oromanf zräses fof "be ranzo änfiyokwr, ah? ... bä moba nrä? ... mä*
nznrugr?"
nafa-fis   oroman=f   zrä\ses/   fof
3.POSS-husband old.man=ERG.SG 2|3SG:SBJ>3SG.FEM:OBJ:IRR:PFV/ask EMPH
be   ra=nzo   än\fiyok/wr   ah (.) bä
2SG.ERG what=ONLY 2|3SG:SBJ>2|3PL:OBJ:NPST:IPFV:VENT/make ah (.) 2.ABS
moba   n\rä/   (.) mä   nzn\rugr/
where.ABL 2SG:SBJ:NPST:IPFV/be (.) where 2SG:SBJ:RPST:IPFV/sleep
'Her husband, the old man, asked her "Hey, just what have you been up to?
Where are you coming from? Where have you slept?"'

56 *"mä kwa! bä fof zämnzeré ... zbärma."*
mä   kwa bä fof   zä\mnzer/é   (.) zbär=ma
where FUT MED EMPH 1SG:SBJ:RPST:PFV/fall.asleep (.) night=CHAR
'She replied "Where do you think? I slept there because it got night."'

57 *"nagayaneme znsän zwäfonz. ane gathagathame kkauna mane egathikwroth."*
nagayé=aneme   znsä=n   zwä\fonz/   ane
children=POSS.NSG work=LOC 1SG:SBJ:RPST:PFV/be.caught.by.nightfall DEM
gathagatha=me k-kauna   mane e\gathik/wroth
bad=INS   REDUP-thing which PL:SBJ>2|3PL:OBJ:NPST:IPFV:AND/leave
"'I was caught by nightfall while working for the children sorting those things
which they leave scattered around."'

58 *nafafis miyamr.*
nafa-fis   miyamr
3.POSS-husband ignorance
'Her husband was clueless.'

59 *fi thé enthorakwa ... mnz kabe fof ... nima thäzigrthma*
fi   fthé en\thorak/wa   (.) mnz kabe fof   (.) nima
3.ABS when 2|3PL:SBJ:PST:IPFV:VENT/arrive (.) house people EMPH (.) QUOT
thä\zigrthm/a
2|3PL:SBJ:PST:PFV/look
'At that time the house owners returned to the village. They looked around and
said,'

60 *"nä tmatm ffé nzŋawänzr ... manema kabe zä naf nzyanathr?"*
    nä   tmatm fefe nz=ŋa\wä/nzr   (.) mane=ma   kabe zä
    INDF event   real IPST=2|3SG:SBJ:NPST:IPFV/happen (.) which=CHAR man PROX
    naf   nz=ya\na/thr
    3SG.ERG IPST=2|3SG:SBJ>3SG.MASC:OBJ:NPST:IPFV/eat
    ' "Something terrible has just happened. From which village was the man who
    she ate here?"'

61 *äniyaka zbär zf zukwinzrmth zfkonzrmth.*
    än\yak/a   zbär zf   zu\kwi/nzrmth
    2|3PL:SBJ:PST:IPFV:VENT/walk night IMM 2|3PL:SBJ>3SG.FEM:OBJ:PST:DUR/argue
    zf\ko/nzrmth
    2|3PL:SBJ>3SG.FEM:OBJ:PST:DUR/tell
    'In the night, they came right here and they cursed her and told her.'

62 *zäbrimath "mon kwa wäfiyokwre? bänema kabe z nzirärkwr ... z nzyanathr."*
    zä\brim/ath   mon kwa wä\fiyok/wre
    2|3PL:SBJ:PST:PFV/return how FUT 1PL:SBJ>:3SG.FEM:OBJ:NPST:IPFV/make
    bäne=ma   kabe z   nz=y\rärk/wr   (.) z
    RECOG=CHAR man ALR IPST=2|3SG:SBJ>3SG.MASC:OBJ:NPST:IPFV/mess.up (.) ALR
    nzyanathr
    IPST=2|3SG:SBJ>3SG.MASC:OBJ:NPST:IPFV/eat
    'They returned and said "What are we going to do with her? She already messed
    up this man. She already ate him."'

63 *wati bthan kabe thfrärm ... kabe firran mane thwamnzrm.*
    wati bthan kabe thf\rä/rm   (.) kabe firra=n   mane
    then magic man 2|3PL:SBJ:PST:DUR/be (.) men firra=LOC who
    thwa\m/nzrm
    2|3PL:SBJ:PST:DUR/be
    'Okay, there were sorcerers living in Firra.'

64 *wati, ttmatm äfiyokwrth. ttmatm zwafiyokwrmth*
    wati t-tmatm   ä\fiyok/wrth   t-tmatm
    then REDUP-action 2|3PL:SBJ>2|3PL:OBJ:NPST:IPFV/make REDUP-action
    zwa\fiyok/wrmth
    2|3PL:SBJ>3SG.FEM:PST:DUR/make
    'Okay, they make their magic things. They were doing this to her.'

65 *fam wäfiyokwrth näbinzo "mnime n zräföfe." ... nima tmatmr rä*
    fam   wä\fiyok/wrth   näbi=nzo mni=me n
    thought 2|3PL:SBJ>3SG.FEM:NPST:IPFV/make one=ONLY fire=INS IMN
    zrä\föf/e   (.) nima   tmatm=r
    1PL:SBJ>3SG.FEM:OBJ:IRR:PFV/burn (.) like.this action=PURP

\rä/
3SG.FEM:SBJ:NPST:IPFV/be
'They came up with a plan "We will burn her with fire." This was the plan.'

66   *wati, bthan tmatmme nafane fam zwarmänwrmth.*
     wati bthan tmatm=me nafane   fam   zwa\rmän/wrmth
     then magic action=INS 3SG.POSS though 2|3PL:SBJ>3SG.FEM:IO:PST:DUR/close
     'Okay, they were distracting her mind with magic.'

67   *wärmänwath e ane bafen keke kwamätrakwrm bänema fam z zürmänth.*
     wä\rmän/wath   e   ane baf=en   keke
     2|3PL:SBJ>3SG:OBJ:IO:NPST:IPFV/close until DEM RECOG=LOC NEG
     kwa\mätrak/wrm   bäne=ma   fam   z
     SG:SBJ:PST:DUR/come.out RECOG=LOC thought ALR
     zü\rmän/th
     2|3PL:SBJ>3SG.FEM:IO:ITER/close
     'They were distracting her so that she did not come out of that place, because her thoughts were always distracted.'

68   *wtri we z zära nima "z zwemarth ane yam fiyoksin."*
     wtri we z   zä\r/a   nima z   zwe\mar/th
     fear also ALR 3SG.FEM:SBJ:PST:IPFV/be QUOT ALR 2|3PL:SBJ>1SG:OBJ:RPST:PFV/see
     ane yam fiyok-si=n
     DEM event make-NMLZ=LOC
     'She was also afraid and thought "They already know that I have done this."'

69   *mni wthomonwrth yfö mä zfrärm.*
     mni w\thomon/wrth   yfö mä zf\rä/rm
     fire 2|3PL:SBJ>3SG.FEM:NPST:IPFV/pile.up.fire hole where 3SG.FEM:SBJ:PST:DUR/be
     'They piled up the fire wood where the entrance was.'

70   *mni wthomonwath a zräföfth.*
     mni w\thomon/wath   a
     fire 2|3PL:SBJ>3SG.FEM:PST:IPFV/pile.up.fire until
     zrä\föf/th
     2|3PL:SBJ>3SG.FEM:OBJ:IRR:PFV/burn
     'They piled it up and they set it on fire.'

71   *fi yame yrsifnzo zukonzrm boba wämne yfön fof.*
     fi   yame yr-si=f=nzo   zu\ko/nzrm
     3.ABS mat weave-NMLZ=ERG=ONLY SG:SBJ>3SG.FEM:OBJ:PST:DUR/become
     boba   wämne yfö=n   fof
     MED.ABL tree hole=LOC EMPH
     'She was preoccupied with weaving the mat there in the tree hole.'

72   *nafafis bana krebnaf krekaris "u" mni u kwan fof.*

nafa-fis   bana kre\bnaf/   kre\karis/   u mni
3.POSS-husband poor 2|3SG:SBJ:IRR:PFV/wake.up 2|3SG:SBJ:IRR:PFV/hear u fire
u.kwan   fof
sound.of.strong.wind EMPH
'Her husband woke up and heard it:"uh" the sound of the fire.'

73 *kafar wäsü sukogrm mrab fren.*
    kafar wäsü   su\kogr/m   mrab   fr=en
    big   tree.species 3SG.MASC:SBJ:PST:DUR/stand bamboo grove=LOC
    'The big wäsü tree was standing there in a bamboo grove.'

74 *waisamen ... waisamen ane kar yf rä mobo zwamnzrm ... mrab fr thden.*
    waisamen (.) waisamen ane kar   yf   \rä/   mobo
    waisamen (.) waisamen DEM place name 3SG.FEM:SBJ:NPST:IPFV/be where.ALL
    zwa\m/nzrm   (.) mrab   fr   thd=en
    3SG.FEM:SBJ:PST:DUR/dwell (.) bamboo grove middle=LOC
    'Waisamen ... Waisamen is the name of that place where she was living ... in the
    middle of a bamboo grove.'

75 *krär ... nafafis zräs "be ranzo kayé thwanfiyokwr?"*
    krä\r/   (.) nafa-fis   zrä\s/   be
    2|3SG:SBJ:IRR:PFV/do (.) 3.POSS-husband 2|3SG:SBJ>3SG.FEM:IRR:PFV/ask 2SG.ERG
    ra=nzo   kayé   thwan\fiyok/wr
    what=ONLY yesterday 2|3SG:SBJ>2|3PL:OBJ:RPST:IPFV:VENT/make
    'He got up. Her husband asked "Just what have you done to them yesterday?"'

76 *"ra kwa thanfiyokwé?"*
    ra   kwa than\fiyok/wé
    what FUT 1SG:SBJ>2|3PL:OBJ:RPST:IPFV:VENT/make
    'She replied "What do you think I have done?"'

77 *"ra kwan we rä ah?"*
    ra   kwan we \rä/   ah
    what sound also 3SG.FEM:SBJ:NPST:IPFV/be ah
    'He asked "and what is that sound, eh?"'

78 *"nzukar banafa borbor bana sathor kma borbor u kwan zfrärm zufsgwrm fof."*
    nzu-kar   bana=fa borbor   bana sa\thor/   kma
    1SG.POSS-place poor=ABL thunderstorm poor 3SG.MASC:RPST:PFV/arrive POT
    borbor   u kwan   zf\rä/rm
    thunderstorm roaring.sound 3SG.FEM:SBJ:PST:DUR/be
    zu\fsg/wrm   fof
    SG:SBJ>3SG.FEM:OBJ:PST:DUR/blow EMPH
    'She replied "The thunderstorm is coming from my poor village. It must be the
    sound of the storm blowing."'

79 *mni kwarsirm. mni komnzo zöfthé zethkäfa.*
mni kwa\rsi/rm   mni komnzo zöfthé ze\thkäf/a
fire SG:SBJ:PST:DUR/burn fire just   before SG:SBJ:PST:PFV/start
'It was the fire burning. The fire which has just started to burn.'

80 *nima säzigrm nafafis bana fof zänmätra fof mni zbo z zamara.*
nima   srä\zigrm/   nafa-fis   bana fof
like.this 3SG.MASC:SBJ:IRR:PFV/look 3.POSS-husband poor EMPH
zän\mätr/a   fof   mni zbo   z   za\mar/a
SG:SBJ:PST:PFV/exit EMPH fire PROX.ALL ALR SG:SBJ>3SG.FEM:OBJ:PST:PFV/see
'He looked around. Her poor husband stepped outside and saw the fire close by.'

81 *rürä fthé zagathifa nima sathfärako.*
rürä   fthé   za\gathif/a   nima
alone when SG:SBJ>3SG.FEM:OBJ:PST:PFV/leave like.this
sa\thfär/ako
3SG.MASC:SBJ:PST:PFV:AND/jump
'That was when he left her alone. He jumped out.'

82 *nima fi fthé sathfärako yakäsü ... trtha zuthorakwrm.*
nima   fi   fthé   sa\thfär/ako   yak=ä=sü   (.) trtha
like.this 3.ABS when 3SG.MASC:SBJ:PST:PFV:AND/jump run=ASSOC=ETC (.) life
zu\thorak/wrm
SG:SBJ>3SG.FEM:OBJ:PST:DUR/search
'When he jumped out in a rush, he was running for his life.'

83 *foba näbi fthé zanmatha fof.*
foba   näbi fthé   zan\math/a   fof
DIST.ABL one   when SG:SBJ:PST:PFV:VENT/ran EMPH
'From there, he ran for good.'

84 *emoth fäth nima ämnzr oten.*
emoth fäth nima   ä\m/nzr   ote=n
girl   DIM like.this 2|3PL:SBJ:NPST:IPFV/dwell ote=LOC
'The daughters are living there in Ote.'

85 *komnzo zena bobo rä. ane kar we nä fof rä trikasi kar fof.*
komnzo zena bobo   \rä/   ane kar   we   nä   fof
still   today MED.ABL 3SG.FEM:SBJ:NPST:IPFV/be DEM village also INDF EMPH
\rä/   trik-si   kar   fof
3SG.FEM:SBJ:NPST:IPFV/be tell-NMLZ village EMPH
'This place is still there and there is also a story about that place.'

86 *dödö fr rä kafar dödö fr zbo thden rä.*
dödö   fr   \rä/   kafar dödö   fr
tree.species grove 3SG.FEM:SBJ:NPST:IPFV/be big   tree.species grove

zbo thd=en \rä/
3SG.FEM:SBJ:NPST:IPFV/be middle=LOC 3SG.FEM:SBJ:NPST:IPFV/be
'The is a dödö grove (Melaleuca sp), a big dödö grove about halfway.'

87 *näbüwä thé zanmatha ote. emoth fäthnm thrätrif*
näbi-wä fthé zan\math/a ote emoth fäth=nm
one=EMPH when SG:SBJ:PST:PFV:VENT/run ote girl DIM=DAT.NSG
thrä\trif/
2|3SG:SBJ>2|3PL:IO:IRR:PFV/tell
'Then he ran off for good to Ote. He told the girls: '

88 *"beŋame ausi ... bzaföfth ... nafanemäwä!"*
be-ŋame ausi (.) b=za\föf/th (.)
2NSG.POSS-mother old woman (.) MED=2|3PL:SBJ>3SG.FEM:OBJ:PST:PFV/burn (.)
nafane=ma=wä
3SG.POSS=CHAR=EMPH
' "Your mother, the old woman ... they burned her there! It was all her own fault!"'

89 *"kafar yam zwafiyokwr ... kabe nä z swanathr!"*
kafar yam zwa\fiyok/wr (.) kabe nä z
big event 2|3SG:SBJ>3SG.FEM:OBJ:RPST:IPFV/make (.) man INDF ALR
swa\na/thr
2|3SG:SBJ>3SG.MASC:OBJ:RPST:IPFV/eat
' "She has made a big mistake. She ate a man!"'

90 *fi nimanzo fefe yarako.*
fi nima=nzo fefe ya\r/ako
3.ABS like.this=ONLY really 3SG.MASC:SBJ:PST:IPFV:AND/be
'He had left just like this.'

91 *fi nima mni zewaräfa ... ŋarsira*
fi nima mni ze\waräf/a (.) ŋa\rsir/a
but like.this fire SG:SBJ:PST:PFV/burn.down (.) SG:SBJ:PST:IPFV/burn
'But the fire burned down ... it was burning'

92 *ŋarsira kma zräzigrm "moba kwa krämätré? moba?"*
ŋa\rsir/a kma zrä\zigrm/ moba kwa
SG:SBJ:PST:IPFV/burn POT 3SG.FEM:SBJ:IRR:PFV/burn where.ABL FUT
krä\mätr/é moba
1SG:SBJ:IRR:PFV/exit where.ABL
'It was burning and she tried to escape and said "Where will I get out? Where?"'

93 *näbi fefe zaföfath ŋarsira eee kwot zäbtha.*
näbi fefe za\föf/ath ŋa\rsir/a eee
one really 2|3PL:SBJ>3SG.FEM:PST:PFV/burn.down SG:SBJ:PST:IPFV/burn until

kwot zä\bth/a
properly SG:SBJ:PST:PFV/finish
'They really burned her for good. The fire burned until she was finished.'

94   *brbrnzo fof n zäthba bafen ... ymden fof.*
brbr=nzo fof n zä\thb/a baf=en (.) ymd=en fof
spirit=ONLY EMPH IMN SG:SBJ:PST:PFV/enter RECOG=LOC (.) bird=LOC EMPH
'Only her spirit was about to enter that bird.'

95   *"kuka kuka" fä mane wänor "kuka kuka"*
kuka kuka fä mane wä\nor/ kuka kuka
kuka kuka DIST who 3SG.FEM:SBJ:NPST:IPFV/shout kuka kuka
' "kuka kuka" the one that shouts out "kuka kuka" over there.'

96   *krärth ane bthan woga ane kuka kuka zrämgth krätr.*
krä\r/th ane bthan woga ane kuka kuka
2|3PL:SBJ:IRR:PFV/do DEM magic man DEM kuka kuka
zrä\mg/th krä\tr/
2|3PL:SBJ>3SG.FEM:IRR:PFV/shoot 2|3SG:SBJ:IRR:PFV/fall
'They got up. The sorcerers shot that *kuka kuka* bird and it fell down.'

97   *wati, fefe zaföfath ane fobo fä zäbtha.*
wati fefe za\föf/ath ane fobo fä
then really 2|3PL:SBJ>3SG.FEM:PST:PFV/burn.down DEM DIST.ALL DIST
zä\bth/a
SG:SBJ:PST:PFV/finish
'They burned the bird over there until that it was finished.'

98   *ane thrma mni fthé zäbtha wati nagawa ŋabrigwa sir*
ane thrma mni fthé zä\bth/a wati nagawa ŋa\brig/wa
DEM after fire when SG:SBJ:PST:PFV/finish then nagawa SG:SBJ:PST:IPFV/return
si=r
eye=PURP
'After the fire had finished, Nagawa went back to see.'

99   *"komnzo rä o z kwarsir mnin?"*
komnzo \rä/ o z kwa\rsir/ mni=n
sill 3SG.FEM:SBJ:NPST:IPFV/be or ALR SG:SBJ:RPST:IPFV/burn fire=LOC
'He asked himself "Is she still alive or did she burn in the fire?"'

100   *ŋabrigwa bobomr we waisam wäsü thé sanmara "watik fi nafazfthenwä"*
ŋa\brig/wa bobomr we waisam (.) wäsü thé
SG:SBJ:PST:IPFV/return until also waisam (.) wäsü when
san\mar/a watik fi nafa-zfth=en=wä
SG:SBJ:PST:PFV:VENT/see then 3.ABS 3.POSS-fault=LOC=EMPH
'He walked until Waisam. When he saw the wäsü tree he said "Well, it was her own fault."'

101 *yanzo bobo yanora ... nafaŋareanema ... wati, fi näbi zäbrima.*
ya=nzo   bobo   ya\nor/a   (.) nafa-ŋare=ane=ma   (.)
cry=ONLY MED.ALL 3SG.MASC:SBJ:PST:IPFV/shout (.) 3.POSS-woman=POSS=CHAR (.)
wati fi   näbi zä\brim/a
then 3.ABS one SG:SBJ:PST:PFV/return
'He was crying badly for his wife. Then he returned for good.'

102 *zbo yamnzr ane woga oten. emoth fäthä ämnzr.*
zbo   ya\m/nzr   ane woga ote=n   emoth fäth=ä
PROX.ALL 3SG.MASC:SBJ:NPST:IPFV/dwell DEM man ote=/Loc girl   DIM=ASSOC.PL
ä\m/nzr
2|3PL:SBJ:NPST:IPFV/dwell
'That man lives here in Ote. He lives together with his daughters.'

103 *watik kabeyé komnzo fä nomai sumarwre ymarwre fthé*
watik kabe=yé   komnzo fä   nomai su\mar/wrth
then man=ERG.NSG still   DIST always 2|3PL:SBJ>3SG.MASC:OBJ:RPST:IPFV/see
y\mar/wre   fthé
1NSG:SBJ>3SG.MASC:OBJ:RPST:IPFV/see when
'The people still see him there, we see him when...'

104 *fä ŋaritakwr nima firrafo yak we nima ŋabrigwr*
fä   ŋa\ritak/wr   nima firra=fo \yak/
DIST 2|3SG:SBJ:NPST:IPFV/cross like.this firra=ALL 3SG.MASC:SBJ:NPST:IPFV/return
we nima ŋa\brig/wr

'he goes across the river and when he goes to Firra and also when he returns that same way again.'

105 *tnz fäth ane kabe yé*
tnz   fäth ane kabe \yé/
short DIM DEM man 3SG.MASC:NPST:IPFV/be
'He is a short guy.'

106 *ane nzürna ŋareane ... zokwasi nimame fof rä fof*
ane nzürna ŋare=ane   (.) zokwasi nima=me   fof
DEM nzürna woman=POSS (.) speech   like.this=INS EMPH
\rä/   fof
3SG.FEM:SBJ:NPST:IPFV/be EMPH
'This nzürna woman's story really happened like this.'

107 *mane bobo firran zwamnzrm.*
mane bobo   firra=n   zwa\m/nzrm
who MED.ALL firra=LOC 3SG.FEM:SBJ:PST:DUR/dwell
'The nzürne who was living there in Firra.'

108 *tüfr yam nä ffé thwafiyokwrm*
tüfr yam nä ffé thwa\fiyok/wrm
many event INDF really SG:SBJ>2|3PL:OBJ:PST:DUR/make
'She did many things, '

109 *fi fathfa ane fof wäfiyokwa*
fi fath=fa ane fof wä\fiyok/wa
but clear.place=ABL DEM EMPH SG:SBJ>3SG.FEM:OBJ:PST:IPFV/make
'but she did this one thing in public.'

110 *nä karma kabe mane yanatha mogarkamma.*
nä kar=ma kabe mane ya\na/tha
INDF village=CHAR man who SG:SBJ>3SG.MASC:OBJ:PST:IPFV/eat
mogarkam=ma.
mogarkam=CHAR
'Eating this man from another village from Mogarkam.'

111 *nafane zokwasi ... ane trikasi fobonzo wythk fof brä ... ane nzürna ŋareanema.*
nafane zokwasi (.) ane trik-si fobo=nzo
3SG.POSS words (.) DEM tell-NMLZ DIST.ALL=ONLY
w\ythk/ fof b=\rä/ (.) ane
3SG.FEM:SBJ:NPST:IPFV/come.to.end EMPH MED=3SG.FEM:SBJ:NPST:IPFV/be (.) DEM
nzürna ŋare=ane=ma
nzürna woman=POSS.SG=CHAR
'Her story story finishes there, the one about that nzürna woman.'

112 *watik, fobo fof zräkoré.*
watik fobo fof zrä\kor/é
then DIST.ALL EMPH 1SG:SBJ>3SG.FEM:OBJ:IRR:PFV/speak
'Well, I have told it from there.'

113 *nä karen nima nä buné bänema ...*
nä kar=en nima nä.bun=é bäne=ma (.)
INDF village=LOC like.this INDF=ERG.NSG RECOG=CHAR
'In other villages, others can tell'

114 *nä nzürna ŋare zokwasi trikasi bä räro fi ane kar woga mane erä fi ane miyatha erä.*
nä nzürna ŋare zokwasi trik-si bä \rä/ro fi
INDF nzürna woman words tell-NMLZ MED 3SG.FEM:SBJ:NPST:IPFV:AND/be but
ane kar woga mane e\rä/ fi ane miyatha
DEM village man who 2|3PL:SBJ:NPST:IPFV/be 3.ABS DEM knowledgeable
e\rä/
2|3PL:SBJ:NPST:IPFV/be
'other nzürna stories there. But it is those other village people who know about these.'

115   *nzefe nzüwäbragwé nima ni miyatha nrä.*

nze=wä   nz=wä\brag/wé   nima   ni
1SG.ERG=EMPH IPST=1SG:SBJ>3SG.FEM:OBJ:NPST:IPFV/follow like.this 1NSG

miyatha   n\rä/
knowledgeable 1PL:SBJ:NPST:IPFV/be

'I just followed the story as we know it.'

116   *nzekaren ane yam kwafiyokwrm nzenme ŋafyé mä thwamnzrm.*

nze-kar=en   ane yam kwa\fiyok/wrm   nzenme   ŋafe=yé
1NSG.POSS-village=LOC DEM event SG:SBJ:PST:DUR/make 1NSG.POSS father=ABS.NSG

mä   thwa\m/nzrm
where 2|3PL:SBJ:PST:DUR/dwell

'She was doing this in our village, where our fathers were living'

117   *ŋafyé we nzenm natrikwath.*

ŋafe=yé   we nzenm   na\trik/wath
father=ERG.NSG also 1NSG.DAT 2|3PL:SBJ>1PL:IO:PST:IPFV/tell

'and our fathers also told us about it.'

118   *nima zbo zf zakoré ... fof zäbthé.*

nima   zbo   zf   za\kor/é   (.) fof
like.this PROX.ALL IMM 1SG:SBJ>3SG.FEM:OBJ:RPST:PFV/speak (.) EMPH

zä\bth/é.
1SG:SBJ>3SG.FEM:OBJ:RPST:PFV/finish

'I said it like this and I finished it.'   [tci20120901-01]

Sample text: Kwafar

Kwafar

The following text was prompted by my question "Where did the yams come from?" It was told by Abia Bai. The text should be seen as a compendium rather than a single storyline. It was recorded as my fieldtrip in 2013 came to an end. During the previous weeks, I had talked with Abia many times about different topics and he promised to tell me these stories properly in the context of a recording session.

The text can be cut into three storylines, which I have been told independently by others. The first part is the *Kwafar* myth. *Kwafar* is a place off the coast between the island of New Guinea and the Australian continent. According to the story, there was a large *wäsi* tree at *kwafar* and the people of different tribes and languages lived together in this tree. Eventually, the tree burned down and the people started spreading out from there. Many clans of the Morehead district have an apical ancestor who came from *kwafar*. One of the many myths located at *Kwafar* involves two brothers, who went hunting in the area. The brothers came across a mysterious being which devours the bodies of those people who have died in the fire. The two brothers try to shoot the creature, but only the older brother is successful. As his arrow pierces the creature, a flood of water bursts out of the wound. In recent versions of the myth, the younger brother is said to be white like Europeans. He owns a shotgun instead of a bow. He runs south towards what is now Australia. The older brother runs north. He stops the flood by beating the water with branches of *dödö* (Melaleuca sp). At this point, Abia transitions into the second part. This is the story of *Mathkwi*, the apical ancestor of his clan. This story involves many small episodes about the route that *Mathkwi* took and all the things he carried and brought along. The third part is about customs and traditions around yam cultivation and a particular magic stone which Abia's father used to own.

This text can be accessed under: https://zenodo.org/record/1292876

1   *moba zrathkäfe?*
moba   zra\thkäf/e
where.ABL 1DU:SBJ:IRR:PFV/start
'Where do we start?'

2   CD speaking:
wawa moba enrera?
wawa moba   en\rä/ra
yam   where.ABL 2|3PL:SBJ:PST:IPFV:VENT/be
'Where did the yams come from?'

3   *okay, kwa zöbthé zrathkäfe nimame trikasi fof ... kwafar ...*
okay kwa zöbthé zra\thkäf/e   nima=me   trik-si   fof   (.) kwafar (.)
okay FUT first 1DU:SBJ:IRR:PFV/start like.this=INS tell-NMLZ EMPH (.) kwafar (.)
'Okay, first we will start the story really ... with Kwafar.'

4   *nimame fof nzranyan e zbo zrabthe*
nima=me   fof   nzran\yan/   e   zbo
like.this=INS EMPH 1DU:SBJ:IRR:IPFV:VENT/walk until PROX.ALL
zra\bth/e
1DU:SBJ:IRR:PFV/finish
'We will go like this until we finish the story here:'

5   *ra nzigfu enfathwath*
ra   nzigfu   en\fath/wath
what magic.stone 2|3PL:SBJ>2|3PL:OBJ:PST:IPFV:VENT/hold
'about what magic rain stones were they holding'

6   *ra fofosa nzigfu enfathwath?*
ra   fofosa nzigfu   enfathwath
what heart magic.stone 2|3PL:SBJ>2|3PL:OBJ:PST:IPFV:VENT/hold
'and what magic yam stones were they holding.'

7   *watik zbo zf zrabthe aneme fof.*
watik zbo   zf zra\bth/e   ane=me fof
then PROX.ALL IMM 1DU:SBJ:IRR:PFV/finish DEM=INS EMPH
'We will finish with this topic right here.'

8   *trikasi näbi kwa wänyak.*
trik-si   näbi kwa wän\yak/
tell-NMLZ one FUT 3SG.FEM:SBJ:NPST:IPFV:VENT/walk
'In this way, it will come as one story.'

9   *zrethkäfé?*
zre\thkäf/é
1SG:SBJ>3SG.FEM:OBJ:IRR:PFV/start
'Should I start?'

10 *okay, zane mane rä … zane trikasi … ŋafyf bäyf mane ŋatrikwa*
okay zane   mane \rä/   (.) zane   trik-si   (.)
okay DEM:PROX who 3SG.FEM:SBJ:NPST:IPFV/be (.) DEM:PROX tell-NMLZ (.)
ŋafe=f   bäi=f   mane ŋa\trik/wa
father=ERG.SG bäi=ERG.SG who SG:SBJ:PST:IPFV/tell
'As for this one, this story, it was father Bäi who told it.'

11 *nzenm natrikwa … watik ane trikasi fof zena ŋaritakwr.*
nzenm   na\trik/wa   (.) watik ane trik-si   fof   zena
1NSG.DAT SG:SBJ>1PL:IO:PST:IPFV/tell (.) then DEM tell-NMLZ EMPH today
ŋa\ritak/wr
2|3SG:SBJ:NPST:IPFV/cross.over
'He told it to us and today it will pass on.'

12 *trikasi mane rä kwafarma rä.*
trik-si   mane   \rä/   kwafar=ma   \rä/
tell-NMLZ which 3SG.FEM:NPST:IPFV/be kwafar=CHAR 3SG.FEM:NPST:IPFV/be
'This story is about Kwafar.'

13 *"kwafar" ŋafyf nima fof kwatrikwrm "kwafar mane rera thden rera"*
kwafar ŋafe=f   nima fof kwa\trik/wrm   kwafar mane
kwafar father=ERG.SG QUOT EMPH SG:SBJ:PST:DUR/tell kwafar which
\rä/ra   thd=en   \rä/ra
3SG.FEM:SBJ:PST:IPFV/be middle=LOC 3SG.FEM:SBJ:PST:IPFV/be
' "Kwafar", father was telling us, "Kwafar was in the middle."'

14 *zane zena mane bad mane wythk.*
zane   zena mane bad   mane w\ythk/
DEM:PROX today which ground which 3SG.FEM:SBJ:NPST:IPFV/come.to.end
'Here, where this land ends today,'

15 *mazo mä ŋakonzr a australiane bad mä wythk.*
mazo mä   ŋa\ko/nzr   a australia=ane   bad   mä
ocean where 2|3SG:SBJ:NPST:IPFV/become until australia=POSS.SG ground where
w\ythk/
3SG.FEM:SBJ:NPST:IPFV/come.to.end
'where the ocean begins until where the Australian continent ends:'

16 *fä mä fi zfrärm ane kwafar fof … kabe mä kwamosinzrmth.*
fä   mä   fi   zf\rä/rm   ane kwafar fof   (.) kabe   mä
DIST where 3.ABS 3SG.FEM:SBJ:PST:DUR/be DEM kwafar EMPH (.) people where
kwa\mosi/nzrmth
2|3PL:SBJ:PST:DUR/gather
'that's where Kwafar was located and where the people were gathering.'

17   *wäsi warfo thfrugrm.*
     wäsi warfo thf\rugr/m
     wäsi above 2|3PL:SBJ:PST:DUR/sleep
     'People were sleeping on top of the wäsi tree (Ficus elastica).'

18   *wäsi bäne ykonzrth nä bä bikogro ... zärkarä.*
     wäsi bäne   y\ko/nzrth   nä   bä
     wäsi DEM:MED 2|3PL:SBJ>3SG.MASC:OBJ:NPST:IPFV/speak INDF MED
     b=y\kogr/o   (.) zär=karä
     MED=3SG.MASC:NPST:IPFV:AND/stand (.) shade=PROP
     'They call this one wäsi. There is one standing over there ... the one with shade.'

19   *kabe fä fof thwamnzrm fof.*
     kabe fä fof thwa\m/nzrm   fof
     people DIST EMPH 2|3PL:SBJ:PST:DUR/dwell EMPH
     'The people were living there.'

20   *zokwasi ffrümenzo ... nä zfthen thwamnzrm nä thden thwamnzrm nä kerker thwamnzrm.*
     zokwasi f-frü=me=nzo   (.) nä   zfth=en   thwa\m/nzrm
     language REDUP-single=INS=ONLY (.) INDF base=LOC 2|3PL:SBJ:PST:DUR/dwell
     nä   thd=en   thwa\m/nzrm   nä   kerker thwa\m/nzrm
     INDF middle=LOC 2|3PL:SBJ:PST:DUR/dwell INDF tail   2|3PL:SBJ:PST:DUR/dwell
     'They spoke different languages ... some people were living at the base, some people were living in the middle and some people were living up in the branches.'

21   *watik zokwasi ane ffrümenzo kwanafrmth.*
     watik zokwasi ane f-frü=me=nzo   kwa\na/frmth
     then language DEM REDUP-single=INS=ONLY 2|3PL:SBJ:PST:DUR/talk
     'Well, they were speaking different languages.'

22   *nä kayé wäsi ane zäföfa fof ... zästha fof.*
     nä   kayé   wäsi ane zä\föf/a   fof   (.) zä\sth/a
     INDF yesterday wäsi DEM SG:SBJ:PST:IPFV/burn EMPH (.) SG:SBJ:PST:PFV/set.alight
     fof
     EMPH
     'One day that wäsi tree burned down. It really went up in flames.'

23   *nä kabe nima kwakwikwrmth*
     nä   kabe   nima   kwa\kwi/kwrmth
     INDF people like.this 2|3PL:SBJ:PST:DUR/run
     'Some people ran away this way.'

24   *nä kabe nima mnin kwarsirwrmth*
     nä   kabe   nima   mni=n   kwa\rsir/wrmth
     INDF people like.this fire=LOC 2|3PL:SBJ:PST:DUR/burn
     'Some people burned in the fire.'

25 *watik wäsi ane kwot ŋarsira ... zäbtha*
    watik wäsi ane properly kwot   ŋa\rsir/a   (.) zä\bth/a
    then   wäsi DEM properly SG:SBJ:PST:IPFV/burn (.) SG:SBJ:PST:PFV/finish
    'That wäsi tree burned completely. It finished.'

26 *kabe bä mane thwägrm warfo nä mrmr ... fi we nimäwä kwarsirwrmth*
    kabe   bä   mane th\wägr/m   warfo nä mrmr (.) fi   we
    people MED who 2|3PL:SBJ:PST:DUR/be.on.top above INDF inside (.) 3.ABS also
    nima=wä   kwa\rsir/wrmth
    like.this=EMPH 2|3PL:SBJ:PST:DUR/burn
    'The people who lived on top and some who lived inside, they burned.'

27 *watik ... ezi ... kabe ane frümenzo tnägsi zethkäfath ... bä frümenzo thwamnzrm.*
    watik (.) ezi   (.) kabe ane frü=me=nzo   tnäg-si
    then (.) morning (.) people DEM single=INS=ONLY lose-NMLZ
    zä\thkäf/ath   (.) bä frü=me=nzo   thwa\m/nzrm
    2|3PL:SBJ:PST:PFV/start (.) MED single=INS=ONLY 2|3PL:SBJ:PST:DUR/dwell
    'Then, in the morning, the people began to scatter all over the place. They were
    living by themselves.'

28 *watik, mni fthé ŋarsira ... kar ane bramöwä ŋarsira fof ... thgathg zfrärm ... fath
    thefath fath*
    watik mni fthé   ŋa\rsir/a   (.) kar ane bramöwä
    then fire when SG:SBJ:PST:IPFV/burn (.) place DEM all
    ŋa\rsir/a   fof (.) thgathg   zf\rä/rm   (.)
    SG:SBJ:PST:IPFV/burn EMPH (.) scorched.place 3SG.FEM:SBJ:PST:DUR/be (.)
    fath   thefath   fath
    clear.place burned.place clear.place
    'When the fire burned, it burned really the whole area. It became a scorched
    landscape, a clear place.'

29 *watik menzmenz ane fof yabun kafar ... thgathg bänemr ane fof zenfara ...*
    watik menz-menz   ane fof   yabun kafar (.) thgathg   bänemr   ane
    then REDUP-story.man DEM EMPH fat   big   (.) burned.place RECOG.PURP DEM
    fof   zen\far/a   (.)
    EMPH SG:SBJ:PST:PFV/set.off (.)
    'Well, that big, fat creature went to the burned place to get and eat those ones ...'

30 *kabe mane thfthnm kwosi.*
    kabe   mane thf\thn/m   kwosi
    people who 2|3PL:SBJ:PST:DUR/lie.down dead
    'the people who were lying around dead.'

31 *watik ... gwamf ŋatha thäsa ... ezi ... ane ... thefath thgathgen fof ... yaser*
    watik (.) gwam=f   ŋatha thä\s/a   (.) ezi   (.)
    then (.) gwam=ERG.SG dog SG:SBJ>2|3PL:OBJ:PST:IPFV/call.for (.) morning (.)

ane (.) thefath thgathg=en fof (.) yase=r

DEM (.) burned.place scorched.place=LOC EMPH (.) meat=PURP

'Well, Gwam called for the dogs for hunting, in the morning at that scorched place.'

32 *watik ŋatha anenzo fof sathkäfa.*

watik ŋatha ane=nzo fof sa\thkäf/a

then dog DEM=ONLY EMPH SG:SBJ>3SG.MASC:OBJ:PST:PFV/start

'Well, he started hunting with that one dog only.'

33 *ŋatha ane swaruthrm gwam mon nima yarera*

ŋatha ane swa\ru/thrm   gwam mon nima

dog DEM SG:SBJ>3SG.MASC:IO:PST:DUR/bark gwam how like.this

ya\rä/ra

SG:SBJ>3SG.MASC:IO:PST:IPFV/do

'The dog was barking at the creature and Gwam noticed it.'

34 *eda erna kabe kafar yf mane thfrnm … nafangthrwä gwam … muri*

eda e\rn/a   kabe kafar yf mane thf\rn/m (.)

two 2|3DU:SBJ:PST:IPFV/be man big name who 2|3DU:SBJ:PST:DUR/be (.)

nafa-ngth=r=wä   gwam (.) muri

3.POSS-younger.sibling=ASSOC.DU=EMPH gwam (.) muri

'They were two men who had well-known names Gwam with his small brother Muri.'

35 *gwam yara nafanane … muri nafangth*

gwam ya\r/a   nafa-nane (.) muri

gwam 3SG.MASC:SBJ:PST:IPFV/be 3.POSS-older.sibling (.) muri

nafa-ngth

3.POSS-younger.sibling

'Gwam was his older brother and Muri the younger brother.'

36 *wati gwamf ane fof ezi ŋatha thäsa thgathgen e*

wati gwam=f ane fof ezi ŋatha thä\s/a

then gwam=ERG.SG DEM EMPH morning dog SG:SBJ>2|3PL:OBJ:PST:PFV/call.out

thgathg=en e

burned.place until

'Well, that Gwam was calling out for the dogs in that burned place.'

37 *anenzo fof ŋatha yayamgwa … yayamgwa.*

ane=nzo fof ŋatha ya\yamg/wa   (.)

DEM=ONLY EMPH dog SG:SBJ>3SG.MASC:OBJ:PST:IPFV/shock (.)

ya\yamg/wa

SG:SBJ>3SG.MASC:OBJ:PST:IPFV/shock

'That creature shocked the dog, it shocked him.'

38 *ane menznzo fof kabe maf änatha fof*
ane menz=nzo   fof kabe maf   ä\na/tha
DEM story.man=ONLY   EMPH people who.ERG.SG SG:SBJ>2|3PL:OBJ:PST:IPFV/eat
fof
EMPH
'that creature which ate the people.'

39 *fewakaf kwosi thwanathrm*
fewa=kaf   kwosi thwa\na/thrm
stench=PROP   dead SG:SBJ>2|3PL:OBJ:PST:DUR/eat
'It was eating the rotten corpses.'

40 *murif zagr ymarwa fof ... maf yé? gwamf!*
muri=f   zagr y\mar/wa   fof (.) maf
muri=ERG.SG   far   SG:SBJ>3SG.MASC:OBJ:PST:IPFV/see EMPH (.) who.ERG.SG
\yé/   gwam=f
3SG.MASC:SBJ:NPST:IPFV/be gwam=ERG.SG
'Muri was seeing him from a distance ... Who's that? Gwam! (not Muri)'

41 *"ra bäne yé?" nima n samara ... o "ra menzmenz yé?"*
ra   bäne   \yé/   nima   n
what DEM:MED 3SG.MASC:SBJ:NPST:IPFV/be like.this IMN
sa\mar/a   (.) o ra   menz-menz
SG:SBJ>3SG.MASC:OBJ:PST:PFV/see   (.) or what REDUP-story.man
\yé/
3SG.MASC:SBJ:NPST:IPFV/be
' "What is this?" he was about to see it "What creature is this?"'

42 *kabe nrma fi fobo fof ŋagathikwa fof ... ane menzmenz*
kabe   nr=ma   fi   fobo   fof ŋa\gathik/wa   fof (.) ane
people stomach=CHAR   3.ABS DIST.ALL EMPH SG:SBJ:PST:IPFV/stop EMPH (.) DEM
menz-menz
REDUP-story.man
'Because its stomach was full with people, it stopped there ... that creature.'

43 *kabe ane zenthkäfath yak.*
kabe ane zen\thkäf/ath   yak
man DEM 2|3PL:SBJ:PST:IPFV:VENT/start running
'The people (survivors) started running here.'

44 *ŋatha mane kwaruthrm tifr ... yf ŋatha yara ane tifr*
ŋatha mane kwa\ru/thrm   tifr (.) yf   ŋatha ya\r/a   ane
dog   who SG:SBJ:PST:DUR/bark   tifr (.) name dog   3SG.MASC:SBJ:PST:IPFV/be DEM
tifr
tifr
'As for the barking dog, it was Tifr. The dog's name was Tifr.'

45   *wati sathkäfath.*
     wati sa\thkäf/ath
     then 2|3PL:SBJ>3SG.MASC:OBJ:PST:IPFV/start
     'Then, they started engaging the creature.'

46   *kabeyé ane dunzi kma sfruthrmth … keke*
     kabe=yé   ane dunzi kma sf\ru/thrmth   (.) keke
     man=ERG.NSG DEM arrow POT 2|3PL:SBJ>3SG.MASC:OBJ:PST:DUR/shoot (.) NEG
     'The people were trying to shoot arrows at the creature without success.'

47   *gwamf nafangth sräkor "muri! zba känrit nzuzawe! nzefé biruthro."*
     gwam=f   nafa-ngth   srä\kor/
     gwam=ERG.SG 3.POSS-younger.sibling 2|3SG:SBJ>3SG.MASC:OBJ:IRR:PFV/speak
     muri zba   kän\rit/   nzu-zawe   nze=wä
     muri PROX.ABL 2SG:SBJ:IMP:PFV/cross.over 1SG.POSS-side 1SG.ERG=EMPH
     b=y\ru/thro
     MED=SG:SBJ>3SG.MASC:OBJ:NPST:IPFV:AND/shoot
     'Gwam said to his small brother: "Muri! Come over to my side! I will shoot it there."'

48   *naf nima "samg! bänema nä buné fof yruthrth byé keke kwosi yathizr."*
     naf   nima sa\mg/   bäne=ma   nä bun=é
     3SG.ERG QUOT 2SG:SBJ>3SG.MASC:OBJ:IMP:PFV/shoot RECOG=CHAR INDF=ERG.NSG
     fof   y\ru/thrth   b=\yé/
     EMPH 2|3PL:SBJ>3SG.MASC:OBJ:NPST:IPFV/shoot MED=3SG.MASC:SBJ:NPST:IPFV/be
     keke kwosi ya\thiz/r
     NEG dead 3SG.MASC:SBJ:NPST:IPFV/die
     'He replied: "Shoot it! Because others are shooting and it is not dying."'

49   *naf nima: "keke fi miyamr erä fofosa mä rä. nze komnzo zimarwé fof."*
     naf   nima keke fi   miyamr e\rä/   fofosa mä
     3SG.ERG QUOT NEG 3.ABS ignorant 2|3PL:SBJ:NPST:IPFV/be heart where
     \rä/   nze   komnzo
     3SG.FEM:SBJ:NPST:IPFV/be 1SG.ERG only
     z=y\mar/wé   fof
     PROX=1SG:SBJ>3SG.MASC:OBJ:NPST:IPFV/see EMPH
     'He replied: "No, they do not know where the heart is. Only I can see it here."'

50   *zirkn thfrnm. nä bun kwanafrm. nä bun kwanafrm.*
     zirkn   thf\rn/m   nä bun kwa\na/frm   nä bun
     persistent 2|3DU:SBJ:PST:DUR/be INDF   SG:SBJ:PST:DUR/talk INDF
     kwa\na/frm
     SG:SBJ:PST:DUR/talk
     'They were going back and forth. One was talking and then the other was talking.'

51 *watik "ngth biruthé!"*
    watik ngth   b=y\ru/thé
    then younger.sibling   MED=1SG:SBJ>3SG.MASC:OBJ:NPST:IPFV/shoot
    'Well, (Gwam said) "Brother, I shoot it now!"'

52 *"famkaräsü gnräré!" ... nafananaf ane fof*
    fam=karä=sü   gn\rä/ré   (.) nafa-nana=f   ane fof
    thought=PROP=ETC 2SG:SBJ:IMP:IPFV/be (.) 3.POSS-older.brother=ERG.SG DEM EMPH
    '(Muri said) "You must watch out!" His big brother (was the one who shot).'

53 *trikasi nima rä*
    trik-si   nima   \rä/
    tell-NMLZ like.this 3SG.FEM:SBJ:NPST:IPFV/be
    'The story is like this:'

54 *nafangth kma markai näbikarä sfrärm*
    nafa-ngth   kma markai   näbi=karä sf\rä/rm
    3.POSS-younger.sibling POT white.man bow=PROP 3SG.MASC:SBJ:PST:DUR/be
    'His small brother must have had a shotgun.'

55 *watik nafangth mane yara naf keke samga ... nafananafnzo*
    watik nafa-ngth   mane ya\r/a   naf keke
    then 3.POSS-younger.sibling who 3SG.MASC:SBJ:PST:IPFV/be 3SG.ERG NEG
    sa\mg/a   (.) nafa-nana=f=nzo
    SG:SBJ>3SG.MASC:PST:PFV/shoot (.) 3.POSS-older.brother=ERG.SG=ONLY
    'But his small brother did not hit the creature, only his older brother.'

56 *näbi ŋathunza ... zf sfthnm*
    näbi ŋa\thu/nza   (.) zf   sf\thn/m
    bow SG:SBJ:PST:IPFV/fold (.) IMM 3SG.MASC:SBJ:PST:DUR/lie.down
    'He drew the bow while the creature was laying down here,'

57 *yo kwan ... fof sargosira fofosa fefen*
    yo.kwan   (.) fof   sa\rgosi/ra   fofosa ffe=n
    sound.of.arrow (.) EMPH SG:SBJ>3SG.MASC:OBJ:PST:IPFV/penetrate heart real=LOC
    'Wham! The arrow poked right through to the heart.'

58 *no fof zärfetha*
    no   fof   zä\rfeth/a
    water EMPH SG:SBJ:PST:PFV/burst
    'Water bursted out.'

59 *no ane zamatha*
    no   ane   za\math/a
    water DEM SG:SBJ:PST:PFV/run
    'That water was gushing out.'

60 *wati no mane kwakwirm fof*
wati no mane kwa\kwir/m fof
then water which SG:SBJ:PST:DUR/run EMPH
'Well, the water that was flowing'

61 *wäsi zrminz mä ŋanrsira fof ... mni mä ŋanrsira*
wäsi zrminz mä ŋan\rsir/a   fof (.) mni mä
wäsi root where SG:SBJ:PST:IPFV:VENT/burn EMPH (.) fire where
ŋan\rsir/a
SG:SBJ:PST:IPFV:VENT/burn
'to the place where the wäsi roots had burned, where the fire had burned.'

62 *no fä kwanthorthrm fof ... ane zrminz fof*
no fä kwan\thor/thrm   fof (.) ane zrminz fof
water DIST SG:SBJ:PST:DUR:VENT/enter EMPH (.) DEM root EMPH
'The water went inside there ... into those roots.'

63 *nof nä nima thärkothmako. nä nima thänkothma nzezawe.*
no=f nä nima thä\kothm/ako   nä nima
water=ERG INDF like.this SG:SBJ>2|3PL:OBJ:PST:PFV:AND/chase INDF like.this
thän\kothm/a   nze-zawe
SG:SBJ>2|3PL:OBJ:PST:PFV:VENT/chase 1NSG.POSS-side
'The water chased some people that way and it chased others here to our side.'

64 *gwamane nima zenmathath ... muriane nima.*
gwam=ane nima zen\math/ath   (.) muri=ane nima
gwam=POSS.SG like.this 2|3PL:SBJ:PST:PFV:VENT/run (.) muri=POSS.SG like.this
'Gwam's people ran this way. Muri's people ran that way (towards Australia).'

65 *mane ŋankwirwath zentnäthath*
mane ŋankwirwath   zentnäthath
who 2|3PL:SBJ:PST:IPFV:VENT/run 2|3PL:SBJ:PST:PFV:VENT/scatter
'Those who came running started to go in different directions.'

66 *nä enrera bawi.*
nä en\rä/ra   bawi
INDF SG:SBJ:PST:IPFV:VENT/be bawi
'Some came to Bawi.'

67 *wartha nima bämnzr wartha a kondomarin ... smärki.*
wartha nima b=ä\m/nzr   wartha a kondomarin (.)
wartha like.this MED=2|3PL:SBJ:NPST:IPFV/dwell wartha and marind   (.)
smärki
smärki
'Like the Wartha people living there. The Wartha and Marind ... and the Smärki.'

68 *nafanme ... foba fof ŋankwira fof*
   nafanme (.) foba   fof   ŋan\kwi/ra   fof
   3NSG.POSS (.) DIST.ABL EMPH SG:SBJ:PST:IPFV:VENT/run EMPH
   'Their ancestor was coming really from there.'

69 *fi foba fof ŋankwirwath ... bawi*
   fi   foba   fof   ŋan\kwi/rwath   (.) bawi
   3.ABS DIST.ABL EMPH 2|3PL:SBJ:PST:IPFV:VENT/run (.) bawi
   'They came from Bawi.'

70 *watik gwamf fä fof mni ... bäne zafrafa fof no.*
   watik gwam=f   fä   fof   mni (.) bäne
   then   gwam=ERG.SG DIST EMPH fire (.) RECOG.ABS
   za\fraf/a   fof   no
   SG:SBJ>3SG.FEM:OBJ:PST:PFV/extinguish EMPH water
   'Okay, Gwam extinguished the fire there ... I mean the water.'

71 *dödöme zakwra.*
   dödö=me za\kwr/a
   dödö=INS SG:SBJ>3SG.FEM:OBJ:PST:PFV/hit
   'He hit the water with the dödö plant (Melaleuca sp).'

72 *watik no fä fof zäkora ... keke kwa nof zanmäyofa.*
   watik no   fä   fof   zä\kor/a   (.) keke kwa no=f
   then   water DIST EMPH SG:SBJ:PST:IPFV/become (.) NEG FUT water=ERG
   zan\mäyof/a
   SG:SBJ>3SG.FEM:OBJ:PST:PFV:VENT/continue
   'Okay, the water stopped there. It did not continue to come our way.'

73 *fobo fof no ŋagathikwa fof.*
   fobo   fof   no   ŋa\gathik/wa   fof
   DIST.ALL EMPH water SG:SBJ:PST:IPFV/stop EMPH
   'The flood stopped there.'

74 *watik fi mane enrera e ... zwari ... wartha fof.*
   watik fi   mane en\rä/ra   e   (.) zwari (.) wartha fof
   then   3.ABS who   SG:SBJ:PST:IPFV:VENT/be until (.) zwari (.) wartha EMPH
   'Those who came until Zwari (= Bawi) were really the Wartha people.'

75 *watik fä fof zwarin zämsath.*
   watik fä   fof   zwari=n   zä\ms/ath
   then   DIST EMPH zwari=LOC 2|3PL:SBJ:PST:PFV/dwell
   'They settled there in Zwari.'

76 *zokwasi fthé emarwath ffrümenzo ... watik kondomarin nima feräro.*
   zokwasi fthé   e\mar/wath   f-frü=me=nzo   (.)
   language when 2|3PL:SBJ>2|3PL:OBJ:PST:IPFV/see REDUP-single=INS=ONLY (.)

watik kondomarin nima   f=e\rä/ro
then marind   like.this DIST=2|3PL:SBJ:PST:IPFV:AND/be
'When they saw that people spoke different languages, then the Marind moved on that way.'

77 *zena boba wazi fi berä merauken.*
    zena boba   wazi fi   b=e\rä/   merauke=n
    today MED.ABL side 3.ABS MED=2|3PL:SBJ:NPST:IPFV/be merauke=LOC
    'Today, they are on the other side, there in Merauke.'

78 *nä mane erera zwarifa ŋafrezath thoro.*
    nä   mane e\rä/ra   zwari=fa
    INDF who 2|3PL:SBJ:PST:IPFV/be zwari=ABL
    ŋa\frez/ath   thoro
    2|3PL:SBJ:PST:IPFV/come.up.from.river thoro
    'As for others, they came up from Zwari to Thoro.'

79 *watik thoron fä fthé zemarath we nimäwä fof ... zokwasi ffrümenzo.*
    watik thoro=n   fä   fthé ze\mar/ath   we nima=wä   fof (.)
    then thoro=LOC DIST when 2|3PL:SBJ:PST:IPFV/see also like.this=EMPH EMPH (.)
    zokwasi f-frü=me=nzo
    language REDUP-single=INS=ONLY
    'When they looked at themselves in Thoro, it was the same thing again ...
    different languages.'

80 *watik foba zethkäfath nimame kwasogwrmth.*
    watik foba   ze\thkäf/ath   nima=me kwa\sog/wrmth
    then   DIST.ABL 2|3PL:SBJ:PST:IPFV/start like.this 2|3PL:SBJ:PST:DUR/climb
    'Then they began walking from there. They came up this way.'

81 *okay, nä mane enrera bäne ... zwari ... zwarifa e bäne ... tamgakar.*
    okay nä   mane en\rä/ra   bäne   (.) zwari (.) zwari=fa
    okay INDF who 2|3PL:SBJ:PST:IPFV:VENT/be RECOG.ABS (.) zwari (.) zwari=ABL
    e   bäne   . tamgakar
    until RECOG.ABS (.) tamgakar
    'Okay, some came until Zwari. From Zwari until Tamgakar.'

82 *nima bä ämnzr safs*
    nima   bä   ä\m/nzr   safs
    like.this MED 2|3PL:SBJ:NPST:IPFV/dwell safs
    'like the ones who live there in Safs.'

83 *wati fi fä fof thfyakm.*
    wati fi   fä   fof   thf\yak/m
    then 3.ABS DIST EMPH 2|3PL:SBJ:PST:DUR/walk
    'Okay, this is how they were going.'

84 *nzenme mane yanra ... mä ŋankwirwath komo fä ŋanfrezath ... komo.*

nzenme   mane yan\r/a   (.) mä

1NSG./Poss who   3SG.MASC:SBJ:PST:IPFV:VENT/be (.) where

ŋan\kwir/wath   komo fä

2|3PL:SBJ:PST:IPFV:VENT/run komo DIST

ŋan\frez/ath   (.) komo

2|3PL:SBJ:PST:IPFV:VENT/come.up.from.water (.) komo

'As for our ancestor, he was running to Komo. He came up there in Komo.'

85 *nzenme mayawama kabe nä fä thägathizath.*

nzenme   mayawa=ma   kabe nä   fä   thä\gathiz/ath

1NSG.POSS mayawa=CHAR man INDF DIST 2|3PL:SBJ>2|3PL:OBJ:PST:PFV/leave

'Our Mayawa man left some people there.'

86 *we foba ... thden nä kwot we mayawama kabe fof.*

we   foba   (.) thd=en   nä   kwot   we   mayawa=ma   kabe   fof

also DIST.ABL (.) middle=LOC INDF properly also mayawa=CHAR people EMPH

'and again ... halfway he left some more Mayawa people again.'

87 *foba ... baguma kabe ... zena mifnen zämnzr.*

foba   (.) bagu=ma   kabe   (.) zena mifne=n

DIST.ABL (.) bagu=CHAR people (.) today mibini=LOC

z=ä\m/nzr

PROX=2|3PL:SBJ:NPST:IPFV/dwell

'He left some Bagu people there. They live in Mibini today.'

88 *sagara fä thägathinzath. okay fi nima erera ... mogarkam.*

sagara fä   thä\gathinz/ath   okay fi   nima

sagara DIST 2|3PL:SBJ>2|3PL:OBJ:PST:IPFV/leave okay 3.ABS like.this

e\rä/ra   (.) mogarkam

2|3PL:SBJ:PST:IPFV/be (.) mogarkam

'They left some Sagara people there. They used to live in Mogarkam.'

89 *nä mane erera nima erera bäne ... drdr ... nä sagara fof.*

nä   mane e\rä/ra   nima   e\rä/ra   bäne   (.)

INDF who   2|3PL:SBJ:PST:IPFV/be like.this 2|3PL:SBJ:PST:IPFV/be RECOG.ABS (.)

drdr   (.) nä   sagara fof

derideri (.) INDF sagara EMPH

'Others were there in Derideri ... another Sagara clan.'

90 *bagu mane enrera bäne ... mäta.*

bagu mane en\rä/ra   bäne   (.) mäta

bagu who 2|3PL:SBJ:PST:IPFV:VENT/be RECOG.ABS (.) mäta

'The Bagus who were coming, they went to Mäta.'

91   *sagara mane enrera garaita.*
       sagara mane en\rä/ra   garaita
       sagara who   2|3PL:SBJ:PST:IPFV:VENT/be garaita
       'and the Sagaras continued to Garaita.'

92   *mayawa ni zbo zf nnrera.*
       mayawa ni   zbo   zf   nn\rä/ra
       mayawa 1NSG PROX.ALL IMM 1PL:SBJ:PST:IPFV:VENT/be
       'We Mayawas came right here.'

93   *okay nzenme bada ... mrzarane bada mane yanra ... fi fof yanra bäne ... mathkwi.*
       okay nzenme   bada   (.) mrzar=ane   bada   mane
       okay 1NSG.POSS ancestor (.) mrzar=POSS.SG ancestor who
       yan\r/a   (.) fi   fof   yan\r/a
       3SG.MASC:SBJ:PST:IPFV:VENT/be (.) 3.ABS EMPH 3SG.MASC:SBJ:PST:IPFV:VENT/be
       bäne   (.) mathkwi
       RECOG.ABS (.) mathkwi
       'Okay, our ancestor, the Mrzar clan's ancestor who came was Mathkwi.'

94   *yf ane yanra mathkwi!*
       yf   ane yan\r/a   mathkwi
       name DEM 3SG.MASC:SBJ:PST:IPFV:VENT/be mathkwi
       'That was the name, Mathkwi!'

95   *mathkwif ane enfathwa ... wawa fofosa.*
       mathkwi=f   ane en\fath/wa   (.) wawa fofosa
       mathkwi=ERG.SG DEM SG:SBJ>2|3PL:OBJ:PST:IPFV:VENT/hold (.) yam   heart
       'Mathkwi was holding those magic yam stones.'

96   *naf ane ynfathwa fof.*
       naf   ane yn\fath/wa   fof.
       3SG.ERG DEM SG:SBJ>3SG.MASC:OBJ:PST:IPFV:VENT/hold EMPH
       'He was holding that one.'

97   *wati näbi ane komnzo fofosa yara wawama ... nasi ... duga ... biskar ... dagon nä berä fof*
       wati näbi ane komnzo fofosa ya\r/a   wawa=ma (.) nasi
       then one DEM only   heart 3SG.MASC:SBJ:PST:IPFV/be yam=CHAR (.) long.yam
       (.) duga (.) biskar   (.) dagon nä   b=e\rä/   fof
       (.) taro (.) cassava (.) food   INDF MED=2|3PL:SBJ:NPST:IPFV:be EMPH
       'Okay, there was just one stone for yams, long yams, taro, cassava and the other food there.'

99   *watik fi anekarä fof yanra fof.*
       watik fi   ane=karä fof   yan\r/a   fof
       then   3.ABS DEM=PROP EMPH 3SG.MASC:SBJ:PST:IPFV:VENT/be EMPH
       'He came with this one.'

100　*mane yanyaka e … wm bä ythn … zabrta.*
　　mane yan\yak/a　　　　　　　e　(.) wm　bä
　　who　3SG.MASC:SBJ:PST:IPFV/walk until (.) stone MED
　　y\thn/　　　　　　　　　　　　(.) zabrta
　　3SG.MASC:SBJ:NPST:IPFV/lie.down (.) zabrta
　　'As he came to the place where the stone is lying, there at Zabrta,'

101　*fä fof ŋanritakwath fof.*
　　fä　fof　ŋan\ritak/wath　　　　　　fof
　　DIST EMPH 2|3PL:SBJ:PST:IPFV:VENT/cross EMPH
　　'they crossed the river.'

102　*kwanritakwrmth trkren.*
　　kwan\ritak/wrmth　　　　　trkr=en
　　2|3PL:SBJ:PST:DUR:VENT/cross flood=LOC
　　'They were going across during the rainy season.'

103　*watik, nima n fam zära "garaita zawe? keke, nä kabe foba z sfyak."*
　　watik nima n　fam　zä\r/a　　　　　garaita zawe keke nä　kabe foba
　　then　QUOT IMN though SG:SBJ:PST:IPFV/do garaita side　NEG　INDF man DIST.ABL
　　z　sf\yak/
　　ALR 3SG.MASC:SBJ:PST:IPFV/walk
　　'He was thinking: "Should I go to Garaita? No, another man went this way already."'

104　*watik, nima zethkäfa fi … safs.*
　　watik nima　ze\thkäf/a　　　　　fi　(.) safs
　　then　like.this SG:SBJ:PST:PFV/start 3.ABS (.) safs
　　'Then, he started coming this way towards Safs.'

105　*nimame ane zethkäfa mothr mane yanra e … akrimogo.*
　　nima=me　ane ze\thkäf/a　　　　moth=r　　　mane
　　like.this=INS DEM SG:SBJ:PST:PFV/start walking=PURP who
　　yan\r/a　　　　　　　　　　e　(.) akrimogo
　　3SG.MASC:SBJ:PST:IPFV:VENT/be until (.) akrimogo
　　'He started to walk like this, he walked until Akrimogo.'

106　*yam fä fof thremar fof.*
　　yam　fä　fof　thre\mar/　　　　　　　　fof
　　footprint DIST EMPH 2|3SG:SBJ>2|3PL:OBJ:IRR:PFV/see EMPH
　　'He saw footprints there.'

107　*"oh, nä nima z eräro."*
　　oh nä　nima　z　e\rä/ro
　　oh INDF like.this ALR 2|3PL:SBJ:NPST:IPFV:AND/be
　　'He said "Oh, others were walking along here already."'

108 *watik, keräfi foba fof zäzira fof e ... kar yf rä ymnz.*
watik keräfi   foba   fof   zä\zi/ra   fof   e   (.) kar   yf
then   blackpalm DIST.ABL EMPH SG:SBJ:PST:PFV/throw EMPH until (.) place name
\rä/   ymnz
3SG.FEM:SBJ:NPST:IPFV/be ymnz
'Then he shot an arrow from there until ... the name of the place is Ymnz.'

109 *watik, fobo fof "oh, kabe bä yé ... watik, nimame wyak."*
watik fobo   fof   oh kabe bä   \yé/   (.) watik
then   DIST.ALL EMPH oh man MED 3SG.MASC:SBJ:NPST:IPFV/be (.) then
nima=me   w\yak/
like.this=INS 1SG:SBJ:NPST:IPFV/walk
'Okay, there he said: "Oh, there is a man there! Okay, I will go that path then."'

110 *watik foba fof akrimogofa zenfara fof.*
watik foba   fof   akrimogo=fa   zen\far/a   fof
then   DIST.ABL EMPH akrimogo=ABL SG:SBJ:PST:PFV/set.off EMPH
'Okay, he set off from there, from Akrimogo.'

111 *akrimogo ... foba näbi yanyaka. karane yf rä füsari.*
akrimogo (.) foba   näbi yan\yak/   kar=ane   yf
akrimogo (.) DIST.ABL one 3SG.MASC:SBJ:PST:IPFV:VENT/walk place=POSS.SG name
\rä/   füsari
3SG.FEM:SBJ:NPST:IPFV/be füsäri
'From Akrimogo he was coming straight to ... the name of that place is Füsari.'

112 *füsärifa ... rarafü kar ... rarafü karfa ... kafrir fä ttfön zänrita e ... bäne ... zofok.*
füsäri=fa (.) rarafü kar (.) rarafü kar=fa   (.) kafrir fä   ttfö=n
füsäri=ABL (.) rarafü place (.) rarafü place=ABL (.) kafrir DIST creek=LOC
zän\rit/a   e   (.) bäne   (.) zofok
SG:SBJ:PST:PFV:VENT/cross until (.) RECOG.ABS (.) zofok
'From Füsari to Rarafü, from Rarafü to Kafrir, he crossed the creek, until he
arrived at Zofok.'

113 *zofok fä yamthiza.*
zofok fä   ya\mthi/za
zofok DIST 3SG.MASC:SBJ:PST:IPFV/rest
'He rested there in Zofok.'

114 *nabi komnzo bekogr.*
nabi   komnzo b=e\kogr/
bamboo still   MED=2|3PL:SBJ:NPST:STAT/be.standing
'The bamboos are still standing there.'

115 *nabi ŋatr fä fof zurärm zwafrmnzrm.*
nabi ŋatr   fä   fof   zu\rä/rm
bow bowstring DIST EMPH SG:SBJ>3SG.FEM:OBJ:PST:DUR/do

zwa\frm/nzrm
SG:SBJ>3SG.FEM:OBJ:PST:DUR/prepare
'He was fixing his bowstring there.'

116 *zurzirakwa fof.*
zu\rzirak/wa fof
SG:SBJ>3SG.FEM:OBJ:PST:IPFV/tie EMPH
'He tied it properly.'

117 *bäne yanatha ... nasi nömä. nasi nömä yanatha.*
bäne ya\na/tha (.) nasi nömä nasi
RECOG.ABS SG:SBJ>3SG.MASC:OBJ:PST:IPFV/eat (.) long.yam yamcake long.yam
nömä ya\na/tha
yamcake SG:SBJ>3SG.MASC:OBJ:PST:IPFV/eat
'He ate that yamcake (from long yams). He ate the yamcake.'

118 *rfarrfar futhfuth mane erera ... watik, wmr ane fof ŋakwthenzath fof.*
rfar-rfar futh-futh mane e\rä/ra (.) watik wm=r ane
REDUP-crumb REDUP-scraps which SG:SBJ:PST:IPFV/be (.) then stone=PURP DEM
fof ŋa\kwthe/nzath fof
EMPH 2|3PL:SBJ:PST:IPFV/change EMPH
'As for those crumbs, those scraps, they turned into stones.'

119 *zäkwtherath ... watik komnzo berästhgr.*
zä\kwther/ath (.) watik komnzo b=e\räs/thgr
2|3PL:SBJ:PST:PFV/change (.) then still MED=2|3PL:SBJ:NPST:STAT/be.erected
'They changed into stones. They are still sticking out there.'

120 *wm mane yé ... ynfathwa fof no nzigfu ... watik ane fof yräza fof ... zofok kar.*
wm mane \yé/ (.)
stone which 3SG.MASC:SBJ:NPST:IPFV/be (.)
yn\fath/wa fof no nzigfu (.) watik ane
SG:SBJ>3SG.MASC:OBJ:PST:IPFV:VENT/hold EMPH water magic.stone (.) then DEM
fof y\rä/za fof (.) zofok kar
EMPH SG:SBJ>3SG.MASC:OBJ:NPST:IPFV/erect EMPH (.) zofok place
'As for the stone that he held, the rain magic stone, he pushed it in the ground at Zofok.'

121 *watik foba yanyaka bäne ... misa zfth. mäbri misa zfth yrn.*
watik foba yan\yak/a bäne (.) misa.zfth mäbri
then DIST.ABL 3SG.MASC:SBJ:PST:IPFV:VENT/walk RECOG.ABS (.) misa.zfth mäbri
misa.zfth yrn
misa.zfth yrn
'Then he went to Misa Zfth from there. Mäbri, Misa Zfth and Yrn.'

122 *fä zänrsöftha fof ... yanyaka benzü zfth.*
fä   zän\rsöfth/a   fof   (.) yan\yak/a
DIST SG:SBJ:PST:PFV:VENT/descend EMPH (.) 3SG.MASC:SBJ:PST:IPFV:VENT/walk
benzü.zfth
benzü.zfth
'There he came down and walked to Benzü Zfth.'

123 *foba fof ymd threnkaris fof ... afa kfokfo ythama*
foba   fof   ymd thren\karis/   fof   (.) afa.kfokfo
DIST.ABL EMPH bird 2|3SG:SBJ>2|3PL:OBJ:IRR:PFV:VENT/hear EMPH (.) afa kfokfo
ythama
ythama
'From there he heard those birds ... *afa kfokfo* and *ythama*.'[1]

124 *fam zära "kar bä rä. ah, kar töna fobo fof wyak fof."*
fam   zä\r/a   kar bä \rä/   ah kar
thought SG:SBJ:PST:PFV/do place MED 3SG.FEM:SBJ:NPST:IPFV/be ah place
töna   fobo   fof wo\yak/   fof
high.ground DIST.ALL EMPH 1SG:SBJ:NPST:IPFV/walk EMPH
'He thought "There is a place there. Ah, I will go there to the high ground."'

125 *yanyaka fä fof zänrita fof rä kukwrb fr zra ... mnzär fr neba.*
yan\yak/a   fä fof zän\rit/a
3SG.MASC:SBJ:PST:IPFV:VENT/walk DIST EMPH SG:SBJ:PST:PFV:VENT/cross.over
fof   \rä/   kukwrb fr zra   (.) mnzär fr neba
EMPH 3SG.FEM:SBJ:NPST:IPFV/be kukwrb fr swamp (.) mnzär fr opposite
'He walked and crossed the river at Kukwrb Fr swamp opposite from Mnzär Fr.'

126 *wati fä fof yanyaka fof ... mä swanyakm ... mä zänfrefa ... nömä futhfuth ... fä fof*
... ŋantnägwath.
wati fä   fof yan\yak/a   fof   (.) mä
then DIST EMPH 3SG.MASC:SBJ:PST:IPFV:VENT/walk EMPH (.) where
swan\yak/m   (.) mä
3SG.MASC:SBJ:PST:DUR:VENT/walk (.) where
zän\fref/a   (.) nömä   futh-futh   (.) fä   fof
SG:SBJ:PST:PFV:VENT/come.up.from.river (.) yamcake REDUP-scraps (.) DIST EMPH
(.) ŋan\tnäg/wath
(.) 2|3PL:SBJ:PST:IPFV:VENT/lose
'Well, he walked there. and where he was walking, where he came up, he
dropped those crumbs from the yamcake.'

127 *mane yanra e zrä zöfäthak bä brä brä ... zafe ŋazi fr ... nä fof ethn berä*
mane yan\r/a   e   z=\rä/
who 3SG.MASC:SBJ:PST:IPFV:VENT/be until PROX=3SG.FEM:SBJ:NPST:IPFV/be

---

[1]These are: *afa kfokfo* 'Hooded Butcherbird' and *ythama* 'Raggiana Bird-of-Paradise'.

zöfäthak bä   b=\rä/   b=\rä/   (.)
zöfäthak MED MED=3SG.FEM:SBJ:NPST:IPFV/be MED=3SG.FEM:SBJ:NPST:IPFV/be (.)
zafe ŋazi   fr   (.) nä   fof   e\thn/
old coconut stem (.) INDF EMPH 2|3PL:SBJ:NPST:STAT/be.lying
b=e\rä/
MED=2|3PL:SBJ:NPST:IPFV/be
'He walked up right here Zöfäthak, over there by the old coconut trees. There are
some stones lying down there.'

128 *watik nä fä fof ŋantnägwath fof*
     watik nä   fä   fof   ŋan\tnäg/wath   fof
     then INDF DIST EMPH 2|3PL:SBJ:PST:IPFV:VENT/lose EMPH
     'Well, some more crumbs were dropped there.'

129 *fä fof sakuka "oh, zane zf zunthorakwé."*
     fä   fof   sa\kuk/a   oh zane   zf
     DIST EMPH 3SG.MASC:SBJ:PST:PFV/stand oh DEM:PROX IMM
     zun\thorak/wé
     1SG:SBJ>3SG.FEM:OBJ:RPST:IPFV:VENT/search
     'There he stood and said "Oh, this is what I was looking for."'

130 *fz zamara afa kfokfo zakarisa … bäne zakarisa ythama*
     fz   za\mar/a   afa.kfokfo za\karis/a   (.)
     forest SG:SBJ>3SG.FEM:OBJ:PST:PFV/see butcherbird SG:SBJ:PST:PFV/hear (.)
     bäne   za\karis/a   ythama
     RECOG.ABS SG:SBJ:PST:PFV/hear bird.of.paradise
     'He saw the forest, he heard the butcherbird and the bird of paradise.'

131 *watik krenafth "nima wyak. zbo kar rä farem kar."*
     watik kre\nafth/   nima wo\yak/   zbo   kar
     then 2|3SG:SBJ:IRR:PFV/speak like.this 1SG:SBJ:NPST:IPFV/walk PROX.ALL place
     \rä/   farem kar
     3SG.FEM:SBJ:NPST:IPFV/be farem place
     'Then he said "I will go this way. There is a place here, Faremkar."'

132 *watik, fthé yaka bobo, foba krekaris "oh, füthan nä zbo kabe yamnzr."*
     watik fthé \yak/a   bobo   foba   kre\karis/
     then when 3SG.MASC:SBJ:PST:IPFV/walk MED.ALL DIST.ABL 2|3SG:SBJ:IRR:PFV/hear
     oh fütha=n   nä   zbo   kabe ya\m/nzr
     oh fütha=LOC INDF PROX.ALL man 3SG.MASC:SBJ:NPST:IPFV/dwell
     'When he walked there, he heard someone from over there "Oh, a man lives here
     in Fütha."'

133 *we foba krekaris "oh, faremkaren kabe yé."*
     we foba   kre\karis/   oh faremkar=en kabe
     also DIST.ABL 2|3SG:SBJ:IRR:PFV/hear oh faremkar=LOC man

\yé/
3SG.MASC:SBJ:NPST:IPFV/be
'He also heard someone from over there "Oh, a man lives here in Faremkar."'

134   *watik yako.*
watik \yak/o
then   3SG.MASC:SBJ:NPST:IPFV:AND/walk
'Then he walked away.'

135   *faremaneme kabe z sathora.*
farem=aneme   kabe z   sa\thor/a
farem=POSS.NSG man ALR 3SG.MASC:SBJ:PST:PFV/arrive
'The Farem clan's man had already arrived,'

136   *bafane bada fof ... fatamaane.*
baf=ane   bada   fof   (.) fatama=ane
RECOG=POSS.SG ancestor EMPH (.) fatama=POSS.SG
'that one's ancestor, Fatama's ancestor.'

137   *farem thden watik foba fof sräkor "foba fof bä fä fof gnamnzé! ey, fisor bthanen*
      käms!"
farem thd=en   watik foba   fof   srä\kor/
farem middle=LOC then   DIST.ABL EMPH 2|3SG:SBJ>3SG.MASC:OBJ:IRR:PFV/speak
foba   fof   bä   fä   fof   gna\m/nzé   ey fisor bthan=en
DIST.ABL EMPH 2.ABS DIST EMPH 2SG:SBJ:IMP:STAT/dwell hey fisor bthan=LOC
kä\m/s
2SG:SBJ:IMP:PFV/dwell
'In the middle of Farem, he told him from there: "You stay right there! Hey, you
settle at Fisor Bthan!"'

138   *wati we nä sräthoro ... bäne ... wazu.*
wati we nä   srä\thor/o   (.) bäne   (.) wazu
then also INDF 3SG.MASC:SBJ:IRR:PFV:AND/arrive (.) RECOG.ABS (.) wazu
'Then, another one arrived ... that one ... Wazu.'

139   *fä fof sräkor "watik, foba fof käms wazufa!"*
fä   fof   srä\kor/   watik foba   fof
DIST EMPH 2|3SG:SBJ>3SG.MASC:OBJ:IRR:PFV/speak then   DIST.ABL EMPH
kä\m/s   wazu=fa
2SG:SBJ:IMP:PFV/dwell wazu=ABL
'He told him there: "Okay, you settle there at Wazu!"'

140   *watik fthé zamara katan fäth ane zfrärm*
watik fthé za\mar/a   katan fäth ane
then   when SG:SBJ>3SG.FEM:OBJ:PST:PFV/see small DIM DEM
zf\rä/rm
3SG.FEM:SBJ:PST:DUR/be
'He looked at the place. It was a small patch.'

141   *"kwa nzä zä zf kwramnzr? nima ŋabrigwé."*

kwa nzä   zä   zf   kwra\m/nzr   nima   ŋa\brig/wé

FUT 1SG.ABS PROX IMM 1SG:SBJ:IRR:IPFV/dwell like.this 1SG:SBJ:NPST:IPFV/return

' "Will I stay right here? I will go back this way."'

142   *boba fthmäsü zänbrima watik … nasi nömä ane fof tnägsi thenthkäfa rrfar …*
futhfuth.

boba   fthmäsü zän\brim/a   watik (.) nasi   nömä   ane

MED.ABL while   SG:SBJ:PST:PFV:VENT/return then   (.) long.yam yamcake DEM

fof   tnäg-si   then\thkäf/a   r-rfar   (.)

EMPH lose-NMLZ SG:SBJ>2|3PL:OBJ:PST:PFV:VENT/start REDUP-crumb (.)

futh-futh

REDUP-scrap

'While he was coming back from there, he started dropping this yamcake crumbs
… the scraps.'

143   *zä zf e zane zf zethno zerä*

zä   zf   e   zane   zf   z=e\thn/o

PROX IMM until DEM:PROX IMM PROX=2|3PL:SBJ:NPST:STAT:AND/be.lying

z=e\rä/

PROX=2|3PL:SBJ:NPST:IPFV/be

'Right here to these these stones right here.'

144   *fä fof ane futhfuth thuntnägwrm*

fä   fof   ane futh-futh   thun\tnäg/wrm

DIST EMPH DEM REDUP-scrap SG:SBJ>2|3PL:OBJ:PST:DUR:VENT/lose

'Over there he was dropping the scraps.'

145   *nä bä enthn e nima zyaro e masu.*

nä   bä   en\thn/   e   nima

INDF MED 2|3PL:SBJ:NPST:STAT:VENT/be.lying until like.this

z=ya\r/o   e   masu

PROX=3SG.MASC:SBJ:PST:IPFV:AND/be until masu

'There are some stones lying there. and then he walked that way until Masu.'

146   *foba fof sathora "nzukar, zä zf ämnzr!"*

foba   fof   sa\thor/a   nzu-kar   zä   zf

DIST.ABL EMPH 3SG.MASC:SBJ:PST:PFV/arrive 1SG.POSS-place PROX IMM

ä\m/nzr

2|3PL:SBJ:NPST:IPFV/dwell

'He arrived over there and said "This is my place. My people will live right here!"'

147   *watik menz kar ane fof zräkorth bäne … yari.*

watik menz kar   ane fof   zrä\kor/th   bäne   (.) yari

then   myth place DEM EMPH 2|3PL:SBJ>3SG.FEM:OBJ:IRR:PFV/call RECOG.ABS (.) yari

'Well, they call this story place Yari.'

148 *yari sathora fof.*
yari sa\thor/a   fof
yari 3SG.MASC:SBJ:PST:PFV/arrive EMPH
'He had arrived at Yari.'

149 *watik fä fof ... no nzigfukarä fi fof sathora fof.*
watik fä   fof   (.) no nzigfu=karä   fi   fof
then DIST EMPH (.) rain rain.stone=PROP 3.ABS EMPH
sa\thor/a   fof
3SG.MASC:SBJ:PST:PFV:VENT/arrive EMPH
'Over there ... he arrived with the magic rain stone.'

150 *fi mane yanra nzigfu nä fofosa yfathwa fof nasi, wawa, duga, fiskar ... ranzo fä*
dagon eräro.
fi   mane yan\r/a   nzigfu nä   fofosa
3.ABS who 3SG.MASC:SBJ:PST:IPFV:VENT/be rain.stone INDF heart
y\fath/wa   fof nasi   wawa duga fiskar (.)
SG:SBJ>3SG.MASC:OBJ:PST:IPFV/hold EMPH long.yam yam   taro cassava (.)
ra=nzo   fä   dagon e\rä/ro
what=ONLY DIST food 2|3PL:SBJ:NPST:IPFV:AND/be
'As he came, he had this rain stone and another stone ... for long yams, yams,
taro and cassava ... all the crops.'

151 *anekaräsü swamnzrm fof.*
ane=karä=sü   swa\m/nzrm   fof
DEM=PROP=ETC 3SG.MASC:SBJ:PST:DUR/dwell EMPH
'He was staying with these ones.'

152 *fthé wawa thuworthrmth.*
fthé   wawa thu\wor/thrmth
when yam   2|3PL:SBJ>2|3PL:OBJ:PST:DUR/plant
'Whenever the people were planting yams,'

153 *watik sfrärm e wawa taga kwot thkarthé kwafiyokwrmth.*
watik sf\rä/rm   e   wawa taga kwot   thkarthé
then 3SG.MASC:SBJ:PST:DUR/be until yam   leaf properly hard
kwa\fiyok/wrmth
2|3PL:SBJ:PST:DUR/make
'he was there until the yam leaves were becoming dry.'

154 *watik fthé fof wawa taga nä thurtnwrm ... nasi taga ... kemar taga ... taga bäne*
bera biskar duga.
watik fthé   fof   wawa taga nä   thu\rtn/wrm   (.) nasi
then when EMPH yam   leaf INDF SG:SBJ>2|3PL:OBJ:PST:DUR/pull.off (.) long.yam
taga (.) kemar taga (.) taga bäne   b=e\r/a   biskar duga
leaf (.) kemar leaf (.) leaf RECOG.ABS MED=2|3PL:SBJ:PST:IPFV/be cassava taro
'That was when he pulled of some yam leaves, long yam leaves, kemar (type of
yam) leaves and those leaves there ... cassava and taro.'

155   *watik nzigfu mrmr foba sfrärm … ane tagame sumyuknwrm.*
watik nzigfu   mrmr foba   sf\rä/rm   (.) ane taga=me
then   magic.stone inside DIST.ABL 3SG.MASC:SBJ:PST:DUR/be (.) DEM leaf=INS
su\myuk/nwrm
SG:SBJ>3SG.MASC:OBJ:PST:DUR/wrap
'The magic stone was there inside. He was wrapping it with these leaves.'

156   *surdiknwrm … watik wawa zfthen swäzin*
su\rdikn/wrm   (.) watik wawa zfth=en
SG:SBJ>3SG.MASC:OBJ:PST:DUR/tie.around (.) then yam   base=LOC
swä\zin/
2|3SG:SBJ>3SG.MASC:OBJ:ITER/put.down
'He tied them around. Then he used to put it down to the yams.'

157   *sfthnm e wawa fthé thwemar nima thkarthé zäkorth.*
sf\thn/m   e   wawa fthé   thwe\mar/
3SG.MASC:SBJ:PST:DUR/be.lying until yam   when 2|3SG:SBJ:>2|3PL:OBJ:ITER/see
nima   thkarthé zä\kor/th
like.this hard   2|3PL:SBJ:PST:PFV/become
'The stone was lying there until he saw that the leaves became dry.'

158   *watik ausiausi thukonzrm "käthfe kabe!"*
watik ausi-ausi   thu\ko/nzrm   kä\thf/e
then REDUP-old.woman SG:SBJ>2|3PL:OBJ:PST:DUR/say 2PL:SBJ:IMP:PFV/walk
kabe
people
'Then he said to the women: "People, go!"'

159   *ausiausi thfyakm ŋanz ffrümenzoma …*
ausi-ausi   thf\yak/m   ŋanz
REDUP-old.woman 2|3PL:SBJ:PST:DUR/walk garden.row
f-frü=me=nzo=ma   (.)
REDUP-single=INS=ONLY=CHAR (.)
'The women went and took from each patch …'

160   *wawa ane … ebar fr wawa ebar fr kafar*
wawa ane (.) ebar fr   wawa ebar fr   kafar
yam   DEM (.) head stem yam   head stem big
'those yams … the best yams and big yams.'

161   *watik nä ŋanzma wawa näbi nä ŋanzma nä ŋanzma nä ŋanzma nimanzo watik*
watik nä   ŋanz=ma   wawa näbi nä   ŋanz=ma   nä   ŋanz=ma   nä
then INDF garden.row yam   one INDF garden.row INDF garden.row INDF
ŋanz=ma   nima=nzo   watik
garden.row like.this=ONLY then
'one yam from one patch, from another patch, from another patch, from another
patch … just like this.'

162 *mnime thufränzrmth ... watik thufthakwrmth foba ... karome thurzathrmth.*
mni=me thu\frä/nzrmth   (.) watik
fire=INS 2|3PL:SBJ>2|3PL:OBJ:PST:DUR/singe (.) then
thu\fthak/wrmth   foba   (.) karo=me
2|3PL:SBJ>2|3PL:OBJ:PST:DUR/take.out.of.fire DIST.ABL (.) oven=INS
thu\rza/thrmth
2|3PL:SBJ>2|3PL:OBJ:PST:DUR/cook.in.oven
'They were burning the hair off the yams. Then they took them out of the fire and cooked them in the ground oven.'

163 *zizi ane fof thfzänzrmth bobo ... far mä suräzrmth.*
zizi   ane fof thf\zä/nzrmth   bobo   (.) far   mä
afternoon DEM EMPH 2|3PL:SBJ>2|3PL:OBJ:PST:DUR/carry MED.ALL (.) post where
su\räz/rmth
2|3PL:SBJ>3SG.MASC:OBJ:PST:DUR/erect
'In the afternoon, they carried these yams where they had planted a post.'

164 *mathkwi o karawa o kukuma o ote ...*
mathkwi o karawa o kukuma o ote (.)
mathkwi or karawa or kukuma or ote (.)
'Mathkwi or Karawa or Kukuma or Ote ...'

165 *watik ane far fof sfrästhgrm wawa fobo fof thunakwrm.*
watik ane far fof sf\räs/thgrm   wawa fobo   fof
then DEM post EMPH 3SG.MASC:SBJ:PST:DUR/be.erected yam DIST.ALL EMPH
thu\nak/wrm
SG:SBJ>2|3PL:OBJ:PST:DUR/put.down
'Well, that post was standing there and he put the yams down on its base.'

166 *fobo ffé n wawa kwanäbünzrmth ... kwosi kwakonzrmth bänemr e ... tayo tfotfo.*
fobo   ffé   n   wawa kwa\näbü/nzrmth   (.) kwosi
DIST.ALL really IMN yam 2|3PL:SBJ:PST:DUR/decompose (.) rotten
kwa\ko/nzrmth   bänemr   e   (.) tayo tfotfo
2|3PL:SBJ:PST:DUR/become RECOG.PURP until (.) ripe almost
'When those yams were about to fall apart, about to become rotten, the yams (in the ground) were almost ready.'

167 *tayo wawa fthé kwakonzrmth ...*
tayo wawa fthé kwa\ko/nzrmth   (.)
ripe yam when 2|3PL:SBJ:PST:DUR/become (.)
'When the yams were getting ready ...'

168 *rfnaksir bobo zarfa thfrärm ... mäta garaita*
rfnak-si=r   bobo   zarfa thf\rä/rm   (.) mäta garaita
taste-NMLZ=PURP MED.ALL ear 2|3PL:SBJ:PST:DUR/be (.) mäta garaita
'they heard from Mata and Garaita that they started to taste them.'

169 *nafa fthé kwänrfnth ... "ayo!" wrwr fof zefaro ... swänrifthth*

nafa   fthé   kwän\rfn/th   (.) ayo   wrwr   fof

3NSG.ERG when 2|3PL:SBJ:ITER/taste (.) watch.out eastwind EMPH

ze\far/o   (.) swän\rifth/th

SG:SBJ:PST:PFV:AND/set.off (.) 2|3PL:SBJ>3SG.MASC.OBJ:ITER/send

'When tasting the yams, they always shouted "Watch out!!" and the eastwind blew the message here.'

170 *watik we masu karé kwekaristh "oh, nafa z zärfnth."*

watik we   masu kar=é   kwe\karis/th   oh nafa   z

then   also masu place=ERG.NSG 2|3PL:SBJ:ITER/hear oh 3NSG.ERG ALR

zä\rfn/th

2|3PL:SBJ:RPST:PFV/taste

'The Masu people used to hear this and said "Oh, they have started tasting the yams already."'

171 *we kwot we näbikakme we nä wawa thfrärmth katan o kafar ... thuwoknzrmth ... watik kwarzathrmth.*

we   kwot   we   näbi-kak=me   we   nä   wawa thf\rä/rmth

also properly also one-DISTR=INS also INDF yam   2|3PL:SBJ>2|3PL:OBJ:PST:DUR/do

katan o   kafar (.) thu\wok/nzrmth   (.) watik

small or   big   (.) 2|3PL:SBJ>2|3PL:OBJ:PST:DUR/choose (.) then

kwa\rza/thrmth

2|3PL:SBJ>2|3PL:OBJ:PST:DUR/cook.in.oven

'Now they also took some yams, one by one, big or small. They choose some and cooked them in the oven.'

172 *tawar ane thfrärmth ŋazi thurwrmth ... kwot thufathwrmth kobakob*

tawar   ane thf\rä/rmth   ŋazi

yam.pulp DEM 2|3PL:SBJ>2|3PL:OBJ:PST:DUR/do coconut

thu\rw/rmth   (.) kwot   thu\fath/wrmth

2|3PL:SBJ>2|3PL:OBJ:PST:DUR/scrape (.) properly 2|3PL:SBJ>2|3PL:OBJ:PST:DUR/hold

kobakob

round.object

'They took out the yam pulp and mixed it with scraped coconut and then they formed little round balls out of the dough.'

173 *kwarfnakwrmth watik nima kwanrzrmth.*

kwa\rfnak/wrmth   watik nima   kwan\rz/rmth

SG:SBJ:PST:DUR/taste   then   like.this SG:SBJ:PST:DUR:VENT/throw

'Then they tasted the yams and they threw their arms up this way.'

174 *fatr nima thwafiyokwrmth "ayo! farem benm fräro!" ... nima fof*

fatr   nima   thwa\fiyok/wrmth   ayo   farem benm

upper.arm like.this 2|3PL:SBJ>2|3PL:OBJ:PST:DUR/make watch.out farem 2NSG.DAT

f=\rä/ro   (.) nima   fof
DIST=3SG.FEM:SBJ:NPST:IPFV:AND/be (.) like.this EMPH
'They threw the arms up like this and shouted "Watch out! Farem people, this is for you!" like this.'

175 *watik ane fthé kwärit ane tmatm*
     watik ane fthé kwä\rit/   ane tmatm
     then DEM when 2|3SG:SBJ:ITER/pass.by DEM event
     'Each time when that ritual had passed'

176 *rfnaksi tmatm thumarwrmth e ... rrr kwan fthé bäne kwäkorth ... tayo kwot thuwäkwrm*
     rfnak-si   tmatm thu\mar/wrmth   e (.) rrr kwan   fthé
     taste-NMLZ event 2|3PL:SBJ>2|3PL:OBJ:PST:DUR/see until (.) rustling.sound when
     bäne   kwä\kor/th   (.) tayo kwot   thu\wäk/wrm
     RECOG.ABS 2|3PL:SBJ:ITER/become (.) ripe properly 2|3PL:SBJ:PST:DUR/ripen
     'when they saw the tasting rituals, when the yam leaves were rustling, when the yams were ready ...'

177 *watik fthé fof yaka swefafth.*
     watik fthé fof   yaka   swe\faf/th
     then when EMPH digging.stick 2|3PL:SBJ>3SG.MASC:OBJ:ITER/hold
     'that was when they picked up the digging stick and began to harvest.'

178 *anenzo fof ... ane tmatm kwaritakwrm e zbo bäidbo ... bäi kafar zäkora*
     ane=nzo   fof   (.) ane tmatm kwa\ritak/wrm   e   zbo
     DEM=ONLY EMPH (.) DEM event SG:SBJ:PST:DUR/cross.over until PROX.ALL
     bäi=dbo   (.) bäi kafar zä\kor/a
     bäi=ALL.SG (.) bäi big SG:SBJ:PST:PFV/become
     'That was it. That ritual was passed on to Bäi. Bäi had become a big man.'

179 *nafaŋafyf ... nafane ŋafyf ane fof sara fof ... foba fof otef.*
     nafa-ŋafe=f   (.) nafane ŋafe=f   ane fof
     3.POSS-father=ERG.SG (.) 3SG.POSS father=ERG.SG DEM EMPH
     sa\r/a   fof (.) foba   fof   ote=f
     SG:SBJ>3SG.MASC:IO:PST:PFV/give EMPH (.) DIST.ABL EMPH ote=ERG.SG
     'His father and his father passed on this tradition ... all the way from Ote.'

180 *watik naf we ane fof thwamonegwrm no bäne ... no nzigfu a fofosa frä ... dagon fofosa fof.*
     watik naf   we ane fof   thwa\moneg/wrm   no bäne
     then 3SG.ERG also DEM EMPH SG:SBJ>2|3PL:OBJ:PST:DUR/look.after rain RECOG.ABS
     (.) no nzigfu   a   fofosa f=\rä/   (.) dagon fofosa
     (.) rain rain.stone and heart DIST=3SG.FEM:SBJ:NPST:IPFV/be (.) food   heart
     fof
     EMPH
     'He also looked after that rain magic stone and the other stone there ... the magic food stone.'

181   *foba e ni kafar ŋankonzake.*
     foba   e   ni   kafar ŋan\ko/nzake
     DIST.ABL until 1NSG big   1PL:SBJ:NPST:IPFV:VENT/become
     'Later we grew up.'

182   *nzesinenwä ane fof komnzo thfrnm ane eda … eda rokar fof.*
     nze-si=en=wä   ane fof   komnzo thf\rn/m   ane eda (.)
     1NSG.POSS-eye=LOC=EMPH DEM EMPH still   2|3DU:SBJ:PST:DUR/be DEM two (.)
     eda rokar fof
     two things EMPH
     'We still saw those two with our own eyes … those two stones.'

183   *e nama masun ane yam tmatm z zwabrgwre fof.*
     e   nama   masu=n   ane yam   tmatm z
     until recently masu=LOC DEM custom event   ALR
     zwa\brg/wre   fof
     1PL:SBJ>3SG.FEM:OBJ:RPST:IPFV/follow EMPH
     'We have followed this tradition until recently in Masu.'

184   *e watik foba zänbrimake zena mänwä zä namnzr zf … znrä.*
     e   watik foba   zän\brim/ake   zena mä=wä   zä
     until then DIST.ABL 1PL:SBJ:RPST:PFV/return today where=EMPH PROX
     na\m/nzr   zf (.) z=n\rä/
     1PL:SBJ:NPST:IPFV/dwell IMM (.) PROX=1PL:SBJ:NPST:IPFV/be
     'Then we returned from there to where we are living now … right here.'

185   *watik fi fthmäsü kwik … kwosi yara … greg täwdben ane thfrärm.*
     watik fi   fthmäsü   kwik (.) kwosi ya\r/a   (.) greg
     then 3.ABS meanwhile sick (.) dead 3SG.MASC:SBJ:PST:IPFV/be (.) greg
     täw=dben   ane thf\rä/rm
     father=LOC.SG DEM 2|3PL:SBJ:PST:DUR/be
     'In the meanwhile father had become sick and died. Those stones were with Greg's father.'

186   *ane bäne … nzigfu thfrnm edawä.*
     ane bäne   (.) nzigfu   thf\rn/m   eda=wä
     DEM RECOG.ABS (.) magic.stone 2|3DU:SBJ:PST:DUR/be two=EMPH
     'Those were magic stones … those two.'

187   *watik nzenme ŋafe fthmäsü kwosi yara.*
     watik nzenme   ŋafe fthmäsü   kwosi ya\r/a
     then 1NSG.POSS father meanwhile dead 3SG.MASC:SBJ:PST:IPFV/be
     'Well, our father died in the meantime …'

188   *watik foba ni miyamr nrä mafadben zena ethn.*
     watik foba   ni   miyamr n\rä/   mafa=dben zena
     then DIST.ABL 1NSG ignorant 1PL:SBJ:NPST:IPFV/be who=LOC.SG today

e\thn/
2|3PL:SBJ:NPST:IPFV/be.lying
'and since then we do not know with whom these (magic stones) are now.'

189 *z thrifthmath fof*
 z th\rifthm/ath   fof
 ALR 2|3PL:SBJ>2|3DU:OBJ:PST:PFV/hide fof
 'They might have hidden them.'

190 *watik ane bäne mane rera … ane trikasi mane nŋatrikwé fof … ŋafynm badafa ane*
 fof ŋanritakwa fof
 watik ane bäne mane \rä/ra   (.) ane trik-si mane
 then DEM RECOG.ABS which 3SG.FEM:SBJ:PST:IPFV/be (.) DEM tell-NMLZ which
 n=ŋa\trik/wé   fof (.) ŋafe-nm   bada=fa   ane fof
 IPST=1SG:SBJ:NPST:IPFV/tell EMPH (.) father=DAT.NSG ancestor=ABL DEM EMPH
 ŋan\ritak/wa   fof
 SG:SBJ:PST:IPFV/pass EMPH
 'The story, which I have just told, was passed on from the ancestor to the fathers.'

191 *bada aki kwark benrera fof … zath kwark enrera e ŋafydbo we nzedbo fof n zänrita*
 nima
 bada aki   kwark b=en\rä/ra   fof (.)
 ancestor grandfather deceased MED=2|3PL:SBJ:PST:IPFV:VENT/be EMPH (.)
 zath   kwark en\rä/ra   e ŋafe=dbo we
 grandfather deceased 2|3PL:SBJ:PST:IPFV:VENT/be until father=ALL.SG also
 nzedbo fof n zän\rit/a   nima
 1NSG.ALL EMPH ALR SG:SBJ:PST:PFV/pass like.this
 'From the ancestors to the late grandfathers until it came to the fathers. It was
 about to pass to us…'

192 *watik maf keke wäbragwr ane*
 watik maf   keke wä\brag/wr   ane
 then who.ERG.SG NEG 2|3SG:SBJ>3SG.FEM:OBJ:NPST:IPFV/follow DEM
 'but nobody follows (these traditions) anymore.'   [tci20131013-01]

Sample text: Fenz yonasi

Fenz yonasi

This text was recorded from Nakre Abia. The topic of *bthan kabe*, sorcerers or magicians, can be overheard routinely in daily discourse. Much of the talk about sorcercy is speculative and of a very general nature. In contrast, the details and specific actions of sorcerers, let alone accusations, are rarely expressed publically. The only place for open accusations are court cases where there are several mediators and a strict code of conduct which regulates speaking time and turn-taking. It took me long time to find someone who would explain the different beliefs surrounding the actions of sorcerers. This short text was offered to me by Nakre Abia. Her narrative was prompted by a minimal pair, one of which was the word *fenz* 'body liquid'. *Fenz* may refer to puss or to the liquids inside a rotting corpse. Nakre explains that sorcerers visit the gravesites of recently deceased people and extract body parts including the liquid. They take their strength from *fenz yonasi*, the 'drinking of the body liquid'. The following day, I asked her to tell me about this in more detail.

This text can be accessed under: https://zenodo.org/record/1305970

1   *bänema kwa ŋatrikwé ... nzefé.*
      bäne=ma   kwa ŋa\trik/wé   (.) nzefé
      RECOG=CHAR FUT 1SG:SBJ:NPST:IPFV/tell (.) 1SG.ERG.EMPH
      'I will talk about this.'

2   *fenz ane mane ŋonathrth ... kwosifr kabeaneme ... bthan kabeyé.*
      fenz   ane mane ŋo\na/thrth   (.) kwosifr kabe=aneme   (.)
      body.liquid DEM which 2|3PL:SBJ:NPST:IPFV/drink (.) corpse man=POSS.NSG (.)
      bthan kabe=yé
      magic man=ERG.NSG
      'The body fluid that they drink ... the dead people's fluid ... those sorcerers.'

3   *trikasi zrethkäfé*
      trik-si   zre\thkäf/é
      tell-NMLZ 2|3PL:SBJ:IRR:PFV/drink
      'I start the story.'

4   *bthan kabe fthé fenz yonasi ... bänemr zrethkäfth mätraksir.*
      bthan kabe fthé   fenz   yona-si   (.) bänemr   zre\thkäf/th
      magic man when body.liquid drink-NMLZ (.) RECOG.PURP 2|3PL:SBJ:IRR:PFV/start
      mätrak-si=r
      take.out-NMLZ=PURP
      'When the sorcerers drink the body fluids, they start by bringing out this one,'

5   *kzi kwa yafiyokwrth.*
      kzi   kwa ya\fiyok/wrth
      bark.tray FUT 2|3PL:SBJ>3SG.MASC:OBJ:NPST:IPFV/make
      'they make a barktray.'

6   *srafiyokwrth karesama kzi. srärzirth.*
      srafiyokwrth   karesa=ma   kzi
      2|3PL:SBJ>3SG.MASC:OBJ:IRR:IPFV/make paperbark=CHAR barktray
      srä\rzir/th
      2|3PL:SBJ>3SG.MASC:OBJ:IRR:PFV/tie
      'They make a bark tray from the paperbark tree. They tie it'

7   *watik kwa eyak. nima kwosifr fthé ... kabe fthé ynänzüthzrth baden ...*
      watik kwa e\yak/   nima   kwosifr fthé (.) kabe fthé
      then   FUT 2|3PL:SBJ:NPST:IPFV/walk like.this corpse when (.) man when
      y\nänzüth/zrth   bad=en
      2|3PL:SBJ:NPST:IPFV/bury ground=LOC
      'and then they go. When people have buried a corpse in the ground,'

8   *fthé one week srakor ...*
      fthé   one week sra\kor/
      when one week 3SG.MASC:SBJ:IRR:PFV/become
      'after one week has passed,'

9   *fthé fof krefar ane bthan kabe bobo ... fokam znfo, fokam mnzfo ... sikwankwanme zbär thd.*

fthé   fof   kre\far/   ane bthan kabe bobo   (.) fokam
when EMPH 2|3SG:SBJ:IRR:PFV/set.off DEM magic man MED.ALL (.) grave

zn=fo   fokam mnz=fo   (.) sikwankwan=me zbär   thd
place=LOC grave house=LOC (.) secret=INS   night middle

'the sorcerer sets off to go to the grave yard, to the grave house. He goes secretly in the middle of the night.'

10   *kabef keke kwa sremar.*

kabe=f   keke kwa sre\mar/
man=ERG.SG NEG FUT 2|3SG:SBJ>3SG.MASC:OBJ:IRR:PFV/see

'No one will see him.'

11   *süsübäthen kwa yak ... tosinmäre ... kwayanmäre.*

süsübäth=en   kwa \yak/   (.) tosin=märe   (.)
darkness=LOC FUT 3SG.MASC:SBJ:NPST:IPFV/walk (.) flashlight=PRIV (.)

kwayan=märe
light=PRIV

'He will walk in the darkness without a flashlight ... without light.'

12   *kwa yak. yfrsé gwonyamekarä kwa yé.*

kwa \yak/   yfrsé gwonyame=karä kwa
FUT 3SG.MASC:SBJ:NPST:IPFV/walk black clothes=PROP   FUT

\yé/
3SG.MASC:SBJ:NPST:IPFV/be

'He will go and he will wear black clothes.'

13   *keke kwa kwayanthé gwonyamekarä bänema kabef sremar ... kabeyé sremarth*

keke kwa kwayan-thé gwonyame=karä bäne=ma   kabe=f
NEG FUT light-ADJZR clothes=PROP   RECOG=CHAR man=ERG.SG

sre\mar/   (.) kabe=yé
2|3SG:SBJ>3SG.MASC:OBJ:IRR:PFV/see (.) man=ERG.NSG

sre\mar/th
2|3PL:SBJ>3SG.MASC:OBJ:IRR:PFV/see

'No bright clothes because someone might see him ... people might see him.'

14   *watik yfö katanr kwa yarenzr.*

watik yfö   katan=r   kwa ya\re/nzr
then hole small=PURP FUT 3SG.MASC:SBJ:NPST:IPFV/look.around

'Okay, he will look around for a small hole.'

15   *katan yfö fthé zremar ... ebarfa fä fof kwa bäne ythorthr ... nabi a mrrab.*

katan yfö   fthé zre\mar/   (.) ebar=fa fä   fof   kwa
small hole when 2|3SG:SBJ>3SG.FEM:OBJ:IRR:PFV/see (.) head=ABL DIST EMPH FUT

bäne   y\thor/thr   (.) nabi   a
RECOG.ABS 2|3SG:SBJ>3SG.MASC:OBJ:NPST:IPFV/insert (.) bamboo and

mrrab
small.bamboo
'When he sees a small hole, he will insert this small bamboo at the head end of the grave.'

16 *mrrab zbo zanfr byé.*
mrrab   zbo   zanfr b=\yé/
small.bamboo PROX.ALL long MED=3SG.MASC:SBJ:NPST:IPFV/be
'A small bamboo about this long.'

17 *ane fof sräsryöfth bobo yfön.*
ane fof   srä\sryöfth/   bobo   yfö=n
DEM EMPH 2|3SG:SBJ>3SG.MASC:OBJ:IRR:PFV/send MED.ALL hole=LOC
'He will push this one into the hole.'

18 *watik fobo fof srayak.*
watik fobo   fof   sra\yak/
then DIST.ALL EMPH 3SG.MASC:SBJ:IRR:IPFV/walk
'Okay, it will go like this.'

19 *kzi zräzin nabi tonze ... mrrab tonze.*
kzi   zrä\zin/   nabi   tonze (.)
barktray 2|3SG:SBJ>3SG.FEM:OBJ:IRR:PFV/put.down bamboo close (.)
mrrab   tonze
small.bamboo close
'He will put the barktray close to the bamboo ... close to the small bamboo.'

20 *fenzane bäne ... mrrab bäne kwa ... wämneme yrthakunzr.*
fenz=ane   bäne   (.) mrrab   bäne   kwa (.) wämne=me
body.liquid RECOG.ABS (.) small.bamboo RECOG.ABS FUT (.) stick=INS
y\rthaku/nzr
2|3SG:SBJ>3SG.MASC:OBJ:NPST:IPFV/spray
'He sprays the body liquid with that small bamboo ... with that stick.'

21 *watik fenz ane kwa ŋankarkwr naf*
watik fenz   ane kwa ŋan\kark/wr   naf
then body.liquid DEM FUT 2|3SG:SBJ:NPST:IPFV:VENT/pull 3SG.ERG
'He sucks up the body fluid'

22 *fobo fof krayagunzr kzifo.*
fobo   fof   kra\yagu/nzr   kzi=fo
DIST.ALL EMPH 2|3SG:SBJ:IRR:IPFV/pour barktray=ALL
'and he pours it into the barktray.'

23 *nafawatikthmenzo ... ke ka krärtf ... ane kzi*
nafa-watik-th=me=nzo   (.) keke kwa krä\rtf/   (.) ane
3.POSS-enough-ADJZR=INS=ONLY (.) NEG FUT 2|3SG:OBJ:IRR:IPFV/fill.up (.) DEM

kzi
barktray
'There is enough for him. That barktray won't be filled right up.'

24 *fthé zremar nima "watikthmenzo zfrä" mrrab ane sräfum.*
fthé   zre\mar/   nima watik-th=me=nzo
when 2|3SG:SBJ>3SG.FEM:OBJ:IRR:PFV/see QUOT enough-ADJZR=INS=ONLY
zf\rä/   mrrab   ane
3SG.FEM:SBJ:RPST:IPFV/be small.bamboo DEM
srä\fum/
2|3SG:SBJ>3SG.MASC:OBJ:IRR:IPFV/pull.out
'When he looks at it and thinks "That's enough" he pulls out the small bamboo.'

25 *watik kwot zrarmänwr ... yfö. watik krefar fof.*
watik kwot   zra\rmän/wr   (.) yfö watik
then   properly 2|3SG:SBJ>3SG.FEM:OBJ:IRR:IPFV/close (.) hole then
kre\far/   fof
2|3SG:SBJ:IRR:PFV/set.off EMPH
'Then he closes up the hole and leaves the place.'

26 *bäne zrazänzr ... fenz ... kzikaf ... mä ke kwa kabef sremar ane yam fiyoksin*
bäne   zra\zä/nzr   (.) fenz   (.) kzi=kaf
RECOG.ABS 2|3SG:SBJ>3SG.FEM:OBJ:IRR:IPFV/carry (.) body.liquid (.) barktray=PROP
(.) mä   keke kwa kabe=f   sre\mar/   ane yam
(.) where NEG FUT man=ERG.SG 2|3SG:SBJ>3SG.MASC:OBJ:IRR:PFV/see DEM event
fiyok-si=n
do-NMLZ=LOC
'He carries those body fluids with the barktray (to some place) where no one can
see him in doing that thing.'

27 *kwa wrifthzr.*
kwa w\rifth/zr
FUT 2|3SG:SBJ>3SG.FEM:OBJ:NPST:IPFV/hide
'He will hide it.'

28 *watik fi zöbthé zane bäne kramanziknwr ... zzarfa, wämne, bäne ferä ... ymd thäbu
nzabu.*
watik fi zöbthé zane   bäne   kra\manzikn/wr   (.) zzarfa
then   but first DEM:PROX RECOG.ABS 2|3SG:SBJ:IRR:IPFV/prepare (.) ginger
wämne bäne   f=e\rä/   (.) ymd thäbu nzabu
stick RECOG.ABS DIST=2|3PL:SBJ:NPST:IPFV/be (.) bird hair wing
'But first he will prepare some things: ginger, some sticks, and those bird feathers
or wings.'

29   *watik ane thrma ane fof krefar fokamfo.*
watik ane thrma ane fof   kre\far/   fokam=fo
then DEM after DEM EMPH 2|3SG:SBJ:IRR:PFV/set.off grave=ALL
'Okay, after this, he sets off from the grave.'

30   *ane fthé zrarinakwr … kzin. zräbth.*
ane fthé zra\rinak/wr   (.) kzi=n
DEM when 2|3SG:SBJ>3SG.FEM:OBJ:IRR:IPFV/pour (.) barktray=LOC
zrä\bth/
2|3SG:SBJ:IRR:PFV/finish
'He finishes pouring it in the barktray.'

31   *watik yonasir fof zrärifthm.*
watik yona-si=r   fof   zrä\rifthm/
then drink-NMLZ=PURP EMPH 2|3SG:SG:IRR:PFV/hide
'He really hides now for drinking it.'

32   *zöbthé bäneme kwa wrthakunzr … zzarfame bänema gatha miyosé rä.*
zöbthé bäne=me   kwa w\rthaku/nzr   (.) zzarfa=me
first RECOG.=INS FUT 2|3SG:SBJ>3SG.FEM:OBJ:NPST:IPFV/spray (.) ginger=INS
bäne=ma   gatha miyosé \rä/
RECOG=CHAR bad taste 3SG.FEM:SBJ:NPST:IPFV/be
'First, he will sprinkle it with ginger, because it has a bad taste.'

33   *nafane miyo keke namä wärä.*
nafane   miyo keke namä wä\rä/
3SG.POSS taste NEG good 3SG.MASC:IO:NPST:IPFV/be
'Its taste is not good.'

34   *zrarthakunzr zräbth.*
zra\rthaku/nzr   zrä\bth/
2|3SG:SBJ>3SG.FEM:OBJ:IRR:IPFV/spray 2|3SG:SBJ:IRR:PFV/finish
'He finished sprinkling the ginger.'

35   *wati bäne ane kwa yfethakwr … ymd nzabu.*
wati bäne   ane kwa y\fethak/wr   (.) ymd nzabu
then RECOG.ABS DEM FUT 2|3SG:SBJ>3SG.MASC:OBJ:NPST:IPFV/dip.in (.) bird wing
'Then he dips in the bird wing.'

36   *srafethakwr … keke kwa zane touch srarär ane fenzme.*
sra\fethak/wr   (.) keke kwa zane   touch
2|3SG:SBJ>3SG.MASC:OBJ:IRR:IPFV/dip.in (.) NEG FUT DEM:PROX touch
sra\rär/   ane fenz=me
2|3SG:SBJ>3SG.MASC:IO:IRR:IPFV/do DEM body.liquid
'He dip sits in. but he should not touch this here (lips) with the body fluid.'

37 *kwan krakurwr.*
kwan kra\kur/wr
throat 2|3SG:SBJ:IRR:IPFV/split
'It hurts the mouth.'

38 *zrarär kwanen … bänema … thafma … gatha miyoma.*
zra\rär/   kwan=en (.) bäne=ma   (.) thaf=ma   (.) gatha
2|3SG:SBJ:IRR:IPFV/do throat=LOC (.) RECOG=CHAR (.) bitter=CHAR (.) bad
miyo=ma
taste=CHAR
'It will hurt because of it is bitterness … because of its bad taste.'

39 *zrarär … zrafethakwr we … zbo sranakwr … krafigthkwr.*
zra\rär/   (.) zra\fethak/wr   we (.) zbo
2|3SG:SBJ:IRR:IPFV/do (.) 2|3SG:SBJ>3SG.FEM:OBJ:IRR:IPFV/dip.in also (.) PROX.ALL
sra\nak/wr   (.) kra\figthk/wr
2|3SG:SBJ>3SG.MASC:IO:IRR:IPFV/put.down (.) 2|3SG:SBJ:IRR:IPFV/lick
'He dips it in and places the feather here in the mouth and licks it.'

40 *we nimanzo kwot e zräbth ane fenz.*
we nima=nzo   kwot   e   zrä\bth/   ane fenz
also like.this=ONLY properly until 2|3SG:SBJ:IRR:PFV/finish DEM body.liquid
'This way, he will finish all those body fluids.'

41 *fthé zräbth kzi ane kwa yfönzr mnime fewama.*
fthé zrä\bth/   kzi   ane kwa
when 2|3SG:SBJ:IRR:PFV/finish barktray DEM FUT
y\fö/nzr   mni=me fewa=ma
2|3SG:SBJ>3SG.MASC:OBJ:NPST:IPFV/burn fire=INS smell=CHAR
'When he is finished, he will burn the barktray in the fire because of its stench.'

42 *mnime sräföf watik.*
mni=me srä\föf/   watik
fire=INS 2|3SG:SBJ>3SG.MASC:OBJ:IRR:PFV/burn enough
'He burns it in the fire and then its over.'

43 *kräbrim nafane mnzfo.*
krä\brim/   nafane   mnz=fo
2|3SG:SBJ:IRR:PFV/return 3SG.POSS house=LOC
'He returns to his house.'

44 *kwa yrugr e … baf fthé sräbth nima kabe zan miyof.*
kwa y\rugr/   e   (.) baf   fthé
FUT 3SG.MASC:SBJ:NPST:IPFV/sleep until (.) RECOG.ERG.SG when
srä\bth/   nima   kabe zan   miyo=f
2|3SG:SBJ>3SG.MASC:OBJ:IRR:PFV/finish like.this man killing desire=ERG
'He sleeps until when that bloodlust comes over him.'

45 *okay fthé fof krefar.*
okay fthé fof kre\far/
okay when EMPH 2|3SG:SBJ:IRR:PFV/set.off
'Okay, that is when he sets off.'

46 *keke kwa mnzen ane tmatm zrafiyokwr ane yam.*
keke kwa mnz=en ane tmatm zra\fiyok/wr ane yam
NEG FUT house=LOC DEM event 2|3SG:SBJ:IRR:IPFV/make DEM event
'He will not do these things in the house.'

47 *zagr kwa yak ksi karen. bä sramnzr.*
zagr kwa \yak/ ksi kar=en bä
far FUT 3SG.MASC:SBJ:NPST:IPFV/walk bush place=LOC MED
sra\m/nzr
3SG.MASC:SBJ:IRR:IPFV/dwell
'He will go far away to the bush. He will stay there.'

48 *foba fof krefar kabe zanr.*
foba fof kre\far/ kabe zan=r
DIST.ABL EMPH 2|3SG:SBJ:IRR:PFV/set.off man killing=PURP
'It is really from there, that he goes and kills people.'

49 *si kwa zöbthé ŋazübrakwr warfo kabedbo.*
si kwa zöbthé ŋa\zübrak/wr warfo kabe=dbo
eye FUT first 2|3SG:SBJ:NPST:IPFV/pray above man=ALL.ANIM.SG
'First, he will pray to god.'

49 *warfo kabe kwa ykonzr "befe mitafo sabrim! nzun fefe kwagathif!"*
warfo kabe kwa y\ko/nzr befe mitafo
above man FUT 2|3SG:SBJ>3SG.MASC:OBJ:NPST:IPFV/speak 2SG.ERG.EMPH spirit
sa\brim/ nzun fefe
2|3SG:SBJ>3SG.MASC:IO:IMP:PFV/return 1SG.DAT body
kwa\gathif/
2|3SG:SBJ>1SG:IO:IMP:PFV/leave
'He says to god: "You take the spirit! Leave the body for me!"'

50 *watik ane kabe kwa yfänzr.*
watik ane kabe kwa y\fä/nzr
then DEM man FUT 2|3SG:SBJ>3SG.MASC:OBJ:NPST:IPFV/show
'Then he points to this man.'

51 *kabe yf kwa ybräknwr nima "bäi! bäiane mitafo be sabrim! nzun fefe kwagathif!"*
kabe yf kwa y\bräkn/wr nima bäi bäi=ane
man name FUT 2|3SG:SBJ>3SG.MASC:OBJ:NPST:IPFV/call.out QUOT bäi bäi=POSS.SG
mitafo be sa\brim/ nzun fefe
spirit 2SG.ERG 2|3SG:SBJ>3SG.MASC:IO:IMP:PFV/return 1SG.DAT body

kwa\gathif/
2|3SG:SBJ>1SG:IO:IMP:PFV/leave
'He calls out that man's name: "Bäi! You take Bäi's spirit. Leave the body for me!"'

52 *fthé krefar kabef keke kwa sremar bänema …*
  fthé kre\far/   kabe=f keke kwa
  when 2|3SG:SBJ:IRR:PFV/set.off man=ERG.SG NEG FUT
  sre\mar/   bäne=ma (.)
  2|3SG:SBJ>3SG.MASC:OBJ:IRR:PFV/see RECOG=CHAR (.)
  'When he sets off, no man should see him, because'

53 *mnzen fthé srarugr nagayé disturb o ŋare disturb srarär.*
  mnz=en fthé sra\rugr/   nagayé disturb o ŋare disturb
  house=LOC when 3SG.MASC:SBJ:IRR:IPFV/sleep children disturb or woman disturb
  sra\rär/
  2|3SG:SBJ:NPST:IPFV/do
  'if he sleeps in the house, the children or his wife might disturb him.'

54 *watik anema fof krämätr outside nä karfo ksi karen. fä sramnzr.*
  watik ane=ma fof krä\mätr/   outside nä kar=fo ksi
  then DEM=CHAR EMPH 2|3SG:SBJ:IRR:PFV/bring.out outside INDF place=ALL bush
  kar=en fä sra\m/nzr
  place=ALL DIST 3SG.MASC:SBJ:IRR:IPFV/dwell
  'Therefore, he goes out to another place in the bush. He stays there.'

55 *fä ane tmatm kwa kabe yafiyokwr. bthazan yfnzr.*
  fä ane tmatm kwa kabe ya\fiyok/wr   bthazan
  DIST DEM event FUT man 2|3SG:SBJ>3SG.MASC:OBJ:NPST:IPFV/make black.magic
  y\fn/nzr
  2|3SG:SBJ>3SG.MASC:OBJ:NPST:IPFV/hit
  'He makes these things with the man there. He puts black magic on him.'

56 *foba fof krethfär … mobo fthzé … nima … zba fthé roukuma nge srarä.*
  foba fof kre\thfär/   (.) mobo fthzé (.) nima (.) zba
  DIST.ABL EMPH 2|3SG:SBJ:IRR:IPFV/fly (.) where.ALL ever (.) like.this (.) PROX.ABL
  fthé rouku=ma nge sra\rä/
  when rouku=CHAR child 3SG.MASC:SBJ:IRR:IPFV/be
  'From there, he flies away to where ever he wants. It might be a boy from here from Rouku.'

57 *zbär kwa yam zä wäfiyokwr zba krethfär safsfo.*
  zbär kwa yam zä wä\fiyok/wr   zba
  night FUT custom PROX 2|3SG:SBJ>3SG.FEM:OBJ:NPST:IPFV/make PROX.ABL
  kre\thfär/   safs=fo
  2|3SG:SBJ:IRR:IPFV/fly safs=ALL
  'He will do that in the night. He will fly from here to Safs.'

58 *bä ... bthazan srafnzr bthanme srafnzr.*
bä   (.) bthazan   sra\fn/nzr   bthan=me
MED (.) black.magic 2|3SG:SBJ>3SG.MASC:OBJ:IRR:IPFV/hit magic=INS
sra\fn/nzr
2|3SG:SBJ>3SG.MASC:OBJ:IRR:IPFV/hit
'There he puts black magic on someone. He puts a spell on him.'

59 *e ... kränbrim we ane we zbär.*
e   (.) krän\brim/   we ane we zbär
until (.) 2|3SG:SBJ:IRR:PFV:VENT/return also DEM also night
'And then he returns here again in the night.'

60 *keke kwa bä srarugr o srawäkwr.*
keke kwa bä   sra\rugr/   o sra\wäk/wr
NEG FUT MED 3SG.MASC:SBJ:IRR:IPFV/sleep or 3SG.MASC:SBJ:IRR:IPFV/wake
'He will not sleep there or wake up there.'

61 *zbär we kwa ŋanbrigwr keke kwa mothen fi srayak fi krathfänzr.*
zbär we kwa ŋan\brig/wr   keke kwa moth=en fi
night also FUT 2|3SG:SBJ:NPST:IPFV:VENT/return NEG FUT path=LOC 3.ABS
sra\yak/   fi   kra\thfä/nzr
3SG.MASC:SBJ:NPST:IPFV/walk 3.ABS 2|3SG:SBJ:NPST:IPFV/fly
'He will return in the night. He will not walk on the road, but he will fly.'

62 *nima ane wäfiyokwr.*
nima   ane wä\fiyok/wr
like.this DEM 2|3SG:SBJ>3SG.FEM:OBJ:NPST:IPFV/make
'That's what he does.'

63 *fthé sräbth ... kabe bthazan srethkäf watik fä mane kwik erä fof.*
fthé   srä\bth/   (.) kabe bthazan
when 2|3SG:SBJ>3SG.MASC:SBJ:IRR:PFV/finish (.) man black.magic
sre\thkäf/   watik fä mane   kwik e\rä/   fof
2|3SG:SBJ:IRR:PFV/start then DIST who.ABS sick 2|3PL:SBJ:NPST:IPFV/be EMPH
'When he is finished, the black magic will set in. It is then, when they will get really sick.'

64 *keke, taurifo tmatm zrafiyokwr o ŋathafo ... o faso rrokar berä.*
keke tauri=fo   tmatm zra\fiyok/wr   o ŋatha=fo (.) o faso
NEG wallaby=ALL event 2|3SG:SBJ:IRR:IPFV/make or dog=ALL (.) or meat
r-rokar   b=e\rä/
REDUP-stuff MED=2|3PL:SBJ:NPST:IPFV/be
'No, he does that thing to a wallaby or dog ... or to some other animal there.'

65 *ane rrokarfo kwa tmatm yafiyokwr keke kwa nima nä kabedben.*
ane r-rokar=fo   kwa tmatm ya\fiyok/wr   keke
DEM REDUP-stuff=ALL FUT event 2|3SG:SBJ>3SG.MASC:IO:NPST:IPFV/make NEG

kwa nima   nä   kabe=dben
FUT like.this INDF man=LOC.ANIM.SG
'He does that to those animals, not to a man.'

66 *fi ane kabeane mitafo kwa wthorthr.*
    fi   ane kabe=ane   mitafo kwa w\thor/thr
    but DEM man=POSS.SG spirit FUT 2|3SG:SBJ>3SG.FEM:OBJ:NPST:IPFV/enter
    'But it will go inside that man's spirit.'

67 *nä faso rokarfo o fthzé ŋatha zräthb ...*
    nä   faso rokar=fo   o fthzé ŋatha zrä\thb/   (.)
    INDF meat stuff=ALL or ever dog   2|3SG:SBJ:NPST:PFV/enter (.)
    'It goes into some animals or dogs ...'

68 *ra fthzé srarä ... ymd.*
    ra   fthzé sra\rä/   (.) ymd
    what ever 3SG.MASC:SBJ:IRR:IPFV/be (.) bird
    'whatever there may be ... a bird.'

69 *watik ane fof kwa tmatm yafiyokwr ŋatha yafiyokwr nafane yfkaf.*
    watik ane fof   kwa tmatm ya\fiyok/wr   ŋatha
    then DEM EMPH FUT event 2|3SG:SBJ>3SG.MASC:IO:NPST:IPFV/make dog
    ya\fiyok/wr   nafane   yf=kaf
    2|3SG:SBJ>3SG.MASC:IO:NPST:IPFV/make 3SG.POSS name=PROP
    'Well, he makes this thing. He does it do a dog with his (the man's) name.'

70 *nezä kabe kwa kwosi yé. keke ŋatha kwa kwosi srarä yakme.*
    nezä   kabe kwa kwosi \yé/   keke ŋatha kwa kwosi
    in.return man FUT dead 3SG.MASC:SBJ:NPST:IPFV/be NEG dog   FUT dead
    sra\rä/   yakme
    3SG.MASC:SBJ:IRR:IPFV/be quickly
    'As a consequence, the man will die. But the dog will not die quickly.'

71 *mon tariasi fthé kratariwr ŋatha ...*
    mon tari-si   fthé kra\tari/wr   ŋatha (.)
    how weaken-NMLZ when 2|3SG:SBJ:IRR:IPFV/weaken dog   (.)
    'As the dog gets weaker,'

72 *we kabe nimäwä kwa ŋatariwr ...*
    we kabe nima=wä   kwa ŋa\tari/wr   (.)
    also man like.this=EMPH FUT 2|3SG:SBJ:NPST:IPFV/weaken (.)
    'the man will also get weaker.'

73 *kwot e ŋatha fthé zä kwosi srarä kabe bä kwa kwosi yé.*
    kwot   e   ŋatha fthé zä   kwosi sra\rä/   kabe bä kwa
    properly until dog   when PROX dead 3SG.MASC:SBJ:IRR:IPFV/be man MED FUT
    kwosi \yé/
    dead 3SG.MASC:SBJ:NPST:IPFV/be
    'until some time passes. When the dog dies, the man will also die.'

74   *bänema ŋatha ane nafane yfkaf sfrä.*
bäne=ma   ŋatha ane nafane yf=kaf   sf\rä/
RECOG=CHAR dog   DEM 3SG.POSS name=PROP 3SG.MASC:SBJ:RPST:IPFV/be
'Because that dog was with his name.'

75   *nimame ane fof bthan erä ... äfiyokwrth.*
nima=me   ane fof bthan e\rä/   (.)
like.this=INS DEM EMPH magic 2|3PL:SBJ:NPST:IPFV/be (.)
ä\fiyok/wrth
2|3PL:SBJ>2|3PL:OBJ:NPST:IPFV/make
'This is how the magic works, how they do it.'

76   CD: *rma fi ŋonathrth ane fenz?*
rma fi   ŋo\na/thrth   ane fenz
why 3.ABS 2|3PL:SBJ:NPST:IPFV/drink DEM body.liquid
'Why do they drink the body fluids?'

77   *okay, ane fenz mane ŋonathrth tmä naf fof ärithr.*
okay ane fenz   mane ŋo\na/thrth   tmä   naf   fof
okay DEM body.liquid which 2|3PL:SBJ:NPST:IPFV/drink strength 3SG.ERG EMPH
ä\ri/thr
2|3SG:SBJ>2|3PL:IO:NPST:IPFV/give
'Okay, drinking the body fluids gives them strength.'

78   *kwosifr kabeane tmäf fof ezänzr nä karfo.*
kwosifr kabe=ane   tmä=f   fof   e\zä/nzr
corpse man=POSS.SG strength=ERG EMPH 2|3SG:SBJ>2|3PL:OBJ:NPST:IPFV/carry
nä   kar=fo
INDF place=ALL
'The deceased man's strength carries them to another place.'

78   *nä kayé kam kwa emätrakwrth ... kabe kam ... kwosifr kam.*
nä   kayé   kam kwa e\mätrak/wrth   (.) kabe kam (.)
INDF yesterday bone FUT 2|3PL:SBJ>2|3PL:OBJ:NPST:IPFV/take.out (.) man bone (.)
kwosifr kam
corpse bone
'Sometimes they extract a bone, a human bone, a bone from a corpse.'

79   *watik, ane fof thfäsir fof.*
watik ane fof   thfä-si=r   fof
then DEM EMPH fly-NMLZ=PURP EMPH
'That one is really for flying.'

80   *ane kamf kwa yzänzr bobo nä karfo.*
ane kam=f   kwa y\zä/nzr   bobo   nä
DEM bone=ERG FUT 2|3SG:SBJ>3SG.MASC:OBJ:NPST:IPFV/carry MED.ALL INDF

kar=fo
place=ALL
'That bone will carry them away to another place.'

81 *fi fenz ane bänemrnzo rä ... tmä yarisir.*
fi   fenz   ane bänemr=nzo   \rä/   (.) tmä
but body.liquid DEM RECOG.PURP=ONLY 3SG.FEM:SBJ:NPST:IPFV/be (.) strength
yari-si=r
give-NMLZ=PURP
'But the body liquid is just for giving them strength'

82 *kamf fi ane kwa yzänzr bobo nima safs ...*
kam=f   fi   ane kwa y\zä/nzr   bobo
bone=ERG 3.ABS DEM FUT 2|3SG:SBJ>3SG.MASC:OBJ:NPST:IPFV/carry MED.ALL
nima   safs (.)
like.this safs (.)
'The bone will carry there, for example to Safs'

83 *o wämnefr nima zagr kwa ŋathfänzr weam.*
o wämnefr nima   zagr kwa ŋa\thfä/nzr   weam
or wämnefr like.this far   FUT 2|3SG:SBJ:NPST:IPFV/fly weam
'or Wämnefr. He will fly far this way to Weam.'

84 *fthzé bobomrwä arufe krathfänzr ... zagr karfo.*
fthzé bobomr=wä arufe kra\thfä/nzr   (.) zagr kar=fo
ever until=EMPH arufe 2|3SG:SBJ:IRR:IPFV/fly (.) far   place=LOC
'Where ever he wants. He will fly all the way to Arufe, to places far away.'

85 *ane kam ane tmäf kwa yzänzr.*
ane kam ane tmäf   kwa y\zä/nzr
DEM bone DEM strength FUT 2|3SG:SBJ>3SG.MASC:OBJ:NPST:IPFV/carry
'That bone and that strength will carry him,'

86 *kam a fenz.*
kam a   fenz
bone and body.liquid
'the bone and the body fluids.'

87 *eso kafar. anenzo katan trikasi zfrä.*
eso   kafar ane=nzo   katan trik-si   zf\rä/
thank big   DEM=ONLY small tell-NMLZ 3SG.FEM:SBJ:RPST:IPFV/be
'Thank you very much! That was just my small story.'

88 *trikasi nimanzo worä kabeyé mane watrikwrth.*
trik-si   nima=nzo   wo\rä/   kabe=yé   mane
tell-NMLZ like.this=ONLY 1SG:SBJ:NPST:IPFV/be man=ERG.NSG which
wa\trik/wrth
2|3PL:SBJ>1SG:IO:NPST:IPFV/tell
'This is my version, which others were telling me.'

89   *fi srakéwä fthzé kwot kratrikwrth.*
     fi   srak=é=wä   fthzé   kwot   kra\trik/wrth
     but boy=ERG.NSG=EMPH whenever properly 2|3PL:SBJ:IRR:IPFV/tell
     'But the boys talk about this all the time.'

90   *gadmöwä!*
     gadmöwä
     thanks
     'Thank you!'   [tci20130903-04]

List of recordings

Overview

The following table lists the 65 texts which make up the Komnzo text corpus at the present time. The table provides general information about each text: the archive ID, digital object identifier (DOI), title, text genre, length (in min:sec), number of annotation units (records), and number of tokens (words). The archive ID refers to the date on which the recording was made. For example, tci20110810-02 refers to the second recording session on the 10th of August 2011. The corpus contains the following text genres: nrr = narrative, prd = procedural, cvr = conversation, stt = stimulus task, pub = public speech. Moreover, all speakers are listed with their name, age and their section/clan: M = Mayawa, S = Sagara, B = Bagu.

The reader of the digital version of this grammar can simply click on the DOI in the table to access the respective dataset, which contains the audio, video, and transcription files. For the reader of the print version, all material is available under: https://zenodo.org/communities/komnzo. Future changes, especially to the transcription files, will be marked at the Zenodo website with consecutive version numbers of the respective dataset, and each version will receive its own DOI number. A snapshot of all transcription files at the time of the publication of this grammar can be found as a zip-file under: https://zenodo.org/record/1306247.

At the present time, the Komnzo corpus consists of 65 texts with a total of 11hrs and 42min of transcribed material, and around 54,000 words. 34 speakers are featured: 9 female speakers and 25 male speakers covering an age range from 20 to 68.

List of recordings

Table .1: Overview of the text corpus

archive ID	corpus DOI	title	genre	speaker	age	sex	sec	length (mm:ss)	records	tokens
tci20100905	10.5281/zenodo.1218622	kukufia	nrr	Abia Bai	60	m	M	06:00	137	462
tci20110802	10.5281/zenodo.1219532	safak a faikore	nrr	Abia Bai	60	m	M	06:37	144	540
tci20110810-01	10.5281/zenodo.1209855	no kzi	prd	Marua Bai	68	m	M	03:24	76	218
tci20110810-02	10.5281/zenodo.1219876	ruga fiyaf	nrr	Marua Bai	68	m	M	03:24	80	286
tci20110813-09	10.5281/zenodo.1292770	zra frzsi	prd	Daure Kaumb	38	m	M	03:49	64	360
tci20110817-02	10.5281/zenodo.1216887	nge fathasi	prd	Abia Bai	60	m	M	04:44	122	424
tci20111004	10.5281/zenodo.1215730	picture task	stt, cvr	Railey Abia	31	m	M		542	2154
				Taylor Abia	24	m	M	37:24	261	772
				Mae Karembu	25	m	M		5	24
tci20111028-01	10.5281/zenodo.1284365	put project	stt	Nakre Abia	28	f	M	23:08	88	329
tci20111107-01	10.5281/zenodo.1285129	ebar zan	nrr	Maraga Kwozi	63	m	M	11:23	194	941
tci20111107-03	10.5281/zenodo.1284494	crow&jackal	stt	Nakre Abia	28	f	M	06:20	80	251
tci20111119-01	10.5281/zenodo.1291004	faw brigsi	nrr	Abia Bai	60	m	M	10:16	197	798
tci20111119-03	10.5281/zenodo.1300677	fiyafr	nrr	Abia Bai	60	m	M	09:50	202	864
tci20111119-06	10.5281/zenodo.1302995	nzürna trikasi	nrr	Marua Bai	68	m	M	07:57	159	590
				Ronnie Marua	40	m	M		19	54
tci20120805-01	10.5281/zenodo.1291348	yam culture	nrr	Abia Bai	60	m	M	48:50	850	2930
tci20120814	10.5281/zenodo.1291350	babuane trikasi	nrr	Abia Bai	60	m	M	13:46	665	2288
tci20120815	10.5281/zenodo.1299687	nzöyär	nrr	Abia Bai	60	m	M	03:02	74	349
tci20120817-02	10.5281/zenodo.1299697	ythama	nrr	Abia Bai	60	m	M	01:31	49	153
tci20120818	10.5281/zenodo.1299699	ebar zan	nrr	Abia Bai	60	m	M	05:03	91	343
tci20120821-01	10.5281/zenodo.1299705	dö	nrr	Lucy Abia	56	f	S	03:54	81	316
tci20120821-02	10.5281/zenodo.1299707	ruga fiyaf	nrr	Lucy Abia	56	f	S	05:00	115	365

archive ID	corpus DOI	title	genre	speaker	age	sex	sec	length (mm:ss)	records	tokens
tci20120824	10.5281/zenodo.1300789	brubru	prd	Karo Abia	42	m	M	06:35	160	538
tci20120827-03	10.5281/zenodo.1294658	nzürna trikasi	nrr	Kurai Tawéth	42	m	B	11:57	250	869
tci20120901-01	10.5281/zenodo.1294666	nzürna trikasi	nrr	Maraga Kwozi	63	m	M	10:30	238	922
tci20120904-01	10.5281/zenodo.1299316	ŋazi traksi	nrr	Marua Bai	68	m	M	07:21	185	620
tci20120904-02	10.5281/zenodo.1294670	srak brüzsi	nrr	Marua Bai	68	m	M	12:20	278	1020
tci20120906	10.5281/zenodo.1294674	gwfiyar	prd, cvr	Sékri Karémbu / Marua Bai	38 / 68	m / m	M / M	10:36	110 / 96	385 / 376
tci20120909-06	10.5281/zenodo.1300793	masis	nrr	Kaumb Bai	65	m	M	07:12	123	655
tci20120914	10.5281/zenodo.1303336	frfr & kifikifi	prd	Nakre Abia	28	f	M	04:27	66	237
tci20120922-08	10.5281/zenodo.1303977	masu	nrr	Daure Kaumb	38	m	M	06:12	138	592
tci20120922-09	10.5281/zenodo.1303981	sfisam	nrr	Daure Kaumb	38	m	M	02:41	49	237
tci20120922-19	10.5281/zenodo.1304219	ymäd zfth	nrr	Daure Kaumb	38	m	M	02:17	44	222
tci20120922-21	10.5281/zenodo.1304230	säfifok	nrr	Daure Kaumb	38	m	M	02:44	48	249
tci20120922-23	10.5281/zenodo.1304450	nabi	prd	Masen Abia	35	m	M	07:56	111	515
tci20120922-24	10.5281/zenodo.1304456	mni	nrr, cvr	Masen Abia / Steven Karémbu	35 / 28	m / m	M / M	09:12	90 / 39	389 / 177
tci20120922-25	10.5281/zenodo.1305034	zuzi	nrr	Alice Karo	38	f	S	04:12	56	305
tci20120922-26	10.5281/zenodo.1294676	dagon dradr	nrr, cvr	Moses Marua / Marua Bai / Daure Kaumb	50 / 68 / 38	m / m / m	M / M / M	11:38	30 / 64 / 145	155 / 209 / 610
tci20120924-01	10.5281/zenodo.1305050	daru	nrr	Trafe Kaumb	29	f	M	05:19	69	285
tci20120924-02	10.5281/zenodo.1305055	zokwasi	nrr	Abraham Maembu	45	m	S	02:53	47	186
tci20120925	10.5281/zenodo.1292778	picture task	stt, cvr	Mae Kapa / Kaumb Bai / Mea Abia	46 / 65 / 55	m / m / m	M / M / M	42:59	431 / 256 / 19	1726 / 1060 / 68
tci20120929-02	10.5281/zenodo.1305062	wath frmnzsi	nrr	Sitau Karémbu	42	m	M	05:46	102	468

archive ID	corpus DOI	title	genre	speaker	age	sex	sec	length (mm:ss)	records	tokens
tci20121001	10.5281/zenodo.1294680	*wawa mnz*	prd	Abia Bai	60	m	M	12:13	222	926
tci20121008-03	10.5281/zenodo.1305430	*dobakwr*	nrr, prd	Moses Marua / Marua Bai	50 / 68	m / m	M / M	04:13	28 / 17	103 / 84
tci20121019-04	10.5281/zenodo.1305436	*se zokwasi*	pub	Abia Bai / Sékri Karémbu / Sitau Karémbu	60 / 38 / 42	m / m / m	M / M / M	27:40	267 / 81 / 51	1367 / 334 / 221
tci20130822-08	10.5281/zenodo.1305440	*ŋarake znsä*	prd, cvr	Janet Abia / Lucy Abia	26 / 56	f / f	M / S	05:15	55 / 41	211 / 186
tci20130823-06	10.5281/zenodo.1305922	garden	cvr	Caspar Mokai / Steven Karémbu	35 / 28	m / m	S / M	21:29	117 / 259	441 / 1056
tci20130823-08	10.5281/zenodo.1305942	*fathasi*	nrr	Wafine Mokai / Yufai Karémbu	32 / 24	f / m	M / M	06:07	85 / 77	296 / 283
tci20130901-04	10.5281/zenodo.1305946	*bthan kabe*	cvr	Nakre Abia / Mbai Karo	28 / 20	f / m	M / M	14:12	177 / 22	761 / 72
tci20130903-01	10.5281/zenodo.1305960	*kut*	prd	Maembu Kwozi	35	m	M	05:59	66	168
tci20130903-02	10.5281/zenodo.1305962	*kata*	nrr	Maembu Kwozi	35	m	M	01:30	27	92
tci20130903-03	10.5281/zenodo.1305964	*fiyaf trikasi*	nrr	Maembu Kwozi	35	m	M	09:24	193	681
tci20130903-04	10.5281/zenodo.1305970	*fenz yonasi*	nrr	Nakre Abia	28	f	M	07:16	151	629
tci20130905-02	10.5281/zenodo.1305977	*ŋoti*	nrr	Maembu Kwozi	35	m	M	05:36	124	424
tci20130907-02	10.5281/zenodo.1292845	plant walk	cvr, prd	Nakre Abia / Janet Abia	28 / 26	f / f	M / M	63:37	763 / 732	2709 / 2371
tci20130911-03	10.5281/zenodo.1305987	*mary*	nrr	Mabata Abraham	40	f	M	04:41	93	394
tci20130914-01	10.5281/zenodo.1305989	*ŋatr rziraksi*	prd	Kaumb Bai	65	m	M	03:01	61	307
tci20130923-01	10.5281/zenodo.1306003	*yem/kwras*	nrr	Alice Abia	34	f	M	04:17	72	272
tci20130927-06	10.5281/zenodo.1292871	old times	cvr	Marua Bai / Caspar Mokai	68 / 35	m / m	M / S	20:20	383 / 63	1696 / 217

archive ID	corpus DOI	title	genre	speaker	age	sex	sec	length (mm:ss)	records	tokens
tci20131004-05	10.5281/zenodo.1306007	sota	cvr	Nakre Abia	28	f	M		65	392
				Railey Abia	31	m	M		17	100
				Dorothy Railey	28	f	B	05:54	25	155
				Yufai Karémbu	24	m	M		8	33
				Ester Railey	12	f	M		6	12
				Ronnie Marua	40	m	M		11	45
tci20131008-01	10.5281/zenodo.1306009	tūtū	nrr	Kaumb Bai	65	m	M	03:23	49	186
				Abia Bai	60	m	M		7	31
tci20131013-01	10.5281/zenodo.1292876	kwafar	nrr	Abia Bai	60	m	M	25:00	514	1900
tci20131013-02	10.5281/zenodo.1292878	ausi bada	nrr	Abia Bai	60	m	M	16:51	346	1205
tci20131103-08	10.5281/zenodo.1306013	se zokwasi	pub	Ako Koko	55	m	S	14:58	214	991
tci20150906-10	10.5281/zenodo.1294682	srak brüzsi	nrr	Abia Bai	60	m	M	18:43	414	1271
tci20150916-03	10.5281/zenodo.1306019	nümgar	nrr	Sékri Karémbu	38	m	M		140	473
				Nakre Abia	28	f	M	09:50	30	71
				Mea Abia	55	m	M		20	83
tci20150919-05	10.5281/zenodo.1294712	ausi	nrr, cvr	Lucy Abia	56	f	S		375	1397
				Sékri Karémbu	38	m	M	18:40	30	109
				Nakre Abia	28	f	M		20	55
TOTAL								11:42:44	13.333	53.625

References

Anderson, Stephen R. 1992. *A-Morphous Morphology*. Cambridge: Cambridge University Press.

Andrews, Avery. 2007a. Relative clauses. In Timothy Shopen (ed.), *Language typology and syntactic description, volume II: Complex constructions (2nd edition)*, 206–236. Cambridge: Cambridge University Press.

Andrews, Avery. 2007b. The major functions of the noun phrase. In Timothy Shopen (ed.), *Language typology and syntactic description, volume I: Clause structure (2nd edition)*, 132–223. Cambridge: Cambridge University Press.

Arka, I Wayan. 2012. Projecting morphology and agreement in Marori, an isolate of Southern New Guinea. In Nicholas Evans & Marian Klamer (eds.), *Melanesian languages on the edge of Asia: Challenges for the 21st century.* (Language Documentation & Conservation Special Publication No. 5). Manoa: University of Hawai'i Press.

Arkadiev, Peter M. 2008. Thematic roles, event structure, and argument encoding in semantically aligned languages. In Mark Donohue & Søren Wichmann (eds.), *The typology of semantic alignment*, 101–117. Oxford: Oxford University Press.

Ayres, Mary C. 1983. *This side, that side: Locality and exogamous group definition in Morehead area, Southwestern Papua*. Chicago: University of Chicago dissertation.

Baerman, Matthew. 2012. Paradigmatic chaos in Nuer. *Language* 88(3). 467–494.

Baerman, Matthew, Greville G. Corbett, Dunstan Brown & Andrew Hippisley. 2006. *Surrey Typological Database on Deponency*. Surrey Morphology Group. University of Surrey. URL: http://dx.doi.org/10.15126/SMG.15/1.

Baker, Mark. 1996. *The polysynthesis parameter*. Oxford: Oxford University Press.

Ballard, Chris. 2010. Synthetic histories: Possible futures for Papuan Pasts. *Reviews in Anthropology* 39(4). 232–257.

Bickel, Balthasar. 2011. Grammatical relations typology. In Jae J. Song (ed.), *The Oxford handbook of linguistic typology*, 399–444. Oxford: Oxford University Press.

Biggs, Bruce. 1963. A non-phonemic central vowel type in Karam, a "Pygmy" language of the Schrader Mountains, Central New Guinea. *Anthropological Linguistics* 5(4). 13–17.

Blake, Barry. 1994. *Case*. Cambridge: Cambridge University Press.

Blevins, Juliette. 1995. The syllable in phonological theory. In John A. Goldsmith (ed.), *The handbook of phonological theory*, 206–244. Cambridge: Basil Blackwell.

Blevins, Juliette & Andrew Pawley. 2010. Typological implications of Kalam predictable vowels. *Phonology* 27. 1–44.

Boevé, Alma & Marco Boevé. 2003. *Arammba grammar essentials*. Ukarumpa: SIL Unpublished Ms.

References

Bybee, Joan L. 2010. Markedness: Iconicity, economy and frequency. In Jae J. Song (ed.), *Handbook of linguistic typology*, 131–147. Oxford: Oxford University Press.

Bybee, Joan L. & Östen Dahl. 1989. The creation of tense and aspect systems in the languages of the world. *Studies in Language* 13(1). 51–103.

Bybee, Joan L., Revere Perkins & William Pagliuca. 1994. *The evolution of grammar: Tense, aspect, and modality in the languages of the world.* Chicago: The University of Chicago Press.

Caballero, Gabriela & Alice C. Harris. 2012. A working typology of multiple exponence. In Ferenc Kiefer, Mária Ladányi & Péter Siptár (eds.), *Current issues in morphological theory: (ir)regularity, analogy and frequency. Selected papers from the 14th International Morphology Meeting, Budapest, 13-16 May 2010*, 163–188. Amsterdam; Philadelphia: John Benjamins.

Carroll, Matthew. 2017. *The Ngkolmpu Language – with special reference to distributed exponence.* Canberra: Australian National University dissertation.

Chappell, John. 2005. Geographic changes of coastal lowlands in the Papuan past. In Andrew Pawley, Attenborough Robert, Jack Golson & Robin Hide (eds.), *Papuan pasts: Cultural, linguistic and biological histories of Papuan-speaking peoples*, 525–540. Canberra: Pacific Linguistics.

Clifton, John M., Geoff Dyall & Paul O'Rear. 1991. *The linguistic situation south of the Fly River, Western Province.* Ukarumpa: SIL Unpublished Ms.

Comrie, Bernard. 1976. *Aspect: An introduction to the study of verbal aspect and related problems.* Cambridge: Cambridge University Press.

Comrie, Bernard & Michael Cysouw. 2012. New Guinea through the eyes of WALS. *Language and Linguistics in Melanesia* 30(1). 65–94.

Comrie, Bernard & Sandra A. Thompson. 2007. Lexical nominalization. In Timothy Shopen (ed.), *Language typology and syntactic description, volume III: Grammatical categories and the lexicon (2nd edition)*, 334–381. Cambridge: Cambridge University Press.

Coulmas, Florian. 1982. Some remarks on Japanese deictics. In Jürgen Weissenborn & Wolfgang Klein (eds.), *Here and there: Cross-linguistic studies on deixis and demonstration*, 209–223. Amsterdam; Philadelphia: John Benjamins.

Cristofaro, Sonia. 2004. Past habituals and irrealis. In Yuri A. Lander, Vladimir A. Plungian & Anna Y. Urmanchieva (eds.), *Irrealis and irreality*, 256–272. Moscow: Gnosis.

Croft, William. 1991. *Syntactic categories and grammatical relations: The cognitive organization of information.* Chicago: The University of Chicago Press.

de Vries, Lourens. 2005. Towards a typology of tail–head linkage in Papuan languages. *Studies in Language* 29(2). 363–384.

Diessel, Holger. 1999. The morphosyntax of demonstratives in synchrony and diachrony. *Linguistic Typology* 3(1). 1–49.

Dik, Simon C. 1997. *The theory of functional grammar, part I: The structure of the clause.* K. Hengeveld (ed.). Berlin; New York: Mouton de Gruyter.

Dingemanse, Mark. 2012. Advances in the cross-linguistic study of ideophones. *Language and Linguistics Compass* 6(10). 654–672.

Dixon, R. M. W. 1972. *The Dyirbal language of North Queensland.* Cambridge: Cambridge University Press.

Dixon, R. M. W. 2003. Demonstratives: A cross-linguistic typology. *Studies in Language* 27(1). 61–112.

Donohue, Mark. 2008. Complexities with restricted numeral systems. *Linguistic Typology* 12(3). 423–429.

Drabbe, Peter. 1955. *Spraakkunst van het Marind: Zuidkust Nederlands Nieuw-Guinea. Studia Instituti Anthropos, volume 11.* Wien-Mödling: Missiehuis St. Gabriel.

Dryer, Matthew S. 2007. Word order. In Timothy Shopen (ed.), *Language typology and syntactic description, volume I: Clause structure (2nd edition)*, 61–130. Cambridge: Cambridge University Press.

Evans, Nicholas. Forthcoming. *A grammar of Nen.*

Evans, Nicholas. 1995. *A grammar of Kayardild: With historical-comparative notes on Tangkic.* Berlin; New York: Mouton de Gruyter.

Evans, Nicholas. 1997. Sign metonymies and the problem of flora-fauna polysemy in Australian languages. In Darrell T. Tryon & Michael Walsh (eds.), *Boundary rider: Essays in honour of Geoffrey O'Grady*, 133–153. Canberra: Pacific Linguistics.

Evans, Nicholas. 2009. Two pus one makes thirteen: Senary numerals in the Morehead-Maro region. *Linguistic Typology* 13(2). 321–335.

Evans, Nicholas. 2010. Semantic typology. In Jae J. Song (ed.), *The Oxford handbook of linguistic typology*, 504–533. Oxford: Oxford University Press.

Evans, Nicholas. 2012a. Even more diverse than we had thought: The multiplicity of Trans-Fly languages. In Nicholas Evans & Marian Klamer (eds.), *Melanesian languages on the edge of Asia: Challenges for the 21st century* (Language Documentation & Conservation Special Publication No. 5), 109–149. Manoa: University of Hawai'i Press.

Evans, Nicholas. 2012b. Nen assentives and the problem of dyadic parallelisms. In Andrea C. Schalley (ed.), *Practical theories and empirical practice: Facets of a complex interaction*, 159–183. Amsterdam; Philadelphia: John Benjamins.

Evans, Nicholas. 2014. Positional verbs in nen. *Oceanic Linguistics* 53(2). 225–255.

Evans, Nicholas. 2015a. Inflection in Nen. In Matthew Baerman (ed.), *The oxford handbook of inflection.* Oxford: Oxford University Press.

Evans, Nicholas. 2015b. Valency in Nen. In Andrej L. Malchukov & Bernard Comrie (eds.), *Valency classes in the world's languages*, 1049–1096. Berlin; New York: Walter de Gruyter.

Evans, Nicholas. 2017. Quantification in Nen. In Denis Paperno & Edward Keenan (eds.), *Handbook of quantification in natural language, volume II*, 571–607. New York: Springer.

Evans, Nicholas, I Wayan Arka, Matthew Carroll, Christian Döhler, Eri Kashima, Emil Mittag, Kyla Quinn, Jeff Siegel, Philip Tama & Charlotte van Tongeren. 2017. The languages of Southern New Guinea. In Bill Palmer (ed.), *The languages and linguistics of the New Guinea area*, 641–774. Berlin; Boston: Walter de Gruyter.

Evans, Nicholas & Alan C. Dench. 1988. Multiple case-marking in Australian languages. *Australian Journal of Linguistics* 8(1). 1–47.

Evans, Nicholas & Alan C. Dench. 2006. Introduction. In Felix K. Ameka, Alan C. Dench & Nicholas Evans (eds.), *Catching language: The standing challenge of grammar writing*, 1–40. Berlin; New York: Mouton de Gruyter.

Evans, Nicholas & Julia C. Miller. 2016. Nen. *Journal of the International Phonetic Association* 46(3). 331–349.

Evans, Nicholas & Hans-Jürgen Sasse. 2002. Introduction. In Nicholas Evans & Hans-Jürgen Sasse (eds.), *Problems of polysynthesis*, 1–13. Berlin: Akademie Verlag.

Fedden, Sebastian O. 2011. *A grammar of Mian*. Berlin; Boston: Walter de Gruyter.

Fillmore, Charles. 1968. The case for case. In Emmon Bach & Robert T. Harms (eds.), *Universals in linguistic theory*, 1–25. London: Holt, Rinehart & Winston.

Foley, William A. 1986. *The Papuan languages of New Guinea*. Cambridge: Cambridge University Press.

Foley, William A. 2000. The languages of New Guinea. *Annual Review of Anthropology* 29. 357–404.

Frawley, William. 1992. *Linguistic semantics*. Hillsdale: Lawrence Erlbaum Associates.

Garde, Murray. 2013. *Culture, interaction and person reference in an Australian language: An ethnography of Bininj Gunwok communication*. Amsterdam; Philadelphia: John Benjamins.

Geniušienė, Emma. 1987. *The typology of reflexives*. Berlin; New York: Mouton de Gruyter.

Givón, Talmy. 1994. Irrealis and the subjunctive. *Studies in Language* 18(2). 265–337.

Givón, Talmy. 2001. *Syntax: An introduction, volume II*. Amsterdam; Philadelphia: John Benjamins.

Goddard, Cliff. 1985. *A grammar of Yankunytjatjara*. Alice Springs: Institute of Aboriginal Development.

Golson, Jack. 2005. Introduction to the chapters on archaeology and ethnology. In Andrew Pawley, Attenborough Robert, Jack Golson & Robin Hide (eds.), *Papuan pasts: Cultural, linguistic and biological histories of Papuan-speaking peoples*, 221–234. Canberra: Pacific Linguistics.

Grummit, John & Janell Masters. 2012. *A survey of the Tonda sub-group of languages*. Ukarumpa: SIL Electronic Survey Report 2012-018. URL: http://www.sil.org/silesr/2012/silesr2012-018.pdf.

Gurevich, Olga. 2006. *Constructional morphology: The Georgian version*. Berkley: University of California dissertation.

Hale, Kenneth L. 1976. The adjoined relative clause in Australia. In R. M. W. Dixon (ed.), *Grammatical categories in Australian languages*, 78–105. Canberra: Australian Institute of Aboriginal Studies.

Hammarström, Harald. 2009. Whence the Kanum base-6 numeral system? *Linguistic Typology* 13(2). 305–319.

Hartzler, Margaret. 1983. Mode, aspect, and foregrounding in Sentani. *Language & Linguistics in Melanesia* 14. 175–194.

Haspelmath, Martin. 1997. *Indefinite pronouns*. Oxford: Clarendon.

Haspelmath, Martin. 2001. The European linguistic area: Standard Average European. In Martin Haspelmath, Wulf Oesterreicher & Wolfgang Raible (eds.), *Language typology and language universals* (Handbücher zur Sprach- und Kommunikationswissenschaft), 1492–1510. Berlin; New York: Mouton de Gruyter.

Haspelmath, Martin. 2007. Coordination. In Timothy Shopen (ed.), *Language typology and syntactic description, volume II: Complex constructions (2nd edition)*, 1–51. Cambridge: Cambridge University Press.

Haspelmath, Martin. 2013. Negative indefinite pronouns and predicate negation. In Matthew Dryer & Martin Haspelmath (eds.), *The world atlas of language structures online*. Leipzig: Max Planck Institute for Evolutionary Anthropology. URL: http://wals.info/chapter/115.

Haspelmath, Martin & Thomas Müller-Bardey. 2004. Valency change. In Geert Booij, Christian Lehmann & Joachim Mugdan (eds.), *Morphologie / Morphology. Ein internationales Handbuch zur Flexion und Wortbildung / An international handbook on inflection and word-formation*, chap. 107, 1130–1145. Berlin; New York: Mouton de Gruyter.

Heath, Jeffrey. 1984. *Functional grammar of Nunggubuyu*. Canberra: Australian Institute of Aboriginal Studies.

Heine, Bernd & Tania Kuteva. 2005. *Language contact and grammatical change*. Cambridge: Cambridge University Press.

Hercus, Luise & Jane Simpson. 2002. Indigenous placenames: An introduction. In Luise Hercus & Jane Simpson (eds.), *The land is a map*, 1–23. Canberra: Pacific Linguistics.

Himmelmann, Nikolaus P. 1996. Demonstratives in narrative discourse. In Barbara Fox (ed.), *Studies in anaphora*, 205–254. Amsterdam; Philadelphia: John Benjamins.

Hitchcock, Garrick. 2004. *Wildlife is our gold: Political ecology of the Torassi River borderland, southwest Papua New Guinea*. Brisbane: University of Queensland dissertation.

Hitchcock, Garrick. 2009. William Dammköhler's third encounter with the Tugeri (Marind-Anim) – manuscript XX. *The Journal of Pacific History* 44(1). 89–97.

Hopper, Paul J. 1979. Aspect and foregrounding in discourse. In Talmy Givón (ed.), *Discourse and syntax*, 213–241. New York: Academic Press.

Hopper, Paul J. 1990. Where do words come from? In William Croft, Keith Denning & Suzanne Kemmer (eds.), *Studies in typology and diachrony: Papers presented to Joseph H. Greenberg on his 75th birthday*, 151–160. Amsterdam; Philadelphia: John Benjamins.

Keenan, Edward L. & Matthew S. Dryer. 2007. Passives in the world's languages. In Timothy Shopen (ed.), *Language typology and syntactic description, volume I: Clause structure (2nd edition)*, 325–361. Cambridge: Cambridge University Press.

Kemmer, Suzanne. 1993. *The middle voice*. Amsterdam; Philadelphia: John Benjamins.

Kennedy, Christopher & Louise McNally. 2005. Scale structure, degree modification, and the semantics of gradable predicates. *Language* 81(2). 345–381.

Knauft, Bruce M. 1993. *South coast New Guinea cultures: History, comparision, dialectic*. Cambridge: Cambridge University Press.

König, Ekkehard. 1991. *The meaning of focus particles: A comparative perspective*. London & New York: Routledge.

Kubota, Yusuke. 2010. Marking aspect along a scale: The semantics of *-te iku* and *-te kuru* in Japanese. *Semantics and Linguistic Theory* 20. 128–146.

Lichtenberk, Frantisek. 1983. *A grammar of Manam* (Oceanic Linguistics Special Publications No. 18). Manoa: University of Hawai'i Press.

Lichtenberk, Frantisek. 1991. Semantic change and heterosemy in grammaticalization. *Language* 67(3). 475–509.

Lichtenberk, Frantisek. 2000. Inclusory pronominals. *Oceanic Linguistics* 39(1). 1–32.

Luraghi, Silvia. 2001. Syncretism and the classification of semantic roles. *STUF – Language Typology and Universals* 54(1). 35–51.

Luraghi, Silvia. 2003. *On the meaning of prepositions and cases: The expression of semantic roles in Ancient Greek*. Amsterdam; Philadelphia: John Benjamins.

MacGregor, William. 1890. *Annual report on British New Guinea from 1st July 1889 to 30th June 1890 with appendices*. Brisbane: Govt Printer. URL: http://nla.gov.au /nla.obj-82702440.

MacGregor, William. 1896. *Annual report on British New Guinea from 1st July 1895 to 30th June 1896 with appendices*. Brisbane: Govt Printer. URL: http://nla.gov.au /nla.obj-82720595.

Makihara, Miki & Bambi B. Schieffelin. 2007. Cultural processes and linguistic mediations: Pacific explorations. In Miki Makihara & Bambi B. Schieffelin (eds.), *Consequences of contact: Language ideologies and sociocultural transformations in Pacific societies*, 3–30. Oxford: Oxford University Press.

Matthews, Peter H. 1974. *Morphology: An introduction to the theory of word-structure*. Cambridge: Cambridge University Press.

Meakins, Felicity & Rachel Nordlinger. 2014. *A grammar of Bilinarra: an Australian Aboriginal language of the Victoria River District (NT)*. Berlin; New York: Mouton de Gruyter.

Mel'čuk, Igor. 1973. The structure of linguistics signs and possible formal-semantic relations between them. In Rey-Debove Josette (ed.), *Recherches sur les systèmes signifiants: symposium de varsovie*, 103–135. The Hague; Paris: Mouton.

Merlan, Francesca. 1981. Land, language and social identity in Aboriginal Australia. *Mankind Quarterly* 13. 133–148.

Merlan, Francesca. 1985. Split intransitivity: Functional oppositions in intransitive inflection. In Johanna Nichols & Tony Woodbury (eds.), *Grammar inside and outside the clause: Some approaches to theory from the field*, 324–362. Cambridge: Cambridge University Press.

Merlan, Francesca. 2001. Form and Context in Jawoyn placenames. In Jane Simpson, David Nash, Mary Laughren, Peter Austin & Barry Alpher (eds.), *Forty years on: Ken Hale and Australian languages*, 367–383. Canberra: Pacific Linguistics.

Mithun, Marianne. 1991. Active/agentive case marking and its motivations. *Language* 67(3). 510–546.

Mithun, Marianne. 2009. Polysynthesis in the Arctic. In Marc-Antoine Mahieu & Nicole Tersis (eds.), *Variations on polysynthesis: The Eskimo-Aleut languages*, 3–18. Amsterdam; Philadelphia: John Benjamins.

Mühlhäusler, Peter. 2006. Naming languages, drawing language boundaries and maintaining languages with special reference to the linguistic situation in Papua New Guinea. In Denis Cunningham, David E. Ingram & Kenneth Sumbuk (eds.), *Language diversity in the Pacific: Endangerment and survival*, 24–39. Clevedon: Multilingual Matters.

Murray, John H. P. 1912. *Papua or British New Guinea*. London: T. Fisher Unwin. URL: https://archive.org/details/papuaorbritishne00murr.

Ochs Keenan, Elinor & Bambi B. Schieffelin. 1976. Topic as a discourse notion. In Charles N. Li (ed.), *Subject and topic*, 335–384. New York: Academic Press.

Olsson, Bruno. 2013. *Iamitives: Perfects in Southeast Asia and beyond*. Stockholm: Stockholms Universitet MA thesis.

Olsson, Bruno. 2017. *The Coastal Marind language*. Singapore: Nanyang Technological University dissertation.

Paijmans, Kees. 1970. Land evaluation by air photo interpretation and field sampling in Australian New Guinea. *Photogrammetria* 26(2-3). 77–100.

Paijmans, Kees, D. H. Blake & P. Bleeker. 1971. Land systems of the Morehead-Kiunga area. In Kees Paijmans, D. H. Blake, P. Bleeker & J. R. McAlpine (eds.), *Land resources of the Morehead-Kiunga area, territory of Papua and New Guinea (Land Research Series No. 29)*, 19–45. Melbourne: Commonwealth Scientific & Industrial Research Organization, Australia.

Pawley, Andrew. 1966. *The structure of Karam*. Auckland: University of Auckland dissertation.

Pawley, Andrew. 2005. Introduction to the chapters on historical linguistics. In Andrew Pawley, Attenborough Robert, Jack Golson & Robin Hide (eds.), *Papuan pasts: cultural, linguistic and biological histories of Papuan-speaking peoples*, 1–14. Canberra: Pacific Linguistics.

Pawley, Andrew, Simon P. Gi, Ian S. Majnep & John Kias. 2000. Hunger acts on me: the grammar and semantics of bodily and mental process expressions in Kalam. *Oceanic Linguistics Special Publications, Grammatical Analysis: Morphology, Syntax, and Semantics* (29). 153–185.

Pawley, Andrew, Attenborough Robert, Jack Golson & Robin Hide. 2005. *Papuan pasts: Cultural, linguistic and biological histories of Papuan-speaking peoples*. Canberra: Pacific Linguistics.

Pollard, Carl J. & Ivan A. Sag. 1987. *Information-based syntax and semantics*. Stanford: Center for the Study of Language & Information.

Ray, Sidney H. 1907. Papuan languages west of the Fly river. In Sidney H. Ray (ed.), *Linguistics*, vol. III (Reports of the Cambridge Anthropological Expedition to Torres Straits), 291–301. Cambridge University Press.

Ray, Sidney H. 1923. The Languages of the western division of Papua. *Journal of the Royal Anthropological Institute of Great Britain and Ireland* 53. 332–360.

Ray, Sidney H. 1926. *A comparative study of the Melanesian Island languages*. Cambridge: Cambridge University Press.

Reesink, Ger. 1987. *Structures and their functions in Usan: A Papuan language of Papua New Guinea*. Vol. 13 (Studies in Language companion series). Amsterdam; Philadelphia: John Benjamins.

Reesink, Ger. 2009. A connection between Bird's Head and (Proto) Oceanic. In Bethwyn Evans (ed.), *Discovering history through language*, 181–192. Canberra: Pacific Linguistics.

Ross, Malcolm. 2005. Pronouns as a preliminary diagnostic for grouping Papuan languages. In Andrew Pawley, Attenborough Robert, Jack Golson & Robin Hide (eds.), *Papuan pasts: Cultural, linguistic and biological histories of Papuan-speaking peoples*, 15–66. Canberra: Pacific Linguistics.

Rumsey, Alan. 1990. Wording, meaning, and linguistic ideology. *American Anthropologist* 92(2). 346–361.

Saeed, John I. 1984. *The syntax of focus and topic in Somali*. Hamburg: Helmut Buske.

Sarsa, Risto. 2001. *Studies in Wára verb morphology*. Helsinki: University of Helsinki MA thesis.

Sasse, Hans-Jürgen. 2002. Recent activity in the theory of aspect: accomplishments, achievements, or just non-progressive state. *Linguistic Typology* 6(2). 199–271.

Schachter, Paul & Timothy Shopen. 2007. Parts-of-speech systems. In Timothy Shopen (ed.), *Language typology and syntactic description, volume I: Clause structure (2nd edition)*, 1–60. Cambridge: Cambridge University Press.

Schultze-Berndt, Eva. 2000. *Simple and complex verbs in Jaminjung*. Nijmegen: Katholieke Universiteit Nijmegen dissertation.

Siegel, Jeff. 2014. The morphology of tense and aspect in Nama, a Papuan language of Southern New Guinea. *Open Linguistics* 1. 211–231.

Silverstein, Michael. 1976. Hierarchy of features and ergativity. In R. M. W. Dixon (ed.), *Grammatical categories in Australian languages*, 112–171. Canberra: Australian Institute of Aboriginal Studies.

Silverstein, Michael. 1979. Language structure and linguistic ideology. In Paul Clyne, Williams Hanks & Carol Hofbauer (eds.), *The elements: A parasession on linguistic units and levels*, 193–247. Chicago: Chicago Linguistic Society.

Singer, Ruth. 2001. *The inclusory construction in Australian languages*. Melbourne: The University of Melbourne honours thesis.

Smith, Carlota. 1997. *The parameter of aspect (2nd edition)*. Dordrecht: Kluwer.

Sutton, Peter. 1978. *Wik: Aboriginal society, territory and language at Cape Keerweer, Cape York Peninsula*. Brisbane: University of Queensland dissertation.

Thompson, Sarah A., Robert E. Longacre & Shin J.J. Hwang. 2007. Adverbial clauses. In Timothy Shopen (ed.), *Language typology and syntactic description, volume II: Complex constructions (2nd edition)*, 237–300. Cambridge: Cambridge University Press.

Turner-Lister, Robert & J. B. Clark. 1935. *A dictionary of the Motu language of Papua (2nd edition by P. Chatterton)*. Sydney: Pettifer.

Usher, Timothy & Edgar Suter. 2015. The Anim languages of Southern New Guinea. *Oceanic Linguistics* 54(1). 110–142.

van Enk, Gerrit & Lourens de Vries. 1997. *The Korowai of Irian Jaya: Their language in its cultural context* (Oxford Studies in Anthropological Linguistics). Oxford: Oxford University Press.

White, John P. & James F. O'Connell. 1982. *A prehistory of Australia, New Guinea and Sahul*. Sydney: Academic Press.

Wichmann, Søren & Jan Wohlgemuth. 2008. Loan verbs in a typological perspective. In Thomas Stolz, Dik Bakker & Rosa Salas Palomo (eds.), *Aspects of language contact: New theoretical, methodological and empirical findings with special focus on Romancisation processes*, 89–121. Berlin; New York: Mouton de Gruyter.

Williams, Francis E. 1936. *Papuans of the Trans-Fly*. Oxford: Clarendon Press.

Wurm, Stephen A. 1971. Notes on the linguistic situation of the Trans-Fly area. In Thomas E. Dutton, Clemens L. Voorhoeve & Stephen A. Wurm (eds.), *Papers in new guinea linguistics 14*, 115–172. Canberra: Pacific Linguistics.

Wurm, Stephen A. 1975. *New Guinea area languages and language study, 1: Papuan languages and the New Guinea linguistic scene*. Canberra: Pacific Linguistics.

Zwicky, Arnold & Geoffrey Pullum. 1983. Cliticization vs. inflection: English *n't*. *Language* 59(3). 502–513.

Name index

Language index

Language index

Wèré, 1, 22[11], 37–42, 184, 185, 355[9]

Subject index

www.ingramcontent.com/pod-product-compliance
Lightning Source LLC
Chambersburg PA
CBHW081112160426
42814CB00035B/291